Adobe®
PHOTOSHOP® CS6
COMPREHENSIVE

Adobe® PHOTOSHOP® CS6

COMPREHENSIVE

Joy L. Starks

Alec Fehl

COURSE TECHNOLOGY
CENGAGE Learning™

SHELLY
CASHMAN
SERIES®

Australia • Brazil • Japan • Korea • Mexico • Singapore • Spain • United Kingdom • United States

COURSE TECHNOLOGY
CENGAGE Learning

Adobe® Photoshop® CS6: Comprehensive
Joy L. Starks, Alec Fehl

Editor-in-Chief: Marie Lee

Executive Editor: Kathleen McMahon

Senior Product Manager: Emma Newsom

Associate Product Manager: Crystal Parenteau

Editorial Assistant: Sarah Ryan

Director of Marketing: Cheryl Costantini

Marketing Manager: Adrienne Fung

Marketing Coordinator: Michael Saver

Print Buyer: Julio Esperas

Director of Production: Patty Stephan

Content Project Manager: Jennifer Feltri-George

Developmental Editor: Amanda Brodkin

QA Manuscript Reviewers: Danielle Shaw

Copyeditor: Foxxe Editorial

Proofreader: Kim Kosmatka

Indexer: Rich Carlson

Art Director: Jackie Bates, GEX Publishing Services

Cover and Text Design: Lisa Kuhn, Curio Press, LLC

Cover Photo: Tom Kates Photography

Compositor: PreMediaGlobal

For product information and technology assistance, contact us at
Cengage Learning Customer & Sales Support, 1-800-354-9706

For permission to use material from this text or product,
submit all requests online at **cengage.com/permissions**
Further permissions questions can be emailed to
permissionrequest@cengage.com

Library of Congress Control Number: 2012947751
ISBN-13: 978-1-133-52592-9
ISBN-10: 1-133-52592-X

Course Technology
20 Channel Center Street
Boston, Massachusetts 02210
USA

Adobe, the Adobe logos, and Photoshop are either registered trademarks or trademarks of Adobe Systems Incorporated in the United States and/or other countries. THIS PRODUCT IS NOT ENDORSED OR SPONSORED BY ADOBE SYSTEMS INCORPORATED, PUBLISHER OF PHOTOSHOP.

Cengage Learning is a leading provider of customized learning solutions with office locations around the globe, including Singapore, the United Kingdom, Australia, Mexico, Brazil, and Japan. Locate your local office at:
international.cengage.com/region

Cengage Learning products are represented in Canada by Nelson Education, Ltd.

For your course and learning solutions, visit **www.cengage.com**

To learn more about Course Technology,
visit **www.cengage.com/coursetechnology**

Purchase any of our products at your local college bookstore or at our preferred online store **www.cengagebrain.com**

Printed in the United States of America
2 3 4 5 6 7 18 17 16 15

Adobe
PHOTOSHOP® CS6
COMPREHENSIVE

Contents

Appendices

Preface

The Shelly Cashman Series® offers the finest textbooks in computer education. We are proud of the fact that our previous Photoshop® books have been so well received. With each new edition of our Photoshop® books, we have made significant improvements based on the comments made by instructors and students. The Adobe® Photoshop® CS6 books continue with the innovation, quality, and reliability you have come to expect from the Shelly Cashman Series®.

For this Photoshop® CS6 text, the Shelly Cashman Series® development team carefully reviewed our pedagogy and analyzed its effectiveness in teaching today's student. Students today read less, but need to retain more. They not only need to be able to perform skills, but to retain those skills and know how to apply them to different settings. Today's students need to be continually engaged and challenged to retain what they're learning.

With this Photoshop® CS6 text, we continue our commitment to focusing on the user and how they learn best.

Objectives of This Textbook

Adobe® Photoshop® CS6: Comprehensive is intended for a course that offers an introduction to Photoshop® and image editing. No previous experience with Adobe® Photoshop® CS6 is assumed, and no mathematics beyond the high school freshman level is required.

The objectives of this book are:

- To teach the fundamentals and more advanced features of Adobe® Photoshop® CS6 using student-focused exercises

- To expose students to image editing and graphic design fundamentals

- To develop an exercise-oriented approach that promotes learning by doing

- To encourage independent study and to help those who are working alone

The Shelly Cashman Approach

A Proven Pedagogy with an Emphasis on Project Planning

Each chapter presents a practical problem to be solved, within a project planning framework. The project orientation is strengthened by the use of Plan Ahead boxes, that encourage critical thinking about how to proceed at various points in the project. Step-by-step instructions with supporting screens guide students through the steps. Instructional steps are supported by the Q&A, Experimental Step, and BTW features.

A Visually Engaging Book that Maintains Student Interest

The step-by-step tasks, with supporting figures, provide a rich visual experience for the student. Call-outs on the screens that present both explanatory and navigational information provide students with information they need, when they need to know it. Each chapter presents a real-world, photo scenario with current topics and new CS6 features.

Supporting Reference Materials (Quick Reference, Appendices)

The appendices provide additional information about the application at hand, such as the Help Feature and customizing the application, as well as a new appendix, For Mac Users. With the Quick Reference, students can quickly look up information about a single task, such as keyboard shortcuts, and find page references of where in the book the task is illustrated.

Integration of the World Wide Web

The World Wide Web is integrated into the Photoshop CS6 learning experience by (1) BTW annotations; and (2) a Quick Reference Summary Web page.

End-of-Chapter Student Activities

Extensive end of chapter activities provide a variety of reinforcement opportunities for students where they can apply and expand their skills through individual and group work. To complete some of these assignments, you will be required to use the Data Files for Students. Visit http://www.cengage.com/ct/studentdownload for detailed access instructions or contact your instructor for information about accessing the required files.

New To This Edition

Completely Updated for CS6 Features

This edition reflect all of the new CS6 features, including the new Content-Aware Patch and Move, the new Crop Tool, the new Blur gallery and others!

Mac User Support

A new appendix, For Mac Users, provides information and details for students on a Mac where instructions may differ.

Publishing to a Web Server

A new appendix discusses considerations and instructions for publishing to a web server.

New Images

Updated photos in chapter project reflect topics of interest and are geared towards today's students.

Instructor Resources

The Instructor Resources include both teaching and testing aids that can be accessed via the Instructor Resouce CD or at www.cengage.com/login.

Instructor's Manual Includes lecture notes summarizing the chapter sections, figures and boxed elements found in every chapter, teacher tips, classroom activities, lab activities, and quick quizzes in Microsoft Word files.

Syllabus Easily customizable sample syllabi that cover policies, assignments, exams, and other course information.

Data Files for Students Illustrations for every figure in the textbook in electronic form. Visit www.cengage.com/ct/studentdownload for detailed instructions.

PowerPoint Presentations A multimedia lecture presentation system that provides slides for each chapter. Presentations are based on chapter objectives.

Solutions to Exercises Includes solutions for all end-of-chapter and chapter reinforcement exercises.

Test Bank & Test Engine Test Bank includes 112 questions for every chapter, featuring objective-based and critical thinking question types, including page number references and figure references, when appropriate. Also included is the test engine, ExamView, the ultimate tool for your objective-based testing needs.

Additional Activities for Students Consists of Chapter Reinforcement Exercises, which are true/false, multiple-choice, and short answer questions that help students gain confidence in the material learned.

Learn Online

CengageBrain.com is the premier destination for purchasing or renting Cengage Learning textbooks, ebooks, eChapters and study tools, at a significant discount (eBooks up to 50% off Print). In addition, CengageBrain.com provides direct access to all digital products including eBooks, eChapters and digital solutions (i.e. CourseMate, SAM) regardless of where purchased. The following are some examples of what is available for this product on www.cengagebrain.com.

Student Companion Site Quizzing, learning games and activities are available for no additional cost at www.cenagebrain.com to help reinforce chapter terms and concepts.

Adobe Photoshop CS6 CourseMate CourseMate with ebook for Adobe Photoshop CS6 keeps today's students engaged and involved in the learning experience. Adobe Photoshop CS6 CourseMate includes an integrated, multi-media rich and eBook, and a variety of interactive learning tools, including quizzes, activities, videos, and other resources that specifically reinforce and build on the concepts presented in the chapter. These interactive activities are tracked within CourseMate's Engagement Tracker, making it easy to assess students' retention of concepts. All of these resources enable students to get more comfortable using technology and help prepare students to use the Internet as a tool to enrich their lives. Available at the Comprehensive level in Spring 2013.

CourseNotes

Course Technology's CourseNotes are six-panel quick reference cards that reinforce the most important and widely used features of a software application in a visual and user-friendly format. CourseNotes serve as a great reference tool during and after the course. CourseNotes are available for software applications, such as Microsoft Office 2010, Word 2010, PowerPoint 2010, Excel 2010, Access 2010, and Windows 7. There are also topic-based CourseNotes available for Best Practices in Social Networking, Hot Topics in Technology, and Web 2.0. Visit www.cengage.com/ct/coursenotes to learn more!

course|notes™
quick reference guide

About Our Covers

The Shelly Cashman Series is continually updating our approach and content to reflect the way today's students learn and experience new technology. This focus on student success is reflected on our covers, which feature real students from Naugatuck Valley Community College using the Shelly Cashman Series in their courses, and reflect the varied ages and backgrounds of the students learning with our books. When you use the Shelly Cashman Series, you can be assured that you are learning computer skills using the most effective courseware available.

Textbook Walk-Through

Plan Ahead boxes prepare students to create successful projects by encouraging them to think strategically about what they are trying to accomplish before they begin working.

BTW

Screen Resolution
If your system has a high-resolution monitor with a screen resolution of 1280 × 800 or higher, lowering that resolution to 1024 × 768 might cause some images to be distorted because of a difference in the aspect ratio. If you want to keep your high-resolution setting, be aware that the location of on-screen tools might vary slightly from the book.

Overview

As you read this chapter, you will learn how to edit the photo shown in Figure 1–1a on the previous page by performing these general tasks:

- Customize the workspace.
- Display and navigate a photo at various magnifications.
- Crop a photo effectively.
- Create and modify a border.
- Stroke a selection.
- Resize and print a photo.
- Save, close, and then reopen a photo.
- Add stroked text to the photo.
- Save a photo for the Web.
- Use Photoshop Help.

Plan Ahead

General Project Guidelines

When editing a photo, the actions you perform and decisions you make will affect the appearance and characteristics of the finished product. As you edit a photo, such as the one shown in Figure 1–1a, you should follow these general guidelines:

1. **Find an appropriate image or photo.** Keep in mind the purpose and the graphic needs of the project when choosing an image or photo. Decide ahead of time on the file type and decide if the image will be used on the Web. An eye-catching graphic image should convey a theme that is understood universally. The photo should grab the attention of viewers and draw them into the picture, whether in print or on the Web.

2. **Determine how to edit the photo to highlight the theme.** As you edit, use standard design principles, and keep in mind your subject, your audience, the required size and shape of the graphic, color decisions, the rule of thirds, the golden rectangle, and other design principles. Decide which parts of the photo portray your message and which parts are visual clutter. Crop the photo as needed.

3. **Identify finishing touches that will further enhance the photo.** The overall appearance of a photo significantly affects its ability to communicate clearly. You might want to add text or a border.

4. **Prepare for publication.** Resize the photo as needed to fit the allotted space. Save the photo on a storage medium, such as a hard drive, USB flash drive, or CD. Print the photo or publish it to the Web.

When necessary, more specific details concerning the above guidelines are presented at appropriate points in the chapter. The chapter also will identify the actions performed and decisions made regarding these guidelines during the creation of the edited photo shown in Figure 1–1b on the previous page.

BTW

By The Way Boxes
For a complete list of the BTWs found in the margins of this book, visit the BTW chapter resource on the student companion site located at www.cengagebrain.com.

Starting Photoshop

If you are using a computer to step through the project in this chapter, and you want your screen to match the figures in this book, you should change your screen's resolution to 1024 × 768. For information about how to change a screen's resolution, read Appendix F, the Changing Screen Resolution appendix.

To Start Photoshop

The following steps, which assume Windows 7 is running, start Photoshop, based on a typical installation. You may need to ask your instructor how to start Photoshop for your computer.

Textbook Walk-Through

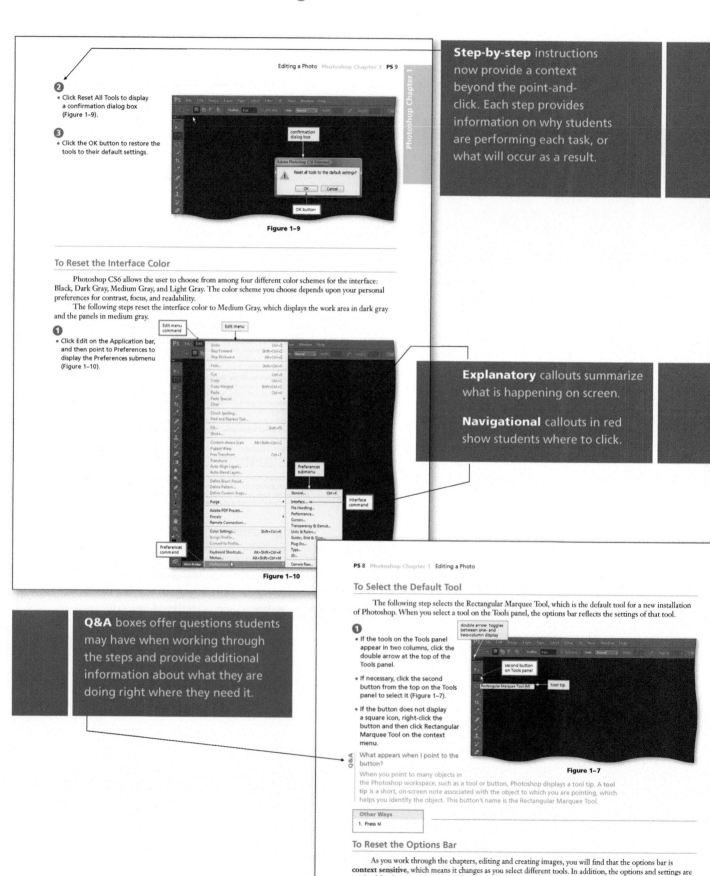

2
- Click Reset All Tools to display a confirmation dialog box (Figure 1–9).

3
- Click the OK button to restore the tools to their default settings.

confirmation dialog box

OK button

Figure 1–9

Step-by-step instructions now provide a context beyond the point-and-click. Each step provides information on why students are performing each task, or what will occur as a result.

To Reset the Interface Color

Photoshop CS6 allows the user to choose from among four different color schemes for the interface: Black, Dark Gray, Medium Gray, and Light Gray. The color scheme you choose depends upon your personal preferences for contrast, focus, and readability.

The following steps reset the interface color to Medium Gray, which displays the work area in dark gray and the panels in medium gray.

1
- Click Edit on the Application bar, and then point to Preferences to display the Preferences submenu (Figure 1–10).

Edit menu command

Edit menu

Preferences submenu

Preferences command

Interface command

Explanatory callouts summarize what is happening on screen.

Navigational callouts in red show students where to click.

Figure 1–10

Q&A boxes offer questions students may have when working through the steps and provide additional information about what they are doing right where they need it.

To Select the Default Tool

The following step selects the Rectangular Marquee Tool, which is the default tool for a new installation of Photoshop. When you select a tool on the Tools panel, the options bar reflects the settings of that tool.

1
- If the tools on the Tools panel appear in two columns, click the double arrow at the top of the Tools panel.

- If necessary, click the second button from the top on the Tools panel to select it (Figure 1–7).

- If the button does not display a square icon, right-click the button and then click Rectangular Marquee Tool on the context menu.

double arrow toggles between one- and two-column display

second button on Tools panel

Rectangular Marquee Tool (M)   tool tip

Q&A What appears when I point to the button?

When you point to many objects in the Photoshop workspace, such as a tool or button, Photoshop displays a tool tip. A tool tip is a short, on-screen note associated with the object to which you are pointing, which helps you identify the object. This button's name is the Rectangular Marquee Tool.

Figure 1–7

Other Ways
1. Press M

To Reset the Options Bar

As you work through the chapters, editing and creating images, you will find that the options bar is **context sensitive**, which means it changes as you select different tools. In addition, the options and settings are retained for the next time you use Photoshop. To match the figures in this book, you should reset the options bar, using a context menu, each time you start Photoshop. A **context menu**, or **shortcut menu**, appears when you right-click some objects in the Photoshop workspace. The menu displays commands representing the active

BTW

Q&A
For a complete list of the Q&As found in many of the step-by-step sequences in this book, visit the Q&A chapter resource on the student companion site located at www.cengagebrain.com.

Customizing the Photoshop Workspace

The screen in Figure 1–3 on the previous page shows how the Photoshop workspace looks the first time you start Photoshop after installation on most computers. Photoshop does not open a blank or default photo automatically; rather, the Application bar and the options bar appear across the top of the screen with a work area below the options bar. The Tools panel is displayed on the left; other panels are displayed on the right and across the bottom. The work area and panels are referred to collectively as the **workspace**.

As you work in Photoshop, the panels, the selected tool, and the options bar settings might change. Therefore, if you want your screen to match the figures in this book, you should restore the default workspace, select the default tool, and reset the options bar. In addition, users might change the default color for the workspace. For more information about how to change other advanced Photoshop settings, see the Changing Screen Resolution appendix.

Because of a default preference setting, each time you start Photoshop, the Photoshop workspace is displayed the same way it was the last time you used Photoshop. If you (or another user) move the panels while working in Photoshop, they will appear in their new locations the next time you start Photoshop. You can create and save your own workspaces, or use Photoshop's saved workspaces that show groups of panels used for certain tasks. For example, the Painting workspace displays the Brush panel, the Brush presets panel, and the Swatches panel, among others — all of which you would need when painting. You will learn more about panels later in this chapter. Similarly, if values on the options bar are changed or a different tool is selected, they will remain changed the next time you start Photoshop. If you want to return the workspace to its default settings, follow these steps each time you start Photoshop.

To Select the Essentials Workspace

The default workspace, called Essentials, displays commonly used panels. The following steps select the Essentials workspace and reset its default values.

1

- Click Window on the Application bar to display the Window menu.

- Point to Workspace on the Window menu to display the Workspace submenu (Figure 1–4).

Experiment

- Click each of the workspaces that are displayed in the list to view the different panel configurations. Notice that Photoshop displays a check mark on the menu, next to the chosen workspace. When you are finished, click Window on the Application bar and then point to Workspace again to display the submenu.

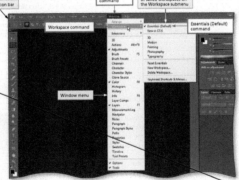

Figure 1–4

Experiment Steps within our step-by-step instructions, encourage students to explore, experiment, and take advantage of the features of the Photoshop CS6 user interface. These steps are not necessary to complete the projects, but are designed to increase the confidence with the software and build problem-solving skills.

Textbook Walk-Through

Other Ways boxes that follow many of the step sequences explain the other ways to complete the task presented.

To Select the Default Tool

The following step selects the Rectangular Marquee Tool, which is the default tool for a new installation of Photoshop. When you select a tool on the Tools panel, the options bar reflects the settings of that tool.

1

- If the tools on the Tools panel appear in two columns, click the double arrow at the top of the Tools panel.

- If necessary, click the second button from the top on the Tools panel to select it (Figure 1–7).

- If the button does not display a square icon, right-click the button and then click Rectangular Marquee Tool on the context menu.

Q&A What appears when I point to the button?

When you point to many objects in the Photoshop workspace, such as a tool or button, Photoshop displays a tool tip. A tool tip is a short, on-screen note associated with the object to which you are pointing, which helps you identify the object. This button's name is the Rectangular Marquee Tool.

Figure 1–7

Other Ways

1. Press M

To Reset the Options Bar

As you work through the chapters, editing and creating images, you will find that the options bar is **context sensitive**, which means it changes as you select different tools. In addition, the options and settings are retained for the next time you use Photoshop. To match the figures in this book, you should reset the options bar, using a context menu, each time you start Photoshop. A **context menu**, or **shortcut menu**, appears when you right-click some objects in the Photoshop workspace. The menu displays commands representing the active ... the options bar using a context menu.

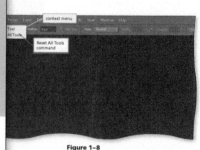

Figure 1–8

Chapter Summary

In this chapter, you gained a broad knowledge of Photoshop. First, you learned how to start Photoshop. You were introduced to the Photoshop workspace. You learned how to open a photo, change the magnification, zoom, and display rulers. You learned about design issues related to the placement of visual points of interest. You then learned how to crop a photo to eliminate extraneous background. After you added a blended border, you resized the image and added text. Once you saved the photo, you learned how to print it. You used the Save for Web command to optimize and save a Web version. You learned how to use Adobe Help to research specific help topics. Finally, you learned how to quit Photoshop.

The items listed below include all the new Photoshop skills you have learned in this chapter:

1. Start Photoshop (PS 4)
2. Select the Essentials Workspace (PS 6)
3. Select the Default Tool (PS 8)
4. Reset the Options Bar (PS 8)
5. Reset the Interface Color (PS 9)
6. Open a File (PS 11)
7. Save a File in the PSD Format (PS 20)
8. Use the Zoom Tool (PS 24)
9. Use the Navigator Panel (PS 26)
10. Minimize the Navigator Panel (PS 27)
11. Use the Hand Tool (PS 28)
12. Change the Magnification (PS 29)
13. Display Rulers (PS 30)
14. Crop a Photo (PS 33)
15. Create a Selection (PS 35)
16. Stroke a Selection (PS 36)
17. Modify a Selection (PS 39)
18. Switch Foreground and Background Colors (PS 40)
19. Deselect (PS 41)
20. Save a File with the Same File Name (PS 42)
21. Close a File (PS 42)
22. Open a Recent File (PS 43)
23. Resize the Image (PS 45)
24. Select the Horizontal Type Tool (PS 47)
25. Set Font Options (PS 47)
26. Insert Text (PS 48)
27. Stroke Text (PS 50)
28. Save a File with a Different Name (PS 51)
29. Print a Photo (PS 52)
30. Preview using the Save for Web Dialog Box (PS 53)
31. Choose a Download Speed (PS 54)
32. Preview the Photo on the Web (PS 55)
33. Save the Photo for the Web (PS 56)
34. Access Photoshop Help (PS 58)
35. Use the Help Search Box (PS 58)
36. Quit Photoshop (PS 60)

Chapter Summary includes a concluding paragraph, followed by a listing of the tasks completed within a chapter together with the pages on which the step-by-step, screen-by-screen explanations appear.

Apply Your Knowledge

Reinforce the skills and apply the concepts you learned in this chapter.

Editing a Photo in the Photoshop Workspace

Instructions: Start Photoshop and perform the customization steps found on pages PS 6 through PS 10. Open the Apply 1-1 Water Park file in the Chapter 01 folder from the Data Files for Students. Visit www.cengage.com/ct/studentdownload for detailed instructions or contact your instructor for information about accessing the required files.

First, you will save the photo in the PSD format, then you will crop the photo, add a white border, and save the edited photo, as shown in Figure 1–87 on the next page. Next, you will resize the photo for printing and print one copy. Finally, you will reopen your edited photo, and then you will optimize it for the Web, save it, and close it.

Continued >

15. Select using the Lasso Tool (PS 100)
16. Subtract from a Selection using the Magic Wand Tool (PS 102)
17. Select using the Elliptical Marquee Tool (PS 105)
18. Subtract Noncontiguous Pixels of the Same Color (PS 106)
19. Duplicate and Scale (PS 107)
20. Reselect (PS 108)

21. Fit Screen (PS 110)
22. Crop a Selection (PS 110)
23. Save a Photo in the PDF Format (PS 112)
24. Create a New Keyboard Shortcut (PS 114)
25. Test a New Keyboard Shortcut (PS 117)
26. Return to the Default Settings for Keyboard Shortcuts (PS 118)

Apply Your Knowledge

Reinforce the skills and apply the concepts you learned in this chapter.

Moving and Duplicating Selections

Instructions: Start Photoshop and perform the customization steps found on pages PS 6 through PS 10. Open the Apply 2-1 Bread file in the Chapter 02 folder from the Data Files for Students and save it, in the PSD file format, as Apply 2-1 Bread Edited. Visit www.cengage.com/ct/studentdownload for detailed instructions or contact your instructor for information about accessing the required files.

You will create a grocery advertisement featuring bakery items. First, you will select individual items from within the file, and then you will transform and move them so that the finished design looks like Figure 2–72. You will place the rest of the images from back to front.

Figure 2–72

Textbook Walk-Through

Photoshop Chapter 1

STUDENT ASSIGNMENTS

7. To create the border:

  a. If necessary, press the D key to select the default colors. Press the x key to reverse the foreground and background colors, so that white displays over black on the Tools panel.

  b. Press CTRL+A to select all of the photo.

  c. Use the Select menu to modify the border to 100 pixels.

  d. Use the Stroke command on the Edit menu to stroke the selection with white.

  e. Press CTRL+D to clear your selection when you are finished creating the border.

8. Press CTRL+S to save the Apply 1-1 Water Park Edited photo with the same file name in the same location.

9. Use the Image menu to resize the photo width to 5 inches wide to create a custom-sized photo for printing.

10. Save the resized file as Apply 1-1 Water Park for Print.

11. Print the photo and then close the file. If Photoshop displays a dialog box about saving again, click the No button.

12. Open the Apply 1-1 Water Park for Print file using the Open Recent list.

13. Save the photo for the Web, displaying it in the 4-Up tab. Select the preview that looks the best for your download speed.

14. Preview the optimized photo in your browser. Close the browser.

15. Save the optimized file with the name, Apply-1-1-Water-Park-for-Web.

16. Close the Apply 1-1 Water Park for Print file without saving it and quit Photoshop.

Extend Your Knowledge

Extend the skills you learned in this chapter and experiment with new skills. You may need to use Help to complete the assignment.

Exploring Crop Tool Options

Instructions: Start Photoshop and perform the customization s[...]
PS 10. Open the Extend 1-1 Arc de Triomphe file in the Chapte[...]
Students and save it on your storage device as Extend 1-1 Arc d[...]
format. Visit www.cengage.com/ct/studentdownload
for detailed instructions or contact your instructor for
information about accessing the required files.

  The photo (Figure 1–88) is to be added to a book
about Paris; therefore, the structure should be centered,
straightened, and display in a 5 × 7 format.

> **Extend Your Knowledge** projects at the end of each chapter allow students to extend and expand on the skills learned within the chapter. Students use critical thinking to experiment with new skills to complete each project.

STUDENT ASSIGNMENTS

Extend Your Knowledge *continued*

Perform the following tasks:

1. Use Help to read about the Crop Tool's Straighten button and the Aspect Ratio button.

2. Select the Crop Tool. On the options bar, click the Straighten button, and then drag in the photo, across a line that should be straight in the upper portion of the monument.

3. Use the 'Select a preset aspect ratio' button to choose a 5 × 7 forced ratio. Drag a corner cropping handle inward, keeping the arc within the grid. Drag the picture to center it within the cropping area.

4. Click the 'Delete cropped pixels' check box, if necessary, and then crop the photo.

5. Review Table 1–4 on page PS 38. Use the commands on the Modify submenu to set the border options of your choice. Stroke the selection with a color of your choice.

6. After viewing the resulting border, use the History panel to go back to the photo's cropped state.

7. Repeat Steps 5 and 6 several times to experiment with different border widths and colors, then apply the border that best complements the photo and save the changes to the photo.

8. Close the photo and quit Photoshop.

Make It Right

Analyze a project and correct all errors and/or improve the design.

> **Make It Right** projects call on students to analyze a file, discover errors in it, and fix them using the skills they learned in the chapter.

Changing a Photo's Focus and Optimizing It for the Web

Instructions: Start Photoshop and perform the customization steps found on pages PS 6 through PS 10. Open the Make It Right 1-1 Young Stars file in the Chapter 01 folder from the Data Files for Students and save it on your storage device as Make It Right 1-1 Young Stars Edited in the PSD file format. Visit www.cengage.com/ct/studentdownload for detailed instructions or contact your instructor for information about accessing the required files.

  Members of your Astronomy Club have selected the Young Stars photo (Figure 1–89) for the club's Web site. You are tasked with editing the photo to focus more clearly on the cluster of stars and its trailing dust blanket, and then optimizing the photo for the Web.

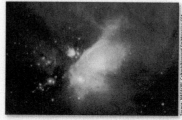

Source: NASA/JPL-Caltech/Harvard-Smithsonian CfA

Figure 1–89

  View the photo in different screen modes and at different magnifications. Keeping the rule of thirds and the golden rectangle concepts in mind, crop the photo to change its focal point and resave it. Then save the photo for the Web as Make-It-Right-1-1-Young-Stars-for-Web.

6. Select a different tool so the cropping handles no longer are displayed.

7. Save the photo again with the same name.

8. Close the file and open it again using the Recent submenu.

9. Press CTRL+A to select all of the photo.

10. To create the border, do the following:

    a. On the Select menu, point to Modify, and then click Border.

    b. When the Border Selection dialog box is displayed, type 100 in the Width Box. Click the OK button.

    c. On the Select menu, open the Modify submenu, and then click Smooth.

    d. When the Smooth Selection dialog box is displayed, type 50 in the Sample Radius box to smooth the corners. Click the OK button.

    e. Press SHIFT+F5 to access the Fill command.

    f. When the Fill dialog box is displayed, click the Use box arrow and then click White in the list.

    g. Click the Mode box arrow and then click Normal in the list, if necessary.

    h. If necessary, type 100 in the Opacity box. Click the OK button.

    i. Press CTRL+D to deselect the border.

11. Save the photo again.

12. Use the Print One Copy command on the File menu to print a copy of the photo.

13. Close the document window.

14. Quit Photoshop.

15. Submit the assignment in the format specified by your instructor.

In the Lab

In the Lab assignments require students to utilize the chapter concepts and techniques to solve problems on a computer.

Lab 3: Preparing a Photo for the Web

Problem: As an independent consultant in Web site design, you have been hired by the Pineapple Growers Association to prepare a photo of an exotic pineapple growing in a field for use on the association's Web site. The edited photo is displayed in Figure 1–92.

Note: To complete this assignment, you will be required to use the Data Files for Students. Visit www.cengage.com/ct/student-download for detailed instructions or contact your instructor for information about accessing the required files.

Instructions: Perform the following tasks:
Start Photoshop. Perform the customization steps found on pages PS 6 through PS 10. Open the file, Lab 1-3 Pineapple, from the Chapter 01 folder of the Data Files for Students. Save the file in the PSD format with the name Lab 1-3 Pineapple Edited. Resize the photo to 500 pixels wide. Zoom to 50% magnification. Search Photoshop Help for help related to optimization. Read about optimizing for the Web. Print a copy of the help topic and then close the Adobe Help window.

    Use the Save for Web dialog box to view the 4-Up tab. Choose the best-looking preview. Select the connection speed of

Figure 1–92

Continued >

Textbook Walk-Through

In the Lab *continued*

your Internet connection. Save the Web version of the photo using the name, Lab-1-3-Pineapple-for-Web. For extra credit, upload the Web version to a Web server. See Appendix C for information on publishing to a Web server. See your instructor for ways to submit this assignment.

Cases and Places

Apply your creative thinking and problem-solving skills to design and implement a solution.

Note: To complete these assignments, you may be required to use the Data Files for Students. Visit www.cengage.com/ct/studentdownload for detailed instructions or contact your instructor for information about accessing the required files.

1: Crop a Photo for a Class Directory

Academic

As a member of your high school reunion committee, it is your task to assemble the class photo directory. You are to edit a high school student photo and prepare it for print in the reunion directory. The photo needs to fit in a space 1.75 inches high and 1.33 inches wide. Each photo needs to have approximately .25 inches above the head. After starting Photoshop and resetting the workspace, select the photo, Case 1-1 Student, from the Chapter 01 folder of the Data Files for Students. Save the photo on your USB flash drive storage device as Case 1-1 Student Edited, using the PSD format. Resize the photo to match the requirements. Use the rulers to help you crop the photo for .25 inches above the top of the student's head. Save the photo again and print a copy for your instructor.

2: Create a Photo for a Social Networking Site

Personal

You would like to place a photo of your recent tubing adventure on your social networking page. The photo you have is of two people. You need to crop out the other person who is tubing. After starting Photoshop and resetting the workspace, select the photo, Case 1-2 Tubing, from the Chapter 01 folder of the Data Files for Students. Save the photo on your USB flash drive storage device as Case 1-2 Tubing Edited, using the PSD format. Crop the photo to remove one of the tubes, keeping in mind the rule of thirds, the golden rectangle, and the direction of the action. Save the photo for the Web and upload it to Facebook or another Web server as directed by your instructor.

3: Creating a Photo for a Brochure

Professional

You are an intern with an event planning business. The company is planning to send out a trifold brochure about local churches and chapels used for weddings. The photo named Case 1-3 Chapel is located in the Chapter 01 folder of the Data Files for Students. Save the photo on your USB flash drive storage device as Case 1-3 Chapel Edited, using the PSD format. Resize the photo to be 3.5 inches wide. Create a black border of 10 pixels. Save the file again and print a copy for your instructor.

Found within the Cases and Places exercises, the **Personal** activities call on students to create an open-ended project that relates to their personal lives.

Adobe®
PHOTOSHOP® CS6
COMPREHENSIVE

1 | Editing a Photo

Objectives

You will have mastered the material in this chapter when you can:

- Start Photoshop and customize the Photoshop workspace

- Open a photo

- Identify parts of the Photoshop workspace

- Explain file types

- View a photo using the Zoom Tool, Navigator panel, and the Hand Tool

- Display rulers

- Crop a photo using the rule of thirds overlay

- Save a photo for both print and the Web

- Create a border

- Open a recent file

- Resize a photo

- Insert text and stroke

- Print a photo

- Access Photoshop Help

- Close a file and quit Photoshop

1 | Editing a Photo

What Is Photoshop CS6?

Photoshop CS6 is a popular image-editing software program produced by Adobe Systems Incorporated. **Image-editing software** refers to computer programs that allow you to create and modify **digital images**, or pictures in electronic form. One type of digital image is a digital **photograph**, or **photo**, which is a picture taken with a camera and stored as a digitized file. The photo then is converted into a print or a slide, or used in another file. Other types of digital images include scanned images, or electronic forms of original artwork created from scratch. Digital images are used in graphic applications, advertising, print publishing, and on the Web. Personal uses include private photos, online photo sharing, scrapbooking, blogging, and social networking, among others. Image-editing software, such as Photoshop, can be used for basic adjustments such as rotating, cropping, or resizing, as well as for more advanced manipulations, such as airbrushing, retouching, photo repair, changing the contrast of images and balancing or combining elements of different images. Because Photoshop allows you to save multilayered, composite images and then return later to extract parts of those images, it works well for repurposing a wide variety of graphic-related files.

Photoshop CS6 is part of the **Adobe Creative Suite 6** and comes packaged with most of the suite versions. It also is sold and used independently as a stand-alone application. Photoshop CS6 is available for both the PC and Macintosh computer platforms. Photoshop CS6 Extended includes all of the features of Photoshop CS6 and some new features for working with 3D imagery, motion-based content, and advanced image analysis. The chapters in this book use Photoshop CS6 on the PC platform, running the Windows 7 operating system; however, Photoshop looks very similar on the Windows and the Mac operating systems. Both versions present the same tools and similar menus. One of the main differences is in the approach to shortcut keys. Windows uses the CTRL key to access many of the shortcuts in the Adobe Creative Suite; MacOS uses the CMD key represented by the symbol ⌘ and sometimes the OPT key represented by the symbol ⌥. As system dialog boxes are presented in the chapters, the corresponding steps for Mac users are presented in Appendix G, the For Mac Users appendix.

To illustrate the features of Photoshop CS6, this book presents a series of chapters that use Photoshop to edit photos similar to those you will encounter in academic and business environments, as well as photos for personal use.

Project Planning Guidelines

The process of editing a photo requires careful analysis and planning. As a starting point, choose a photo that correctly expresses your desired subject or theme. Once the theme is determined, analyze the intended audience. Define a plan for editing that enhances the photo, eliminates visual clutter, improves color and contrast, and corrects defects. Always work on a duplicate of an original image. Finally, determine the file format and print style that will be most successful at delivering the message. Details of these guidelines are provided in Appendix A, Project Planning Guidelines. In addition, each chapter in this book provides practical applications of these planning considerations.

Project — Postcard Graphic

BTW

What's New in CS6?
Photoshop CS6 has many new features, including an advanced cropping tool, Content Aware Move and Patch tools, Paragraph and Character Style panels, a new Blur gallery, as well as many others. To see more, press the F1 key and then click the What's new link.

A **postcard** is a rectangular piece of mail intended for writing and sending without an envelope. People use postcards for greetings, announcements, reminders, and business contacts. Many times, a postcard is an effective marketing tool used to generate prospective leads at a relatively low cost. One of the most popular uses for postcards involves pictures. Businesses and organizations produce a postcard with a photo or graphic on one side and a short description with room to write a brief correspondence on the other. People purchase picture postcards to mail to friends or to serve as reminders of their vacation. Sometimes a picture postcard is mailed to attract attention and direct people to Web sites or business locations. A postcard graphic must portray clearly its message or theme in an eye-catching manner, keeping in mind the relevant audience.

Most postcards are rectangular, at least 3½ inches high and 5 inches long — some are larger. A common size is 4 inches by 6 inches. A picture postcard might contain text printed over the picture or a border to add interest. A graphic designed for a postcard should be of high quality, use strong color, and deliver a message in the clearest, most attractive, and most effective way possible.

The project in this chapter uses Photoshop to enhance a photograph of an eagle and add text to create a postcard for use by a wildlife park. The original photo is displayed in Figure 1–1a. The edited photo is displayed in Figure 1–1b. The enhancements will emphasize the eagle by positioning the scene to make the layout appear more visually appealing and to crop some of the background. A gray border will frame the scene. Text will be added to identify the location. Finally, the photo will be resized to fit on a postcard and then optimized for the park's Web site.

(a) Original photo

(b) Edited photo

source: NASA

Figure 1–1

BTW

Screen Resolution
If your system has a high-resolution monitor with a screen resolution of 1280 × 800 or higher, lowering that resolution to 1024 × 768 might cause some images to be distorted because of a difference in the aspect ratio. If you want to keep your high-resolution setting, be aware that the location of on-screen tools might vary slightly from the book.

Overview

As you read this chapter, you will learn how to edit the photo shown in Figure 1–1a on the previous page by performing these general tasks:

- Customize the workspace.
- Display and navigate a photo at various magnifications.
- Crop a photo effectively.
- Create and modify a border.
- Stroke a selection.
- Resize and print a photo.
- Save, close, and then reopen a photo.
- Add stroked text to the photo.
- Save a photo for the Web.
- Use Photoshop Help.

Plan Ahead

General Project Guidelines

When editing a photo, the actions you perform and decisions you make will affect the appearance and characteristics of the finished product. As you edit a photo, such as the one shown in Figure 1–1a, you should follow these general guidelines:

1. **Find an appropriate image or photo.** Keep in mind the purpose and the graphic needs of the project when choosing an image or photo. Decide ahead of time on the file type and decide if the image will be used on the Web. An eye-catching graphic image should convey a theme that is understood universally. The photo should grab the attention of viewers and draw them into the picture, whether in print or on the Web.

2. **Determine how to edit the photo to highlight the theme.** As you edit, use standard design principles, and keep in mind your subject, your audience, the required size and shape of the graphic, color decisions, the rule of thirds, the golden rectangle, and other design principles. Decide which parts of the photo portray your message and which parts are visual clutter. Crop the photo as needed.

3. **Identify finishing touches that will further enhance the photo.** The overall appearance of a photo significantly affects its ability to communicate clearly. You might want to add text or a border.

4. **Prepare for publication.** Resize the photo as needed to fit the allotted space. Save the photo on a storage medium, such as a hard drive, USB flash drive, or CD. Print the photo or publish it to the Web.

When necessary, more specific details concerning the above guidelines are presented at appropriate points in the chapter. The chapter also will identify the actions performed and decisions made regarding these guidelines during the creation of the edited photo shown in Figure 1–1b on the previous page.

BTW

By The Way Boxes
For a complete list of the BTWs found in the margins of this book, visit the BTW chapter resource on the student companion site located at www.cengagebrain.com.

Starting Photoshop

If you are using a computer to step through the project in this chapter, and you want your screen to match the figures in this book, you should change your screen's resolution to 1024 × 768. For information about how to change a screen's resolution, read Appendix F, the Changing Screen Resolution appendix.

To Start Photoshop

The following steps, which assume Windows 7 is running, start Photoshop, based on a typical installation. You may need to ask your instructor how to start Photoshop for your computer.

1

- Click the Start button on the Windows 7 taskbar to display the Start menu.

- Type `Photoshop CS6` as the search text in the 'Search programs and files' text box, and watch the search results appear on the Start menu (Figure 1–2).

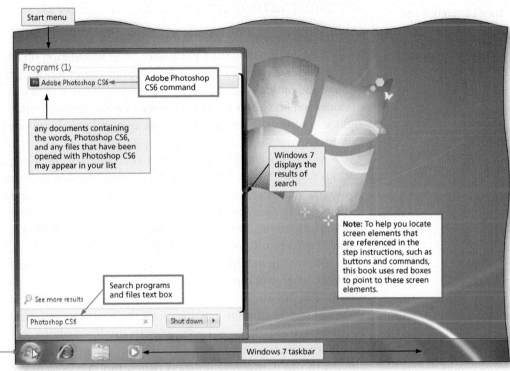

Start menu

Programs (1)

Adobe Photoshop CS6 ⟵ Adobe Photoshop CS6 command

any documents containing the words, Photoshop CS6, and any files that have been opened with Photoshop CS6 may appear in your list

Windows 7 displays the results of search

Note: To help you locate screen elements that are referenced in the step instructions, such as buttons and commands, this book uses red boxes to point to these screen elements.

See more results

Search programs and files text box

Photoshop CS6   ✕   Shut down ▶

Start button

Windows 7 taskbar

Figure 1–2

2

- Click Adobe Photoshop CS6 in the search results on the Start menu to start Photoshop.

- After a few moments, when the Photoshop window is displayed, if the window is not maximized, click the Maximize button next to the Close button on the Application bar to maximize the window (Figure 1–3).

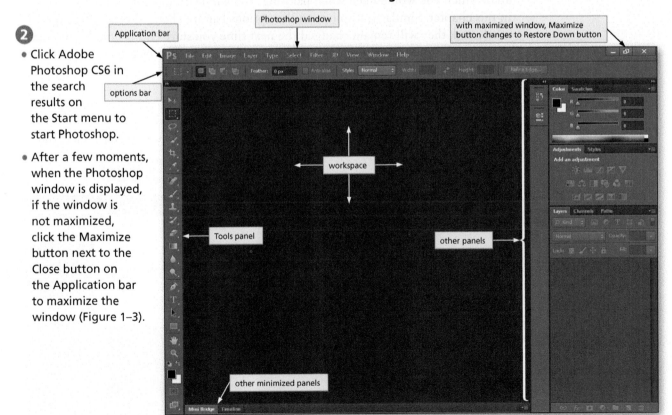

Application bar

Photoshop window

with maximized window, Maximize button changes to Restore Down button

options bar

workspace

Tools panel

other panels

other minimized panels

Figure 1–3

Other Ways

1. Double-click Photoshop icon on desktop, if the icon is present

2. Click Adobe Photoshop CS6 on Start menu

For a detailed example of this procedure using the Mac operating system, refer to the steps on page APP 76 of the For Mac Users appendix at the end of this book.

Customizing the Photoshop Workspace

The screen in Figure 1–3 on the previous page shows how the Photoshop workspace looks the first time you start Photoshop after installation on most computers. Photoshop does not open a blank or default photo automatically; rather, the Application bar and the options bar appear across the top of the screen with a work area below the options bar. The Tools panel is displayed on the left; other panels are displayed on the right and across the bottom. The work area and panels are referred to collectively as the **workspace**.

As you work in Photoshop, the panels, the selected tool, and the options bar settings might change. Therefore, if you want your screen to match the figures in this book, you should restore the default workspace, select the default tool, and reset the options bar. In addition, users might change the default color for the workspace. For more information about how to change other advanced Photoshop settings, see the Changing Screen Resolution appendix.

Because of a default preference setting, each time you start Photoshop, the Photoshop workspace is displayed the same way it was the last time you used Photoshop. If you (or another user) move the panels while working in Photoshop, they will appear in their new locations the next time you start Photoshop. You can create and save your own workspaces, or use Photoshop's saved workspaces that show groups of panels used for certain tasks. For example, the Painting workspace displays the Brush panel, the Brush presets panel, and the Swatches panel, among others — all of which you would need when painting. You will learn more about panels later in this chapter. Similarly, if values on the options bar are changed or a different tool is selected, they will remain changed the next time you start Photoshop. If you want to return the workspace to its default settings, follow these steps each time you start Photoshop.

To Select the Essentials Workspace

The default workspace, called Essentials, displays commonly used panels. The following steps select the Essentials workspace and reset its default values.

1
- Click Window on the Application bar to display the Window menu.

- Point to Workspace on the Window menu to display the Workspace submenu (Figure 1–4).

🔍 **Experiment**
- Click each of the workspaces that are displayed in the list to view the different panel configurations. Notice that Photoshop displays a check mark on the menu, next to the chosen workspace. When you are finished, click Window on the Application bar and then point to Workspace again to display the submenu.

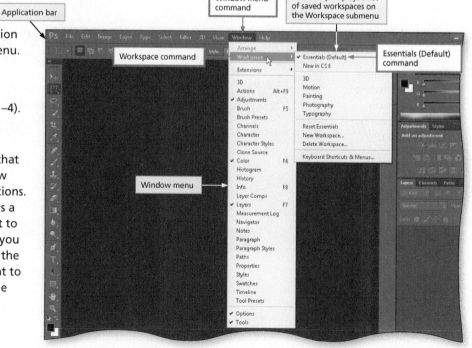

Figure 1–4

2

- Click Essentials (Default) on the Workspace submenu to select the default workspace panels.

- Click Window on the Application bar and then point to Workspace again to display the submenu (Figure 1–5).

Q&A

What does the New Workspace command do?

The New Workspace command displays a dialog box where you can create a new workspace based on the currently displayed panels. You also can delete a workspace from the Workspace submenu.

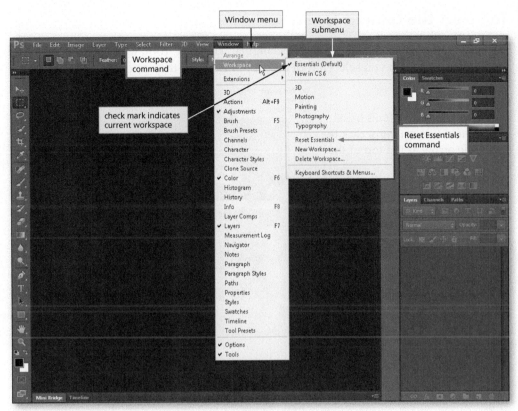

Figure 1–5

3

- Click Reset Essentials to restore the workspace to its default settings and reposition any panels that might have been moved (Figure 1–6).

Q&A

My screen did not change. Did I do something wrong?

If Photoshop is a new installation on your system, you might notice few changes on your screen.

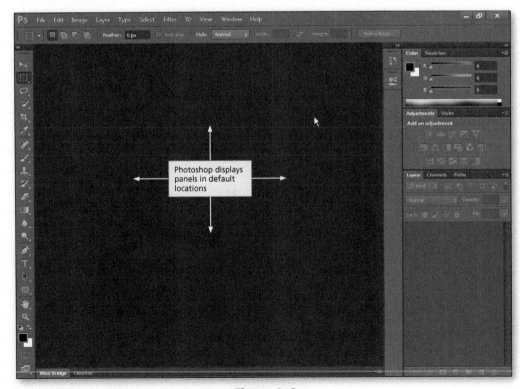

Figure 1–6

To Select the Default Tool

The following step selects the Rectangular Marquee Tool, which is the default tool for a new installation of Photoshop. When you select a tool on the Tools panel, the options bar reflects the settings of that tool.

- If the tools on the Tools panel appear in two columns, click the double arrow at the top of the Tools panel.

- If necessary, click the second button from the top on the Tools panel to select it (Figure 1–7).

- If the button does not display a square icon, right-click the button and then click Rectangular Marquee Tool on the context menu.

Q&A What appears when I point to the button?

When you point to many objects in the Photoshop workspace, such as a tool or button, Photoshop displays a tool tip. A **tool tip** is a short, on-screen note associated with the object to which you are pointing, which helps you identify the object. This button's name is the Rectangular Marquee Tool.

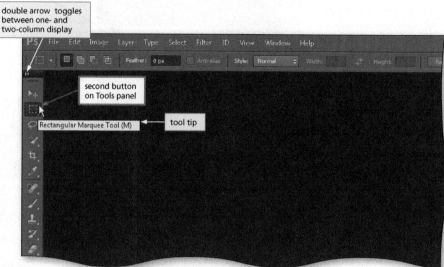

Figure 1–7

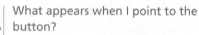

Other Ways

1. Press M

To Reset the Options Bar

As you work through the chapters, editing and creating images, you will find that the options bar is **context sensitive**, which means it changes as you select different tools. In addition, the options and settings are retained for the next time you use Photoshop. To match the figures in this book, you should reset the options bar, using a context menu, each time you start Photoshop. A **context menu**, or **shortcut menu**, appears when you right-click some objects in the Photoshop workspace. The menu displays commands representing the active tool, selection, or panel.

The following steps reset all tool settings in the options bar using a context menu.

- Right-click the Rectangular Marquee Tool icon on the options bar to display its context menu (Figure 1–8).

Q&A Why is my icon elliptical?

It is possible that a previous user has used the Elliptical Marquee Tool. Press SHIFT+M to return to the Rectangular Marquee Tool.

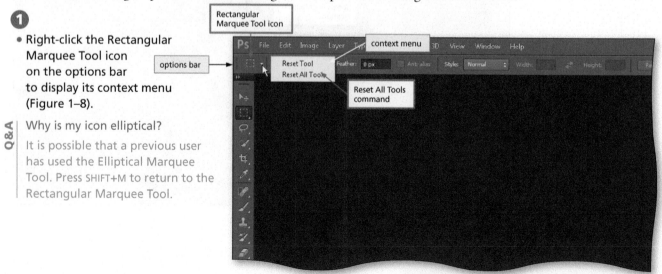

Figure 1–8

2

- Click Reset All Tools to display a confirmation dialog box (Figure 1–9).

3

- Click the OK button to restore the tools to their default settings.

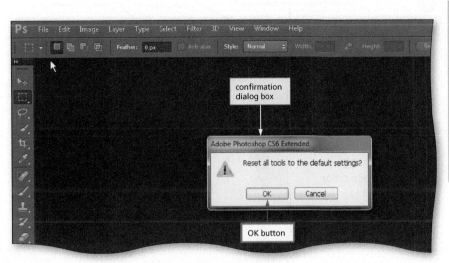

Figure 1–9

To Reset the Interface Color

Photoshop CS6 allows the user to choose from among four different color schemes for the interface: Black, Dark Gray, Medium Gray, and Light Gray. The color scheme you choose depends upon your personal preferences for contrast, focus, and readability.

The following steps reset the interface color to Medium Gray, which displays the work area in dark gray and the panels in medium gray.

1

- Click Edit on the Application bar, and then point to Preferences to display the Preferences submenu (Figure 1–10).

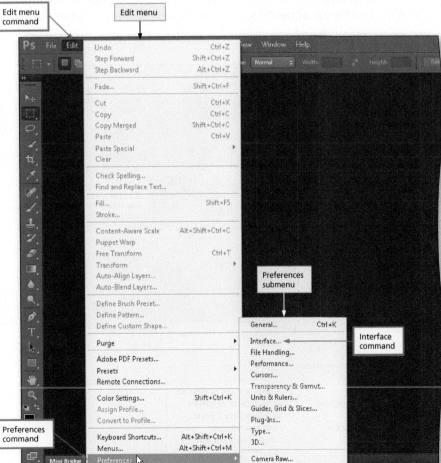

Figure 1–10

2

• Click Interface on the Preferences submenu to display the Preferences dialog box.

• In the Appearance area, click the third button, Medium Gray, to change the interface color (Figure 1–11).

Q&A

What other preferences can I change?

You can change things such as the color of certain display features, the number of states in the History panel, and the unit of measure, among others.

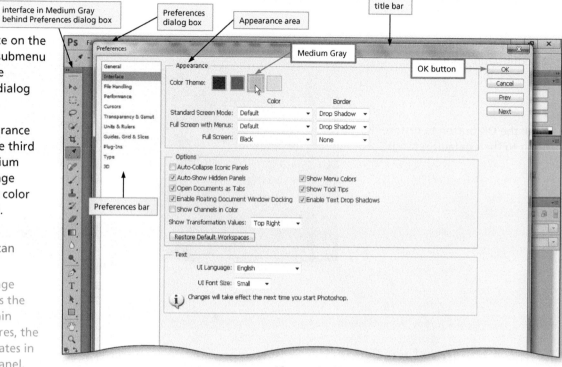

Figure 1–11

Experiment

• One at a time, click each of the four color schemes and notice how the interface changes. You can drag the title bar of the Preferences dialog box to move it out of the way, if necessary.

3

• Click the OK button in the Preferences dialog box to close the dialog box and return to the Photoshop workspace (Figure 1–12).

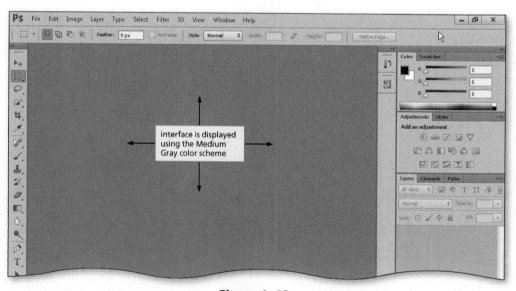

Figure 1–12

Other Ways

1. Press CTRL+K, click Interface on Preferences bar, click desired color scheme, click OK button

2. Right-click any button on vertical dock of panels, click Interface Options, click desired color scheme, click OK button

Opening a Photo

To open a photo in Photoshop, it must be stored as a digital file on your computer system or on an external storage device. To **open** a photo, you bring a copy of the file from the storage location to the screen where you can **edit**, or make changes to, the photo. The changes do not become permanent, however, until you **save** or store the changed file on a storage device. The photos used in this book are included in the Data Files for Students. Visit www.cengage.com/ct/studentdownload for detailed instructions or contact your instructor for information about accessing the required files. Your instructor may designate a different location for the photos.

Find an appropriate image or photo.
Sometimes a person or business gives you a specific photo to use in a project. Other times, you are assigned a theme and asked to find or take the photo. An eye-catching graphic image should convey a visual message that is not expressed easily with words. Keep the audience in mind as you choose a photo. Photos generally fall into one of four categories:

- In advertising, a photo might show a product, service, result, model, or benefit.

- In a public service setting, a photo might represent a topic of interest, nature, signage, buildings, or a photo of historical importance.

- In industry, a photo might display a process, product, work organization, employee, facility, layout, equipment, safety, result, or culture.

- For personal or journalistic use, a photo might be a portrait, scenery, action shot, or event.

Plan Ahead

To Open a File

The following steps open the Eagle file from the Data Files for Students. Visit www.cengage.com/ct/studentdownload for detailed instructions or contact your instructor for information about accessing the required files.

- Click File on the Application bar to display the File menu (Figure 1–13).

Q&A Do I need the Data Files for Students?

You will need the Data Files for Students to complete the activities and exercises in this book. See your instructor for information on how to acquire the necessary files.

Q&A Can I use a shortcut key to open a file?

Yes, the shortcut keys are displayed on the menu. In this textbook, the shortcut keys also are displayed at the end of each series of steps in the Other Ways box.

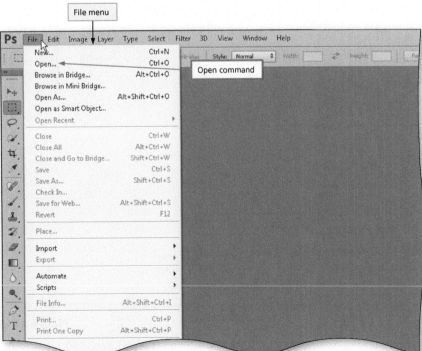

Figure 1–13

2

- Click Open on the File menu to display the Open dialog box.

- Click the Look in box arrow to display a list of the available storage locations on your system (Figure 1–14).

Q&A

What do the other buttons in the Open dialog box do?

To the right of the Look in box arrow are buttons to help you navigate folders, create folders, and change the view. Links to common storage locations are found in the Navigation pane on the left.

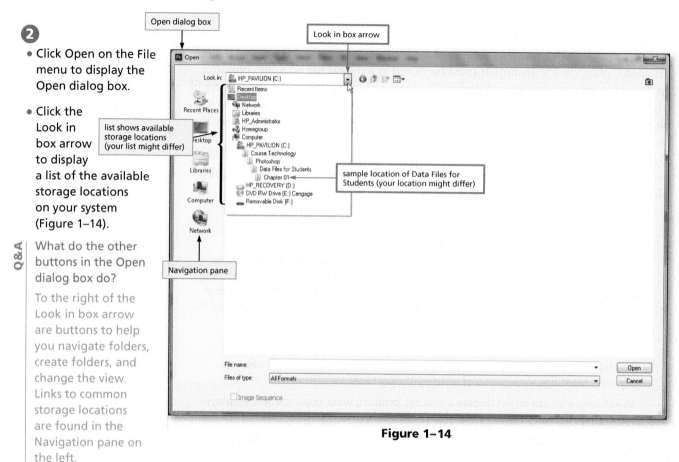

Figure 1–14

3

- Click the storage location of the Data Files for Students, as specified by your instructor, to display its contents (Figure 1–15).

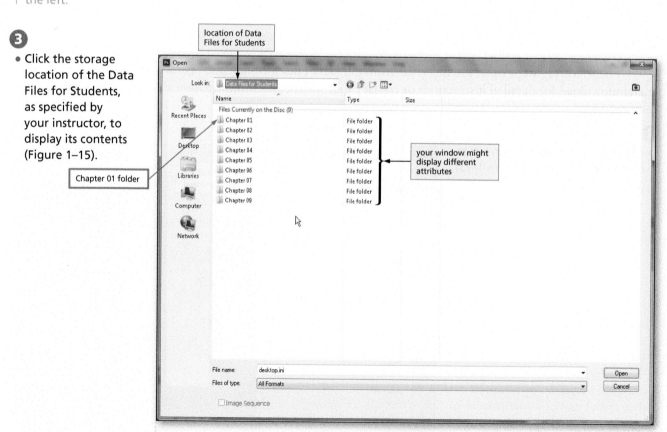

Figure 1–15

4

- Double-click the Photoshop folder and then double-click the Chapter 01 folder.

- Click the file, Eagle, to select the file to be opened (Figure 1–16).

Q&A Why is my file list different?

Your list might vary. In addition, the files in Figure 1–16 are displayed in List view. Click the View Menu button to verify your view.

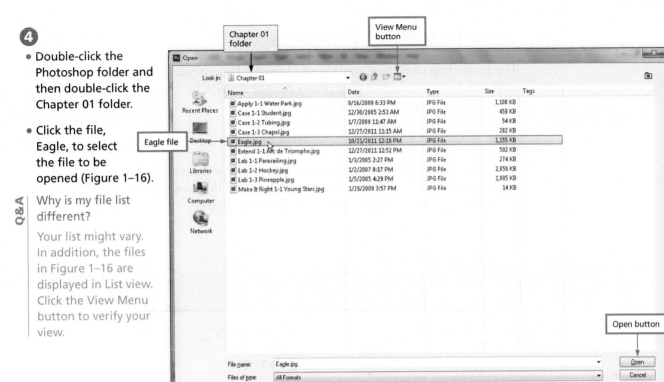

Figure 1–16

5

- Click the Open button to open the selected file and display the photo in the Photoshop workspace (Figure 1–17).

Q&A Can I edit a printed photo?

Most of the images you will use in this book already are stored in digital format; however, when you have a print copy of a picture, rather than a digital file stored on your system, it sometimes is necessary to scan the picture using a scanner. A **scanner** is a device used to convert a hard copy into a digital form for storage, retrieval, or other electronic purposes. Photoshop allows you to bring a copy from the scanner directly into the workspace.

Figure 1–17

 For a detailed example of this procedure using the Mac operating system, refer to the steps on pages APP 77 through APP 79 of the For Mac Users appendix.

Other Ways

1. Press CTRL+O, select file, click Open button

2. In Windows, right-click file, click Open with, click Adobe Photoshop CS6

The Photoshop Workspace

The Photoshop workspace consists of a variety of components to make your work more efficient and to make your photo documents look more professional. The following sections discuss these components.

The Application Bar

The Application bar appears at the top of the workspace (Figure 1–18). The Application bar contains the application button and the menu. On the far right side of the Application bar are the common window clip controls.

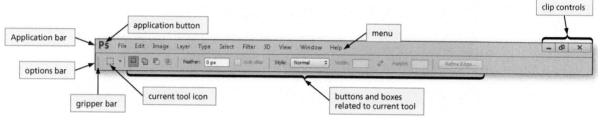

Figure 1–18

Hidden Menu Commands
When Photoshop first is installed, all of the menu commands within a menu appear when you click the menu name. To hide seldom-used menu commands, you can click the Menus command on the Edit menu and follow the on-screen instructions. A **hidden command** does not appear immediately on a menu.

Show All Menu Items
If menu commands have been hidden, a Show All Menu Items command will appear at the bottom of the menu list. Click the Show All Menu Items command, or press and hold the CTRL key when you click the menu name to display all menu commands, including hidden ones.

The menu displays the Photoshop menu names. Each **menu** contains a list of commands you can use to perform tasks such as opening, saving, printing, and editing photos. To display a menu, such as the View menu, click the View menu name on the Application bar. If you point to a command on a menu that has an arrow on its right edge, a **submenu**, or secondary menu, displays another list of commands. (See Figure 1–10 on page PS 9).

The Options Bar

The options bar (Figure 1–18) appears below the Application bar. Sometimes called the control panel, the options bar contains buttons and boxes that allow you to perform tasks more quickly than when using the Application bar and related menus. Most buttons on the options bar display words or images to help you remember their functions. When you point to a button or box on the options bar, a tool tip is displayed below the mouse pointer. The options bar changes to reflect the tool currently selected on the Tools panel. For example, a tool related to text might display a font box on the options bar, whereas a tool related to painting will display a brush button. The selected tool always appears as an icon on the left side of the options bar. As each tool is discussed, the associated options bar will be explained in more detail.

You can **float**, or move, the options bar in the workspace by dragging the gray gripper bar on the left side of the options bar. You can **dock** or reattach the options bar below the Application bar by resetting the workspace. To hide or show the options bar, click Options on the Window menu.

The Tools Panel

On the left side of the workspace is the Tools panel. The Tools panel is a group of **tools**, or buttons, organized into a toolbar. As with the options bar, you can float, dock, hide, or show the Tools panel. Each tool on the Tools panel displays a **tool icon**. When you point to the tool icon, a tool tip displays the name of the tool, including its shortcut key. You can expand some tools to show hidden tools beneath them. Expandable tools display a small triangle in the lower-right corner of the tool icon. Click and hold the tool button or right-click to see or select one of its hidden tools from the context menu. The default tool names and their corresponding shortcut keys are listed in Figure 1–19.

When you click a tool on the Tools panel, Photoshop selects the button and changes the options bar as necessary. When using a tool from the Tools panel, the mouse pointer changes to reflect the selected tool.

The Tools panel is organized by purpose. At the very top of the panel is a button to display the panel in two columns, followed underneath by the gripper bar. Below that, the selection tools appear, then the crop and slice tools, followed by retouching, painting, drawing and type, annotation, measuring, and navigation tools. At the bottom of the Tools panel are buttons to set colors, create a quick mask, and change screen modes.

As each tool is introduced throughout this book, its function and options bar characteristics will be explained further.

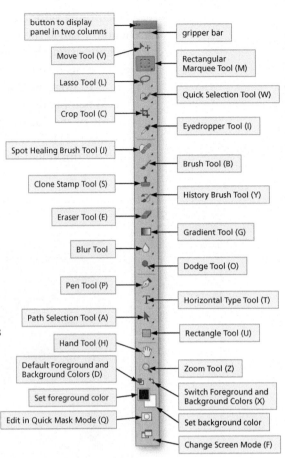

Figure 1–19

The Document Window

The **document window** is the windowed area within the workspace that displays the active file or image. The document window contains the document window tab, the display area, scroll bars, and a status bar (Figure 1–20).

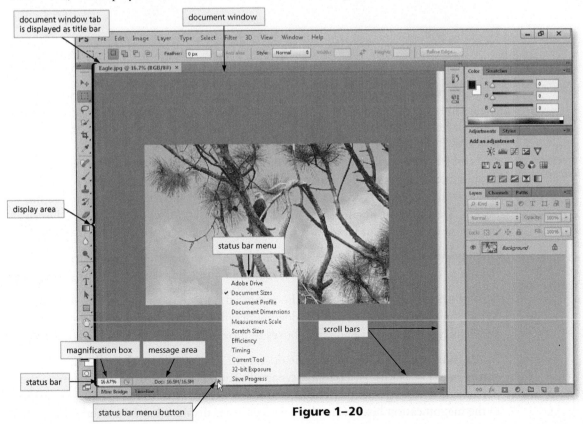

Figure 1–20

Document Window Tab When a file is open, Photoshop displays a **document window tab** at the top of the document window that shows the name of the file, the magnification, the color mode, and a Close button. If you have multiple files open, each has its own document window tab.

To **float** the document window in the display area, drag the document window tab. When the document window is floating, the document Window tab expands across the top of the document window and displays Minimize, Maximize, and Close buttons (Figure 1–21). To **dock** the document window again, or lock it in its previous location, drag the document window tab close to the options bar.

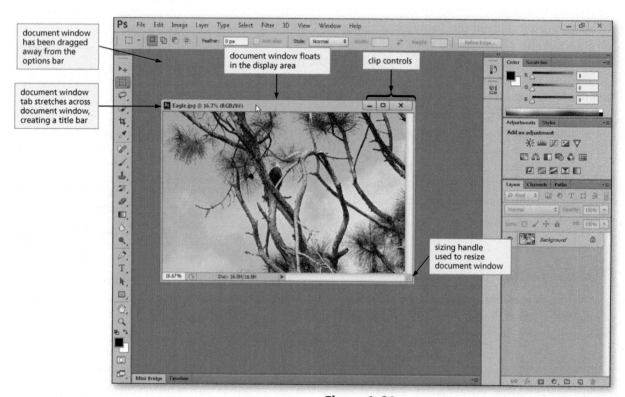

document window has been dragged away from the options bar

document window floats in the display area

clip controls

document window tab stretches across document window, creating a title bar

Eagle.jpg @ 16.7% (RGB/8#)

sizing handle used to resize document window

16.67%   Doc: 16.5M/16.5M

Figure 1–21

To **minimize** a document window, drag the document window tab away from the options bar so that the window floats, and then click the Minimize button. A minimized document window does not appear in the workspace; rather, it appears as a second Photoshop button on the Windows taskbar.

In Photoshop, a maximized document window fills the entire screen; you cannot see the menus or panels. To **maximize** a document window, drag the document window tab away from the options bar so that it floats, and then click the Maximize button. To return the document window to a floating state, click the Restore Down button on the document window title bar.

Display Area The **display area** is the portion of the document window that displays the photo or image. You perform most tool tasks and edit the photo in the display area.

Scroll Bars **Scroll bars** appear on the right and bottom of the document window. When the photo is bigger than the document window, the scroll bars become active and display scroll arrows and scroll boxes to move the image up, down, left, and right.

Status Bar Across the bottom of the document window, Photoshop displays the **status bar**. The status bar contains a magnification box. **Magnification** refers to the percentage of enlargement or reduction on the screen. For example, a 50% indication in the magnification box means the entire photo is displayed at 50 percent of its actual size. Changing the magnification does not change the size of the photo physically; it merely displays it on the screen at a different size. You can type a new percentage in the magnification box to display a different view of the photo.

Next to the magnification box is the **message area**. Messages can display information about the file size, the current tool, or the document dimensions. When you first start Photoshop, the message area displays information about the document size in storage.

On the right side of the status bar is the status bar menu button, which, when clicked, displays a status bar menu (Figure 1–20 on page PS 15). You use the status bar menu to change the message area or to change to other versions of the document.

Your installation of Photoshop might display rulers at the top and left of the document window. You will learn about rulers later in this chapter.

Panels

A **panel** is a collection of graphically displayed choices and commands related to a specific tool or feature, such as those involving colors, brushes, actions, or layers (Figure 1–22). Panels help you monitor and modify your work. Each panel displays a panel tab with the name of the panel and a panel menu button. When you click the panel menu button, also called the panel menu icon, Photoshop displays a context-sensitive panel menu that allows you to make changes to the panel. Some panels have a status bar across the bottom. A panel can display buttons, boxes, sliders, scroll bars, or drop-down lists.

BTW

Panels vs. Palettes
In previous versions of the Adobe Creative Suite, the panels were called palettes. In all of the CS6 applications, panels can be grouped, stacked, or docked in the workspace, just as palettes were.

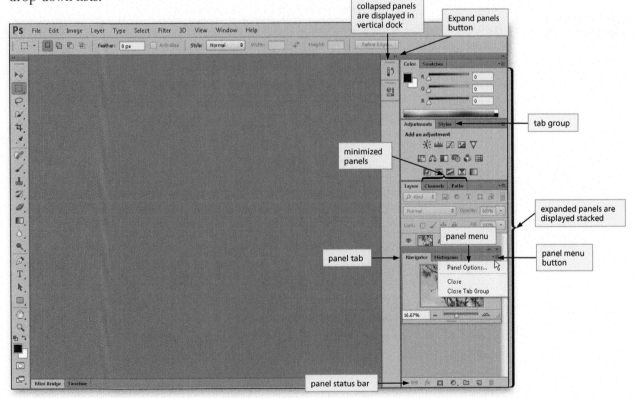

Figure 1–22

Several panels appear in the Essentials workspace. Some panels are expanded to display their contents, and are grouped by general purpose. A **panel group** or **tab group** displays several panels horizontally. The panel group is docked vertically on the right side of the workspace. Other open panels are displayed along the bottom or as icons or buttons in a vertical dock between the document window and the expanded panels. Panels are **collapsed** when they appear as an icon or button, or **expanded**

More Panel Options
If you want to display panels as buttons rather than as minimized or expanded pallets, right-click the panel tab, and then click Collapse to Icons on the context menu. A panel icon displays the name of the panel and its associated icon as a button.

Adobe Bridge
When organizing your photos into folders, or if you want to rate your photos, it might be more convenient to use Adobe Bridge CS6. See Appendix E, the Using Adobe Bridge CS6 appendix, for more information.

when they display their contents. Panels are **minimized** when they display only their tab. To collapse or expand a panel group, click the double arrow at the top of the panel or double-click its tab. To close a panel, click Close on the panel menu. To redisplay the panel, click the panel name on the Window menu or use a panel shortcut key.

You can arrange and reposition panels either individually or in groups. To move them individually, drag their tabs; to move a group, drag the area to the right of the tabs. To float a panel in the workspace, drag its tab outside of the vertical dock. You can create a **stack** of floating panels by dragging a panel tab to a location below another floating panel and docking it.

Sometimes you might want to hide all the panels to display more of the document window. To hide all panels, press the TAB key. Press the TAB key again to display the panels.

Photoshop comes with 29 panels, described in Table 1–1. As each panel is introduced throughout this book, its function and characteristics will be explained further.

Table 1–1 Photoshop Panels

Panel Name	Purpose
3D	To show the 3D layer components, settings, and options of the associated 3D file — available in Photoshop Extended only
Actions	To record, play, edit, and delete individual actions
Adjustments	To create nondestructive adjustment layers with color and tonal adjustments
Brush	To select preset brushes and design custom brushes
Brush Presets	To create, load, save, and manage preset brush tips
Channels	To create and manage channels
Character	To provide options for formatting characters
Character Styles	To create, load, save, and manage character styles
Clone Source	To set up and manipulate sample sources for the Clone Stamp Tools or Healing Brush Tools
Color	To display the color values for the current foreground and background colors
Histogram	To view tonal and color information about an image
History	To jump to any recent state of the image created during the current working session
Info	To display color values and document status information
Layer Comps	To display multiple compositions of a page layout
Layers	To show and hide layers, create new layers, and work with groups of layers
Mini Bridge	To assist in navigating folders and files, and to access other modules in the suite
Measurement Log	To record measurement data about a measured object — available in Photoshop Extended only
Navigator	To change the view or magnification of the photo using a thumbnail display
Notes	To insert, edit, and delete notes attached to files
Options	To display options and settings for the currently selected tool
Paragraph	To change the formatting of columns and paragraphs
Paragraph Styles	To create, load, save, and manage paragraph styles
Paths	To manipulate each saved path, the current work path, and the current vector mask
Properties	To display characteristics about the file and to assist in creating precise, editable pixel- and vector-based masks
Styles	To view and select preset styles
Swatches	To select and store colors that you need to use often
Timeline	To create a sequence of images or frames, displayed as motion over time
Tools	To select tools
Tool Presets	To save and reuse tool settings

File Types

A **file type** refers to the internal characteristics of digital files; it designates the operational or structural characteristics of a file. Each digital file, graphic or otherwise, is stored with specific kinds of formatting related to how the file appears on the screen, how it prints, and the software it uses to do so. Computer systems use the file type to help users open the file with the appropriate software. A **file extension**, in most computer systems, is a three- or four-letter suffix after the file name that distinguishes the file type. For example, Eagle.jpg refers to a file named Eagle with the extension and file type JPG. A period separates the file name and its extension. When you are exploring files on your system, you might see the file extensions as part of the file name, or you might see a column of information about file types.

Graphic files are created and stored using many different file types and extensions. The type of file sometimes is determined by the hardware or software used to create the file. Other times, the user has a choice in applying a file type and makes the decision based on the file size, the intended purpose of the graphic file — such as whether the file is to be used on the Web — or the desired color mode.

Several common graphic file types are listed in Table 1–2.

Table 1–2 Graphic File Types		
File Extension	**File Type**	**Description**
BMP	Bitmap	BMP is a standard Windows image format used on DOS and Windows-compatible computers. BMP format supports many different color modes.
EPS	Encapsulated PostScript	EPS files can contain both bitmap and vector graphics. Almost all graphics, illustration, and page-layout programs support the EPS format, which can be used to transfer PostScript artwork between applications.
GIF	Graphics Interchange Format	GIF commonly is used to display graphics and images on Web pages. It is a compressed format designed to minimize file size and electronic transfer time.
JPG or JPEG	Joint Photographic Experts Group	JPG files commonly are used to display photographs on Web pages. JPG format supports many different color modes. JPG retains all color information in an RGB image, unlike GIF format. Most digital cameras produce JPG files.
PDF	Portable Document Format	PDF is a flexible file format based on the PostScript imaging model that is cross-platform and cross-application. PDF files accurately display and preserve fonts, page layouts, and graphics. PDF files can contain electronic document search and navigation features such as hyperlinks.
PSD	Photoshop Document	PSD format is the default file format in Photoshop and the only format that supports all Photoshop features. Other Adobe applications can import PSD files directly and preserve many Photoshop features because of the tight integration among Adobe products.
RAW	Photoshop Raw	RAW format is a flexible file format used for transferring images between applications and computer platforms. There are no pixel or file size restrictions in this format. Documents saved in the Photoshop Raw format cannot contain layers.
TIF or TIFF	Tagged Image File Format	TIF is a flexible bitmap image format supported by almost all paint, image-editing, and page-layout applications. This format often is used for files that are to be exchanged between applications or computer platforms. Most desktop scanners can produce TIF images.

BTW

File Extensions
The default setting for file extensions in Photoshop is to use a lowercase three-letter extension. If you want to change the extension, do the following: Press SHIFT+CTRL+S to access the Save As dialog box. In the File name text box, type the file name, period, and new extension within quotation marks. Click the Save button.

BTW

File Name Characters
A file name can have a maximum of 260 characters, including spaces. The only invalid characters are the backslash (\), forward slash (/), colon (:), asterisk (*), question mark (?), quotation mark ("), less than symbol (<), greater than symbol (>), and vertical bar (|).

BTW

Saving Files
While Photoshop is saving your file, it briefly displays a Working in Background shape. In addition, your USB drive might have a light that flashes during the save process. The new file name appears on the document window tab.

Saving a Photo

As you make changes to a file in Photoshop, the computer stores it in memory. If you turn off the computer or if you lose electrical power, the file in memory is lost. If you plan to use the photo later, you must save it on a storage device such as a USB flash drive, hard disk, or in cloud storage.

While you are editing, to preserve the most features such as layers, effects, masks, and styles, Photoshop recommends that you save photos in the **PSD format**. PSD, which stands for Photoshop Document Format, is the default file format for files created from scratch in Photoshop, and supports files up to 2 gigabytes (GB) in size. The PSD format also maximizes portability among other Adobe versions and applications.

To Save a File in the PSD Format

The following steps save the photo on a USB flash drive using the file name, Eagle Edited. In addition to saving in the PSD format, you will save the photo with a new file name and in a new location, so that the original photo is preserved in case you need to start again. Even though you have yet to edit the photo, it is a good practice to save a copy of the file on your personal storage device early in the process. A **folder** is a specific location on a storage medium, represented visually by a file folder icon. Folders are good ways to organize files. In this book, you will create a folder for each chapter.

1

- With a USB flash drive connected to one of the computer's USB ports, click File on the Application bar to display the File menu (Figure 1–23).

Q&A
Do I have to save to a USB flash drive?

No. You can save to any device or folder.

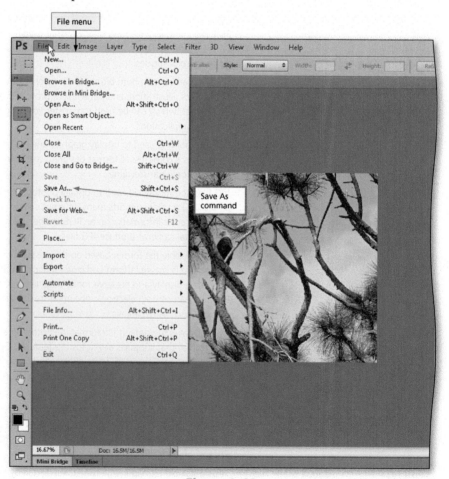

Figure 1–23

2

- Click Save As to display the Save As dialog box.

- Type `Eagle Edited` in the File name text box to change the file name. Do not press the ENTER key after typing the file name.

- Click the Save in box arrow to display the list of available drives (Figure 1–24).

 Q&A

What if my USB flash drive has a different name or letter?

It is very likely that your USB flash drive will have a different name and drive letter and be connected to a different port. Verify that the device in your list is correct.

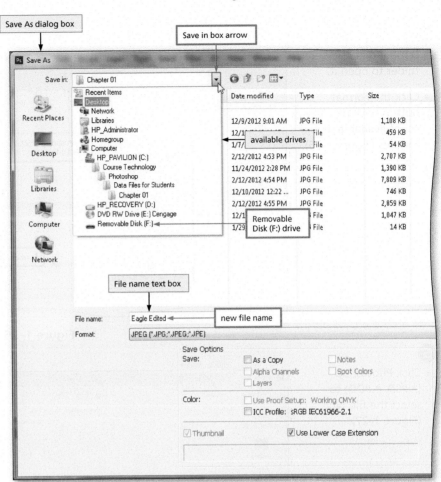

Figure 1–24

3

- Click Removable Disk (F:), or the name of your USB flash drive, in the list of available storage devices to select that drive as the new save location.

- Click the Create New Folder button on the Save As dialog box toolbar to create a new folder on the selected storage device.

- When the new folder appears, type `Chapter 01` to change the name of the folder, and then press the ENTER key (Figure 1–25).

Q&A

Why is my list of drives arranged and named differently?

The size of the Save As dialog box and your computer's configuration determine how the list is displayed and how the drives are named.

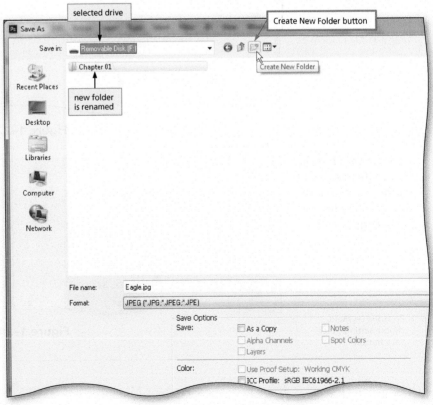

Figure 1–25

● Double-click the new folder to open it.

● Click the Format button to display the list of available file formats (Figure 1–26).

Do I have to use the same file name?

It is good practice to identify the relationship of this photo to the original by using at least part of the original file name with some notation about its status.

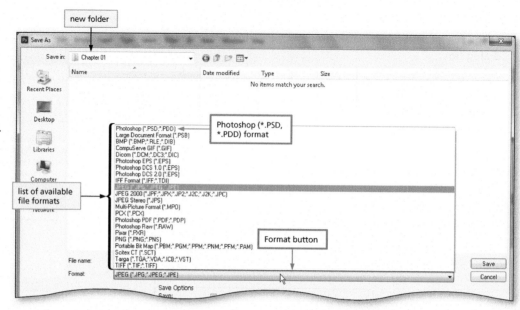

Figure 1–26

❺

● Click Photoshop (*.PSD, *.PDD) to select the file type (Figure 1–27).

What is PDD?

The **PDD format** is used with images created by Photo Deluxe and other software packages. Some older digital cameras produce files with a PDD extension as well.

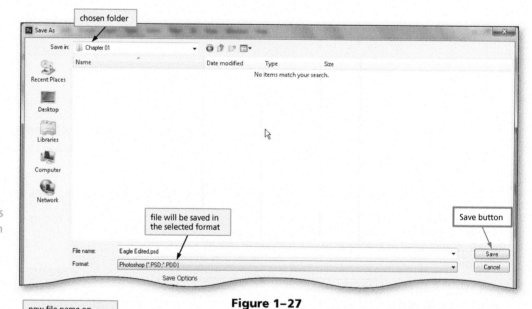

Figure 1–27

❻

● Click the Save button to save the document on the selected drive with the new file name (Figure 1–28).

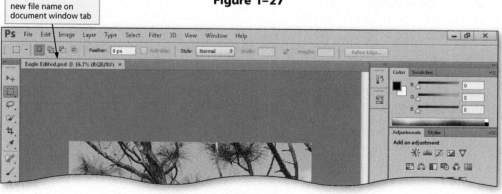

Other Ways

1. Press SHIFT+CTRL+S, choose settings, click Save button

Figure 1–28

For a detailed example of this procedure using the Mac operating system, refer to the steps on pages APP 79 through APP 80 of the For Mac Users appendix.

Viewing Photos

Photoshop allows you to view photos in many different ways, by adjusting the document window and by using different tools and panels. Using good navigation techniques to view images can help you edit the details of a photo or check for problems. For example, you might want to zoom in on a specific portion of the photo or move to a different location in a large photo. You might want to use a ruler to measure certain portions of the photo. Or you might want to view the image without the distraction of the panels and menu. Zooming, navigating, scrolling, and changing the screen mode are some ways to view the document window and its photo.

Zooming

To make careful edits in a photo, you sometimes need to change the magnification, or **zoom**. Zooming allows you to focus on certain parts of the photo, such as a specific person in a crowd scene or details in a complicated picture. A magnification of 100% means the photo is displayed at its actual size. Zooming in enlarges the percentage of magnification of the photo; zooming out reduces the magnification. Note that zooming does not change the size of the photo; it merely changes the appearance of the photo in the document window.

The Zoom Tool button displays a magnifying glass icon on the Tools panel. You also can press the z key to select the Zoom Tool. Choosing one over the other is a matter of personal choice. Most people use the shortcut key. Others sometimes choose the button because of its proximity to the mouse pointer at the time.

When you use the Zoom tool, each click magnifies the image to the next preset percentage. When positioned in the photo, the Zoom Tool mouse pointer displays a magnifying glass, with either a plus sign, indicating an increase in magnification, or a minus sign, indicating a decrease in magnification. Right-clicking with the Zoom Tool in the photo displays a context menu with options to zoom in or zoom out, among others.

Figure 1–29 displays the Zoom Tool options bar, with buttons to zoom in and out. Other options include check boxes used when working with multiple photos, displaying the actual pixels, fitting the entire photo on the screen, filling the screen, and displaying the photo at its print size.

BTW

Ways to Zoom
There are many ways to zoom, including the Zoom tool, the Zoom buttons, the magnification box, and the Navigator panel. How you zoom depends on your personal preference and whether you want to change the current tool.

BTW

Scrubby Zoom
If you click the Scrubby Zoom check box, you can drag to the left in the image to zoom out, or to the right to zoom in.

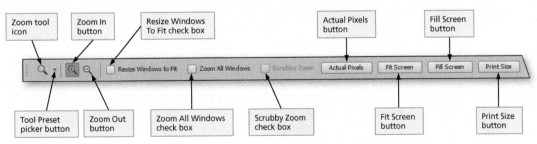

Figure 1–29

To Use the Zoom Tool

The following steps zoom in on the eagle for careful editing later in the chapter.

1

- Click the Zoom Tool button on the Tools panel to select the Zoom Tool.

- Move the mouse pointer into the document window to display the magnifying glass mouse pointer (Figure 1–30).

Why does my mouse pointer display a minus sign?

Someone may have previously zoomed out and the setting has carried over. Click the Zoom In button on the options bar.

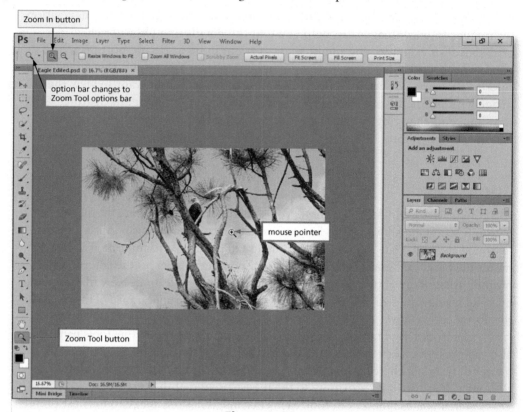

Zoom In button

option bar changes to Zoom Tool options bar

mouse pointer

Zoom Tool button

Figure 1–30

2

- Click the eagle three times to zoom in (Figure 1–31).

Experiment

- On the options bar, click the Zoom In button and then click the photo. Click the Zoom Out button and then click the photo. ALT+click the photo to zoom in the opposite direction from the options bar setting. Zoom to 50% magnification.

Other Ways

1. Press Z, click document window

2. Press CTRL+PLUS SIGN (+) or CTRL+MINUS SIGN (-)

3. On View menu, click Zoom In or Zoom Out

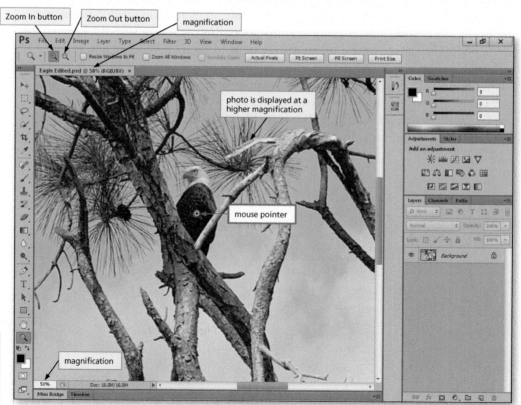

Zoom In button

Zoom Out button

magnification

photo is displayed at a higher magnification

mouse pointer

magnification

Figure 1–31

The Navigator Panel

Another convenient way to zoom and move around the photo is to use the Navigator panel. The Navigator panel (Figure 1–32) is used to change the view of your document window using a thumbnail display. To display the Navigator panel, select Navigator from the Window menu.

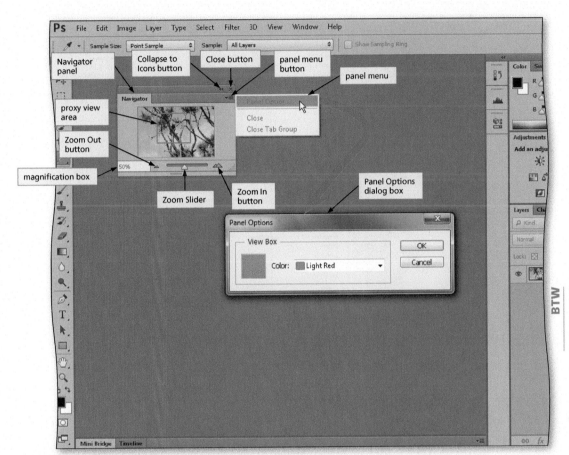

Figure 1–32

The rectangle with the red border in the Navigator panel is called the **proxy view area** or **view box**, which outlines the currently viewable area in the window. Dragging the proxy view area changes the portion of the photo that is displayed in the document window. In the lower portion of the Navigator panel, you can type in the desired magnification, or you can use the slider or buttons to increase or decrease the magnification.

In Figure 1–32, the Navigator panel menu appears when you click the panel menu button. The Panel Options command displays the Panel Options dialog box.

BTW

Moving Panels
If you want to move a panel to the workspace, as is shown in Figure 1-32, simply drag the panel tab.

BTW

Quick Reference
For a table that lists how to complete the tasks covered in this book using the mouse, menus, context menus and keyboard, see the Quick Reference Summary at the back of the book or visit the student companion site located at www.cengagebrain.com.

To Use the Navigator Panel

The following steps display and use the Navigator panel to reposition the view of the photo using the proxy view area.

1

● Click Window on the Application bar to display the Window menu (Figure 1–33).

Q&A

What two panels are already on the vertical dock of panels?

In the Essentials workspace, the History panel and Properties panel appear on the dock.

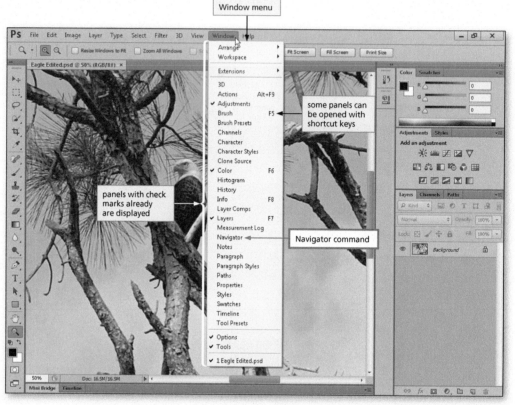

Figure 1–33

2

● Click Navigator on the Window menu to display the Navigator panel (Figure 1–34).

Q&A

Why would I choose the Navigator panel over other methods of moving around the screen?

When you are using a different tool on the Tools panel, such as a text tool or brush tool, it is easier to use the Navigator panel to zoom in or out and move around in the photo. That way, you do not have to change to the Zoom Tool, perform the zoom, and then change back to your editing tool.

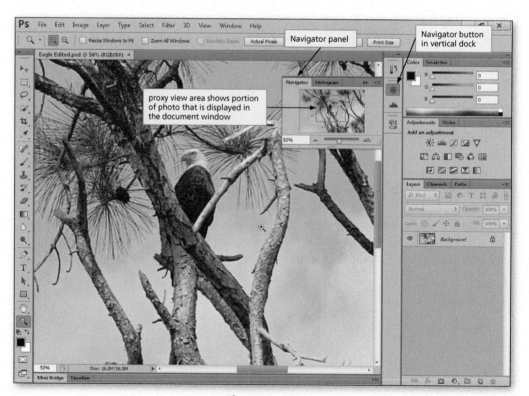

Figure 1–34

3

- Drag the proxy view area on the Navigator Panel to display the upper-right portion of the photo (Figure 1–35).

🔍 **Experiment**

- Drag the proxy view area to display different portions of the photo. Drag the Zoom Slider and try clicking the Zoom In and Zoom Out buttons on the Navigator panel. When you are finished, return to 50% magnification, and drag the proxy view area to display the upper-right portion of the photo.

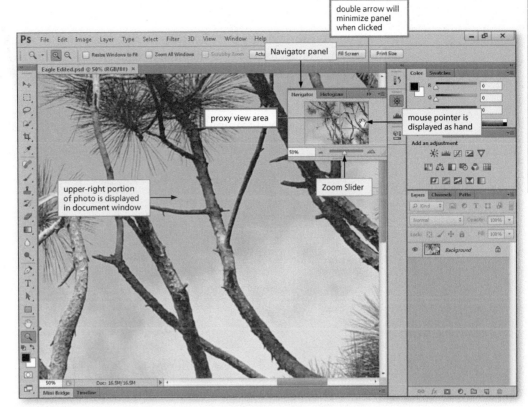

Figure 1–35

To Minimize the Navigator Panel

The following step minimizes the Navigator panel so that it is displayed as a button in the vertical dock of buttons. In the right portion of the panel's title bar, the double arrow, sometimes called the Collapse to Icons button, minimizes a panel.

1

- Click the double arrow at the top of the Navigator panel (Figure 1–36).

Q&A

How would I move or close the panel?

To move the panel, drag the panel tab. To close the panel, click Close on the panel menu, or if the panel is floating, click the panel's Close button.

Figure 1–36

Other Ways

1. On vertical dock, click Navigator button

The Hand Tool

You also can use the Hand Tool to move around in the photo if the photo has been magnified to be larger than the document window. To use the Hand Tool, click the Hand Tool button on the Tools panel, and then drag in the display area of the document window.

The Hand Tool options bar (Figure 1–37) displays boxes and buttons to assist you in scrolling and manipulating the document window.

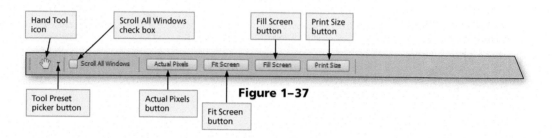

Figure 1–37

To Use the Hand Tool

The following step uses the Hand Tool to view a different part of the photo.

1

- Click the Hand Tool button on the Tools panel to select the Hand Tool.

- Drag in the document window to display the center portion of the photo (Figure 1–38).

What is the other tool grouped with the Hand Tool?

Grouped with the Hand Tool is the Rotate View Tool. It is used to rotate the entire image, nondestructively, for fine editing.

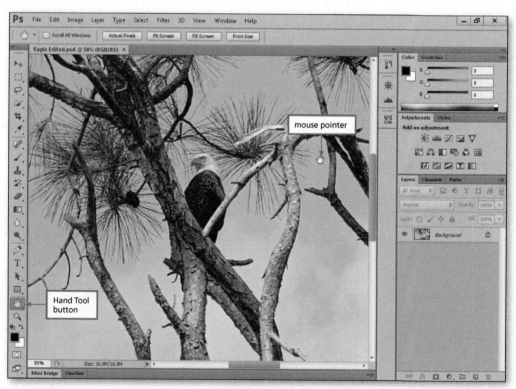

Figure 1–38

Other Ways

1. Press H, drag photo

To Change the Magnification

The following steps use the Magnification box on the status bar to change the magnification.

1
• Double-click the Magnification box on the status bar to select the current magnification (Figure 1–39).

magnification selected in Magnification box

status bar

Figure 1–39

2
• Type 20 and then press the ENTER key to change the magnification (Figure 1–40).

photo is displayed at new magnification

magnification is changed

Figure 1–40

Other Ways

1. On Navigator panel, type percentage in Magnification box

To Display Rulers

To make careful edits in a photo, sometimes it is necessary to use precise measurements in addition to zooming and navigating. In these cases, you should change the Photoshop document window to view the rulers. **Rulers** appear on the top and left sides of the document window. Rulers help you position images or elements precisely. As you move your mouse pointer over a photo, markers on the ruler display the mouse pointer's position.

The following steps display the rulers in the document window.

1
- Click View on the Application bar to display the View menu (Figure 1–41).

Q&A What unit of measurement do the rulers use?

Rulers display inches by default, but you can right-click a ruler to change the increment to pixels, centimeters, or other units of measurement.

Figure 1–41

2
- Click Rulers to display the rulers in the document window (Figure 1–42).

Q&A Is the photo really 42 × 26 inches?

The resolution from photos taken with digital cameras is measured in **megapixels** or millions of pixels. The more megapixels you have, the better the photo resolution; however, it translates to very large print sizes. You will resize the photo later in the chapter.

Figure 1–42

Other Ways
1. Press CTRL+R

Screen Modes

To change the way the panels, bars, and document window appear, Photoshop includes three **screen modes**, or ways to view the document window. The Change Screen Mode button is located at the bottom of the Tools panel (Figure 1–42) and toggles among the screen modes. Standard screen mode displays the Application bar, document window, scroll bars, and visible panels. Full screen mode displays only the image and rulers, if they are visible, on a black background. Full screen mode with menu enlarges the document window to fill the workspace with no title bar, status bar, or scroll bars. A fourth way to view the screen is to hide the panels using the TAB key. Pressing the TAB key again redisplays the panels.

Choosing a mode depends on what you are trying to accomplish. While editing a single photo, standard screen mode may be the best, especially for beginners. If you are working on multiple files, screen space is at a premium and you might want to use one of the full screen modes.

Editing the Photo

Editing, or making corrections and changes to a photo, involves a wide variety of tasks such as changing or emphasizing the focus of interest, recoloring portions of the photo, correcting defects, adding new artwork, or changing the file type for specific purposes. Editing also is called **post-processing**, because it includes actions you take after the picture has been processed by the camera or scanner.

Table 1–3 suggests typical categories and types of edits you might perform on photos; there are many others. These edits commonly overlap, and, when performed in combination, they can even create new editing varieties. You will learn more about edits as you work through the chapters in this book.

Table 1–3 Photo Edits	
Category	**Types of Edits**
Transformations	Cropping, slicing, changing the aspect, rotating, leveling, mirroring, warping, skewing, distorting, flipping, and changing the perspective
Enhancements and Layering	Filters, layers, clones, borders, artwork, text, animation, painting, morphing, ordering, styles, masks, cutaways, selections, depth perception, anti-aliasing, moves, shapes, rasterizing
Color	Correction, contrast, blending, modes and systems, separations, screening, levels, ruling, trapping, matching, black and white
Correction	Sharpening, red-eye, tears, correcting distortion, retouching, reducing noise, blur, dodge, burn
File Type	Camera raw, print, Web, animated images
Resolution	Resampling, resizing, collinear editing, interpolation, editing pixel dimensions and document sizes

Editing the Eagle Edited photo will involve three steps. First, you will crop the photo to remove excessive background. Next, you will add a border and stroke it with color. Finally, you will resize the photo to fit the intended use and size requirements, inserting text for the postcard.

BTW

Screen Modes
You also can use the View menu to change Screen Modes as well as pressing the F key on the keyboard.

BTW

Cropping
To evaluate an image for cropping, make a printout. Using two L shapes cut from paper, form a size and shape rectangle to isolate a portion of the image. Draw lines on the printout to use as a guide when cropping in Photoshop.

BTW

When Not to Crop
At times, cropping the photo is not desirable. For example, when you are working with older photos that convey a specific setting or location, the background might contain details that help evoke the setting, such as furniture, clothing worn by people in the background, or toys or vehicles from a particular time period. Retaining these details can help viewers recall the time and place of the original photo.

Determine how to edit the photo to highlight the theme.
You always should perform editing with design principles in mind. Look at your photo carefully. Are there parts that detract from the central figure? Would the theme be illustrated better by only displaying a portion of the photo? If you want to emphasize a single object on a fairly solid background, you might need to crop, or trim, extraneous space around the object. Decide which parts of the photo portray your message and which parts are visual clutter.

- Use the rule of thirds to position visual lines.
- Crop the photo to remove excess background.
- Rotate the photo if necessary.

BTW

Rotate and Crop
You can rotate the image around the cropping area by moving the mouse pointer just outside of one of the cropping handles. When the mouse pointer changes to a curved arrow, drag to rotate. If you are using the Perspective Crop Tool, the rotation mouse pointer rotates the crop area rather than the image.

BTW

Straighten and Crop
If you click the Straighten button on the options bar, you can drag a line in the crop area. The image will rotate to match the angle of the line. This is useful when the image is out of alignment. You should try to drag across a natural line within the image.

BTW

Trimming vs. Cropping
The Trim command also crops an image by removing unwanted portions of the photo, but in a different way from the Crop Tool. The Trim command, on the Image menu, trims surrounding transparent pixels or background pixels of the color you specify.

Cropping

The first step in editing the eagle photo is to **crop**, or cut away, some of the extra sky and branches so the photo focuses on the eagle. Photographers try to compose and capture images full-frame, which means the object of interest fills the dimensions of the photo. When that is not possible, photographers and graphic artists crop the photo either to create an illusion of full-frame, to fit unusual shapes in layouts, or to make the image more dramatic. From a design point of view, sometimes it is necessary to crop a photo to straighten an image, remove distracting elements, or simplify the subject. The goal of most cropping is to make the most important feature in the original photo stand out. Cropping sometimes is used to convert a digital photo's proportions to those typical for traditional photos.

Most photographers and graphic artists use the **rule of thirds**, also called the principle of thirds, when placing the focus of interest. Imagine that the scene is divided into thirds both vertically and horizontally. The intersections of these imaginary lines suggest four positions for placing the focus of interest. The position you select depends on the subject and its presentation in the photo. For instance, there might be a shadow, path, or visual line you wish to include. In the case of moving objects, you generally should leave space in front of them, into which they theoretically can move. When eyes are involved, it is better to leave space on the side toward which the person or animal is looking, so they do not appear to look directly out of the setting.

Because the eagle photo will be used on a postcard, the photo's orientation should be **landscape**, or horizontal. In most cases, you should try to crop to a rectangular shape with an approximate short-side to long-side ratio of 5:8. Sometimes called the **golden rectangle**, a 5:8 ratio emulates natural geometric forms such as flowers, leaves, shells, and butterflies. Most digital cameras take pictures with a similar ratio.

The Crop Tool allows you to select the portion of the photo you wish to retain. Photoshop automatically displays handles and a rule of thirds overlay for further adjustments, if necessary. Then, when you press the ENTER key, the rest of the photo is cropped, or removed. You can choose to permanently delete the cropped pixels on the options bar. The cropping handles continue to appear until you choose another tool.

The Crop Tool is grouped with the Perspective Crop Tool. In a **perspective crop**, when you drag one of the cropping handles, the other handles stay in place, which creates a distortion.

The Crop Tool options bar displays boxes and buttons to assist cropping activities (Figure 1–43). You can specify the aspect ratio, or the exact height and width of the crop. The options bar also contains buttons to rotate or straighten the photo, as well as a View button menu to change the overlay grid.

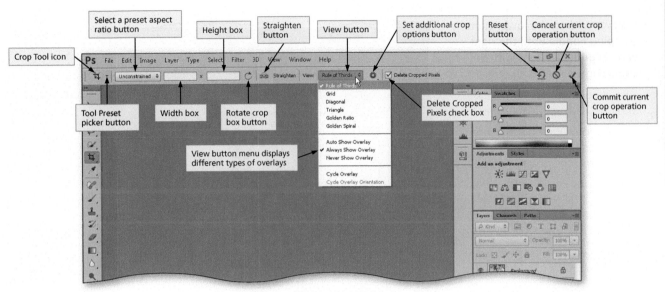

Figure 1–43

To Crop a Photo

To make the eagle the focus of the photo, the extra background will be cropped to provide a line of sight to the left, keeping as much of the tree as possible. The following steps crop the photo of the eagle.

1

- Click the Crop Tool button on the Tools panel to select the Crop Tool.

- Click the photo to display the rule of thirds grid.

- If necessary, click the Delete Cropped Pixels check box on the options bar, so that it displays a check mark (Figure 1–44).

Experiment

- On the options bar, click the View button, and then, one at a time, choose different overlays. Click the photo to display the overlay each time. When you are finished, click the View button again and then click Rule of Thirds.

Figure 1–44

- SHIFT+CTRL+drag the lower-right cropping handle until the right vertical gridline aligns with the eagle (Figure 1–45).

Why should I hold down the SHIFT and CTRL keys while dragging?

SHIFT+CTRL+dragging maintains the aspect ratio of both the grid overlay and the image.

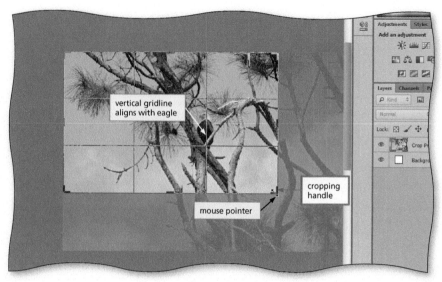

Figure 1–45

- Within the cropping area, drag the photo straight up, until the upper-right intersection of the grid is centered over the eagle (Figure 1–46).

What if I change my mind or make a mistake when cropping?

If you make a mistake while dragging the cropping area and want to start over, you can click the Cancel current crop operation button or press the ESC key, which cancels the selection. If you already have performed the crop and then change your mind, you have several choices. You can click the Undo command on the Edit menu, or you can press CTRL+Z to undo the last edit.

Figure 1–46

- Press the ENTER key to complete the crop (Figure 1–47).

🔍 **Experiment**

- If you want to practice cropping, drag a cropping handle again. After each crop, press CTRL+Z to undo the crop.

Other Ways

1. Press C, drag in photo, on options bar click 'Commit current crop operation' button

2. Select portion of image, on Image menu click Crop, press ENTER key

Figure 1–47

To Select the Default Tool Again

If you do not want to use the Crop Tool any longer, or you do not want to see the cropping handles, select any other tool on the Tools panel. The following step selects the default tool again, as you did at the beginning of the chapter.

1 On the Tools panel, click the Rectangular Marquee Tool button to select the tool.

Creating a Border

A **border** is a decorative edge on a photo or a portion of a photo. Photoshop provides many ways to create a border, ranging from simple color transformations around the edge of the photo to predefined decorated layers to stylized photo frames.

A border helps define the edge of the photo, especially when the photo might be set on colored paper or on a Web page with a background texture. A border visually separates the photo from the rest of the page, while focusing the viewer's attention. Rounded borders soften the images in a photo. Square borders are more formal. Decorative borders on a static photo can add interest and amusement but easily can detract from the focus on a busier photo. **Blended borders** are not a solid fill; rather, they blend a fill color from the outer edge toward the middle, sometimes providing a three-dimensional effect. A border that complements the photo in style, color, and juxtaposition is best. In the eagle photo, you will create a border using selections of 75 black pixels with 25 pixels of overlapping white. A **pixel** is an individual dot of light that is the basic unit used to create digital images.

BTW | **Selections**
When you select all, Photoshop displays the photo with a marquee around all four edges. The selection tools on the Tools panel also can help you make selections in the photo. The Rectangular Marquee, Lasso, Quick Selection, and Magic Wand tools will be discussed in Chapter 2.

> **Identify finishing touches that will further enhance the photo.**
> Adding a border or decorative frame around a photo sometimes can be an effective way to highlight or make the photo stand out on the page. A border should frame the subject, rather than become the subject. If a border is required by the customer or needed for layout placement, choose a color and width that neither overwhelms nor overlaps any detail in the photo. Using a border color that complements one of the colors already in the photo creates a strong, visually connected image. For more information about graphic design concepts, read Appendix B, Graphic Design Overview.

Plan Ahead

To Create a Selection

Specifying or isolating an area of your photo for editing is called making a **selection**. Selecting specific areas allows you to edit and apply special effects to portions of your image, while leaving the unselected areas untouched.

Selections can be simple shapes such as rectangles or ovals, or unusually shaped areas of a photo, outlining specific objects. Selections can be the entire photo or as small a portion as one pixel. A selection displays a marquee in Photoshop. A **marquee** is a flashing or pulsating border, sometimes called marching ants.

In the case of the Eagle Edited photo, you will make a selection around the edge of the photo to create a border. The steps on the next page select the photo.

1

- On the Application bar, click Select to display the Select menu (Figure 1–48).

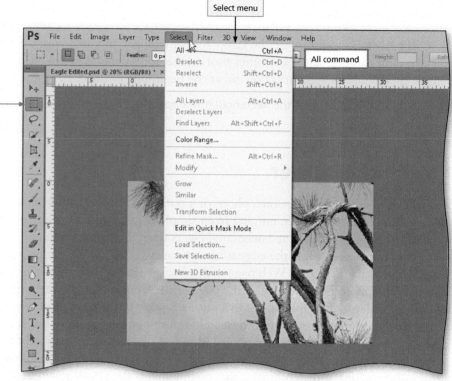

Figure 1–48

2

- On the Select menu, click the All command to display the selection marquee around the entire photo (Figure 1–49).

Q&A | Am I selecting all of the photo?
You are identifying the pixels along the edge of the image. Some commands apply to all of the pixels within the selection border, such as copying, deleting, or filling; other commands, such as stroking, apply only to the pixels along the edge of the selection.

Figure 1–49

Other Ways

1. To select all, press CTRL+A

To Stroke a Selection

A **stroke** is a colored outline or edge. When stroking a selection, you must specify the number of pixels to include in the stroke and the desired color. You also must decide whether to apply the stroke outside the selection border, inside the selection border, or centered on the selection border. Other stroke settings include blending modes and opacity, which you will learn about in a later chapter. The following steps stroke a selection.

1

• With the photograph still selected, click Edit on the Application bar to display the Edit menu (Figure 1–50).

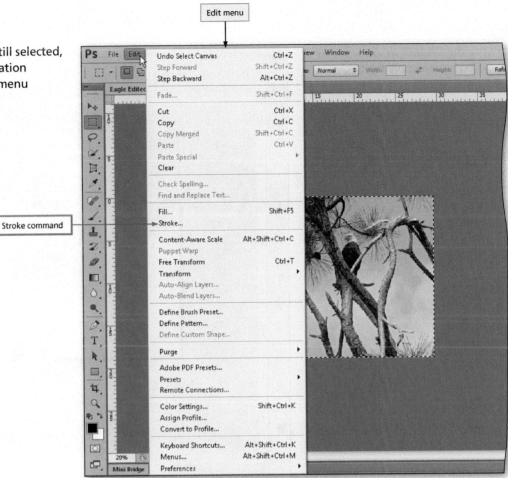

Figure 1–50

2

• Click Stroke to display the Stroke dialog box.

• Type   75   in the Width box (Figure 1–51).

Q&A

Do I need to select a color?

No, the default value is the foreground color, black. If your foreground color is not black, click the Cancel button, press the D key to choose the default colors and start again with Step 1.

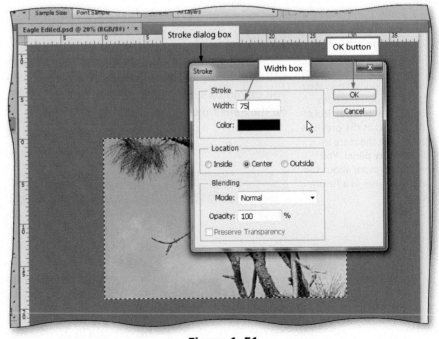

Figure 1–51

3

- Click the OK button in the Stroke dialog box to apply the stroke (Figure 1–52).

Q&A

What does the asterisk mean in the document window tab?

The asterisk means you have made changes to the photo since your last save. Once you save the file, the asterisk no longer is displayed.

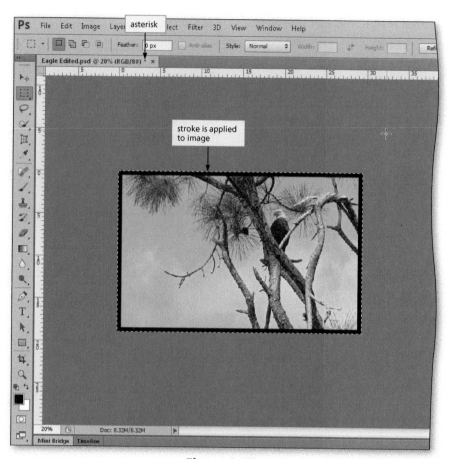

Figure 1–52

BTW

Reviewing Your Edits
Each edit or state of the photo is recorded sequentially in the History panel. If you want to step back through the edits or go back to a particular state, such as the previous crop, click the state in the History panel. You will learn more about the History panel in a future chapter.

Modifying Selections

You can modify the selection in several different ways. In the eagle photo, you will modify the selection border by increasing the number of pixels along the border so you can add a second color at that location. Table 1–4 displays the Modify commands on the Select menu.

Table 1–4 Modify Commands	
Type of Modification	**Result**
Border	This command allows you to select a width of pixels, from 1 to 200, to be split evenly on either side of the existing selection marquee.
Smooth	This command allows you to select a number of pixels in a radius around the selection. Photoshop adds or removes pixels in that radius to smooth sharp corners and jagged lines, reducing patchiness.
Expand	The border is increased by a number of pixels from 1 to 100.
Contract	The border is decreased by a number of pixels from 1 to 100.
Feather	This command creates a feather edge with a width from 0 to 250 pixels.

To Modify a Selection

The following steps modify the selection by changing the border selection area.

1

- On the Application bar, click Select, and then point to Modify to display the Modify submenu (Figure 1–53).

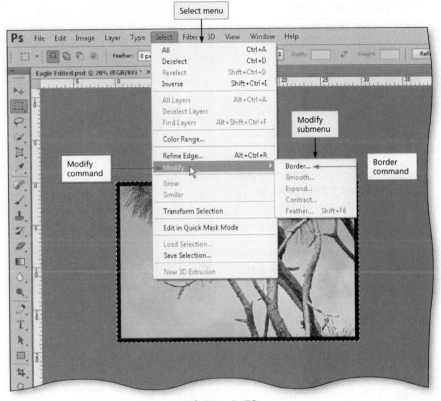

Figure 1–53

2

- Click Border on the Modify submenu to display the Border Selection dialog box.

Q&A Could I use the Contract command to contract the selection?

No, you must specify the border first. The Contract command is **grayed out**, or **unavailable**, so you cannot select it, before choosing the Border command.

- Type 50 in the Width box to create a border selection on each side of the marquee (Figure 1–54).

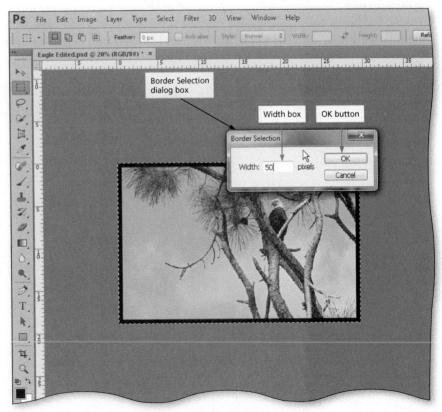

Figure 1–54

● Click the OK button in the Border Selection dialog box to define the selection (Figure 1–55).

Q&A

My display shows two marquees around the photo. Did I do something wrong?

No. Your version of Photoshop might be using a different screen mode or resolution.

Experiment

● To practice smoothing the border, click the Select menu, point to Modify, and then click Smooth. Enter a value in the Sample Radius box and then click the OK button. Notice the change in the marquee. Press CTRL+Z to undo the Smooth command.

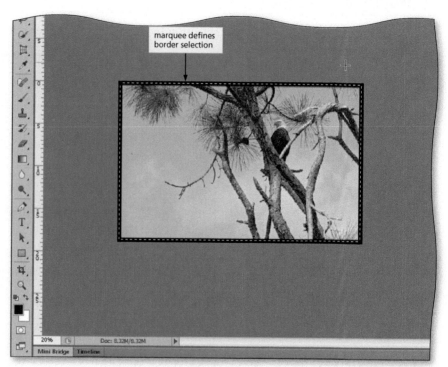

marquee defines border selection

Figure 1–55

To Switch Foreground and Background Colors

On the Tools panel, the default foreground color is black and the default background color is white. Photoshop uses the default foreground color in strokes, fills, and brushes — in the previous steps when you stroked, the pixels became black. To create a rounded gray border, you will use a white, overlapping stroke. The following step switches the foreground and background colors so white is over black.

● Click the Switch Foreground and Background Colors button to reverse the colors (Figure 1–56).

white over black

Switch Foreground and Background Colors button

Switch Foreground and Background Colors (X)

Other Ways

1. Press X

Figure 1–56

To Stroke Again

To create the gray border, you will stroke the selection again, this time with white, and using a narrower width.

1 Click Edit on the Application bar to display the Edit menu.

2 Click Stroke to display the Stroke dialog box.

3 Type 25 in the Width box to set the width of the stroke.

4 Click the OK button to apply the stroke (Figure 1–57).

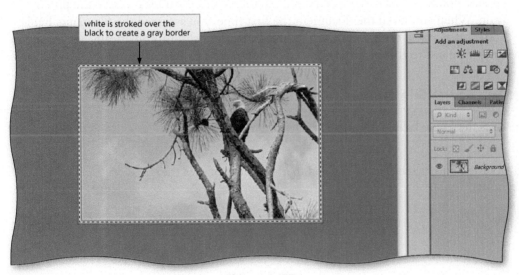

white is stroked over the black to create a gray border

Figure 1–57

To Deselect

Because the border is complete, you should remove the selection indicator, or **deselect** it, so the marquee no longer appears. The following step removes the selection.

1
- Click Select on the Application bar, and then click Deselect to remove the selection (Figure 1–58).

selection no longer is displayed

Figure 1–58

Other Ways	**PS**
1. Press CTRL+D	

To Switch Foreground and Background Colors Again

The following step switches the foreground and background colors back to black over white.

 On the Tools panel, click the Switch Foreground and Background Colors button again to reverse the colors.

Saving a Photo with the Same File Name

Because you have made many edits to the photo, it is a good idea to save the photo again. When you saved the document the first time, you assigned the file name, Eagle Edited. When you use the following procedure, Photoshop automatically assigns the same file name to the photo, and it is stored in the same location.

To Save a File with the Same File Name

The following step saves the Eagle Edited file with the changes you made.

- On the Application bar, click File to display the File menu, and then click Save to save the photo with the same file name.

Other Ways

1. Press CTRL+S

To Close a File

The following step closes the Eagle Edited document window without quitting Photoshop.

- Click the Close button on the document window tab (Figure 1–59) to close the document window and the image file.

- If Photoshop displays a dialog box asking you to save again, click the No button.

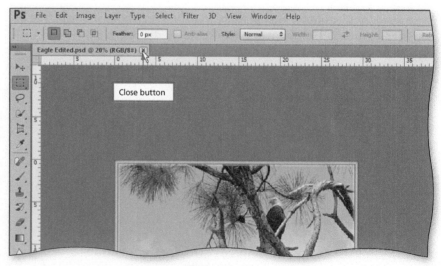

Figure 1–59

 For a detailed example of this procedure using the Mac operating system, refer to the steps on page APP 81 of the For Mac Users appendix.

Other Ways

1. Press CTRL+W   2. On File menu, click Close

Break Point: If you wish to take a break, this is a good place to do so. You can quit Photoshop now. To resume at a later time, start Photoshop, and continue following the steps from this location forward.

Opening a Recent File in Photoshop

Once you have created and saved a document, you may need to retrieve it from your storage medium. For example, you might want to edit the photo further or print it. Photoshop maintains a list of recently used files to give you quick access to them for further editing. The list is maintained from session to session.

To Open a Recent File

Earlier in this chapter, you saved your edited photo on a USB flash drive, using the file name, Eagle Edited. The following steps open the Eagle Edited file using the Open Recent list.

1

- Click File on the Application bar and then point to Open Recent to display the Open Recent submenu (Figure 1–60).

Q&A

What does the Clear Recent File List command do?

If you click the Clear Recent File List command, your Recent list will be emptied. To open a file, you then would have to click Open on the File menu and navigate to the location of the file.

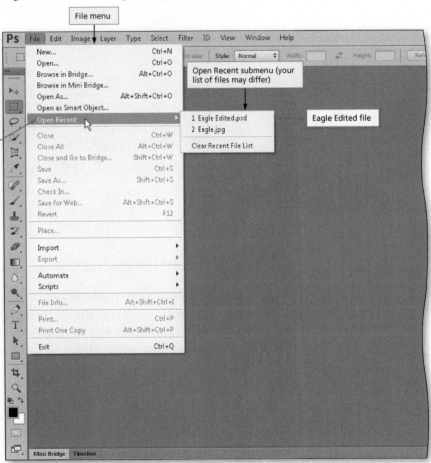

Figure 1–60

2

• Click the Eagle Edited file to open it.

• If necessary, change the magnification to 25% (Figure 1–61).

Eagle Edited photo again is displayed

25% magnification

Figure 1–61

BTW

Document Size
Cropping reduces the storage size of the document, which is the size of the saved, flattened file in Adobe Photoshop format. The document window status bar displays the new document size after cropping.

Changing Image Sizes

Sometimes it is necessary to resize an image to fit within certain space limitations. **Resize** means to scale or change the dimensions of the photo. Zooming in or dragging a corner of the document window to change the size is not the same as actually changing the dimensions of the photo. Resizing in a page layout program, such as Publisher, QuarkXPress, or InDesign, merely stretches the pixels. In Photoshop, resizing means adding to or subtracting from the number of pixels.

Photoshop uses a mathematical process called **interpolation**, or **resampling**, when it changes the number of pixels. The program interpolates or calculates how to add new pixels to the photo to match those already there. Photoshop samples the pixels and reproduces them to determine where and how to enlarge or reduce the photo.

When you resize a photo, you must consider many things, such as the type of file, the width, the height, and the resolution. **Resolution** refers to the number of pixels per inch, printed on a page or displayed on a monitor. Not all photos lend themselves to resizing. Some file types lose quality and sharpness when resized. Fine details cannot be interpolated from low-resolution photos. Resizing works best for small changes where exact dimensions are critical. If possible, it usually is better to take a photo at the highest feasible resolution or rescan the image at a higher resolution rather than resize it later.

In those cases where it is impossible to create the photo at the proper size, Photoshop helps you resize or **scale** your photos for print or online media.

Plan
Ahead

Prepare for publication.
Keep in mind the golden rectangle of well-designed photos and the limitations of your space. Resize the photo. Print a copy and evaluate its visual appeal. If you are going to publish the photo to the Web, determine the following:

- Typical download speed of your audience

- Browser considerations

- Number of colors

- File type

Finally, save the photo with a descriptive name indicating its completion.

To Resize the Image

Because the eagle photo will be printed on a postcard at a specific size, you will change the height to 4 inches. The following steps resize the image to create a custom-sized photo for printing.

1

- Click Image on the Application bar to display the Image menu (Figure 1–62).

Q&A What is the difference between Image Size and Canvas size?

Increasing the canvas size adds space around an existing image. Decreasing the canvas size is the same as cropping.

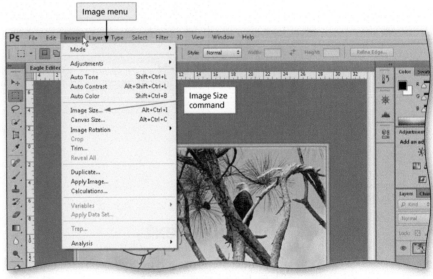

Figure 1–62

2

- Click Image Size to display the Image Size dialog box.

- In the Document Size area, double-click the value in the Height box and then type   4   to replace the previous value (Figure 1–63).

Q&A Why did the width change?

When you change the width or height, Photoshop automatically adjusts the other dimension to maintain the proportions of the photo. Your exact width might differ slightly depending on how closely you cropped the original photo.

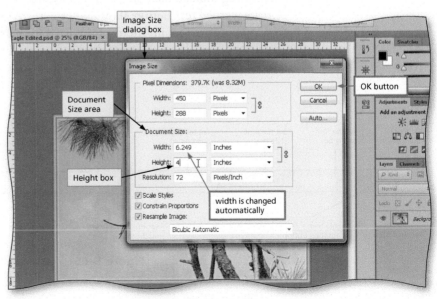

Figure 1–63

- Click the OK button to finish resizing the image.

- Change the magnification to 100% (Figure 1–64).

Experiment

- Click the status bar menu button and then click Document Dimensions to verify that the image size has been changed. Then, click the status bar menu button again and then click Document Sizes to redisplay the document size.

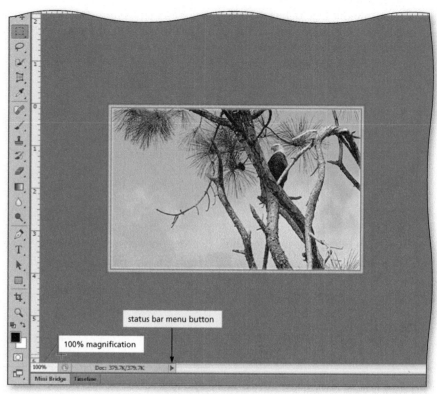

Figure 1–64

Other Ways

1. Press ALT+CTRL+I, change settings, click OK button

Inserting Text

The next steps use a type tool to create text for the postcard. On the Tools panel, the default type tool is the Horizontal Type Tool. The options bar for the Horizontal Type Tool (Figure 1–65) includes boxes and buttons typical of those found in a word processing toolbar, including font family, font style, font size, and justification. A Create warped text button allows you to create text in specialized formations, similar to the WordArt tool in Microsoft Word. On the right side of the options bar are buttons to cancel and commit editing changes. In a future chapter, you will learn about the Character and Paragraph panels that provide additional tools for manipulating text.

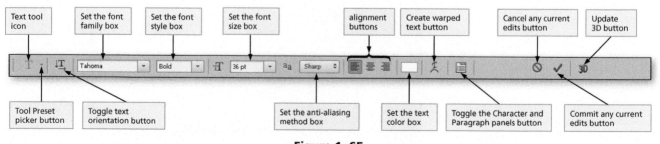

Figure 1–65

To Select the Horizontal Type Tool

The following step selects the Horizontal Type Tool on the Tools panel.

1

- Click the Horizontal Type Tool on the Tools panel to select it (Figure 1–66).

- If the solid T icon does not appear on the button, right-click the button to display its context menu, then click Horizontal Type Tool in the list.

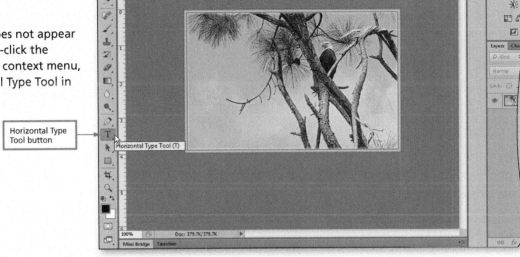

Horizontal Type Tool button

Horizontal Type Tool (T)

Figure 1–66

Other Ways
1. Press T

To Set Font Options

The following steps select font settings on the options bar. In addition to the font and alignment options, when you click the 'Set the text color' box, Photoshop uses color picker tools, such as a color field and color model boxes, to help you select the text color.

1

- On the options bar, click the 'Set the font family' box arrow to display the list of font families.

- Scroll in the list to display the Tahoma font family (Figure 1–67).

Set the font family box arrow

list of available fonts

Tahoma font family

scroll box

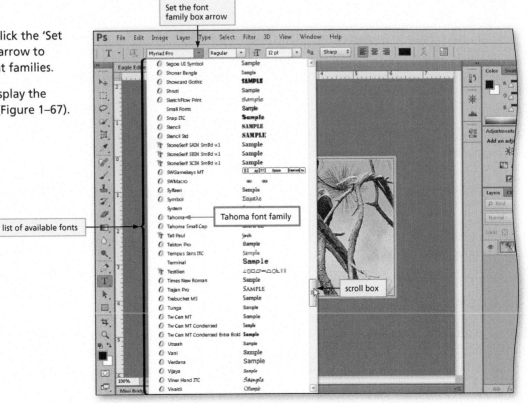

Figure 1–67

2

- Click Tahoma or a similar font in the list.

- Click the 'Set the font style' box arrow to display the list of font styles (Figure 1–68).

Q&A Why does the list not include other styles, such as italics?

Available font styles depend on the chosen font and the capability of the printer to reproduce that font. This font has only regular and bold styles.

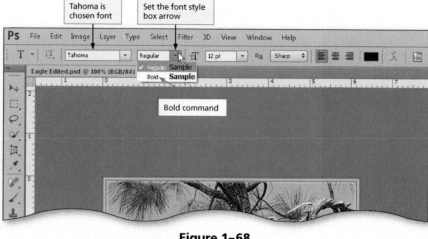

Figure 1–68

3

- Click Bold to choose a bold font style.

- Select the value in the 'Set the font size' box, and then type 36 to replace the size (Figure 1–69).

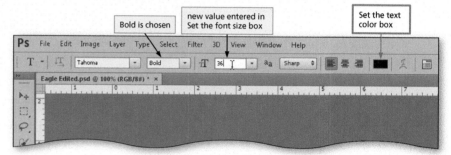

Figure 1–69

4

- Click the 'Set the text color' box to open the Color Picker (Text Color) dialog box.

- Click a white color in the upper-left corner of the color field (Figure 1–70).

Q&A What do the numerical boxes indicate?

Each color mode uses a numerical method called a color model, or color space, to describe the color. Some companies use specific numbers to create exact colors for branding purposes.

5

- Click the OK button in the Color Picker (Text Color) dialog box to apply white as the text color on the options bar.

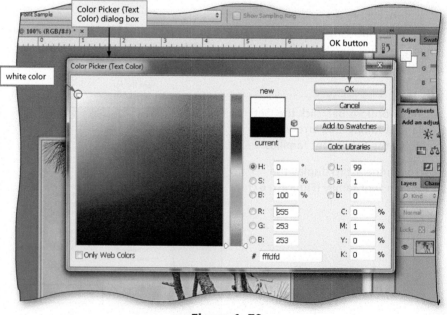

Figure 1–70

To Insert Text

With the type tool selected, you drag a bounding box in the document window to insert text. A **bounding box** is similar to a text box in other applications, with a dotted outline and sizing handles. As you drag, the mouse pointer changes to a small, open book outline. After typing the text in the bounding box, you use the 'Commit any current edits' button to complete the entry. Then, if the size of the bounding box needs to be adjusted, you can drag the sizing handles. The mouse pointer becomes an insertion point when positioned over the text. You will learn about other type tools and features in a later chapter.

The following steps enter text on the postcard.

1

- With the Horizontal Type Tool still selected, drag a bounding box in the lower-right portion of the photo, approximately 2.5 inches wide and 2 inches tall, as shown in Figure 1–71.

Q&A What is the new notation on the Layers panel?

When you create a bounding box, Photoshop separates the text from the rest of the picture in its own layer. You will learn more about layers in a future chapter.

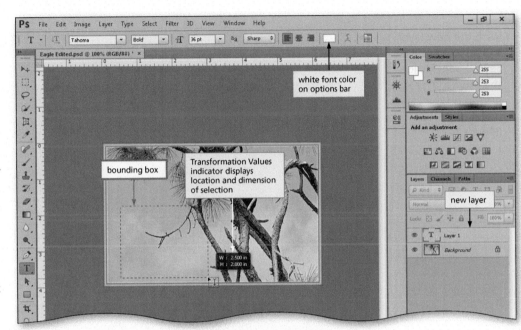

Figure 1–71

2

- Type National and then press the ENTER key.

- Type Wildlife and then press the ENTER key.

- Type Park to complete the text (Figure 1–72).

Q&A Can I make changes and corrections to the text?

Yes, you can click anywhere in the text box, use the ARROW keys, the BACKSPACE key, and the DELETE key just as you do in word processing. If your bounding box is too small, you can drag the sizing handles.

Figure 1–72

3

- On the options bar, click the 'Commit any current edits' button to finish the new layer.

To Stroke Text

Earlier in this chapter, you added a stroke of color to a selection as you created a border for the postcard. The following steps stroke the text with black to make the letters stand out. You will use the Layer Style dialog box to create the stroke.

1

- With the new layer still selected on the Layer's panel, click the 'Add a layer style' button on the Layers panel status bar (Figure 1–73).

Q&A

Could I use the Stroke command on the Edit menu to stroke text?

No. The Stroke command on the Edit menu is for selections only. Because this is an entire layer, you need to use a layer style.

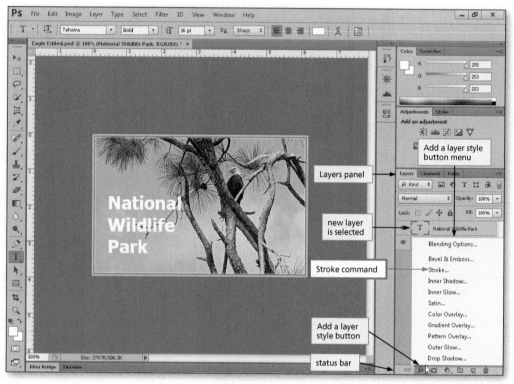

Figure 1–73

2

- Click Stroke in the list of layer styles to display the Layer Style dialog box.

- Type 1 in the Size box to create 1 pixel of black stroke (Figure 1–74).

Q&A

What should I do if my color does not appear as black?

Black is the default color; however, a previous user on your computer may have changed the color. Click the Color box to display a Color Picker dialog box. Click black and then click the OK button.

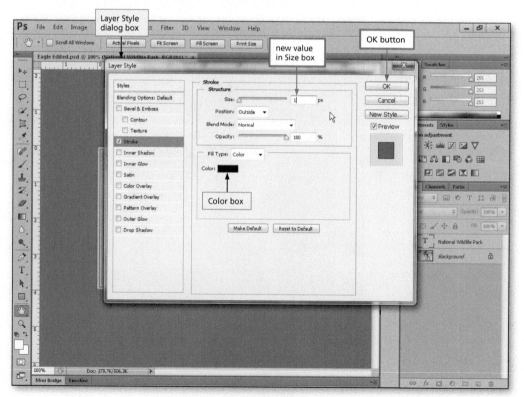

Figure 1–74

- Click the OK button in the Layer Style dialog box to accept the settings and add the stroke (Figure 1–75).

- Press the D key to reset the default colors on the Tools panel.

Figure 1–75

To Save a File with a Different Name

Many graphic designers will save multiple copies of the same photo with various edits. Because this photo has been resized to print properly, you need to save it with a different name, as performed in the following step.

- Click File on the Application bar and then click Save As to display the Save As dialog box.

- In the Save As dialog box, type Eagle Resized with Text in the File name text box.

- If necessary, click the Save in box arrow and then click Removable Disk (F:), or the location of your USB flash drive and appropriate folder in the list.

- If necessary, click the Format button and then click Photoshop (*.PSD, *.PDD) to select the format type (Figure 1–76).

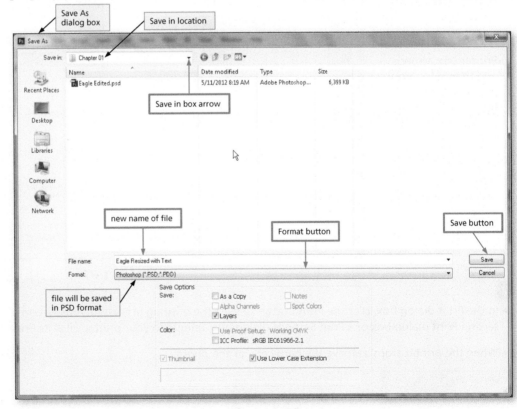

Figure 1–76

- Click the Save button to save the image with the new name.

- If Photoshop displays a Photoshop Format Options dialog box, click the OK button to accept the settings and close the dialog box.

Printing a Photo

The photo now can be printed, saved, taken to a professional print shop, or sent online to a printing service. A printed version of the photo is called a **hard copy** or **printout**. You can print one copy using the Print One Copy command on the File menu, or to display the Print dialog box, you can click Print on the File menu, which offers you more printing options.

The Print One Copy command sends the printout to the default printer. If you are not sure which printer is your default printer, choose the Print command. In the Print dialog box, click the Printer box arrow and choose your current printer. You will learn more about the Print dialog box in Chapter 2.

To Print a Photo

The following steps print the photo created in this chapter.

1

- Ready the printer according to the printer instructions.

- Click File on the Application bar, and then click Print to display the Print dialog box.

- If necessary, click the Printer box arrow and then select your printer from the list. Do not change any other settings (Figure 1–77).

Q&A

Does Photoshop have a Print button?

No. Photoshop's Print commands are available on the File menu or by using shortcut keys.

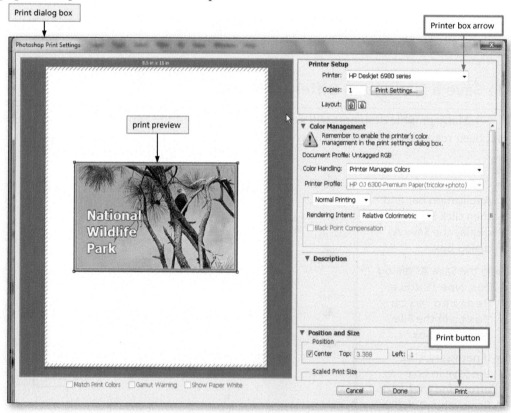

Figure 1–77

2

- In the Print dialog box, click the Print button to start the printing process. If your system displays a second Print dialog box or a Print Settings dialog box, unique to your printer, click its Print button.

- When the printer stops, retrieve the hard copy of the photo.

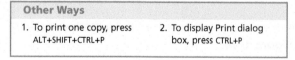

Other Ways	
1. To print one copy, press ALT+SHIFT+CTRL+P	2. To display Print dialog box, press CTRL+P

Saving a Photo for Use on the Web

When preparing photos for the Web, you often need to compromise between the quality of the display and the file size. Web users do not want to wait while large photos load from Web servers to their individual computer systems. To solve this problem, Photoshop provides several commands to compress the file size of an image while optimizing its online display quality. Additionally, Photoshop allows you to save the photo in a variety of formats such as **GIF**, which is a compressed graphic format designed to minimize file size and electronic transfer time, or as an **HTML** (Hypertext Markup Language) file, which contains all the necessary information to display your photo in a Web browser.

Therefore, you have two choices in Photoshop for creating Web images: the Zoomify command and the Save for Web command. When you **zoomify**, you create a high-resolution image for the Web, complete with a background and tools for navigation, panning, and zooming. To zoomify, click Export on the File menu and then click Zoomify. In the Zoomify Export dialog box, you set various Web and export options. Photoshop creates the HTML code and accompanying files for you to upload to a Web server.

If you do not want the extra HTML files for the background, navigation, and zooming, you can create a single graphic file by using the Save for Web command. The resulting graphic can be used on the Web or on a variety of mobile devices.

Optimization is the process of changing the photo to make it most effective for its purpose. The Save for Web command allows you to preview optimized images in different file formats, and with different file attributes, for precise optimization. You can view multiple versions of a photo simultaneously and modify settings as you preview the image.

BTW

Reviewing the HTML Code
If you want to review the HTML code later, you can either open the file in Photoshop, access the Save for Web dialog box, and then click the Preview button; or, you can double-click the HTML file to open it in a browser, click View on the Browser's menu bar, and then click Source.

To Preview using the Save for Web Dialog Box

To optimize the eagle photo for use on the Web, you need to make decisions about the file size, and how long it might take to load on a Web page, as you preview the image. These kinds of decisions must take into consideration the audience and the nature of the Web page. For example, Web pages geared for college campuses probably could assume a faster download time than those that target a wide range of home users. An e-commerce site that needs high-quality photography to sell its product will make certain choices in color and resolution.

The hardware and software of Web users also is taken into consideration. For instance, if a Web photo contains more colors than the user's monitor can display, a browser might **dither**, or approximate, the colors that it cannot display, by blending colors that it can. Dithering might not be appropriate for some Web pages, because it increases the file size and, therefore, causes the page to load more slowly.

Many other appearance settings play a role in the quality of Web graphics, some of which are subjective in nature. As you become more experienced in Photoshop, you will learn how to make choices about dithering, colors, texture, image size, and other settings.

The step on the next page uses the Save for Web command to display previews for four possible Web formats.

● With the Eagle Resized with Text photo open, click File on the Application bar to display the File menu and then click Save for Web to display the Save for Web dialog box.

● Click the 4-Up tab to display four versions of the photo (Figure 1–78).

Why are there four frames?

Photoshop displays four previews — the original photo and three others that are converted to different resolutions to optimize download times.

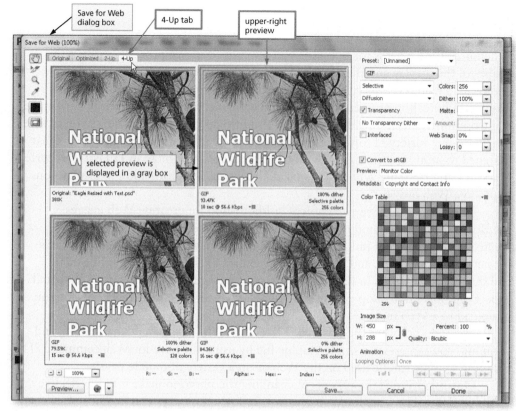

Figure 1–78

Other Ways

1. Press ALT+SHIFT+CTRL+S

To Choose a Download Speed

For faster downloads when the photo is displayed as a Web graphic, you can choose a download speed that will be similar to that of your target audience. The **annotation area** below each preview in the Save for Web dialog box provides optimization information such as the size of the optimized file and the estimated download time using the selected modem speed. You will learn more about other settings in the Save for Web dialog box in a later chapter.

The following steps change the download speed to 512 kilobytes per second (Kbps).

● Click the upper-right preview, if necessary, to choose a high quality version of the photo.

● In the annotation area below the upper-right preview, click the 'Select download speed' button to display the list of connection speeds (Figure 1–79).

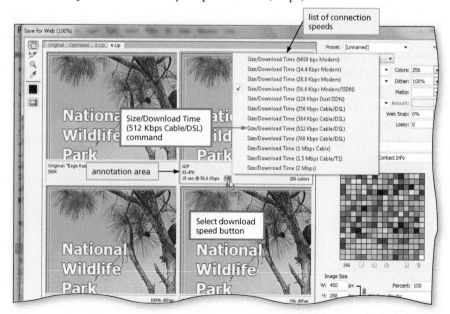

Figure 1–79

2

- In the list, click Size/Download Time (512 Kbps Cable/DSL) or another appropriate speed (Figure 1–80).

Q&A

How fast will the picture download?

In Figure 1–78, the speed was 18 seconds at 56.6 Kbps. At 512 Kbps, the photo will download in 3 seconds, as shown in Figure 1–80. Your download times might differ slightly.

Experiment

- Click the Select download speed button to display the list of connection speeds and then click various connection speeds to see how the download times are affected. When finished, click Size/Download Time (512 Kbps Cable/DSL) in the list.

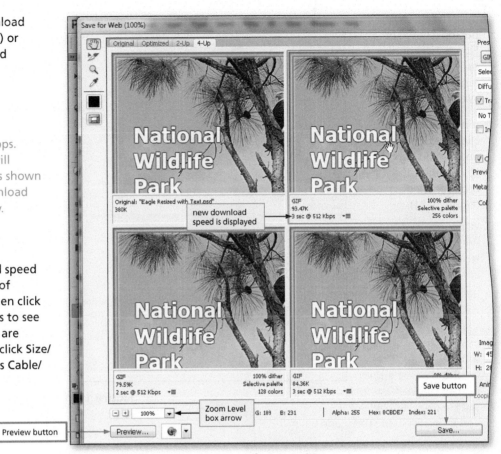

Figure 1–80

Other Ways

1. Right-click annotation area, select download speed

BTW

Save for Web Preview
If you want the entire photo to display in the Save for Web dialog box, click the Zoom Level box arrow and then click Fit in View.

To Preview the Photo on the Web

Before uploading a photo to the Web, it is always a good idea to preview it to check for errors. When Photoshop displays a Web preview of any photo, it also displays the characteristics of the file and the HTML code used to create the preview. The steps on the next page preview the image in a browser.

1

- Click the Preview button (shown in Figure 1–80 on the previous page) to display the photo in a Web browser.

- If necessary, double-click the browser's application bar to maximize the browser window (Figure 1–81).

Q&A

When I clicked the Preview button, the HTML code displayed in Notepad. Should it open in a browser?

If Photoshop cannot detect a default browser on your system, you may have to click the box arrow next to the Preview button (Figure 1–80), and then click Edit List to add your browser.

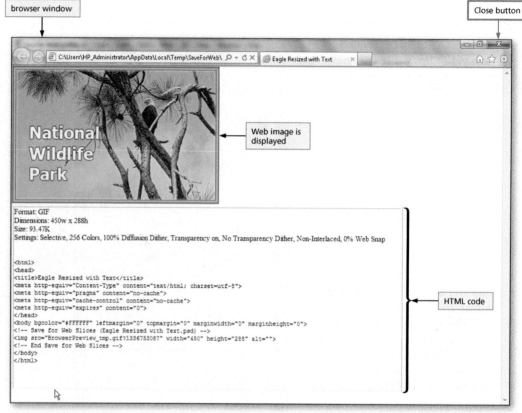

Figure 1–81

Q&A

How would I use the HTML code?

As a Web designer, you might copy and paste the code into a text editor or Web creation software, replacing BrowserPreview with the name of the file. After saving, the code, the HTML file, and the photo would need to be uploaded to a server.

2

- Click the Close button on the browser's application bar to close the browser window. If necessary, click the Adobe Photoshop CS6 button on the Windows taskbar to return to the Save for Web dialog box.

BTW

Saving for Web
In the Save Optimized As dialog box, you can click the Format button to choose one of three ways to save for the Web. The Images only option saves the photo itself in a Web-friendly format as a GIF file. The HTML only option saves the coding that creates the Web page, but not the photo. The HTML and Images option saves the Web page and creates an accompanying folder named Images to go with the Web page file. Inside the Images folder is a GIF version of the photo.

BTW

CS6 Device Central
Device Central, available in Photoshop CS6, the extended version, enables you to preview how Photoshop files will look on a variety of mobile devices. An emulator or mock-up displays the device and preview. Photoshop supports most cell phone displays, portable electronic devices, and MP3 players with video. In the Device Central window, you can adjust settings for lighting, scaling, and alignment.

To Save the Photo for the Web

When you click the Save button in the Save for Web dialog box, Photoshop displays the Save Optimized As dialog box, where you will name the Web file. The following steps save the Photo for the Web.

1

- In the Save for Web dialog box (Figure 1–80 on page PS 55), click the Save button to display the Save Optimized As dialog box.

- Type `Eagle-for-Web` in the File name text box.

- If necessary, click the Save in box arrow and then click Removable Disk (F:), or the location of your USB flash drive. Double-click the appropriate folder in the list (Figure 1–82).

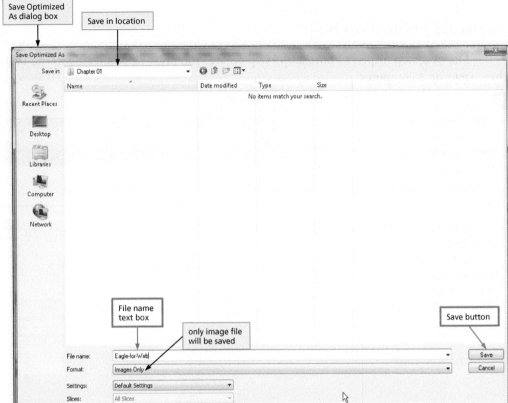

Figure 1–82

 Q&A Why are the words in the file name hyphenated?

For ease of use, it is standard for Web graphics to have no spaces in their file names.

2

- Click the Save button in the Save Optimized As dialog box to save the file.

Photoshop Help

At anytime while you are using Photoshop, you can get answers to questions by using **Photoshop Help.** You activate Photoshop Help either by clicking Help on the Application bar or by pressing the F1 key. The Help menu includes commands to display more information about your copy of Photoshop, as well as a list of how-to guides for common tasks. The Photoshop Online Help command connects you, through the Adobe Photoshop Support Center on the Web, to a wealth of assistance, including tutorials with detailed instructions accompanied by illustrations and videos. Used properly, this form of online assistance can increase your productivity and reduce your frustration by minimizing the time you spend learning how to use Photoshop. Additional information about using Photoshop Help is available in Appendix D, the Using Photoshop Help appendix.

BTW

Community Help
Community Help is an integrated Web environment that includes Photoshop Help and gives you access to community-generated content moderated by Adobe and industry experts. Comments from users help guide you to an answer.

To Access Photoshop Help

The next step displays Photoshop Help online. You must be connected to the Web if you plan to perform these steps on a computer.

1

- With Photoshop open on your system, press the F1 key to access the Photoshop Help / Help and tutorials page.

- If necessary, double-click the application bar to maximize the window (Figure 1–83).

Q&A

My page looks different. Did I do something wrong?

No. Adobe updates the Help pages frequently. Your page will differ.

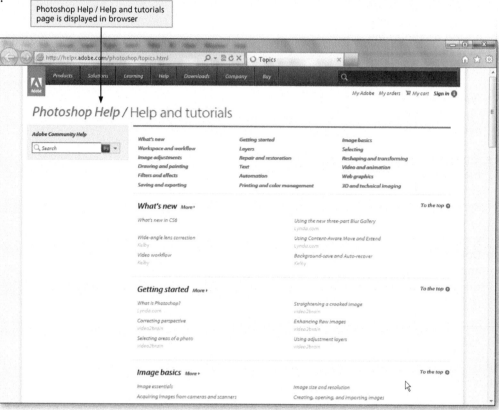

Photoshop Help / Help and tutorials page is displayed in browser

Figure 1–83

Other Ways

1. On Help menu, click Photoshop Online Help

To Use the Help Search Box

The Search box allows you to type words or phrases about which you want additional information and help, such as cropping or printing images. When you press the ENTER key, Photoshop Help responds by displaying a list of topics related to the word or phrase you typed.

The following steps use the Search box to obtain information about the Tools panel.

1

- Click the Search box and then type `Tools panel` to enter the search topic (Figure 1–84).

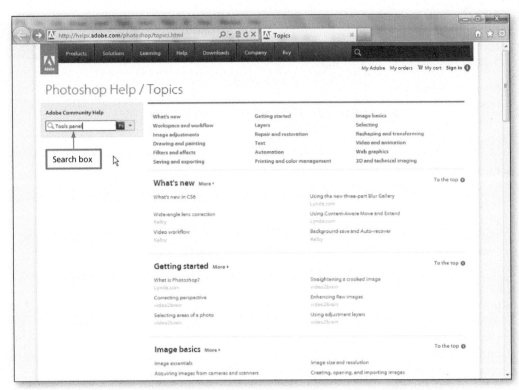

Figure 1–84

2

- Press the ENTER key to display the relevant links (Figure 1–85).

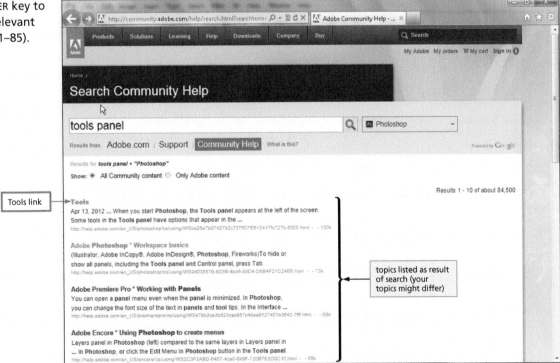

Figure 1–85

Close button

3

- Click the link, Tools, to display the contents (Figure 1–86).

- Scroll as necessary to read the information about tools.

 Experiment

- Click other links to view more information, or search for other topics using the Search box.

4

- In the browser application bar, click the Close button to close the window, and then, if necessary, click the Adobe Photoshop CS6 button on the taskbar to return to Photoshop.

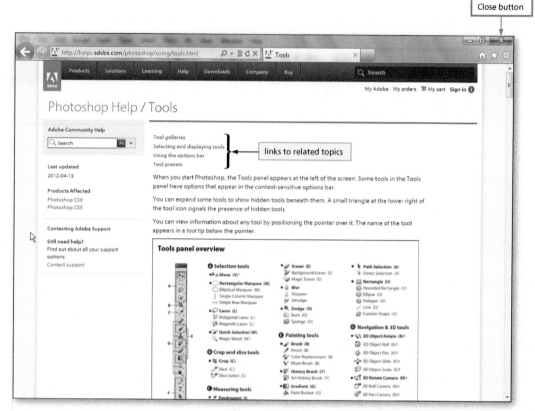

Figure 1–86

Other Ways

1. On Help menu, click Photoshop Online Help, enter search topic

---

To Quit Photoshop

The following step quits Photoshop and returns control to Windows.

1

- Click the Close button on the right side of the Application bar to close the window.

- If Photoshop displays a dialog box asking you to save changes, click the No button.

 For a detailed example of this procedure using the Mac operating system, refer to the steps on page APP 82 of the For Mac Users appendix.

Other Ways

1. On File menu, click Exit
2. Press CTRL+Q

Chapter Summary

In this chapter, you gained a broad knowledge of Photoshop. First, you learned how to start Photoshop. You were introduced to the Photoshop workspace. You learned how to open a photo, change the magnification, zoom, and display rulers. You learned about design issues related to the placement of visual points of interest. You then learned how to crop a photo to eliminate extraneous background. After you added a blended border, you resized the image and added text. Once you saved the photo, you learned how to print it. You used the Save for Web command to optimize and save a Web version. You learned how to use Adobe Help to research specific help topics. Finally, you learned how to quit Photoshop.

The items listed below include all the new Photoshop skills you have learned in this chapter:

1. Start Photoshop (PS 4)
2. Select the Essentials Workspace (PS 6)
3. Select the Default Tool (PS 8)
4. Reset the Options Bar (PS 8)
5. Reset the Interface Color (PS 9)
6. Open a File (PS 11)
7. Save a File in the PSD Format (PS 20)
8. Use the Zoom Tool (PS 24)
9. Use the Navigator Panel (PS 26)
10. Minimize the Navigator Panel (PS 27)
11. Use the Hand Tool (PS 28)
12. Change the Magnification (PS 29)
13. Display Rulers (PS 30)
14. Crop a Photo (PS 33)
15. Create a Selection (PS 35)
16. Stroke a Selection (PS 36)
17. Modify a Selection (PS 39)
18. Switch Foreground and Background Colors (PS 40)
19. Deselect (PS 41)
20. Save a File with the Same File Name (PS 42)
21. Close a File (PS 42)
22. Open a Recent File (PS 43)
23. Resize the Image (PS 45)
24. Select the Horizontal Type Tool (PS 47)
25. Set Font Options (PS 47)
26. Insert Text (PS 48)
27. Stroke Text (PS 50)
28. Save a File with a Different Name (PS 51)
29. Print a Photo (PS 52)
30. Preview using the Save for Web Dialog Box (PS 53)
31. Choose a Download Speed (PS 54)
32. Preview the Photo on the Web (PS 55)
33. Save the Photo for the Web (PS 56)
34. Access Photoshop Help (PS 58)
35. Use the Help Search Box (PS 58)
36. Quit Photoshop (PS 60)

Apply Your Knowledge

Reinforce the skills and apply the concepts you learned in this chapter.

Editing a Photo in the Photoshop Workspace

Instructions: Start Photoshop and perform the customization steps found on pages PS 6 through PS 10. Open the Apply 1-1 Water Park file in the Chapter 01 folder from the Data Files for Students. Visit www.cengage.com/ct/studentdownload for detailed instructions or contact your instructor for information about accessing the required files.

First, you will save the photo in the PSD format, then you will crop the photo, add a white border, and save the edited photo, as shown in Figure 1–87 on the next page. Next, you will resize the photo for printing and print one copy. Finally, you will reopen your edited photo, and then you will optimize it for the Web, save it, and close it.

Continued >

Source: Mali Jones

Figure 1–87

Perform the following tasks:

1. On the File menu, click Save As. When Photoshop displays the Save As dialog box, navigate to your storage device and then double-click the appropriate folder, if necessary. In the File name box, type `Apply 1-1 Water Park Edited`. Click the Format button and choose the PSD file format. Click the Save button to save the file.

2. Use the Zoom Tool to zoom the photo to 50% magnification, if necessary.

3. Use the Hand Tool to reposition the photo in the workspace to view different areas of the zoomed photo.

4. Use the Navigator panel to zoom out to 16.67%.

5. Use the Crop Tool to crop the photo, retaining the top patio of the water slide and the child on the right slide as shown in Figure 1–87. When using the Crop Tool, you might want to use the 'Rotate the crop box between portrait and landscape orientation' button. Include more water than sky. Use the rule of thirds guide to position the child in the lower-right intersection. (*Hint:* If your cropping selection does not look correct, you can press the ESC key to clear the selection before you press the ENTER key. Immediately after cropping the photo, you can click Undo on the Edit menu to undo the crop action.)

6. Select a different tool so the cropping handles no longer are displayed.

7. To create the border:

   a. If necessary, press the D key to select the default colors. Press the x key to reverse the foreground and background colors, so that white displays over black on the Tools panel.

   b. Press CTRL+A to select all of the photo.

   c. Use the Select menu to modify the border to 100 pixels.

   d. Use the Stroke command on the Edit menu to stroke the selection with white.

   e. Press CTRL+D to clear your selection when you are finished creating the border.

8. Press CTRL+S to save the Apply 1-1 Water Park Edited photo with the same file name in the same location.

9. Use the Image menu to resize the photo width to 5 inches wide to create a custom-sized photo for printing.

10. Save the resized file as Apply 1-1 Water Park for Print.

11. Print the photo and then close the file. If Photoshop displays a dialog box about saving again, click the No button.

12. Open the Apply 1-1 Water Park for Print file using the Open Recent list.

13. Save the photo for the Web, displaying it in the 4-Up tab. Select the preview that looks the best for your download speed.

14. Preview the optimized photo in your browser. Close the browser.

15. Save the optimized file with the name, Apply-1-1-Water-Park-for-Web.

16. Close the Apply 1-1 Water Park for Print file without saving it and quit Photoshop.

Extend Your Knowledge

Extend the skills you learned in this chapter and experiment with new skills. You may need to use Help to complete the assignment.

Exploring Crop Tool Options

Instructions: Start Photoshop and perform the customization steps found on pages PS 6 through PS 10. Open the Extend 1-1 Arc de Triomphe file in the Chapter 01 folder from the Data Files for Students and save it on your storage device as Extend 1-1 Arc de Triomphe Edited in the PSD file format. Visit www.cengage.com/ct/studentdownload for detailed instructions or contact your instructor for information about accessing the required files.

    The photo (Figure 1–88) is to be added to a book about Paris; therefore, the structure should be centered, straightened, and display in a 5 × 7 format.

Figure 1–88

Continued >

Extend Your Knowledge *continued*

Perform the following tasks:

1. Use Help to read about the Crop Tool's Straighten button and the Aspect Ratio button.

2. Select the Crop Tool. On the options bar, click the Straighten button, and then drag in the photo, across a line that should be straight in the upper portion of the monument.

3. Use the 'Select a preset aspect ratio' button to choose a 5 × 7 forced ratio. Drag a corner cropping handle inward, keeping the arc within the grid. Drag the picture to center it within the cropping area.

4. Click the 'Delete cropped pixels' check box, if necessary, and then crop the photo.

5. Review Table 1–4 on page PS 38. Use the commands on the Modify submenu to set the border options of your choice. Stroke the selection with a color of your choice.

6. After viewing the resulting border, use the History panel to go back to the photo's cropped state.

7. Repeat Steps 5 and 6 several times to experiment with different border widths and colors, then apply the border that best complements the photo and save the changes to the photo.

8. Close the photo and quit Photoshop.

Make It Right

Analyze a project and correct all errors and/or improve the design.

Changing a Photo's Focus and Optimizing It for the Web

Instructions: Start Photoshop and perform the customization steps found on pages PS 6 through PS 10. Open the Make It Right 1-1 Young Stars file in the Chapter 01 folder from the Data Files for Students and save it on your storage device as Make It Right 1-1 Young Stars Edited in the PSD file format. Visit www.cengage.com/ct/studentdownload for detailed instructions or contact your instructor for information about accessing the required files.

Members of your Astronomy Club have selected the Young Stars photo (Figure 1–89) for the club's Web site. You are tasked with editing the photo to focus more clearly on the cluster of stars and its trailing dust blanket, and then optimizing the photo for the Web.

Source: NASA/JPL–Caltech/Harvard-Smithsonian CFA

Figure 1–89

View the photo in different screen modes and at different magnifications. Keeping the rule of thirds and the golden rectangle concepts in mind, crop the photo to change its focal point and resave it. Then save the photo for the Web as Make-It-Right-1-1-Young-Stars-for-Web.

In the Lab

Design and/or create a project using the guidelines, concepts, and skills presented in this chapter. Labs are listed in order of increasing difficulty.

Lab 1: Cropping a Photo and Adding a Smooth Border

Problem: An extreme sports magazine has accepted the submission of your parasailing photo, but they would like you to crop the photo more, add a smooth border, and resize it. The edited photo is displayed in Figure 1–90.

Note: To complete this assignment, you will be required to use the Data Files for Students. Visit www.cengage.com/ct/ studentdownload for detailed instructions or contact your instructor for information about accessing the required files.

Figure 1–90

Instructions: Perform the following tasks:

1. Start Photoshop.

2. Click Window on the application bar, point to Workspace, and then click Essentials (Default). Repeat the process and click Reset Essentials to reset the Essentials workspace.

3. Select the second button on the Tools panel to reset the Tools panel.

4. Right-click the Rectangular Marquee Tool icon on the options bar, and then click Reset all Tools to reset the options bar.

5. Press the D key to select the default colors. If black is not over white at the bottom of the Tools panel, click the Switch foreground and background colors button.

6. Open the file, Lab 1-1 Parasailing, from the Chapter 01 folder of the Data Files for Students or from a location specified by your instructor.

7. Click Save As on the File menu, and then type the new file name, Lab 1-1 Parasailing Edited. Navigate to your storage location, if necessary. Click the Format button and choose the PSD format. Click the Save button.

8. Use the Magnification box to zoom the photo to 25% magnification, if necessary.

9. If the rulers do not appear, press CTRL+R to view the rulers.

10. Select the Crop Tool. Click the photo to display the rule of thirds grid. SHIFT+drag the lower-right cropping handle until the sail is positioned at the upper-right intersection of the rule of thirds grid.

11. Press the ENTER key. If your crop does not seem correct, click the Undo command on the Edit menu and repeat Step 10.

12. Select another tool so the cropping handles no longer are displayed.

13. Save the photo again.

14. Press CTRL+A to select all of the photo. Click Select on the Application bar, point to Modify to display the Modify submenu, and then click Border to display the Border Selection dialog box. Type 100 in the Width box, and then click the OK button.

Continued >

In the Lab *continued*

15. Display the Modify submenu again, and click Smooth. Type 50 in the Smooth Radius box, and then click the OK button to create a second marquee with smoothed corners.

16. If white is not the foreground color, press the x key to switch the foreground and background colors. Click Edit on the Application bar and then click Stroke. Type 50 in the Width box. Click the Inside option button in the Location area. Click the OK button to stroke the selection. Press CTRL+D to deselect.

17. Click the Image Size command on the Image menu. When the Image Size dialog box is displayed, in the Document Size area, type 4 in the Width box. Click the OK button.

18. Press CTRL+S to save the file again.

19. Use the Print One Copy command on the File menu to print a copy of the photo.

20. Close your file and quit Photoshop.

21. Send the photo as an e-mail attachment to your instructor, or submit it in the format specified by your instructor.

In the Lab

Lab 2: Creating a Smoothed Border

Problem: The local hockey team is preparing a flyer to advertise its next game. The marketing department would like you to take one of the pictures from the last game and crop it to show just the face-off players and the official. Because the flyer will be printed on white paper, you should create a white border, so the photo blends into the background and adds to the ice rink effect. The edited photo is displayed in Figure 1–91.

Figure 1–91

Note: To complete this assignment, you will be required to use the Data Files for Students. Visit www.cengage.com/ct/studentdownload for detailed instructions or contact your instructor for information about accessing the required files.

Instructions: Perform the following tasks:

1. Start Photoshop. Perform the customization steps found on pages PS 6 through PS 10.

2. Open the file, Lab 1-2 Hockey, from the Chapter 01 folder of the Data Files for Students or from a location specified by your instructor.

3. Use the Save As command on the File menu to save the file on your storage device with the name, Lab 1-2 Hockey Edited, in the PSD format.

4. Click the Zoom Tool button on the Tools panel. Click the official in the photo to center the photo in the display. Zoom as necessary so you can make precise edits.

5. Crop the picture to display only the official and the two hockey players ready for the face-off. The vertical line of the hockey stick and the visual line of the official should be positioned using the rule of thirds.

6. Select a different tool so the cropping handles no longer are displayed.

7. Save the photo again with the same name.

8. Close the file and open it again using the Recent submenu.

9. Press CTRL+A to select all of the photo.

10. To create the border, do the following:

   a. On the Select menu, point to Modify, and then click Border.

   b. When the Border Selection dialog box is displayed, type 100 in the Width Box. Click the OK button.

   c. On the Select menu, open the Modify submenu, and then click Smooth.

   d. When the Smooth Selection dialog box is displayed, type 50 in the Sample Radius box to smooth the corners. Click the OK button.

   e. Press SHIFT+F5 to access the Fill command.

   f. When the Fill dialog box is displayed, click the Use box arrow and then click White in the list.

   g. Click the Mode box arrow and then click Normal in the list, if necessary.

   h. If necessary, type 100 in the Opacity box. Click the OK button.

   i. Press CTRL+D to deselect the border.

11. Save the photo again.

12. Use the Print One Copy command on the File menu to print a copy of the photo.

13. Close the document window.

14. Quit Photoshop.

15. Submit the assignment in the format specified by your instructor.

In the Lab

Lab 3: Preparing a Photo for the Web

Problem: As an independent consultant in Web site design, you have been hired by the Pineapple Growers Association to prepare a photo of an exotic pineapple growing in a field for use on the association's Web site. The edited photo is displayed in Figure 1–92.

Note: To complete this assignment, you will be required to use the Data Files for Students. Visit www.cengage.com/ct/student-download for detailed instructions or contact your instructor for information about accessing the required files.

Instructions: Perform the following tasks:
Start Photoshop. Perform the customization steps found on pages PS 6 through PS 10. Open the file, Lab 1-3 Pineapple, from the Chapter 01 folder of the Data Files for Students. Save the file in the PSD format with the name Lab 1-3 Pineapple Edited. Resize the photo to 500 pixels wide. Zoom to 50% magnification. Search Photoshop Help for help related to optimization. Read about optimizing for the Web. Print a copy of the help topic and then close the Adobe Help window.

    Use the Save for Web dialog box to view the 4-Up tab. Choose the best-looking preview. Select the connection speed of

Figure 1–92

Continued >

In the Lab *continued*

your Internet connection. Save the Web version of the photo using the name, Lab-1-3-Pineapple-for-Web. For extra credit, upload the Web version to a Web server. See Appendix C for information on publishing to a Web server. See your instructor for ways to submit this assignment.

Cases and Places

Apply your creative thinking and problem-solving skills to design and implement a solution.

Note: To complete these assignments, you may be required to use the Data Files for Students. Visit www.cengage.com/ct/studentdownload for detailed instructions or contact your instructor for information about accessing the required files.

1: Crop a Photo for a Class Directory

Academic

As a member of your high school reunion committee, it is your task to assemble the class photo directory. You are to edit a high school student photo and prepare it for print in the reunion directory. The photo needs to fit in a space 1.75 inches high and 1.33 inches wide. Each photo needs to have approximately .25 inches above the head. After starting Photoshop and resetting the workspace, select the photo, Case 1-1 Student, from the Chapter 01 folder of the Data Files for Students. Save the photo on your USB flash drive storage device as Case 1-1 Student Edited, using the PSD format. Resize the photo to match the requirements. Use the rulers to help you crop the photo for .25 inches above the top of the student's head. Save the photo again and print a copy for your instructor.

2: Create a Photo for a Social Networking Site

Personal

You would like to place a photo of your recent tubing adventure on your social networking page. The photo you have is of two people. You need to crop out the other person who is tubing. After starting Photoshop and resetting the workspace, select the photo, Case 1-2 Tubing, from the Chapter 01 folder of the Data Files for Students. Save the photo on your USB flash drive storage device as Case 1-2 Tubing Edited, using the PSD format. Crop the photo to remove one of the tubes, keeping in mind the rule of thirds, the golden rectangle, and the direction of the action. Save the photo for the Web and upload it to Facebook or another Web server as directed by your instructor.

3: Creating a Photo for a Brochure

Professional

You are an intern with an event planning business. The company is planning to send out a trifold brochure about local churches and chapels used for weddings. The photo named Case 1-3 Chapel is located in the Chapter 01 folder of the Data Files for Students. Save the photo on your USB flash drive storage device as Case 1-3 Chapel Edited, using the PSD format. Resize the photo to be 3.5 inches wide. Create a black border of 10 pixels. Save the file again and print a copy for your instructor.

2 | Using Selection Tools and Shortcut Keys

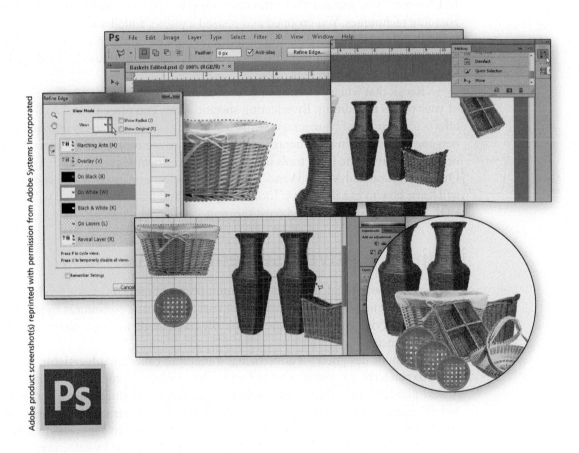

Objectives

You will have mastered the material in this chapter when you can:

- Explain the terms layout, perspective, and storyboard
- Describe selection tools
- Select objects using the marquee tools
- Move and duplicate selections
- Use the History panel
- Use the Grow command and Refine Edges to adjust selections
- Employ the lasso tools
- Subtract areas from selections
- Use grids, guides, and snapping
- Select objects using the Quick Selection and Magic Wand Tools
- Print to a PDF file
- Use, create, and test new keyboard shortcuts

2 | Using Selection Tools and Shortcut Keys

Introduction

In Chapter 1, you learned about the Photoshop interface, as well as navigation and zooming techniques. You cropped and resized a photo, added a border and text, and saved the photo for both Web and print media. You learned about Online Help, along with opening, saving, and printing photos. This chapter continues to emphasize those topics and presents some new ones.

Recall that when you make a selection, you are specifying or isolating an area of your photo for editing. By selecting specific areas, you can edit and apply special effects to portions of your image, while leaving the unselected areas untouched. The new topics covered in this chapter include the marquee tools used to select rectangular or elliptical areas, the lasso tools used to select free-form segments or shapes, and the Quick Selection and Magic Wand Tools used to select consistently colored areas. You will learn how to use the Move Tool to duplicate and scale. Finally, you will print to a PDF file and create a new keyboard shortcut.

Project — Advertisement Graphic

An advertisement, or ad, is a form of communication that promotes a product or service to a potential customer. An advertisement tries to persuade consumers to purchase a product or service. An advertisement typically has a single message directed toward a target audience.

A graphic designed for advertising, sometimes called an **advertising piece**, needs to catch the customer's eye and entice him or her to purchase the product. A clear graphic with strong contrast, item repetition, and visual lines tells the story and enhances text that might be added later. Chapter 2 illustrates the creation of a retail store advertising piece. You will begin with the image in Figure 2–1a that shows individual wicker baskets. You then will manipulate the image by selecting, editing, and moving the objects to produce a more attractive layout, creating Figure 2–1b for use in the advertisement.

Overview

As you read this chapter, you will learn how to create the advertisement graphic shown in Figure 2–1b by performing these general tasks:

- Select portions of the photo.
- Copy, move, and scale selections.
- Eliminate white space in and among objects in selected areas.
- Retrace editing steps using the History panel.
- Refine edges of selections.
- Print to a PDF file.
- Create a new shortcut key.

(a) Original image   **(b) Edited image**

Figure 2–1

Plan
Ahead

General Project Guidelines

When editing a photo, the actions you perform and decisions you make will affect the appearance and characteristics of the finished product. As you edit a photo, such as the one shown in Figure 2–1a, you should follow these general guidelines:

1. **Choose the correct tool.** When you need to copy and paste portions of your photo, consider carefully which Photoshop selection tool to use. You want the procedure to be efficient and produce a clear image. Keep in mind the shape and background of the photo you want to copy, as well as your expertise with various tools.

2. **Plan your duplications.** Use a storyboard or make a list of the items you plan to duplicate, and then decide whether it will be an exact duplication or a manipulated one, called a **transformed copy**. The decision depends on the visual effect you want to achieve and the customer requirements.

3. **Use grids and guides.** When you are working with exact measurements, close cropping and moving, or just want to align things easily, use grids and guides to display nonprinting lines across the document window. Use the Photoshop snapping function to align selections. Visual estimations of size and location are easier to perceive when using these guides.

4. **Create files in portable formats.** You might have to distribute your artwork in a variety of formats, depending on its use. Portability is an important consideration. It usually is safe to begin work in the Photoshop PSD format and then use the Save as command or Print command to convert your work to the PDF format. PDF files are platform and software independent.

When necessary, more specific details concerning the above guidelines are presented at appropriate points in the chapter. The chapter also will identify the actions performed and decisions made regarding these guidelines during the creation of the edited photo shown in Figure 2–1b.

Creating an Advertising Piece

Figure 2–2 illustrates the design decisions made to create the advertising piece. Using an attractive layout containing multiple objects is a good marketing strategy; such a piece visually and subconsciously can encourage the viewer to purchase more than one item. **Layout** refers to placing visual elements into a pleasing and understandable arrangement; in the basket advertisement, the layout is suggestive of how the product or products might look in a buyer's home. Advertising artists and product designers try to determine how the target consumer will use the product and group objects accordingly in the layout.

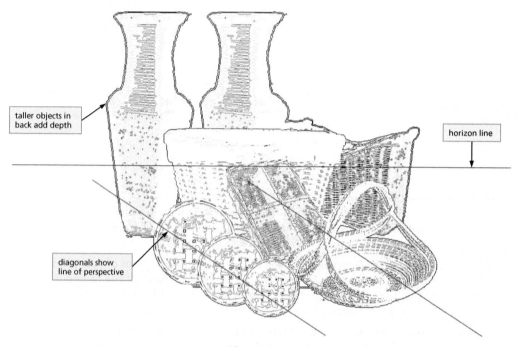

taller objects in back add depth

horizon line

diagonals show line of perspective

Figure 2–2

From a design point of view, creating visual diagonal lines creates perspective. **Perspective** is the technique photographers, designers, and artists use to create the illusion of three dimensions on a flat or two-dimensional surface. Perspective is a means of fooling the eye by making it appear as if there is depth or receding space in an image. Adjusting the sizes and juxtaposing the objects creates asymmetrical balance and visual tension between the featured products. For example, in Figure 2–2, the height of the tall baskets leads the viewer's eye to the background, as does the diagonal alignment of smaller pieces in front of the larger ones.

The **horizon line** in perspective drawing is a virtual horizontal line across the picture. The placement of the horizon line determines from where the viewer seems to be looking, such as down from a high place or up from close to the ground. In the basket advertisement, the horizon line runs across the middle of the drawing.

Using white space, or nonimage area, is effective in directing the viewer to notice what is important. The products grouped this way are, in a sense, framed by the white space.

This product layout also helps other members of the design team when it is time to make decisions about type placement. The group of products can be shifted up or down, as one image, to accommodate the layout and text, including the font sizes, placement, title, description, and price information. Recall that the rule of thirds offers a useful means to make effective layouts for images and text.

Designing a preliminary layout sketch, similar to Figure 2–2, to help you make choices about placement, size, perspective, and spacing, is referred to as creating a **storyboard** or **rough**.

To Start Photoshop

If you are stepping through this project on a computer and you want your screen to match the figures in this book, then you should change your computer's resolution to 1024 × 768 and reset the panels, tools, and colors. For more information about how to change the resolution on your computer and other advanced Photoshop settings, read Appendix F, the Changing Screen Resolution appendix.

The following steps, which assume Windows 7 is running, start Photoshop based on a typical installation. You may need to ask your instructor how to start Photoshop for your system.

1 Click the Start button on the Windows 7 taskbar to display the Start menu and then type Photoshop CS6 in the 'Search programs and files' box.

2 Click Adobe Photoshop CS6 in the list to start Photoshop.

3 If the Photoshop window is not maximized, click the Maximize button next to the Close button on the Application bar to maximize the window.

To Reset the Workspace

As discussed in Chapter 1, it is helpful to reset the workspace so that the tools and panels appear in their default positions. The following steps select the Essentials workspace.

1 Click Window on the Application bar to display the Window menu, and then point to Workspace to display the Workspace submenu.

2 Click Essentials (Default) on the Workspace submenu to select the default workspace panels.

3 Click Window on the Application bar, and then point to Workspace again to display the list.

4 Click Reset Essentials to restore the workspace to its default settings and reposition any panels that may have been moved.

To Reset the Tools and the Options Bar

Recall that the Tools panel and the options bar retain their settings from previous Photoshop sessions. The following steps select the Rectangular Marquee Tool and reset all tool settings in the options bar.

1 If the tools in the Tools panel appear in two columns, click the double arrow at the top of the Tools panel.

2 If necessary, click the Rectangular Marquee Tool button on the Tools panel to select it.

3 Right-click the Rectangular Marquee Tool icon on the options bar to display the context menu, and then click Reset All Tools. When Photoshop displays a confirmation dialog box, click the OK button to restore the tools to their default settings.

To Set the Interface and Default Colors

Recall that Photoshop retains the interface color scheme, as well as the foreground and background colors, from session to session. The following steps set the interface to Medium Gray and the foreground and background colors to black over white.

1 Click Edit on the Application bar to display the Edit menu. Point to Preferences and then click Interface on the Preferences submenu to display the Preferences dialog box.

② If necessary, click the third button, Medium Gray, to change the interface color scheme.

③ Click the OK button to close the Preferences dialog box.

④ Press the D key to reset the default foreground and background colors. If black is not over white on the Tools panel, press the X key.

To Open a File

To open a file in Photoshop, it must be stored as a digital file on your computer system or on an external storage device. To complete this assignment, you will be required to use the Data Files for Students. Visit www.cengage.com/ct/studentdownload for detailed instructions or contact your instructor for information about accessing the required files. The following steps open the Baskets file from the Data Files for Students.

① With the Photoshop window open, click File on the Application bar, and then click Open to display the Open dialog box.

② In the Open dialog box, click the Look in box arrow to display the list of available locations, and then click the location of the Photoshop Data Files for Students.

③ Double-click the Chapter 02 folder to display its contents. Double-click the file, Baskets, to open it.

④ When Photoshop displays the image in the document window, if the magnification shown on the status bar is not 60%, double-click the magnification box on the document window status bar, type 60, and then press the ENTER key to change the magnification (Figure 2–3).

BTW

Document Window Status Bar
The status bar of the document window in Figure 2–3 shows the current document size. To display the document dimensions, click the status bar menu button, and then click Document Dimensions.

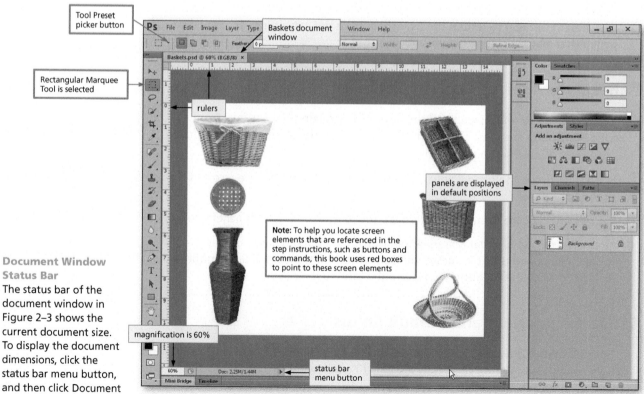

Figure 2–3

To View Rulers

The following steps display the rulers in the document window to facilitate making precise measurements.

1 If the rulers are not shown on the top and left sides of the document window, press CTRL+R to display the rulers in the workspace.

2 If necessary, right-click the horizontal ruler and then click Inches on the context menu to display the rulers in inches.

To Save a Photo

Even though you have yet to edit the photo, it is a good practice to save the file on your personal storage device early in the process. The following steps save the photo with the name Baskets Edited in a new folder named Chapter 02.

1 With your USB flash drive connected to one of the computer's USB ports, click File on the Application bar to display the File menu and then click Save As to display the Save As dialog box.

2 In the File name text box, type `Baskets Edited` to rename the file. Do not press the ENTER key after typing the file name.

3 Click the Save in box arrow, and then click Removable Disk (F:), or the location associated with your USB flash drive, in the list, if necessary.

4 On the Save As dialog box toolbar, click the Create New Folder button to create a new folder on the selected storage device.

5 When the new folder appears, type `Chapter 02` to change the name of the folder, and then press the ENTER key. Double-click the new folder to open it.

6 Click the Save button in the Save As dialog box to save the file in the new folder.

The Marquee Tools

The **marquee tools** allow you to draw a marquee that selects a portion of the document window. Marquee tools are useful when the part of an image or photo that you wish to select fits into a rectangular or an elliptical shape. Photoshop has four marquee tools that appear in a context menu when you click the tool and hold down the mouse button, or when you right-click the tool. You can select any of the marquee tools from this context menu. Recall that Photoshop offers the added flexibility of selecting a tool with a single letter shortcut key. Pressing the M key activates the current marquee tool.

The Rectangular Marquee Tool is the default marquee tool that selects a rectangular or square portion of the image or photo. The Elliptical Marquee Tool allows you to select an ellipsis, oval, or circular area.

Dragging with the Rectangular or Elliptical Marquee Tools creates a marquee drawn from a corner. If you press the SHIFT key while dragging a marquee, Photoshop constrains the proportions of the shape, creating a perfect square or circle. If you press the ALT key while drawing a selection, Photoshop creates the marquee from the center. Pressing SHIFT+ALT starts from the center and constrains the proportions.

BTW

Marquee Tool Selection
If you are using a different tool and want to activate the marquee tools, you can click the Rectangular Marquee Tool button on the Tools panel or press the M key on the keyboard to select the tool. Once the tool is selected, pressing SHIFT+M toggles between the Rectangular and Elliptical Marquee tools. You must choose the Single Row and Single Column Marquee tools from the context menu – there are no keyboard shortcuts.

The Single Row Marquee Tool allows you to select a single row of pixels. The Single Column Marquee Tool allows you to select a single column of pixels. A single click in the document window then creates the selection. Because a single row or column of pixels is so small, it is easier to use these two marquee tools at higher magnifications.

Plan Ahead

Choose the correct tool.
When you need to copy, paste, and move portions of your photo, consider carefully which selection tool to use. You want the procedure to be efficient and produce a clear image. Keep in mind the following as you choose a selection tool:

• The shape of the selection

• The background around the selection

• The contrast between the selection and its surroundings

• The proximity of the selection to other objects

• Your expertise in using the tool

• The availability of other pointing devices, such as a graphics tablet

• The destination of the paste

Table 2–1 describes the four marquee tools.

BTW

Single Row and Single Column Marquee Tools
To create interesting backgrounds, wallpapers, and color ribbons using the Single Row or Single Column Marquee tools, choose a colorful photo and create a single row or single column marquee. Press CTRL+T to display the bounding box. Then drag the sizing handles until the selection fills the document window.

Table 2–1 The Marquee Tools

Tool	Purpose	Shortcut	Button
Rectangular Marquee	Selects a rectangular or square portion of the document window	M SHIFT+M toggles to Elliptical Marquee	
Elliptical Marquee	Selects an elliptical, oval, or circular portion of the document window	M SHIFT+M toggles to Rectangular Marquee	
Single Row Marquee	Selects a single row of pixels in the document window	(none)	
Single Column Marquee	Selects a single column of pixels in the document window	(none)	

The options bar associated with each of the marquee tools contains many buttons and settings to draw effective marquees (Figure 2–4). The options bar displays an icon for the chosen marquee on the left, followed by the Tool Preset picker. The Tool Preset picker allows you to save and reuse toolbar settings.

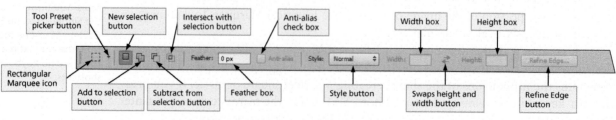

Figure 2–4

The next four buttons to the right adjust the selection. When selected, the New selection button allows you to start a new marquee.

The 'Add to selection' button draws a rectangle or ellipsis and adds it to any current selection. The 'Add to selection' button is useful for selecting the extra corners of an L-shaped object or for shapes that do not fit within a single rectangle or ellipsis. To activate the 'Add to selection' button, you can click it on the options bar, or press and hold the SHIFT key while dragging a second selection. When adding to a selection, the mouse pointer changes to a crosshair with a plus sign.

The 'Subtract from selection' button allows you to deselect or remove a portion of an existing selection. The new rectangle or ellipsis is removed from the original selection. It is useful for removing block portions of the background around oddly shaped images, or for deselecting ornamentation in an object. To activate the 'Subtract from selection' button, you can click it on the options bar, or press and hold the ALT key while dragging. When subtracting from a selection, the mouse pointer changes to a crosshair with a minus sign.

The 'Intersect with selection' button allows you to draw a second rectangle or ellipsis across a portion of the previously selected area, resulting in a selection border only around the area in which the two selections overlap. To activate the 'Intersect with selection' button, you click it on the options bar, or hold down the SHIFT and ALT keys while dragging. When creating an intersection, the mouse pointer changes to a crosshair with an X.

To the right of the selection buttons, the options bar displays a Feather box. **Feathering** softens the edges of the selection. In traditional photography, feathering is called **vignetting,** which creates a soft-edged border around an image that blends into the background. Feathering sometimes is used in wedding photos or when a haloed effect is desired. The width of the feather is measured in pixels. When using the Elliptical Marquee Tool, you can further specify blending by selecting the Anti-alias check box. **Anti-aliasing** softens the block-like, staircase look of rounded corners. Figure 2–5 shows a rectangle with no feathering, one with 10 pixels of feathering, an ellipsis with no anti-aliasing, and one created with a check mark in the Anti-alias check box.

BTW

The Tool Preset Picker
Most tools display a Tool Preset picker on the options bar. When you click the button, Photoshop displays a list of settings used during the current Photoshop session or previously saved options bar settings. The list makes it easier to save and reuse tool settings. You can load, edit, and create libraries of tool presets in conjunction with the Tool Presets panel. To choose a tool preset, click the Tool Preset picker in the options bar, and then select a preset from the list.

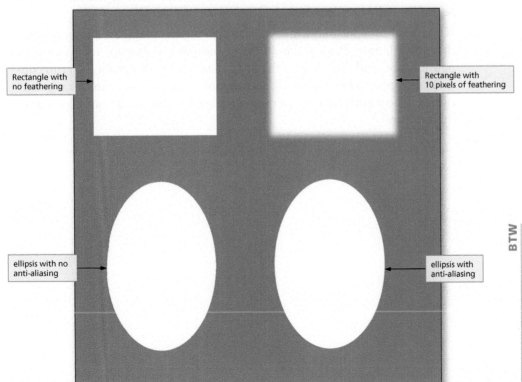

Rectangle with no feathering

Rectangle with 10 pixels of feathering

ellipsis with no anti-aliasing

ellipsis with anti-aliasing

Figure 2–5

BTW

Anti-Aliasing
Anti-aliasing is available for the Elliptical Marquee Tool, the Lasso Tool, the Polygonal Lasso Tool, the Magnetic Lasso Tool, and the Magic Wand Tool. You must specify this option before applying these tools. Once a selection is created, you cannot add anti-aliasing.

BTW

Scrubby Sliders
You can drag some options bar labels in Photoshop. When you point to the label, a **scrubby slider** that looks like a pointing finger appears. Dragging the scrubby slider changes the value in the accompanying text box on the options bar. For example, the Feather box label on the Rectangular Marquee Tool options bar is a scrubby slider.

BTW

Layers
A layer is a portion of the image superimposed, or separated, from other parts of the document. Think of layers as sheets of clear film stacked one on top of the other. In Chapter 3, you will learn how to change the composition of an image by changing the order and attributes of layers.

BTW

Deleting Selections
You can delete a selection by pressing the DELETE key on the keyboard. Photoshop will display a Fill dialog box. Click the OK button. If you delete by accident, press CTRL+Z to bring the selection back.

When using the Rectangular Marquee Tool or the Elliptical Marquee Tool, you can click the Style button (Figure 2–4 on page PS 76) to choose how the size of the marquee selection is determined. A Normal style sets the selection marquee proportions by dragging. A Fixed Ratio style sets a height-to-width ratio using decimal values. For example, to draw a marquee twice as wide as it is high, enter 2 for the width and 1 for the height, and then drag in the photo. A Fixed Size style allows you to specify exact pixel values for the marquee's height and width. Photoshop enables the Width box and Height box when you choose a style other than Normal. A button between the two boxes swaps the values, if desired.

Sometimes you need to make subtle changes to a selection marquee. For example, if the border or edge of a selection seems to be jagged or hazy, or if the colors at the edge of a selection bleed slightly across the marquee, you can use the Refine Edge button. When clicked, it opens a dialog box in which you can increase or decrease the radius of the marquee, change the contrast, and smooth the selection border.

Once you have drawn a marquee, you can choose from other options for further manipulation of the selected area. Right-clicking a selection displays a context menu that provides access to many other useful commands such as deselecting, reselecting, or selecting the **inverse**, which means selecting everything in the image outside of the current selection. The context menu also enables you to create layers, apply color fills and strokes, and make other changes that you will learn about in future chapters.

If you make a mistake or change your mind when drawing a marquee, you can do one of three things:

1. If you want to start over, and the New selection button is selected on the options bar, you can click somewhere else in the document window to deselect the marquee; then simply draw a new marquee. Deselecting also is available as a command on the Select menu and on the context menu. The shortcut for deselecting is CTRL+D.

2. If you have already drawn the marquee but want to move or reposition it, and the New selection button is selected on the options bar, you can drag the selection to the new location.

3. If you want to reposition while you are creating the marquee, do not release the mouse button. Press and hold the SPACEBAR key, drag the marquee to the new location, and then release the SPACEBAR key. At that point, you can continue dragging to finish drawing the marquee. Repositioning in this manner can be done while using any of the four selection adjustment buttons on the options bar.

To Use the Rectangular Marquee Tool

The following step selects the tall basket in the lower-left corner of the Baskets Edited image using the Rectangular Marquee Tool. You will use the Elliptical Marquee Tool later in this chapter.

- With the Rectangular Marquee Tool selected on the Tools panel, drag to draw a rectangle around the tall basket in the lower-left corner to create a marquee selection. Drag close to the basket itself, as shown in Figure 2–6.

Experiment

- Practice drawing rectangular and elliptical marquees. Press SHIFT+M to switch between the two. SHIFT+DRAG to look at the effects. Press and hold the SPACEBAR key while you drag to reposition the current marquee. When you are finished, redraw a rectangle around the basket.

Q&A

What was the black box that appeared as I created the marquee?

That was the Transformation Values indicator to help show you exactly where you are in the image.

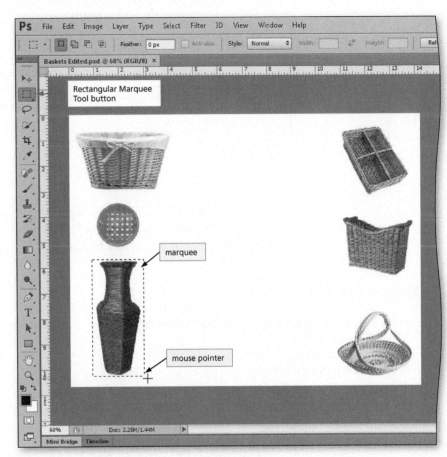

Figure 2–6

Other Ways

1. Press M key or SHIFT+M until Rectangular Marquee Tool is active, drag selection

The Move Tool

The Move Tool on the Photoshop Tools panel is used to move or make other changes to selections. Activating the Move Tool by clicking the Move Tool button, or by pressing the V key on the keyboard, enables you to move the selection border and its contents by dragging in the document window. When you first use the Move Tool, the mouse pointer displays a black arrowhead with scissors. To move the selection in a straight line, press and hold the SHIFT key while dragging. If you press and hold the ALT key while dragging, you duplicate or move only a copy of the selected area, effectively copying and pasting the selection. While duplicating, the mouse pointer changes to a black arrowhead with a white arrowhead behind it.

When you move selections, you need to be careful about overlapping images. As you will learn in Chapter 3, Photoshop might layer or overlap portions of images when you move them. While that sometimes is preferred when creating collages or composite images, it is undesirable if an important object is obscured. Close tracing while creating selections and careful placement of moved selections will prevent unwanted layering.

The Move Tool options bar displays tools to help define the scope of the move (Figure 2–7). Later, as you learn about layers, you will use the Auto-Select check box to select layer groupings or single layers. The Show Transform Controls check box causes Photoshop to display transformation controls on the selection. The align and distribute buttons and the Auto-Align Layers button also are used with layers. The 3D mode buttons transform a 3-D selection.

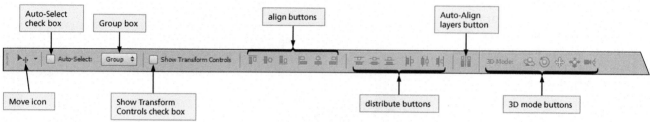

Figure 2–7

As you use the Move Tool throughout this chapter, be careful to position your mouse pointer inside the selection before moving. Do not try to move a selection by dragging its border. If you drag a border by mistake, press the ESC key.

To Use the Move Tool

The following steps use the Move Tool to move the basket up and to the right.

1

- With the basket still selected, click the Move Tool button on the Tools panel to activate the Move Tool.

- If necessary, on the options bar, click the Auto-Select check box so it does not display a check mark. If necessary, click the Show Transform Controls check box so it does not display a check mark (Figure 2–8).

Q&A

Are there any other tools nested with the Move Tool?

No, the Move Tool does not have a context menu. Tools with a context menu display a small black rectangle in the lower-right corner.

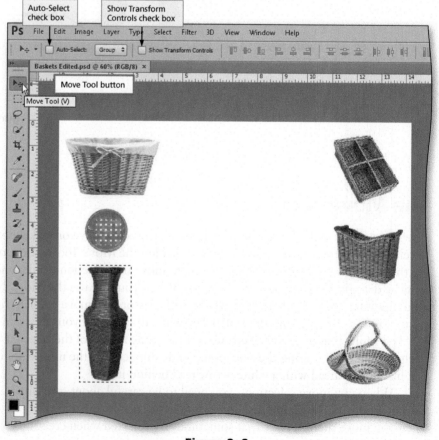

Figure 2–8

2

• Position your mouse pointer over the basket, within the marquee. Drag the selection to a position in the upper-center portion of the photo (Figure 2–9). Do not press any other keys.

Q&A

My document window shows a black square. What did I do wrong?

It is possible that the default colors on your system were changed by another user. Press CTRL+Z to undo the move. Press the D key to select the default foreground and background colors. If black is not on top at the bottom of the Tools panel, press the X key to exchange the black and white colors.

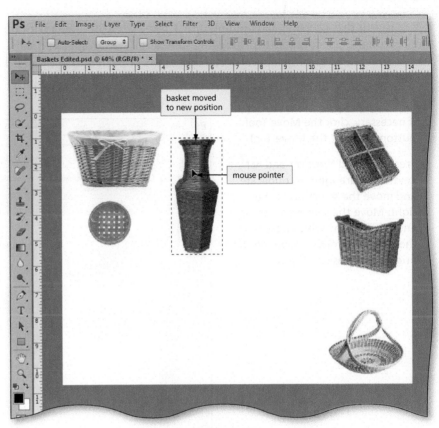

Figure 2–9

Other Ways

1. Press V, drag selection

Plan your duplications.

Creating a storyboard, either by hand or by using software, allows you to plan your image and make decisions about copies and placement. Some graphic artists annotate each copy in the storyboard with information about size, shape, location, and the tool they plan to use (Figure 2–2 on page PS 72). For example, when you paste or drag a new copy of an image into a photo, you have two choices. You can keep the copy as an exact duplicate, or you can transform the copy. The choice depends on the visual effect you want to achieve and the customer requirements. Notating those requirements on your storyboard ahead of time will facilitate creating your image.

Use an exact copy of a logo or border to create a tiled background. Commercial applications may create duplications to represent growth; or several duplications beside each other can emphasize a brand. Sometimes artists will duplicate an item several times when creating a quick sketch or a rough draft. Across photos, exact duplicates maintain consistency and product identification.

Transforming a copy or section provides additional flexibility and diversity. You might want to create the illusion of multiple, different items to promote sales. Scaling, skewing, warping, and distorting provide interest and differentiation, and sometimes can correct lens errors. Flipping, rotating, or changing the perspective of the copy adds visual excitement to reproductions and creates the illusion of three dimensions.

Plan Ahead

To Duplicate a Selection

Recall that pressing and holding the ALT key while dragging with the Move Tool creates a copy, or duplicates, the selection. SHIFT+dragging moves the selection in a straight line. Using both the SHIFT and ALT keys while dragging duplicates and moves the copy in a straight line. The following step accesses the Move Tool and creates a copy of the selected basket.

- If necessary, click the Move Tool button to select the Move Tool.

- Press and hold the SHIFT and ALT keys while dragging to duplicate and move the selection to the right. Move the selection just far enough that the white portion of the selection does not overlap the original tall basket (Figure 2–10).

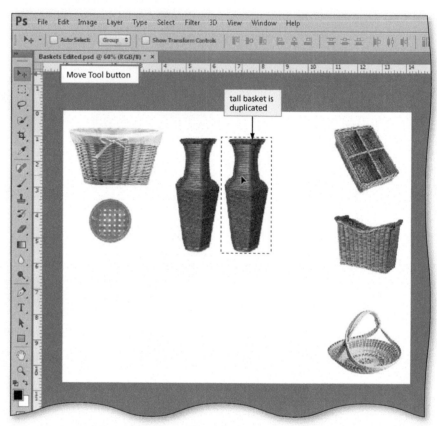

Figure 2–10

Other Ways

1. Press CTRL+C, press CTRL+V, press V, drag selection
2. Press V, ALT+drag selection

To Deselect

The following step deselects the baskets.

 On the Select menu, click Deselect.

The Quick Selection Tool

The Quick Selection Tool draws a selection quickly using the mouse. As you drag, Photoshop creates a selection automatically, expanding outward to find and follow the defined edges in the image. The Quick Selection Tool is nested with the Magic Wand Tool on the Tools panel. You can access either tool from the context menu or by pressing the W key; if the Magic Wand Tool has been used previously, press SHIFT+W to access the Quick Selection Tool.

Dragging a quick selection is almost like painting a stroke with a brush. The Quick Selection Tool does not create a rectangular or oval selection; rather, it looks for a contrast in color and aligns the selection border to that contrast. It is most useful for isolated objects or parts of an image that contain a contrasting background. When using the Quick Selection Tool, the mouse pointer changes to a brush tip that displays a circle with a centered cross inside. You can decrease or increase the size of the brush tip by using the LEFT BRACKET ([) or RIGHT BRACKET (]) keys respectively, or by using the options bar.

The Quick Selection Tool options bar (Figure 2–11) displays the size of the brush and contains some of the same buttons as other selection tools. It also contains an Auto-Enhance check box that reduces roughness in the selection boundary when the box is checked.

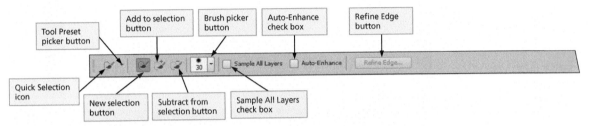

Figure 2–11

To Use the Quick Selection Tool

The following steps use the Quick Selection Tool to select the basket in the middle on the right.

1

- Click the Quick Selection Tool button on the Tools panel to select it. If the tool icon does not display a brush, right-click the button and then click Quick Selection Tool on the context menu.

- On the options bar, click the New selection button, if necessary.

- Click the Auto-Enhance check box so it displays a check mark (Figure 2–12).

Q&A

What does the Auto-Enhance feature do?

Auto-Enhance reduces the block-like edges in the selection border and adjusts the selection further toward the edges of the image.

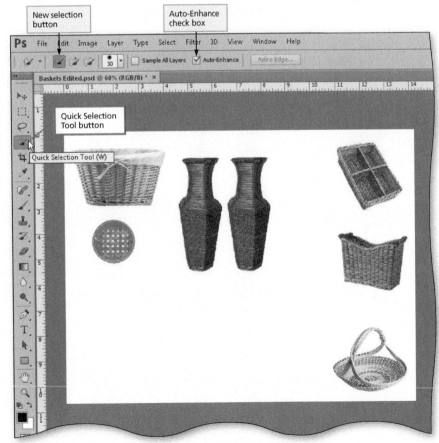

Figure 2–12

2

- Move the mouse pointer to the lower-right corner of the middle basket on the right, and then slowly drag up and left to select only the basket (Figure 2–13).

Q&A

What should I do if I make a mistake with the Quick Selection Tool?

If you make a mistake and want to start over, you can deselect by pressing CTRL+D, and then begin again.

Experiment

- Practice resizing the mouse pointer by using the LEFT BRACKET ([) key to decrease the size or the RIGHT BRACKET (]) key to increase the size.

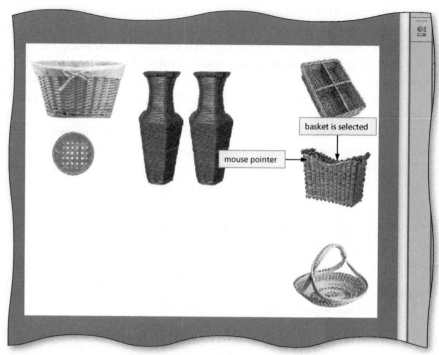

Figure 2–13

Other Ways

1. Press W or SHIFT+W until Quick Selection Tool is active, drag selection

To Move a Selection

The following steps move the basket using the Move Tool. If you make a mistake while moving, press CTRL+Z and then move the basket again.

1 On the Tools panel, click the Move Tool button to select the tool.

2 Drag the selection left and slightly up, as shown in Figure 2–14. Do not press any other keys.

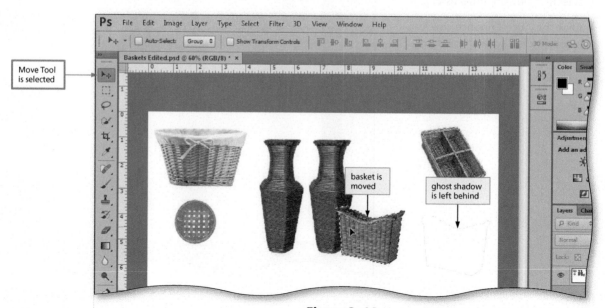

Figure 2–14

The History Panel

The History panel appears when you click the History button on the vertical dock of minimized panels. The History panel records each step, called a **state**, as you edit a photo (Figure 2–15). Photoshop displays the initial state of the document at the top of the panel. Each time you apply a change to an image, the new state of that image is added to the bottom of the panel. Each state lists the name of the tool or command used to change the image.

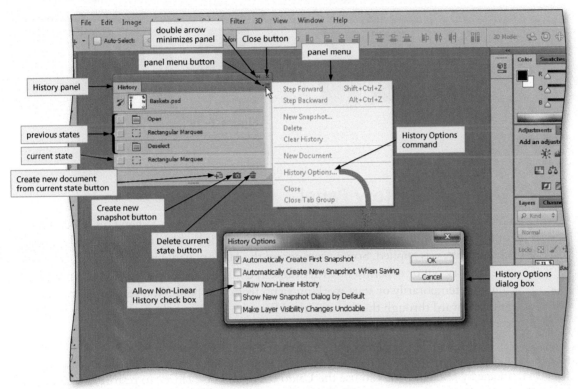

Figure 2–15

Like the Navigator panel that you learned about in Chapter 1, the History panel also has a panel menu where you can clear all states, change the history settings, or dock the panel. Buttons on the History panel status bar allow you to create a new document from a state, save the selected state, or delete it. The panel can be minimized by clicking the History button on the vertical dock or by clicking the double arrow at the top of the panel. To redisplay a minimized History panel, click the History button on the vertical dock, or choose it from the Window menu.

BTW

Using the History Panel Menu
The History panel menu has commands you can use to step forward and step backward through the listed states on the History panel.

To Display the History Panel

The following step displays the History panel.

1

- Click the History button on the vertical dock of minimized panels (Figure 2–16).

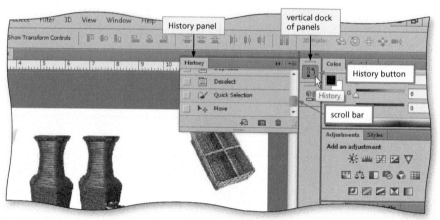

Figure 2–16

BTW

The History Panel
The History panel will list a Duplicate state when you use the ALT key to copy a selection. The word Paste will appear next to the state when you use the Copy and Paste commands from the keyboard or from the menu. The Copy command alone does not affect how the image looks; it merely sends a copy to the system Clipboard. Therefore, it does not appear as a state.

Using the History Panel

You can use the History panel in several different ways. When you select one of the states, Photoshop displays the image the way it looked at that point, when that change first was applied. Some users access the History panel to undo mistakes. Others use it to try out or experiment with different edits. By clicking a state, you can view the state temporarily or start working again from that point. You can step forward and backward through the states in the History panel by clicking them, or by pressing CTRL+SHIFT+Z or CTRL+ALT+Z, respectively.

Selecting a state and then changing the image in any way eliminates all the states in the History panel that came after it; however, if you select a state and change the image by accident, you can use the Undo command or CTRL+Z to restore the eliminated states. If you select the Allow Non-Linear History check box in the History Options dialog box (Figure 2–15 on the previous page) deleting a state deletes only that state.

You can use the History panel to jump to any recent state of the image created during the current working session by clicking the state. Alternatively, you also can give a state a new name, called a **snapshot**. Naming a snapshot identifies a state and distinguishes it from other states. Snapshots are stored at the top of the History panel and make it easy to compare effects. For example, you can take a snapshot before and after a series of transformations. Then, by clicking between the two snapshots in the History panel, you can see the total effect, or choose the before snapshot and start over. To create a snapshot, right-click the state and then click New Snapshot on the context menu, or click the Create new snapshot button on the History panel status bar. Snapshots do not save with the image; closing an image deletes its snapshots.

Not all steps appear in the History panel. For instance, changes to panels, color settings, actions, and preferences are not displayed in the History panel, because they are not changes to a particular image.

By default, the History panel lists the previous 20 states. You can change the number of remembered states by changing a preference setting (see the Changing Screen Resolution appendix). Photoshop deletes older states automatically to free more memory. Once you close and reopen the document, all states and snapshots from the last working session are cleared from the panel.

To Undo Changes Using the History Panel

Notice in Figure 2–14 on page PS 84 that a shadow appears in the previous location of the basket. This shadow, called a ghost shadow, sometimes occurs when using any of the selection tools, especially when fringe pixels are faded — they were not included in the selection marquee. Therefore, you need to return to the previous state and try again. The following step uses the History Panel to undo the Move command.

1

- If necessary, scroll down in the History panel to display the last few states.

- Click the Quick Selection state in the History panel to go back one step and undo the move (Figure 2–17). Do not press any other keys.

Q&A | Could I have pressed CTRL+Z to undo the move?

Yes, if you only need to undo one step, pressing CTRL+Z will work. If you need to go back more than one step, you can press CTRL+ALT+Z or use the History panel.

Q&A | What is the box to the left of each state?

When selected, that box sets the source for painting a clone-like image using the Art History Brush Tool.

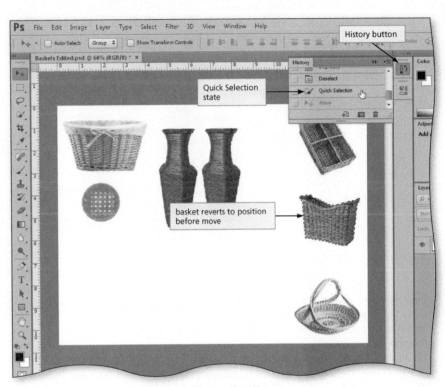

Figure 2–17

Other Ways
1. Press CTRL+ALT+Z

To Minimize the History Panel

Recall in Chapter 1 that you minimized the Navigator panel by clicking the double arrow at the top of the panel. You also can minimize a panel by clicking the panel button on the vertical dock, as demonstrated in the following step.

1 Click the History button to minimize the panel.

BTW

Moving Among History Panel States
Photoshop uses many function keys to move easily among the states in the History panel. To step forward, press SHIFT+CTRL+Z. To step backward, press CTRL+ALT+Z. You also can use the History panel menu to step forward and backward.

Refining Edges

Each of the selection tools has a Refine Edge button located on its options bar, as shown in Figure 2–11 on page PS 83. Clicking the Refine Edge button displays a dialog box where you can make choices about improving selections with jagged edges, soft transitions, hazy borders, or fine details, and improve the quality of a selection's edges. Additionally, it allows you to view the selection on different backgrounds to facilitate editing (Figure 2–18 on the next page).

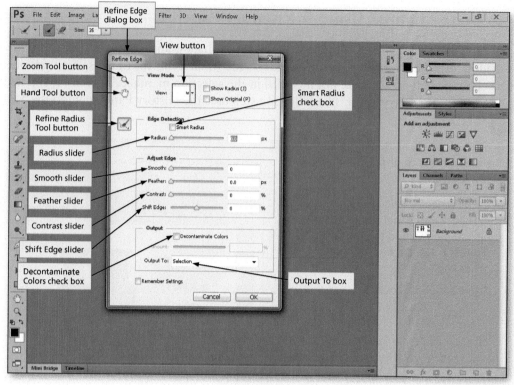

Figure 2–18

Flipping Selections
When you flip a selection, Photoshop creates a mirror image with a horizontal flip, or an upside-down version of the selection with a vertical flip. Flipping is available on the Edit menu and its Transform submenu or on the context menu when you right-click a selection. Flip transformations do not have to be committed.

Table 2–2 displays some of the controls in the Refine Edge dialog box and their functions.

Table 2–2 Controls and Buttons in the Refine Edge Dialog Box	
Control or Button	**Function**
View Mode	Allows you to choose the background of the selection and show the radius, original, or both views
Smart Radius check box	Adjusts the radius edges automatically
Radius slider	Adjusts the size of the selection boundary by pixels
Smooth slider	Reduces irregular areas in the selection boundary to create a smoother outline with values from 0 to 100 pixels
Feather slider	Softens the edges of the selection for blending into backgrounds using values from 0 to 250 pixels
Contrast slider	Sharpens the selection edges to remove any hazy or extraneous pixels, sometimes called fuzzy artifacts or noise; increasing the contrast percentage can remove excessive noise near selection edges caused by a high radius setting
Shift Edge	Moves soft-edged borders helping remove or include background colors from selection edges
Decontaminate Colors check box	Replaces fringe color
Output To	Sets the output to a mask, layer, or new document
Remember Settings check box	Saves all settings in the dialog box for use on another selection
Zoom Tool button	Zooms selection in or out
Hand Tool button	Moves portion of the document window that is displayed
Refine Radius Tool button	Precisely adjusts the border area in which edge refinement occurs; pressing SHIFT+E toggles to the Erase Refinements Tool button
Erase Refinements Tool button	Precisely adjusts the border area in which edge refinement occurs; pressing SHIFT+E toggles to the Refine Radius Tool button

The various settings in the Refine Edge dialog box take practice to use intuitively. The more experience you have adjusting the settings, the more comfortable you will feel with the controls. To improve selections for images on a contrasting background, you should first increase the radius and then increase the contrast to sharpen the edges. For grayscale images or selections where the colors of the object and the background are similar, try smoothing first, then feathering. For all selections, you might need to adjust the Contract/Expand slider.

To Refine Edges

The following steps refine the edge of the selection.

1

- On the Tools panel, click the Quick Selection Tool button to select it (Figure 2–19).

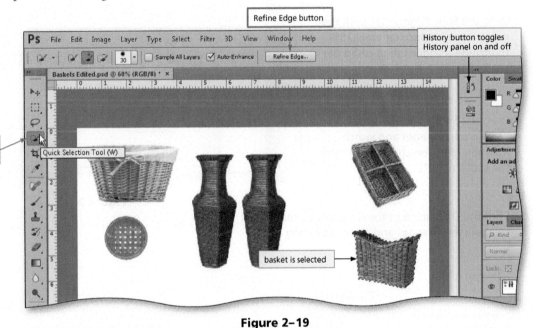

Figure 2–19

2

- On the Quick Selection Tool options bar, click the Refine Edge button to display the Refine Edge dialog box.

- Click the View button to display the refine edge views (Figure 2–20).

  Experiment

- One at a time, click each of the views and notice how the background of the document window changes. Drag the title bar of the dialog box, if necessary to move the dialog box out of the way.

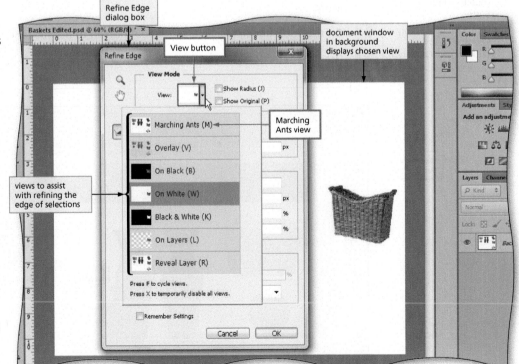

Figure 2–20

- Double-click Marching Ants to view the selection as a marquee.

- Drag the Radius slider until the Radius box displays approximately 20 pixels to increase the radius of the selection.

- Drag the Contrast slider until the Contrast box displays 40% to increase the contrast between the selection and its surrounding.

- Drag the Shift Edge slider until the percentage is approximately 75% to include a wider range of border colors (Figure 2–21).

 **Experiment**

- Drag the Shift Edge slider to various percentages and watch how the selection changes. Return the slider to 75%.

- Click the OK button in the Refine Edge dialog box to apply the changes and close the dialog box.

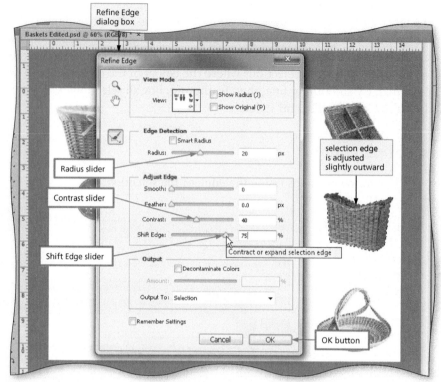

Figure 2–21

Other Ways

1. Press ALT+CTRL+R, choose settings, click OK button

2. Right-click selection, click Refine Edge, choose settings, click OK button

3. On Select menu, click Refine Edge, choose settings, click OK button

To Move Again

The following steps move the basket again, this time without leaving behind a shadow.

1 On the Tools panel, click the Move Tool button to activate the Move Tool.

2 Drag the selection left and slightly up, as shown in Figure 2–22.

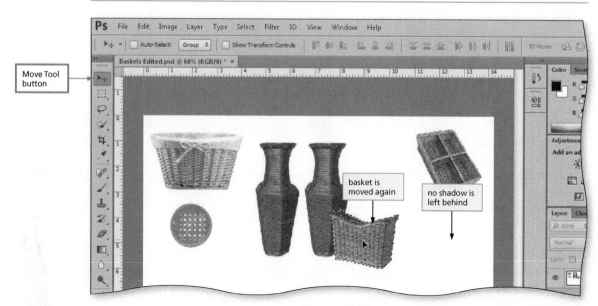

Figure 2–22

To Deselect Using a Shortcut Key

The following step deselects the selection using a shortcut key.

1 Press CTRL+D to deselect.

To Zoom

To facilitate selecting other baskets, the following steps zoom to the upper-left portion of the document window.

1 On the Tools panel, click the Zoom Tool button to select the tool.

2 Click the upper-left corner of the document window twice to zoom that portion of the window to 100% (Figure 2–23).

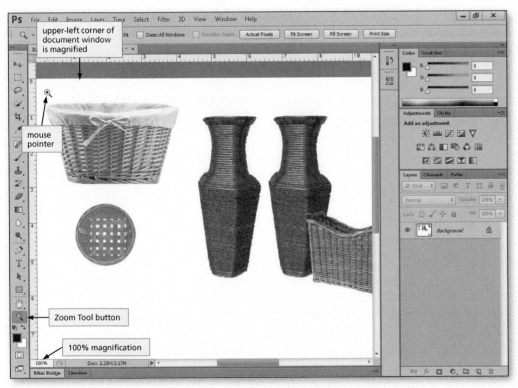

Figure 2–23

The Lasso Tools

The **lasso tools** draw freehand selection borders around objects. The lasso tools provide more flexibility than the marquee tools with their standardized shapes, and might be more suitable than the Quick Selection Tool when the object has a noncontrasting background. Photoshop provides three kinds of lasso tools. The first is the default Lasso Tool, which allows you to create a selection by using the mouse to drag around any object in the document window. You select the Lasso Tool button on the Tools panel. You then begin to drag around the desired area. When you release the mouse, Photoshop connects the selection border to the point where you began dragging, finishing the loop. The Lasso Tool is useful for a quick, rough selection.

BTW

Lasso Tool Selection
If you are using a different tool, and want to activate a lasso tool, you can click the Lasso Tool button on the Tools panel or press the L key on the keyboard to select the Lasso Tool. After selecting the Lasso Tool, pressing SHIFT+L cycles through the three lasso tools.

BTW

Completing Lassos
To complete a selection using the Lasso tool, simply release the mouse button. To complete a selection using the Polygonal Lasso or Magnetic Lasso, double-click. Alternatively, you can move the mouse pointer close to the starting point. When a small circle appears on the edge of the mouse pointer, single-click to complete the lasso.

The Polygonal Lasso Tool is similar to the Lasso Tool in that it draws irregular shapes in the image; however, the Polygonal Lasso Tool uses straight line segments. To use the Polygonal Lasso Tool, choose the tool, click in the document window, release the mouse button, and then move the mouse in straight lines, clicking each time you turn a corner. When you get back to the beginning of the polygon, double-click to complete the selection.

The Magnetic Lasso Tool allows you to click close to the edge of the object you want to select. The Magnetic Lasso Tool tries to find the edge of the object by looking for the nearest color change. It then attaches the marquee to the pixel on the edge of the color change. As you move the mouse, the Magnetic Lasso Tool follows that color change with a magnetic attraction. The Magnetic Lasso Tool's marquee displays fastening points on the edge of the object. You can create more fastening points by clicking as you move the mouse, to force a change in direction or to adjust the magnetic attraction. When you get all the way around the object, you click at the connection point to complete the loop, or double-click to have Photoshop connect the loop for you. Because the Magnetic Lasso Tool looks for changes in color to define the edges of an object, it might not be as effective to create selections in images with a busy background or images with low contrast. Each of the lasso tools displays its icon as the mouse pointer.

Table 2–3 describes the three lasso tools.

Table 2–3 The Lasso Tools			
Tool	**Purpose**	**Shortcut**	**Button**
Lasso	Used to draw freeform loops, creating a selection border	L SHIFT+L toggles through all three lasso tools	
Polygonal Lasso	Used to draw straight lines, creating segments of a selection border	L SHIFT+L toggles through all three lasso tools	
Magnetic Lasso	Used to draw a selection border that snaps to the edge of contrasting color areas in the image	L SHIFT+L toggles through all three lasso tools	

Each of the lasso tools displays an options bar similar to the marquee options bar, with buttons to add to, subtract from, and intersect with the selection; the ability to feather the border; and, an Anti-alias check box to smooth the borders of a selection (Figure 2–24). Unique to the Magnetic Lasso Tool options bar, however, is a Contrast box to enter the **contrast**, or sensitivity of color that Photoshop evaluates in making the path selection. A higher value detects only edges that contrast sharply with their surroundings; a lower value detects lower-contrast edges. The Width box causes the Magnetic Lasso Tool to detect edges only within the specified distance from the mouse pointer. A Frequency box allows you to specify the rate at which the lasso sets fastening points. A higher value anchors the selection border in place more quickly. A tablet pressure button on the right changes the pen width when using a graphic drawing tablet instead of a mouse.

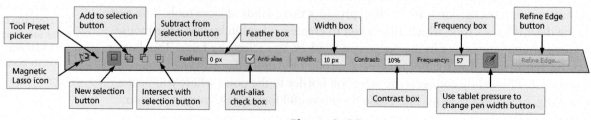

Figure 2–24

To Select using the Polygonal Lasso Tool

The following steps select the upper-left, lined basket by drawing lines around it with the Polygonal Lasso Tool. You will use the other lasso tools later in the chapter.

1

- In the document window, scroll as necessary to display the lined basket in the upper-left corner.

- Right-click the Lasso Tool button on the Tools panel to display the context menu (Figure 2–25).

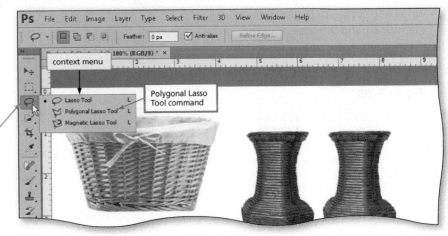

Figure 2–25

2

- Click Polygonal Lasso Tool to activate the lasso.

- If necessary, on the options bar, click the New selection button (Figure 2–26).

Experiment

- Practice using the Polygonal Lasso Tool to draw a triangle by doing the following: in a blank area of the photo, click to begin; move the mouse pointer to the right; and then click to create one side. Move the mouse pointer up, and then click to create a second side. Move the mouse pointer to the beginning point, and then click to complete the lasso. When you are finished experimenting, press CTRL+D to deselect.

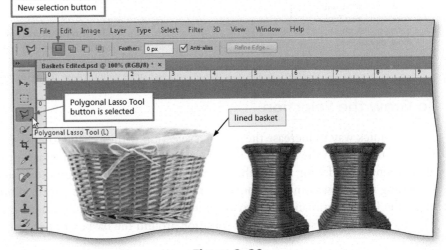

Figure 2–26

3

- Using the tip of the black arrow on the mouse pointer, click the top of the lined basket near the left side.

- Move the mouse pointer to the right to create the first line.

- Click the upper-right corner of the basket at a location before the basket's edge begins to curve downward (Figure 2–27).

Q&A Can I reposition the starting point if I make a mistake?

Yes. Press the ESC key and then start again.

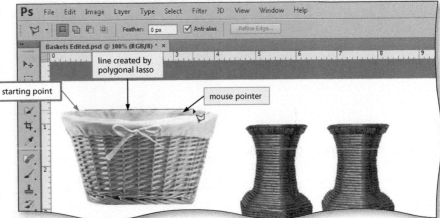

Figure 2–27

- Continue creating line segments by moving the mouse pointer and clicking each time you need to change direction.

- When you complete the lines all the way around the basket, move the mouse pointer until a small circle is visible, and then click to complete the selection (Figure 2–28).

Q&A

What was the small circle that appeared when I moved close to the beginning of the polygonal lasso?

When the mouse pointer moves close to where you started the polygonal lasso, Photoshop displays a small circle, which means you can single-click to complete the lasso. Otherwise, you have to double-click to complete the lasso.

Figure 2–28

Other Ways

1. Press L or SHIFT+L until Polygonal Lasso Tool is active, click photo, move mouse

BTW

The Similar Command
The Similar command increases the selection to include pixels throughout the selection, not just adjacent ones, which fall within the specified tolerance range. Choosing the Similar command more than once will increase the selection in increments.

To Grow the Selection

A quick way to increase the size of a selection without using the Refine Edge dialog box is to use the Grow command on the Select menu. The Grow command will increase, or grow, the selection border to include all adjacent pixels falling within the tolerance range as specified on the options bar of most selection tools. Choosing the Grow command more than once will increase the selection on increments. Similar to refining the edge, the Grow command helps to avoid leaving behind a shadow when you move the selection.

The following steps grow the selection around the basket, to prevent a shadow when moving.

- Click Select on the Application bar to display the Select menu (Figure 2–29).

Q&A

Will I notice a big difference after I use the Grow command?

You might not see the subtle change in the selection marquee; however, growing the border helps ensure that you will not leave behind a shadow when you move the selection.

- Click Grow to increase the selection border.

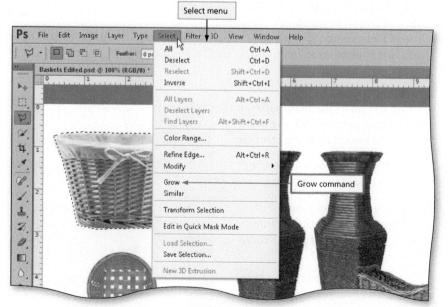

Figure 2–29

To Save using a Shortcut Key

The following step saves the image again, with the same file name, using a shortcut key.

1 Press CTRL+S to save the Baskets Edited file with the same name.

Break Point: If you wish to take a break, this is a good place to do so. To resume at a later time, start Photoshop, open the file called Baskets Edited, select the upper-left basket, and continue following the steps from this location forward.

Grids, Guides, and Snapping

Photoshop can show a **grid** of lines that appears as an overlay on the image. The grid is useful for laying out elements symmetrically or positioning them precisely. The grid can appear as nonprinting lines or dots. To display the grid, click Show on the View menu and then click Grid.

> **Use grids and guides.**
> Showing grids in your document window gives you multiple horizontal and vertical lines with which you can align selections, copies, and new images. Grids also can help you match and adjust sizes and perspective.
>   Create guides when you have an exact margin, location, or size in mind. Because selections will snap to guides, you easily can create an upper-left corner to use as a boundary when you move and copy. Grids and guides do not print and are turned on and off without difficulty.

**Plan
Ahead**

A **guide** is a nonprinting ruler line or dashed line that graphic designers use to align objects or mark key measurements. To create a guide, you turn on the ruler display and then drag from the horizontal ruler at the top of the document window or from the vertical ruler at the left side of the document window. When you release the mouse, a light, blue-green line appears across the image.

Table 2–4 displays various ways to manipulate guides.

Table 2–4 Manipulating Guides	
Action	**Steps**
Change color and style	Double-click guide.
Clear all guides	On the View menu, click Clear Guides.
Convert between horizontal and vertical guide	Select the Move Tool, ALT+click guide.
Create	Drag from ruler into document window, or, on the View menu, click New Guide, and then enter the orientation and position.
Lock in place	On the View menu, click Lock Guides.
Move	Select the Move Tool, and then drag the guide to a new location.
Remove	Select the Move Tool, and then drag the guide to the ruler.
Snap guide to ruler tick	SHIFT+drag the ruler.
Turn on/off display	On the Application bar, click View Extras, and then click Show Guides, or, on the View menu, point to Show, and then click Guides; or press CTRL+SEMICOLON (;).

BTW

Displaying Extras
On the View menu is an Extras command with which you can show or hide selection edges, guides, target paths, slices, annotations, layer borders, and smart guides. You also can use CTRL+H to show or hide those items.

The term **snapping** refers to the ability of objects to attach to, or automatically align with, a grid or guide. For example, if you select an object in your image and begin to move it, as you get close to a guide, the object's selection border will attach itself to the guide. It is not a permanent attachment. If you do not want to leave the object there, simply keep dragging. To turn on or off snapping, click Snap on the View menu.

In a later chapter, you will learn about smart guides that automatically appear when you draw a shape or move a layer. Smart guides further help align shapes, slices, selections, and layers. The Changing Screen Resolution appendix describes how to set guide and grid preferences using the Edit menu.

To Display a Grid

The following steps display the grid.

• On the Application bar, click View to display the View menu, and then point to Show to display the Show submenu (Figure 2–30).

Q&A

What does the Show Extras Options command do?

That command displays a dialog box where you can choose to display many different options such as grids, guides, layer edges, brush previews, and others. The choices you make then directly affect the Extras command on the View menu.

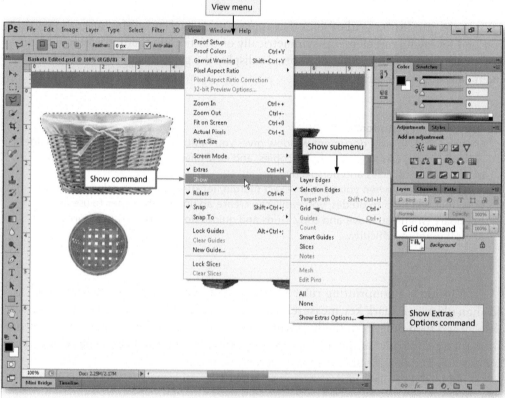

Figure 2–30

• Click the Grid command to display the grid (Figure 2–31).

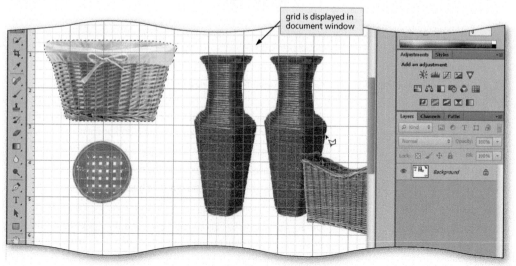

Figure 2–31

Other Ways

1. Press CTRL+APOSTROPHE (')

To Turn Off the Grid Display

The display of a grid is a **toggle**, which means that you turn it off in the same manner that you turned it on; in this case, with the same command.

1 On the Application bar, click View to display the View menu, and then point to Show to display the Show submenu.

2 Click Grid to remove the check mark and remove the grid from the display.

To Create a Guide

The following steps will create a guide to help you position the lined basket on the same horizontal plane as the previous basket.

- Position the mouse pointer in the horizontal ruler at the top of the document window.

- Drag down to create a guide, and stop at 6 inches as measured on the vertical ruler (Figure 2–32).

Q&A What is the black box that appears as I drag?

It is a mouse pointer tool tip that shows the location as you drag.

- Release the mouse button.

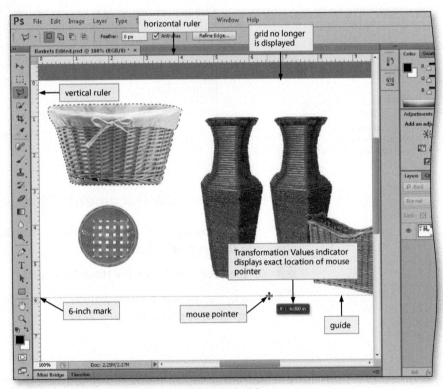

Figure 2–32

Other Ways

1. To show or hide guides, press CTRL+SEMICOLON (;)

2. To show or hide guides, point to Show on View menu, click Guides

3. To create guide, on View menu click New Guide, enter value, click OK button

---

BTW

Transformation Values Indicator
You can change the display of the Transformation Values indicator, or turn it off completely, by clicking Edit on the Application bar, pointing to Preferences, and then clicking Interface. In the Preferences dialog box, click the Show Transformation Values box arrow and then click the desired location of the indicator or click Never in the list.

To Snap a Selection to the Guide

The following steps move the selection, snapping it to the guide.

- Press the V key to activate the Move Tool.

- Slowly drag the selection to a location in front of the tall baskets until the bottom of the selection snaps to the guide (Figure 2–33).

2

- Press CTRL+D to deselect.

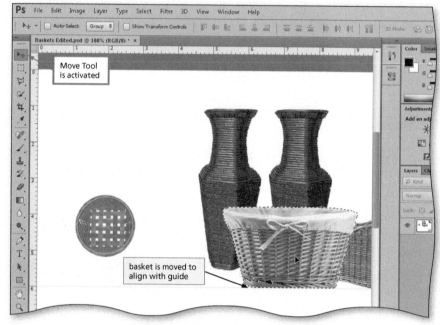

Other Ways

1. To turn on or off snapping, press SHIFT+CTRL+SEMICOLON (;)

Figure 2–33

To Reposition the Document Window

The following steps reposition the document window so that you can select the basket in the upper-right corner.

1 On the Tools panel, click the Hand Tool button.

2 Drag in the document window down and left until the basket in the upper-right corner is displayed, as shown in Figure 2–34.

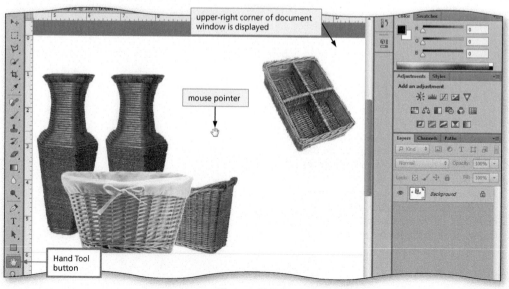

Figure 2–34

To Select using the Magnetic Lasso Tool

The following steps use the Magnetic Lasso Tool to select the divided basket in the upper-right corner of the document window. Recall that the Magnetic Lasso Tool selects by finding the edge of a contrasting color and creating fastening points.

● Right-click the current lasso tool button, and then click Magnetic Lasso Tool to select it from the context menu.

● If necessary, on the options bar, click the New selection button to select the tool.

● Click the lower-left corner of the basket to start the selection (Figure 2–35).

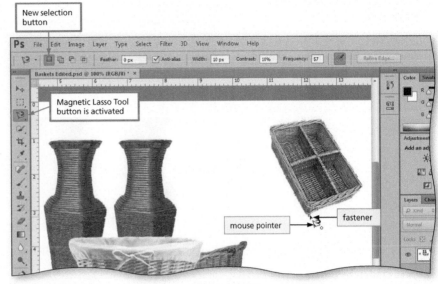

Figure 2–35

● Move, rather than drag, the mouse pointer slowly along the bottom edge of the basket to create a selection marquee (Figure 2–36).

Q&A How do I correct a mistake?

As you use the Magnetic Lasso Tool, if you make a mistake, press the ESC key and begin again.

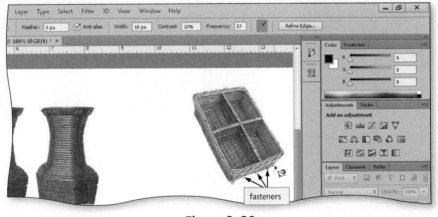

Figure 2–36

● Continue moving the mouse pointer around the edge of the basket. Click the mouse when turning a corner to create an extra fastening point.

● When you get to the lower-left corner again, double-click to finish the lasso (Figure 2–37).

Q&A When I double-clicked, the selection disappeared. What did I do wrong?

If your mouse pointer is exactly on the fastening point, a small circle indicates you are back at the beginning. In that case, a single-click finishes the lasso. If your selection disappears, press CTRL+Z to undo the double-click; the selection then should appear as shown in Figure 2–37.

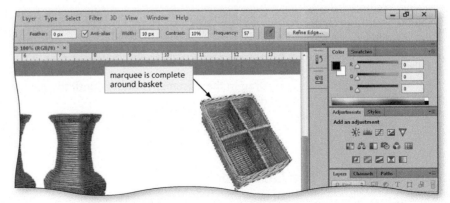

Figure 2–37

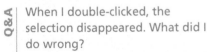

Other Ways

1. Press L or SHIFT+L until Magnetic Lasso Tool is active, click photo, move mouse

To Move a Selection using a Shortcut Key

The following steps move the selection.

- Press the V key to activate the Move Tool.

- Slowly drag the selection to a location in front of the other baskets as shown in Figure 2–38.

Should I redo the move if a shadow is left behind?

You can press CTRL+Z to undo the move and then use the Grow command on the Select menu; however, later in the chapter you will crop the photo, which will remove any shadows that are left behind.

- Press CTRL+D to deselect.

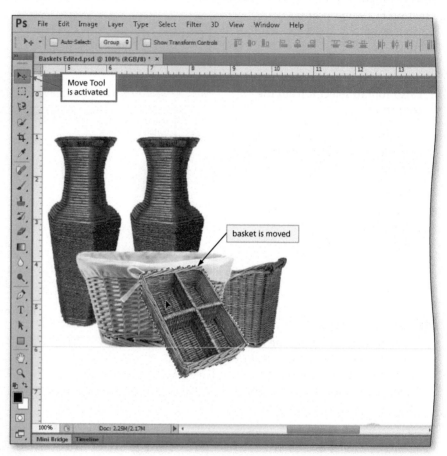

Figure 2–38

Nudging Selections
Instead of dragging to move a selection, you can use the arrow keys on the keyboard to move in small increments in a process called **nudging**.

To Navigate using a Shortcut Key

The following steps reposition the document window so that you can select the basket in the lower-right corner.

1 Press the H key to activate the Hand Tool.

2 Drag in the document window until the handled basket in the lower-right corner is displayed.

To Select using the Lasso Tool

The following steps use the Lasso Tool to create a selection by dragging around the object. As you will notice, the Lasso Tool leaves white space around the basket and inside the handle.

1

- Right-click the current lasso tool button on the Tools panel to display the context menu and then click Lasso Tool to select it.

- If necessary, on the options bar, click the New selection button to select the tool.

- Drag partway around the handled basket to start the lasso. Do not release the mouse button (Figure 2–39).

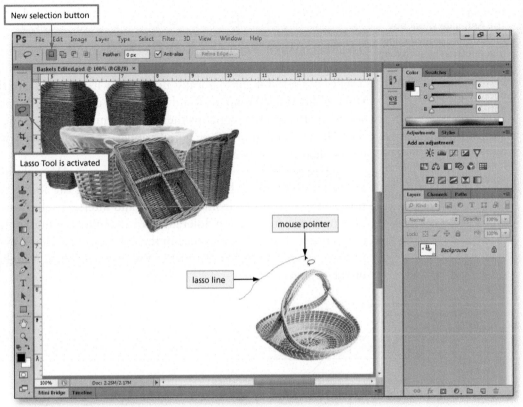

Figure 2–39

2

- Continue dragging around the basket to create a completed lasso, and then release the mouse button to finish the loop (Figure 2–40).

Q&A

How will I know if the lasso is complete?

When you release the mouse button, Photoshop completes the Lasso Tool selection, no matter where you are in the image.

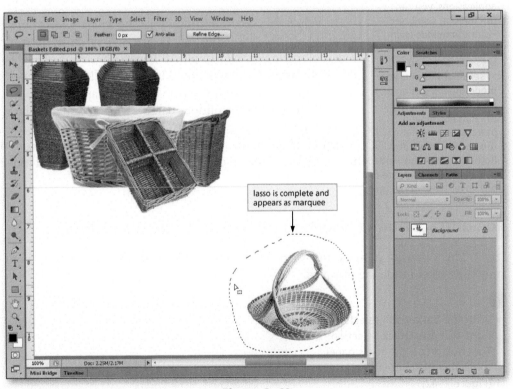

Figure 2–40

Other Ways

1. Press L or SHIFT+L until Lasso Tool is active, drag selection

BTW

Anti-Aliasing
The Anti-alias check box smooths the jagged edges of a selection by softening the color transition between edge pixels and background pixels. While anti-aliasing is useful when cutting, copying, and pasting selections to create composite images, it might leave behind a shadow after cutting or moving a selection.

The Magic Wand Tool

The Magic Wand Tool lets you select a consistently colored area with a single click. For example, if you wanted to select the blue sky in an image, clicking with the Magic Wand Tool would select it automatically, no matter what the shape of the blue area. When you use the Magic Wand Tool and click in the image or within a selection, Photoshop selects every pixel that contains the same or similar colors as the location you clicked. The Magic Wand Tool mouse pointer appears as a small line with a starburst on the end, similar to a magic wand.

The Magic Wand Tool options bar (Figure 2–41) contains the same selection adjustment buttons as the marquee tools, including the ability to create a new selection, add to or subtract from a selection, and intersect selections. The Magic Wand Tool options bar also has a Tolerance box that allows you to enter a value that determines the similarity or difference in the color of the selected pixels. A low value selects the few colors that are very similar to the pixel you click. A higher value selects a broader range of colors.

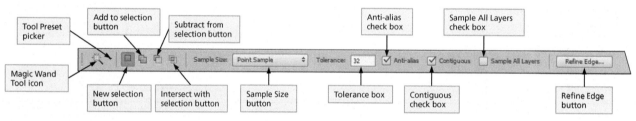

Figure 2–41

BTW

Cutting and Pasting
Just as you do in other applications, you can use the Cut, Copy, and Paste commands from the Edit menu or shortcut keys to make changes to selections. Unless you predefine a selection area by dragging a marquee, the Paste command pastes to the center of the document window. Both the commands and the shortcut keys create a new layer when they copy or paste.

When checked, the Contiguous check box selects only adjacent areas with the same color. Otherwise, Photoshop selects all pixels in the entire image that use the same color. Finally, the Sample All Layers check box selects colors using data from all visible layers. Otherwise, the Magic Wand Tool selects colors from the active layer only. You will learn about layers in a future chapter.

Besides using the options bar, the Magic Wand Tool can be used with many shortcut keys. Holding the SHIFT key while clicking adds to a Magic Wand Tool selection. Holding the ALT key while clicking subtracts from the selection. Holding the CTRL key while dragging with the Magic Wand Tool moves the selection.

To Subtract from a Selection using the Magic Wand Tool

The following steps use the Magic Wand Tool to eliminate the white background in the selection, leaving only the basket inside the marquee.

- With the basket still selected, right-click the Quick Selection Tool button on the Tools panel to display the context menu (Figure 2–42).

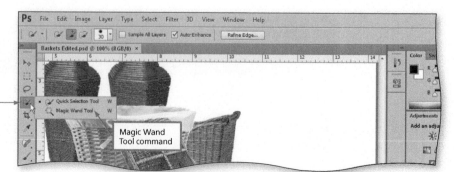

Figure 2–42

2

- Click Magic Wand Tool to activate it.

- On the options bar, click the 'Subtract from selection' button. Click the Anti-alias check box so it does not display a check mark.

- If necessary, type 32 in the Tolerance box, and, if necessary, click to display a check mark in the Contiguous check box (Figure 2–43).

Q&A

Could I press the W key to choose the Magic Wand Tool?

Yes, if the Magic Wand Tool appears on the Tools panel, you can press the W key to activate it; however, if the Quick Selection Tool appears on the Tools panel, you have to press SHIFT+W.

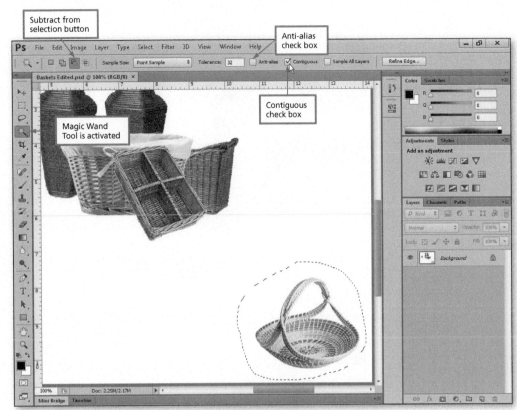

Figure 2–43

3

- Using the tip of the Magic Wand Tool mouse pointer, click the white space outside the basket, but inside the selection marquee, to remove the white color from the selection (Figure 2–44).

Q&A

What is the minus sign next to the mouse pointer?

The minus sign appears whenever you choose to subtract from a selection. A plus sign would indicate an addition to the selection, and an X indicates an intersection. Photoshop displays these signs so you do not have to glance up at the options bar to see which button you are using while you drag the selection.

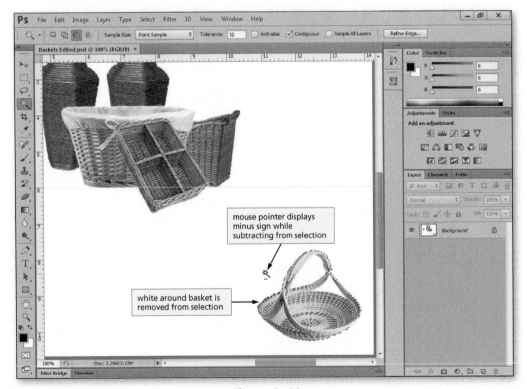

Figure 2–44

● Click the white spaces inside the basket's handle to remove them from the selection (Figure 2–45).

Q&A

Could I have removed the Contiguous check mark and just clicked the white area to remove all white areas?

Yes, but doing so would remove pixels because there is some white on the basket itself. It was better to remove the contiguous white spaces around the basket and within the handles.

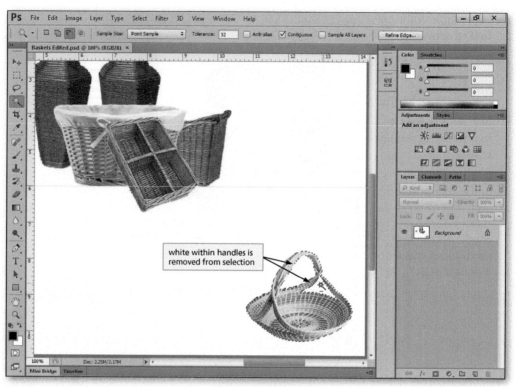

white within handles is removed from selection

Figure 2–45

Other Ways

1. Press W or SHIFT+W until Magic Wand Tool is active, click 'Subtract from selection' button, click selection

2. Select Magic Wand Tool, ALT+CLICK selection

3. Select Magic Wand Tool, right-click photo, click Subtract From Selection

To Move the Basket

The following steps move the basket.

1 Press the V key to activate the Move Tool.

2 Drag the basket to a location to the right of the previous selection, as shown in Figure 2–46.

3 Press CTRL+D to deselect.

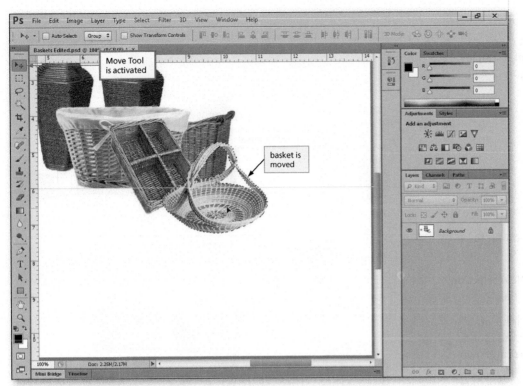

Figure 2–46

To Select using the Elliptical Marquee Tool

The following steps use the Elliptical Marquee Tool to draw a circle around the final basket to select it. Recall that SHIFT+dragging with a marquee tool maintains proportions, in this case creating a circle rather than an oval. In addition, you can press and hold the SPACEBAR key to move a selection while you create it.

1

- Scroll to the left until the entire round basket is displayed (Figure 2–47).

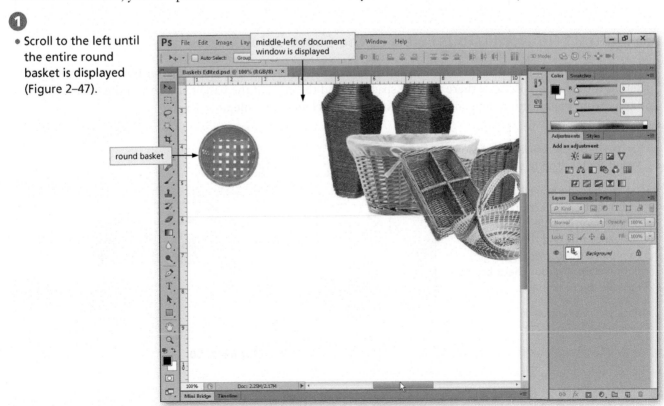

Figure 2–47

2

● Right-click the current marquee tool on the Tools panel to display the context menu (Figure 2–48).

Figure 2–48

3

● Click Elliptical Marquee Tool to activate the tool.

● If necessary, click the New selection button on the options bar.

● Position the mouse pointer at the upper-left edge of the round basket and then SHIFT+drag down and to the right to create a circle selection. Do not release the SHIFT key or mouse button.

● If necessary, press and hold the SPACEBAR key and then drag the selection into position.

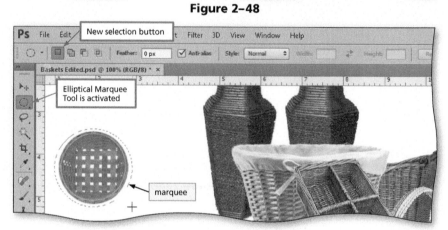

Figure 2–49

● Release the mouse button before releasing the SHIFT and SPACEBAR keys (Figure 2–49).

To Subtract Noncontiguous Pixels of the Same Color

The following step uses the Magic Wand Tool and the 'Subtract from selection' button to remove white pixels in the selection. Because there is white space around the edge of the basket and within the basket, you will subtract from the selection noncontiguously. You also will change the tolerance level.

1

● On the Tools panel, click the Magic Wand Tool button to select it.

● On the options bar, click the 'Subtract from selection' button if necessary. Double-click the Tolerance box and then type 10 to replace the current setting. Click the Contiguous check box to remove its check mark.

● Click the white area in the selection (Figure 2–50).

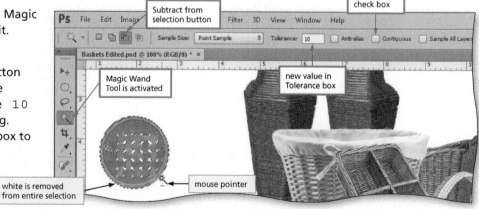

Figure 2–50

 How does the tolerance setting work?

In this selection, some of the edges of the basket are quite light. You do not want to leave them behind as a shadow when you move the basket; therefore, you are subtracting a more narrow range of color — the pixels that are closest in color to the strong white background.

To Move the Round Basket

The following steps move the round basket.

1 Press the V key to activate the Move Tool.

2 Drag the selection to a location in front of the lined basket as shown in Figure 2–51. Do not deselect.

Move Tool is activated

basket is moved

Figure 2–51

BTW

Resizing
Photoshop allows you to apply some transformations to entire images or photos, rather than just selections. For example, you can change the size of the photo or rotate the image using the Image menu. You then can enter dimensions or rotation percentages on the submenu and subsequent dialog boxes.

To Duplicate and Scale

The following steps create a smaller copy of the selected basket. When you click the Show Transform Controls check box on the Move Tool options bar, Photoshop displays a bounding box with sizing handles. To resize, drag one of the sizing handles. To resize proportionally, SHIFT+drag one of the sizing handles. When you change the size of a selection, it is called **scaling**.

1

- With the Move Tool still selected, ALT+drag the selection to a location slightly down and to the right of the original selection. The copy will overlap the original round basket slightly.

- On the options bar, click the Show Transform Controls check box to display a check mark (Figure 2–52).

Q&A Could I just use the Copy and Paste commands?

Yes, however those commands create a new layer in the photo and increase the file size.

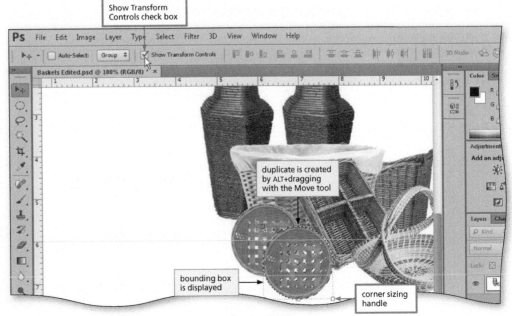

Show Transform Controls check box

duplicate is created by ALT+dragging with the Move tool

bounding box is displayed

corner sizing handle

Figure 2–52

● SHIFT+drag a corner sizing handle toward the center of the basket to scale it down approximately 10 percent smaller (Figure 2–53).

Q&A Why did the options bar change?

The options bar changed to the Transform options bar — an options bar not associated with any one specific tool. You will learn more about the Transform options bar in a future chapter.

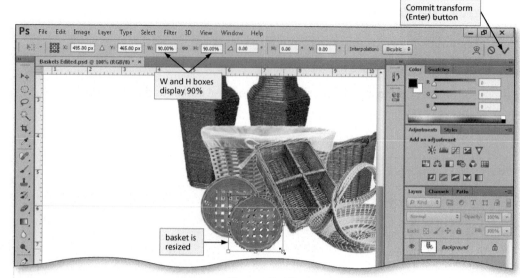

Figure 2–53

Q&A How do I know what 10 percent smaller is?
You can drag until the option bars display approximately 90% in the W and H boxes.

● On the options bar click the 'Commit transform (Enter)' button to accept the transformation.

● Press CTRL+D to deselect.

To Reselect

When you deselect on purpose or by accident, you can return to the previous selection by using the **Reselect** command. The following steps reselect the copy of the round basket.

❶
● Click Select on the Application bar to display the Select menu (Figure 2–54).

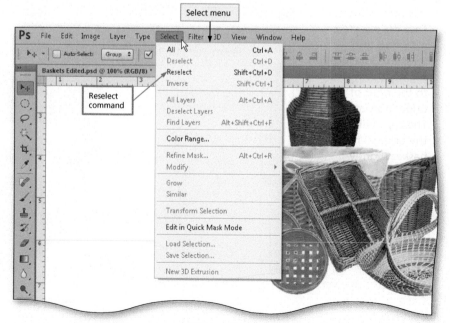

Figure 2–54

2

● Click Reselect
to display the
previous selection
(Figure 2–55).

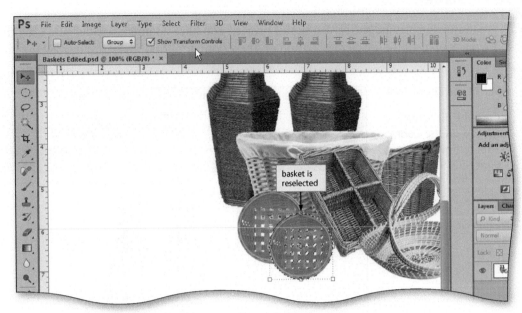

Figure 2–55

To Create and Scale Another Copy

The following steps create another copy of the basket.

1 Select the Move Tool if necessary. ALT+drag the selection to a location slightly down
and right of the previous selection. The copy will overlap slightly.

2 SHIFT+drag a corner sizing handle to scale the selection down by approximately
10 percent (Figure 2–56).

3 On the options bar, click the 'Commit transform (Enter)' button to accept the
transformation, and then deselect.

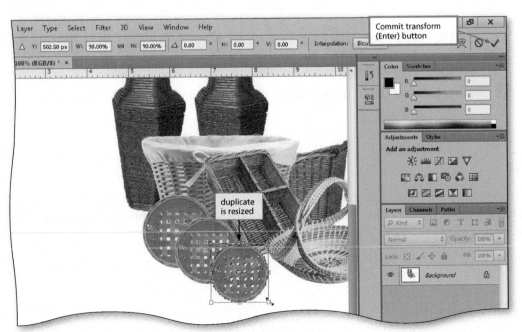

Figure 2–56

To Fit Screen

In moving around the screen in this project, you have zoomed, scrolled and used the Hand Tool. The following step uses the Fit Screen button on the Zoom Tool options bar to display the entire document window.

● Select the Zoom Tool.

● Click the Fit Screen button on the Zoom Tool options bar (Figure 2–57).

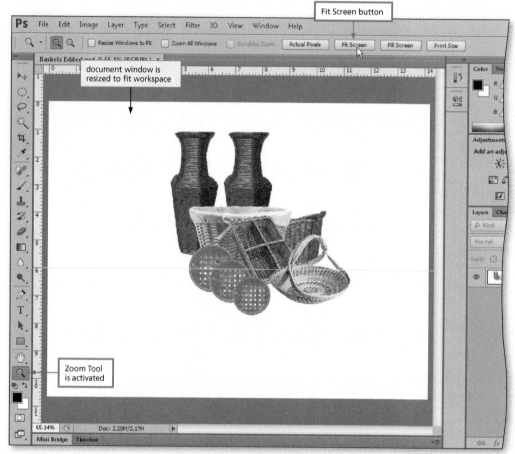

Figure 2–57

Other Ways

1. Press CTRL+0 (zero)
2. On View menu, click Fit on Screen

To Turn Off Guides using a Shortcut Key

The following step turns off the display of the green ruler guide.

❶ Press CTRL+SEMICOLON (;) to turn off the display of guides.

To Crop a Selection

Finally, you will crop the advertisement to center the baskets, including a minimal amount of border space. In Chapter 1, you activated the Crop Tool and then adjusted the size of the selection. In the following steps, you will select first, and then crop.

1

- Press SHIFT+M to select the Rectangular Marquee Tool.

- Drag a rectangular marquee that leaves an even amount of white space on all four sides of the baskets.

- Press the C key to activate the Crop Tool (Figure 2–58).

Q&A Why did I have to use SHIFT+M to activate the Rectangular Marquee Tool?

Previously, the Elliptical Marquee Tool had been selected. Pressing the M key would have activated it. Pressing SHIFT+M toggles through all of the marquee tools.

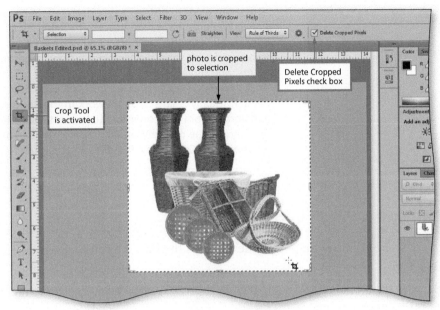

Figure 2–58

2

- On the options bar, click the Delete Cropped Pixels check box so it displays a check mark, if necessary.

- Press the ENTER key twice to accept the cropping selection and to complete the crop.

- Press the M key to return to the Rectangular Marquee Tool.

To Save Again

The following step saves the image again, with the same file name, using a shortcut key.

1 Press CTRL+S to save the Baskets Edited file with the same name.

Break Point: If you wish to take a break, this is a good place to do so. To resume at a later time, start Photoshop, open the file named Baskets Edited, and continue following the steps from this location forward.

Creating PDF Files

The final step is to create a PDF file of the advertising image for document exchange. **PDF** stands for **Portable Document Format**, a flexible file format based on the PostScript imaging model that is compatible across platforms and applications. PDF files accurately display and preserve fonts, page layouts, and graphics. There are two ways to create a PDF file in Photoshop. First, you can save the file in the PDF format. Alternatively, you can use the Print command to create the PDF format, allowing you to make some changes to the settings before saving.

Plan
Ahead

Create files in portable formats.
You might need to distribute your artwork in a variety of formats for customers, print shops, Webmasters, and e-mail attachments. The format you choose depends on how the file will be used, but portability is always a consideration. The document might need to be used with various operating systems, monitor resolutions, computing environments, and servers.

It is a good idea to discuss with your customer the types of formats he or she might need. It usually is safe to begin work in the Photoshop PSD format and then use the Save as command or Print command to convert the files. PDF is a portable format that can be read by anyone on the Web with a free reader. The PDF format is platform and software independent. Commonly, PDF files are virus free and safe as e-mail attachments.

To Save a Photo in the PDF Format

The following steps save the photo in the PDF format for ease of distribution.

- Click File on the Application bar, and then click Save As to display the Save As dialog box.

- Click the Format button to display the various formats you can use to save Photoshop files (Figure 2–59).

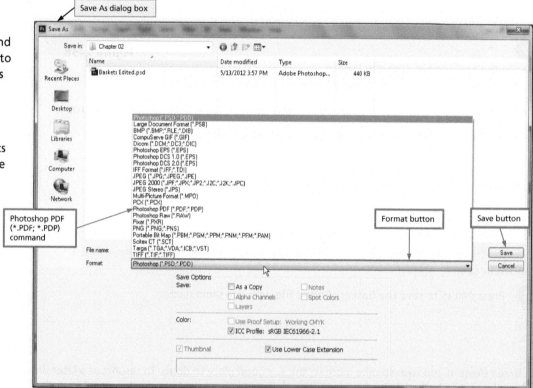

Figure 2–59

- Click Photoshop PDF (*.PDF;*.PDP) in the list to select the PDF format, and then click the Save button to continue the saving process (Figure 2–60).

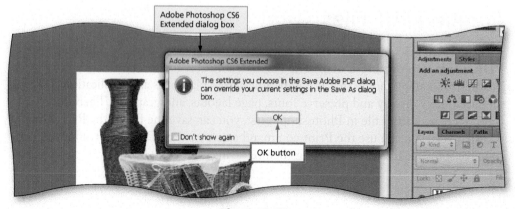

Figure 2–60

● Click the OK button to display the Save Adobe PDF dialog box (Figure 2–61).

Q&A

The Save Adobe PDF dialog box did not appear. What happened?

If you have multiple windows open on your system, the dialog box might be behind some of the other windows. In that case, minimize the other windows until the dialog box appears.

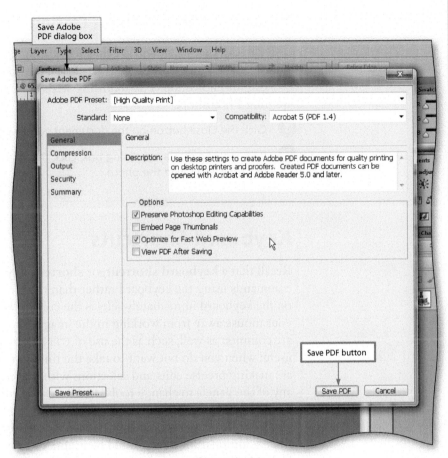

Figure 2–61

● Click the Save PDF button to continue the saving process and display a second Save Adobe PDF dialog box (Figure 2–62).

Q&A

Will the PDF version have the same name?

Yes. After you save the file, you will see the name Baskets Edited.pdf on the document window tab because Photoshop can edit PDF files directly. The file also can be viewed with Adobe Acrobat or any PDF reader.

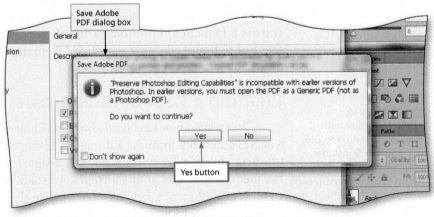

Figure 2–62

● Click the Yes button to finish saving.

Other Ways

1. Press CTRL+P, click Document box arrow, click Adobe PDF, click Print

To Close a Photo without Closing Photoshop

Recall that when you are finished editing a photo or file, you should close it to help save system resources. You can close a photo after you have saved it and continue working in Photoshop. The following steps close the Baskets Edited.pdf file without quitting Photoshop.

1 Click the Close button on the document window tab to close the Baskets Edited.pdf file.

2 If Photoshop displays a dialog box, click the No button to ignore the changes since the last time you saved the photo.

Keyboard Shortcuts

Recall that a **keyboard shortcut**, or **shortcut key**, is a way to activate menu or tool commands using the keyboard rather than the mouse. For example, pressing the L key on the keyboard immediately selects the current lasso tool without having to move your mouse away from working in the image. Shortcuts that combine two keystrokes are common as well, such as the use of CTRL+A to select an entire image. Shortcuts are useful when you do not want to take the time to traverse the menu system or when you are making precise edits and selections with the mouse and do not want to go back to any of the panels to change tools or settings. A Quick Reference summary describing Photoshop's keyboard shortcuts is included in the back of the book.

While many keyboard shortcuts already exist in Photoshop, there might be times when additional shortcuts would be useful. For instance, the Single Row and Single Column Marquee Tools have no shortcut key. If you frequently use those tools, adding the Single Row and Single Column Marquee Tools to the M keyboard shortcut might be helpful. Photoshop allows users to create, customize, and save keyboard shortcuts in one of three areas: menus, panels, and tools. When you create keyboard shortcuts, you can add them to Photoshop's default settings, save them in a personalized set for retrieval in future editing sessions, or delete them from your system.

Creating a Keyboard Shortcut

To create a new keyboard shortcut, Photoshop provides a dialog box interface, which is accessible from the Edit menu. Using that dialog box, you can select one of the three shortcut areas. Then you can assign a shortcut key or combination of keys. For menu commands, your shortcut keystrokes must include a combination of the CTRL key or a function key followed by a single keyboard character. When creating shortcuts for tools, you must use a single alphabetic character. To avoid conflicting duplications, Photoshop immediately warns you if you have chosen a keyboard shortcut used somewhere else in the program.

To Create a New Keyboard Shortcut

In the following steps, you will create a shortcut to display the Essentials workspace. While that command is accessible on the Window menu, a shortcut would save time when you need to choose the workspace.

1

- Click Edit on the Application bar to display the Edit menu, and then click Keyboard Shortcuts to display the Keyboard Shortcuts and Menus dialog box.

- Click the Shortcuts For box arrow, and then click Application Menus in the list, if necessary.

- In the Application Menu Command list, scroll down, and then click the triangle to the left of the Window command to display the list of Window menu commands (Figure 2–63).

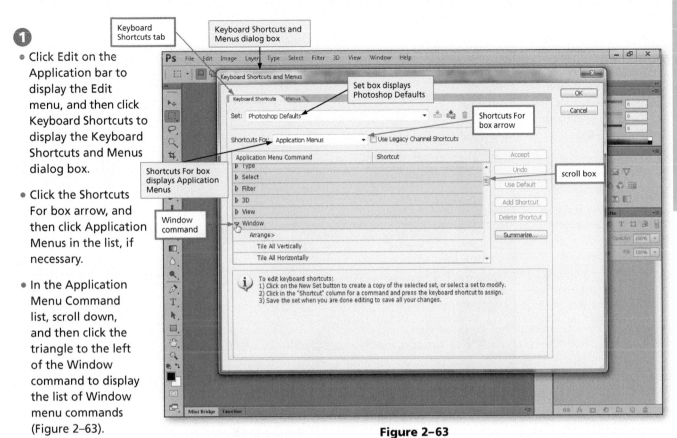

Figure 2–63

2

- Scroll down to display Workspace under the Window menu commands, and then click Essentials (Default) to display a shortcut key box (Figure 2–64).

Q&A

How are the buttons at the top of the dialog box used?

The 'Save all changes to the current set of shortcuts' button allows you to name the set for future retrieval. The 'Create a new set based on the current set of shortcuts' button creates a copy of the current keyboard shortcut settings. The 'Delete the current set of shortcuts' button deletes the set.

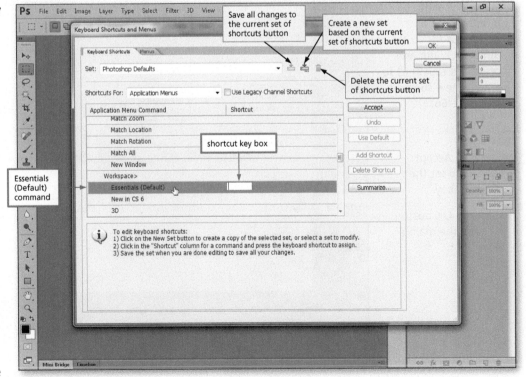

Figure 2–64

● Press the F12 key to enter a new shortcut keystroke for the Essentials (Default) command (Figure 2–65).

How can I find out which shortcuts keys still are available?

When you click the Summarize button, Photoshop creates a Web page with all of the keyboard shortcuts in the set. You can save that file on your system or print it.

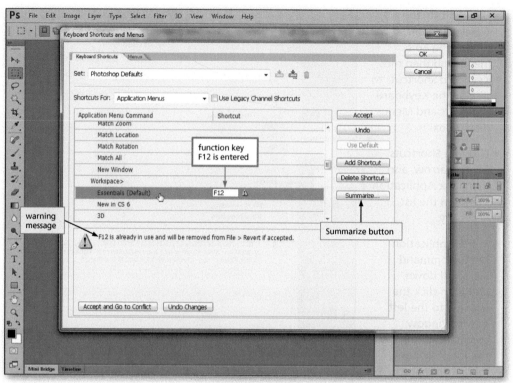

Figure 2–65

● Because Photoshop warns you that the F12 key already is being used as a shortcut for a different command, press CTRL+SLASH (/) to enter a new shortcut (Figure 2–66).

● Click the Accept button to set the shortcut key.

● Click the OK button to close the dialog box.

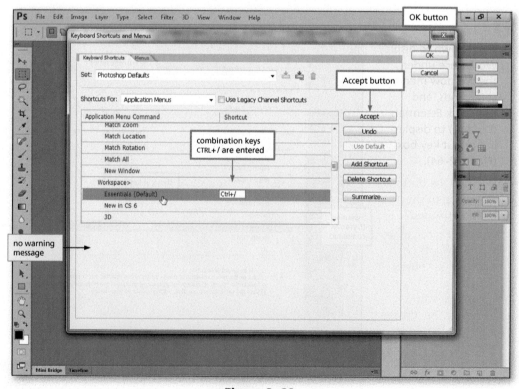

Figure 2–66

Other Ways

1. Press ALT+SHIFT+CTRL+K, edit settings, click OK button

To Test a New Keyboard Shortcut

The next steps test the new keyboard shortcut.

1

- Click Window on the Application bar and point to Workspace to verify the shortcut key assignment (Figure 2–67).

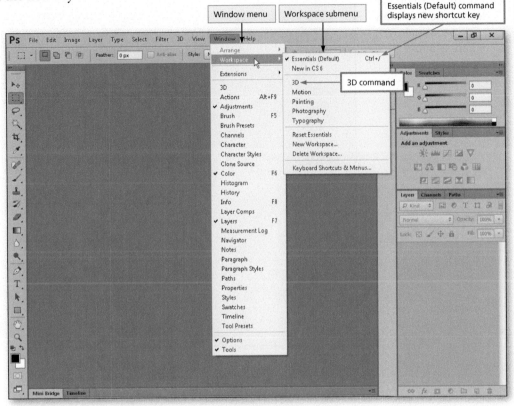

Figure 2–67

2

- Click the 3D command to change to the 3D workspace (Figure 2–68).

Q&A

Will the new shortcut become permanent?

The new shortcut will be saved on your system in the Photoshop Defaults (modified) set. That set will be in effect the next time you start Photoshop. If you want to remove it, you can edit that specific shortcut, or delete the set by clicking the 'Delete the current set of shortcuts' button.

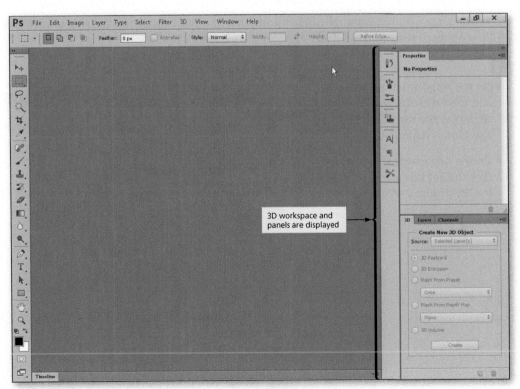

Figure 2–68

- Press CTRL+SLASH (/) to test the shortcut and display the Essentials workspace again (Figure 2–69).

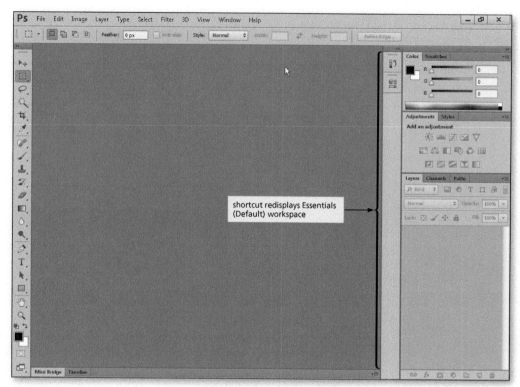

shortcut redisplays Essentials (Default) workspace

Figure 2–69

To Return to the Default Settings for Keyboard Shortcuts

It is a good idea, especially in a lab situation, to reset the keyboard shortcuts to their default settings. The following steps restore the default shortcut keys.

- On the Application bar, click Edit, and then click Keyboard Shortcuts to display the Keyboard Shortcuts and Menus dialog box.

- On the Keyboards Shortcuts tab, click the Set box arrow to display the list (Figure 2–70).

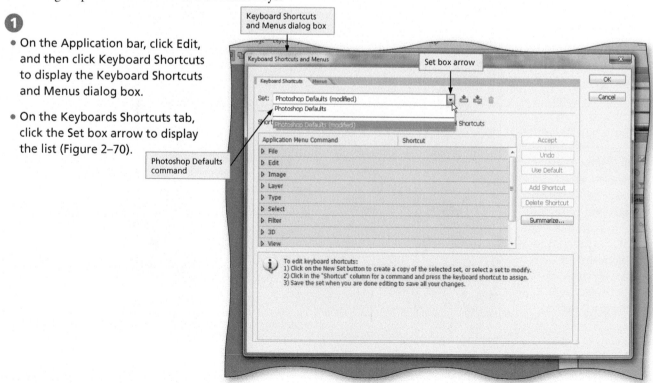

Keyboard Shortcuts and Menus dialog box

Set box arrow

Photoshop Defaults command

Figure 2–70

2

- Click Photoshop Defaults to choose the default settings for shortcuts (Figure 2–71).

3

- When Photoshop displays a message asking if you want to save your changes, click the No button so your previous changes are not saved.

- In the Keyboard Shortcuts and Menus dialog box, click the OK button to close the dialog box.

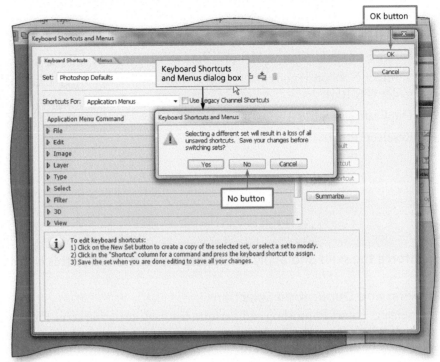

Figure 2–71

To Quit Photoshop using a Shortcut Key

The following step quits Photoshop and returns control to Windows.

1 Press CTRL+Q to quit Photoshop.

Chapter Summary

In this chapter, you learned how to use selection tools, including the marquee tools, the lasso tools, the Quick Selection Tool, and the Magic Wand Tool. You learned about the History panel and its states. You worked with the 'Subtract from selection' command, the Refine Edge dialog box, and the Grow command to edit the selection border. You used the Move Tool to move and copy selections and scaled them. Each of the tools and commands had its own options bar with settings to control how the tool or command worked. You used a guide to help align objects. Finally, you saved the photo as a PDF file, and you learned how to create and test a new keyboard shortcut.

The items listed below include all the new Photoshop skills you have learned in this chapter:

1. Use the Rectangular Marquee Tool (PS 79)
2. Use the Move Tool (PS 80)
3. Duplicate a Selection (PS 82)
4. Use the Quick Selection Tool (PS 83)
5. Display the History Panel (PS 86)
6. Undo Changes using the History Panel (PS 87)
7. Refine Edges (PS 89)

8. Select using the Polygonal Lasso Tool (PS 93)
9. Grow the Selection (PS 94)
10. Display a Grid (PS 96)
11. Create a Guide (PS 97)
12. Snap a Selection to the Guide (PS 98)
13. Select using the Magnetic Lasso Tool (PS 99)
14. Move a Selection using a Shortcut Key (PS 100)

15. Select using the Lasso Tool (PS 100)
16. Subtract from a Selection using the Magic Wand Tool (PS 102)
17. Select using the Elliptical Marquee Tool (PS 105)
18. Subtract Noncontiguous Pixels of the Same Color (PS 106)
19. Duplicate and Scale (PS 107)
20. Reselect (PS 108)
21. Fit Screen (PS 110)
22. Crop a Selection (PS 110)
23. Save a Photo in the PDF Format (PS 112)
24. Create a New Keyboard Shortcut (PS 114)
25. Test a New Keyboard Shortcut (PS 117)
26. Return to the Default Settings for Keyboard Shortcuts (PS 118)

Apply Your Knowledge

Reinforce the skills and apply the concepts you learned in this chapter.

Moving and Duplicating Selections

Instructions: Start Photoshop and perform the customization steps found on pages PS 6 through PS 10. Open the Apply 2-1 Bread file in the Chapter 02 folder from the Data Files for Students and save it, in the PSD file format, as Apply 2-1 Bread Edited. Visit www.cengage.com/ct/studentdownload for detailed instructions or contact your instructor for information about accessing the required files.

You will create a grocery advertisement featuring bakery items. First, you will select individual items from within the file, and then you will transform and move them so that the finished design looks like Figure 2–72. You will place the rest of the images from back to front.

Figure 2–72

Perform the following tasks:

1. Because the checkered tablecloth is in the very back of the arrangement, you will start with it. Use the Rectangular Marquee Tool to select the checkered tablecloth.

2. Use the Move Tool to move the tablecloth to the top-center portion of the page. Do not deselect the tablecloth.

3. With the Move Tool still selected, click the Show Transform Controls check box to display a check mark. To distort the tablecloth and make it appear in perspective, CTRL+drag each of the lower corner sizing handles down and outward. Do not overlap any of the bread items. The result should be a trapezoid shape, as shown in Figure 2–72. If you make a mistake, press the ESC key and start again. When you are satisfied with the shape, press the ENTER key to confirm the transformation. Do not deselect.

4. The croissant is the back-most item in the arrangement. Use the Polygonal Lasso Tool to select the croissant. (*Hint:* The croissant is the lower-right item in the Apply 2-1 Bread image.) Right-click the Quick Selection Tool button on the Tools panel, and then click Magic Wand Tool. On the options bar, click the 'Subtract from selection' button, then click the white area around the croissant to remove it.

5. Use the Move Tool to move the croissant to the upper-right portion of the tablecloth. ALT+drag a second croissant to a location below and to the left of the first, as shown in Figure 2–72. (*Hint:* Do not drag the center reference point.) Press CTRL+D to deselect it.

6. Repeat Steps 4 and 5 to select and move the French bread.

7. ALT+drag the French bread to the right to create a duplicate.

8. Select and move the remaining bread items until you are satisfied with the arrangement. For each bread item, use a selection tool that will approximate the shape of the bread. On the options bar, use the 'Add to selection' and 'Subtract from selection' buttons as necessary. Use the Magic Wand Tool to remove white space around the selection before moving it.

9. Right-click the Rectangular Marquee Tool button on the Tools panel, then click Elliptical Marquee Tool. Use the Elliptical Marquee Tool to select the Sale button. (*Hint:* Press and hold the SHIFT key as you select to maintain a perfect circle.)

10. Move the Sale button to the lower-right portion of the advertisement.

11. Use the Crop Tool to select the portion of the image to use for the final advertisement. (*Hint:* The remaining white space is unnecessary.)

12. Save the Apply 2-1 Bread Edited file, and then close Photoshop.

13. Submit the assignment in the format specified by your instructor.

Extend Your Knowledge

Extend the skills you learned in this chapter and experiment with new skills. You may need to use Help to complete the assignment.

Separating Objects from the Background

Instructions: Start Photoshop and perform the customization steps found on pages PS 6 through PS 10. Open the Extend 2-1 Flowers file in the Chapter 02 folder from the Data Files for Students and save it, in the PSD format, as Extend 2-1 Flowers Edited. Visit www.cengage.com/ct/studentdownload for detailed instructions or contact your instructor for information about accessing the required files.

The original flower image displays the flowers in their natural settings, with various colors in the background. After moving the frame and making a copy, you will select the flowers while preventing background colors from straying into the selection. Finally, you will position each flower in front of a frame, as shown in Figure 2–73.

Figure 2–73

Perform the following tasks:

1. Use the Elliptical Marquee Tool to select the oval frame. (*Hint:* For more careful placement, while dragging to create the selection, you can press the SPACEBAR key to adjust the location of the drag and then release it to continue drawing the marquee.) Be careful to select only the frame, and eliminate any white around the edge of the selection using the Magic Wand Tool and the 'Subtract from selection' button.

2. Drag the selection to a location below the left side of the word, Flowers. Do not be concerned if you leave a slight shadow behind. On the Move Tool options bar, if necessary, click to display a check mark in the Show Transform Controls check box. SHIFT+drag a corner sizing handle to scale the selection approximately 10 percent bigger. (*Hint:* You also can increase the selection to 110 percent in both the Width and Height boxes.) Press the ENTER key to commit the transformation.

3. With the frame still selected, SHIFT+ALT+drag to create a duplicate and place it to the right of the original. (*Hint:* Recall that using the SHIFT key keeps the duplicate aligned with the original.)

4. Use appropriate selection tools to select the upper flower and its stem. (*Hint:* Use the Magic Wand Tool with a tolerance setting of 50 to select the contiguous pink and then add to the selection using other tools.) Click the 'Intersect with selection' button to combine selected areas, if necessary. Do not include the background.

5. To ensure that the selection does not have any stray pixels around its border, use the Refine Edge dialog box to refine the edge by increasing the radius to 7 px.

6. As you create the selection, if necessary, press CTRL+ALT+Z to step back through the editing history and return the image to an earlier state.

7. Move the selected flower onto the left frame and resize as necessary.

8. Repeat Steps 4 through 7 for the lower flower and the right frame. If you make an error, display the History panel and then click a previous state.

9. Crop the image to include only the word, Flowers, and the two framed flowers. Save the changes.

10. Use the Magic Wand Tool to select the blue color in the word, Flowers. (*Hint:* To select all of the letters, you will have to remove the check mark in the Contiguous box.) If parts of the image other than the word, Flowers, appear within the marquee, use the 'Subtract from selection' button to remove them.

11. Use Photoshop Help to investigate how to soften the edges of selections. Use the Refine Edge dialog box to soften the edges. Expand the selection and feather the edges.

12. Use Photoshop Help to investigate how to stroke a selection or layer with color. With the letters selected, use the Stroke command on the Edit menu to display the Stroke dialog box. Stroke the selection with a white color, 5 pixels wide, on the outside of the selection.

13. Save your changes, close the file, and then quit Photoshop. Send the revised photo to your instructor as an e-mail attachment.

Make It Right

Analyze a project and correct all errors and/or improve the design.

Correcting an Error in a Photo

Instructions: Start Photoshop and perform the customization steps found on pages PS 6 through PS 10. Open the Make It Right 2-1 Footballs file in the Chapter 02 folder from the Data Files for Students and save it as Make It Right 2-1 Footballs Edited. Visit www.cengage.com/ct/ studentdownload for detailed instructions or contact your instructor for information about accessing the required files.

A coworker has made an error when trying to make a duplicate of the football (Figure 2–74). The duplicate on the right included some white space around the football, which overlaps the football on the left. In addition, the football on the right should be bigger because it is closer in the picture. Use selection tools as necessary, along with the 'Add to selection' and 'Subtract from selection' buttons, to select only the football (and its shadow) on the right. Refine the edge. ALT+drag with the Move Tool to create a duplicate and place it over the top of the football on the left. Select the football on the right again. Display the transform controls and scale the selection to be approximately 10 percent bigger.

Save the project again. Submit the revised document in the format specified by your instructor.

Figure 2–74

In the Lab

Design and/or create a project using the guidelines, concepts, and skills presented in this chapter. Labs are listed in order of increasing difficulty.

Lab 1: Using Keyboard Shortcuts to Create a Logo

Problem: You are an intern with the Parks and Recreation department for the city. They are planning to create T-shirts for their summer youth program. Your supervisor has provided a file with some individual graphics about activities in the park. You are to move and place the graphics to form the logo shown in Figure 2–75. He reminds you that the T-shirt manufacturer needs a PDF file.

Figure 2–75

Note: To complete this assignment, you will required to use the Data Files for Students. Visit www.cengage.com/ct/studentdownload for detailed instructions or contact your instructor for information about accessing the required files.

Instructions: Perform the following tasks:

1. Start Photoshop. Set the default workspace, and reset all tools and colors.

2. Press CTRL+O to open the Lab 2-1 Park T-shirt file from the Chapter 02 folder of the Data Files for Students, or from a location specified by your instructor.

3. Press SHIFT+CTRL+S to display the Save As dialog box. Save the file on your storage device with the name, Lab 2-1 Park T-shirt Edited.

4. If the photo does not appear at 25% magnification, press CTRL+PLUS SIGN (+) or CTRL+HYPHEN (-) to zoom in or out as necessary.

5. Drag from the horizontal ruler to create a guide at 3.25 inches, which you will use to align the graphics.

6. To select and move the kite:

   a. Press SHIFT+L until the Polygonal Lasso Tool is selected.

   b. On the options bar, click the New selection button, if necessary.

Continued >

c. Click a corner of the kite to start the selection. Continue clicking corners to create straight line segments around the kite. When you are finished, double-click to finish the selection.

d. On the Select menu, click Grow to expand the selection slightly.

e. Press the v key to access the Move Tool. Drag the kite to a location in front of the red circle, snapping the bottom of the kite to the ruler guide. It is OK to leave behind a slight shadow, as the logo will be cropped later in the steps.

f. Press CTRL+D to deselect.

7. To select and move the bat:

a. Press SHIFT+L until the Lasso Tool is selected.

b. On the options bar, click the New selection button, if necessary.

c. Drag to create a selection around the bat.

d. Press SHIFT+W until the Magic Wand Tool is selected.

e. ALT+click the white area around the bat, within the selection. Recall that pressing the ALT key while clicking activates the 'Subtract from selection' button on the options bar; the mouse pointer displays a minus sign.

f. Press the v key to access the Move Tool. Drag the bat to a location in front of the kite, as shown in Figure 2–75 on the previous page, snapping the bottom of the bat to the ruler guide.

g. Press CTRL+D to deselect.

8. To select and move the ball:

a. Press SHIFT+M until the Elliptical Marquee Tool is selected.

b. On the options bar, click the New selection button, if necessary.

c. SHIFT+drag to create a circular selection around the ball. Avoid including any white space around the ball. If necessary, press the SPACEBAR key while dragging to position the selection marquee.

d. Press the v key to access the Move Tool. Drag the ball to a location in front of the kite as shown in Figure 2–75, snapping the ball to the ruler guide.

e. If you make a mistake while selecting or moving the ball, click the History button on the vertical dock of panels to display the History panel. Click a previous state and begin to select or move again.

f. Press CTRL+D to deselect.

9. To select and move the remote control airplane:

a. Press the z key to activate the Zoom Tool, and then click the airplane several times to zoom in.

b. Press SHIFT+L until the Magnetic Lasso Tool is selected.

c. On the options bar, click the New selection button, if necessary.

d. Click a corner of the airplane. Slowly move the mouse pointer around the airplane, creating fasteners along the edge. Click at each corner to create an extra fastener. When you get close to the beginning fastener, move your mouse pointer until a small circle appears, and then click to complete the lasso.

e. On the options bar, click the Refine Edge button to display the Refine Edge dialog box. Drag the Shift Edge slider to 75%, and then click the OK button to close the dialog box.

    f. Press the Z key and then ALT+click to zoom out as necessary. Scroll to display the red circle and the remote control airplane.

    g. Press the V key to access the Move Tool. Drag the airplane to a location in front of the kite as shown in Figure 2–75 on page PS 125.

    h. Deselect.

10. To select and move the tennis racquet:

    a. Press CTRL+PLUS SIGN (+) several times to zoom in on the racquet, scrolling as necessary.

    b. Press SHIFT+W until the Quick Selection Tool is selected.

    c. On the options bar, click the New selection button, if necessary.

    d. Slowly drag from the handle, upward, to create a selection around the racquet. If you make a mistake, deselect and begin again.

    e. Press SHIFT+W until the Magic Wand Tool is selected. On the options bar, select the value in the Tolerance box and then type 10 to replace it. If necessary, click to remove the check mark in the Contiguous check box.

    f. ALT+click a white area within the selection. Be careful not to click the strings of the racquet.

    g. Press CTRL+ HYPHEN (-) to zoom out as necessary.

    h. Press the V key to access the Move Tool. Drag the racquet to a location in front of the kite as shown in Figure 2–75, snapping the bottom of the racquet to the ruler guide.

    i. Deselect.

11. Press CTRL+S to save the file with the same name. If Photoshop displays a Photoshop Format Options dialog box, click the OK button.

12. To crop:

    a. Press SHIFT+M until the Rectangular Marquee Tool is selected.

    b. SHIFT+drag around the red circle to create a square selection.

    c. Press the C key to crop. On the options bar, if necessary, click the Delete Cropped Pixels check box so it displays a check mark. Press the ENTER key twice to crop the selection.

13. To create the PDF file:

    a. Press SHIFT+CTRL+S to open the Save as dialog box.

    b. Click the Format button to display the various formats.

    c. Click Photoshop PDF (*.PDF;*.PDP) in the list to select the PDF format, and then click the Save button to continue the saving process, saving the file with the same name.

    d. When Photoshop displays a dialog box, click the OK button to display the Save Adobe PDF dialog box. Click the Save PDF button to continue the saving process.

    e. When Photoshop displays the Save Adobe PDF dialog box, click the Yes button to finish saving.

14. Quit Photoshop by pressing CTRL+Q.

15. Send the PDF file as an e-mail attachment to your instructor, or submit it in the format specified by your instructor.

Continued >

In the Lab

Lab 2: Creating a Graphic from Back to Front

Problem: A local author has asked for your help in creating a book cover graphic about clock collecting. He has several photos of clocks that he wants placed in specific locations and in varied sizes. The final graphic is shown in Figure 2–76.

Note: To complete this assignment, you will required to use the Data Files for Students. Visit www.cengage.com/ct/studentdownload for detailed instructions or contact your instructor for information about accessing the required files.

Figure 2–76

Instructions: Perform the following tasks:

1. Start Photoshop. Set the default workspace and reset all tools.

2. Open the file, Lab 2-2 Clocks, from the Chapter 02 folder of the Data Files for Students, or from a location specified by your instructor.

3. Use the Save As command to save the file on your storage device with the name Lab 2-2 Clocks Edited.

4. To select and transform the round clock:

   a. Use the Elliptical Marquee Tool to select the round clock (the lower-right clock). If necessary, use the Magic Wand Tool and the Subtract from selection button to remove any white from around the edge of the clock.

   b. Use the Move Tool to move it to a location in the center of the white area.

   c. Show the transform controls and enlarge the selection approximately 500 percent as shown on the options bar. Do not let it overlap any of the other clocks. Drag a side handle to make the clock more round. When you are satisfied with the clock's appearance, deselect it.

5. To select and transform the mantle clock:

   a. Use the Lasso Tool to select the mantle clock (the lower-left clock). Use the Magic Wand Tool and the 'Subtract from selection' button to remove the white areas from around the selection. Grow the selection to avoid leaving a shadow.

   b. Use the Move Tool to move the mantle clock to a location just below the round clock face and slightly to the left.

   c. Display the transform controls and enlarge the selection to match Figure 2–76.

6. To select and resize the grandfather clock:

   a. Use the Rectangular Marquee Tool to select the grandfather clock. Use the Magic Wand Tool and the 'Subtract from selection' button to remove the white areas from around the selection.

   b. Use the Move Tool to move the grandfather clock to a location in front of and on the right side of the round clock face.

   c. Display the transform controls and enlarge the selection to match Figure 2–76. Notice that the clock is not perfectly straight. Move the mouse pointer to a location just outside the selection. When the mouse pointer changes to a curved double-arrow, drag to rotate the clock slightly to make it look like it is standing on a flat surface. (*Hint:* Turning on the grid display will help align the clock.) When you are satisfied with the transformation, deselect it.

7. To select and transform the wall clock:

   a. Use the Lasso Tool to select the wall clock. Use the Magic Wand Tool and the 'Subtract from selection' button to remove any white from around the edge of the clock.

   b. Use the Move Tool to move it to a location in the upper-left corner of the scene, as shown in Figure 2–76.

   c. Display the bounding box and enlarge the selection, and then deselect it.

8. Save the file and then submit the document, shown in Figure 2–76, in the format specified by your instructor.

In the Lab

Lab 3: Creating a Money Graphic

Problem: Your local bank is starting an initiative to encourage children to open a savings account using their loose change. The bank would like a before and after picture showing how money can grow with interest.

Note: To complete this assignment, you will required to use the Data Files for Students. Visit www. cengage.com/ct/studentdownload for detailed instructions or contact your instructor for information about accessing the required files.

Instructions: Perform the following tasks:

1. Start Photoshop. Set the default workspace and reset all tools.

2. Open the file, Lab 2-3 Coins, from the Chapter 02 folder of the Data Files for Students, or from a location specified by your instructor.

3. Use the Save As command to save the file on your storage device with the name Lab 2-3 Coins Edited.

4. Use the Elliptical Marquee Tool to select the quarter. (*Hint:* While dragging, if your selection marquee does not match the quarter exactly, press and hold the SPACEBAR key to move the selection.) Once the quarter is selected, ALT+drag to create several duplicate copies. As you create the duplicates, display the transform controls on the options bar, and then right-click the selection to display the context menu. Use the context menu commands to distort, rotate 90° CW, and apply perspective.

5. Use the Magnetic Lasso tool to select the dime. ALT+drag to create several duplicate copies. As you create the duplicates, use the transform control sizing handle to move, scale, and drag a corner to create a slight distortion.

6. Use the Quick Selection Tool to select the nickel. ALT+drag to create several duplicate copies. As you create the duplicates, use the transform controls to change some of the copies.

7. Use the Magic Wand Tool to select the penny. Create several copies. Your document should resemble Figure 2–77.

8. Save the file again, and submit it in the format specified by your instructor.

Figure 2–77

Cases and Places

Apply your creative thinking and problem-solving skills to design and implement a solution.

Note: To complete this assignment, you will required to use the Data Files for Students. Visit www.cengage.com/ct/studentdownload for detailed instructions or contact your instructor for information about accessing the required files.

1: Design a Poster for the Computer Lab

Academic

The computer lab at your school wants a poster reminding students to save their work often. The department chair has asked you to create a graphic of a computer mouse that seems to be eating data. He has taken a picture of a mouse from the lab and started the poster for you. A file named Case 2-1 Poster is located in the Chapter 02 folder of the Data Files for Students. Start Photoshop and use the selection tools to select the mouse. Flip the mouse horizontally. Then, using the Subtract from selection button, remove the white part around the selection. Also, remove the dark gray bottom portion of the mouse from the selection. With the top portion of the mouse selected, warp the selection up and away from the bottom part of the mouse to simulate an open mouth. Move the selection close to the 0 and 1 data pattern. Save a copy of the poster as a PDF and send it as an e-mail attachment to your instructor.

2: Create a New Shortcut

Personal

You have decided to create a new keyboard shortcut to reset all tools, rather than having to move the mouse to the options bar, right-click, and then choose to reset all tools. Because other family members work on your computer system, you would like to save the new shortcut in a separate set for your personal use. You also would like to see a complete listing of the Photoshop shortcuts for your system. Access the Keyboard Shortcuts and Menus dialog box. Click the Shortcuts For box arrow, and then click Panel Menus in the list. Scroll down and double-click Tool Presets, and then click Reset All Tools in the list. Enter the shortcut, CTRL+SLASH (/). Click the 'Create a new set based on the current set of shortcuts' button, and save the shortcuts with your name. Click the Summarize button and save the summary as My Shortcut Summary. When the summary displays in the browser, print a copy for your records.

3: Create a Grocery Store Flyer

Professional

You have been hired to create an advertisement for a grocery store flyer about citrus fruits that are on sale. Search the Web for samples of fruit displays, noting the ones that look most appealing. A file named Case 2-3 Fruits is located in the Chapter 02 folder of the Data Files for Students. Start Photoshop and reset the workspace, tools, and colors. Use selection tools to select the various fruits and move them into an attractive display. Create duplicates of fruits and resize the copies as necessary. Keep in mind the horizon line and perspective.

3 | Working with Layers

Objectives

You will have mastered the material in this chapter when you can:

- Use the Layers panel and change options
- Create a layer via cut
- Rename layers and set identification colors
- Hide, view, and rearrange layers
- Arrange and consolidate document windows
- Create a new layer from another image or selection
- Transform selections and layers

- Use the Eraser, Magic Eraser, and Background Eraser Tools
- Create layer masks
- Make level adjustments and opacity changes
- Apply adjustments using the Adjustments panel
- Add a layer style
- Use the Clone Stamp Tool
- Flatten a composite image

3 | Working with Layers

Introduction

Whether it is adding a new person to a photograph, combining artistic effects from different genres, or creating 3D animation, the concept of layers in Photoshop allows you to work on one element of an image without disturbing the others. You might think of layers as sheets of clear film stacked one on top of another. You can see through transparent areas of a layer to the layers below. The nontransparent, or opaque, areas of a layer are solid and obscure the content of the layers beneath. You can change the composition of an image by changing the order and attributes of layers. In addition, special features, such as adjustment layers, layer masks, fill layers, and layer styles, allow you to create sophisticated effects.

Another tool that graphic designers use when they want to recreate a portion of another photo is the Clone Stamp Tool. As you will learn in this chapter, the Clone Stamp Tool takes a sample of an image and then applies, as you draw, an exact copy of that image to your document.

Graphic designers use layers and clones, along with other tools in Photoshop, to create **composite** images that combine or merge multiple images and drawings to create a new image, also referred to as a **montage**. Composite images illustrate the power of Photoshop to prepare documents for businesses, advertising, marketing, and media artwork. Composite images such as navigation bars can be created in Photoshop and used on the Web along with layered buttons, graphics, and background images.

Project — Room Furnishing

Chapter 3 uses Photoshop to create a composite image from several photographs by using layers. Specifically, it begins with a photo of an empty room and creates a composite image by inserting layers of furniture, a plant, a painting, and other decorative pieces to create a complete room design (Figure 3–1). The enhancements will show how the room will look when furnished. Wood flooring will replace the carpeting; a sofa, lamp, table, and other decorations will be added. Finally, adjustment layers will give the room eye appeal.

(a) Original image

(b) Edited image

Figure 3–1

Overview

As you read this chapter, you will learn how to create the composite room shown
in Figure 3–1b by performing these general tasks:

- Create a layer via cut.
- Insert layers from new images.
- Use the eraser tools.
- Add a layer mask.
- Create layer adjustments and apply layer styles.
- Clone an image.
- Flatten the image.
- Save the photo with and without layers format.

General Project Guidelines

When editing a photo, the actions you perform and decisions you make will affect the appearance and characteristics of the finished product. As you edit a photo, such as the one shown in Figure 3–1 on the previous page, you should follow these general guidelines:

1. **Gather your photos and plan your layers.** The graphics you choose should convey the overall message of your composite image. Choose high-quality photos with similar lighting characteristics. Create an ordered list of the layers you plan to include. Select images that are consistent with the visual effect you want to achieve as well as with customer requirements.

2. **Evaluate the best way to move outside images into the composite.** Sometimes it is easier to create a selection first and move the selection into the composite image as a layer. Other times, you may want to bring in the entire image and then erase or mask portions of the image. Once the layer exists, choose the correct tool for making edits and erasures.

3. **Create layer adjustments.** Fine-tune your layers by creating layer adjustments. Look at each layer and evaluate how it fits into the background scene. Experiment with different adjustment tools until the layer looks just right. Decide whether to use destructive or nondestructive edits. Keep in mind the standard tonal dimensions of brightness, saturation, and hue.

4. **Edit layer styles.** Add variety to your layers by including layer styles such as shadow, glow, emboss, bevel, overlay, and stroke. Make sure the layer style does not overwhelm the overall image or detract from previous layer adjustments.

When necessary, more specific details concerning the above guidelines are presented at appropriate points in the chapter. The chapter also will identify the actions performed and decisions made regarding these guidelines during the creation of the edited photo shown in Figure 3–1.

Creating a Composite

Creating a composite with visual layers is a powerful effect. Photographers sometimes try to achieve this effect by using a sharp focus on objects in the foreground against an out-of-focus background. Others stage their photos with three layers of visual action. For example, at a baseball game, a person in the stands (foreground) may be observing a close call at first base (middle ground), while outfielders watch from afar (background). When those kinds of photographic techniques cannot be achieved, graphic artists use **composition techniques,** the layering of images and actions. Not only can you make realistic changes to parts of a photo, but you also can add additional images and control their placement, blending, and special effects. In addition, you can make changes to a layer, independent of the layer itself, which is extremely helpful in composite production.

Simple layers may incorporate new objects or new people. Layer effects create adjustments, add blending modes, or edit the coloring, fill, and opacity of the layer. Masks conceal or reveal part of a layer. All of the layering techniques are **nondestructive,** which means that no pixels are changed in the process; the effect is applied over the image or layer to create the change. Adding layers increases the file size of a Photoshop document, but that increase is justified by the value and flexibility layers provide. When you are finished working with layers, you can flatten the Photoshop document to reduce the file size. You will learn about flattening later in this chapter.

When an image duplication is required and layering a new copy does not achieve the required effect, some graphic artists **clone,** or reproduce, an image by painting a copy into the scene. As with masks, cloning allows you to control exactly how much of the image you want to use — even down to the smallest pixel. You also can use cloning to remove minor imperfections in a photo or to clone over intricate elements that do not fit into the picture.

The steps in this chapter create a composite image with layers, layer effects, adjustments, masks, and cloning.

To Start Photoshop

If you are stepping through this project on a computer and you want your screen to match the figures in this book, then you should change your computer's resolution to 1024 × 768 and reset the panels, tools, and colors. For more information about how to change the resolution on your computer, and other advanced Photoshop settings, read the Changing Screen Resolution appendix.

The following steps, which assume Windows 7 is running, start Photoshop based on a typical installation. You may need to ask your instructor how to start Photoshop for your system.

1 Click the Start button on the Windows 7 taskbar to display the Start menu, and then type `Photoshop CS6` in the 'Search programs and files' box.

2 Click Adobe Photoshop CS6 in the list to start Photoshop.

3 If the Photoshop window is not maximized, click the Maximize button next to the Close button on the Application bar to maximize the window.

To Reset the Workspace

As discussed in Chapter 1, it is helpful to reset the workspace so that the tools and panels appear in their default positions. The following steps select the Essentials workspace.

1 Click Window on the Application bar to display the Window menu and then point to Workspace to display the Workspace submenu.

2 Click Essentials (Default) on the Workspace submenu to select the default workspace panels.

3 Click Window on the Application bar, and then point to Workspace again to display the list.

4 Click Reset Essentials to restore the workspace to its default settings and reposition any panels that may have been moved.

To Reset the Tools and the Options Bar

Recall that the Tools panel and the options bar retain their settings from previous Photoshop sessions. The following steps select the Rectangular Marquee Tool and reset all tool settings in the options bar.

1 If the tools in the Tools panel appear in two columns, click the double arrow at the top of the Tools panel.

2 If necessary, click the Rectangular Marquee Tool button on the Tools panel to select it.

3 Right-click the Rectangular Marquee Tool icon on the options bar to display the context menu, and then click Reset All Tools. When Photoshop displays a confirmation dialog box, click the OK button to restore the tools to their default settings.

To Set the Interface and Default Colors

Recall that Photoshop retains the interface color scheme, as well as the foreground and background colors, from session to session. The following steps set the interface to Medium Gray and the foreground and background colors to black over white.

1 Click Edit on the Application bar to display the Edit menu. Point to Preferences and then click Interface on the Preferences submenu to display the Preferences dialog box.

2 Click the third button, Medium Gray, to change the interface color scheme.

3 Click the OK button to close the Preferences dialog box.

4 Press the D key to reset the default foreground and background colors.

To Open a File

To open a file in Photoshop, it must be stored as a digital file on your computer system or on an external storage device. The photos used in this book are stored in the Data Files for Students. Visit www.cengage.com/ct/studentdownload for detailed instructions or contact your instructor for information about accessing the required files.

The following steps open the Room file from the Data Files for Students.

1 With the Photoshop window open, click File on the Application bar, and then click Open to display the Open dialog box.

2 In the Open dialog box, click the Look in box arrow to display the list of available locations, and then navigate to the storage location of the Data Files for Students.

3 Double-click the Photoshop folder and then double-click the Chapter 03 folder to open it. Double-click the file, Room, to open it.

4 When Photoshop displays the image in the document window, if the magnification shown on the status bar is not 33.33%, double-click the magnification box on the document window status bar, type 33.33 and then press the ENTER key to change the magnification (Figure 3–2).

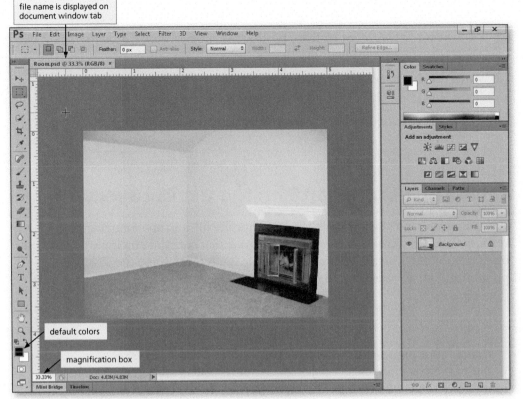

Figure 3–2

To View Rulers

The following steps display the rulers in the document window to facilitate
making precise measurements.

1 If the rulers are not shown on the top and left sides of the document window, press
CTRL+R to display the rulers in the workspace.

2 If necessary, right-click the horizontal ruler and then click Inches on the context menu
to display the rulers in inches.

To Save a Photo

Even though you have yet to edit the photo, it is a good practice to save the
file on your personal storage device early in the process. The following steps save the
photo with the name Room Edited in a new folder named Chapter 03.

1 With your USB flash drive connected to one of the computer's USB ports, click File on
the Application bar to display the File menu and then click Save As to display the Save
As dialog box.

2 In the File name text box, type `Room Edited` to rename the file. Do not press the
ENTER key after typing the file name.

3 Click the Save in box arrow and then click Removable Disk (F:), or the location
associated with your USB flash drive, in the list, if necessary.

BTW

Layer Comps

Graphic artists often create multiple versions, or compositions, of their work. A **layer comp** is a single view of the page layout with specific visible layers and attributes. You can use layer comps to demo versions of your composition to customers or colleagues, or simply to jump back and forth between different views and layers of your document. Similar to the History panel's snapshot, a layer comp takes a picture of the composite, using the Layers panel to show a particular stage of development.

④ On the Save As dialog box toolbar, click the Create New Folder button to create a new folder on the selected storage device.

⑤ When the new folder appears, type Chapter 03 to change the name of the folder, and then press the ENTER key. Double-click the new folder to open it.

⑥ Click the Save button in the Save As dialog box to save the file in the new folder.

Creating a Composite Image using Layers

Photoshop has many tools to help create composite images, photomontages, and collages. A composite, or composite image, is one that combines multiple photographs or images to display in a single combined file. Graphic artists use the newer term, **photomontage**, to refer to both the process and the result of creating a composite from photos.

Plan Ahead

> **Gather your photos and plan your layers.**
> One of the keys to successful image compositions is finding the best source material with similar lighting situations and tonal qualities. Choose high-quality photos and images that convey your overall message. Make sure you have permission to use the images if they are not original photographs taken by you or provided to you by a colleague or client. Obtain several versions of the same photo, if possible, including photos from different angles and with different lighting situations. Make two copies of each photo and store one as a backup. Crop unwanted portions of the photos before adding them as new layers.

BTW

Layer Comps vs. History Snapshots

Layer comps include the visibility, position, and appearance of layers, not the edited steps. In addition, layer comps are saved with the document, whereas History panel snapshots are not. You can export layer comps to separate graphic or PDF files for easy distribution.

BTW

Layer Comps Panel

The Layer Comps panel includes a status bar with buttons to move back and forth through the comps, to update comps from the current view, to create them, and to delete them. The Layer Comps menu has some of those same commands, as well as others to duplicate a layer comp and set its properties.

Layers

One of the most powerful tools in Photoshop is layering. A **layer** is a section within a Photoshop document that you can manipulate independently from the rest of the document. Layers can be stacked one on top of the other, resembling sheets of clear film, to form a composite image.

Layers have been used by business and industry for years. Cartoonists create layers of physical transparencies to help with animation. The medical field uses overlays to illustrate anatomical features. Virtual simulations use layers to display processes. With Photoshop, layers are easy to create and export for these kinds of applications.

Recall that you used selections in Chapter 2 to move, copy, and scale portions of a photo. Layers can perform all of the same functions performed by selecting, while providing added features. The most powerful feature of layers is the ability to revisit a portion of the image to make further changes, even after deselecting. Layers can be created, copied, deleted, displayed, hidden, merged, locked, grouped, repositioned, and flattened. Layers can be composed of images, patterns, text, shapes, colors, or filters. You can use layers to apply special effects, correct or colorize pictures, repair damaged photos, or import text elements. In previous chapters, you worked with images in a flat, single layer called the Background layer. In this chapter, you will create, name, and manipulate multiple layers on top of the Background layer.

Many layer manipulations are performed using the Layers panel, which lists all the layers, groups, and layer effects in an image (Figure 3–3). Each time you insert a layer onto an image, the new layer is added above the current layer, or to the top of the panel. The default display of a layer on the Layers panel includes a visibility

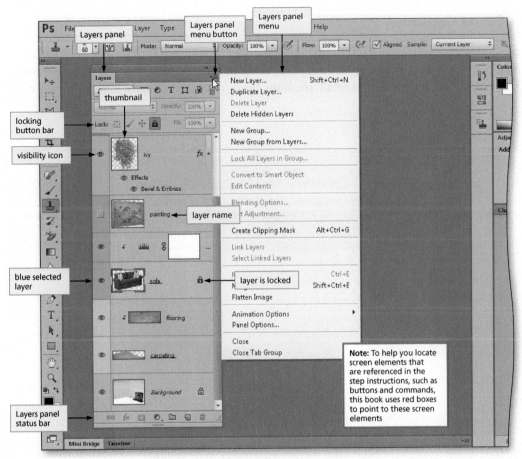

Figure 3–3

icon, a thumbnail of the layer, and the layer's name. To the right of the layer's name, a locking icon or other special effect notations might appear.

Photoshop allows you to **lock** three different components of layers. The 'Lock transparent pixels' button confines editing to opaque layer portions. The 'Lock image pixels' button prevents modification of the layer's pixels using paint tools. The Lock position button prevents the layer from being moved. The Lock all button enables all three ways of locking the layer. A lock icon appears to the right of the name on the Layers panel on locked layers.

The Layers panel is used in several different manners: to show and hide layers, create new layers, and work with groups of layers. You can access additional commands and attributes by clicking the Layers panel menu button or by right-clicking a layer. The Layers panel defines how layers interact. As you use the buttons and boxes on the Layers panel, each will be explained.

While Photoshop allows background editing, as you have done in previous chapters, the Background layer cannot be moved, nor can its transparency be changed. In other words, the Background layer fills the document window, and there is no layer behind the background. Partially locked by default, the Background layer displays a hollow lock (Figure 3–3). If you want to convert the Background layer into a fully editable layer, double-click the layer on the Layers panel, and then click the OK button in the New Layer dialog box.

When working with layers, it is important to make sure you know which layer you are editing by looking at the active layer on the Layers panel or by looking at the layer name, appended to the file name on the document window tab. Many other layer commands appear on the Layer menu, including those for making adjustments to the layer, creating layer masks, grouping layers, and other editing and placement commands.

To Change Layers Panel Options

The Panel Options command, accessible from the Layers panel menu, allows you to change the view and size of the thumbnail related to each layer. A thumbnail displays a small preview of the layer on the Layers panel. The Panel Options dialog box allows you to choose small, medium, large, or no thumbnails. The following steps select a medium-sized thumbnail of each layer.

1

- Click the Layers panel menu button to display the Layers panel menu (Figure 3–4).

Q&A

Do I have to display thumbnails?

No, but displaying a thumbnail of each layer allows you to see easily what the layer looks like and helps you to be more efficient when editing a layer. To improve performance and save monitor space, however, some Photoshop users choose not to display thumbnails.

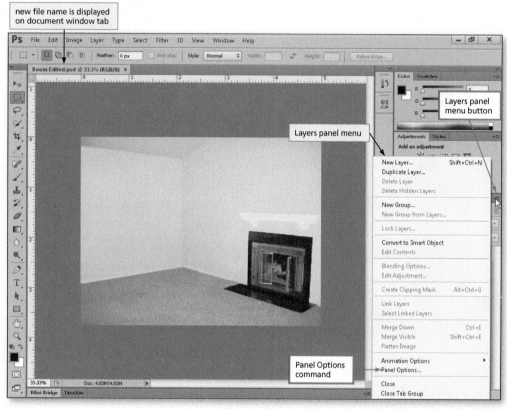

Figure 3–4

2

- Click Panel Options on the menu to display the Layers Panel Options dialog box.

- Click the medium thumbnail to select it.

- Click the Layer Bounds option button, if necessary, to change the look and feel of the Layers panel (Figure 3–5).

Q&A

How does the Layer Bounds option change the interface?

The Layer Bounds option causes the Layers panel to display only the layer, restricting the thumbnail to the object's pixels on the layer.

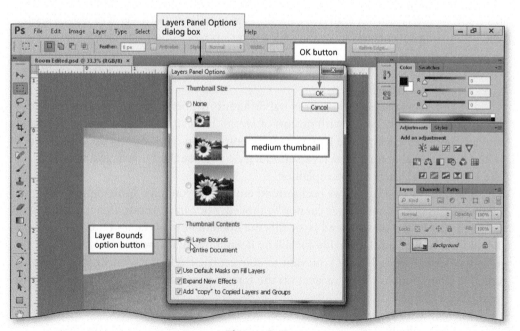

Figure 3–5

3

- Click the OK button to close the Layers Panel Options dialog box (Figure 3–6).

Q&A

Should I see a difference on the Layers panel?

Yes. Unless a previous user had already changed it, the size of the thumbnail should have changed on the Layers panel. Layer bounds will not appear until you create a layer other than the Background layer.

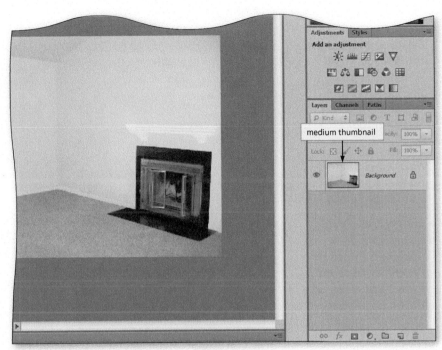

Figure 3–6

Creating a Layer via Cut

There are several ways to create a new layer. You can:

- Isolate a portion of the image and then cut or make a layer copy
- Create a new layer by copying from a different image
- Duplicate a layer that already exists
- Create a new, blank layer on which you can draw or create text

When you add a layer to an image, a new layer appears above, or on top of, the currently selected layer, creating a **stacking order**. By default, Photoshop names and numbers layers sequentially; however, you can rearrange the stacking order to change the appearance of the image. The final appearance of an edited Photoshop document is a view of the layer stack from the top down. In the document window, the layers at the top of the Layers panel appear in front of the layers at the bottom of the panel.

BTW

Deleting Layers
To delete a layer permanently, right-click the layer name and then click Delete Layer on the context menu, or activate the layer and press the DELETE key.

To Create a Layer via Cut

The steps on the next page create a new layer that includes only the carpeting on the floor. You will use the Quick Selection Tool to select the area and then use the Layer Via Cut command to isolate the floor from the rest of the photo, creating a new layer. You will manipulate the new layer, later in the chapter.

1

● On the Tools panel, select the Quick Selection Tool button. If the Magic Wand Tool is selected, press SHIFT+W to toggle to the Quick Selection Tool.

● If necessary, click the New selection button on the options bar to start a new selection.

● In the photo, drag slowly from the upper-left corner of the carpeting to the lower-right corner of the photo to select only the carpeting (Figure 3–7).

Q&A

Why did Photoshop change to the 'Add to selection' button on the options bar?

Once you create a new selection, the most common task is to add more to the selection, so Photoshop selects that button automatically. If you want to start over, you can select the New selection button again.

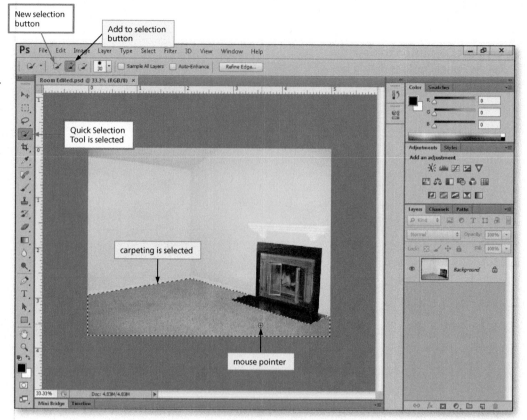

Figure 3–7

2

● Right-click the selection to display the context menu (Figure 3–8).

Q&A

Could I use the New Layer command?

No. The New Layer command creates a blank layer.

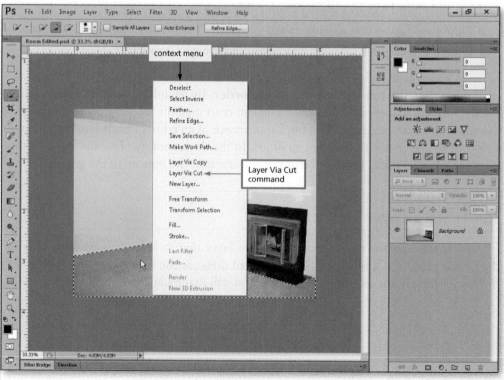

Figure 3–8

3

- Click Layer Via Cut on the context menu to create the new layer (Figure 3–9).

Q&A

What is the difference between Layer Via Cut and Layer Via Copy?

The Layer Via Cut command differs from the Layer Via Copy command in that it removes the selection from the background. Future edits to the Background, such as changing the color or lighting, will not affect the cut layer.

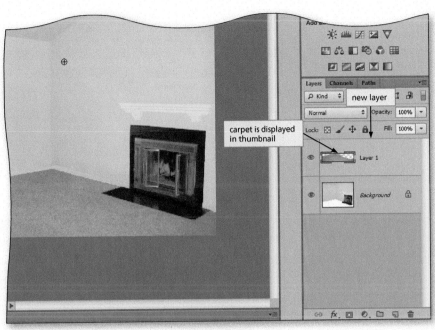

Figure 3–9

Other Ways	
1. Create selection, on Layer menu, point to New, click Layer Via Cut	2. Create selection, press SHIFT+CTRL+J

To Rename a Layer

It is a good practice to give each layer a unique name so you can identify it more easily. The name of the active layer appears on the Layers panel and on the title bar of the document window. The following steps rename a layer.

1

- On the Layers panel, double-click the name of the layer you want to rename, in this case Layer 1 (Figure 3–10).

Figure 3–10

2

- Type carpeting to replace the current name of the layer, and then press the ENTER key to rename the layer (Figure 3–11).

Figure 3–11

Other Ways

1. On Layer menu, click Rename Layer, enter new name, press ENTER key

To Assign a Color to a Layer

Photoshop allows you to give each layer its own color identification. Assigning a color helps you recognize relationships among layers. For example, if two of your layers display objects in the sky, you might assign those two layers a blue identification color so you quickly could see which layers were related to the sky. The color appears around the visibility icon on the left side of the layer. The following steps assign a color to a layer.

1

- Right-click the carpeting layer to display its context menu (Figure 3–12).

Q&A

Does it make any difference exactly where I right-click?

No. You can right-click anywhere on the layer. If you click the area around the visibility icon, Photoshop displays a shorter context menu with only color and hide/show options.

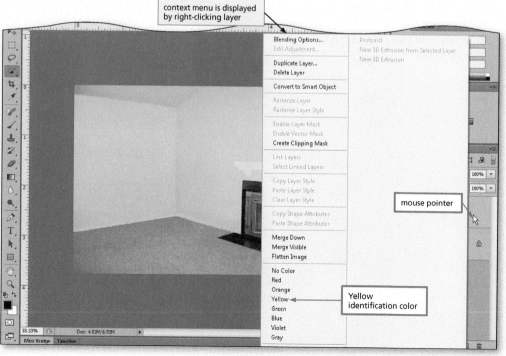

Figure 3–12

2

- Click Yellow in the list to choose a yellow identification color (Figure 3–13).

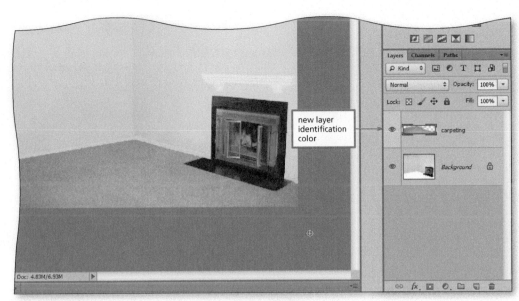

Figure 3–13

Other Ways

1. Right-click visibility area, click color

To Hide and Show a Layer

Sometimes you want to hide a layer to view other layers and make editing decisions. The visibility icon is a button that toggles the visibility of the layer on and off. The following steps hide and show the Background layer.

1

- Click the 'Indicates layer visibility' button to the left of the Background layer to hide the layer in the document window and hide the visibility icon (Figure 3–14).

Q&A

What is the checkerboard effect in the carpeting layer?

The checkerboard effect represents blank portions of the document window that are transparent.

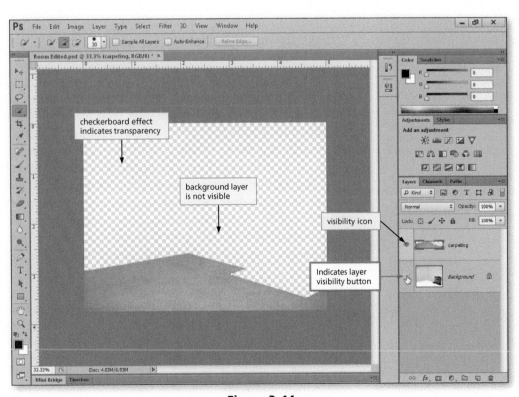

Figure 3–14

2

● Click the 'Indicates layer visibility' button again to show the Background layer in the document window and display the visibility icon (Figure 3–15).

Q&A

What is the white area on the Background layer thumbnail?

When you cut or delete from a locked layer, such as the Background layer, the default background color shows through; in this case, it is the default white color. Because other layers will eclipse the white, you do not have to remove it.

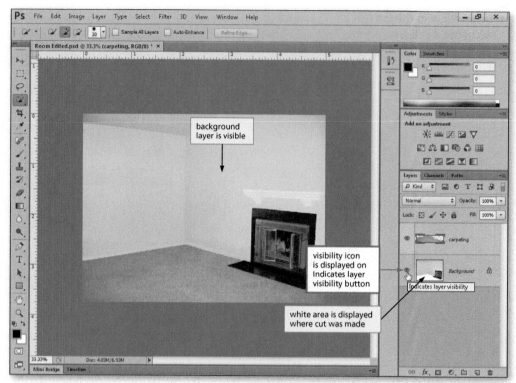

background layer is visible

visibility icon is displayed on Indicates layer visibility button

white area is displayed where cut was made

Indicates layer visibility

Figure 3–15

Other Ways

1. Right-click visibility icon, click Hide this layer or Show this layer

2. On Layer menu, click Hide Layers or Show Layers

BTW

Layer Selection
Sometimes a menu or panel will cover the Layers panel, or a layer might be scrolled out of sight. You always can identify which layer you are working with by looking at the document window tab. The name of the current layer appears in parentheses.

Creating a Layer from Another Image

When you create composite images, you might want to create layers from other images. It is important to choose images that closely match or complement color, lighting, size, and perspective if you want your image to look natural. While you can adjust disparate images to improve how well they match, it is easier to start with as close a match as possible, ideally with similar lighting situations and tonal qualities.

Many sources exist for composite images, and they come in many different file types and sizes. For example, you can use your own digital photos, scanned images, images from royalty-free Web sites, or you can draw your own. If you use a photo or image from the Web, make sure you have legal rights to use the image. Means of obtaining legal rights include getting permission from the photographer or artist to use the image or purchasing the rights, through a contract, from an online store.

Plan Ahead

Evaluate the best way to move outside images into the composite.
If the desired portion of the outside image is selected easily, such as a rectangle, oval or polygon, then select and copy it. Paste it in the composite image to create a layer. If the desired portion of the outside image is not easy to select, drag the entire image into the composite, creating a layer. Then, use eraser tools to eliminate the unwanted portion of the layer. That way, you have not changed the original image, should you need to return to it later.

The basic process of creating a new layer from another image involves opening a second image, selecting the area you want to use, and then moving it to the original photo in a drag-and-drop, or cut-and-paste, fashion. Once the layer exists in the destination photo, you might need to do some editing to remove portions of the layer, to resize it, or to make tonal adjustments.

To Open a Second Image

To add a sofa as a layer to the Room Edited image, you will need to open a new file, Sofa, from the Data Files for Students, or from a location specified by your instructor. The following steps open the Sofa file, which is stored in the PSD format.

① Press CTRL+O to display the Open dialog box.

② In the Open dialog box, if necessary, click the Look in box arrow, and then navigate to the Chapter 03 folder of the Data Files for Students or a location specified by your instructor.

③ Double-click the file named Sofa to open it (Figure 3–16).

Figure 3–16

Displaying Multiple Files

Photoshop offers many different ways to arrange and view document windows when more than one file is open. You also can create a custom workspace by moving and manipulating document windows manually.

For example, you might want to display two document windows, horizontally or vertically, in order to drag and drop from one image to another. You might want to compare different versions or views of photos beside each other in the document window. Or, when creating a panorama, you might want to preview how certain photos will look side by side.

When you are finished viewing multiple document windows in the workspace, you can **consolidate** them, or view only one window at a time.

To Arrange Document Windows

The following steps display the Room Edited and Sofa windows beside each other using the Arrange submenu on the Window menu.

1

● On the Application bar, click Window and then point to Arrange to display the Arrange submenu (Figure 3–17).

Q&A Why are some of the arrangements grayed out?

Because you have only two document windows open, the only arrangements enabled are the ones that display two windows.

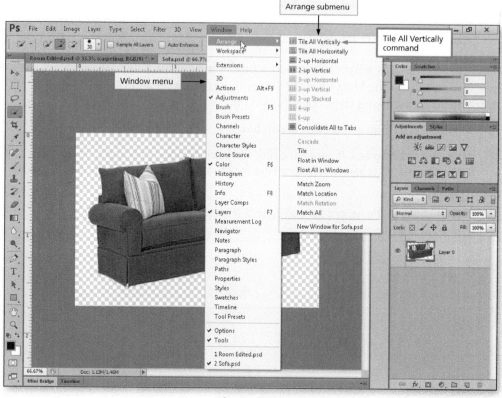

Figure 3–17

2

● Click Tile All Vertically in the submenu to display the windows beside each other (Figure 3–18).

Q&A What is the difference between Tile All Vertically and 2-up Vertical?

When you have only two document windows open, there is no difference. If you have more than two document windows open, Tile All Vertically will open all the windows; 2-up Vertical will open only the two most recently used document windows.

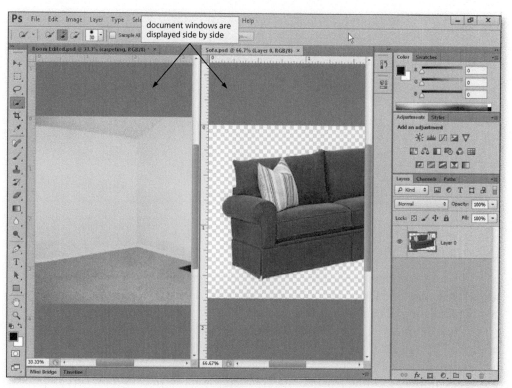

Figure 3–18

To Create a Layer by Dragging an Entire Image

When you drag a selection from one document window to the other, Photoshop creates a new layer in the destination document window, above the currently selected layer. If you want to include the entire image from the source window, use the Move Tool to drag from any location in the source window to the destination window. Dragging between document windows is an automatic duplication rather than a true move out of one window and into the other. The original, source image remains unchanged.

The following step moves the entire image from the source window, Sofa, to the destination window, Room Edited.

1

• Press the v key to activate the Move Tool.

• Drag the sofa image into the Room Edited window and drop it in the room (Figure 3–19).

Q&A

Why is the sofa so much bigger in its own document window?

The sofa is the same size; the magnification of the windows is different.

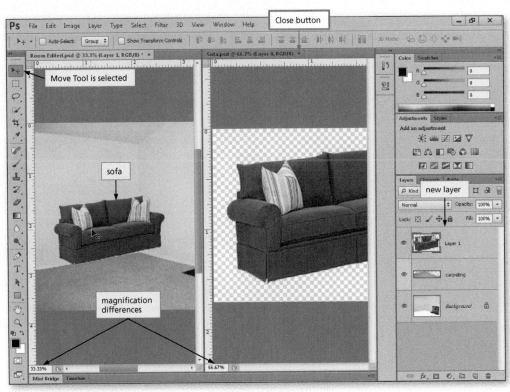

Figure 3–19

Other Ways

1. In source window, on Edit menu click Copy, in destination window on Edit menu click Paste

To Close the Sofa Document Window

Because you are finished with the Sofa image, the following step closes the Sofa window.

1 Click the Close button on the Sofa document window tab. If Photoshop asks you to save the file again, click the No button.

BTW

Consolidate Windows
Sometimes, after viewing multiple document windows, you might want to view only one window at a time. In that case, right-click the tab at the top of the Room Edited document window to display the context menu and then click Consolidate All to Here to view that document window alone. The Arrange submenu has a Consolidate All to Tabs command that has the same effect.

To Move a Layer in the Document Window

If there is no marquee selection, the Move Tool moves the entire current layer when you drag. The following step moves the sofa to a new location.

1

- With the new layer still selected on the Layers panel, and the Move Tool still selected on the Tools panel, drag the sofa to a position along the left wall, on the floor (Figure 3–20).

Q&A

Is it acceptable for some of the sofa to disappear off the edge of the document window?

Yes. Your goal is to make it look as natural as possible, as if it is sitting on the floor.

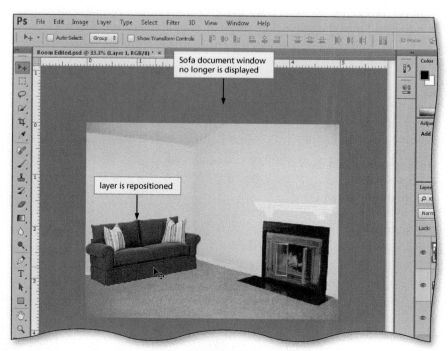

Figure 3–20

To Name and Color the Sofa Layer

The following steps rename the new layer and assign it a color.

1 On the Layers panel, double-click the name of the layer, Layer 1. Type `sofa` and then press the ENTER key to name the layer.

2 Right-click the layer to display the context menu, and then click Blue in the list to choose a blue identification color (Figure 3–21).

BTW

Layer Boundaries
The settings you chose in the Layer Panel Options dialog box appear in Figure 3-21. Only the portion of the layer that contains an image is displayed in the medium-sized thumbnails because of the Layer Bounds setting.

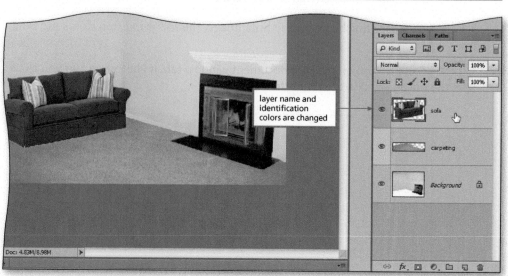

Figure 3–21

To Save the File

Because you have created layers and made changes to the image, it is a good idea to save the file again. The following step saves the file again.

1 Press CTRL+S to save the Room Edited file with the same name. If Photoshop displays a dialog box about compatibility, click the OK button.

Break Point: If you wish to stop working through the chapter at this point, you can quit Photoshop now and then resume the project at a later time by starting Photoshop, opening the file named Room Edited and continuing to follow the steps from this location forward.

Creating a Layer by Dragging a Selection

Sometimes you do not want to move an entire image from one window to another. When you want to move only a part of an image, you create a selection, as you learned in Chapter 2 and then move the selection to the destination window. Once the selection exists in the destination window, you might need to do some editing, such as scaling, erasing, or adjusting.

To Open the Painting Image

The following steps open a file named Painting.

1 Press CTRL+O to display the Open dialog box.

2 Click the Look in box arrow, and then navigate to the Chapter 03 folder of the Data Files for Students, or a location specified by your instructor.

3 Double-click the file named Painting to open it.

To Select the Painting

When adding the painting image to the Room Edited image, you will not need the surrounding wall. The following steps select the painting using the Rectangular Marquee Tool.

1 If necessary, right-click the current marquee tool and then click Rectangular Marquee Tool on the context menu to select it.

2 If necessary, click the New selection button on the options bar to start a new selection.

3 Drag around the painting, including the gold frame and matte. Avoid including the wall in the selection. If you make a mistake while selecting, press the ESC key and then begin again (Figure 3–22 on the next page).

BTW

Smart Objects
You can convert a layer into a smart object, which is a nondestructive layer that does not change the original pixels. Smart Objects are useful for warping, scaling, or rotating both raster and vector graphic layers. To convert a layer into a smart object, right-click the layer, and then click Convert to Smart Object on the context menu.

BTW

JPG File Type
The Painting image is stored as JPG file. Recall that JPG stands for Joint Photographic Experts Group and is the file type typically generated by digital cameras. JPG format supports many different color modes. JPG retains all color information in an RGB image, unlike GIF format.

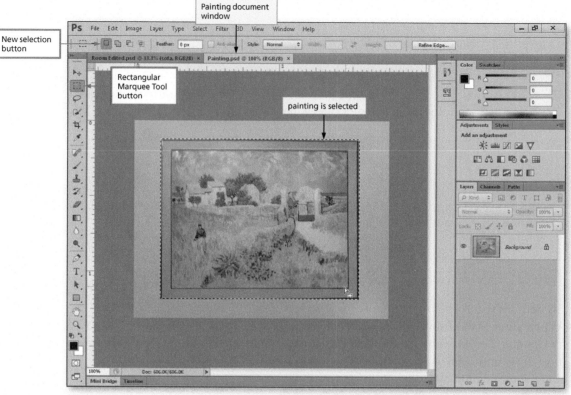

Figure 3–22

To Create a Layer by Dragging a Selection

The following steps move the selection. To facilitate dragging the selection between windows, you will view the windows above and below one another.

- On the Application bar, click Window, point to Arrange to display the submenu and click the Tile All Horizontally command to display the windows above and below one another (Figure 3–23).

Experiment

- Open a third file and then try some of the other configurations on the Arrange submenu. When you are done, close the third file. Repeat Step 1.

Figure 3–23

2

- Press the v key to activate the Move Tool.

- Drag the selection and drop it in the Room Edited window (Figure 3–24).

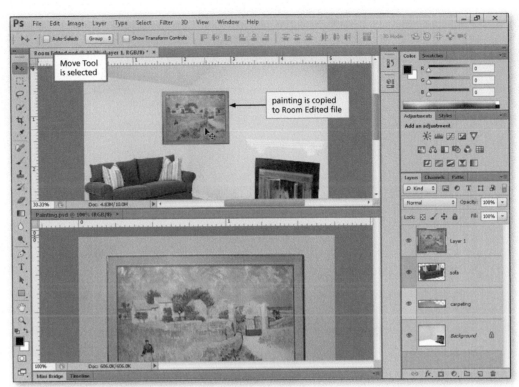

Figure 3–24

To Close the Painting Window

The next step closes the Painting window.

1 Click the Close button on the Painting document window tab. If Photoshop displays a dialog box asking if you want to save the changes, click the No button.

To Name and Assign a Color to the Painting Layer

The following steps rename the new layer and assign an identification color.

1 Double-click the name, Layer 1, on the Layers panel and then type `painting` and press the ENTER key to rename the layer.

2 Right-click the layer and then click Red to assign an identification color.

To Position the Painting Layer

The following steps move the painting to a location above the sofa.

1 Press the v key to active the Move Tool, if necessary.

2 Drag the painting to a location above the sofa, as shown in Figure 3–25 on the next page.

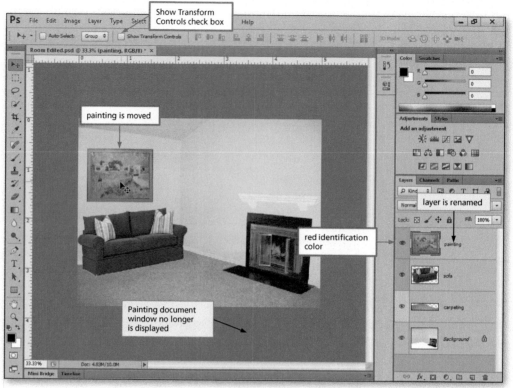

Figure 3–25

The Transformation Commands

In Photoshop, the word **transform** refers to changing the appearance of a selection by altering its shape, size, or other physical characteristics. To choose a transformation command, click the Edit menu, point to Transform, and then click the desired transformation. Alternatively, you can click Transform Selection on the context menu that is displayed when you right-click a selection.

Table 3–1 lists the types of transformations you can perform on a selection, the techniques used to perform a particular transformation, and the result of the transformation. Many of the commands also appear on the context menu when you right-click the bounding box. If you choose free transform, you must use the mouse techniques to perform the transformation.

Table 3–1 Transformation Commands

Using the Menu	Using the Mouse (Free Transform)	Using the Transform Options Bar	Result
Scale	Drag a sizing handle on the bounding box. SHIFT+drag to scale proportionately. ALT+drag to scale opposite sides at the same time.	To scale numerically, enter percentages in the Width and Height boxes, shown as W and H, on the options bar. Click the Link icon to maintain the aspect ratio.	Selection is displayed at a different size.
Rotate 180° Rotate 90° CW Rotate 90° CCW (CW stands for clockwise. CCW stands for counterclockwise.)	Move the mouse pointer outside the bounding box border. It becomes a curved, two-headed arrow. Drag in the direction you want to rotate. SHIFT+drag to constrain the rotation to 15° increments.	In the Set Rotation box, shown as a compass on the options bar, type a positive number for clockwise rotation or a negative number for counterclockwise rotation.	Selection is rotated or revolved around the reference point.

Table 3–1 Transformation Commands *(continued)*

Using the Menu	Using the Mouse (Free Transform)	Using the Transform Options Bar	Result
Skew	Right-click selection and then click Skew. Drag a side of the bounding box. ALT+drag to skew both vertically and horizontally.	To skew numerically, enter decimal values in the horizontal skew and vertical skew boxes, shown as H and V on the options bar.	Selection is tilted or slanted either horizontally or vertically.
Distort	Right-click selection and then click Distort. Drag a corner sizing handle to stretch the bounding box.	Enter new numbers in the location, size, rotation, and skew boxes.	Selection is larger on one edge than on the others.
Perspective	Right-click selection and then click Perspective. Drag a corner sizing handle to apply perspective to the bounding box.	Enter new numbers in the size, rotation, and skew boxes.	The selection appears larger on one edge than on the others, giving the larger edge the appearance of being closer to the viewer.
Warp	When the warp mesh is displayed, drag any line or point.	Click the Custom box arrow. Click a custom warp.	Selection is reshaped with a bulge, arch, warped corner, or twist.
Flip Horizontal Flip Vertical	Flipping is available only on the menu.	Flipping is available only on the menu.	Selection is turned upside down or mirrored.

Figure 3–26 displays a painting in its original state and with various transformation effects applied (Figure 3–26).

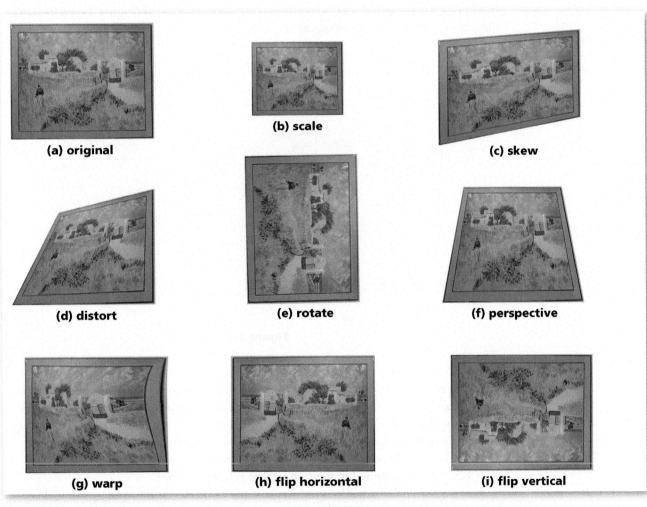

(a) original   **(b) scale**   **(c) skew**   **(d) distort**   **(e) rotate**   **(f) perspective**   **(g) warp**   **(h) flip horizontal**   **(i) flip vertical**

Figure 3–26

Transform is not a tool on the Tools panel; however, Photoshop displays a Transform options bar that contains boxes and buttons to help you with your transformation (Figure 3–27). To display the Transform options bar, create a selection and then do one of the following things: click Free Transform on the Edit menu, click a sizing handle, or press CTRL+T. Recall that if you are using the Move Tool, you also can click the Show Transform Controls check box. As you start to transform, Photoshop displays the Transform options bar.

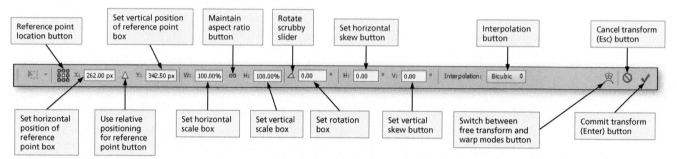

Figure 3–27

Rotating
When the bounding box is displayed, you can rotate the selection by dragging just outside of the corner. The mouse pointer changes to a double-headed, curved arrow as shown in Figure 3-28.

BTW

When you choose to transform, Photoshop displays a **bounding box**, or border with eight sizing handles around the selection. A small reference point appears in the center of the selection as a small circle with a crosshair symbol. A **reference point** is a fixed pivot point around which transformations are performed (Figure 3–28). You can move a reference point by dragging it.

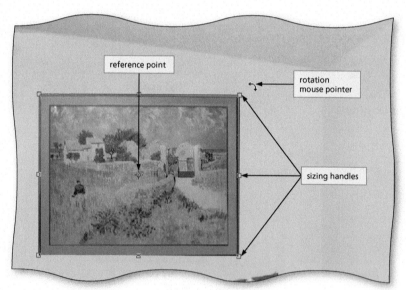

Figure 3–28

On the left side of the Transform options bar, Photoshop displays the 'Reference point location' button. Each of the nine squares on the button corresponds to a point on the bounding box. The default middle square represents the center reference point. To select a different reference point, click a different square on the 'Reference point location' button. By selecting one of the nine preset locations, any transformation, such as rotating, is applied in relation to that reference point.

The X and Y boxes allow you to place the reference point at an exact pixel location in the document window by entering horizontal and vertical values. When you enter a value in one of those boxes, Photoshop moves the entire selection. If you click the 'Use relative positioning for reference point' button, located between the X and Y boxes, the movement of the selection is relative to the current location.

The W and H boxes allow you to scale the width and height of the selection. When you click the 'Maintain aspect ratio' button between the W and H boxes, the aspect ratio of the selection is maintained.

To the right of the scale boxes is a Set rotation box. Entering a positive number rotates, or turns, the selection clockwise; a negative number rotates the selection counterclockwise.

The H and V boxes, to the right of the Set rotation box, set the horizontal and vertical skews of the selection, measured in degrees. A positive number skews the selection to the right; a negative number skews it to the left.

A unique feature is the ability to drag labels to change the box values. For example, if you drag the H, Y, W, or other labels, the values in the text boxes change. The interactive labels, called **scrubby sliders,** appear when you position the mouse pointer over the label. When you point to any of the scrubby sliders on the Transform options bar, the mouse pointer changes to a hand with a double-headed arrow, indicating the ability to drag. Dragging to the right increases the value; dragging to the left decreases the value. Holding the SHIFT key while dragging the scrubby slider accelerates the change by a factor of 10. Many options bars use scrubby sliders.

On the far right of the Transform options bar are three buttons. The first one switches between the Transform options bar and the Warp options bar. After you are finished making transformations, you commit changes, or apply the transformations by pressing the ENTER key or by clicking the Commit transform (Enter) button. **Committing** the transformation is the same as saving it. If you do not want to make the transformation, press the ESC key or click the Cancel transform (Esc) button.

After transforming a selection, you either must commit or cancel the transformation before you can perform any other action in Photoshop.

To Transform by Skewing

The following steps display the transformation controls and make the painting appear more natural in the setting by skewing the layer.

1

• Press CTRL+T to display the bounding box and the Transform options bar (Figure 3–29).

Q&A
Should I make a selection before pressing CTRL+T?

In this case, you are transforming the entire layer, so no selection is necessary. Photoshop displays the bounding box around the edges of the layer itself.

Figure 3–29

2

- Right-click the selection to display the context menu with the list of transformations (Figure 3–30).

When should I use skew rather than perspective?

You should use skew when the selection or layer is titled or slanted either horizontally or vertically. Use perspective when you want the selection or layer to appear closer or further away in the setting.

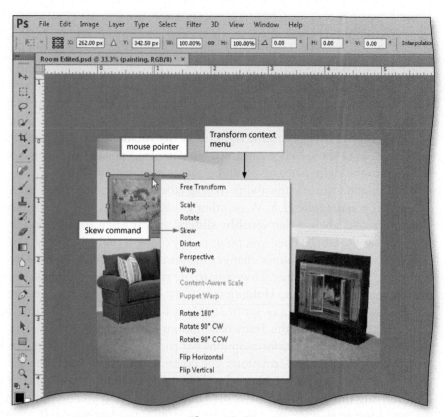

Figure 3–30

3

- Click Skew on the context menu to activate skewing.

- Drag the upper-left sizing handle up until the top of the painting is parallel with the top of the wall.

- Drag the lower-right sizing handle up until the bottom of the painting is parallel with the top of the sofa (Figure 3–31).

4

- Press the ENTER key to commit the transformation.

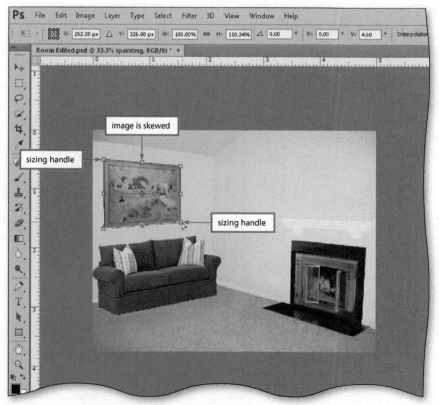

Other Ways

1. On Edit menu, point to Transform, click Skew, drag bounding box sizing handle

Figure 3–31

To Open the Coffee Table Image

The following step opens a file named Coffee Table in preparation for the next series of steps.

1 Open the Coffee Table file from the Chapter 03 folder of the Data Files for Students, or a location specified by your instructor.

To Create the Coffee Table Layer

The following steps create the coffee table layer.

1 On the Application bar, click Window, point to Arrange, and then click Tile All Horizontally to display the windows above and below one another.

2 With the Coffee Table window still active, click the Move Tool button on the Tools panel, if necessary.

3 Drag the entire coffee table image and drop it in the Room Edited window (Figure 3–32).

4 Close the Coffee Table document window. If Photoshop displays a dialog box asking if you want to save the changes, click the No button.

BTW

PNG File Type
The Coffee Table image is stored as PNG file. Recall that PNG stands for Portable Network Graphics and is a cross-platform file type similar to GIF. It differs in that you can control the opacity of transparent colors. PNG files **interlace**, or fill in, faster on Web pages.

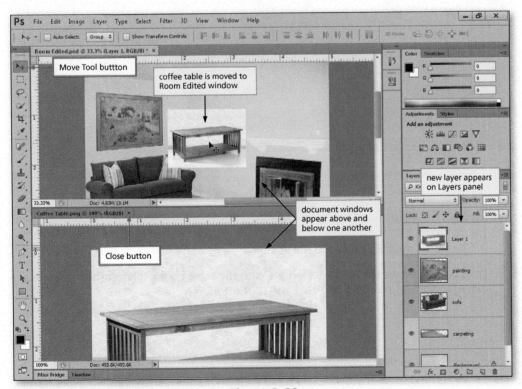

Figure 3–32

To Rename and Color the Coffee Table Layer

The following steps rename the new layer and assign an identification color.

1 Rename the layer `coffee table`.

2 Assign a Gray identification color to the layer.

3 With the Move Tool still selected, drag the layer to a location in front of the sofa (Figure 3–33).

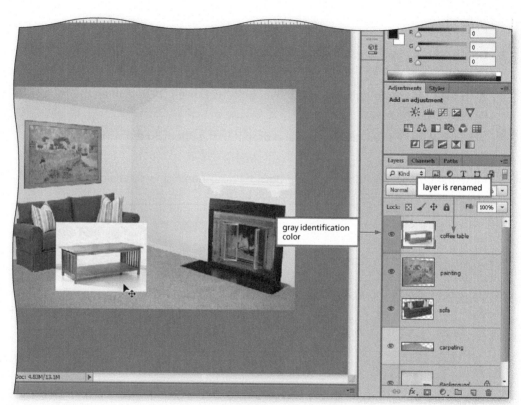

Figure 3–33

To Save the File

The following step saves the file again.

1 Press CTRL+S to save the Room Edited file with the same name. If Photoshop displays a dialog box about compatibility, click the OK button.

Break Point: If you wish to stop working through the chapter at this point, you can quit Photoshop now and then resume the project at a later time by starting Photoshop, opening the file named Room Edited and continuing to follow the steps from this location forward.

The Eraser Tools

In the painting layer, you eliminated the painting's background before moving it by using a selection technique. At other times, however, a new layer still might have extra color or objects that are not appropriate for the composite image. The image might be shaped oddly, making selecting tedious, or there might be other images in the background that come along with the selection and are not easily eliminated using the marquee selection technique you used previously. In those cases, dragging the image into a layer and then erasing part of that layer gives you more freedom and control in how the layer appears.

On the Tools panel, when you right-click the Eraser Tool button, Photoshop displays the three eraser tools. To alternate among the three eraser tools, press SHIFT+E. To access the eraser tools after using a different tool, press the E key.

The eraser tools are described in Table 3–2.

Table 3–2 Eraser Tools			
Tool	**Purpose**	**Shortcut**	**Button**
Eraser Tool	Erases pixels beneath the cursor or brush tip	E SHIFT+E toggles through all three eraser tools	
Background Eraser Tool	Erases sample color from the center of the brush	E SHIFT+E toggles through all three eraser tools	
Magic Eraser Tool	Erases all similarly colored pixels	E SHIFT+E toggles through all three eraser tools	

When using the eraser tools, it is best to erase small portions at a time. That way each erasure is a separate state on the History panel. If you make mistakes, you can click earlier states on the panel. Small erasures also can be undone. To undo an erasure, press CTRL+Z, or click Edit on the Application bar, and then click Undo Eraser.

Using the Magic Eraser Tool

The Magic Eraser Tool erases all similarly colored pixels with one click. The Magic Eraser Tool options bar (Figure 3–34) gives you the choice of erasing contiguous or noncontiguous pixels and allows you to enter a tolerance value to define the range of erasable color. A lower tolerance erases pixels within a range of color values very similar to the pixel you click. A higher tolerance erases pixels within a broader range. Recall that the Anti-alias check box creates a smooth edge that can apply to both selecting and erasing. **Opacity** refers to the level at which you can see through a color to reveal the layer beneath it. When using the eraser tools, an opacity setting of 100% completely erases pixels. A lower opacity partially erases pixels.

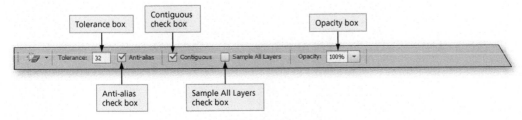

Figure 3–34

To Display Only the Current Layer

Some users find it easier to erase in a layer when only that layer appears in the document window. The following step hides all but the current layer by ALT+clicking the visibility icon.

- On the Layers panel, ALT+click the coffee table layer visibility icon, so only the coffee table is displayed.

- Press the z key to activate the Zoom Tool, and then click the coffee table several times to zoom in (Figure 3–35).

- If necessary, scroll the document window so that the entire coffee table is visible.

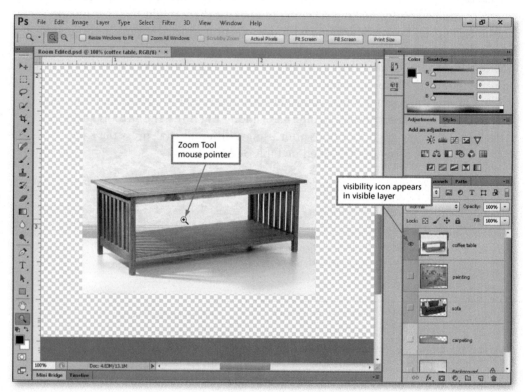

Figure 3–35

To Erase using the Magic Eraser Tool

The following steps use the Magic Eraser Tool to remove the blue wallpaper background from the coffee table image layer.

- Right-click the Eraser Tool button on the Tools panel to display the context menu (Figure 3–36).

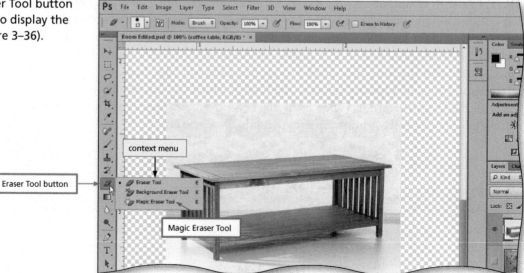

Figure 3–36

2

- Click Magic Eraser Tool to select it.

- If necessary, click the Anti-alias check box so it displays a check mark.

- Click the Contiguous check box so it does not display a check mark (Figure 3–37).

Q&A

Why do I need to remove the Contiguous check mark?

You want to erase all occurrences of the wallpaper color, even those that are not connected continuously, such as those in between the slats of the coffee table.

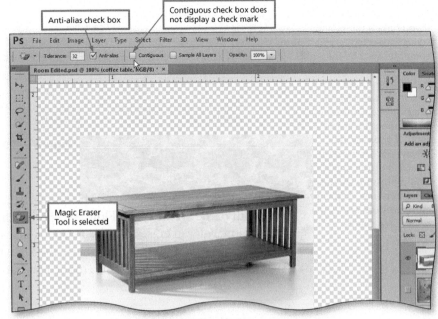

Figure 3–37

3

- Click the wallpaper to delete all of the blue color.

- If some blue remains in your layer, click it (Figure 3–38).

Q&A

How should I position the Magic Eraser Tool mouse pointer?

Position the lower-left tip of the eraser over the pixel color to erase.

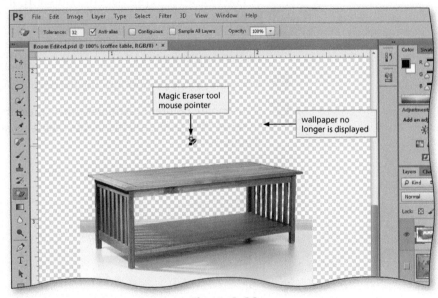

Figure 3–38

Other Ways

1. Press SHIFT+E until Magic Eraser Tool is selected, click photo

Using the Eraser Tool

The Eraser Tool changes pixels in the image as you drag through them. On most layers, the Eraser Tool simply erases the pixels or changes them to transparent, revealing the layer beneath. On a locked layer, such as the Background layer, the Eraser Tool changes the pixels to the current background color.

The Eraser Tool options bar (Figure 3–39 on the next page) displays a Mode box in which you can choose one of three shapes for erasure: brush, block, and pen. The brush shape gives you the most flexibility in size, and many different brush tips are available. The default brush tip is a circle. Block mode is a hard-edged, fixed-sized square with no options for changing the opacity or flow; however, it does give you quick access to a square to erase straight lines and corners. The pencil mode is similar to the brush mode, except that the pencil does not spread as much into adjacent pixels.

Pressure Buttons
If you have a tablet and stylus connected to your computer system, the pressure you apply to the stylus can indicate the opacity or size of your brush stroke. For example, when using the eraser tools, if you click the Always use Pressure for Opacity button, applying a light pressure creates a lighter erasure. Applying more pressure erases the color more deeply.

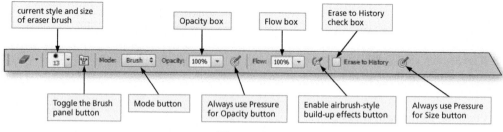

current style and size of eraser brush

Opacity box

Flow box

Erase to History check box

Toggle the Brush panel button

Mode button

Always use Pressure for Opacity button

Enable airbrush-style build-up effects button

Always use Pressure for Size button

Figure 3–39

As with the Magic Eraser Tool options bar, an Opacity box allows you to specify the depth of the erasure. The Flow box specifies how quickly the erasure is performed. In addition, you can erase to a saved state or snapshot in the History panel.

As you erase with the brush shape, the RIGHT BRACKET (]) and LEFT BRACKET ([) keys increase and decrease the size of the eraser, respectively.

To Select the Eraser Tool and Resize the Mouse Pointer

The following steps select the Eraser Tool in preparation for erasing more of the layer.

1 Right-click the Magic Eraser Tool button on the Tools panel, and then click Eraser Tool on the context menu.

2 Move the mouse pointer into the document window.

3 If the mouse pointer is extremely small, press the RIGHT BRACKET (]) key several times to resize the eraser until the mouse pointer changes from a dot to a small circle (Figure 3–40).

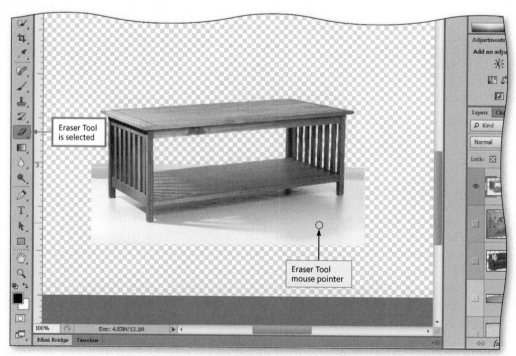

Eraser Tool is selected

Eraser Tool mouse pointer

Figure 3–40

To Erase using the Eraser Tool

The following steps erase the floor using the Eraser Tool.

- Drag the mouse across a portion of the floor to erase it. Do not drag across the coffee table (Figure 3–41).

Q&A How should I position the Eraser Tool mouse pointer?

By default, the Eraser Tool mouse pointer appears as a circle. When you click or drag, Photoshop erases everything within the circle. You can change the size of the mouse pointer using the bracket keys.

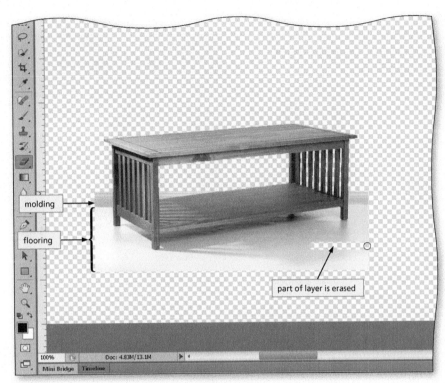

molding

flooring

part of layer is erased

Figure 3–41

- Continue dragging to erase more of the floor and the molding, using the LEFT BRACKET ([) and RIGHT BRACKET (]) keys to change the size of your eraser. Do not erase completely along the very edge of the coffee table (Figure 3–42).

Experiment

- Drag a short erasure over the coffee table that creates an error. Then press CTRL+Z to undo the erasure.

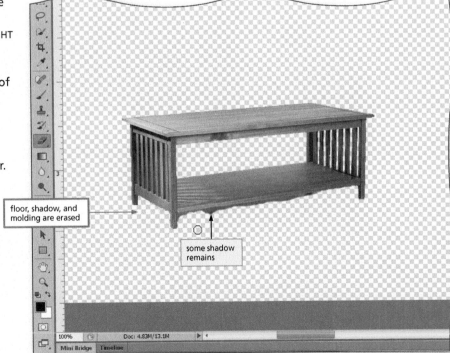

floor, shadow, and molding are erased

some shadow remains

Figure 3–42

To Erase using the Block Mouse Pointer

The following steps delete flooring and shadows that are very close to the coffee table using a block mouse pointer.

- Click the Mode button on the options bar to display its list (Figure 3–43).

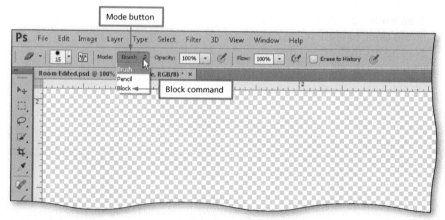

Figure 3–43

2

- Click Block to choose a block mouse pointer.

- Drag close to the coffee table to erase the rest of the flooring and shadows (Figure 3–44).

Q&A

I cannot get close enough to the edge to erase. What should I do?

You can zoom in to erase more closely, or use the Magic Eraser Tool, contiguously, with a high tolerance level. When you get close, you can press and hold the SHIFT key while dragging to create a straight line of erasure.

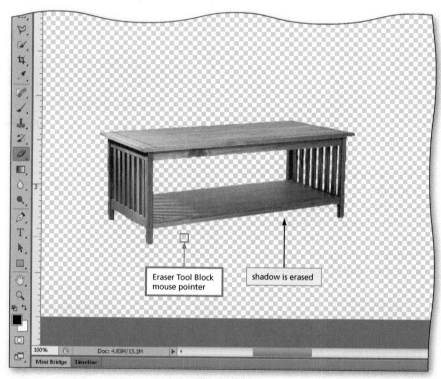

Figure 3–44

Other Ways

1. Press SHIFT+E until Eraser Tool is selected, click document

To View All Layers

The following steps show all of the layers.

1 ALT+click the visibility icon on the visible layer, in this case the coffee table, to show all of the layers.

2 If you see pixels that need to be erased, click them, zooming and scrolling as necessary.

To Transform by Changing the Perspective

The following steps transform the coffee table layer to make it fit the perspective of the room.

1

- With the coffee table layer still selected, press CTRL+T to turn on the bounding box.

- Right-click within the bounding box to display the context menu and then select Perspective.

- Drag the left-center sizing handle down to change the perspective so that the horizontal lines of the coffee table parallel the lines of the sofa (Figure 3–45).

2

- Press the ENTER key to confirm the transformation.

- If necessary, use the Move Tool to drag the coffee table to a location centered in front of the sofa.

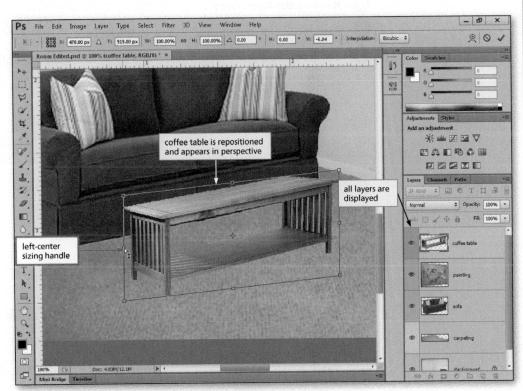

Figure 3–45

Other Ways

1. On Edit menu, point to Transform, click Perspective, drag bounding box sizing handle

To Create the Ivy Layer

To create the ivy layer, you will open the file and then move the entire image into the Room Edited document window.

1 Open the Ivy file from the Chapter 03 folder of the Data Files for Students, or from a location specified by your instructor.

2 On the Application bar, click Window, point to Arrange, and then click Tile All Vertically to display the windows beside each other.

3 With the Ivy window still active, click the Move Tool button on the Tools panel, if necessary.

4 Drag the entire ivy image and drop it in the Room Edited window.

5 Close the Ivy document window. If Photoshop displays a dialog box asking if you want to save the changes, click the No button.

BTW

TIFF File Type
The Ivy file is stored as a TIF file. The TIF, or TIFF, is a flexible raster image format. A raster image is a digital image represented by a matrix of pixels. TIFF stands for Tagged Image File Format and is a common file format for images acquired from scanners and screen capture programs. Because TIF files are supported by virtually all paint, image-editing, and page-layout applications, it also is a versatile format for cross-platform applications.

To Rename and Color the Ivy Layer

The following steps rename the new layer and assign an identification color.

1 Rename the layer `ivy`.

2 Assign a Green identification color to the layer.

3 Zoom to 50 percent magnification and scroll to display the entire layer (Figure 3–46).

Figure 3–46

The Background Eraser Tool
The Background Eraser Tool samples the hot spot and then, as you drag, it deletes that color wherever it appears inside the brush. The Background Eraser Tool overrides the lock transparency setting of a layer.

Using the Background Eraser Tool

The Background Eraser Tool erases the background while maintaining the edges of an object in the foreground, based on a set color that you choose for the background. The Background Eraser Tool samples the color in the center of the mouse pointer, called the **hot spot**. As you drag, the tool erases that color, leaving the rest of the layer intact. You release the mouse button and drag again to sample a different color. On the Background Eraser Tool options bar (Figure 3–47), you can use the tolerance setting to control the range of colors that will be erased, sample the color selections, and adjust the sharpness of the boundaries by setting limits. The three sampling buttons on the Background Eraser Tool options bar sample in different ways. When you use the Sampling: Continuous button, it samples colors and erases continuously as you drag, the Sampling: Once button erases only the areas containing the color you first click, and the Sampling: Background Swatch button erases only areas containing the current color on the Tools panel, Color panel, or Swatches panel.

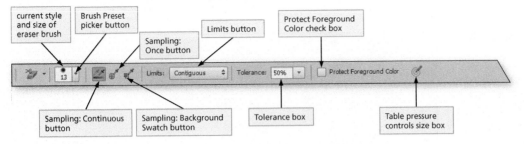

Figure 3–47

To Erase using the Background Eraser Tool

The following steps use the Background Eraser Tool to remove the paneling from behind the ivy plant. If you make a mistake while erasing, click the previous state on the History panel or press CTRL+Z and begin erasing again.

1

- With the ivy layer still selected, right-click the Eraser Tool button on the Tools panel and then click Background Eraser Tool on the context menu to select the tool.

- On the options bar, click the Sampling: Once button to erase only the areas containing the color you first click.

- Click the Limits button to display its list (Figure 3–48).

Figure 3–48

2

- Click Discontiguous to choose the setting.

- Enter 25 in the Tolerance box, and then press the ENTER key to lower the Tolerance setting, which will erase a more narrow range of color.

- Move the mouse pointer to the document window, and then press the RIGHT BRACKET (]) key several times to increase the size of the eraser, if necessary (Figure 3–49)

What does discontiguous mean?

Discontiguous refers to noncontiguous pixels, or pixels of the same color that are not physically located together. In the ivy layer, parts of the brown panel appear behind the ivy and are not adjacent to the other brown paneling.

Figure 3–49

3

- Position the center of the mouse pointer directly over a portion of the paneling.

- Click and hold the mouse button. Drag across the layer, including the ivy, to erase some of the paneling (Figure 3–50).

What is the purpose of the Protect Foreground Color check box?

When checked, the Protect Foreground Color check box gives you even more control of the background erasing. When colors are very similar, you can ALT+click the color you want to keep, then drag the color you want to erase.

Figure 3–50

4

- Position the mouse pointer directly over a portion of the paneling.

- Click and hold the mouse button. Drag to erase the rest of the paneling.

- If some color remains, zoom as necessary to position your mouse directly over any remaining shadow or color of the paneling. Click and drag to erase the rest of the color (Figure 3–51).

all paneling is erased

Figure 3–51

To Finish the Ivy Layer

The following steps erase the rest of the background and resize the ivy layer.

1 With the ivy layer still selected on the Layers panel, use a combination of eraser tools and techniques in the document window to erase the white portion of the layer and the chair rail molding.

2 Press CTRL+T to display the Transform bounding box, and then SHIFT+drag a corner sizing handle to scale the size of the selection down to approximately 35 percent. Press the ENTER key to commit the transformation.

3 Move the layer to a location on the left side of the fireplace mantel (Figure 3–52).

background is removed and layer is scaled and repositioned

Figure 3–52

To Add a Pole Lamp to the Room

The following steps add a pole lamp layer to the room.

1 Open the file named Pole Lamp from the Chapter 03 folder of the Data Files for Students or from a location specified by your instructor.

2 Use the techniques you have learned to create a new layer and place the pole lamp in the Room Edited document window.

3 Name the new layer `pole lamp` and color the layer orange.

4 Close the Pole Lamp document window.

To Rearrange Layers

The following steps rearrange the layers on the Layers panel, moving the pole lamp layer below the sofa layer, so the pole lamp appears behind the end of the sofa.

- Select the pole lamp layer on the Layers panel, if necessary.

- Press CTRL+LEFT BRACKET ([) several times to move the layer down and place it below the sofa layer on the Layers panel.

- In the document window, move the pole lamp to the right end of the sofa, in the corner of the room (Figure 3–53).

🔍 **Experiment**

- Drag individual layers on the Layers panel to new locations in the stack, and watch how that changes the document window. When you are finished, rearrange the layers to appear as shown in Figure 3–53.

Figure 3–53

- Reposition the pole lamp layer as necessary.

Other Ways	
1. To move a layer up, press CTRL+RIGHT BRACKET (])	2. Drag layer on Layers panel, drop between other layers

To Add Mantel Decorations to the Room

The following steps add a mantel decoration layer to the room.

1 On the Layers panel, click the top layer to select it, so the new layer will appear on top.

2 Open the file named Mantel Decorations from the Chapter 03 folder of the Data Files for Students, or from a location specified by your instructor.

3 Use the techniques you have learned to create a new layer and edit it as necessary; you may want to scale to 50% and adjust the perspective.

4 Place the mantel decorations on the mantel in the Room Edited document window.

5 Name the new layer `mantel decorations` and color the layer violet.

6 Close the Mantel Decorations document window, and zoom to 33.33% magnification (Figure 3–54).

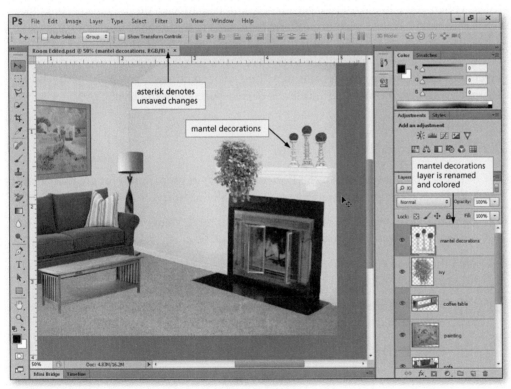

BTW

Saving Files
Photoshop displays an asterisk (*) on the document window tab to denote changes have been made to the file (Figure 3–54). Once you save the file, the asterisk no longer is displayed.

Figure 3–54

To Save the File

Many layers have been added to the composite image. The following step saves the file.

1 Save the Room Edited file with the same name.

Break Point: If you wish to stop working through the chapter at this point, you can quit Photoshop now and then resume the project at a later time by starting Photoshop, opening the file named Room Edited and continuing to follow the steps from this location forward.

Layer Masks

BTW

Default Colors and Layer Masks
When you apply a mask to a layer, or select a previously created mask on the Layers panel, Photoshop automatically inverts the default colors. White is used to reveal portions of the mask. Black is used to hide portions of the mask. Double-check the colors in the lower portion of the Tools panel when working with masks.

Another way to edit layers is by creating a mask. A **mask** is an overlay that hides portions of a layer; it also can protect areas of the layer from inadvertent editing. For example, in a graphic of an exotic animal, you might want to mask all of the area except the animal, rather than permanently delete the background. Or, if you wanted to layer a musical score over the top of a piano graphic, you might mask the edges of the paper so the notes look like they blend into the piano. A mask does not alter the layer as the Eraser Tool does; it merely overlays a template to conceal a portion of the layer. That way, if you change your mind and need to display more of the layer, you can. Nothing has been erased permanently. With the Eraser Tool, you would have to delete the layer, open a backup copy, recreate the layer, and then begin to edit again. With masks, you simply edit the mask.

Photoshop provides two types of masks. **Layer masks** or **pixel masks** are resolution-dependent bitmap images, created with the painting or selection tools. **Vector masks** are resolution independent, created with a pen or shape tool. In this chapter, you will create a layer mask.

When you add a mask, a layer mask thumbnail appears on the Layers panel in **grayscale**, which means each pixel in the mask uses a single shade of gray on a scale from black to white. When selecting the layer mask thumbnail, the default colors change to white over black and the eraser tools are inactive. To mask, you paint on the layer with black. If you change your mind and want to unmask, you paint with white. Painting with gray displays various levels of transparency in the layer.

Manipulating Masks
Once you have created a mask, you might want to perform other manipulations on the mask. For example, if you want to unlink a mask to move it independently of its layer, click the link icon on the Layers panel. To unlink a mask temporarily, SHIFT+click the link icon. If you want to mask the entire layer completely, you can ALT+click the 'Add layer mask' button. In that case, you would paint with white in the mask to reveal portions of the mask. To make the mask permanent and reduce overall file size, apply the mask using a command on the mask's context menu.

To Open the Potted Plant File

The following steps open the Potted Plant file in preparation for creating a layer mask, and uses a copy and paste process to place the plant in the room.

1. Open the file named Potted Plant from the Chapter 03 folder of the Data Files for Students or from a location specified by your instructor.

2. With the Potted Plant window active, press CTRL+A to select all, and then press CTRL+C to copy the entire image.

3. Click the Room Edited document window tab to make the window active. Press CTRL+V to paste the copied image from the Windows clipboard.

4. Name the new layer `potted plant` and color the layer green.

5. Close the Potted Plant document window.

To Create a Layer Mask

The following steps mask the plant in the potted plant layer to reveal only the pot. That way, potential decorators can see what the room would look like with and without the plant. As you create the layer mask, you will use the Brush Tool to brush over the parts of the image to mask.

Moving Masks
To move the mask, first click the link icon on the Layers panel to unlink the mask from the layer. Select the Move Tool. Then, in the document window, drag the layer to reposition it. When the mask is positioned correctly, click between the layer and layer mask on the Layers panel to relink them.

1

- With the potted plant layer selected, zoom to 100 percent.

- Click the 'Add layer mask' button on the Layers panel status bar to create a layer mask (Figure 3–55).

Q&A

What is the new notation on the Layers panel?

Photoshop adds a layer mask thumbnail to the selected layer on the panel. The link icon **links**, or connects, the mask to the layer. A link icon appears between the layer thumbnail and the mask thumbnail. Also, notice that the default color swatches on the Tools panel are reversed.

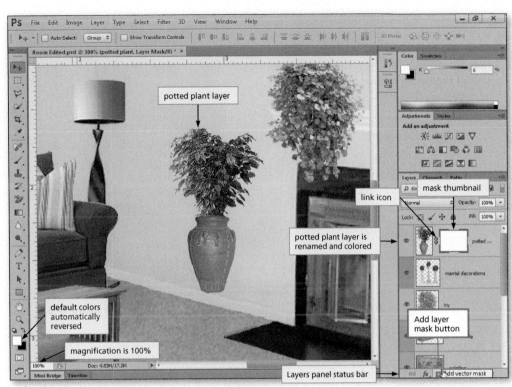

Figure 3–55

2

- Press the X key to choose black over white, which creates a mask.

- Press the B key to activate the brush and then move the mouse pointer into the document window.

- Press the RIGHT BRACKET (]) key to increase the size of the brush's circle, as necessary.

- Drag the mouse across the plant itself. Do not drag the pot (Figure 3–56).

Q&A

Did I erase the plant?

No, you still can see the plant in the layer thumbnail on the Layers panel. You only masked the plant out of view.

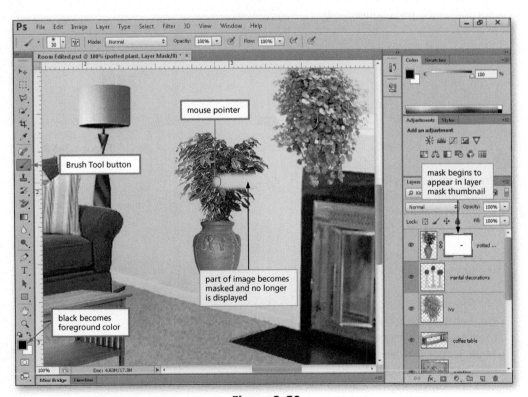

Figure 3–56

3

- Continue dragging through the layer to remove everything except the pot. Zoom the magnification and adjust the size of the brush mouse pointer, as necessary (Figure 3–57).

Q&A

Why does the layer mask use a brush tip mouse pointer?

Layer masks use painting techniques to mask out portions of the image.

Figure 3–57

To Correct a Masking Error

The following steps create a masking error and then unmask the area by painting with white.

1

- Drag across the pot to mask a portion of the pot (Figure 3–58).

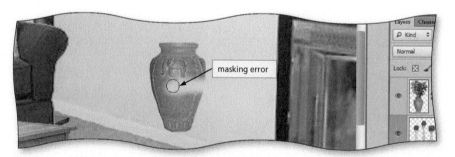

Figure 3–58

2

- Press the x key to switch the foreground and background colors so you are painting with white, which restores the image.

- Drag across the same portion of the pot to unmask it (Figure 3–59).

Experiment

- On the Layers panel, right-click the mask and then click Disable Layer Mask. Notice the entire potted plan appears and the mask has an X through it. Right-click the mask again and then click Enable Layer Mask.

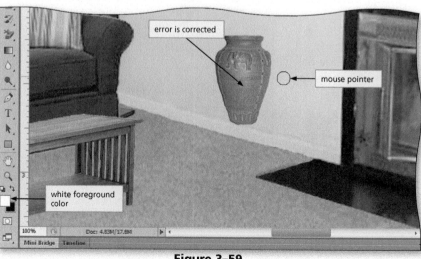

Figure 3–59

To Move the Potted Plant

The following step moves the potted plant to the right side of the fireplace.

1 Select the Move Tool and drag the potted plant to the floor on the right side of the fireplace. Scroll as necessary.

Fine-Tuning Layers

Sometimes layers need special adjustments to better fit into their new surroundings in the document window. This fine-tuning usually involves **tonal adjustments** that affect the color, lighting, opacity, level, or fill; **style adjustments** such as special effects or blends; or **filter adjustments** that let you apply pictures, tiles, or patterns. With the correct adjustment, a layer can be made to look like it was an original part of the image, maintaining a consistency of appearance for the overall composite image.

Create layer adjustments. Layer adjustments allow you to fine-tune your layers. Evaluate layers to see if a change in levels, brightness, saturation, or hue would help them to fit more naturally into the background scene. Use nondestructive edits when possible, so that if you are not satisfied with the adjustment, you can remove it.

Plan Ahead

When you do not want to alter the pixels in an image permanently, you can create an extra layer in which to make changes while preserving the original pixels. An **adjustment layer** is a new layer added to the image to affect a large-scale tonal change. You can create adjustment layers for the entire composite image or just a specific layer.

Adjustment layers have several advantages. They are nondestructive, which means you can experiment with various settings and reedit the adjustment layer at any time. Adjustment layers reduce the amount of damage you do to an image by making direct edits. You can copy adjustments to other layers and images, saving time and maintaining consistency.

If you want to make permanent tonal, style, or filter changes to the pixels themselves, you can edit the layer directly. Features such as opacity, fill, and blending modes can be changed on the Layers panel. These changes can be undone using the History panel, but they become permanent when you save the image.

Making an Opacity Change to a Layer

Some adjustment tools specific to layers are located on the Layers panel. (See Figure 3-60 on the next page.) The Opacity box allows you to change the opacity or transparency of a layer. You can control exactly how solid the objects on a specific layer appear. For example, if you wanted to display an American flag superimposed over a memorial or monument, you might change the flag layer's opacity to 50 percent. The monument easily would be visible through the flag.

The Fill box changes the fill of a layer's opacity as well, but it only changes the pixels in the layer rather than changing any applied layer styles or blending modes. Adjusting the fill percentage sometimes is called changing the **interior opacity**. If you have no layer styles or blending modes, you can use either the Opacity or Fill box.

The Blending mode button displays a list of blending modes for the selected layer or layers. **Blending modes** define how an object interacts with other objects, such as the Background layer.

BTW

Pop-Up Sliders
If there is a triangle next to a text box in the Photoshop interface, you can click it to display a **pop-up slider**. Drag the slider to the desired value. Click outside the slider or press the ENTER key to close the slider box. To cancel the changes, press the ESC key.

BTW

Panel Boxes
The Opacity and Fill boxes can be changed in one of three ways. You can drag the scrubby slider label. When you click the box arrow, a pop-up slider is displayed to adjust the percentage. You also can type a percentage in either box.

To Make an Opacity Change to a Layer

The following step lightens the mantel decorations by lowering the opacity, to make them fit better into the room design.

- Zoom to display the mantel decorations in the document window at 100% magnification.

- On the Layers panel, click to select the mantel decorations layer.

- On the Layers panel, point to the word, Opacity, and then drag the scrubby slider to the left until the Opacity box displays 85% to lower the opacity (Figure 3–60).

Experiment

- Click the Blending mode button and choose a blending mode such as Hard Light or Linear Burn. Experiment with other blending modes. When you are done, click the Blending mode button and then click Normal in the list.

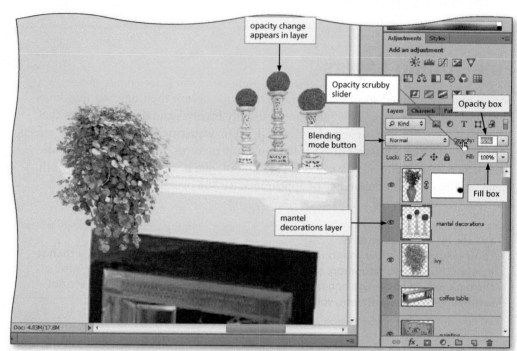

Figure 3–60

Adjustments and Properties

Tools that nondestructively adjust image lighting and shading are located on the Adjustments panel (Figure 3–61).

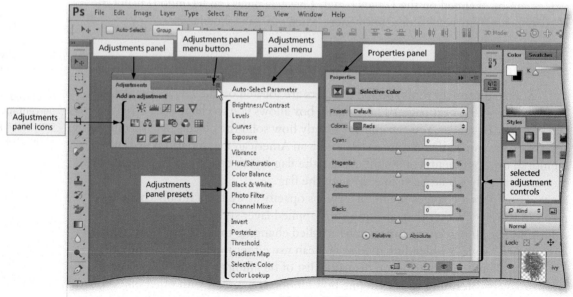

Figure 3–61

Clicking an **adjustment icon,** or preset, also displays the Properties panel and its settings for the specific adjustment, including channel selectors, eyedroppers, sliders, and input boxes, among others. Buttons on the Properties panel status bar allow you to specify visibility, delete the adjustment, or create a **clip** that applies the adjustment to a layer rather than the entire image.

Some adjustments also can display their settings using a dialog box, if accessed from outside the Adjustments panel with a shortcut key or a menu command. Table 3–3 displays a list of the Adjustments available on the Adjustments panel. Many of the adjustments also are available through the Adjustments panel menu (Figure 3–61), through the Layers menu on the application bar, or through a button on the Layers panel.

Table 3–3 Adjustments Panel Icons

Adjustment	Description	Shortcut (if available)	Icon
Brightness/Contrast	Changes general brightness (shadows and highlights) and overall contrast (tonal range)		
Levels	Adjusts color balance for shadows, midtones, highlights, and color channels	CTRL+L	
Curves	Adjusts individual points in the tonal range of black to white	CTRL+M	
Exposure	Changes exposure, which adjusts the highlights; changes offset, which darkens the shadows and midtones; changes gamma, which adjusts the midtones		
Vibrance	Adjusts vibrance and color saturation settings so shifting to primary colors, or clipping, is minimized		
Hue/Saturation	Changes hue, saturation, and lightness of entire image or specific colors	CTRL+U	
Color Balance	Adjusts the overall midtone of colors in an image	CTRL+B	
Black & White	Converts a color image to grayscale	ALT+SHIFT+CTRL+B	
Photo Filter	Simulates effects of using a filter in front of a camera lens		
Channel Mixer	Modifies and adjusts individual color channels		
Color Lookup	Remaps every color using a lookup table or predetermined style		
Invert	Converts every color to its inverse or opposite	CTRL+I	
Posterize	Specifies the number of tonal levels in each channel		
Threshold	Converts images to high-contrast black and white		
Selective Color	Changes the mixture of colors in each of the primary color components		
Gradient Map	Maps colors to a specified gradient fill		

Level Sliders
In the Levels dialog box, the Input Level sliders on each end map the black point (on the left) and white point (on the right) to the settings of the Output sliders. The middle Input slider adjusts the gamma or midtone in the image, changing the intensity values of the middle range of gray tones without dramatically altering the highlights and shadows. As you move any of the Input Level sliders, the black point, midtone, and white point change in the Output sliders; all the remaining levels are redistributed.

Level Adjustments

A **level adjustment** is one way to make tonal changes to shadows, midtones, and highlights. A **shadow** is a darkened shade in an image. A **midtone**, also called **gamma**, is the midpoint gray between shadows and highlights. A **highlight** is a portion of an image that is strongly illuminated and may appear as the lightest or whitest part of the image. To change levels, Photoshop uses black, gray, and white sliders to adjust any or all of the three tonal input levels. A **histogram**, or frequency distribution bar chart, indicates the amount of color in the tonal ranges. When adjusting levels using the histogram, a general guideline is to drag the black-and-white sliders to the first indication, or outlier, of strong tonal change in the histogram. Then, experiment with the gray slider to change the intensity value of the middle range of gray tones without dramatically altering the highlights and shadows. Becoming proficient at adjusting levels takes practice. Furthermore, adjustments are subjective; the impact of some effects is a matter of opinion.

To Make a Levels Adjustment

In the sofa layer of the image, you will adjust the levels to make the layer better fit into the picture. The following steps make level adjustments to the sofa.

1

• Select the sofa layer on the Layers panel and scroll the document window to display the sofa.

• Click the Levels icon on the Adjustments panel to display the level settings and options on the Properties panel.

• Click the Clip to Layer button on the Properties panel status bar to adjust only the sofa layer (Figure 3–62).

Experiment

• Drag the three Levels Input sliders below the histogram to see how they affect the appearance of the sofa layer.

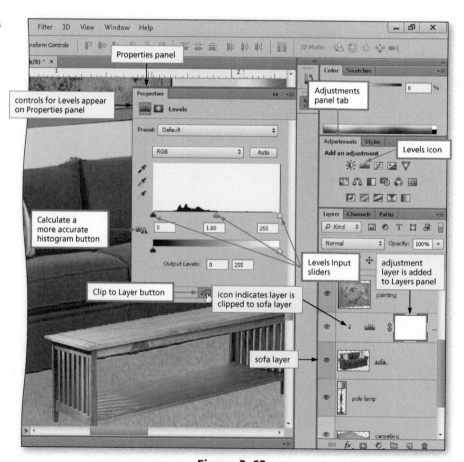

Figure 3–62

2

- Click the 'Calculate a more accurate histogram' button to make the level change more visible.

- Below the histogram display, drag the white Levels Input slider to approximately 223, aligning it with the first visible increase on the right side of the histogram to adjust the highlights.

- Drag the black Levels Input slider to approximately 30, aligning it with the first visible increase on the left side of the histogram to adjust the shadows.

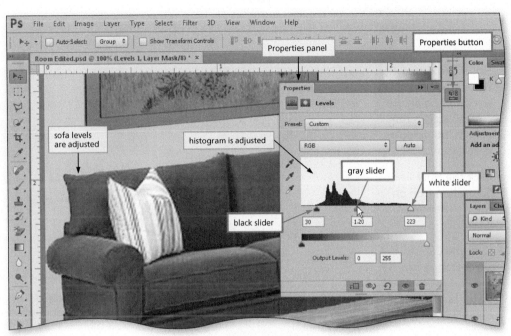

Figure 3–63

- Drag the gray Levels Input slider to 1.20 to adjust the midtone colors (Figure 3–63).

Q&A My visible changes were at different levels. Did I do something wrong?

No, your histogram might differ, depending on your previous erasures.

3

- Click the Properties button on the vertical dock to collapse the Properties panel and complete the adjustment.

Q&A Did the Layers panel change?

Yes, you will see an extra layer created just above the sofa layer, with a clipping symbol to imply the relationship (Figure 3-64 on the next page).

 Experiment

- Click the visibility icon of the new levels layer to notice the change in the sofa. Click it again to redisplay the level adjustment.

Other Ways

1. Press CTRL+L, adjust levels, click OK button

2. On Image menu, point to Adjustments, click Levels, adjust levels, click OK button

Hue and Saturation

Another way to adjust a layer or image is to change the hue or saturation. **Hue** is the shade of a color in an image. **Saturation** is the intensity of a hue and is highly dependent upon the chosen color model, but in general, pastels have low saturation, and bright colors have high saturation. You will learn more about color models and the color wheel in later chapters and by reading Appendix B, the Graphic Design Overview appendix.

BTW

Other Level Adjustments
The three eyedroppers in the Levels area allow you to select the values for shadow, midtone, and highlight from the image itself. To do so, click the eyedropper and then click the location in the image that you want use. Once selected, that color becomes the slider value.

To Adjust the Hue and Saturation

The following steps adjust the hue and saturation of the coffee table layer.

1

- Select the coffee table layer and scroll to display the coffee table in the document window, if necessary.

- Click the Hue/ Saturation icon on the Adjustments panel.

- Click the Clip to Layer button on the Properties panel status bar to adjust only the selected layer.

- Drag the Hue slider to +5. Drag the Saturation slider to –5. Drag the Lightness slider to –10 (Figure 3–64).

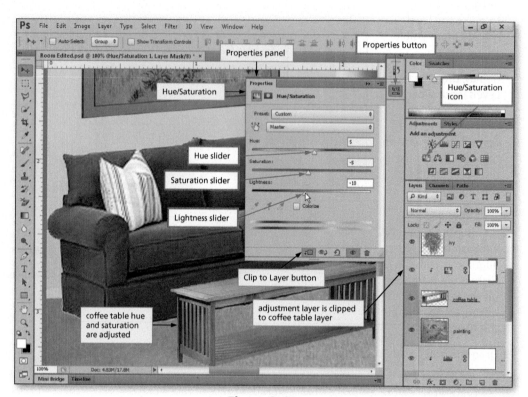

Figure 3–64

Experiment

- Drag the sliders to view the effect of hue and saturation settings to the layer. When you are done experimenting, drag the sliders to the settings listed in the step.

2

- Click the Properties button on the vertical dock to collapse the Properties panel and complete the adjustment.

Other Ways
1. Select layer, press CTRL+U, drag sliders, click OK button.   2. On Layer menu, point to New Adjustment Layer, click Hue/Saturation, edit settings

To Fit the Image on Screen

In previous chapters, you changed the magnification by using a box on the status bar and by using the Navigator panel. The View menu also offers several settings to change the magnification. The following steps use a command to change the magnification, to display the picture as large as possible while still fitting on the screen, in preparation for adjusting the Background layer.

• Click View on the Application
bar to display the View menu
(Figure 3–65).

Q&A

What does the Actual Pixels
command do?

The Actual Pixels command
displays the document window so
that one image pixel equals exactly
one monitor pixel, allowing you to
see the maximum amount of detail
available in your image.

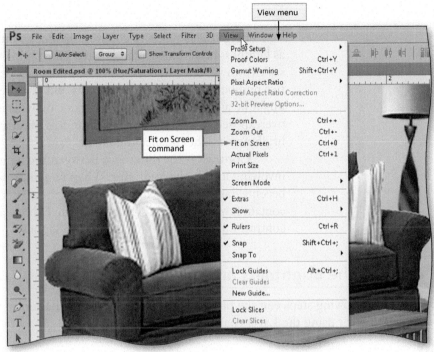

Figure 3–65

2

• Click Fit on Screen to display
the entire photo at the largest
magnification (Figure 3–66).

Figure 3–66

Other Ways
1. Press CTRL+0 (zero)

Brightness and Contrast

Brightness refers to color luminance or intensity of a light source, perceived as lightness or darkness in an image. Photoshop measures brightness on a sliding scale from –150 to +150. Negative numbers move the brightness toward black. Positive numbers compress the highlights and expand the shadows. For example, the layer might be an image photographed on a cloudy day; conversely, the image might appear overexposed by having been too close to a photographer's flash. Either way, editing the brightness might enhance the image.

Contrast is the difference between the lightest and darkest tones in an image, involving mainly the midtones. When you increase contrast, the middle-to-dark areas become darker, and the middle-to-light areas become lighter. High-contrast images contain few color variations between the lightest and darkest parts of the image; low-contrast images contain more tonal gradations.

To Adjust the Brightness and Contrast

The following steps edit the brightness and contrast of the Background layer, this time creating the adjustment layer using the Layers panel.

1

- Scroll in the Layers panel as necessary to select the Background layer.

- On the Layers panel status bar, click the 'Create new fill or adjustment layer' button to display the list of adjustments (Figure 3–67).

Q&A

What is the difference between clicking the Brightness/Contrast button on the Adjustments panel and clicking the 'Create new fill or adjustment layer' button?

There is no difference when adjusting the brightness or contrast. The list of adjustments accessed from the Layers panel includes a few more settings than the Adjustments panel.

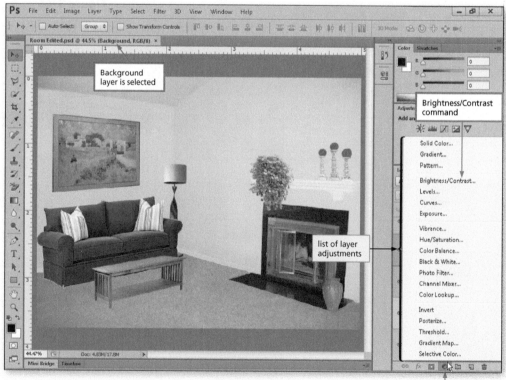

Figure 3–67

2

- Click Brightness/ Contrast in the list to display the settings on the Properties panel.

- Click the Clip to Layer button on the Properties panel status bar to adjust only the Background layer.

- Drag the Brightness slider to 10 and the Contrast slider to −10 to brighten the room (Figure 3–68).

 Experiment

Drag the sliders to various locations and note how the document window changes. When you are finished, drag the Brightness slider to +10 and the Contrast slider to −10.

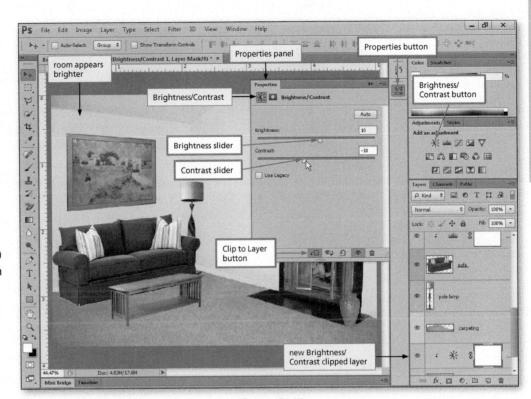

Figure 3–68

2

- Collapse the Properties panel.

Other Ways
1. On Adjustments panel, click Brightness/ Contrast icon, adjust settings
2. On Layer menu, point to New Adjustment Layer, click Brightness/Contrast, click OK, adjust settings

Layer Styles

Similar to a layer adjustment, a **layer style** is applied to a layer rather than changing the layer's actual pixels. Layer styles, or layer effects, alter the appearance of the layer by adding depth, shadow, shading, texture, or overlay. A layer can display multiple styles or effects.

Plan Ahead

Edit layer styles.

Layer styles add dimension, texture, and definition to your layers. Styles such as shadow, glow, emboss, bevel, overlay, and stroke commonly distinguish the layer rather than making it fit in. Choose the settings carefully and think about direction, angle, distance, and spread. Make sure the layer style does not overwhelm the overall image or detract from previous layer adjustments.

BTW

Copying and Moving Layer Styles
To copy a layer style, right-click the source layer and then click Copy Layer Style on the context menu. Right-click the destination layer and then click Paste Layer Style. To move a layer style, drag the fx icon from one layer to another on the Layers panel.

Styles vs. Adjustments
Layer styles are special effects such as shadows, glows, and overlays. Styles appear attached to a layer on the Layers panel. An adjustment applies color, level, and tonal changes on its on layer.

Bevels
A bevel adds depth to an image by creating an angle between an edge and a shadow that softens the look. A bevel increases the 3D look of an image.

Table 3–4 lists the layer styles.

Table 3–4 Layer Styles

Style	Description
Drop Shadow	Creates a shadow behind the layer
Inner Shadow	Creates a shadow inside the edges of the layer
Inner Glow	Adds a glow around the inside edge of the layer
Outer Glow	Adds a glow around the outside edge of the layer
Bevel and Emboss	Adds highlights and shading to a layer
Satin	Applies interior shading to create a satin finish
Color Overlay	Adds a color over the layer
Gradient Overlay	Inserts a gradient in front of the layer
Pattern Overlay	Fills the layer with a pattern
Stroke	Outlines the layer with a color, gradient, or pattern

Each of the layer styles has its own set of options and properties. Table 3–5 describes some of the layer style options. The options apply to many of the styles.

Table 3–5 Layer Style Options

Option	Description
Angle	Sets a degree value for the lighting angle at which the effect is applied
Anti-alias	Blends the edge pixels of a contour or gloss contour
Blend Mode	Determines how a layer style blends with its underlying layers
Color	Assigns the color of a shadow, glow, or highlight
Contour	Allows you to create rings of transparency such as gradients, fades, beveling and embossing, and sculpting
Depth	Sets the depth of a bevel or pattern
Distance	Specifies the offset distance for a shadow or satin effect
Fill Type	Sets the content of a stroke
Global Light	Allows you to set an angle to simulate the direction of the light
Gloss Contour	Creates a glossy, metallic appearance on a bevel or emboss effect
Gradient	Indicates the gradient of a layer effect
Highlight or Shadow Mode	Specifies the blending mode of a bevel or emboss highlight or shadow
Jitter	Varies the color and opacity of a gradient
Layer Knocks Out Drop Shadow	Controls the drop shadow's visibility in a semitransparent layer
Noise	Assigns the number of random elements in the opacity of a glow or shadow
Opacity	Sets the opacity or transparency
Pattern	Specifies the pattern
Position	Sets the position of a stroke
Range	Controls which portion or range of the glow is targeted for the contour
Size	Specifies the amount of blur or the size of the shadow
Soften	Blurs the results of shading to reduce unwanted artifacts
Source	Specifies the source for an inner glow
Style	Specifies the style of a bevel or emboss

Hide Layer Styles
If you want to hide the notation of the Layer styles on the Layers panel, click the 'Reveals layer effects in the panel' button. To redisplay the style, click the button again.

Delete Layer Styles
If you want to delete a layer style, right-click the layer style, and then click Clear Layer Style on the context menu.

When a layer has a style applied to it, an fx icon appears to the right of the layer's name on the Layers panel. You can expand the icon on the Layers panel to view all of the applied effects and edit them when changing the style.

As you can tell from Table 3–4 and Table 3–5, there are a large number of layer styles and settings in Photoshop.

To Apply a Layer Style

The following steps apply a layer style to the ivy. You will create an inner bevel to give the ivy more depth.

1
- On the Layers panel, select the ivy layer.

- Click the 'Add a layer style' button on the Layers panel status bar to display the menu (Figure 3–69).

Q&A

Will I see much change in the document window?

It depends on the magnification — at larger magnifications, you will see more change. The printed image will display more depth in the ivy.

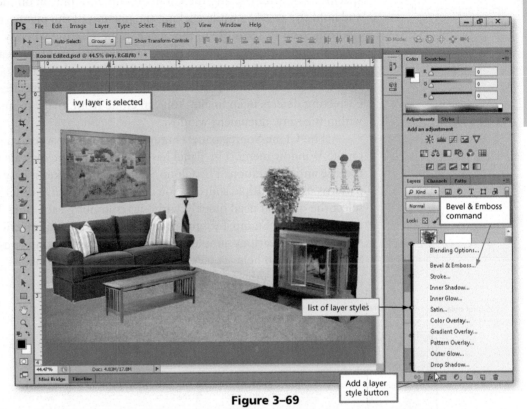

Figure 3–69

2
- Click Bevel & Emboss to display the Layer Style dialog box.

- In the Layer Style dialog box, enter 50 in the Depth box to decrease the strength of the shading.

- Enter 10 in the Size box and 5 in the Soften box to edit the bevel (Figure 3–70).

3
- Click the OK button to close the Layer Style dialog box.

 Experiment

- To view the difference that the adjustment has made, press CTRL+Z to undo the step and then press CTRL+Z again to redo the step.

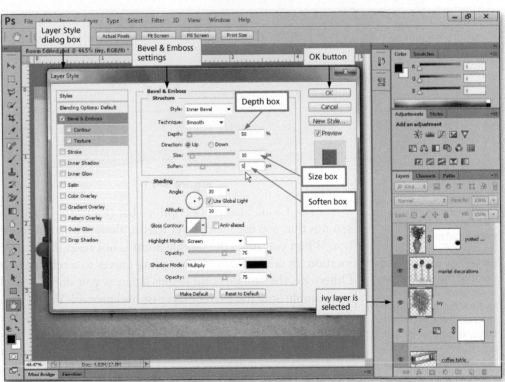

Figure 3–70

Other Ways

1. On Layer menu, point to Layer Style, click desired style, edit | settings in Layer Style dialog box, click OK button

The Clone Stamp Tool

The Clone Stamp Tool reproduces portions of an image, changing the pixels in a specific area. After clicking the Clone Stamp Tool button on the Tools panel, you press and hold the ALT key while clicking the portion of the picture that you want to copy. Photoshop takes a **sample** of the image, remembering where you clicked. You then move the mouse pointer to the position where you want to create the copy. As you drag with the brush, the image is applied. Each stroke of the tool applies more of the sample. The Clone Stamp Tool is useful for duplicating specific parts of an object or correcting defects in an image. You can clone from image to image, or clone locations within the same document window.

The Clone Source panel (Figure 3–71) appears when you click Clone Source on the Window menu. The panel has options to rotate or scale the sample, or specify the size and orientation. The Clone Source panel makes it easy to create variegated patterns using multiple sources. You can create up to five different clone sources to select the one you need quickly, without resampling each time. For example, if you are using the Clone Stamp Tool to repair several minor imperfections in an old photo, you can select your various samples first, and then use the sources as needed. The Clone Source panel also helps you create unique clones positioned at different angles and perspectives from the original.

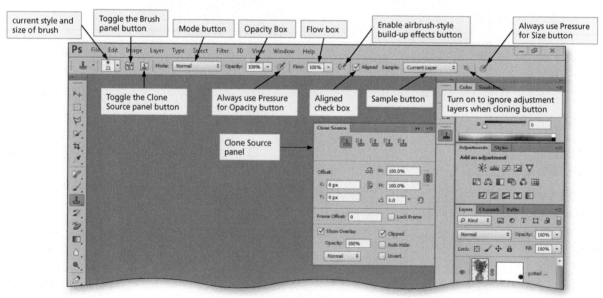

Figure 3–71

The Clone Stamp Tool options bar (Figure 3–71) displays some of the same settings that you used with layer masks, along with an Aligned check box and Sample box. When you align, the sample point is not reset if you start dragging in a new location; in other words, the sampling moves to a relative point in the original image. Otherwise, the sample point begins again as you start a new clone. The default value is to sample only the current layer or background. When you select All Layers in the Sample box, the clone displays all layers. One restriction when using the Clone Stamp Tool from one image to another is that both images have to be in the same color mode, such as RGB or CMYK. The color mode of an image appears on the document window tab. You will learn more about color modes in a later chapter.

Grouped with the Clone Stamp Tool, a second kind of stamp, the Pattern Stamp Tool, allows you to paint with a pattern chosen from Photoshop's pattern library. A **pattern** is a repeated or tiled image, used to fill a layer or selection. On the Pattern Stamp Tool options bar, a Pattern Picker box arrow displays installed patterns. You can import additional patterns into the Pattern Picker box.

To Open the Flooring File and Arrange the Windows

To finish the composite image of the room, you will replace the carpeting with wood flooring. The following steps open the Flooring file.

1 Open the Flooring file from the Chapter 03 folder of the Data Files for Students or from a location specified by your instructor.

2 Tile All Horizontally to arrange the windows above and below one another.

3 Drag the border between the two document windows so more of the Room Edited window is displayed. Scroll in the Room Edited window to display the carpeting.

4 Select the carpeting layer.

To Create a New Blank Layer

The following steps create a new blank layer that clips the carpeting layer, in preparation for cloning.

1

- ALT+click the visibility icon on the carpeting layer to display only the carpeting.

- Press SHIFT+CTRL+N to display the New Layer dialog box.

- Name the layer, flooring.

- Click to display a check mark in the Use Previous Layer to Create Clipping Mask check box.

- Choose a yellow identification color. Do not change the mode or opacity (Figure 3–72).

2

- Click the OK button to close the New Layer dialog box.

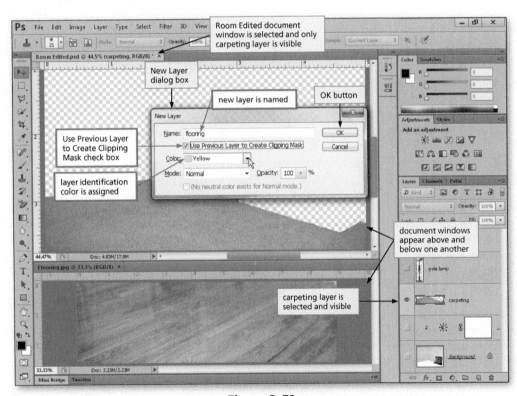

Figure 3–72

To Create a Clone

Using the Clone Stamp Tool, you will sample the Flooring image and then clone it to the carpeted area in the Room Edited image, as shown in the following steps. As you clone the flooring, adjust the magnification of the image to view the corners and small areas clearly. If you make a mistake while cloning, press CTRL+Z to undo the most recent clone stroke or access the History panel and click a previous state, then begin cloning again.

1

- Click the Flooring document window tab to make the window active.

- Click Window on the Application bar, and then click Clone Source to display the Clone Source panel.

- On the Clone Source panel, click the Invert check box to remove its check mark, if necessary.

- On the Tools panel, right-click the Clone Stamp Tool button to display its context menu (Figure 3–73).

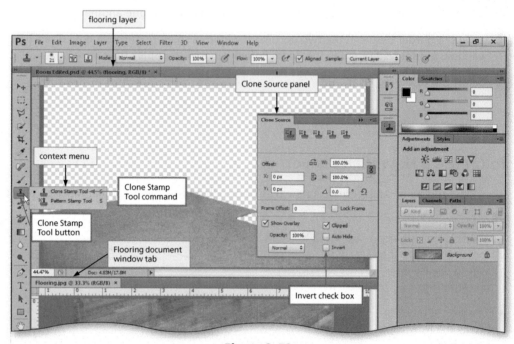

Figure 3–73

2

- Click Clone Stamp Tool to select it.

- On the options bar, click the Aligned check box so it displays a check mark, if necessary.

- Click the Clone Source button on the vertical dock to collapse the panel.

- Move the mouse pointer to the Flooring document window and ALT+click the left-middle edge of the flooring to select the sampling point (Figure 3–74).

How do I know if I indicated the clone source correctly?

As you ALT+click, the Clone Stamp Tool displays a crosshair mouse pointer and the Clone Source panel displays the source of the clone.

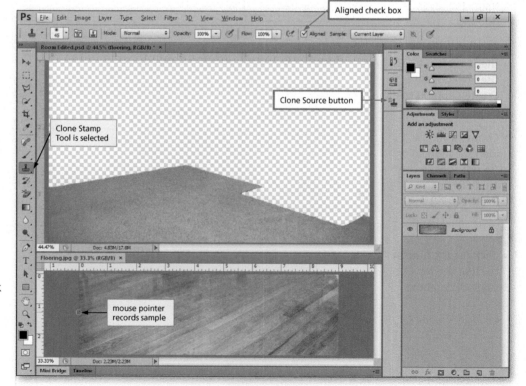

Figure 3–74

3

- Click the Room Edited document window tab to make it active.

- With the flooring layer still selected, and the carpeting layer visible, move the mouse pointer into the document window. Adjust the size of the mouse pointer as necessary.

- Drag from the upper-left corner of the carpeting down to the lower-left corner to create the first stroke of the clone (Figure 3–75).

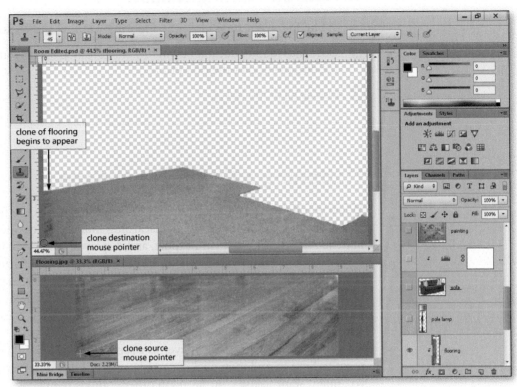

Figure 3–75

4

- Working from left to right, drag to replace the carpeting. Zoom, scroll, and adjust the pointer size as necessary to fill in corners. Use short strokes, so if you make a mistake, you can press CTRL+Z to undo the error. Do not resample (Figure 3–76).

Q&A

What is the purpose of the Aligned check box?

When checked, the Aligned check box allows you to use short strokes as you clone. The clone will not start over if you lift the mouse button to drag in another location. Aligning is good for cloning areas with a pattern.

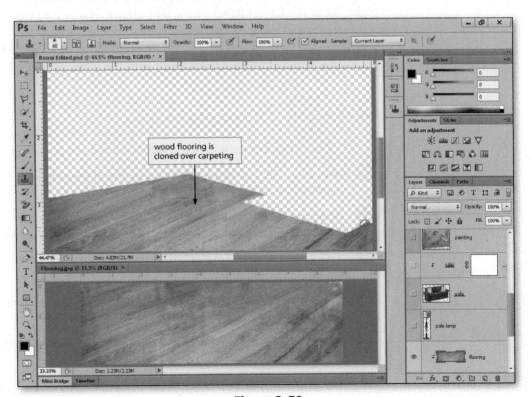

Figure 3–76

Other Ways

1. From another tool, press S key, ALT+click sample, drag clone

2. From Pattern Stamp Tool, press SHIFT+S, ALT+click sample, drag clone

To Close the Flooring Window

The following steps close the Flooring window and redisplay all the layers.

1 Close the Flooring document window. If Photoshop asks if you want to save changes to the document, click the No button.

2 Display all of the layers.

Flattening a Composite Image

When you **flatten** a composite image, Photoshop reduces the file size by merging all visible layers into the background, discarding hidden layers, and applying masks. A flattened file is easier to print, export, and display on the Web. It is a good practice, however, to save the layered version in PSD format before flattening in case you want to make further changes to the file. It is very important to remember that once a file is flattened and saved, no changes can be made to individual layers. If you flatten an image and then change your mind, if the file still is open, you can click the previous state on the History panel to restore all of the layers.

If you want to save each layer as a separate file, click File on the Application bar, point to Scripts, and then click Export Layers to Files. This script is useful if you think you might want to use your layers in other composite images.

The Layer menu displays a Flatten Image command and has many of the same choices as the Layers panel menu. The choice of which to use is a matter of personal preference and the location of your mouse pointer at the time. After saving the composite image, you will use the Layer menu to flatten the visible layers. Finally, you will save the flattened file in TIFF format with the name, Room TIFF.

To Save the Composite Image

The following steps save the Room Edited image with its layers.

1 With your USB flash drive connected to one of the computer's USB ports, click File on the Application bar and then click Save As.

2 When the Save As dialog box is displayed, type `Room Composite` in the File name text box. Do not press the ENTER key after typing the file name.

3 If necessary, click the Format box arrow and then choose Photoshop (*.PSD, *.PDD) in the list.

4 If necessary, click the Save in box arrow and then click Removable Disk (F:), or the location associated with your USB flash drive, in the list.

5 Click the Save button in the Save As dialog box. If Photoshop displays an options dialog box, click the OK button.

To Flatten a Composite Image

The following steps use the Layer menu to flatten the composite image.

1

• Click Layer on the Application bar to display the Layer menu (Figure 3–77).

file is renamed

Layer menu

Flatten Image command

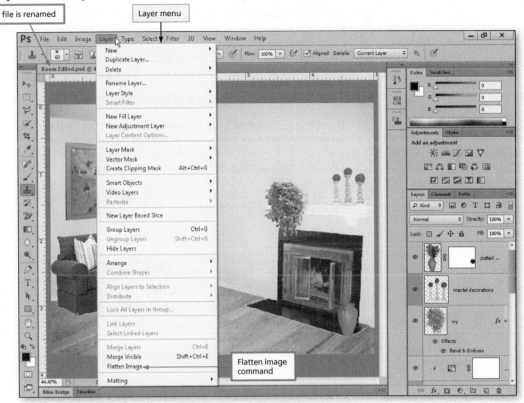

Figure 3–77

2

• Click Flatten Image on the Layer menu to combine all of the layers (Figure 3–78).

Q&A

What is the difference between flatten and merge?

The Merge command flattens specific layers together. The Flatten command uses all of the layers and merges into a Background layer.

image appears without layers

Figure 3–78

Other Ways	
1. Right-click any layer, click Flatten Image	2. Click Layers panel menu button, click Flatten Image

To Save a File in the TIFF Format

The following steps save the flattened image as a TIFF file.

① With your USB flash drive connected to one of the computer's USB ports, click File on the Application bar and then click Save As.

② When the Save As dialog box is displayed, type `Room TIFF` in the File name text box. Do not press the ENTER key after typing the file name.

③ Click the Format box arrow and then click TIFF (*.TIF, *TIFF) in the list.

④ If necessary, click the Save in box arrow and then click Removable Disk (F:), or the location associated with your USB flash drive, in the list.

⑤ Click the Save button in the Save As dialog box.

⑥ When Photoshop displays the TIFF Options dialog box, click the OK button to finish saving the file (Figure 3–79).

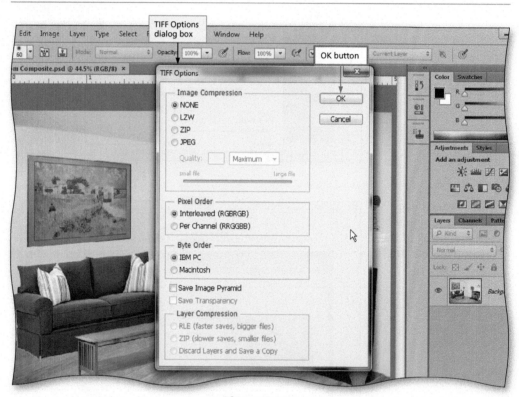

Figure 3–79

To Print the Room TIFF Image

The following steps print a copy of the Room TIFF image on the default printer. If you are unsure which printer is set as your default, use the Print command rather than the Print one Copy command so you can choose your printer.

① Ready the printer according to the printer instructions.

② Click File on the Application bar and then click Print One Copy on the File menu to print the image on the default printer.

To Close the Document Window and Quit Photoshop

The final steps close the document window and quit Photoshop.

1 Click the Close button in the document window.

2 If Photoshop displays a dialog box, click the No button to ignore the changes since the last time you saved the photo.

3 Quit Photoshop.

Chapter Summary

In virtually decorating a room, you gained a broad knowledge of Photoshop's layering capabilities. First, you were introduced to the concept of layers. You created a layer via cut, a layer from another image, and a layer from a selection, using the Layers panel to set options, select, rename, color, view, and hide layers. You then used the eraser tools to erase unneeded portions of a layer. You learned how to hide portions of layers and fine-tuned layers with layer masks, adjustments, and styles. Finally, you used the Clone Stamp Tool to add wood flooring into the composite image. The file was flattened and saved in the TIF format.

The items listed below include all the new Photoshop skills you have learned in this chapter:

1. Change Layers Panel Options (PS 142)
2. Create a Layer via Cut (PS 143)
3. Rename a Layer (PS 145)
4. Assign a Color to a Layer (PS 146)
5. Hide and Show a Layer (PS 147)
6. Arrange Document Windows (PS 150)
7. Create a Layer by Dragging an Entire Image (PS 151)
8. Move a Layer in the Document Window (PS 152)
9. Create a Layer by Dragging a Selection (PS 154)
10. Transform by Skewing (PS 159)
11. Display Only the Current Layer (PS 164)
12. Erase using the Magic Eraser Tool (PS 164)
13. Erase using the Eraser Tool (PS 167)
14. Erase using the Block Mouse Pointer (PS 168)
15. Transform by Changing the Perspective (PS 169)
16. Erase using the Background Eraser Tool (PS 171)
17. Rearrange Layers (PS 174)
18. Create a Layer Mask (PS 176)
19. Correct a Masking Error (PS 178)
20. Make an Opacity Change to a Layer (PS 180)
21. Make a Levels Adjustment (PS 182)
22. Adjust the Hue and Saturation (PS 184)
23. Fit the Image on Screen (PS 184)
24. Adjust the Brightness and Contrast (PS 186)
25. Apply a Layer Style (PS 189)
26. Create a New Blank Layer (PS 191)
27. Create a Clone (PS 192)
28. Flatten a Composite Image (PS 195)

Apply Your Knowledge

Reinforce the skills and apply the concepts you learned in this chapter.

Creating Layers in a Poster

Instructions: Start Photoshop and perform the customization steps found on pages PS 6 through PS 10. Open the file named Apply 3-1 Storage History from the Data Files for Students. Visit www.cengage.com/ct/studentdownload for detailed instructions or contact your instructor for information about accessing the required files.

The purpose of this exercise is to create a composite poster showing the history of external storage devices by creating layers. The edited photo is displayed in Figure 3–80.

Perform the following tasks:

1. Press SHIFT+CTRL+S to open the Save As dialog box. Enter the name, Apply 3-1 Storage History Composite. Do not press the ENTER key. Click the Format box arrow and then select the Photoshop PSD format, if necessary. Click the Save in box arrow and then select your USB flash drive location. Click the Save button to save the file in the PSD format. If Photoshop displays an Options dialog box, click the OK button.

Figure 3–80

Table 3–6 lists the other files, layer names, identification colors, and manipulations that you will use in this assignment.

File Name	Layer Name	Layer Color	Layer Manipulations
Table 3–6 Storage Device Layers			
Apply 3-1 CD	CD	Violet	Layer Style | Outer Glow
Apply 3-1 Flash Drive	flash drive	Green	Layer Style | Inner Glow Mask lid
Apply 3-1 Zip Disk	zip disk	Orange	Layer Style | Bevel and Emboss
Apply 3-1 Tape	tape	Yellow	Adjustments | Hue 10, –10, 0
Apply 3-1 Cassette Tape	cassette tape	Yellow	Adjustments | Brightness/Contrast
Apply 3-1 Small Floppy	small floppy	Blue	erase background and rotate
Apply 3-1 Medium Floppy	medium floppy	Blue	erase background and rotate
Apply 3-1 Large Floppy	large floppy	Blue	erase background and rotate
Apply 3-1 Punched Card	punched card	Red	clone

2. To create the CD layer:

   a. Press CTRL+O to display the Open dialog box. Navigate to the Data Files for Students and then double-click the file named Apply 3-1 CD to open it.

   b. On the Application bar, click Window, point to Arrange to display the Arrange submenu, and then click Tile All Horizontally to arrange the document windows. Press the v key to activate the Move Tool. Drag the image from the Apply 3-1 CD document window into the Apply 3-1 Storage History Composite document window. Close the Apply 3-1 CD file.

c. Name and color the layer as directed in Table 3–6.

d. Click the 'Add a layer style' button on the Layers panel status bar, and then click Outer Glow. Change the Opacity to 75% and the Size to 150 px. Use the default values for all other settings.

e. Resize the CD, if necessary, and position it as shown in Figure 3–80.

3. To create the flash drive layer:

a. Press CTRL+O to display the Open dialog box. Navigate to the Data Files for Students and then open the file named Apply 3-1 Flash Drive.

b. On the Application bar, click Window, point to Arrange and then click Tile All Horizontally to arrange the document windows.

c. Drag the flash drive image into the Apply 3-1 Storage History Composite document window. Close the Apply 3-1 Flash Drive file.

d. Name and color the layer.

e. Click the 'Add a layer style' button on the Layers panel status bar, and then click Inner Glow. Change the Opacity to 75% and the Size to 25 px. Use the default values for all other settings.

f. Resize the flash drive and position it as shown in Figure 3–80.

g. Click the 'Add a layer mask' button. Press the X key to switch the default colors to black over white, if necessary. Press the B key to access the brush and then paint over the lid to mask it.

4. To create the zip disk layer:

a. Open the file, Apply 3-1 Zip Disk.

b. Arrange the document windows side by side.

c. Drag the image from the new window into the Storage History Composite document window. Close the Apply 3-1 Zip Disk file.

d. Name and color the layer.

e. Click the 'Add a layer style' button on the Layers panel status bar, and then click Bevel & Emboss. Click the Style button and then click Inner Bevel, if necessary. Change the Size to 90 px. Use the default values for all other settings.

f. Resize the zip disk, if necessary, and position it as shown in Figure 3–80.

5. To create the tape layer:

a. Open the file, Apply 3-1 Tape. Press CTRL+A to select the entire image. Press CTRL+C to copy the image to the clipboard.

b. Paste the image into the Apply 3-1 Storage History Composite document window. Close the Apply 3-1 Tape file.

c. Name and color the layer.

d. Click the Hue/Saturation icon on the Adjustments panel to display the settings. On the panel's status bar, click the Clip to Layer button. Adjust the Hue to 10, the Saturation to –10 and the Lightness to 0. Click the Adjustments button in the vertical dock to collapse the Adjustments panel.

e. Resize the tape, if necessary, and position it as shown in Figure 3–80.

Continued >

Apply Your Knowledge *continued*

6. To create the cassette tape layer:

   a. Open the file, Apply 3-1 Cassette Tape.

   b. Arrange the document windows and drag the image from the new window into the Apply 3-1 Storage History Composite document window. Close the Apply 3-1 Cassette Tape file.

   c. Name and color the layer.

   d. On the Adjustments panel, click the Brightness/Contrast icon and then click the Clip to Layer button. Adjust the Brightness to 35.

   e. Click the Adjustments button in the vertical dock to collapse the Adjustments panel.

7. To create the floppy disk layers:

   a. One at a time open each of the floppy disk files listed in Table 3–6 on page PS 198.

   b. Copy and paste each image into the Storage History Composite document window.

   c. Name and color each layer.

   d. Use the eraser tools to erase extraneous background.

   e. Position and rotate the images as shown in Figure 3–80 on page PS 198.

8. To clone the punched card:

   a. Select the Background layer. Create a new layer by pressing CTRL+SHIFT+N. Name the layer, punched card. Do not check the Use previous Layer to Create Clipping Mask check box. Choose a red identification color. Do not change the mode or opacity. Click the OK button to close the New Layer dialog box. Press CTRL+LEFT BRACKET ([) to move the punched card layer below the Background layer. ALT+click the visibility icon on the punched card layer to display only that layer.

   b. Open the file, Apply 3-1 Punched Card.

   c. Arrange the document windows above and below one another.

   d. Press the s key to activate the Clone Stamp Tool. On the options bar, click to display the Aligned check mark, if necessary.

   e. ALT+click in the punched card document window, close to the upper-left corner.

   f. Drag in the Apply 3-1 Storage History Composite document window to create a clone.

   g. Repeat Steps e and f to create four more clones at various locations in the window. (*Hint:* in this montage, it is okay for part of a cloned image to run off the edge of the document window.)

9. Close the Apply 3-1 Punched Card window.

10. On the Layers panel of the Apply 3-1 Storage History Composite window, click the 'Indicates layer visibility' button beside each layer to display the layers.

11. Save the file again by pressing CTRL+S.

12. On the Layers panel, click the Layers panel menu button to display the menu. Click Flatten Image on the menu to flatten all of the layers.

13. Press SHIFT+CTRL+S to open the Save As dialog box. Type Apply 3-1 Storage History Complete in the Name box. Click the Format box arrow and then click TIFF in the list. Click the Save button. If Photoshop displays a dialog box, click the OK button.

14. Turn in a hard copy of the photo to your instructor.

15. Quit Photoshop.

Extend Your Knowledge

Extend the skills you learned in this chapter and experiment with new skills. You may need to use Help to complete the assignment.

Exploring Layer Comps

Instructions: Start Photoshop. Set the default workspace, default colors, and reset all tools. To complete this assignment, you will be required to use the Data Files for Students. Visit www.cengage.com/ct/studentdownload for detailed instructions or contact your instructor for information about accessing the required files. Open the file Extend 3-1 Marketing Graphic from the Chapter 03 folder of the Data Files for Students.

The purpose of this exercise to create layer comps of a product box for client evaluation. The current graphic has layers for the background, inside, and outside of the box. You are to insert the trophy graphic and scale it to fit the box, then create layer comps showing the inside and the outside. The edited photo is shown in Figure 3–81.

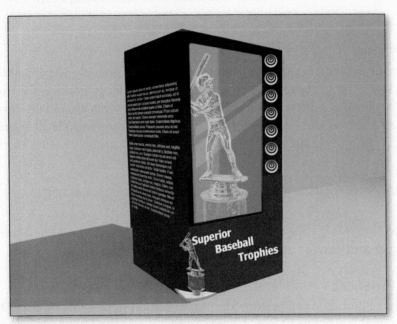

Figure 3–81

Perform the following tasks:

1. Save the file with the name, Extend 3-1 Marketing Graphic Composite. If necessary, click the Format box arrow and then select the Photoshop PSD format. Click the Save in box arrow and then select your USB flash drive location. Click the Save button. If Photoshop displays a Format Options dialog box, click the OK button.

2. Show and hide the various layers using the visibility icon to gain familiarity with the graphic.

3. Make the Background layer and inside layer visible; hide all other layers. Select the inside layer.

4. Open the Extend 3-1 Trophy file from the Chapter 03 folder of the Data Files for Students. Use the Arrange Documents button to display the windows side by side.

5. Use the Move Tool to drag the trophy from its own window into the Extend 3-1 Marketing Graphic Composite document window. Scale the trophy to fit in the box. Make the outside

Continued >

Extend Your Knowledge *continued*

layer visible and make sure the trophy can be seen through the opening in the outer box. Name the layer, trophy.

6. Make the front panel layer visible and select it. At the top of the Layers panel, adjust the Fill setting so the layer looks more transparent, as if it were plastic.

7. Make the gleam layer visible. Adjust the Opacity and Fill settings as necessary. Save the file.

8. Use Photoshop Help to learn about Layer Comps. Also read the BTW boxes on page PS 140. Open the Layer Comps panel and create the layer comps described in Table 3–7.

Table 3–7 Marketing Graphic Layer Comps	
Layer Comp Name	**Visible Layers**
Empty Box	Background, inside
Inner Box with Trophy	Background, inside, trophy
Outer Box with Trophy	Background, inside, trophy, outside, shadow
Complete Graphic	All layers

9. Save the file again.

10. For extra credit, copy the trophy layer and scale it to approximately 30 percent of its original size. In the Layers panel, move the layer above the outside layer. Position the trophy in the lower-middle portion of the box. Warp the layer to make it wrap around the corner of the box. Create a layer comp named Complete with Wrapped Logo and include all layers.

11. Submit this assignment in the format specified by your instructor.

Make It Right

Analyze a project and correct all errors and/or improve the design.

Correcting Layer Errors

Instructions: Start Photoshop and perform the customization steps found on pages PS 6 through PS 10. To complete this assignment, you will be required to use the Data Files for Students. Visit www.cengage.com/ct/studentdownload for detailed instructions or contact your instructor for information about accessing the required files. Open the Make It Right 3-1 Park file from the Chapter 03 folder of the Data Files for Students.

The photo has layers that are invisible, layers that need transformation, and layers that need to be moved, trimmed, and adjusted for levels (Figure 3–82).

Perform the following tasks:
Save the file on your storage device in the PSD format with the name, Make It Right 3-1 Park Composite. For each invisible layer, reveal the layer, correct any order problem by dragging the layer to an appropriate position on the Layers panel, erase or mask parts of the layer as necessary, and move the layer to a logical position.

Use the Adjustments panel and tools such as Levels, Brightness/Contrast, and Hue/Saturation to create adjustment layers. (*Hint:* Be sure to click the Clip to Layer button on the Adjustments panel status bar, so the adjustment will apply to that layer only.) Make any other adjustments or layer style changes that you deem necessary. Save the file again and submit it in the format specified by your instructor.

Figure 3–82

In the Lab

Design and/or create a project using the guidelines, concepts, and skills presented in this chapter. Labs are listed in order of increasing difficulty.

Lab 1: Using the Clone Stamp Tool and Creating a Layer with Outer Glow

Problem: The marketing agency that you work for has asked you to edit the latest advertisement for Qintara perfume. You decide to use Photoshop's layering capabilities to insert the image of the perfume bottle. You also decide to clone the Q of the logo multiple times to create a stylistic band of color across the advertisement. A sample of the advertisement is displayed in Figure 3–83.

Note: To complete this assignment, you will be required to use the Data Files for Students. Visit www.cengage.com/ct/studentdownload for detailed instructions or contact your instructor for information about accessing the required files.

Continued >

Figure 3–83

Instructions: Perform the following tasks:

1. Start Photoshop. Set the default workspace, default colors, and reset all tools.

2. Open the file Lab 3-1 Perfume from the Chapter 03 folder of the Data Files for Students.

3. Click View on the Application bar and then click Fit on Screen to view the entire image at the largest possible magnification.

4. Click the Save As command on the File menu. Type `Lab 3-1 Perfume Edited` as the file name. If necessary, click the Format box arrow and then click PSD in the list. Browse to your USB flash drive storage device. Click the Save button. If Photoshop displays a Format Options dialog box, click the OK button.

5. On the Layers panel, select the layer named, slogan. In the document window, use the Move Tool to move the layer to the lower portion of the image.

6. Open the Lab 3-1 Bottle file from the Chapter 03 folder from the Data Files for Students. Arrange the files horizontally. Select the entire bottle image and then drag a copy to the Lab 3-1 Perfume Edited window.

7. In the Lab 3-1 Perfume Edited window, name the new layer and set an identification color. Close the Lab 3-1 Bottle document window.

8. On the Layers panel status bar, use the 'Add layer mask' button to create a layer mask in the bottle layer. (*Hint:* Make sure you have black over white for the foreground and background colors.) Use the Brush Tool with black to mask the area around the bottle.

9. Click the 'Add a layer style' button on the Layers panel status bar, and then click Outer Glow. When the Layer Style dialog box is displayed, type `25` in the Size box, and then click the OK button.

10. Select the Background layer. Click the Clone Stamp Tool on the Tools panel. ALT+click the top of the letter Q in the logo. Move the mouse pointer down and to the right. Drag to create a clone of the Q.

11. Repeat Step 10, creating multiple, overlapped clones of the letter Q as shown in Figure 3–83 on the previous page. Use short strokes. If you make a mistake, press CTRL+Z and drag again.

12. When you are satisfied with your clones, flatten the image.

13. Save the file again and submit the assignment in the format specified by your instructor.

In the Lab

Lab 2: Creating a Toy Company Advertisement

Problem: You are to create a composite photo for a toy company by adding and adjusting layers, as shown in Figure 3–84.

Note: To complete this assignment, you will be required to use the Data Files for Students. Visit www.cengage.com/ct/studentdownload for detailed instructions or contact your instructor for information about accessing the required files.

Figure 3–84

Instructions: Perform the following tasks:

1. Start Photoshop. Perform the customization steps found on pages PS 6 through PS 10.

2. Open the Lab 3-2 Robot Background file from the Chapter 03 folder of the Data Files for Students and save it on your USB flash storage device with the file name Lab 3-2 Robot Composite.

3. To clone over the shadow on the right side of the image:

   a. Select the Clone Stamp Tool. On the options bar, click the Aligned check box so it does not display a check mark.

   b. ALT+click the ground approximately one inch below the shadow to create the sample for the clone. Drag over the shadowed area, including any rocks, to create a cloned area and hide the shadow. (*Hint*: Use the LEFT BRACKET ([) and RIGHT BRACKET (]) keys to adjust the size of the mouse pointer as needed.)

4. To create a sky layer:

   a. Use the Magic Wand Tool and the 'Add to selection' button to select all of the sky.

   b. On the Layer menu, point to New, and then click Layer Via Cut.

   c. On the Layers panel, double-click the new layer name and type sky to rename the layer. Right-click the visibility icon and select Blue in the list.

5. To add the robot body:

   a. Open the Lab 3-2 Robot Body file from the Chapter 03 folder of the Data Files for Students.

   b. Using the Window menu, arrange the windows side by side.

   c. Use the Move Tool to drag the robot body from the Lab 3-2 Robot Body document window to the Lab 3-2 Robot Composite document window. (*Hint:* Holding down the SHIFT key as you drag automatically centers the image and creates a new layer.) After creating the layer, close the Lab 3-2 Robot Body document window.

   d. Name the layer, robot, and use a violet identification color.

6. Repeat Step 4 to add the shadow graphic using the file, Lab 3-2 Robot Shadow file. Position it behind the robot near the feet, as shown in Figure 3–84. Name the layer, shadow, and use a gray identification color. Close the Lab 3-2 Robot Shadow document window.

Continued >

7. To move the shadow behind the robot, on the Layers panel, drag the shadow layer just below the robot layer.

8. Repeat Step 4 to add the earth graphic using the file, Lab 3-2 Robot Earth file. Position it in the upper-right corner of the scene. Name the layer, earth, and use a green identification color.

9. Repeat Step 4 to add the title graphic using the file, Lab 3-2 Robot Title file. Position the words centered above the robot's head. Name the layer, title, and use a yellow identification color.

10. To create an adjustment layer and make the background appear more like a moonscape:

   a. On the Layers panel, select the Background layer.

   b. On the Adjustments panel, click the Hue/Saturation icon to display the settings on the Properties panel.

   c. On the Properties panel status bar, click the Clip to Layer button to create a new adjustment layer for the background.

   d. Change the Hue to +20 and the Saturation to –80.

   e. Click the Properties button on the vertical dock of panels to collapse the panel.

11. To create an adjustment layer and make the sky layer appear black:

   a. Select the sky layer.

   b. On the Adjustments panel, click the Brightness/Contrast icon to display the settings on the Properties panel. Click the Clip to Layer button. Click the Use Legacy check box so it displays a check mark.

   c. Drag both the Brightness and Contrast sliders to the left to create a black sky.

   d. Click the Properties button on the vertical dock of panels to collapse the panel.

12. To add a layer effect to the title layer:

   a. Select the title layer.

   b. Click the 'Add a layer style' button on the Layers panel status bar, and then click Stroke to display the Layer Style dialog box. (*Hint:* You can read about the Stroke command in Photoshop Help.) Reposition the Layer Style dialog box title bar so you can view title in the document window.

   c. In the Layer Style dialog box, click the Color box to display the Color Picker (Stroke Color) dialog box. Reposition the dialog box so you can view the robot in the document window, if necessary.

   d. Click one of the yellow eyes of the robot to select the yellow color. (*Hint:* The mouse pointer looks like an eyedropper when selecting a color.)

   e. Click the OK button to close the dialog box and then click the OK button to close the Layer Style dialog box.

13. Save the composite file again with all the layers.

14. Right-click any layer on the Layers panel and then click Flatten Image.

15. Press SHIFT+CTRL+S to open the Save As dialog box. Type Lab 3-2 Robot Complete in the Name box. Click the Format box arrow and then click TIFF in the list. Click the Save in box arrow, and then click Removable Disk (F:) or the location associated with your USB flash drive, in the list. Click the Save button. If Photoshop displays a dialog box, click the OK button.

16. Quit Photoshop.

In the Lab

Lab 3: Creating a Contest Entry with Layers

Problem: You would like to enter your hamster in a creative pet photo contest. You decide to use Photoshop's layering capabilities to dress up your hamster, as shown in Figure 3–85.

Note: To complete this assignment, you will be required to use the Data Files for Students. Visit www.cengage.com/ct/studentdownload for detailed instructions or contact your instructor for information about accessing the required files.

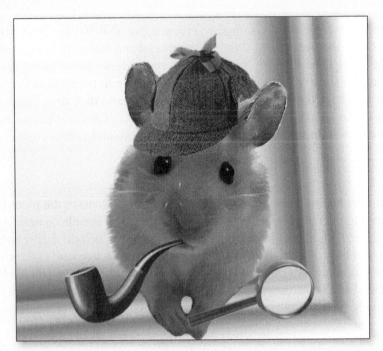

Figure 3–85

Instructions: Perform the following tasks:

Start Photoshop. Set the default workspace, default colors, and reset all tools. Open the file Lab 3-3 Hamster from the Chapter 03 folder of the Data Files for Students. Rename the file, Lab 3-3 Hamster Composite and save it as a PSD file on your file storage device.

Open the Lab 3-3 Pipe file, arrange the windows, and then drag a copy to the Lab 3-3 Hamster Composite window. Set the layer properties. Close the Lab 3-3 Pipe document window. Remove the background around the pipe. Scale and position the layer as necessary. Adjust the perspective. Repeat the process for the Lab 3-3 Magnifying Glass file. Reposition the layers as necessary.

Repeat the process for the Lab 3-3 Hat file, scaling the layer as necessary, and place it on top of the hamster's head. Select the right third (back) of the hat and create a layer via cut. On the Layers panel, set the properties and move the back of hat layer, below the hamster layer, so that part of the hat appears behind the hamster's ear.

Make any other adjustments to the layers that you feel would enhance the photo. When you are satisfied with your layers, save the image again. Flatten the image, save it as a TIFF file, and submit a copy to your instructor.

Cases and Places

Apply your creative thinking and problem-solving skills to design and implement a solution.

Note: To complete this assignment, you will be required to use the Data Files for Students. Visit www.cengage.com/ct/studentdownload for detailed instructions or contact your instructor for information about accessing the required files.

1: Clone within the Same Document

Academic

Earlier in this chapter, a suggestion was made to create a flag with 50 percent opacity superimposed over a memorial. Open the files named Case 3-1 Memorial and Case 3-1 Flag, located in the Chapter 03 folder of the Data Files for Students. (Alternatively, locate or take a photo of a memorial in your city or a building on your campus. If necessary, obtain permission to use a digital photo or scan the image.) Arrange the windows. Select only the flag and then drag it as a new layer into the memorial photo. Resize the layer to fit across the memorial. Change the opacity to 50 percent. Make other corrections as necessary. Save the composite photo and print a copy.

2: Create a Graphic with Opacity Changes

Personal

You recently took a photo of a deer at the local forest preserve. To make the picture more interesting, you decide to create a layer and clone the deer. Open the photo named Case 3-1 Deer, located in the Chapter 03 folder of the Data Files for Students. Click the Layer command on the Application bar, point to New, and then click Layer. Click the Background layer, choose the Clone Stamp Tool, and take a sample of the middle of the deer. Click the new layer and clone the deer. On the Edit menu, click Free Transform and resize the cloned deer so it appears to be farther away. Flip the clone horizontally. Save the file as Case 3-2 Deer Cloned on your storage device.

3: Create a Greeting Card Graphic with Masking

Professional

You have been hired as an intern with a greeting card company. You were given several photos to use in preparing holiday cards. The file named Case 3-3 Santa Scene is located in the Chapter 03 folder of the Data Files for Students. You want to use only the figure of Santa Claus on the front of a card. Save the photo in the PSD format on your USB flash drive storage device as Case 3-3 Santa Layered. Create a rectangular marquee selection around the figure. Use the Layer Via Cut command and name the new layer, Santa. Hide the background. Create a layer mask, painting with black to display only the figure. Print the photo with the background hidden.

4 Drawing and Painting with Color

Adobe product screenshot(s) reprinted with permission from Adobe Systems Incorporated

Objectives

You will have mastered the material in this chapter when you can:

- Create a Photoshop document from scratch using the Painting workspace
- Differentiate between color modes
- Apply gradients using the Gradient Tool
- Create smart objects
- Select colors using the Swatches panel
- Paint and draw using Photoshop brushes

- Adjust the hardness and diameter settings of brushes
- Load new custom shapes
- Use a Color Picker dialog box
- Differentiate among the shape tools, modes, and settings
- Create a custom shape
- Sample colors with the Eyedropper Tool
- Create and use a character style

4 | Drawing and Painting with Color

Introduction

In both academic and business environments, you will be called upon to create graphics from scratch using the tools and techniques available in Photoshop. While many sources of graphics, such as clip art and stock photos, are widely available, some are copyrighted, rights-controlled, or expensive to buy. Others have to be edited so extensively that it might be easier to start from scratch. Still others simply do not fit the particular circumstances for the required project. By creating an original graphic, you solve many of the problems that result when attempting to use ready-made images. If you have good artistic and drawing skills, and an input device such as a graphics tablet, the kinds of graphics you can create are unlimited.

Another way to design graphics is to start from scratch and add images that are digital photographs or scans. That way, your image has the best of both worlds — combining the texture and lines of drawing with the realism of actual photographs. In Photoshop, working from scratch to create an image or illustration is better when the subject is conceptual, imaginative, less formal, or open to interpretation. Beginning with a digital photo is better when the subject is living, tangible, for sale, or more formal; photography does not risk loss of meaning through interpretation. Regardless of the approach you choose, you need to know how to use the drawing and painting tools in Photoshop.

Project — Creating a Poster

Chapter 4 uses Photoshop to create a poster for a jazz club. The poster incorporates brush strokes, text, a gradient, a graphic, and other shapes. The completed image appears in Figure 4–1. Nearly all posters, magazines, and catalogs on the market today are full-color and are printed using a four-color process (CMYK), providing bright color shades and an eye-catching look. CMYK is an acronym for the four-color process used in printing, cyan, magenta, yellow, and black. You will use colors from the CMYK color mode.

Posters commonly are used outdoors in large venues, so it is important to use large text. People will be seeing the poster while in motion, for example while driving or walking by; therefore, eye-catching graphics and straight-to-the-point messages are essential.

Figure 4–1

Overview

As you read this chapter, you will learn how to create the poster shown in Figure 4–1 on the previous page by performing these general tasks:

- Create a new file, starting with a blank canvas.
- Apply a gradient background.
- Choose colors using a variety of tools and dialog boxes.
- Insert real images combined with drawn images.
- Use brushes to draw and paint.
- Draw custom shapes.
- Create a character style for customized text.

Plan Ahead

General Project Guidelines

When editing a photo, the actions you perform and decisions you make will affect the appearance and characteristics of the finished product. As you create a poster, such as the one shown in Figure 4–1, you should follow these general guidelines:

1. **Plan your layout and gather necessary photos.** As you plan your layout of original graphics, create the storyboard and the graphic from the back to the front. Decide on the background first, then layers, followed by foreground objects or text. The graphics you choose should convey the overall message, incorporating high-quality photos with similar lighting characteristics. Keep in mind the customer requirements. For professional-looking graphics, adhere to the general principles of alignment, contrast, repetition, and proximity.

2. **Choose colors purposefully.** Consider the cost of full-color printing, paper, shelf life, and customer requirements when choosing your colors. Try to repeat colors that already exist in incorporated images. Some clients already may have colors that help brand their publications. Consult with the client and print shops for the correct color numbers and the plan for printing. Unless you want a rainbow special effect, limit your colors to two or three on a contrasting background.

3. **Design your brush strokes.** Photoshop brushes imitate the actions of artistic paint brushes. By varying the settings, such as tip shape, hardness, and so on, you can add creative effects to your work.

4. **Use predefined shapes for tangible objects.** Use shapes rather than freehand drawings when you are trying to create a graphic that represents a tangible object. Shapes allow you to maintain straight lines, even corners, constrained proportions, and even curves. Except when intentionally creating a randomized pattern, try to align shapes with something else in the graphic, or parallel to the edge of the publication.

5. **Apply effective text styles and strokes.** Although many graphics include text as a means to educate and inform, text often becomes a creative element itself in the design. The first rule of text is to choose a font that is easy to read. No matter how creative the font style is, if the customer cannot make out the words, the message fails. Avoid using more than two different fonts on the same page or graphic. As a second font, use either the same font at a different size or a highly contrasting font. Keep similar text components in proximity to each other. For example, do not split the address, phone number, and Web page address onto different parts of the page. Use a stroke of color around the text for a more distinctive look that stands out.

When necessary, more specific details concerning the preceding guidelines are presented at appropriate points in the chapter. The chapter also will identify the actions performed and decisions made regarding these guidelines during the creation of the composite image shown in Figure 4–1.

BTW

Composite Images
Photoshop documents that combine drawing and painting effects with photographs and other elements are sometimes called composite images, or comps.

Creating a New File

In this chapter, you will create a new Photoshop document starting with a blank canvas. Photoshop allows you to customize the attributes of file name, image size, resolution, color mode, and background when creating a new document image. Alternatively, Photoshop provides several groups of attributes that are preset. The new image size can be set in pixels, inches, or centimeters, among other units. You can set the width and height independently. When setting the resolution of an image, you specify the number of **pixels per inch** (**ppi**), or **pixels per centimeter** (**ppc**), on the printed page.

A **color mode**, or **color method**, determines the number of colors and combinations of colors used to display and print the image. Each color mode incorporates a numerical method called a **color model** or **color space** to describe the color. Photoshop bases its color modes on the color models that are commonly used when publishing images. Color modes also directly affect the file size of an image. As you will learn in this chapter, choosing a color mode determines which Photoshop tools and file formats are available.

When choosing a color mode, you must take into consideration many factors, including purpose, printing options, file size, number of colors, and layers that may be flattened in later conversions between color modes. Common color modes include RGB, CMYK, LAB, Indexed, and Grayscale, among others. See Appendix B, the Graphic Design Overview appendix, at the back of this book for more details about each of the color modes.

RGB (red, green, blue) is an additive color mode because its colors are created by adding together different wavelengths of light in various intensities. Also called **24-bit color**, RGB color mode is used typically for images that are reproduced on monitors, projectors, slides, transparencies, and the Web.

CMYK (cyan, magenta, yellow, black) is a subtractive color mode because its colors are created when light strikes an object or image and the wavelengths are absorbed. Also called the **four-color process**, the CMYK color mode is used by most desktop printers and commercial printing businesses.

A **gamut**, or **color gamut**, is the range of printed or displayed colors. The color gamut on your monitor might not be the same as on your printer. For example, the RGB color mode displays a wider range of discernible colors than does CMYK. When you print an RGB image from your monitor, it must be reproduced with CMYK inks on your printer. The gamut of reproducible ink colors is smaller than what we see with our eyes, and any color that cannot be printed is referred to as **out of gamut**. In Photoshop, you will see an out of gamut warning if you select colors that have to be converted from RGB to CMYK. If you plan to send your image to a professional print shop, be sure to get details about color modes, models, and gamuts before the image is printed.

Once you choose a color mode, you also can set a bit depth. The **bit depth**, also called **pixel depth** or **color depth**, measures how much color information is available for displaying or printing each pixel in an image. The word **bit** stands for binary digit. A bit depth of eight means that Photoshop assigns eight binary settings for each color.

Photoshop's **color management system** (**CMS**) translates colors from the color space of one device into a device-independent color space. The process is called **color mapping** or **gamut mapping**.

BTW

Converting Between Modes
In Photoshop, you easily can convert from one color mode to another using the Mode command on the Image menu. As you choose a new color mode, Photoshop will inform you of any problems converting the image.

BTW

LAB Color
Three basic parameters make up the LAB color mode. First, the lightness of the color is measured from 0 (indicating black) to 100 (indicating white). The second parameter represents the color's position between magenta and green — negative values indicate green, whereas positive values indicate magenta. Finally, the third parameter indicates a color's position between yellow and blue — negative values indicate blue, whereas positive values indicate yellow.

BTW

Indexed Color
When converting to Indexed color, Photoshop builds a **color lookup table (CLUT)**, which stores and indexes the colors in the image. If a color in the original image does not appear in the table, Photoshop chooses the closest one, or dithers the available colors, to simulate the color. Indexed color mode therefore limits the panel of colors to reduce file size yet maintain visual quality.

To Start Photoshop

The following steps, which assume Windows 7 is running, start Photoshop based on a typical installation. You may need to ask your instructor how to start Photoshop for your system.

1 Click the Start button on the Windows 7 taskbar to display the Start menu and then type `Photoshop CS6` in the 'Search programs and files' box.

2 Click Adobe Photoshop CS6 in the list to start Photoshop.

3 If the Photoshop window is not maximized, click the Maximize button next to the Close button on the Application bar to maximize the window.

BTW

Colors on the Web
The Web typically uses a six-digit hexadecimal number to represent its color mode. Hexadecimal is a numbering system based on groups of 16, using the numbers 0 through 9 and the letters A through F. In decimal numbers, used for color modes other than the Web, three separate numbers are used for each of the 256 available colors per channel.

To Reset the Tools and the Options Bar

The following steps select the Rectangular Marquee Tool and reset all tool settings on the options bar.

1 If the tools in the Tools panel appear in two columns, click the double arrow at the top of the Tools panel.

2 If necessary, click the Rectangular Marquee Tool button on the Tools panel to select it.

3 Right-click the Rectangular Marquee Tool icon on the options bar to display the context menu, and then click Reset All Tools. When Photoshop displays a confirmation dialog box, click the OK button to restore the tools to their default settings.

To Set the Interface and Default Colors

Recall that Photoshop retains the interface color scheme, as well as the foreground and background colors from session to session. The following steps set the interface to Medium Gray and the foreground and background colors to black over white.

1 Click Edit on the Application bar to display the edit menu. Point to Preferences and then click Interface on the Preferences submenu to display the Preferences dialog box.

2 Click the third button, Medium Gray, to change the interface color scheme.

3 Click the OK button to close the Preferences dialog box.

4 Press the D key to reset the default foreground and background colors. If black is not over white on the Tools panel, press the X key.

To Select the Painting Workspace

The Painting workspace displays the Brush Presets, Swatches, and Layers panels open and on top of their panel grouping. Later in the chapter, this workspace will be helpful when choosing brushes and colors. The following steps select the Painting workspace.

1

- Click Window on the Application bar, and then point to Workspace to display the Workspace submenu (Figure 4–2).

 Experiment

- Click different workspace options on the Workspace submenu to see how the panels and layout change. When you are finished, display the Workspace submenu again.

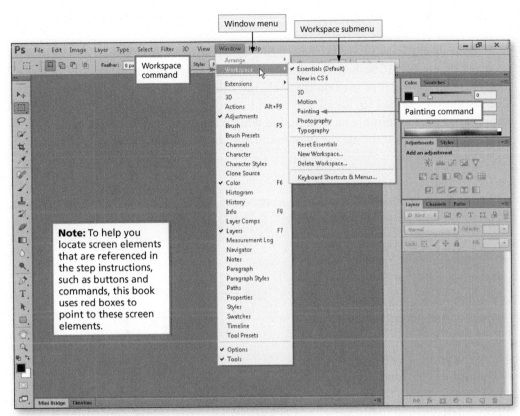

Figure 4–2

2

- Click Painting on the Workspace submenu to choose the Painting workspace (Figure 4–3).

Q&A

What kind of changes will I notice in the workspace?

You should see a different set of panels along the right side of the workspace.

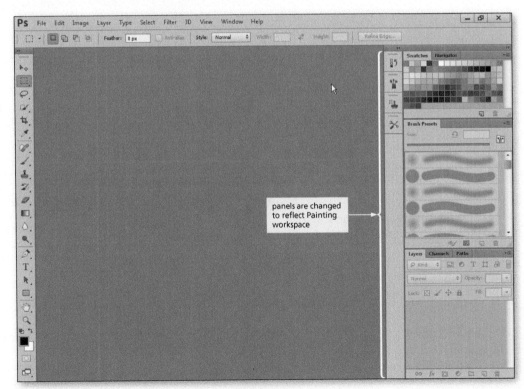

Figure 4–3

To Start a New Photoshop File

In a real business situation, the printing of the poster would be outsourced to a print shop for printing on paper that is 24×36 inches; therefore, you will use that size canvas. Because the graphic will be printed professionally, rather than used on the Web, the color mode will be CMYK and the bit depth will be eight. The resolution will be 150. Recall that resolution refers to the number of pixels per inch, printed on a page or displayed on a monitor. The background will be transparent at the beginning.

The following steps use the New command on the File menu and set the attributes for a new document image.

1

- Click File on the Application bar, and then click New to display the New dialog box.

- Type Jazz Poster in the Name text box to replace the default name.

- If necessary, click the Preset box arrow, and then click Custom in the list.

- Click the Width unit box arrow to display the list of units (Figure 4–4).

My settings are different. Did I do something wrong?

No, your settings might differ. Photoshop imports the settings from the last copy performed on your system, in case you want to create a new file from something you copied to the Clipboard.

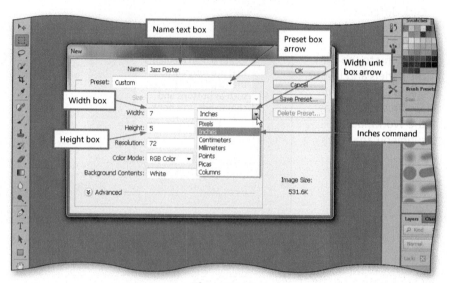

Figure 4–4

 Experiment

- Click the Preset box arrow, and then click one of the preset sizes. Notice how the width, height, and other settings change. When you are finished, click the Preset box arrow, and then click Custom.

2

- Click Inches in the list to select the unit.

- Double-click the Width box, and then type 24 to enter a value of 24 inches wide.

- Double-click the Height box, and then type 36 to enter a value of 36 inches high.

- Double-click the value in the Resolution box, and then type 150 to enter the resolution.

- Click the Color Mode box arrow to display its list (Figure 4–5).

Why are we using 150 in the resolution box?

At higher resolutions, the file size becomes very large, without adding very much quality. For example, if you change the resolution to 300, this poster file size would be more than 300 megabytes.

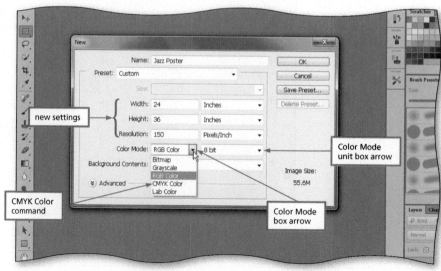

Figure 4–5

3

- Click CMYK Color in the list to choose the CMYK Color mode.

- If necessary, click the Color Mode unit box arrow, and then click 8 bit in the list.

- Click the Background Contents box arrow to display the available backgrounds (Figure 4–6).

Q&A My screen shows Advanced settings. Do I need to edit those settings?

No. The Hide/Show Advanced Options button displays Advanced settings for color profile and aspect ratios. You will leave those at their default values.

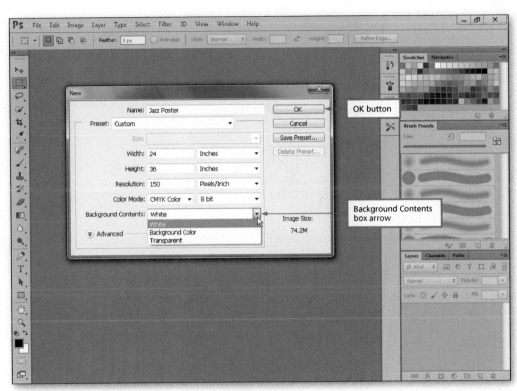

Figure 4–6

4

- Click Transparent in the list to set the background to transparent (Figure 4–7).

Q&A What does the Save Preset button do?

Once you choose a color mode, Photoshop displays an approximate image size on the right side of the New dialog box, based on your settings. If you find that you commonly use those specific settings, you could click the Save Preset button and give your attributes a name. In future sessions, you then could choose the preset from a list.

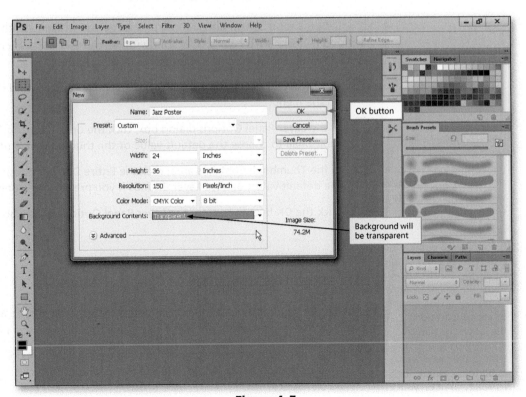

Figure 4–7

5

- Click the OK button to close the dialog box.

- If the rulers do not appear in the document window, press CTRL+R.

- Click View on the Application bar, and then click Fit on Screen to enlarge the canvas to fit the document workspace (Figure 4–8).

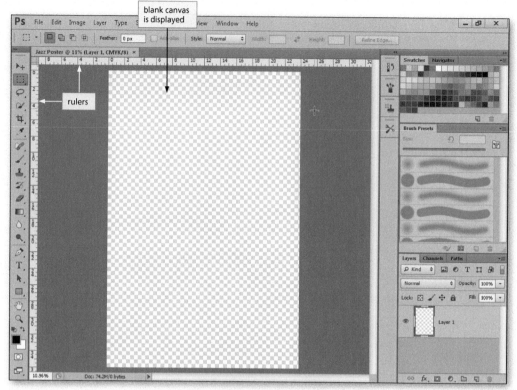

Figure 4–8

Other Ways

1. Press CTRL+N, set attributes, click OK button

2. To fit on screen, press CTRL+0

To Reset the Layers Panel Display

In Chapter 3, you chose to display large thumbnails on the Layers panel, as you learned to work with layers. The following steps reset the Layers panel display to its default value, which matches the figures in this chapter.

1 On the Layers panel, click the Layers panel menu button, and then click Panel Options on the menu.

Background Layer
When you start a new file, the Background Layer is replaced with Layer 1 and the layer is not locked, so you can begin to create content immediately.

2 In the Layer Panel Options dialog box, click the option button for the smallest thumbnail to choose the default value or the thumbnail size of your choosing.

3 In the Thumbnail Contents area, click the Entire Document option button to choose the default value, or click Layer Bounds if you prefer to see only the layer content.

4 Click the OK button to close the Layer Panel Options dialog box.

Image Sizes
For very large publications, reduce the magnification to see the entire image in the document window. The larger the dimensions of your publication, the larger the file size. Photoshop imposes no limit to the size of your publication, except for its ability to fit on your storage device. System resources may be slower in larger documents.

To Save a Document

Even though the document has a name in the document window tab, it is not saved on a storage device. The next steps save the file with the name Jazz Poster.

1 With your USB flash drive connected to one of the computer's USB ports, click File on the Application bar to display the File menu, and then click Save As to display the Save As dialog box.

2 If necessary, in the File name text box, type `Jazz Poster` to rename the file. Do not press the ENTER key after typing the file name.

3 Click the Save in box arrow, and then click Removable Disk (F:) or the location associated with your storage device in the list, if necessary.

4 On the Save As dialog box toolbar, click the Create New Folder button to create a new folder on the selected storage device.

5 When the new folder appears, type `Chapter 04` to change the name of the folder, and then press the ENTER key. Double-click the new folder to open it.

6 Click the Format button and then choose Photoshop (*.PSD;*.PDD) in the list.

7 Click the Save button in the Save As dialog box to save the file. If Photoshop displays a compatibility dialog box, click the OK button.

Gradients

A **gradient**, or **gradient fill**, is a graphic effect consisting of a smooth blend, change, or transition from one color to another. Although there is potential for overuse with gradients, subtle gradients add depth and texture to a graphic or Web page. Shade-to-shade gradients sometimes seem elegant and emotive. They can emulate how light strikes real-world surfaces. Vertical gradients help the eyes to move further down the page. Graphic artists usually save bright, multi-striped gradients for smaller portions of a page, such as a heading, or when they intentionally want to overwhelm the viewer.

Plan your layout and gather necessary photos.
Recall that a storyboard is a preliminary layout sketch used to help plan graphics placement, size, perspective, and spacing. Using a storyboard allows you to create an original graphic from the back to the front.

- As you start on the graphic, fill the background with color, unless the graphic will become part of another publication.

- For busy foregrounds, keep the background simple, with perhaps one color. If text will be used, keep in mind that anything in the darker half of the color spectrum will need light text and vice versa.

- Use black backgrounds sparingly — they are most effective for starkness and special effects.

- For extra depth or perspective, consider using a gradient. A gradient can create depth, add visual interest, or highlight a portion of an image. Use colors that will match colors in your graphic or those desired by the customer. The direction of the gradient should either lead viewers toward a specific focal point or entice them to turn the page.

Typically used as a graduated blend between two colors, the direction of a gradient transition can be top to bottom, bottom to top, side to side, or a variety of other shapes and diagonals. You can apply gradients to the entire image or a selected portion of an image. Photoshop offers many preset gradient fills, or you can create your own using the Gradient Tool.

To create a gradient, click the Gradient Tool button on the Tools panel. If you right-click the Gradient Tool button, its context menu includes the Gradient Tool, the Paint Bucket Tool, and the 3D Material Drop Tool.

The Gradient options bar (Figure 4–9 on the next page) allows you to set the style, blending mode, and other attributes for the gradient fill.

BTW

Gradient Colors
Gradients work best with RGB or CMYK colors. The Gradient Tool cannot be used with the Bitmap or Index color modes.

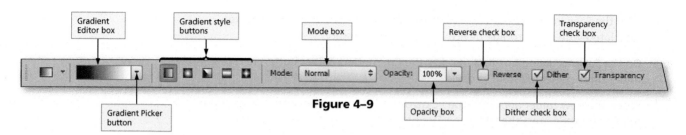

Figure 4–9

On the Gradient Tool options bar, the Gradient Editor button displays the Gradient Editor dialog box, commonly called the Gradient Editor. It allows you to fine-tune and define a new gradient by modifying a copy of an existing gradient or preset, or by choosing colors to create a new blend.

To the right of the Gradient picker button are the gradient styles or shades. A **gradient style** is the way the colors are arranged with regard to the reflection of light in the gradient. Table 4–1 displays the five gradient styles available.

Table 4–1 Gradient Styles	
Gradient	**Style**
Linear	Shades from the starting point to the ending point in a straight line
Radial	Shades from the starting point to the ending point in a circular pattern
Angle	Shades in a counterclockwise sweep around the starting point
Reflected	Shades using symmetric linear gradients on either side of the starting point
Diamond	Shades from the starting point outward in a diamond pattern — the ending point defines one corner of the diamond

The Mode button controls how the colors of the gradient affect the pixels in the image. Some modes apply full color; others randomize, calculate, darken, or lighten to create specific effects. You will learn more about blending modes in a future chapter.

Further right on the Gradient options bar, Photoshop includes an Opacity box to set the percentage of opacity, a Reverse check box to reverse the order of colors in the gradient fill, a Dither check box to create a smoother blend with less banding, and a Transparency check box to create a transparency mask for the gradient fill.

To Select the Gradient Tool and Style

To create a gradient in the Jazz Poster image, you will select the Gradient Tool and then choose a gradient style from the options bar.

- Right-click the Gradient Tool button or the Paint Bucket Tool button on the Tools panel to display the context menu (Figure 4–10).

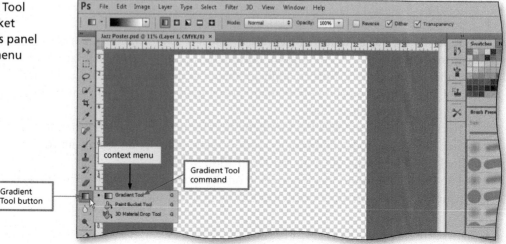

Figure 4–10

2

- Click Gradient Tool to select it.

- On the Gradient options bar, click the Reflected Gradient button to select the gradient style (Figure 4–11).

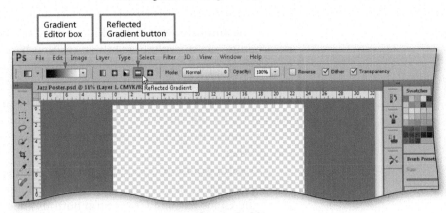

Figure 4–11

Gradient Presets

When you click the Gradient Editor button on the options bar, Photoshop displays the Gradient Editor dialog box (Figure 4–12). In the Gradient Editor dialog box, the Presets area contains 16 predefined gradients called **presets** and a menu button. When clicked, the menu button displays choices for thumbnail size and other gradient presets. Photoshop has 10 sets or **libraries** of additional gradients to create a wide variety of special fill effects. When you choose one of the additional sets, Photoshop will ask if you want to replace or append the new gradient library. The Presets menu button also displays a Reset Gradients command, which changes the presets back to the default list.

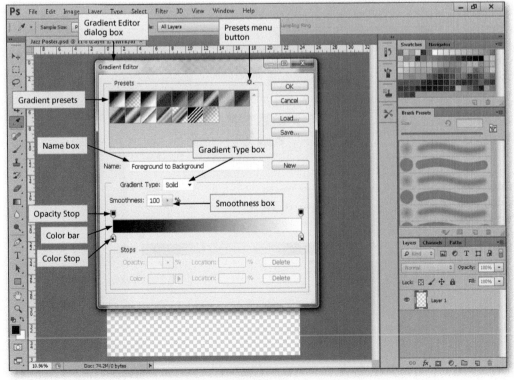

Figure 4–12

The **smoothness** setting (Figure 4–12 on the previous page) is a percentage determining the smoothness of the transition between color bands. A setting of 100% indicates an equally weighted transition in color pixels. When you use lower transition values, the gradient colors will appear more pixilated, with abrupt transitions in the color bands. This effect is even more evident when creating gradients of nonadjacent colors in the color spectrum. When working with a noise gradient, the Smoothness box becomes a Roughness box that indicates how vividly the colors transition between one another.

A **solid gradient** is one that uses the color spectrum to transition the gradient from one color to another. If you choose a solid gradient, Opacity Stop buttons appear above the Color bar, and Color Stop buttons appear below it. Clicking a Color Stop button opens a dialog box in which you can choose a new color. If you adjust the colors, a small diamond, called the Color Midpoint button, appears below the color bar. It indicates the place in the gradient where the display is an even mix of the starting and ending colors. By placing Color Stop buttons very close together in the Gradient Editor, you can reduce the gradient effect and produce strong, distinct bands of color for exciting and creative special effects.

A **noise gradient** is a gradient that contains randomly distributed color specks within the range of colors that you specify. If you choose a noise gradient, the color bar is adjusted by dragging sliders. Noise gradients also display options for restricting color, setting the transparency, and randomizing the colors.

If the gradient you create is one that you plan to use several times, you can name it in the Name box and then click the New button to save it as a gradient file within Photoshop. In subsequent sessions, you then can load the saved gradient to use it again.

To Edit the Gradient

The following steps use the Gradient Editor to choose a gradient preset for the poster.

- On the options bar, click the Gradient Editor box (see Figure 4–11) to display the Gradient Editor dialog box.

- In the Presets area, click the Blue, Yellow, Blue preset button to display the gradient (Figure 4–13).

Experiment

- Click each of the various presets in the Gradient Editor dialog box, and watch how the color settings vary. When you are finished, click the Blue, Yellow, Blue button again.

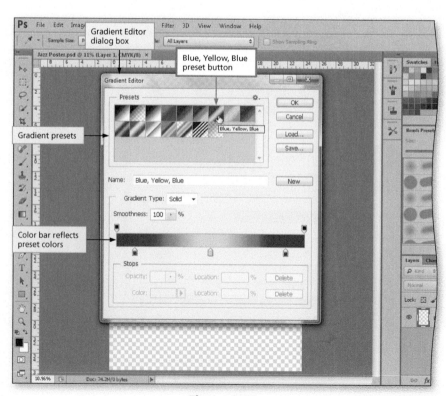

Figure 4–13

2

• To reduce the amount of yellow in the gradient, drag the left color stop button to 25 as noted in the Location box (Figure 4–14).

Q&A I have trouble dragging to exactly 25. Is there another way?

You can type 25 in the Location box if you do not want to drag.

Q&A Why should I use 25 percent?

In this case, the solid blue will continue through the first 25 percent of the color; the gradient then will begin 25 percent of the way in.

 Experiment

• Double-click a Stop button to open the Color Picker (Stop Color) dialog box and notice the various color bars and numeric color boxes. Click the Cancel button to close the dialog box.

Figure 4–14

3

• Drag the right color stop button to 75 as noted in the Location box (Figure 4–15).

Q&A Am I using 75 percent to balance the 25 percent used previously?

Yes, at the end of the gradient, the shading will stop at 75 percent; the last 25 percent will be a solid color.

 Experiment

• Click below the color bar at a location away from a color stop. Notice that Photoshop adds another color stop button for further fine-tuning of the colors and gradient. Press CTRL+Z to undo the addition. Reset the color stops to 25 and 75 if necessary.

4

• Click the OK button to close the dialog box.

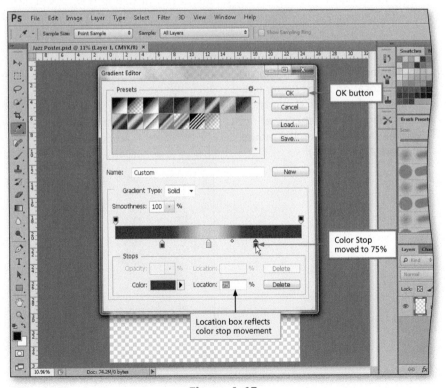

Figure 4–15

To Edit Gradient Colors

If you wanted to edit the colors further, you would perform the following steps using the Gradient Editor dialog box.

1. On the options bar, click the Gradient Editor box to display the Gradient Editor dialog box.

2. Choose a preset.

3. Double-click the left Color Stop button below the gradient bar to display the Color Picker (Stop Color) dialog box. Choose a color and click the OK button to return to the Gradient Editor.

4. Double-click the right Color stop button below the gradient bar to display the Color Picker (Stop Color) dialog box. Choose a color and click the OK button to return to the Gradient Editor.

5. To change the transition, drag the Color Midpoint button.

6. To add a new color, double-click a blank area below the Color bar and select a color.

7. To delete a color, click the Color Stop button, and then click the Delete button.

To Draw the Gradient

The final step in creating a gradient background for the poster is to draw or apply the gradient. To apply the gradient, you drag in the image or selected area, beginning at the point where you want the base color to begin. For linear and radial gradients, you drag in the direction of the desired transition — the rate of transition is dependent on the settings in the Gradient Editor dialog box, as well as on the Transform options bar. The following steps create a diagonal gradient.

- In the document window, drag from a location in the upper-left corner of the canvas, down and right diagonally, to the lower-right corner. Do not release the mouse button (Figure 4–16).

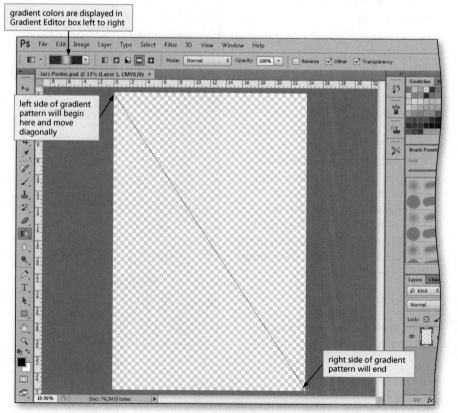

Figure 4–16

②

- Release the mouse button to apply the gradient (Figure 4–17).

🔎 **Experiment**

- Click another style button on the Gradient options bar. Drag in the document window to display a different style gradient. Press CTRL+Z to return to the gradient shown in Figure 4–17.

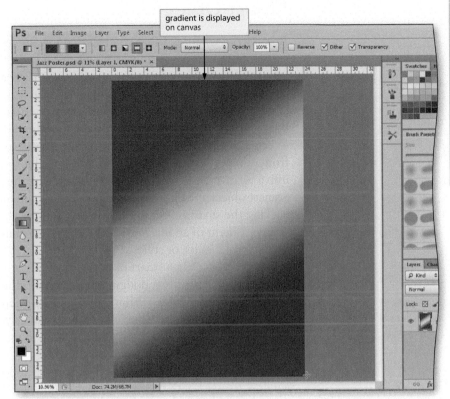

Figure 4–17

To Set Layer Properties

The following steps name the layer and set its identification color.

① Double-click the name of the layer, Layer 1, on the Layers panel. Type `gradient background` and then press the ENTER key to replace the name.

② Right-click the 'Indicates layer visibility' button, and then click Blue in the list to change the layer's identification color (Figure 4–18).

BTW

Gradient Directions
You can create a gradient at any straight line, angle, or position. If you start and end in the extreme corners of the frame, the gradient appears across the entire area. To leave the corners solid and start the gradient more toward the center, drag and end closer to the middle of the area. To constrain the line angle to a multiple of 45°, hold down the SHIFT key as you drag.

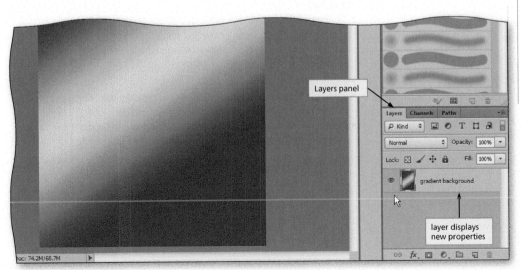

Figure 4–18

Smart Objects

Recall from Chapter 3 that you inserted new images into a document by opening a second file and using various copy, paste, and edit techniques. That insertion became a new layer, independent of its source file; the layer allowed full editing. A **smart object** is an image that is embedded as a linked layer to its source, rather than copied. Embedding an image provides several advantages. For example, transformations on a smart object do not affect the actual original pixel data, which is called **nondestructive editing**. When you embed a smart object from a nonnative file format, such as vector artwork from Adobe Illustrator or Adobe InDesign, Photoshop transforms image information into a format it can recognize without altering the native data. Additionally, you can edit a smart object and choose to update all of the linked instances automatically by double-clicking the smart object icon on the Layers panel. A smart object layer preserves the source content of an image with all its original characteristics, separately from any filters, masks, edits, or styles.

When editing a smart object, you cannot perform operations that alter pixel data — such as painting, dodging, burning, or cloning. However, because a smart object is similar to a file within a file, resizing keeps the maximum resolution. For example, you can resize the file as many times as you want without degrading the image. In a later chapter, you will learn how to use smart objects with filters, for additional nondestructive editing.

Embedded smart objects display a special bounding box in the document window to assist with transformations. Table 4–2 displays transformation tasks you can perform on smart objects.

Table 4–2 Smart Object Transformations

Task	Steps
To adjust the center point	Perform one of the following: • Drag the center point to a new location. • Click a location handle on the Center Point icon on the options bar.
To move	Perform one of the following: • Avoiding the handles, edges, and the center point of the bounding box, drag anywhere in the bounding box. • Enter a value in the location boxes on the options bar.
To reposition	Perform one of the following: • Position the mouse pointer inside the bounding box of the placed image and drag. • On the options bar, enter a value for X to specify the distance between the center point of the placed image and the left edge of the image. Enter a value for Y to specify the distance between the center point of the placed image and the top edge of the image.
To rotate	Perform one of the following: • Position the mouse pointer outside of the bounding box. When the mouse pointer displays a curved arrow, drag to rotate freely. • Enter a value in degrees for the Rotation option on the options bar. The image rotates around the displayed center point.
To scale	Drag one of the corner handles of the bounding box or enter values for W and H on the options bar. When dragging, press and hold the SHIFT key to constrain proportions.
To skew	CTRL+drag a side handle of the bounding box.
To warp	Click Edit on the Application bar, point to Transform, and then click Warp. Choose a warp from the Warp Style context menu on the options bar.

To Create a Smart Object using the Place Command

The following steps use the Place command to embed an image within the Jazz Poster file as a smart object. The image is stored in the Data Files for Students. Visit www.cengage.com/ct/studentdownload for detailed instructions or contact your instructor for information about accessing the required files.

Besides creating a smart object, the Place command can be used to ensure exact placement of selections. If you use a simple copy and paste, the pasted selection will appear in the center of the destination window. A placed copy, however, will appear in the same location from the source window to the destination window; a bird in the sky, for example, will appear in the sky rather than in the center of the new image.

1

- Click File on the Application bar, and then click Place to display the Place dialog box.

- Click the Look in box arrow to display the list of available locations, and then navigate to the Photoshop Data Files for Students.

- Double-click the Chapter 04 folder to open it (Figure 4–19).

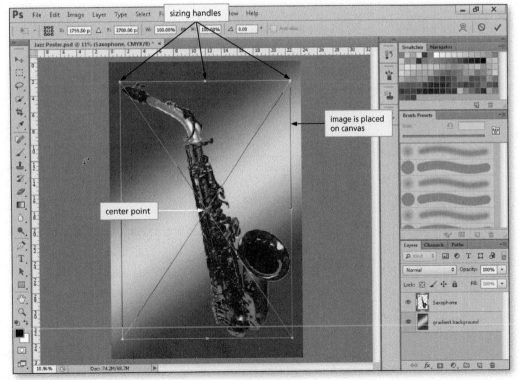

Figure 4–19

2

- Double-click the file named Saxophone to place it in the image (Figure 4–20).

Q&A What changed on the Layers panel?

The new layer automatically takes on the name of the document with which it is linked, in this case, Saxophone.

 Experiment

- On the Layers panel, double-click the layer thumbnail to open the image file itself. Click the Close button on the document tab to close the image file and return to the original file.

Figure 4–20

To Transform the Smart Object

The following steps resize and move the smart object.

1

- On the options bar, click the 'Maintain aspect ratio' button. Double-click the text in the Height box, and then type 67.00% to enter the height.

- Avoiding the handles, edges, and the center point of the Place bounding box, drag the placed image down and left, until the lower-left corner aligns with the corner of the poster (Figure 4–21).

Q&A

Could I drag a handle to resize the placed image?

Yes, you can SHIFT+drag the upper-right sizing handle down and to the left, until the top of the saxophone is aligned at approximately the 15-inch mark on the vertical ruler. Photoshop also displays a small, floating, black box noting the location as you drag.

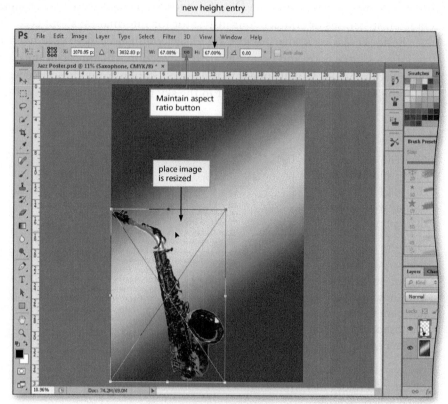

Figure 4–21

2

- Click the Commit transform (Enter) button on the options bar to finish the transformation and hide the bounding box.

- Right-click the new layer to display its context menu, and then click Gray in the list to set an identification color for the saxophone layer.

Q&A

What changed on the Layers panel?

The thumbnail now displays a smart object notation. The name of the placed file becomes the layer name in the current file.

Other Ways

1. On options bar, enter position and size of placed object

To Save the File

Because you have created a gradient and placed an image, it is a good idea to save the file again.

1 Press CTRL+S to save the Jazz Poster file with the same name.

Break Point: If you wish to take a break, this is a good place to do so. You can quit Photoshop now. To resume at a later time, start Photoshop, open the file called Jazz Poster, and continue following the steps from this location forward.

Painting with Brushes

The brush tools change the color of pixels in an image by painting. The Brush and Pencil tools work like their traditional counterparts, applying color with strokes. The Color Replacement Tool replaces a selected color with a new color. Recall that the Gradient Tool creates blends between colors. The Paint Bucket Tool fills similarly colored areas with the foreground color. The History Brush Tool paints a copy of the selected state or snapshot into the current image or layer. The Art History Brush Tool paints with stylized strokes that simulate the look of different paint styles, using a selected state or snapshot. The Mixer Brush Tool simulates realistic painting techniques, such as blending canvas colors and varying paint wetness. By specifying how each tool applies or modifies the color, you can create an endless number of possibilities. You can apply color gradually, with soft or hard edges, with small or large brush tips, and with various brush dynamics and blending properties, as well as by using brushes of different shapes. You even can simulate spraying paint with an airbrush.

In the next section, you first will choose a color from the Swatches panel and create a new layer for the border decoration. Then, you will select the Brush Tool and panel, edit the Brush settings, and finally draw the border on the new layer. You will repeat the process for a second layer of brush strokes using a star tip, accessed from the Brush Presets panel.

The Swatches Panel

The Swatches panel stores colors for repeated use (Figure 4–22). To choose a foreground color, click a color in the Swatches panel. To choose a background color, CTRL+click a color in the Swatches panel. The Swatches panel menu allows you to add more color libraries, or change the settings of the current panel for different projects.

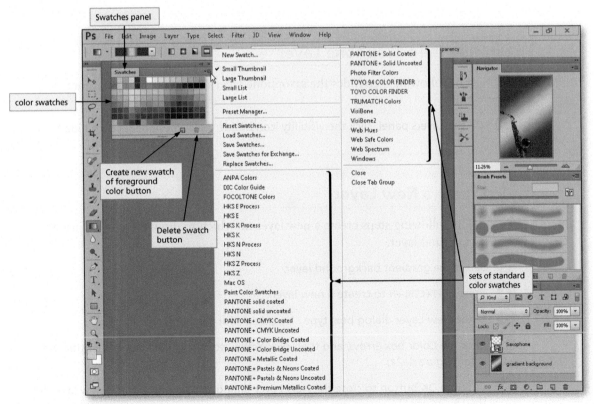

Figure 4–22

<table>
<tr><td>Plan
Ahead</td><td>

Choose colors purposefully.

Choose two or three colors that fit with your client's colors or that match a color that already exists in an image in your layout. Limiting the number of colors creates a stronger brand or identity. The main color should be the one that viewers will remember when they look away. Colors two and three should either contrast or complement the main color to balance the design. Complementary colors create gray, white, or black when mixed in proper proportions, or are found opposite one another on a standard color wheel.

</td></tr>
</table>

To Choose a Color on the Swatches Panel

The following step chooses a foreground color using the Swatches panel. You will use the color later as you create a brushed border.

- On the Swatches panel, in the second row, click the color CYMK Yellow to change the foreground color (Figure 4–23).

 **Experiment**

- Point to various colors on the Swatches panel to display their tool tip names.

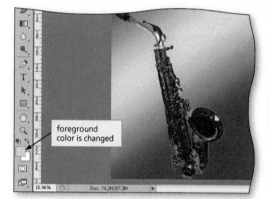
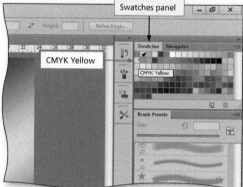

Figure 4–23

To Hide the Saxophone Layer

The following step hides the saxophone layer to allow painting without distraction.

1 On the Layers panel, click the visibility icon beside the saxophone layer to hide the layer.

To Create a New Layer

The following steps create a new layer on which to draw the border, just above the background layer.

1 Select the gradient background layer.

2 Press SHIFT+CTRL+N to create a new layer.

3 In the New Layer dialog box, type border for the name.

4 Click the Color box arrow, and then click Yellow to change the layer's identification color (Figure 4–24).

5 Click the OK button to close the New Layer dialog box and display the new layer on the Layers panel.

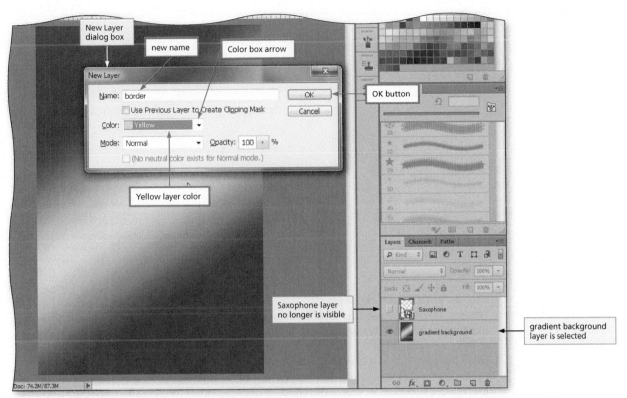

Figure 4–24

The Brush Tool

The Brush Tool paints the current foreground color on an image with strokes of color as you drag. When you click the Brush Tool button on the Tools panel, the Brush options bar appears (Figure 4–25).

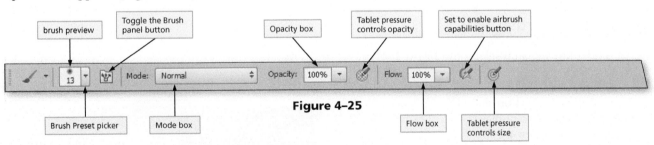

Figure 4–25

Similarly to the Gradient picker, the Brush Preset picker displays the current set of brush tips and settings, such as brush size and hardness. Next to the Brush Preset picker is the Toggle the Brush panel button, which shows and hides the Brush panel. The Mode box arrow displays brush blending modes when clicked, and the Opacity box allows you to specify the degree of transparency. Entering a value in the Flow box specifies how quickly the paint is applied. A lower number applies paint more slowly. The airbrush button enables airbrush capabilities.

In addition to the options bar, several panels used with brushes help you choose and adjust brush settings. Each panel has a button menu to change the size of the thumbnail previews, to create, choose, or append new brushes, as well as reset options. Table 4–3 on the next page lists the panels and their respective purposes.

BTW

Related Tools
The Pencil and Color Replacement tools are related closely to the Brush Tool. The only difference between the Pencil and Brush Tool is that the Brush Tool paints with an anti-aliased or smooth edge, and the Pencil Tool draws with an aliased or rough edge. The Color Replacement Tool replaces specific colors when you paint over a targeted color with a corrective color.

Table 4–3 Panels Used with Brushes			
Panel	**Access**	**Contents**	**Purpose**
Brush Panel	Window | Brush or F5 or Toggle the Brush panel button	Paint options, brush settings, brush tip shapes, stroke preview	To select or modify a brush or to design custom brushes
Brush Presets Panel	Window | Brush Presets	Brush tip and stroke preview, size settings	To choose a preset brush and adjust its size
Brush Preset Picker	Brush Preset picker on Brush options bar	Brush tip preview, size setting, hardness settings	A small panel to quickly choose or verify a brush preset using the options bar

Plan Ahead

Design your brush strokes.
When choosing a brush tip, keep in mind the basic shape of your brush strokes or marks. Use the Brush panel to choose a Brush Preset or Brush Tip shape. Consider the brush shape you want to use such as round, square, or patterned. Think about the density or thickness you wish to see in the brush stroke, as indicated in black, gray, and white in the brush tip preview. Finally think about the style before choosing a brush tip. Many brushes are points (flat, blunt, rounded, or angled); others are brushed, spattered, or stroked with various edges.

Once you have chosen a brush tip, adjust settings for the beginning, middle, and end of the brush stroke. For the beginning, choose an appropriate tip, color, shape, rotation, hardness, spacing, and diameter. For the middle of the stroke, set the shape dynamics, such as pen pressure and tilt, texture, flow, brush edge, distortion, noise, and scattering. For the end of the brush stroke, set the fading effect.

To Select the Brush Tool

The following step selects the Brush Tool on the Tools panel.

- Right-click the current brush tool on the Tools panel to display the context menu (Figure 4–26).

- Click Brush Tool in the list to select it and to display the Brush options bar.

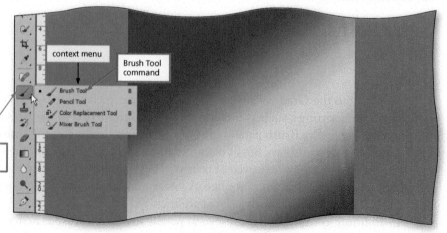

Figure 4–26

The Brush Panel

The Brush panel (Figure 4–27) displays settings such as brush tips, painting characteristics, angles, and spacing, among others. To display the Brush panel, you can click the Toggle the Brush panel button on the Brush options bar (shown in Figure 4–25 on page PS 231), click Brush on the Window menu, click the Brush panel button on the vertical dock, or press the F5 key. Once the Brush panel is displayed, you can click the Brush panel menu button to display a list of available commands.

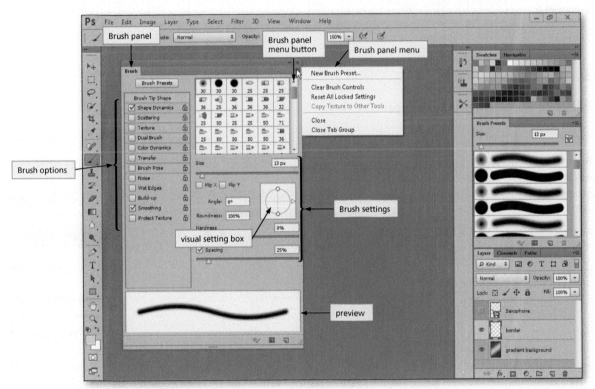

Figure 4–27

The Brush panel allows you to customize preset brush tips. For example, you can set the diameter, which scales the size of the brush tip. The **brush size** is the diameter of the brush tip measured in pixels. The **flip boxes** change the direction of the brush tip on the specified axis. For example, a brush tip that displays a leaf image with the stem down would display the leaf with the stem up if the Flip X check box were checked. **Brush angle** is a measurement of degrees of flat rotation. Positive numbers rotate the brush tip counterclockwise; negative numbers rotate the brush tip clockwise. For example, a brush tip of a raindrop with the pointed end straight up would point left if rotated 90 degrees, counterclockwise. The **roundness** percentage specifies the ratio between the brush's short and long axes. Adjusting the roundness makes the brush tip appear to rotate on its vertical axis in a 3D fashion. A value of 100% indicates a full view or circular brush tip. A value of 0% indicates a sideways view or linear brush tip as if you were painting with a wide brush turned on its side. Values between 0% and 100% represent partial view or elliptical brush tips. For example, a star brush tip set at 50% roundness creates a star that tips backward from the top. Additionally, several settings, such as the angle, rotation, roundness, or height can be changed by dragging in the visual setting box.

BTW

Brush Tips
A brush tip has specific characteristics such as size, shape, and hardness. When you use the Brush Tool, the tip creates the shape that paints in the document window.

BTW

Saving Brush Settings
If you change the size, shape, or hardness of a preset brush, the change is temporary; the next time you choose that brush, it reverts to its original settings. If you use a certain brush tip and characteristics often, you might use the New Brush preset command on the Brush panel menu, which saves your settings as a named brush tip.

The Spacing slider controls the **spacing** or distance between the brush marks in a stroke. The lower the percentage, the closer together the brush tips are within the stroke. For example, a snowflake brush tip set at 1% spacing would display a snowflake shape connected to another snowflake shape. Higher percentages — up to 1000% — space the brush tips farther apart as you drag. For example, a spacing value of 200% would create snowflakes all across the brush stroke with some space in between each one. When the Spacing check box is deselected, the speed at which you drag or paint determines the spacing.

Solid brush tips have a hardness setting that indicates the amount of anti-aliasing for the Brush Tool. **Hardness** is a percentage value indicating how solid the edge of the brush stoke appears.

To Display the Brush Panel

The following step displays the Brush panel.

1

• Click the Brush button on the vertical dock of collapsed panels to display the Brush panel (Figure 4–28).

Q&A

What is the best way to access the Brush panel?

The best way is the way that seems efficient or natural to you. If your mouse pointer happens to be near the menu, perhaps clicking Brush on the Window menu might be the best way. If you commonly use function keys, pressing the F5 key may seem most natural.

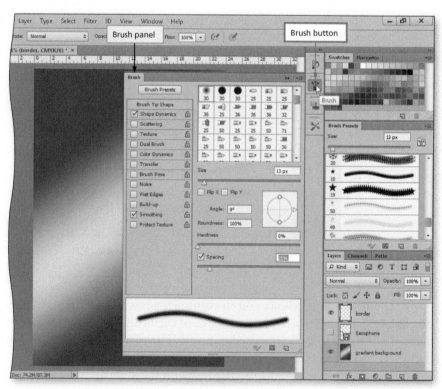

Figure 4–28

Other Ways

1. On Window menu, click Brush
2. Click Toggle the Brush panel button
3. Press F5

Brush Options

When you choose a Brush option, settings specific to that painting dynamic appear on the Brush panel. Table 4–4 displays some of the options not previously mentioned, along with their settings and descriptions.

Table 4–4 Brush Shape Options		
Option	**Setting**	**Description**
Shape Dynamics	Jitter	Specifies how the size, angle, or roundness of brush marks vary in a stroke
	Fade	Fades the size of brush marks between the initial diameter and the minimum diameter in the specified number of steps
	Pen Pressure, Pen Tilt, Stylus Wheel, Rotation	Available only with graphic tablets — varies the size of brush marks between the initial diameter and the minimum diameter based on the pen pressure, pen tilt, position of the pen thumbwheel, or rotation of the pen
Scattering	Scatter	Specifies how brush marks are distributed in a stroke — if the Both Axes check box is selected, brush marks are distributed in a radial direction; if the Both Axes check box is deselected, brush marks are distributed perpendicular to the stroke path
	Count	Specifies the number of brush marks applied at each spacing interval
Texture	Invert	Used for patterns — inverts the high and low points in the texture based on the tones in the pattern
	Scale	Specifies the scale of the pattern
	Depth	Specifies how deeply the paint penetrates into the texture
Dual Brush	Mode	Sets a blending mode to use when combining brush marks from the primary tip and the dual tip
Color Dynamics	Hue, Saturation, Brightness, Purity	Specifies a percentage by which the hue, saturation, or brightness of the paint can vary in a stroke
Transfer	Opacity Jitter and Control	Specifies how the opacity of paint varies in a brush stroke
	Flow Jitter and Control	Specifies how the flow of paint varies in a brush stroke
Noise		Adds additional randomness to individual brush tips
Wet Edges		Causes paint to build up along the edges of the brush stroke, creating a watercolor effect
Airbrush		Applies gradual tones to an image, simulating traditional airbrush techniques
Smoothing		Produces smoother curves in brush strokes
Protect Texture		Applies the same pattern and scale to all brush presets that have a texture

BTW

Brush Sets
Sometimes you might want a unique or distinctive brush that is not among the many brush tips available in Photoshop. In that case, you can purchase the design or create it from scratch. Brush tip files have the extension ABR and are available for purchase on the Web.

BTW

The Restore Sample Size Button
When selecting brush tip shapes on the Brush panel, if you change the diameter of a brush tip, Photoshop might display a Restore Sample Size button. The Restore Sample Size button allows you to reset the brush tip back to its default size.

To Select a Brush and Edit Settings

The following step uses the Brush Panel to select a brush and edit the settings.

1

- Scroll in the brush tip shapes as necessary and then click the Sampled Tip 21 brush.

- In the list of paint options, click the Wet Edges check box to emphasize the edges of the brush stroke, and, if necessary, click the Smoothing check box, to produce smoother brush strokes. Uncheck any other checked boxes.

- In the brush options area, drag the Size slider to 350 px, or select the text in the Size box and then type 350px to enter the brush size.

- Drag the Spacing slider to 20%, or select the text in the Spacing box and then type 20% to enter the brush size (Figure 4–29).

Q&A I cannot drag the Size and Spacing sliders to the exact brush sizes. Is there another way to size the brush?

You can select the text in the Size and Spacing boxes and then type the exact size.

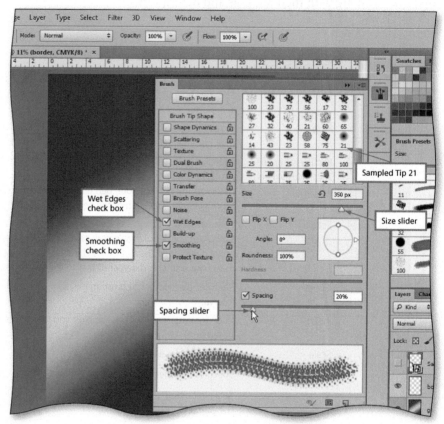

Figure 4–29

Experiment

- Drag the angle icon to rotate the preset and watch how the preview changes. When you are finished, type 0 in the Angle box.

Experiment

- One at a time, click each of the options on the left side of the panel and experiment with dragging the settings to watch how the preview changed. When you are finished, remove the check mark from each of the options except Wet Edges and Smoothing.

Other Ways

1. On Brush Presets panel, select brush tip and size

To Collapse the Brush Panel

The following step collapses the Brush panel.

1 Click the Brush button on the vertical dock of panels to collapse the Brush panel.

To Draw Straight Lines using the Brush Tool

The following steps use the Brush Tool to draw the border. Pressing and holding the SHIFT key with brush strokes creates straight lines. Alternatively, you can click to start a stroke and then SHIFT+click at the ending point, which connects the color in a straight line. If you create a brush stroke that is incorrect, press CTRL+Z and draw again. As you draw with the Brush Tool, the strokes appear with the chosen settings, and in the selected foreground color.

- With the border layer still selected, position the mouse pointer in the upper-left corner of the poster.

- SHIFT+drag to the lower-left corner of the poster to draw in a straight line down the left side (Figure 4–30).

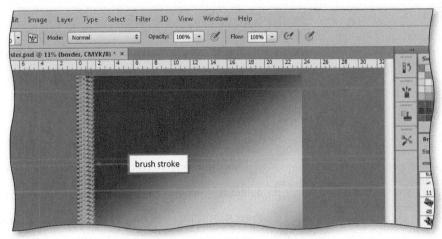

Figure 4–30

❷

- Move the mouse pointer to the lower-right corner of the poster, and SHIFT+click to create a straight line across the bottom (Figure 4–31).

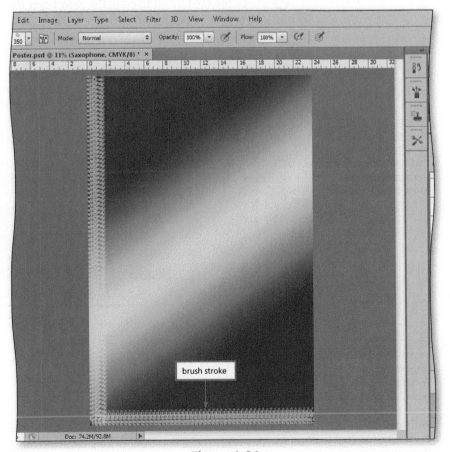

Figure 4–31

To Choose a Color for the Stars

The following step chooses white from the Swatches panel as the color for the stars that you will create later in the chapter.

1 On the Swatches panel, click White in the top row.

To Show the Saxophone Layer

The following step shows the Saxophone layer to help position the stars.

1 On the Layers panel, click the visibility icon beside the Saxophone layer to show the layer.

To Create Another Layer

The following steps create a new layer on which to draw the stars.

1 Select the Saxophone layer so that the new layer will appear above it.

2 Press SHIFT+CTRL+N to display the New Layer dialog box.

3 In the New Layer dialog box, type `stars` for the name. Click the Color box arrow, and then click Green to change the layer's identification color.

4 Click the OK button to close the New Layer dialog box, and display the new layer on the Layers panel (Figure 4–32).

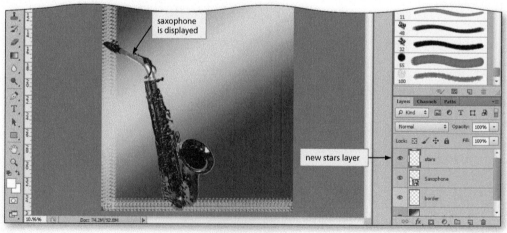

Figure 4–32

The Brush Presets Panel

The Brush Presets panel, which automatically is displayed when using the Painting workspace, allows you quickly to choose a brush and size, without covering any of your workspace (Figure 4–33). These brushes also appear when you click the Brush Preset picker on the options bar. Buttons on the panel help you set the size of the brush, create new brushes, and other functions. In addition to the basic brush tips, Photoshop has 15 other libraries of brush tips that you can append to the panel using the Brush Presets panel menu.

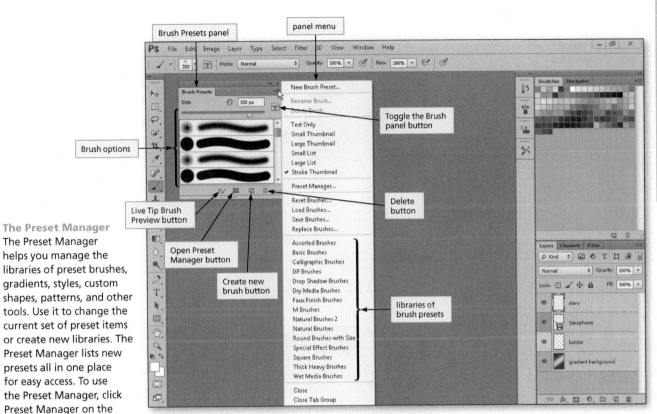

BTW

The Preset Manager
The Preset Manager helps you manage the libraries of preset brushes, gradients, styles, custom shapes, patterns, and other tools. Use it to change the current set of preset items or create new libraries. The Preset Manager lists new presets all in one place for easy access. To use the Preset Manager, click Preset Manager on the Edit menu.

Figure 4–33

To Append a Brush Library

The following steps append a library to the Brush panel.

1

- Click the Brush Presets panel menu button to display its menu (Figure 4–34).

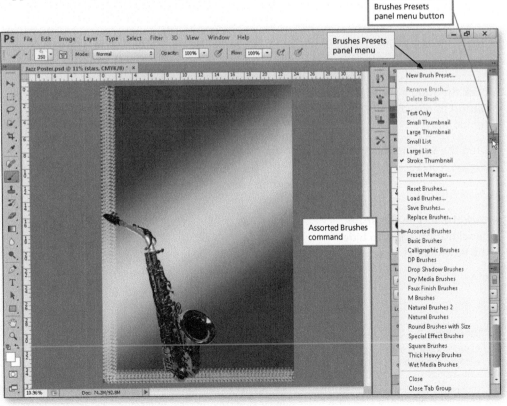

Figure 4–34

2

- Click Assorted Brushes to choose the library and to start the append process (Figure 4–35).

3

- Click the Append button to append the brushes to the panel list.

Figure 4–35

To Select a Brush using the Brush Presets Panel

The following steps select a brush from the Brush Presets panel.

1

- On the Brush Presets panel, scroll down as necessary to the appended brushes, and then select the Star – Large 19 preset.

- Drag the size slider to approximately 200 (Figure 4–36).

Q&A

What is the main difference between the Brush panel and the Brush presets panel?

The Brush panel provides more paint and brush options. The Brush Presets panel is used when you want to choose a brush and size quickly.

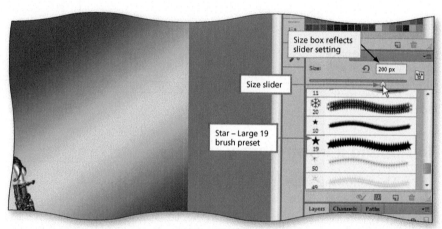

Figure 4–36

2

- Click the Toggle the Brush panel button to display the Brush panel temporarily.

- Drag the Spacing slider to 150% (Figure 4–37).

3

- Click the Toggle the Brush panel button again to hide the Brush panel.

Other Ways

1. Right-click document window, choose brush, edit settings

2. On options bar, click Brush Preset picker button, choose brush, edit settings

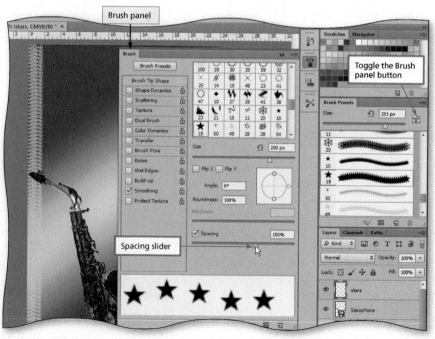

Figure 4–37

To Draw Freehand using the Brush Tool

You will use the Brush Tool to draw stars coming out of the saxophone bell in a freehand style. Remember that if you make a mistake while creating the brush strokes, press CTRL+Z to undo, then begin again.

● With the stars layer still selected, drag in a sweeping motion from the bell of the saxophone, up and to the left as shown in Figure 4–38.

Q&A

If I wanted to change the size of the star, is there an easy way?

Yes. As you did with the Eraser Tool, press the LEFT BRACKET ([) key to reduce the size of the brush. Press the RIGHT BRACKET (]) key to enlarge the size of the brush.

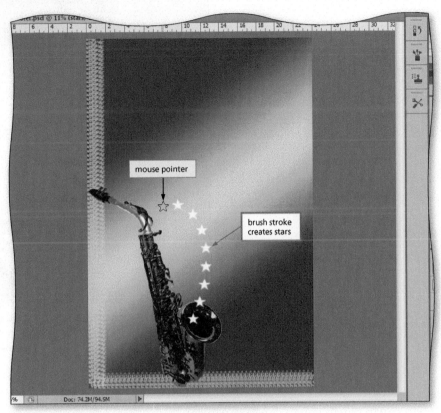

Figure 4–38

● Create a second stroke, up from the bell of the saxophone, to the right at approximately a 45-degree angle. The stroke should not be a perfectly straight line (Figure 4–39).

Experiment

● On the options bar, click the 'Enable airbrush-style build-up effects' button on the options bar. In a remote place on the document window, press and hold the mouse button for several seconds to build up ink. Experiment with drawing a stroke. When you are finished, press CTRL+Z to undo the stroke. Click the 'Enable airbrush-style build-up effects' button again to turn it off.

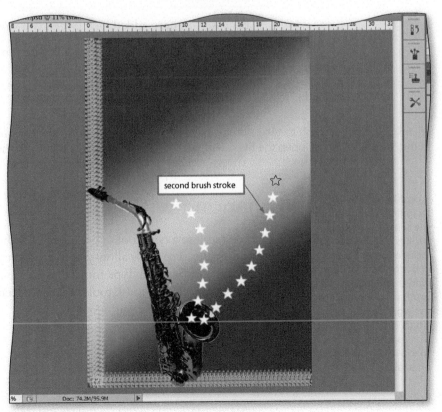

Figure 4–39

● Create a third stroke, from the bell of the saxophone, up and curved to the right as shown in Figure 4–40.

Figure 4–40

To Save the File

Because you have added new layers, you should save the file again.

❶ Press CTRL+S to save the Jazz Poster file with the same name.

Break Point: If you wish to take a break, this is a good place to do so. You can quit Photoshop now. To resume at a later time, start Photoshop, open the file called Jazz Poster, and continue following the steps from this location forward.

BTW

Graphics Tablet
Dragging, without using the SHIFT key, creates strokes of color that may include corners, curves, and arcs. Graphic designers who create many freehand brush strokes sometimes use a graphics tablet, which is an input device that uses a stylus, or specialized mouse, to draw on a tablet surface.

Enhancing with Text

The next steps use a type tool to create text for the poster. Recall from Chapter 1 that Photoshop's four type tools allow you to create text in different ways. When you use the Horizontal or Vertical Type tools, Photoshop automatically creates a new layer in the Layers panel. The mask tools create a selection in the shape of the text on the current layer rather than creating a new one.

**Plan
Ahead**

Apply effective text styles and strokes.
A font or typeface defines the appearance and shape of the letters, numbers, and special characters used in text. The fonts you use create the look, feel, and style of your graphic publications.

- For a more historical, retro, formal, or literary look and feel, use a serif font. Serif means flourish, and indicates that the letters will contain small intersecting lines, sometimes called appendages, at the end of characters.

- For a more modern feel, use sans serif, which means without flourish, and displays in block-like letters without appendages.

- If you use more than one font family, choose contrasting fonts. Fonts that are too similar appear to be design errors.

- If you use different sizes of the same font family, choose sizes that deliberately are different — not close in size. Do not use more than three sizes of the same font on the same page.

- Use strokes or outlines around the lettering when the text has high priority in the graphic, and you want a distinctive look. White strokes make dark text stand out; conversely, black strokes around light-colored text help delineate the text and make it stand out.

To Create Horizontal Guides

The following steps create guides from the horizontal ruler to help place and draw text on the poster. As you drag to create a guide, watch the vertical ruler, which displays numbers for every two inches and large tick marks every one inch. The guide will appear as a dotted line over the tick marks on the vertical ruler.

1 Drag from the horizontal ruler down to approximately the 15-inch mark on the vertical ruler to create a guide at 15 inches.

2 Repeat the process to create four more guides at approximately 10, 5.5, 3, and 1 inches (Figure 4–41).

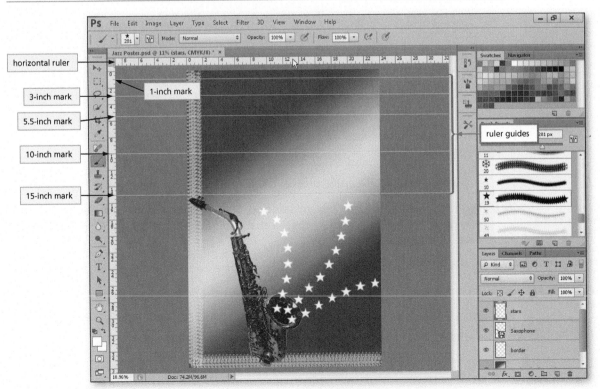

Figure 4–41

To Select the Horizontal Type Tool and Set Font Options

The following steps select font settings on the options bar.

1 On the Tools panel, select the Horizontal Type Tool.

2 On the options bar, click the 'Set the font family' box arrow to display the list of font families. Scroll as necessary, and then click Myriad Pro or a similar font in the list.

3 Select the text in the 'Set the font size' box and then type 175 to replace it.

4 Click the 'Set the anti-aliasing method' button, and then choose Sharp in the list.

5 Click the Center text button (Figure 4–42).

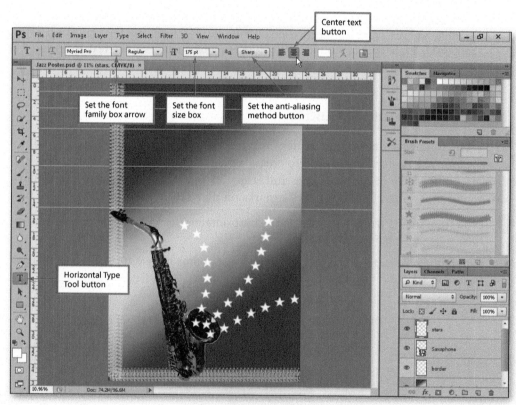

Figure 4–42

To Insert Text

The following steps enter text on the poster.

1 With the Horizontal Type Tool still selected, drag a bounding box between the upper two guides — at 1 inch and 3 inches — that extends from the left edge to the right edge of the poster.

2 In the bounding box, type The stars come out and then press the ENTER key.

3 Click the 'Commit any current edits' button on the options bar to accept the text.

4 Drag a bounding box between the upper two guides — at 3 inches and 5.5 inches — that extends from the left edge to the right edge of the poster.

Adjusting Text
To adjust the size of the text bounding box, drag the sizing handles. Later, if you need to edit the text, you select the layer and select the Type Tool. The mouse pointer then becomes a cursor when positioned over the text.

5   Type at the to complete the second line.

6   Click the 'Commit any current edits' button on the options bar to accept the text.

7   To set the identification color of the new text layers, one at a time, right-click the text layer on the Layers panel, and then click Orange on the context menu (Figure 4–43).

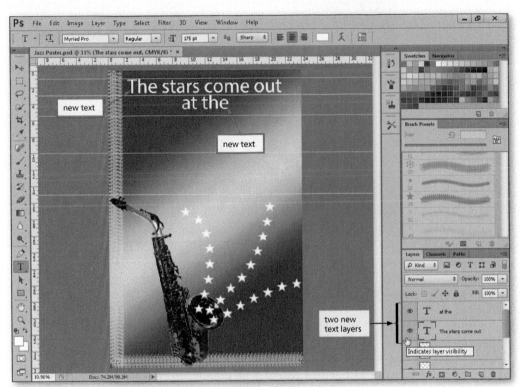

Figure 4–43

To Insert More Text

The following steps create more text for the poster.

1   With the Horizontal Type Tool still selected, change the font size to 110 on the options bar.

2   Drag a bounding box, approximately 10 inches wide and 7 inches tall in the lower-right corner of the poster as shown in Figure 4–44 on the next page.

3   In the bounding box, type Fridays & and then press the ENTER key.

4   Type Saturdays and then press the ENTER key.

5   Type 8:00 pm to complete the third line (Figure 4–44).

6   Click the 'Commit any current edits' button on the options bar to accept the text.

7   Set the identification color of the new layer to Orange.

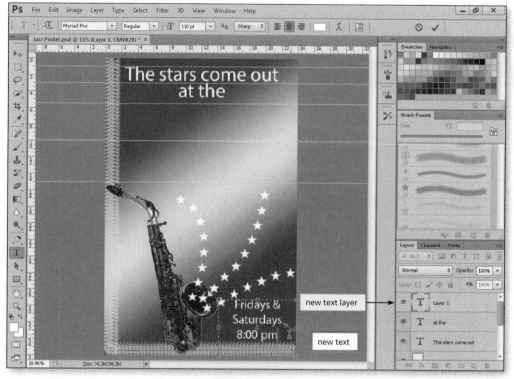

Figure 4–44

BTW

Quick Reference
For a table that lists how to complete the tasks covered in this book using the mouse, context menu, and keyboard, see the Quick Reference Summary at the back of this book.

Character and Paragraph Styles

Photoshop CS6 has two new panels, the Character Styles panel and the Paragraph Styles panel (Figure 4–45), to help you save text styles for future use. Using the Character Styles panel, you can create and apply character styles, which are sets of specific characteristics with which you may be familiar from word processing — features such as font, font size, bold, italic, underline, color, and case. You can name the style and apply it as needed as you work with text. The Paragraph Styles panel includes all of the character style settings plus indentures, vertical spacing, baseline shift, and other settings affecting paragraphs only. Buttons on each panel's status bar help you set advanced text features, such as fractions, ligatures, kerning, and tracking, that you will learn about in future chapters, and apply the changes to the current style shown on the options bar. Once you name and store the style, it is easy to reuse whenever you need it.

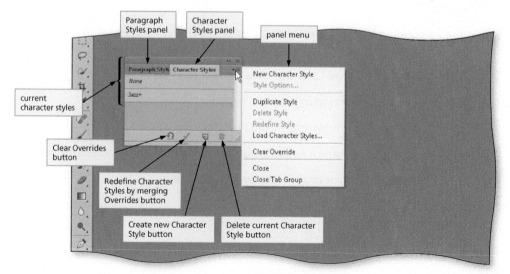

Figure 4–45

As you create a character style, you will select a font color for the character style, ensuring that the color stays with the style and overrides any settings on any of the other panels or the options bar. When you want to identify or edit a color, Photoshop displays a Color Picker dialog box as shown in Figure 4–46. The Color Picker dialog box, also generically called the Color Picker, includes a clickable color field and color bar. Text boxes allow you to identify color model numbers. In addition, the Color Picker displays the original color and a preview of any change. Color Pickers appear when you click a Color box on any panel or options bar, or when you click a Color Stop button.

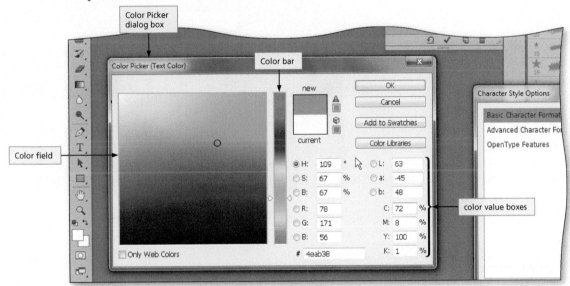

Figure 4–46

To Create a Character Style

The following steps create a character style named Jazz for use in two different text boxes on the poster.

1

- Click Window on the Application bar, and then click Character Styles to display the Character Styles panel (Figure 4–47).

Is the Character Styles panel a part of any named workspace?

Yes. As you will learn in a future chapter, the Typography workspace automatically shows many panels having to do with text.

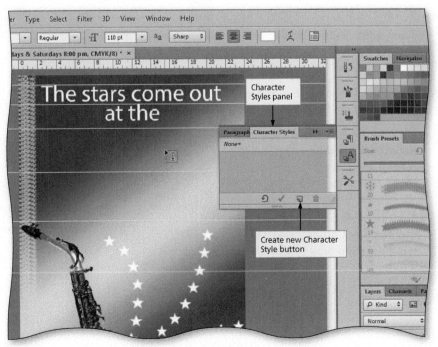

Figure 4–47

• Click the Create new Character Style button on the Character Styles panel status bar to add a new character style to the panel (Figure 4–48).

Figure 4–48

• Double-click the new style, Character Style 1, to display the Character Style Options dialog box.

• Select the text in the Style Name text box, and then type Jazz to rename the new style.

• Click the Font Family box arrow, and then click Lucida Handwriting or a similar font in the list.

• Type 300 in the 'Set the font size' box to choose a large font size.

• Click the Case box arrow, and then click All Caps in the List.

• Click the Faux Bold and Faux Italic check boxes to select them (Figure 4–49).

Experiment

• Point to other boxes to view their tool tips. Click other formats in the left navigation area to view the options.

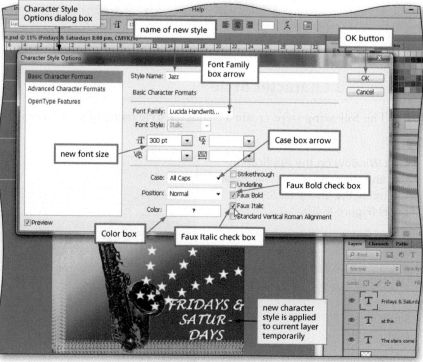

Figure 4–49

4

- Click the Color box to display the Color Picker (Text Color) dialog box.

- In the Color field, click a white color in the upper-left corner (Figure 4–50).

Q&A

Why did Photoshop display a question mark in the Color box?

The question mark is a reminder that you need to verify or set the color in order for the character style to override settings on the options bar — especially if you use the character style at other times and locations; that way, it will also be a pure white.

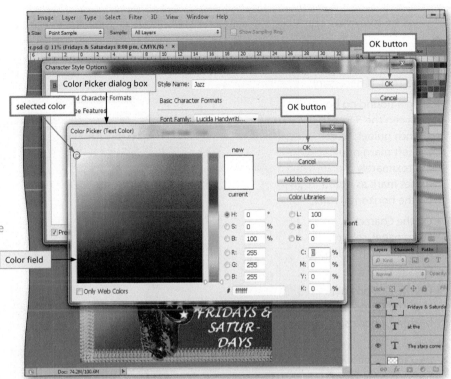

Figure 4–50

5

- Click the OK button in the Color Picker (Text Color) dialog box to finish choosing the color.

- Click the OK button in the Character Style Options dialog box to save the settings.

- Because the new style is applied to the current layer, click None on the Character Styles panel to remove the new style from the Fridays & Saturdays layer (Figure 4–51).

Figure 4–51

To Use a Style

The following steps use the character style, Jazz, as you create more text boxes on the poster.

1

- Select the Horizontal Type Tool, if necessary.

- Drag a bounding box between the 5.5- and 10-inch guides, from the left margin to approximately the 20 inches mark as noted on the horizontal ruler.

- On the Character Styles panel, select Jazz, and then collapse the panel.

- On the options bar click the Center text button, if necessary.

- Type J ZZ with two spaces between the J and the first Z (Figure 4–52).

Q&A

My text is different. Did I do something wrong?

Your settings may differ. Press CTRL+Z to undo the text. Change the font size to 300, if necessary. Click the Color box on the options bar and choose white. Then, retype the letters.

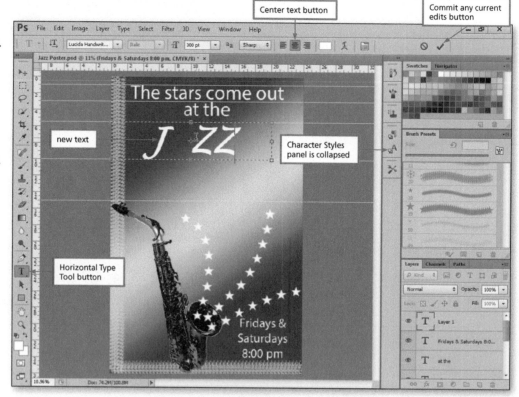

Figure 4–52

2

- Click the 'Commit any current edits' button on the options bar to accept the text.

- Drag a second bounding box between the 10- and 15-inch guides, from the left margin to approximately the 23-inch mark as noted on the horizontal ruler.

- On the options bar click the 'Right align text' button.

- Type C FE with two spaces between the C and the F (Figure 4–53).

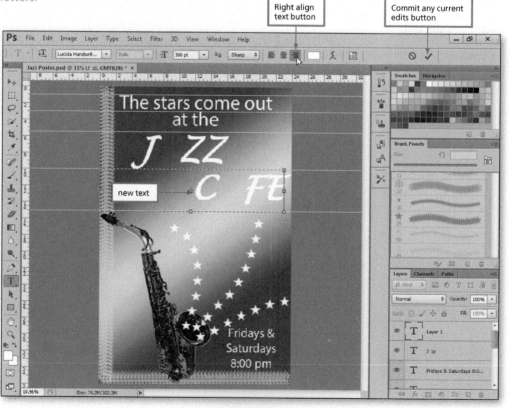

Figure 4–53

❸

- Click the 'Commit any current edits' button on the options bar to accept the text.

- Set the identification color of the new text layers to Orange.

To Create a Stroke Layer

Recall that you used layer styles to stroke text in Chapter 1. You also stroked a border using the Edit menu. By using the **Stroke layer style**, you can keep the stroke separate from the rest of the layer, which allows you to copy, remove, or change the stroke. The following steps create a stroke layer on the first poster text box.

❶ On the Layers panel, select the, The stars come out, text layer.

❷ Click the 'Add a layer style' button on the Layers panel status bar to display the list of layer styles, and then click Stroke to display the Layer Style dialog box.

❸ Drag the 'Set width of stroke' slider to 10 pixels to increase the size of the stroke (Figure 4–54).

❹ Click the OK button to apply the stroke.

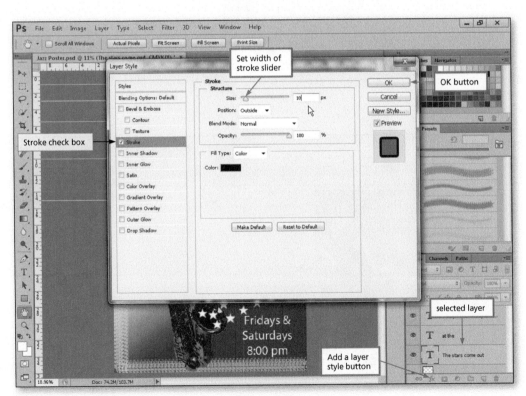

Figure 4–54

To Copy a Layer Style

If you have a layer style, such as a stroke that you want to repeat on another layer, you can copy the style rather than go into the Layer Style dialog box again. The following steps copy the stroke layer style to the other text layers.

- On the Layers panel, right-click the text layer, The stars come out, to display the context menu (Figure 4–55).

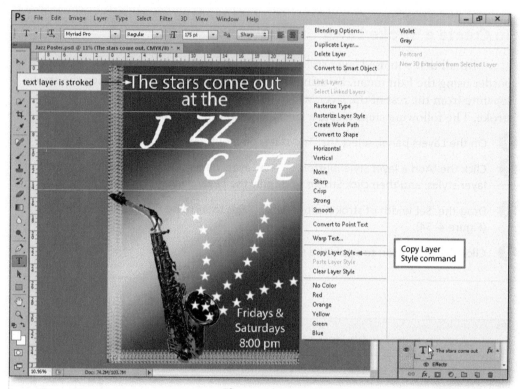

Figure 4–55

- Click Copy Layer Style on the context menu to copy the style to the Clipboard.

- Right-click the, at the, text layer to display the context menu (Figure 4–56).

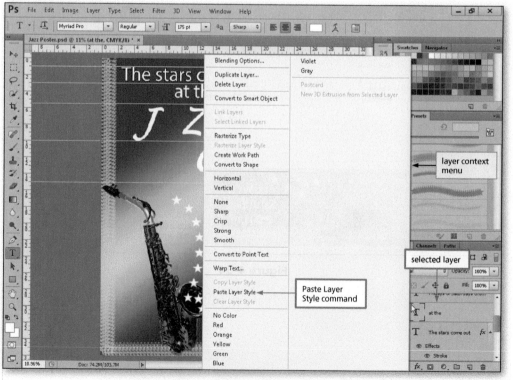

Figure 4–56

3

- Click Paste Layer Style on the context menu to paste the layer style (Figure 4–57).

Figure 4–57

4

- Repeat the paste process for the other three text layers.

- Collapse the Character Styles panel (Figure 4–58).

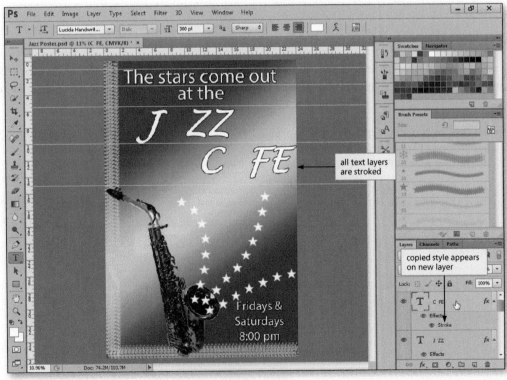

Figure 4–58

Other Ways

1. On Layer menu, point to Layer Style, click Copy Layer Style or Paste Layer Style

BTW

Color Sampler Tool
If you right-click the Eyedropper Tool button on the Tools panel, you can choose the Color Sampler tool from the context menu. Clicking with the Color Sampler tool displays the color mode values in the Info panel. You can click to select up to four color samples per image.

Sampling Colors

The Eyedropper Tool samples an existing color in a graphic or panel to assign a new foreground or background color. When you click a color using the Eyedropper Tool, Photoshop sets a new foreground color on the Tools panel and Color panel. When you ALT+click a color, Photoshop sets a new background color.

The Eyedropper options bar (Figure 4–59) allows you to change the sample size and create a color sample from the active image or from anywhere else in the Photoshop window. The Sample Size box list contains several choices. The default size, Point Sample, samples the precise color of the pixel you click. The other sample sizes, such as 3 by 3 Average and 5 by 5 Average, sample the color of the pixel, where you click along with the surrounding pixels, and then calculate an average color value of the area.

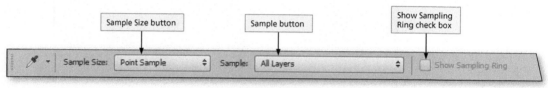

Figure 4–59

Sampling a color ensures that you will match the color without having to enter color values or make selections in other dialog boxes or panels.

Other tools grouped with the Eyedropper Tool are the 3D Material Eyedropper Tool, the Color Sampler Tool, the Ruler Tool, the Note Tool, and the Count Tool. You will learn more about these tools in later chapters.

To Use the Eyedropper Tool

The following steps select the Eyedropper Tool and then sample the blue color from the gradient shape for use in an upcoming shape. Using a color from the gradient maintains color consistency in all parts of the poster.

1

• On the Tools panel, right-click the Eyedropper Tool button to display its context menu (Figure 4–60).

Q&A

What is the difference between the Eyedropper Tool and the Color Sampler Tool?

The Eyedropper tool picks up the color and displays it at the bottom of the Tools panel. The Color Sampler Tool only displays information about the color in an Info panel.

Figure 4–60

2

• Click Eyedropper Tool to select it.

• Move the mouse pointer into the document window and then click the dark blue color in the gradient to set a new foreground color (Figure 4–61).

Q&A

Why did my Eyedropper tool set the background color instead of the foreground color?

It may be that someone has reversed your foreground and background colors. To fix the problem, press the F6 key to display the Color panel and then click the 'Set foreground color' button, which appears as a square color swatch on the left side of the panel.

Figure 4–61

Other Ways

1. Press I, click color

Shapes

One of the more creative uses for Photoshop is drawing shapes. A **shape** is a specific figure or form that can be drawn or inserted into an image. A shape is usually a **vector object** or **vector shape**, which means it does not lose its sharp lines or anti-aliasing if it is resized or reshaped. A vector object is made up of lines and curves defined by mathematical vectors or formulas. Photoshop provides five standard shapes, a variety of custom shapes, and the ability to create new shapes using a path. A path is a special kind of vector shape that you will learn about in a later chapter.

Plan Ahead

Use predefined shapes for tangible objects.
If your goal is to create a graphic that the viewer will recognize right away, start with a predefined shape. This approach is a necessity if you do not have a drawing tablet or if your artistic skills are limited. Shapes allow you to maintain straight lines, even corners, constrained proportions, and consistent curves. To create unique graphics, shapes can be scaled, distorted, skewed, warped, shadowed, and combined in many ways. Using shapes does not limit your creativity, however. Try experimenting with combinations and transformations of shapes to create graphics with perspective, horizon lines, and alignment.

The Shape Tool options bar (Figure 4–62) contains buttons to choose shapes; to add, subtract, and intersect shapes; and to choose shape styles, modes, and colors. If you select a custom shape, the options bar displays a Shape box, allowing you to choose from a panel of customized shapes and append new libraries of shapes. Besides the traditional shapes of lines, rectangles, and an ellipse, you can create freeform shapes, equilateral polygons, rounded rectangles, and custom shapes.

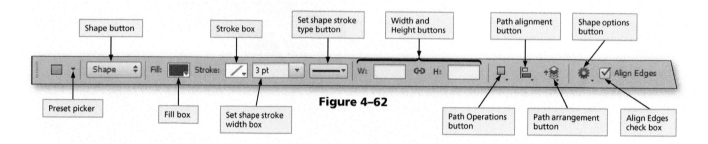

Figure 4–62

The Shape Button
In Photoshop CS6, the Shape button has a menu that replaces the previous Shape, Path, and Pixels buttons.

Table 4–5 explains the process for creating some common shapes that are not immediately available on the Tools panel; however, the kinds of shapes you can create by combining settings is almost endless.

Table 4–5 How to Create Common Shapes	
Shape	**Directions**
Circle	Use the Oval Tool and SHIFT+drag in the document window to create a circle.
Diamond	Use the Polygon tool and enter 4 in the Sides box on the options bar. Drag straight down in the document window.
Heart	Use the Custom Shape tool and choose a heart using the Custom Shape picker.
Parallelogram	Use the Rectangle Tool and drag in the document window to create a rectangle. Press CTRL+T to access transformations. Right-click the rectangle and then click Perspective on the context menu. Drag the upper-middle sizing handle to the right or left.
Right Triangle	Use the Rectangle tool and SHIFT+drag in the document window to create a square. Select the Delete Anchor Point Tool on the Tools panel, and then click on a corner of the square.
Square	Use the Rectangle Tool and SHIFT+drag in the document window to create a square.
Star	Use the Polygon Tool and enter the desired number of points on the star in the Sides box on the options bar. Click the Geometry options button on the options bar, and then click Stars.
Triangle	Use the Polygon Tool and enter 3 in the Sides box on the options bar.

Shape Layers
When you choose Shape on the Shape button menu, Photoshop creates a shape layer. A **shape layer** is a vector object that occupies its own layer. Because shape layers are moved, resized, aligned, and distributed easily, they are useful for creating Web graphics. You can draw multiple shapes on a single layer.

On each of the shape options bar, a special Geometry options button displays context sensitive settings for each of the shapes. Table 4–6 displays the geometry options, the shape or shapes with which they are associated, and a description of their functions.

Table 4–6 Geometry Options for Shapes

Options	Applicable Shape(s)	Description
Arrowheads, Width, Length, Concavity	Line	Adds arrowheads to a line, specifies the proportions of the arrowhead as a percentage of the line width, specifies concavity value defining the amount of curvature on the widest part of the arrowhead
Circle	Ellipse	Constrains to a circle
Curve Fit	Freeform Pen	Controls how sensitive the final path is to the movement of the mouse or stylus based on a value between 0.5 and 10.0 pixels — a higher value creates a simpler path with fewer anchor points
Proportional or Defined Proportions	Rectangle, Rounded Rectangle, Ellipse, Custom Shape	Renders proportional shape based on the values you enter in the W (width) and H (height) boxes
Defined Size	Custom Shape	Renders a custom shape based on the size specifications
Fixed Size	Rectangle, Rounded Rectangle, Ellipse, Custom Shape	Renders a fixed size based on the values you enter in the W (width) and H (height) text boxes
From Center	Rectangle, Rounded Rectangle, Ellipse Custom Shape	Renders the shape from the center
Magnetic	Freeform Pen	Draws a path that snaps to the edges of defined areas, allowing the user to define the range and sensitivity of the snapping behavior, as well as the complexity of the resulting path
Pen Pressure	Freeform Pen	When working with a stylus tablet, an increase in pen pressure causes the width to decrease
Radius	Rounded Rectangle, Polygon	For rounded rectangles, specifies the corner radius; for polygons, specifies the distance from the center of a polygon to the outer points
Rubber Band	Pen	Previews path segments as you draw
Sides	Polygon	Specifies the number of sides in a polygon
Smooth Corners or Smooth Indents	Polygon	Renders the shape with smooth corners or indents
Snap to Pixels	Rectangle, Rounded Rectangle	Snaps edges of a rectangle or rounded rectangle to the pixel boundaries
Square	Rectangle, Rounded Rectangle	Constrains to a square
Star	Polygon	Creates a star from the specified radius — a 50% setting creates points that are half the total radius of the star; a larger value creates sharper, thinner points; a smaller value creates fuller points
Unconstrained	Rectangle, Rounded Rectangle, Ellipse, Custom Shape	Does not constrain shapes

BTW

Resizing Shapes
To resize a shape, press CTRL+T to display the shape's bounding box. Resize the shape by dragging the sizing handles, then press the ENTER key.

To Choose the Custom Shape Tool

The following steps select the Custom Shape Tool.

1
- Right-click the Shape Tool on the Tools panel to display its context menu (Figure 4–63).

Figure 4–63

2
- Click Custom Shape Tool to select the tool and to display the Shape Tools options bar (Figure 4–64).

Figure 4–64

Other Ways

1. Press SHIFT+U until Custom Shape appears on Tools panel

To Append Shape Presets

The following steps append a new library of custom shapes to the Custom Shape Tool options bar.

1

- Click the Shape box to display its list.

- Click the list's menu button to display the choices (Figure 4–65).

Q&A Should I click the Shape box or the Shape box arrow?

You can click either one.

Q&A What is the panel that appears when I click the Shape box?

On some options bars, clicking a button will cause a pop-up panel to appear, similar to the one in Figure 4–65. These pop-up panels may contain buttons, boxes, sliders, lists, and a menu button for more choices.

Figure 4–65

2

- Click Music in the list to choose the library of preset shapes (Figure 4–66).

3

- Click the Append button to append the shapes.

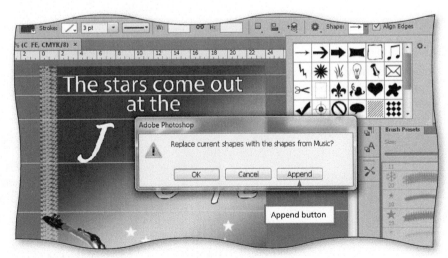

Figure 4–66

Other Ways

1. Point to Presets on Edit menu, click Preset Manager, press CTRL+7, click menu button, choose library

To Create a Shape

The following steps draw an eighth note on the poster.

1

- If necessary, scroll down in the list of custom shapes to display the appended shapes.

- Click the Eighth Note shape to select it (Figure 4–67).

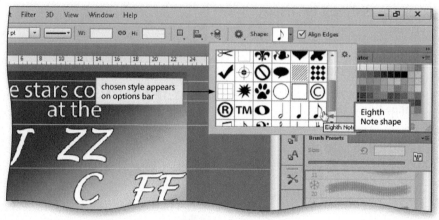

Figure 4–67

2

- On the options bar, click the Stroke box to display its choices.

- Click the Gradient button and then click the Black, White gradient to choose a gradient, black and white stroke (Figure 4–68).

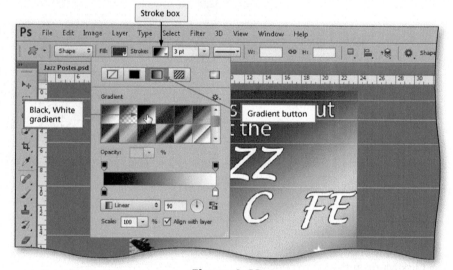

Figure 4–68

3

- On the options bar, select the value in the 'Set shape stroke width' box and then type 20 pt to set the stroke width (Figure 4–69).

Figure 4–69

4

- In the document window, drag to create a large eighth note, approximately 11 inches tall and 6 inches wide.

- Select the Move Tool and move the shape to a location to fill in the A of the word, Jazz (Figure 4–70).

Q&A

My eighth note does not show the blue fill. Did I do something wrong?

It may be that your monitor is set to a different resolution. With the eighth note layer still selected, click the 'Set shape stroke width' box arrow. Drag the slider in small increments to the left until your fill is blue.

Figure 4–70

To Set Layer Properties

The following steps name the shape layer and set its identification color.

1 Double-click the name, Shape 1, in the Layers panel. Type `eighth note` to replace the name and press the ENTER key.

2 Right-click the visibility icon, and then click Violet in the list to change the layer's identification color.

To Duplicate a Shape Layer

The steps on the next page duplicate the eighth note layer, adding a new graphical element to the poster.

1

- Right-click the eighth note layer on the Layers panel to display the context menu (Figure 4–71).

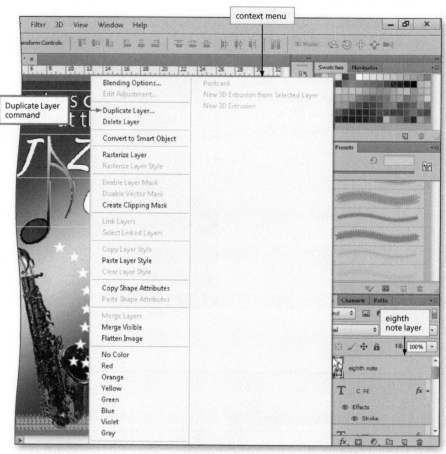

Figure 4–71

2

- Click Duplicate Layer to display the Duplicate Layer dialog box (Figure 4–72).

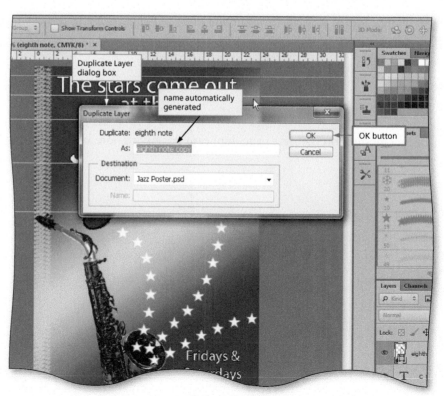

Figure 4–72

3

- Click the OK button to name the new layer with the default name.

- Select the Move Tool and move the second eight note to fill in the A of the word, Cafe (Figure 4–73).

Figure 4–73

To Hide Guides

The following step hides the guides for a better view of the poster.

1 Click View on the Application bar, point to Show, and then click Guides to hide the guides (Figure 4–74).

Figure 4–74

To Save the File

The poster is complete. You will save the file once again before flattening the layers.

1 Press SHIFT+S and save the file with the same name.

To Flatten and Save the File

The following steps flatten the image and save it as a TIFF file.

1 On the Layer menu, click the Flatten Image command.

2 Press SHIFT+CTRL+S and save the file with the name, Jazz Poster for Printing, in the TIFF format. When Photoshop displays the TIFF Options dialog box, click the OK button to finish saving the file.

To Print the Poster

1 Prepare the printer according to the printer instructions.

2 Click File on the Application bar, and then click Print to display the Print dialog box.

3 If necessary, click the Printer box arrow and then select your printer from the list. Scroll as necessary to check the 'Scale to Fit Media' check box (Figure 4–75).

4 In the Print dialog box, click the Print button to start the printing process. If your system displays a second Print dialog box or a Print Settings dialog box, unique to your printer, click its Print button.

5 When the printer stops, retrieve the hard copy of the poster.

Figure 4–75

BTW

Photoshop Help
The best way to become familiar with Photoshop Help is to use it. Appendix D includes detailed information about Photoshop Help and exercises that will help you gain confidence in using it.

To Close the Document Window and Quit Photoshop

The final step is to close the document window and quit Photoshop.

1 Press CTRL+Q to close the document window and quit Photoshop.

Chapter Summary

You used many tools and panels in the Painting workspace as you created the poster in this chapter. You started a new file from scratch and used the Gradient Tool to create a colorful backdrop. You placed a graphic and selected a brush to create a border. You chose a color using the Swatches panel. You then appended a brush library and used a different brush tip to draw stars. You created a character style and many text boxes. After using the Eyedropper Tool to select a color, you created a custom shape of an eighth note with a stroke and duplicated it on the poster. Finally, you flattened the image and saved the file.

The items listed below include all the new Photoshop skills you have learned in this chapter:

1. Select the Painting Workspace (PS 214)
2. Start a New Photoshop File (PS 216)
3. Select the Gradient Tool and Style (PS 220)
4. Edit the Gradient (PS 222)
5. Edit Gradient Colors (PS 224)
6. Draw the Gradient (PS 224)
7. Create a Smart Object using the Place Command (PS 227)
8. Transform the Smart Object (PS 228)
9. Choose a Color on the Swatches Panel (PS 230)
10. Select the Brush Tool (PS 232)
11. Display the Brush Panel (PS 234)
12. Select a Brush and Edit Settings (PS 236)
13. Draw Straight Lines using the Brush Tool (PS 237)
14. Append a Brush Library (PS 239)
15. Select a Brush using the Brush Presets Panel (PS 240)
16. Draw Freehand using the Brush Tool (PS 241)
17. Create a Character Style (PS 247)
18. Use a Style (PS 250)
19. Copy a Layer Style (PS 252)
20. Use the Eyedropper Tool (PS 254)
21. Choose the Custom Shape Tool (PS 258)
22. Append Shape Presets (PS 259)
23. Create a Shape (PS 260)
24. Duplicate a Shape Layer (PS 261)

Apply Your Knowledge

Reinforce the skills and apply the concepts you learned in this chapter.

Creating a Book Cover

Instructions: Start Photoshop and perform the customization steps found on pages PS 6 through PS 10. Open the Apply 4-1 Book Cover file from the Chapter 04 folder of the Data Files for Students. Visit www.cengage.com/ct/studentdownload for detailed instructions or contact your instructor for information about accessing the required files.

The purpose of this exercise is to create a composite photo by adding a gradient and custom shape to create a graphic similar to the one shown in Figure 4–76 on the next page.

Perform the following tasks:

1. Use the Save As command to save the image on your USB flash drive as a PSD file, with the file name Apply 4-1 Book Cover Edited. Hide the text layers.

2. Select the Gradient Tool. On the options bar, click the Gradient Editor box. Double-click the left Color Stop button to display the 'Select stop color' dialog box. Click a yellow color on the color bar and then on the color field. Repeat the process to select a light orange color for the right Color Stop. If other Color Stop buttons appear, click them, and then click the Delete button in the Gradient Editor dialog box. When you are finished, click the OK button.

Continued >

Apply Your Knowledge *continued*

Figure 4–76

3. Drag from the upper-left to the lower-right to create the gradient.

4. Use the Place command to place the image named Apply 4-1 Rose, located in the Chapter 04 folder of the Data Files for Students. Resize the placed object to match Figure 4–76.

5. Use the Magic Eraser Tool to erase the black background from the rose layer. If Photoshop displays a Rasterize dialog box, click the OK button.

6. On the Tools panel, right-click the current shape tool, and then click Custom Shape Tool. On the options bar, click the Shape box. When the pop-up panel appears, click the menu button. Click Nature in the list. Append the shapes. Scroll as necessary, and then click the Raindrop shape.

7. On the Tools panel, click the 'Set foreground color' button to access the Color Picker (Foreground Color) dialog box. Click in the color slider to choose blue, and then click a light blue in the color field. Click the OK button.

8. Drag in the document window several times, with varying lengths, to create the raindrops similar to those shown in Figure 4–76. Each raindrop will create its own layer.

9. Click the visibility icon next to both text layers.

10. Save the file again, and then flatten the image.

11. Save the flattened file with the name Apply 4-1 Book Cover Complete in the TIFF format. Submit the file in the format specified by your instructor.

Extend Your Knowledge

Extend the skills you learned in this chapter and experiment with new skills. You may need to use Help to complete the assignment.

Creating a Promotional Movie Poster

Instructions: Start Photoshop and perform the customization steps found on pages PS 6 through PS 10. Open the Extend 4-1 Movie Poster file from the Chapter 04 folder of the Data Files for Students. Visit www.cengage.com/ct/studentdownload for detailed instructions or contact your instructor for information about accessing the required files. The purpose of this exercise is to create a composite photo with various components, similar to Figure 4–77, and to create both a PSD and TIFF version of the final composition.

Figure 4–77

Perform the following tasks:

1. Save the image on your USB flash drive as a PSD file, with the file name Extend 4-1 Movie Poster Edited.

2. Create a gradient at the top of the photo:

   a. Create a new layer named, sky.

   b. With the new layer selected, use the Rectangular Marquee Tool to create a selection that includes the top half of the canvas, down to the horizon line in the photo.

Continued >

c. Select the Gradient Tool and its Linear Gradient style. Click the Gradient Editor box to display the Gradient Editor dialog box. Click the left stop button and sample a dark blue in the photo. Click the right stop button and sample a light blue from the photo. (*Hint:* You might have to drag the dialog boxes out of the way to sample the colors.) Close the Gradient Editor dialog box.

d. SHIFT+drag from the top of the selection to the bottom of the section to create a linear gradient.

3. Create a gradient at the bottom of the photo:

a. Create a new layer and name it footer.

b. With the new layer selected, use the Rectangular Marquee Tool to create a selection that includes the bottom two inches of the photo.

c. Select the Gradient Tool and its Linear Gradient style. Click the Gradient Editor box to display the Gradient Editor. Choose the second preset, named Foreground to Transparent. Close the Gradient Editor dialog box.

d. SHIFT+drag from the bottom of the selection to the top of the section to create a linear gradient.

4. Insert the placeholder text:

a. Open the Extend 4-1 Movie Text file and arrange the two document windows side by side.

b. Use the Move Tool to drag the text into the Extend 4-1 Movie Poster Edited file and position it in the lower part of the photo, as shown in Figure 4–77 on the previous page.

c. Close the Extend 4-1 Movie Text file.

5. Insert the movie rating text:

a. Open the Extend 4-1 Movie Rating file and arrange the two document windows side by side.

b. Use the Move Tool to drag the rating into the Extend 4-1 Movie Poster Edited file and position it below the placeholder text, as shown in Figure 4–77.

c. Close the Extend 4-1 Movie Rating file.

6. Create the movie title text:

a. Select the Horizontal Text Tool. Choose a Serif font like Trajan Pro or Garamond. Set the font size to 100 and select a light shade for the color. Drag a text box across the top of the canvas. Type `The Big City` in the text box.

b. On the Layers panel, use the 'Add a layer style' button to add a stroke to the title using a dark blue or green color sampled from the photo.

7. Create movie subtitle text:

a. Using the Horizontal Text Tool again, with the same font, set the font size to 30. Drag a text box below the title and to the right. Type `A MOVIE ABOUT THE CITY` in the text box.

8. Add the movie reel image:

a. Use Photoshop Help to read about the Place command. Click File on the Application bar, and then click Place. Browse to the file named Extend 4-1 Movie Reel and select it. Click the Place button and then position the movie reel image as shown in Figure 4–78. Press the ENTER key to finish the place.

9. Save the file again and then flatten the image.

10. Press SHIFT+CTRL+S to open the Save As dialog box. Type `Extend 4-1 Movie Poster Complete` in the Name box. Click the Format box arrow, and then click TIFF in the list. Click the Save button. When Photoshop displays the TIFF Options dialog box, click the OK button to finish saving the file.

11. Submit the file in the format specified by your instructor.

Make It Right

Analyze a project and correct all errors and/or improve the design.

Correcting a Cell Phone Ad

Instructions: Start Photoshop and perform the customization steps found on pages PS 6 through PS 10. Open the Make It Right 4-1 Cell Phone file from the Chapter 04 folder of the Data Files for Students. Visit www.cengage.com/ct/studentdownload for detailed instructions or contact your instructor for information about accessing the required files.

The file contains an ad for the Super Chrome 2000 cell phone (Figure 4–78). The client thinks that it is too bland. You are to improve the look of the ad with gradients and brushes.

Figure 4–78

Perform the following tasks:
1. On the violet background layer, create a radial gradient with shades of purple, from the upper right to the lower left, so the radial appears around the cell phone.
2. Add a radial gradient with shades of green from left to right to the shape in the green layer.
3. Add a radial gradient with shades of blue from top to bottom to the shape in the blue layer.
4. On the Layers panel, CTRL+click the super chrome layer thumbnail to select its content. Apply the Chrome preset gradient in a linear style from top to bottom.
5. Repeat Step 4 for the 2000 layer.
6. For a final touch, use the 'Add a layer style' button to add a bevel and a drop shadow to help set the text layers apart from the blue background. Use the default settings for both layer styles.
7. Save the file as Make It Right 4-1 Cell Phone Edited.

In the Lab

Design and/or create a publication using the guidelines, concepts, and skills presented in this chapter. Labs are listed in order of increasing difficulty.

Lab 1: Creating an Advertisement Using Gradients and Shapes

Problem: Your uncle owns a small golf course on the edge of town. He has heard you are studying Photoshop, and he would like you to create an advertisement for him. He plans to place the color ad in a regional golfing magazine; therefore, he wants a high resolution, CMYK file to submit to the publisher. The owner has a file with the appropriate text copy, an image of a golf ball, and an image of a golfer. You need to put it all together, adding a gradient background and inserting a shape. A sample solution is shown in Figure 4–79.

Note: To complete this assignment, you will be required to use the Data Files for Students. Visit www.cengage.com/ct/studentdownload for detailed instructions or contact your instructor for information about accessing the required files.

Figure 4–79

Instructions: Perform the following tasks:

1. Start Photoshop. Set the default workspace, default colors, and reset all tools. Open the file Lab 4-1 Golf Outing from the Chapter 04 folder of the Data Files for Students.

2. Click the Save As command on the File menu. Browse to your USB flash drive storage device. Click the Save button. If Photoshop displays a format Options dialog box, click the OK button.

3. In the Layers panel, click the visibility icons to hide all text layers. Click the Background layer to select it, if necessary.

4. Press the G key to activate the Gradient Tool. If the Paint Bucket Tool is active, press SHIFT+G to toggle to the Gradient Tool.

5. On the Gradient options bar, click the Linear Gradient button, and then click the Gradient Editor box. When Photoshop displays the Gradient Editor dialog box, click the Foreground to

Background preset. Click the Gradient Type box arrow, and then click Solid. Double-click the Smoothness box and then type 100.

6. Below the color bar, double-click the left Color Stop button. When the Color Picker (Stop Color) dialog box is displayed, click blue on the color bar and then click light blue in the color panel. Click the OK button.

7. Below the color bar, double-click the right Color Stop button. When the Color Picker (Stop Color) dialog box is displayed, click yellow on the color bar and then click light yellow in the color panel. Click the OK button.

8. Below the center of the color bar, double-click to create a new Color Stop button. When the Color Picker (Stop Color) dialog box is displayed, orange on the color bar and then click an orange color in the color panel. Click the OK button.

9. Drag the orange Color Stop button slightly to the right until the gradient smoothly transitions from one color to another, similar to that shown in Figure 4–79. Adjust any Color Midpoint diamonds as necessary.

10. Click the OK button in the Gradient Editor dialog box. Draw a gradient by dragging from the upper-right corner of the page in the document window to the lower-left corner. (*Hint:* If you do not like the result and want to redo the gradient, press CTRL+Z to undo the step and then repeat Steps 6 through 9.)

11. In the Layers panel, display the text layers.

12. Use the Place command to place the image named In the Lab 4-1 Golfer, located in the Chapter 04 folder of the Data Files for Students. Position the placed object to match Figure 4–79. Press CTRL+O and then navigate to the file named Lab 4-1 Golf Ball. Open the file.

13. In the Lab 4-1 Golf Ball document window, press CTRL+A to select the entire image. Press CTRL+C to copy the image. Select the Lab 4-1 Golf Outing document window, and then press CTRL+V to paste the image. Close the Lab 4-1 Golf Ball document window. Position the golf ball as shown in Figure 4–79.

14. Increase the magnification as necessary in the Lab 4-1 Golf Outing document window. Press the E key to access the current Eraser Tool. Use the Magic Eraser Tool to erase the blue areas around the golf ball.

15. Resize the golf ball to make it smaller by pressing CTRL+T to display the bounding box. SHIFT+drag a corner sizing handle, and then press the ENTER key. Rename the new layer golf ball.

16. Right-click the current Shape tool button on the Tools panel, and then click Custom Shape Tool on the context menu.

17. On the Shape options bar, click the Shape box. When the pop-up panel is displayed, click the menu button and then click Web in the list. When Photoshop asks if you want to replace or append the shapes, click the Append button. When the new shapes are displayed, scroll as necessary and double-click the Time shape.

18. On the Shape options bar, click the Fill box. When the Fill panel is displayed, select a light gray color. Click the OK button.

19. In the document window, SHIFT+drag to create a clock in the lower-right portion of the image, similar to the one shown in Figure 4–79. On the Layers panel, drag the Opacity slider to make the appearance of the clock more subtle. Rename the layer clock. A border might appear around the edges of the clock. It will disappear when you flatten the image.

20. On the File menu, click Save.

21. On the Layer menu, click Flatten Image. Save the flattened image as Lab 4-1 Golf Outing Complete in the TIFF format.

22. Quit Photoshop. E-mail the file, as an attachment, to your instructor.

In the Lab

Lab 2: Creating a Web Graphic from Scratch

Problem: You have been asked to create a graphic to place on the paper recycling box in your computer lab (Figure 4–80).

Figure 4–80

Instructions: Perform the following tasks:

1. Start Photoshop. Set the default workspace and reset all tools.

2. Click New on the File menu. When the New dialog box is displayed, start with a blank page that is 8.5 inches by 11 inches.

3. Choose the Custom Shape Tool. Click the Shape box on the Shape options bar. When the panel is displayed, click the menu button and then click Symbols in the list. Click to Append the Symbols to the current set. Scroll to display the recycling logo and click it.

4. Click the Fill box on the Shape option bar and select a dark green color.

5. Drag to create a recycling logo that fills the page.

6. Add the text, Paper Only in the middle of the recycling logo.

7. Print the sign on a color printer. Save the file and submit it as specified by your instructor.

Lab 3: Creating a Flyer

Problem: A local bowling alley has asked you to create a simple image with the words, Bowl-O-Rama, above a colorful bowling ball. The address should appear below the bowling ball. A sample image is displayed in Figure 4–81.

Figure 4–81

Instructions: Perform the following tasks:

Start Photoshop. Set the default workspace and reset all tools. Create a new Photoshop file named Lab 4-3 Bowling Flyer and save it to your USB flash drive storage device. The new file should be approximately 8.5 inches wide by 5.5 inches high. Choose a mid-level resolution and use RGB, 8 bit for the color mode.

Create a background layer containing a radial gradient with shades of purple. Drag in the canvas from the middle to the upper-right corner. Create a selection that includes the lower half of the canvas and create a second linear gradient as shown in Figure 4–81. (*Hint:* The Reverse check box on the options bar should not display a check mark.) Create a new layer named shadow and draw a large circle in the middle of the canvas. (*Hint:* Use the Elliptical Marquee Tool and the SHIFT key.) Add a radial gradient using the Foreground to Transparent preset.

In a new layer, use a Shape Tool to create the bowling ball. (*Hint:* On the options bar, click the Shape box and then click the Nebula preset.) Adjust the opacity of the bowling ball. Create the finger holes on the bowling ball. (*Hint:* Reset the default colors to black over white.)

Create the upper text using the appropriate tool, a typeface similar to Cooper Std, and a large size font. (*Hint:* Click the 'Create warped text' button on the options bar and then click the Style box arrow. Choose the Arc style.) Add the lower text. Create the stars in their own layer using an appropriate brush to make a star pattern randomly across the top of the background.

Save the image again, flatten it, and then save it in the TIFF format with the file name, Lab 4-3 Bowling Flyer Complete. Submit it in the format specified by your instructor.

Cases and Places

Apply your creative thinking and problem-solving skills to design and implement a solution.

Note: To complete these assignments, you will be required to use the Data Files for Students. Visit www.cengage.com/ct/studentdownload for detailed instructions or contact your instructor for information about accessing the required files.

1: Create a Character Style

Academic

The Computer Information Technology (CIT) department has asked you to design a stylized font that they can use on all graphics and letterhead. Use the Character Styles panel and create a font that includes your choice of a font family, size, color, faux bold, faux italics, and all caps. Name the character style, CIT. Use the style to create a sample for your instructor.

2: Create a Snow Scene

Personal

Create a new image that is 8 inches wide and 4 inches tall with a medium blue background. Use the RGB color scheme and set the resolution to 72 pixels per inch. Select white from the Swatches panel. Append the Assorted brush presets, if necessary. Select the snowflake 20 preset. Place snowflakes all around the upper portion of the canvas. Select the texture 6, size 32 brush preset and drag to create a bed of snow across the bottom creating a hill on the right. Use the Place command to insert an image of a skier on the hill. The skier image, Case 4-2 Skier, is stored in the Data Files for Students. Use the Ornament 3 brush tip, rotated 90 degrees with a size of 15 pt, to create black small lines at the end of the skis to simulate movement.

3: Create a Special Effects Storyboard

Professional

You are in charge of special effects for a small movie production company. You need to plan a storyboard of special effects for an upcoming action movie. Decide on a theme for your movie. Create a new document that is 11 inches × 8.5 inches. Copy several digital or electronic images onto your blank canvas. Use painting and drawing tools to add at least four of the following special effects to each of the real images: flames, lightning bolts, explosions, tattoos, jet streams, rocket flares, spider webs, sunbursts, or some other effect of your choosing. Save the file and submit it as directed by your instructor.

5 | Enhancing and Repairing Photos

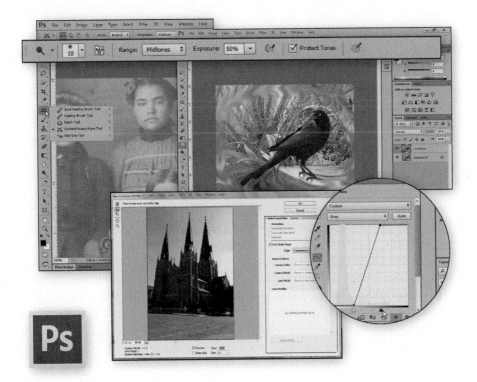

Objectives

You will have mastered the material in this chapter when you can:

- Discuss technical tips for digital cameras and scanners

- Repair documents with aging damage

- Make curve corrections

- Employ Content-Aware technology

- Use new layers for editing and viewing corrections

- Fix red-eye

- Create a vignette

- Correct damage using the healing tools

- Use the Dodge, Burn, and Sponge Tools

- Remove or correct angle and perspective distortions

- Apply blending modes

- Enhance a photo using the Blur, Sharpen, and Smudge Tools

5 | Enhancing and Repairing Photos

Introduction

Repairing and enhancing photos is an important skill for people such as graphic designers, restoration experts, and professional photographers. It is a useful skill for the amateur photographer as well. Many families have old photographs that have been damaged over time, and most people have taken a red-eye photo, a photo that is too light or dark, or one in which the subject is tilted. Freelance photographers, genealogists, family historians, and proud parents all use Photoshop to restore, correct, and improve their photographs.

It is impossible to make every photo look perfect — even with graphic-editing software. Graphics professionals know that a camera lacks the flexibility to rival reality — the tonal range of color is too small. Digital cameras or digital creations cannot reproduce the large number of spectrum colors visible to the human eye. Therefore, enhancing and repairing photos is both an art and a science. Using the digital tools available in Photoshop, you can employ technology to make reparative and restorative changes. Artistically, you need a strong sense of color and design sensibility.

Restoring original documents is a highly skilled art. It takes education, research, and years of practice. When dealing with documents of great value, or when dealing with materials in advanced stages of deterioration, you should consult a professional conservator or restoration service. Many restorers, however, choose to electronically renovate original documents using digital copies. If the document can be scanned or photographed, the original does not have to be disturbed. Photoshop has many tools to help repair and enhance documents.

Project — Enhancing and Repairing Photos

Chapter 5 uses Photoshop to enhance and repair several photographs and documents. A yellowed telegram needs to be repaired and the fold lines removed. A vacation picture has a missing edge. An old family photo contains wrinkles and defects. A photo of a graduate needs to be enhanced by vignetting. A photo of a building needs a perspective correction. A picture of a baby needs to have the red-eye removed. Finally, a nature photo is enhanced artistically. The before and after photos are illustrated in Figure 5–1.

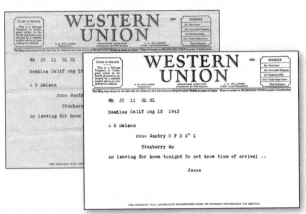

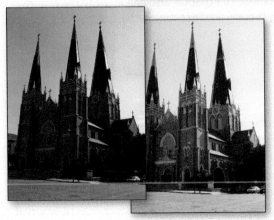

Figure 5–1

Overview

As you read this chapter, you will learn how to enhance and repair the images shown in Figure 5–1 on the previous page by performing these general tasks:

- Remove yellowing.
- Apply blending modes.
- Sharpen images.
- Restore missing portions of a document.
- Repair tears and blemishes.
- Correct red-eye.
- Fix dark spots in a photo.
- Create a vignette.
- Correct lens errors and distortions.
- Use smudging for artistic effect.

Plan Ahead

> **General Project Guidelines**
>
> When editing a photo, the actions you perform and decisions you make will affect the appearance and characteristics of the finished product. As you edit photos, such as the ones shown in Figure 5–1, you should follow these general guidelines:
>
> 1. **Create a high-resolution digital image.** When repairing a printed photo or document, the scanning technique is the most important step in enhancing and repairing the image. Scan using the highest resolution possible with the correct settings. Other image sources may include digital cameras and graphics from the Web. Always work on a copy of the original scan, or create a corrections layer.
>
> 2. **Use Content-Aware techniques for repairs and retouching.** When portions of an image are missing or damaged, the Content-Aware techniques in Photoshop can reproduce them with amazing results. With the various fills, tools, and modes associated with Content-Aware, it is important to use the right tool for the job.
>
> 3. **Heal specific defects.** Remove defects such as yellowing, blemishes, tears, and red-eye to improve legibility and clarity. Restoration professionals attempt to recreate the original look and feel of old documents and photos.
>
> 4. **Correct lens errors.** The final touch is to correct any lens errors. You can correct distortion, angles, blurs, vignetting, perspective errors, keystone distortions, barrel distortions, chromatic aberrations, and scaling.
>
> When necessary, more specific details concerning the preceding guidelines are presented at appropriate points in the chapter. The chapter also will identify the actions performed and decisions made regarding these guidelines during the creation of the edited photos shown in Figure 5–1.

Gathering Images

Recall that a variety of pictures and documents can be imported into Photoshop in different ways. Pictures taken using old photograph-generating devices, such as tintypes, daguerreotypes, and stereographic cameras, as well as those taken with film and instant print cameras, must be scanned using a digital scanner. Many photo-processing services will digitize any type of film onto a photo CD or DVD. Modern digital cameras use simple software to transfer pictures directly into computer systems. Documents and personal papers can be scanned in as images; or, if they are typewritten and easily legible, some scanners can produce digital text files. However, no matter how you generate the image, starting with a high-quality, high-resolution copy is an important step in enhancing and repairing photos and documents.

**Plan
Ahead**

Create a high-resolution digital image.
You may acquire images from a variety of sources:

- Scanners: Considerations that affect the outcome of a scanned image include color, size, and resolution settings of the scanner and the desired file type. When converting an original image to a digital copy, some loss of resolution is inevitable, so you should try to minimize that loss by using correct scanner settings.

- Digital cameras and cell phones: Images can be transferred directly from a digital camera's storage medium to a file or imported into Photoshop, avoiding any loss of resolution. Use the highest possible image file settings. Cell phone images can be e-mailed as well.

- Web: Images downloaded from the Web or sent by e-mail sometimes need enhancement or repair. Make sure you have the legal rights to use the image.

Scanners

A scanner is a peripheral hardware device that scans photos, documents, or even 3D objects, in an optical manner, converting the result to a digital image. Table 5–1 displays some simple tips about using digital scanners that will produce better results. In addition, you should review your scanner documentation carefully.

Table 5–1 Scanner Tips	
Issue	**Tip**
File Type and Mode	Most scanners have a setting related to the type of file you are selecting. Scanners make automatic anti-aliasing adjustments and tonal changes based on the file type you choose. Use the closest possible settings to your original. For example, if you have a text-only document, do not use a setting related to color photos; use the black-and-white or grayscale setting.
Multiple Scans	Do not assume that your first scan is the one you will use. Try scanning with various file types and settings, and at different sizes. Look at a black-and-white scan even if color was your first choice. Keep in mind your final use of the image.
Placement	Place the photo in the upper-left corner of the scanner bed. Align the long side of the original with the long side of the scanner. Use the scanner's preview capability so that the scanner will determine the size and location of the photograph. Use scanner settings to select the exact size rather than the entire scanner bed when possible. After a preview scan, if available, a scaling feature such as Scale to Fit page will produce a bigger copy.
Quality	Always choose the best resolution when scanning an image for use in Photoshop, keeping in mind that an image with higher resolution requires more disk space to store and may be slower to edit and print. Image resolution is a compromise between image quality and file size.
Resolution	The scanner's resolution is a measure of how many dots per inch are scanned. Higher-resolution images can reproduce greater detail and subtler color transitions than lower-resolution images because of the density of the pixels in the images. High-quality images often look good at any print size.
Shading	To maintain the background shading, especially in color, select a setting related to text with pictures rather than just text. A text-only setting can create a picture area that appears as a solid black rectangle.
Size	Use the largest original you can. For instance, an 8 x 10-inch photo will produce a higher-quality 24-inch poster than a 4 x 6-inch photo. Use a reduce or enlarge setting only when absolutely necessary. Keep in mind that, when you print a copy, most printers need at least 1/4-inch margin. A printed copy produced from a scan may lose its edges if the original is the exact size as the paper.
Text	Most scanners have a text or drawing setting, which is appropriate only if your original document contains only black-and-white areas, text, or other solid areas, such as signatures, clip art, line drawings, maps, or blueprints. If you use this setting for a photograph or picture that also contains gray areas, the result may be unsatisfactory.
Tone	If the copy appears too light or too dark, or just appears as solid black, make sure that you have selected the correct file type for the original you are using. Look for darken and lighten settings that might be adjusted.

Digital Cameras

Camera Raw Files
Working with camera raw files allows maximum control for settings such as white balance, tonal range, contrast, color saturation, and sharpening, similar to how photo processors try to fix photos taken by traditional film, reprocessing the negative with different shades and tints. Photoshop displays a special dialog box when working with camera raw photos.

The advent of digital cameras and cell phones with cameras has reduced dramatically the need for the intermediate step of scanning. Images can be transferred directly from the camera's storage medium to a file or imported directly into Photoshop. A digital camera's resolution is measured in megapixels, or millions of dots per inch. It is not uncommon for a digital camera to create photos with eight or more megapixels. Typically, a digital camera processes the pixels using a 24-bit color scheme in the RGB color mode, creating a JPG file. Many photographers prefer to use a feature called Camera Raw, available with advanced digital cameras. **Camera Raw** files are captured with a wider range of colors, and provide minimal in-camera processing. This allows photographers to condense color image information later. Certain digital cameras export images using Windows Image Acquisition (WIA) support. When you use WIA, Photoshop works with Windows and your digital camera or scanner software to import images directly into Photoshop.

Table 5–2 displays some simple tips about digital cameras that will produce better results when working with Photoshop. Again, carefully review your camera's documentation.

Table 5–2 Digital Camera Tips	
Issue	**Tip**
File Type	If possible, set the camera to save files in its own raw file format. The Adobe Web site has a list of cameras supported by Photoshop.
Quality	Use high-capacity memory cards and higher megapixel counts to take more images at a much higher resolution. Use the highest-quality compression setting as well.
Storage	Copy images from the camera to a storage device before editing them in Photoshop. Adobe Bridge can read from most media cards, or you can use the software that comes with your camera.
Lighting and Speed	Experiment with the correlation between light and shutter speeds. Most of the newer digital cameras can take many pictures in a short amount of time, avoiding the shutter lag problem — the delay that occurs between pressing the shutter release button and the actual moment the picture is taken.
Balance	Changing your white balance setting from auto to cloudy when shooting outdoors creates a filtered, richer color, increasing the reds and yellows.
Filters	If possible, use a polarizing filter for landscapes and outdoor shooting. It reduces glare and unwanted reflections. Polarized shots have richer, more saturated colors, especially in the sky. You also can use sunglasses in front of the lens to reduce glare. When shooting through glass, use an infinity focus setting.
Flash	When shooting pictures of people or detailed subjects, use the flash — even outdoors. If available, use the camera's fill flash or flash on mode. That way, the camera exposes the background first and then adds just enough light to illuminate your subject. Keep in mind that most flash mechanisms only have a range of approximately 10 feet.
Settings	When possible, use a plain background, look at your subject in a straight, level manner, and move in as close as possible. Consider the rule of thirds when taking photographs. For busy backgrounds, if your camera has a focus lock feature, center the subject, and push the shutter button halfway down to focus on the subject. Then, move the camera horizontally or vertically away from the center before pressing the shutter button all the way down.
Motion	For moving objects use a fast shutter speed.

Image Resolution
Image resolution is a compromise between image quality ad file size. Resolution is measured by the number of dots per linear inch on a hard copy, or the number of pixels across and down on a display screen. A digital image's file size is proportional to its resolution. Higher resolution gives larger file sizes. Try to optimize images to produce the highest quality image at the lowest file size.

Web Graphics

A vast source of images and documents can be found on the Web. The advantage in using Web graphics is the fact that the pictures and documents already are digitized, so you do not have to manipulate or scan them; neither do you lose any resolution when transferring them to your computer system. The disadvantage of using Web graphics is related to ownership issues. You must obtain permission to use images you download from the Web unless the image is free and unrestricted. You need to scrutinize carefully any Web sites that advertise free graphics. Some cannot be used for business purposes, for reproductions, or for resale. Some illegitimate sites that advertise free downloads also may embed spyware on your system.

Starting and Customizing Photoshop

The following steps start Photoshop and reset the tools, options bar, colors, and interface.

To Start Photoshop

The following steps, which assume Windows 7 is running, start Photoshop based on a typical installation. You may need to ask your instructor how to start Photoshop for your system.

1 Click the Start button on the Windows 7 taskbar to display the Start menu and then type Photoshop CS6 in the 'Search programs and files' box.

2 Click Adobe Photoshop CS6 in the list to start Photoshop.

3 If the Photoshop window is not maximized, click the Maximize button next to the Close button on the Application bar to maximize the window.

To Reset the Tools and the Options Bar

The following steps select the Rectangular Marquee Tool and reset all tool settings on the options bar.

1 If the tools in the Tools panel appear in two columns, click the double arrow at the top of the Tools panel.

2 If necessary, click the Rectangular Marquee Tool button on the Tools panel to select it.

3 Right-click the Rectangular Marquee Tool icon on the options bar to display the context menu, and then click Reset All Tools. When Photoshop displays a confirmation dialog box, click the OK button to restore the tools to their default settings.

To Set the Interface and Default Colors

The following steps set the interface to Medium Gray and the foreground and background colors to black over white.

1 Click Edit on the Application bar to display the Edit menu. Point to Preferences, and then click Interface on the Preferences submenu to display the Preferences dialog box.

② Click the third button, Medium Gray, to change the interface color scheme.

③ Click the OK button to close the Preferences dialog box.

④ Press the D key to reset the default foreground and background colors. If black is not over white on the Tools panel, press the X key.

To Select the Default Workspace

The following steps select the Default workspace.

① Click Window on the Application bar, and then point to Workspace to display the Workspace submenu. Click Essentials (Default) on the Workspace submenu to select the workspace.

② Click Window on the Application bar, and then point to Workspace to display the Workspace submenu again. Click Reset Essentials to reset the workspace.

Restoring Documents

Antique documents, such as licenses, records, letters, and other forms of paper, have some unique aging characteristics that photographs typically do not have. Common document paper is an organic substance composed of cellulose plant fibers that will deteriorate faster than professional photo paper. Rapid deterioration results from the use of production acids that break down the fibers, weakening the paper. Acid deterioration commonly is accompanied by a yellow discoloration caused by the alum-resin sizing agents. High temperatures and moisture compound the problem. Even now, unless the paper is designated as acid-free, archival quality, or permanent, its expected useful life is less than 50 years.

Other types of damage include dry and brittle creases caused by folding or rolling documents; brown spots from water stains or fungus, called **foxing**; brown edges due to airborne pollutants; and the fading of colors caused by light damage, as well as mold, bacteria, improper storage effects, and deterioration caused by animal or insect damage. Handwritten portions of documents are particularly vulnerable. Ink and pencil exposed to significant amounts of sunlight can fade dramatically.

Repairing damage using the Photoshop restoration tools can require some trial and error. Many of the tools work in similar ways, and you might find it more intuitive to use one tool rather than another. It also is possible that in correcting one error, you create another. In this case, use CTRL+Z to undo the last step, or work your way back through the History panel. The effectiveness or obviousness of a repair is subjective, so be willing to experiment to achieve the desired results. The more you work with the Photoshop repair tools, the more proficient you will become with them.

To Open the Telegram File

The first image you will edit is a yellowed telegram from 1942. You will use restorative techniques to correct the discoloration and remove the wrinkles. To complete this assignment, you will be required to use the Data Files for Students. Visit www.cengage.com/ct/studentdownload for detailed instructions or contact your instructor for information about accessing the required files. The following steps open the Telegram file from the Data Files for Students.

1 Press CTRL+O to display the Open dialog box.

2 Open the Telegram file from the Chapter 05 folder of the Data Files for Students or a location specified by your instructor.

3 Press CTRL+R to display the rulers if necessary (Figure 5–2).

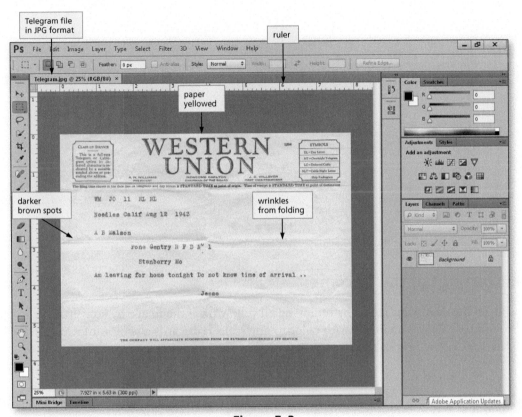

Figure 5–2

To Save the Telegram Repaired File

The following steps save the Telegram file with a new name in the PSD format.

1 With your USB flash drive connected to one of the computer's USB ports, click File on the Application bar to display the File menu, and then click Save As to display the Save As dialog box.

2 In the File name text box, type `Telegram Repaired` to rename the file. Do not press the ENTER key after typing the file name.

3 Click the Save in box arrow, and then click Removable Disk (F:), or the location associated with your USB flash drive, in the list. If you want to create a folder for the photos in Chapter 5, click the Create New Folder button. Then when the new folder is displayed, type a chapter name, such as Chapter 05, and press the ENTER key.

4 Click the Format button to display the list of available file formats, and then click Photoshop (*.PSD, *.PDD) in the list, if necessary.

5 Click the Save button in the Save As dialog box to save the file. If Photoshop displays a dialog box, click the OK button (Figure 5–3 on the next page).

BTW

Layers and the Grayscale Mode
The Grayscale mode conversion only works on a flat file — an image file with no layers; thus, in the Telegram file, you do not create a corrections or edits layer until after you convert it.

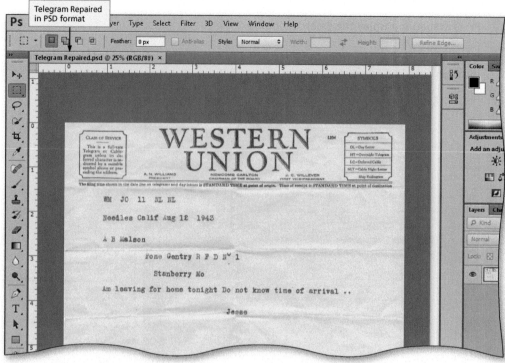

Figure 5–3

To Correct Yellowed Portions of the Document

The following steps begin the document repair by removing all yellow from the image by converting it to Grayscale mode. When Photoshop converts an image with color to grayscale, it discards all color information in the original image. The luminosity of the original pixels is represented by shades of gray in the converted pixels.

• Click Image on the Application bar, then point to Mode to display the Mode submenu (Figure 5–4).

Should I make these changes on a duplicate layer?

The process of converting to Grayscale mode changes all layers. If you had a duplicate layer for corrections, Photoshop would require you to merge before converting to grayscale.

 Experiment

• Click various color modes and watch how the image changes. Press CTRL+Z to undo each one.

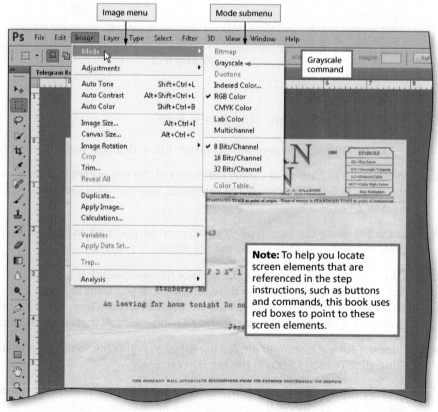

Figure 5–4

2

- Click Grayscale to remove all color. If Photoshop asks if you want to discard all color information, click the Discard button (Figure 5–5).

Q&A

Is this a destructive process?

Yes; however, you can reopen the original file from the Data Files for Students should you need it.

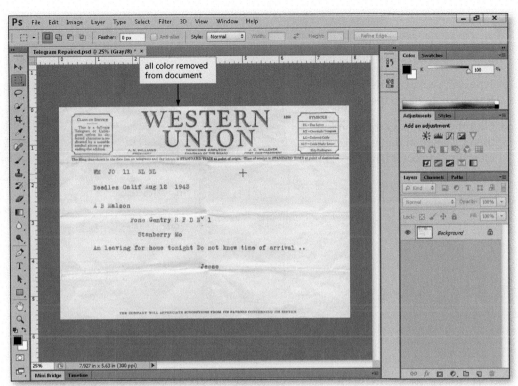

Figure 5–5

To Create a Layer from the Background

The Background layer is locked for direct editing. The following steps change the Background layer into a fully editable layer.

1

- On the Layers panel, right-click the Background layer to display the context menu (Figure 5–6).

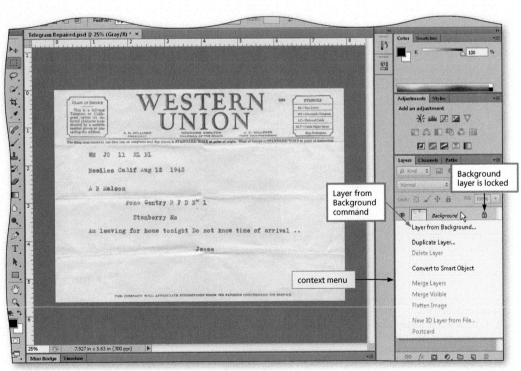

Figure 5–6

- Click Layer from Background to display the New Layer dialog box.

- Type corrections in the Name box to name the layer.

- Click the Color box arrow, and then click Red in the list to set the identification color (Figure 5–7).

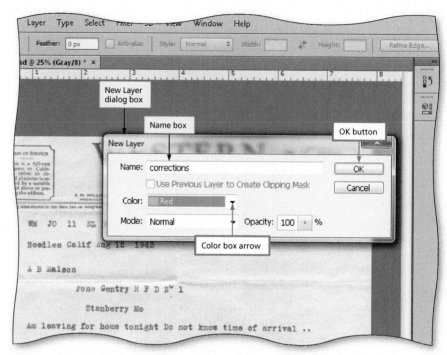

Figure 5–7

- Click the OK button to create the layer (Figure 5–8).

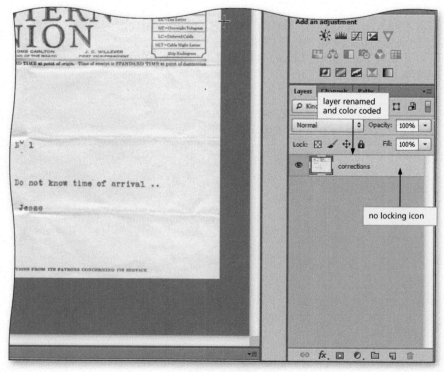

Figure 5–8

Other Ways

1. Double-click Background layer, enter new name (New Layer dialog box), click OK

2. On Layer menu, point to New, click Layer from Background, enter new name (New Layer dialog box), click OK

To Edit Curves

The **curve** of an image is a measure of the brightness value. Adjusting the curve is changing or remapping those brightness values. Similar to the Levels adjustment you learned about in a previous chapter, the Curves adjustment allows you to adjust points throughout the tonal range of an image, from shadows to highlights. Whereas Levels have only three adjustments, with Curves you can make very precise adjustments to individual colors in an image.

The following steps create an adjustment layer and edit the curves.

- On the Adjustments panel, click the Curves icon to display Curves on the Properties panel (Figure 5–9).

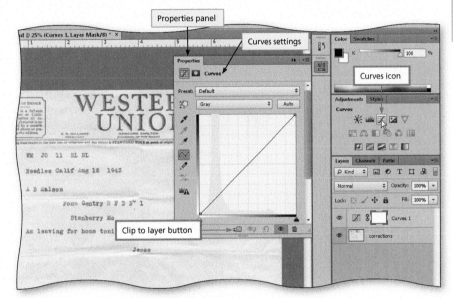

Figure 5–9

- Click the 'Clip to layer' button on the panel status bar to apply the adjustment layer to the current layer.

- Drag the white point slider to the right until most of the gray background is removed from the document.

- Drag the black point slider to the left to remove the glare (Figure 5–10).

 Experiment

- Adjust other settings on the Properties panel to view how they change the image.

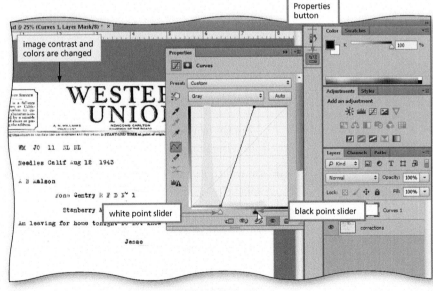

Figure 5–10

- Collapse the Properties panel by clicking the Properties button on the vertical dock of panels.

Other Ways
1. On Layer menu, point to New Adjustment Layer, click Curves, click OK, edit settings   2. On Layers panel, click 'Create new fill or adjustment layer' button, click Curves, edit settings

To Lock Transparent Pixels

The following step locks the transparent pixels of the image so that erasing any dark spots will result in a white area rather than a transparent area.

1

- Select the corrections layer.

- Click the 'Lock transparent pixels' button on the Layers panel to lock the pixels (Figure 5–11).

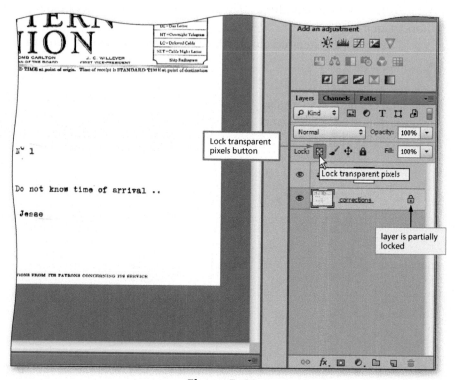

Figure 5–11

To Use the Eraser Tool

Finally, the dark spots in the document will be cleaned using the Eraser Tool in the following steps.

1 On the Tools panel, right-click the current eraser tool, and then click Eraser Tool to select it.

2 Use the LEFT BRACKET ([) or RIGHT BRACKET (]) keys to adjust the size of the eraser brush. With short strokes, drag the remaining dark spots that are not part of the telegram itself. If you make a mistake, press CTRL+Z. Zoom and scroll as necessary.

3 When you are finished, zoom to approximately 25% in order to display the entire document (Figure 5–12).

Other Ways
1. Press E, drag dark spots

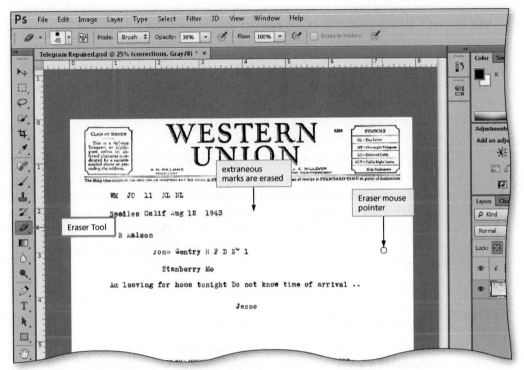

Figure 5–12

To Save and Close the Telegram Repaired File

The following steps save the file again and close it.

1 Press CTRL+S to save the file again. If Photoshop displays a dialog box, click the OK button.

2 Press CTRL+W to close the file without quitting Photoshop.

Break Point: If you wish to take a break, this is a good place to do so. You can quit Photoshop now. To resume at a later time, start Photoshop, and continue following the steps from this location forward.

Content-Aware

Content-Aware is a texture synthesis technology used to edit and repair photos. Using mathematical algorithms, Content-Aware fills the selection with similar nearby content to replicate a portion of an image. By sampling image data from around the area, Content-Aware reconstructs a texture based on the sampled data in order to replicate the area. Texture synthesis is used in computer graphics, digital image editing, 3D computer graphics, and post-production of films.

> **Use Content-Aware techniques for repairs and retouching.**
> When portions of an image are missing or damaged, the Content-Aware techniques in Photoshop can reproduce with amazing results. You can use Content-Aware to fill in portions of an image that are missing, either because the photo was damaged or because the original photo contained an error, or you can remove portions of an image such as a spot on a camera lens or an object that should not be in the scene.

When using Content-Aware techniques, it is common to create a corrections layer on top of the Background layer to hold the newly generated content. Corrections could include spot repair, removing and replacing portions of the image, and correcting the lighting. By creating a corrections layer, or multiple corrections layers, it is easy to compare the original to the corrections and see the difference you have made by showing and hiding various layers. A corrections layer also protects the original in case you want to start again.

To Open the Cactus File

The following step opens a scanned image with a missing edge from the Data Files for Students. Visit www.cengage.com/ct/studentdownload for detailed instructions or contact your instructor for information about accessing the required files.

1 Open the Cactus file from the Chapter 05 folder of the Data Files for Students or a location specified by your instructor (Figure 5–13).

Figure 5–13

To Save the Cactus Repaired File

The following steps save the Cactus file with a new name in the PSD format.

1 Press SHIFT+CTRL+S to open the Save As dialog box, and then navigate to your preferred storage location.

2 In the File name text box, type `Cactus Repaired` to rename the file. Do not press the ENTER key after typing the file name.

3 Click the Format button to display the list of available file formats, and then click Photoshop (*.PSD, *.PDD) in the list, if necessary.

4 Click the Save button to save the file. If Photoshop displays a confirmation dialog box, click the OK button.

To Create a Corrections Layer in the Cactus Repaired File

The following steps create a corrections layer using the Duplicate Layer command.

1 On the Layers panel, right-click the Background layer and then click Duplicate Layer on the context menu.

2 When Photoshop displays the Duplicate Layer dialog box, type `corrections` in the As box and then click the OK button to create the edits layer.

3 Right-click the visibility icon on the corrections layer, and then click Red to assign an identification color.

BTW

Content-Aware and the Fill Dialog Box
When working with the locked Background layer, the DELETE key does not immediately delete a selection to transparency. Photoshop will display the Fill dialog box, offering to fill the selection with a Content-Aware texture or a color. If you are not on the Background layer, you must use the Fill command on the Edit menu.

To Fill using Content-Aware

The following steps fill in a portion of an image using Content-Aware.

1
- With the corrections layer selected, select the Rectangular Marquee Tool on the Tools panel.

- Drag to create a marquee around the white section in the photo (Figure 5–14).

Q&A Could I have selected only the white area?

Yes, but if you include a bit of the edge around the white area, Photoshop has more information with which to create a better Content-Aware fill.

Figure 5–14

• Click Edit on the Application bar to display the menu (Figure 5–15).

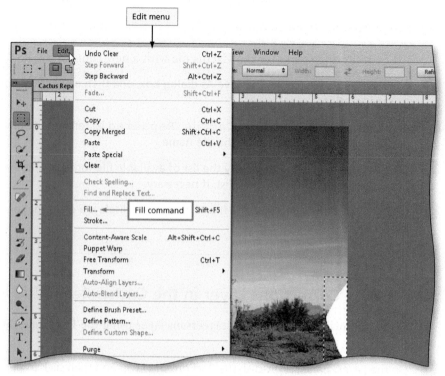

Figure 5–15

• Click Fill on the Edit menu to display the Fill dialog box.

• Click the Use box arrow to display its list (Figure 5–16).

Q&A

What do the Pattern and History commands do?

The Pattern command will display a box to choose from a list of Photoshop created patterns or patterns you have saved. If you choose History in the Use list, Photoshop will fill the selected area with a selected snapshot from the History panel.

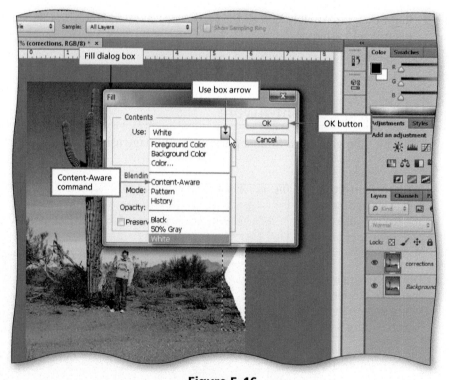

Figure 5–16

4

- Click Content-Aware in the list.

- Click the OK button to fill the selection, thereby replacing the missing portion of the photo (Figure 5–17).

5

- Press CTRL+D to deselect.

missing area recreated

Figure 5–17

Other Ways
1. On selection context menu, click Fill, edit settings, click OK

Retouching Tools

Sometimes photos are damaged or worn from excessive use, age, physical damage, or improper storage. Photoshop has several **retouching tools** that help you touch up spots, tears, wrinkles, and scratches. The retouching tools are organized in the middle of the Tools panel. Table 5–3 on the next page lists some of the tools and their usage. Each of the retouching tools will be explained further as it is used.

Table 5–3 Retouching Tools		
Tool	**Use**	**Button**
Blur Tool	Blurs small portions of the image	
Burn Tool	Darkens areas in an image	
Content-Aware Move Tool	Moves or extends a selection to a new area and then integrates texture, lighting, transparency, and shading to create new content	
Dodge Tool	Lightens areas in an image	
Healing Brush Tool	Removes and repairs imperfections by first taking a sample from another place in the image and then painting an area to match the texture, lighting, transparency, and shading of the sampled pixels to the pixels being healed	
Patch Tool	Repairs imperfections in a selected area of an image by copying a sample or pattern taken from another part of the image — commonly used for larger areas and does not allow brush size selection as with the Healing Brush Tool	
Red Eye Tool	Removes the red tint from all contiguous cells	
Sharpen Tool	Sharpens small portions of an image	
Smudge Tool	Simulates the effect you see when you drag a finger through wet paint	
Sponge Tool	Changes the color saturation of an area	
Spot Healing Brush Tool	Removes blemishes and imperfections by sampling pixels around the spot and then paints with matching texture, lighting, transparency, and shading	

The first set of retouching tools includes five healing or restoration tools to correct imperfections in photos and images. The Spot Healing Brush Tool, the Healing Brush Tool, the Patch Tool, the Content-Aware Move Tool, and the Red Eye Tool are used to make specific kinds of repairs to blemishes, tears, holes, and red-eye problems. As you work with these tools, you will create a corrections layer for each photo in order to protect the original.

Plan Ahead

Heal specific defects.
Defects in photos and documents that are not related to user or lens errors may include the following:

- Physical tears, ragged edges, or missing portions
- Fading due to exposure to light
- Light or dark spots due to aging
- Creasing caused by folding
- Natural aging of paper

It is helpful to make a list of the specific repairs you plan to apply. Create a corrections layer so you can use portions, textures, and colors from the original document for the repairs. Repair smaller areas first. Consider making separate layers for each large repair. Do not be afraid to experiment until the repair is perfect.

To Use the Content-Aware Move Tool

The Content-Aware Move Tool is used to move or extend portions of an image using Content-Aware algorithms. The options bar for the Content-Aware Move Tool displays tools for creating selections and choosing a mode and an adaptation (Figure 5–18). The Move mode replaces both the source and destination area integrating texture, lighting, transparency, and shading to create new content. The Extend mode replaces only the destination area, similarly to a copy command, but with Content-Aware technology. The Extend mode continues an edge or pattern, rather than fills it. Adaptation options control how closely the new area reflects existing image patterns.

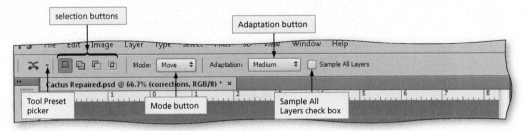

Figure 5–18

The following steps use the Content-Aware Move Tool in Move mode to move a portion of the landscape to cover the tourist in the scene.

1

• On the Tools panel, right-click the current healing brush tool to display the context menu (Figure 5–19).

Figure 5–19

2

- Click Content-Aware Move Tool in the list to select it.

- On the options bar, click the New selection button, if necessary. Click the Mode button and then click Move in the list, if necessary. Deselect the Sample All Layers check box if necessary.

- In the photo, drag an area to the right of the tourist, approximately the same size and shape to create a selection (Figure 5–20).

Figure 5–20

3

- Drag the selection over the top of the tourist and watch while Photoshop creates the new portion of the image (Figure 5–21).

- Press CTRL+D to deselect.

 Q&A My selection was too small to replace all of the tourist. What should I do?

You can undo by pressing CTRL+Z; or, you can create another selection and drag it over the remaining portion of the tourist.

Figure 5–21

To Save and Close the Cactus Repaired File

The following steps save the file again and close it.

1 Press CTRL+S to save the file again.

2 Press CTRL+W to close the file without quitting Photoshop.

The Spot Healing Brush Tool

The Spot Healing Brush Tool removes blemishes and imperfections by sampling pixels around the spot. Photoshop then paints in the image with matching texture, lighting, transparency, and shading. The Spot Healing Brush Tool options bar (Figure 5–22) contains settings for the blending mode of the repair and the sampling methods. Recall that sampling occurs when Photoshop stores the pixel values of a selected spot or area.

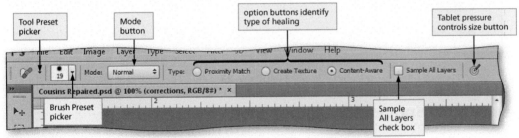

Figure 5–22

In the next steps, you will open a file, save it with a new name, and create a corrections layer in preparation for using the Spot Healing Brush Tool.

To Open the Cousins Image and Save It with a Different Name

The following steps open the Cousins image from the Data Files for Students. Visit www.cengage.com/ct/studentdownload for detailed instructions or contact your instructor for information about accessing the required files.

1 Open the file named Cousins from the Chapter 05 folder of the Data Files for Students, or from a location specified by your instructor.

2 Use the Save As dialog box to save the file on your preferred storage device in the PSD format using the name, Cousins Repaired.

To Create a Corrections Layer in the Cousins Repaired File

The following steps create a corrections layer.

1 On the Layers panel, right-click the Background layer and then click Duplicate Layer on the context menu.

2 When Photoshop displays the Duplicate Layer dialog box, type `corrections` in the As box and then click the OK button to create the edits layer.

3 Right-click the visibility icon on the corrections layer, and then click Red to assign an identification color (Figure 5–23 on the next page).

BTW

Layer from Background
The Layer from Background command renames the background layer in an image and unlocks it. The Duplicate Layer command creates a second, unlocked layer with a copy of the background. Use the latter when you want to maintain the original background layer.

Cousins Repaired
file in PSD format

Figure 5–23

To Repair Damage using the Spot Healing Brush Tool

The following steps use the Spot Healing Brush Tool to fix several small damaged spots. When using the Spot Healing Brush Tool, it is important to use the smallest possible brush tip so that the sample comes from the area directly adjacent to the imperfection.

1

- Zoom in to the upper-right corner of the image.

- Right-click the current healing brush tool on the Tools panel (Figure 5–24).

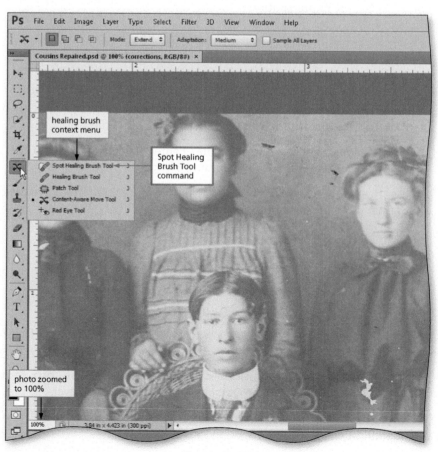

Figure 5–24

2

- Click Spot Healing Brush Tool in the list to select it.

- If necessary on the options bar, click the Mode box arrow, and then click Normal.

- Click the Proximity Match option button, if necessary, to select it.

- In the document window, move the mouse pointer to one of the dark spots on the wall.

- Press the LEFT BRACKET ([) key or the RIGHT BRACKET (]) key until the brush tip is just slightly larger than the spot (Figure 5–25).

  What is a proximity match?

A proximity match uses pixels around the edge of the selection to define the repair.

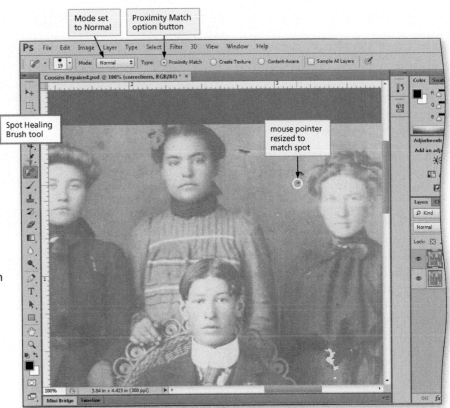

Figure 5–25

3

- Click the spot and then move the mouse pointer away to view the results (Figure 5–26).

  Why does my correction look different?

The size or position of your mouse pointer may have been different, or the color settings on your monitor may be slightly different. If you do not like the result, press CTRL+Z and then try it again.

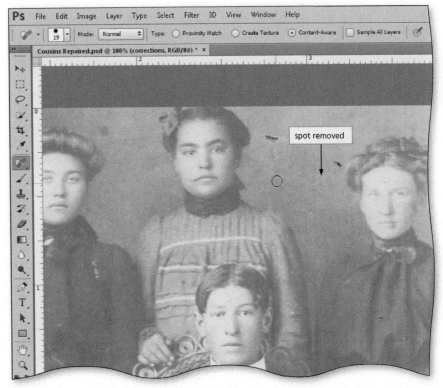

Figure 5–26

4

- Repeat Steps 2 and 3 on the previous page to repair other spots on the wall.

- Point to the scratch on the boy's forehead, and adjust the size of the brush as necessary.

- Drag across the scratch, and then move the mouse pointer away to view the results (Figure 5–27).

Experiment

- Try fixing a large spot in the photo. Notice that the larger the correction, the poorer the quality, as the Spot Healing brush is better suited for small imperfections. Press CTRL+Z to undo the unwanted correction.

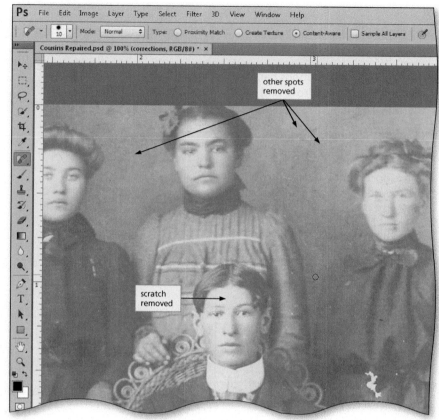

Figure 5–27

Other Ways

1. Press J or SHIFT+J, adjust brush size, click imperfection

The Create Texture Option Button
When contrasting tones or colors are near the area to be repaired, the Create Texture option creates a healing stroke by sampling the pixels inside the selection brush, not just the ones near the edges.

The Content-Aware Option Button
The Content-Aware option button works in the same way as the Fill command. It compares nearby image content to fill the selection using an algorithm, maintaining key details such as shadows and object edges.

The Healing Brush Tool

The Healing Brush Tool is suited for larger areas such as tears or wrinkles. While the Spot Healing Brush Tool samples the surrounding pixels automatically, the Healing Brush Tool requires you to choose the sampled (source) area, as you did with the Clone Tool in a previous chapter. When using the Healing Brush Tool, the Brush Preset picker allows you to set specific characteristics of the brush, including the use of a tablet pen. The Mode box allows you to choose one of several blending modes, or choose to replace the pixels to preserve the grain and texture at the edges of the brush stroke. Additionally, the Healing Brush Tool options bar has an Aligned setting to sample pixels continuously without losing the current sampling point, even if you release the mouse button.

To Sample and Paint using the Healing Brush Tool

The following steps use the Healing Brush Tool to fix a portion of the crease across the middle of the photo.

1

- Press CTRL+0 (zero) to fit the photo on the screen.

- Right-click the Spot Healing Brush Tool button to display the context menu, and then click Healing Brush Tool in the list.

- Click the Aligned check box so it displays a check mark.

- Click the Brush Preset picker on the options bar to display the settings.

- If necessary, drag the Size slider to 19.

- At the bottom of the panel, click the Size button, and then click Off in the list (Figure 5–28).

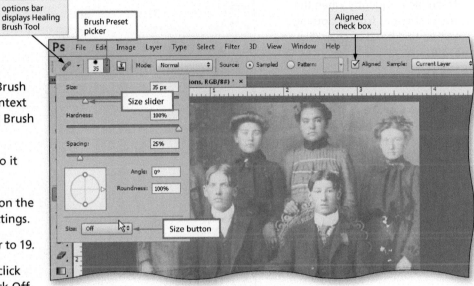

Figure 5–28

Q&A Why should I turn the size off?

The Size box allows you to specify if you will be using pen pressure or a stylus wheel to change the size of the healing brush mouse pointer. Because you changed the diameter of the brush size manually, you do not have to rely on the other methods.

2

- Click the Brush Preset picker again to close the panel.

- To sample the pixels, ALT+click just above the crease, on the right side of the photo.

- Move the mouse pointer straight down to the crease. Using short strokes, drag across a short section of the crease to repair the damage (Figure 5–29).

Q&A What is the difference between the Healing Brush Tool and the Clone Tool?

The Healing Brush Tool does not create an exact copy. It samples the texture, color, and grain of the source and then applies that to the destination, matching the destination surrounding pixels as much as possible.

Figure 5–29

3

- Repeat Step 2 on the previous page to finish repairing the crease. Resample frequently when the image changes from a clothing section to a hand or chair (Figure 5–30).

Q&A

How can I make my corrections look better?

A certain amount of document repair involves trial and error — and patience! Using multiple repair techniques, such as healing, patching, cloning, and Content-Aware, creates better results. Zooming in and resampling frequently also generate better corrections. You will improve with more practice.

Other Ways

1. Press J or SHIFT+J, ALT+click sample, drag flawed areas

crease repaired

Figure 5–30

The Patch Tool

The Patch Tool lets you repair imperfections within a selected area using pixels from another area or by using a pattern. The Patch Tool is more than just a copy-and-paste mechanism, however. Like the Healing Brush Tool, the Patch Tool matches the texture, shading, and lighting of the pixels. When repairing with pixels from the image, select a small area to produce the best results. The Patch Tool can sample pixels from the same image, from a different image, or from a chosen pattern. In Content-Aware mode, the Patch Tool requires you to drag around the damaged area to create a selection. You then move that selection to a location that contains the pixels you want to use as a patch. As you drag to move the selection, Photoshop displays a preview of what the repair will look like. When you release the mouse button, the original selected area is replaced. In Normal mode, the Patch Tool options bar displays settings for the source and destination of the patch, as well as options to adjust the selection or use a pattern to make the patch repair (Figure 5–31).

BTW

Photoshop Help
The best way to become familiar with Photoshop Help is to use it. Appendix D includes detailed information about Photoshop Help and exercises that will help you gain confidence in using it.

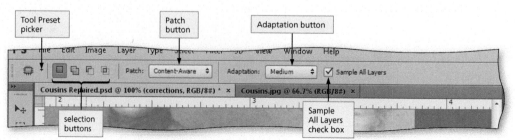

Tool Preset picker

Patch button

Adaptation button

selection buttons

Sample All Layers check box

Figure 5–31

To Patch Areas

The following steps use the Patch Tool to patch a missing portion of the photo.

1

- Zoom to the right side of the photo with 100% magnification, to focus on the missing portions of the lady's dress.

- Right-click the Healing Brush Tool button, and then click Patch Tool in the list.

- On the options bar, click the New selection button, if necessary. Click the Patch button and then click Content-Aware, if necessary (Figure 5–32).

Q&A Could I use the Fill dialog box to replace the missing portion?

Yes, it uses the same Content-Aware technology; however, the Patch Tool has a built-in selection tool, saving you one step.

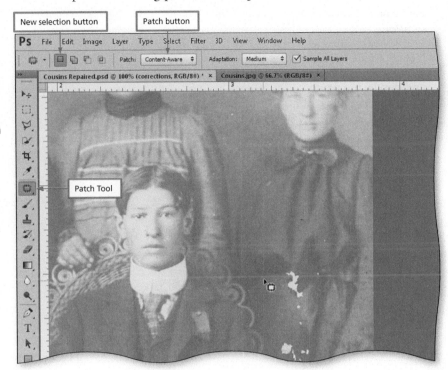

Figure 5–32

2

- Draw around the damaged area to select it (Figure 5–33).

Q&A What is the difference between the Patch Tool and the Content-Aware Move Tool?

When you choose Content-Aware on the Patch Tool options bar, as you did in Step 1, the two tools work the same way. When you click the Patch button on the options bar and choose Normal, the Patch Tool allows you to choose either to drag a damaged area to a good area or the other way around.

Figure 5–33

- Drag the selection to an undamaged area to repair the original location.

- Press CTRL+D to remove the selection and display the patch (Figure 5–34).

Q&A

How do I choose where to drag the selection?

Look for an area in the photo that has undamaged pixels of the same color and texture. When you drag the damage to that area, the Patch Tool will repair the original location using pixels from the destination of the drag.

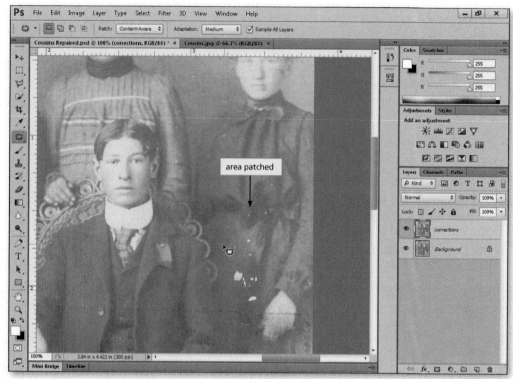

Figure 5–34

Other Ways

1. Press J or SHIFT+J, click Source, drag area, click Destination, drag area

To Repair Other Damage

The final steps repair other damaged areas in the photo. If you make a repair that does not look good, press CTRL+Z, and then try again. Zoom and scroll as necessary.

1 Use a combination of healing brushes and options bar settings to repair any other damaged areas in the photo.

2 Zoom out to display the entire photo (Figure 5–35).

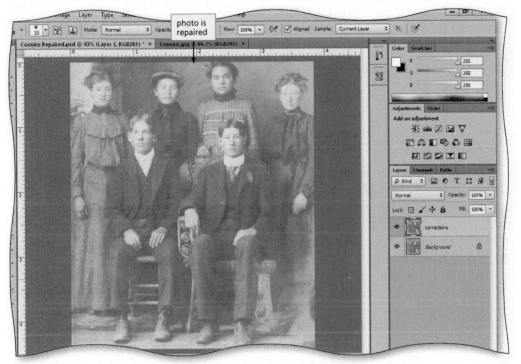

Figure 5–35

To View Corrections

The following step compares the original layer with the corrections layer.

1

- Click the visibility icon on the corrections layer to hide it and view the original image before corrections (Figure 5–36).

- Click the visibility icon on the corrections layer again to view the corrections.

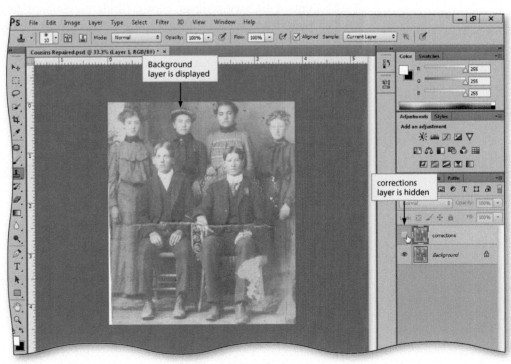

Figure 5–36

To Save and Close the Cousins Repaired File

The following step saves the file again and closes it.

1 Save, and close the file without quitting Photoshop.

BTW

Red-Eye
The amount of red light emerging from the pupil of the eye depends on the amount of melanin in the layers behind the retina. This amount varies strongly between individuals. Light-skinned people with blue eyes have relatively low melanin in the interior surface of the eye, and thus show a much stronger red-eye effect than dark-skinned people with brown eyes. The same holds true for animals.

The Red Eye Tool

In photographs, **red-eye** is a red appearance in the pupils of the subject's eyes. Red-eye occurs in flash photography when the flash of a camera is bright enough to cause a reflection off the retina. Red-eye can be avoided by moving the flash farther away from the lens or by using a more modern camera that has a red-eye reduction feature. In those cameras, the flash goes off twice — once before the picture is taken and then again to take the picture. The first flash causes the pupils to contract, which significantly reduces the red-eye.

Red-eye can be corrected in Photoshop using a specialized tool designed specifically for this problem. The Red Eye Tool removes red-eye in flash photos by recoloring all contiguous red pixels. The Red Eye Tool options bar has settings to change the pupil size and the darken amount. The Red Eye Tool can be used only on photos in the RGB and Lab color formats. It does not work with CMYK color mode.

To Open the Baby File and Save It with a Different Name

The next photo is a picture of a baby that was taken with an older camera that generated red-eye. The following steps open a file named Baby from the Data Files for Students. Visit www.cengage.com/ct/studentdownload for detailed instructions or contact your instructor for information about accessing the required files.

BTW

Red Eye Tool Options Bar
The Red Eye Tool options bar displays options for the pupil size and percentage of darkening. The labels are scrubby sliders.

1 Open the file named Baby from the Chapter 05 folder of the Data Files for Students.

2 Use the Save As dialog box to save the file on your preferred storage device in the PSD format using the name, Baby Repaired.

To Create a Corrections Layer in the Baby Repaired File

The following steps create an edits layer.

1 Duplicate the Background layer and name the new layer, corrections.

2 Create a red identification color on the corrections layer.

3 Zoom to 50% magnification and scroll to display the red-eye problem (Figure 5–37).

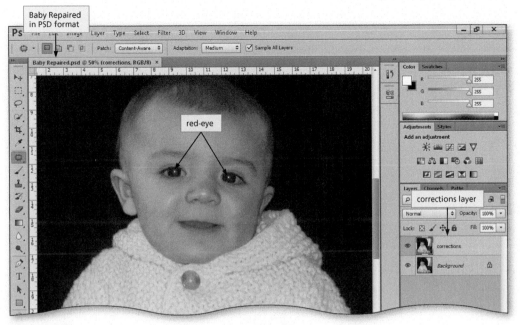

Figure 5–37

To Correct Red-Eye

The following steps remove the red-eye from the photo.

1

- On the Tools panel, right-click the current healing brush tool button, and then click Red Eye Tool in the list.

- On the options bar, drag the Darken Amount scrubby slider to 25%.

- Move the mouse pointer to the girl's eye on the left to display the Red Eye Tool mouse pointer (Figure 5–38).

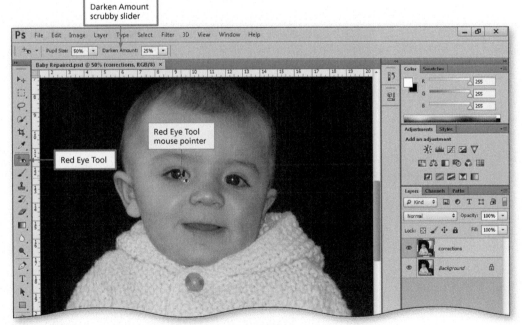

Figure 5–38

Q&A

How does the Darken Amount setting affect the image?

Setting a very low Darken Amount value will make only small changes of color to the eye; conversely, a large value will darken the eye dramatically.

- Click the red portion of the eye to remove the red-eye. Move the mouse pointer to view the result (Figure 5–39).

- Click the other eye to fix the red-eye problem.

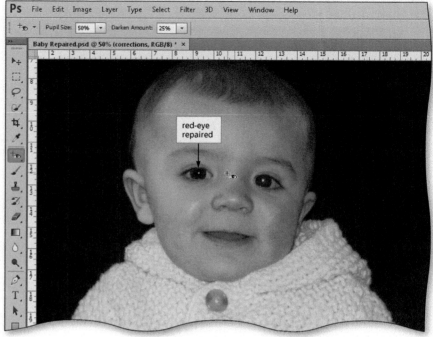

Figure 5–39

Other Ways

1. Press SHIFT+J until Red Eye Tool is active, click red-eye

To Save and Close the Baby Repaired File

The following step saves the file again and closes it.

 Save, and close the file without quitting Photoshop.

Break Point: If you wish to take a break, this is a good place to do so. You can quit Photoshop now. To resume at a later time, start Photoshop, and continue following the steps from this location forward.

The Dodge, Burn, and Sponge Tools

The Dodge Tool is used to lighten areas of an image. The Burn Tool does just the opposite; it darkens areas of an image. Both tools are based on a technique of traditional photography, regulating exposure on specific areas of a print. Photographers reduce exposure to lighten an isolated area on the print, which is called **dodging**. Increasing the exposure to darken areas on a print is called **burning**. Another tool, the Sponge Tool, subtly changes the color saturation of an area, increasing or decreasing the amount of color by a flow percentage.

An Exposure box on the options bar allows you to specify a percentage of dodging or burning. The default value is 50%. A higher percentage in the Exposure box increases the effect (for example, while using the Dodge Tool, a higher exposure results in greater lightening of the image), while a lower percentage reduces it (Figure 5–40). The Dodge, Burn, and Sponge Tools have similar options bars.

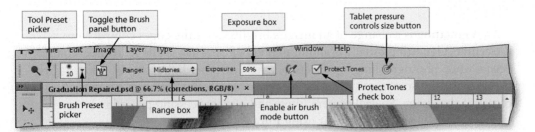

Figure 5–40

To Open the Graduation File and Save It with a Different Name

The next photo is a graduation photo in which you will create a vignette and make corrections. The following steps open a file named Graduation from the Data Files for Students. Visit www.cengage.com/ct/studentdownload for detailed instructions or contact your instructor for information about accessing the required files.

1 Open the file named Graduation from the Chapter 05 folder of the Data Files for Students.

2 Use the Save As dialog box to save the file on your preferred storage device in the PSD format using the name, Graduation Repaired.

To Create a Corrections Layer in the Graduation Repaired File

The following steps create an edits layer.

1 Duplicate the Background layer and name the new layer, corrections.

2 Create a red identification color on the corrections layer (Figure 5–41).

Figure 5–41

Vignetting

Vignetting is a change of an image's brightness at the edges compared to the center. Vignetting usually is an unintended effect, such as the halo effect that occurs when photographing a projection screen or other light source against a dark background, but sometimes it is used as a creative effect to draw attention to the center of the image. Special camera filters and post-processing procedures can create a vignette, but you also can create it using Photoshop.

To Create a Frame for the Vignette

The following steps create an oval in preparation for creating the vignette.

① Right-click the current marquee tool button, and then click Elliptical Marquee Tool on the context menu.

② Drag an oval over the center portion of the image, from the top to the bottom of the image, making sure to include all of the face. While dragging, press and hold the SPACEBAR key to reposition the marquee.

③ On the Select menu, click Inverse to invert the selection (Figure 5–42).

Figure 5–42

To Darken using the Burn Tool

The following steps darken the outer edges of the photo to increase the contrast using the Burn Tool.

1

- If necessary, right-click the Dodge Tool button to display the context menu, and then click Burn Tool to select it.

- If your mouse pointer does not appear as a circle, click the Brush Picker preset on the options bar, and then choose a circular brush.

- Use the RIGHT BRACKET (]) key to increase the size of the brush tip so that it is just larger than the selection, in this case, the entire image.

- Click several times to burn the image, enhancing the contrast of the photo (Figure 5–43).

Q&A Is it OK if my brush extends beyond the edge of the image?

Yes, just make sure you cover the entire image itself.

Q&A Why should I increase the size of the brush to cover the selection?

If your brush is bigger than the selection, clicking once changes the entire selection evenly and does not change the unselected area.

Figure 5–43

2

- Deselect to view the changes.

- Use the LEFT BRACKET ([) key to decrease the size of the brush tip back to a more manageable size.

Other Ways
1. Press O or SHIFT+O, adjust brush size, click imperfection

To Lighten using the Dodge Tool

The following steps use the Dodge Tool to whiten the graduate's teeth.

- Zoom in on the teeth in the image.

- On the Tools panel, select the Quick Selection Tool.

- Drag to create a selection that includes most of the teeth (Figure 5–44).

Figure 5–44

- Right-click the Burn Tool button to display the context menu, and then click Dodge Tool to select it.

- Use the RIGHT BRACKET (]) key to increase the size of the brush tip so that it is just larger than the selection.

- Click several times to dodge the selection (Figure 5–45).

3

- Deselect.

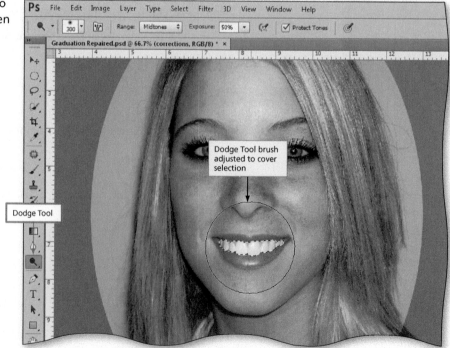

Figure 5–45

To Use the Sponge Tool

The Sponge Tool increases or decreases the color saturation of an area. In grayscale images, the Sponge tool changes the contrast by moving gray levels away from or toward the middle. The following steps use the sponge tool on the irises of the eye to increase the blue color.

1

- Right-click the Dodge Tool button to display the context menu, and then click Sponge Tool to select it.

- On the Sponge Tool options bar, click the Mode button to display its list (Figure 5–46).

Figure 5–46

2

- Click Saturate to choose the mode.

- In the document window, move the mouse pointer to the iris of the graduate's eye.

- Use the BRACKET keys to adjust the size of the brush tip so that it is just larger than the iris.

- Click repeatedly to sponge the image, enhancing the blue contrast of the eye.

- Repeat for the other eye (Figure 5–47).

Q&A

What is the difference between Saturate and Desaturate?

Saturate mode increases the color density and brightens the colors in the selection or image. Desaturate mode dulls the colors, and if sponged enough times, turns the selection or image gray.

Figure 5–47

3

- Deselect to view the changes.

- Compare the Background layer and the Corrections layer by clicking the 'Indicates layer visibility' icon on the corrections layer.

Other Ways

1. Press O or SHIFT+O, adjust brush size, click imperfection

To Save and Close the Graduation Repaired File

The following step saves the file again and closes it.

 Save, and close the file without quitting Photoshop.

Lens Correction Tools

Many kinds of photographic errors can be corrected in Photoshop. The most common mistakes include lens flaws, focus errors, distortions, unintended angle errors, and perspective errors. Every photographer has made an error from time to time.

Plan Ahead

> **Correct lens errors.**
> While modern digital cameras help you correct many user and lighting errors, some **lens correction** is necessary from time to time. If you have a photo that has lens errors, correct these errors after making any color, sharpening, cropping, or healing corrections.

The next series of steps uses the Lens Correction filter to fix some of the lens flaws, distortions, and errors in the Church photo. You can try different settings before committing them permanently to the image. Table 5–4 describes some typical errors and correction methods using the Lens Correction filter.

Table 5–4 Kinds of Distortions

Type of Error	Description	Correction Method
Angle error	An image is crooked or tilted in the photograph	Rotate image
Barrel distortion	A lens defect that causes straight lines to bow out toward the edges of the image	Decrease the barrel effect by negatively removing distortion
Chromatic aberration	Appears as a color fringe along the edges of objects caused by the lens focusing on different colors of light	Increase or decrease the red/cyan fringe or blue/yellow fringe in different planes
Keystone distortion	Wider top or bottom effect that occurs when an object is photographed from an angle or perspective	Correct vertical and/or horizontal perspective error
Pincushion distortion	A lens defect that causes straight lines to bend inward	Decrease the pincushion effect by positively removing distortion
Vignette distortion	A defect where the edges, especially the corners, of an image are darker than the center	Lighten or darken the amount of color at the four corners based on a midpoint in the image

You also can use the Lens Correction filter to rotate an image or fix image perspective caused by vertical or horizontal camera tilt. The filter's image grid makes these adjustments more easily and more accurately than using the Transform command.

Angle and Perspective Errors

While the Crop Tool and warp grids can be used to transform and correct the perspective in an image, the Lens Correction dialog box has the added advantages of allowing very precise measurements and other ways to correct errors. This is useful particularly when working with photos that contain keystone distortion. Keystone distortion in perspective occurs when an object is photographed from an angle. For example, if you take a picture of a tall building from ground level, the edges of the building appear closer to each other at the top than they do at the bottom. Keystone distortions can be corrected by changing the vertical or horizontal perspective in the photo. Angle errors occur when the camera is tilted to the left or right, making objects in the photo appear slanted.

After correcting keystone and angle errors, it is sometimes necessary to scale the image to regain any edges that were clipped by the correction. You also might need to fill in transparent edges created by changing the angle. The Lens Correction dialog box (Figure 5–48) has boxes, sliders, and buttons for correcting the distortions and repairing collateral damage created by the correction.

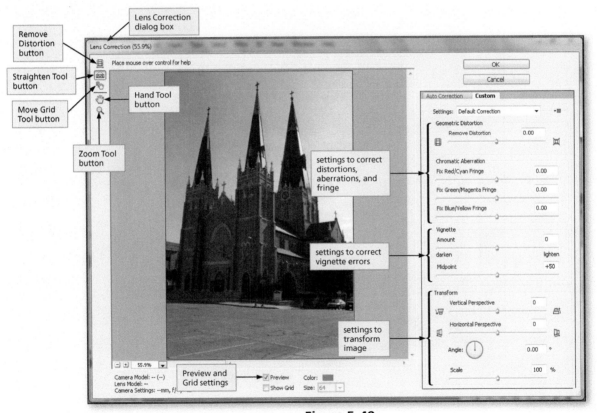

Figure 5–48

To Open the Church File and Save it with a Different Name

The next photo to correct is a church with lens errors. The following steps open a file named Church from the Data Files for Students. Visit www.cengage.com/ct/studentdownload for detailed instructions or contact your instructor for information about accessing the required files.

1. Open the file named Church from the Chapter 05 folder of the Data Files for Students.

2. Use the Save As dialog box to save the file on your preferred storage device in the PSD format using the name, Church Repaired.

To Unlock the Background Layer

Lens corrections must be performed on a single, unlocked layer. The following steps unlock the background layer using the lock icon. Later you will create a corrections layer to adjust the brightness in the photo.

1 On the Layers panel, double-click the lock icon on the Background layer to display the New Layer dialog box.

2 Click the OK button to accept the settings and close the dialog box (Figure 5–49).

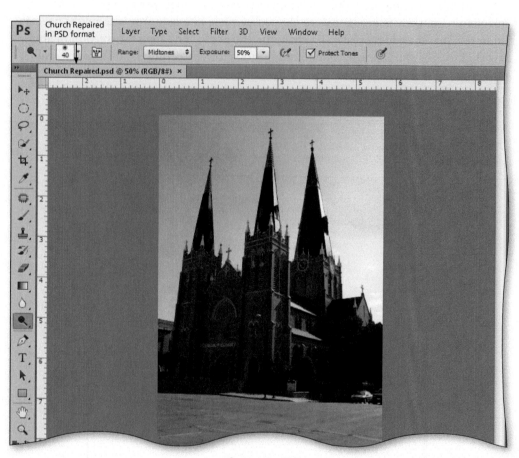

Figure 5–49

BTW

The Lens Correction Dialog Box
The Remove Distortion Tool button corrects barrel and pincushion distortions. The Move Grid Tool button is used to drag the grid lines to any position to help align edges within the image. The Hand Tool button moves or scrolls images that are more than 100 percent magnified.

To Display the Lens Correction Dialog Box

The following steps display the Lens Correction dialog box.

1

- Click Filter on the Application bar to display the Filter menu (Figure 5–50).

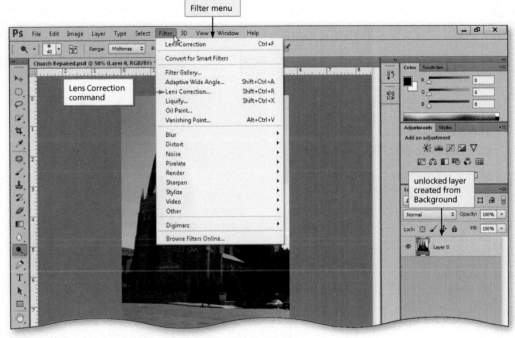

Figure 5–50

2

- Click Lens Correction on the Filter menu to display the Lens Correction dialog box.

- Click the Auto Correction tab, if necessary (Figure 5–51).

Experiment

- Click the Show Grid check box to obtain a visual cue on how much correction you will need to apply. Click the Move Grid Tool button and move the grid so a corner aligns with the top corner of the church. When you are finished evaluating the distortion, click the Show Grid check box again to turn off the grid.

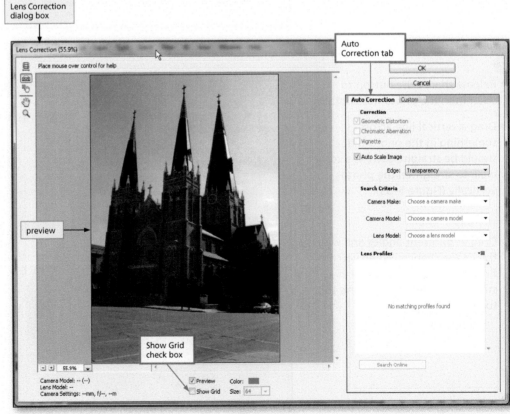

Figure 5–51

Other Ways
1. Press SHIFT+CTRL+R

To Straighten the Photo

To straighten the photo, the following steps use the Straighten Tool in the Lens Correction dialog box.

1

- Click the Straighten Tool button to select it.

- Drag horizontally across something in the photo that should be straight, such as the top of the steps. Do not release the mouse button so you can see the line and readjust as necessary (Figure 5–52).

Q&A

What if my adjustment causes part of my image to disappear?

If that happens, click the Cancel button and open the Lens Correction dialog box again. Drag shorter strokes. You do not have to drag across the entire image to straighten it.

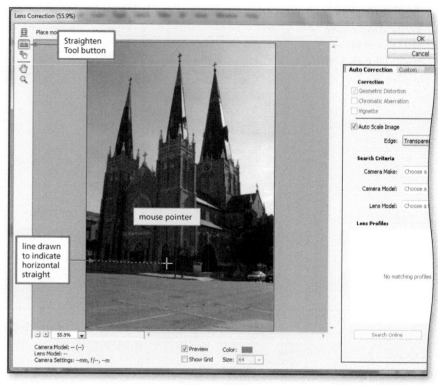

Figure 5–52

2

- Release the mouse button to straighten the photo horizontally.

- Drag a vertical line across something in the photo that should be straight, such as a corner wall, to straighten the photo vertically (Figure 5–53).

Experiment

- Drag at different angles and watch the image change. When you are finished, drag in the image in a straight line, left to right and top to bottom.

Other Ways

1. Click Custom tab (Lens Correction dialog box), drag Angle icon

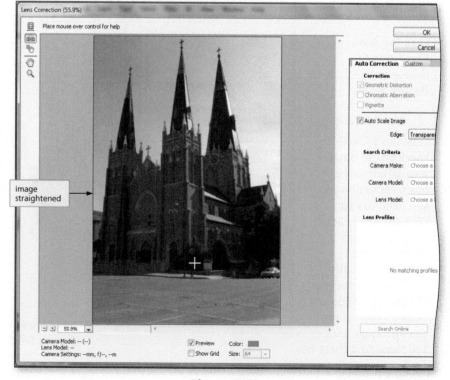

Figure 5–53

To Correct Distortions

The following steps correct keystone distortion in the photo. You also will scale the photo to make sure you include all of the crosses at the top of the church.

- Click the Custom tab to display the correction settings.

- Double-click the Vertical Perspective box, and type -14 to remove the keystone distortion.

- Drag the Scale slider to the left until all of the top cross is visible (Figure 5–54).

Q&A

How do negative values affect the vertical perspective?

A negative value in the Vertical Perspective box brings the top of the picture closer, such as when shooting up from the base of a tall building.

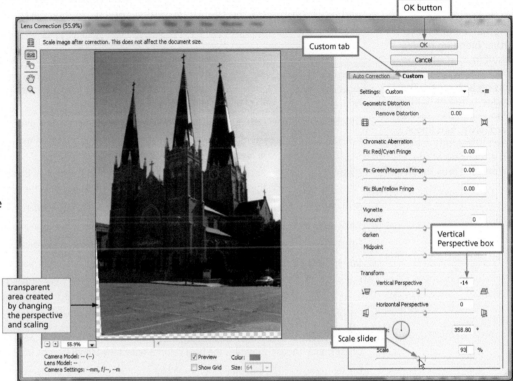

Figure 5–54

 Experiment

- Drag the Vertical Perspective slider back and forth to watch the perspective change in the preview. When you are finished, drag the slider to −14.

2

- Click the OK button to close the Lens Correction dialog box.

Q&A Why do I have transparent areas in the image?

When you correct distortions, Photoshop often has to reduce one side or end of the photo to align the image. You will crop the photo later to remove those areas.

Blending Modes

Blending modes define how an object interacts with other objects, specifically with respect to tonal adjustments. In previous chapters, you used a blending mode such as opacity to edit a layer's transparency. The Mode box appears in the options bar of many tools, as well as on several panels in Photoshop. Typically, it displays a list of blending modes to change how pixels in the image are affected by a color. The default blending mode is Normal, which sometimes is called the **threshold**. Each blending mode works differently, depending on the tool. For example, if you select the Gradient Tool, the blending mode changes how the gradient recolors the pixels as the colors change from one shade to another. The combination of these blending modes with the other settings on the options bar creates an almost infinite number of possibilities.

BTW

Extending the Edges
When you alter the angle or perspective a photo, using the Lens Correction dialog box, you commonly move the edges of the photo, leaving transparency along the edge of the original rectangular shape of the image. Using the Edge button, Photoshop offer choices for filling those transparent areas.

BTW

Blending Modes
Not all modes are available to every color event. The burn-based or darkening blending modes are more appropriate for applying a gradient over another image or layer. Other blending modes result in solid white or black unless the opacity setting is changed. The dodge-based or lighten blending modes such as hard, vivid, and linear, react differently for colors on either side of the 50 percent gray threshold.

Experimenting with the blending modes can give you a better feel for how they work. Photoshop Help has sample images of each of the blending modes. Table 5–5 describes some of the blending modes. As you look through the list, keep in mind that the **base color** is the original color in the image. The **blend color** is the color being applied with the painting or editing tool. The **result color** is the color resulting from the blend. Not all of the blending modes appear on every Mode list.

Table 5–5 Blending Modes

Blending Mode	Description
Normal	Paints each pixel to make it the result color
Dissolve	Used in conjunction with opacity to paint each pixel randomly with the result color
Behind	Paints each pixel in the transparent part of a layer — the Transparency check box must be deselected
Darken	Result color becomes the darker of either the base or blend color — pixels lighter than the blend color are replaced, and pixels darker than the blend color do not change
Multiply	Multiplies the base color by the blend color, resulting in a darker color
Color Burn	Darkens the base color to reflect the blend color by increasing the contrast
Linear Burn	Darkens the base color to reflect the blend color by decreasing the brightness
Darker Color	Result color is the lower value of the base or blend colors
Lighten	Result color becomes the lighter of either the base or blend color — pixels darker than the blend color are replaced, and pixels lighter than the blend color do not change
Screen	Multiplies the inverse of the blend and base colors, resulting in a lighter color
Color Dodge	Brightens the base color to reflect the blend color by decreasing the contrast
Linear Dodge (Add)	Brightens the base color to reflect the blend color by increasing the brightness
Lighter Color	The result color is the higher value of the base or blend colors
Overlay	Preserves the highlights and shadows of the base color as it is mixed with the blend color to reflect the lightness or darkness of the base color
Soft Light	Darkens or lightens the colors depending on the blend color — the effect is similar to shining a diffused spotlight on the image
Hard Light	Multiplies or screens the colors depending on the blend color — the effect is similar to shining a harsh spotlight on the image
Vivid Light	Burns or dodges the colors by increasing or decreasing the contrast depending on the blend color
Linear Light	Burns or dodges the colors by decreasing or increasing the brightness depending on the blend color
Pin Light	Replaces the colors depending on the blend color, creating a special effect
Hard Mix	Changes all pixels to primary colors by adjusting the RGB values
Difference	Looks at the color information in each channel and subtracts either the blend color from the base color, or the base color from the blend color, depending on which has the greater brightness value; blending with white inverts the base color values; blending with black produces no change
Exclusion	Creates an effect similar to, but lower in contrast than, the Difference blending mode
Hue	Creates a result color with the luminance and saturation of the base color, and the hue of the blend color
Saturation	Creates a result color with the luminance and hue of the base color, and the saturation of the blend color
Color	Creates a result color with the luminance of the base color, and the hue and saturation of the blend color
Luminosity	Creates a result color with the hue and saturation of the base color and the luminance of the blend color

To Create a Corrections Layer in the Church Repaired File

The following steps create an edits layer to accommodate the blending mode.

1 Duplicate the Background layer and name the new layer, corrections.

2 Create a red identification color on the corrections layer (Figure 5–55).

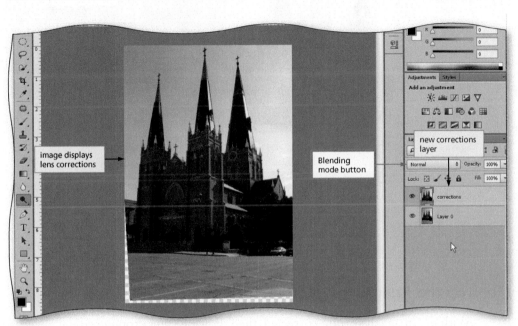

Figure 5–55

To Apply a Blending Mode

The following steps apply the blending mode.

1

• Click the Blending mode button on the Layers panel to display the list (Figure 5–56).

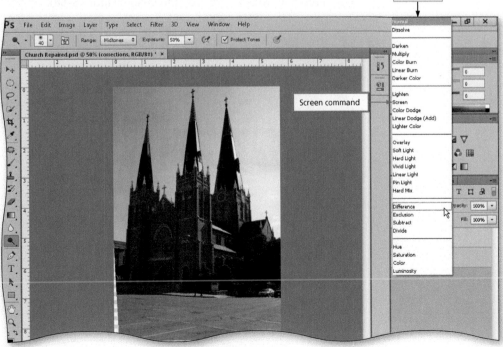

Figure 5–56

2

- Click Screen to set the layer's blending mode to Screen (Figure 5–57).

Why did I choose the Screen blending mode?

The Screen blending mode multiplies the inverse of the blend and base colors, resulting in a lighter color. It is a good mode for correcting exposure in photos that are too dark.

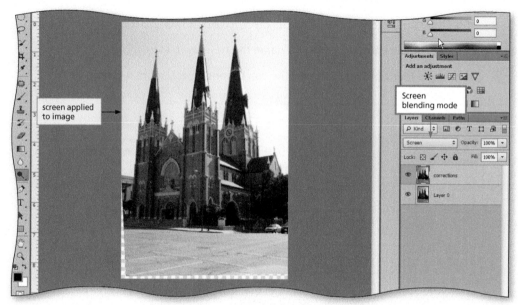

Figure 5–57

To Crop the Image

With the image distortion corrected, the following steps crop the edited image to remove transparent edges and to focus attention on the center building.

1 Select the Crop Tool.

2 Drag from the upper-left corner of the sky down and to the right, to include all of the church and some of the street.

3 Press the ENTER key to crop the image (Figure 5–58).

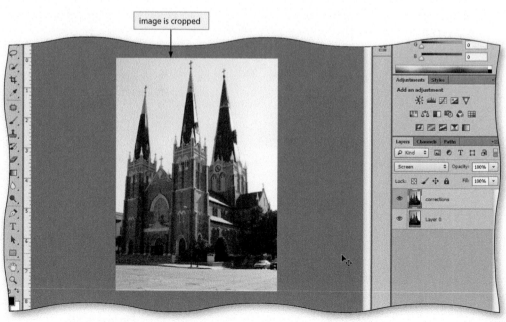

Figure 5–58

To Save and Close the Building Repaired File

The following step saves the file again and closes it.

1 Save and close the file without quitting Photoshop.

Break Point: If you wish to take a break, this is a good place to do so. You can quit Photoshop now. To resume at a later time, start Photoshop, and continue following the steps from this location forward.

The Blur, Sharpen, and Smudge Tools

A final set of tools used to help enhance, restore, and create special effects include the Blur, Sharpen, and Smudge Tools.

The Blur Tool softens hard edges or reduces detail in an image when you drag in the selection or image, by decreasing the color contrast between adjacent pixels. The Blur Tool is used for very subtle changes in small areas. If you are working on a high-resolution image, then the effect of the Blur Tool can be very slight; zooming in on a portion of the photo helps you notice the effect. The options bar includes settings for brush size, mode, and strength. The Sharpen Tool is the opposite of the Blur Tool. It increases contrast along edges to add sharpness. The more you paint over an area with the tool, the greater the sharpen effect. The Smudge Tool picks up color where the stroke begins and pushes it in the direction you drag. The effect is much like finger painting.

The Blur, Sharpen, and Smudge Tools have similar options bars (Figure 5–59).

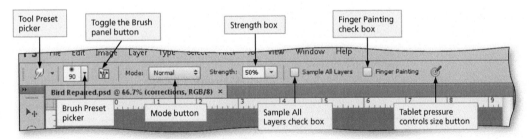

Figure 5–59

To Open the Bird File and Save It with a Different Name

You will use the Blur Tool to enhance a picture of a bird. The following steps open a file named Bird from the Data Files for Students. Visit www.cengage.com/ct/studentdownload for detailed instructions or contact your instructor for information about accessing the required files.

1 Open the file named Bird from the Chapter 05 folder of the Data Files for Students.

2 Use the Save As dialog box to save the file on your preferred storage device in the PSD format using the name, Bird Repaired.

To Create a Corrections Layer in the Bird File

The following steps create a corrections layer to accommodate the blending mode.

1 Duplicate the Background layer and name the new layer, corrections.

2 Create a red identification color on the corrections layer (Figure 5–60).

Figure 5–60

To Smudge

The following steps use the Smudge Tool to create an artistic swirl in the Bird image.

1
- On the Tools panel, right-click the Blur Tool button to display the context menu (Figure 5–61).

Figure 5–61

2

- Click Smudge Tool to select it.

- Press the RIGHT BRACKET (]) key to increase the size of the brush until the options bar displays 80 for the brush size.

3

- Slowly drag a circle around the edge of the image to create a smudge. The smudge will take several seconds to appear (Figure 5–62).

Q&A How do I use the Smudge Tool's options bar?

Figure 5–62

The Smudge Tool's Strength setting modifies the power of the smudge. Setting the Strength to 100% erases nearly all of the existing color. A Strength setting of 15% will give the appearance of trying to smudge dried paint. The Finger Painting check box mimics dipping your finger in the paint color before performing the smudge.

To Use the Sharpen Tool

The following steps sharpen the face of the bird to make it stand out.

1

- Zoom in on the face of the bird.

- Right-click the Smudge Tool and then click Sharpen Tool to select it.

- Adjust the size the Sharpen Tool brush using the BRACKET keys until the brush completely surrounds the face of the bird (Figure 5–63).

Figure 5–63

- Click several times to sharpen the face of the bird (Figure 5–64).

Experiment

- Click the visibility icon on the corrections layer to see the effect of your editing versus the original Background layer. Click it again to turn on the visibility of the corrections.

Figure 5–64

To Save the Bird Repaired File and Quit Photoshop

The final steps are to save the file again and quit Photoshop.

1 Save the file again.

2 Press CTRL+Q to quit Photoshop.

Chapter Summary

To repair and enhance photos, you used healing tools, tools that repaired damage; tools to lighten, darken, straighten, and align; and tools to create artistic effects. You first removed yellowing from a document and used a Curves adjustment to bring it into better focus. You used Content-Aware to fill in a missing portion of a picture and replace another portion. You then repaired scratches and damage to a black-and-white photo. You removed the red-eye from a color photo. Next, you added a vignetting effect. Using the Dodge, Burn, and Sponge Tools, you varied the shading and intensity of selected areas of an image. You opened a building photo that had keystone distortion, which you corrected using the Lens Correction dialog box, and you used a blending mode to lighten the photo. Finally, you used the Sharpen and Smudge Tools to enhance a photo artistically.

The items listed below include all the new Photoshop skills you have learned in this chapter:

1. Correct Yellowed Portions of the Document (PS 284)
2. Create a Layer from the Background (PS 285)
3. Edit Curves (PS 287)
4. Lock Transparent Pixels (PS 288)
5. Fill using Content-Aware (PS 291)
6. Use the Content-Aware Move Tool (PS 295)
7. Repair Damage using the Spot Healing Brush Tool (PS 298)
8. Sample and Paint using the Healing Brush Tool (PS 301)
9. Patch Areas (PS 303)

10. View Corrections (PS 305)
11. Correct Red-Eye (PS 307)
12. Darken using the Burn Tool (PS 311)
13. Lighten using the Dodge Tool (PS 312)
14. Use the Sponge Tool (PS 313)
15. Display the Lens Correction Dialog Box (PS 317)
16. Straighten the Photo (PS 318)
17. Correct Distortions (PS 319)
18. Apply a Blending Mode (PS 321)
19. Smudge (PS 324)
20. Use the Sharpen Tool (PS 325)

Apply Your Knowledge

Reinforce the skills and apply the concepts you learned in this chapter.

Enhancing a Photo for the Web

Instructions: Start Photoshop and perform the customization steps found on pages PS 6 through PS 10. Open the Apply 5-1 Antique file from the Chapter 05 folder of the Data Files for Students. Visit www.cengage.com/ct/studentdownload for detailed instructions or contact your instructor for information about accessing the required files.

The purpose of this exercise is to repair a photo of an antique typewriter and enhance it for use on an auction Web site. The edited photo is shown in Figure 5–65.

Figure 5–65

1. Use the Save As command to save the image on your USB flash drive as a PSD file, with the file name, Apply 5-1 Antique Enhanced.

2. In the Layers panel, right-click the Background layer and then click Duplicate Layer on the shortcut menu.

3. In the Duplicate Layer dialog box, type corrections in the As box, and then click the OK button. Right-click the new layer and choose a red identification color.

4. With the corrections layer selected, click Filter on the Application bar, and then click Lens Correction.

5. When the Lens Correction dialog box is displayed, click the Custom tab, and then edit the following settings:

   a. To adjust the barrel distortion, type 15 in the Remove Distortion box.

   b. To straighten the photo, type 2 in the Angle box.

   c. To correct the keystone distortion, type 50 in the Vertical Perspective box.

   d. To adjust the scale and remove transparent areas in the photo, type 100 in the Scale box.

Continued >

Apply Your Knowledge *continued*

6. Click the OK button in the Lens Correction dialog box.

7. On the Tools panel, right-click the current healing tool button and then click Spot Healing Brush Tool in the list. Use the Spot Healing Brush Tool to correct the damaged area on the wall to the right of the typewriter. Zoom as needed. (*Hint:* Remember to adjust the brush size to be only slightly larger than the damaged area.)

8. Experiment with the healing tools to correct flaws in the white baseboard and remove the small red ball to the left of the table.

9. Right-click the Spot Healing Brush Tool, and then click Healing Brush Tool in the list. On the options bar, click the Mode box arrow and then click Replace.

10. ALT+click a light area in the floor and then, using short strokes, drag through the darker areas in the floor. Resample as necessary.

11. To remove the electrical cord in the photo:

   a. Select the Content-Aware Move Tool. On the options bar, choose the Move mode and the Medium adaptation.

   b. Drag to create a rectangular selection of the floor, approximately the width of the electrical cord. Drag the selection to cover the part of electrical cord that is on the floor.

   c. Drag to create a rectangular selection of the baseboard, approximately the width of the remaining electrical cord. Drag the selection to cover the remaining electrical cord.

   d. Repeat Steps 11b and 11c for the cord and plug on the right side of the image.

12. Press CTRL+S to save the file again. If Photoshop displays an options dialog box, click the OK button.

13. Click File on the Application bar, and then click the Save for Web command. When the Save for Web dialog box is displayed, click the 4-Up tab, if necessary, and then click the best preview for your system. Click the Save button. When the Save Optimized As dialog box is displayed, save the image on your USB flash drive. Photoshop will fill in the name, Apply-5-1-Antique-Enhanced, and the file type for you.

14. Submit this assignment in the format specified by your instructor.

Extend Your Knowledge

Extend the skills you learned in this chapter and experiment with new skills. You may need to use Help to complete the assignment.

Creating a Moving Automobile Photo

Instructions: Start Photoshop and perform the customization steps found on pages PS 6 through PS 10. Open the Extend 5-1 Auto file from the Chapter 05 folder of the Data Files for Students. Visit www.cengage.com/ct/studentdownload for detailed instructions or contact your instructor for information about accessing the required files.

The purpose of this exercise is to edit a photograph of a parked automobile and make it look like it is in motion, creating both PSD and TIF versions of the final image. Many times, it is impossible to take an action photo of an automobile or other subject traveling at a high speed. This technique will show how to take an existing still photo and make it appear to be moving, as in Figure 5–66.

Figure 5–66

Perform the following tasks:

1. Start Photoshop. Set the default workspace and default colors, and reset all tools.

2. Save the image on your USB flash drive as a PSD file, with the file name Extend 5-1 Auto Complete.

3. To create a corrections layer:

   a. Right-click the Background layer and then click Duplicate Layer on the context menu to create a second layer. Name the layer corrections and use a red identification color.

4. To separate the foreground from the background:

   a. Create a selection marquee around the entire car to separate it from the background.

   b. Press CTRL+J or use the Layer via Copy command to place a copy of the automobile on a new layer and assign the layer an appropriate name and color.

5. To create an illusion of speed in the background:

   a. Select the corrections layer. Click Filter on the Application bar, point to Blur, and then click Motion Blur to display the Motion Blur dialog box. (*Hint*: You might want to read about Blur filters in Photoshop Help.)

   b. When the Motion Blur dialog box appears, experiment with the Angle and Distance settings until you are satisfied with the results. Increasing the Distance setting to 100 or more will blur the background enough to hide the sidewalk, so the picture will seem like the car is on a highway. Close the Motion Blur dialog box.

6. To create an illusion of wheel spin:

   a. Select the automobile layer and then create a selection marquee around the front wheel.

   b. Add a Radial Blur to the wheel by clicking Filter on the Application bar. Click Blur on the Filter submenu, and then click Radial Blur to display the Radial Blur dialog box. Select the Spin Blur Method. Experiment with the Amount and Quality settings. When you are satisfied with the effect, close the Radial Blur dialog box and deselect the wheel.

   c. Select the back wheel and then apply the same Radial Blur setting used for the front wheel by pressing CTRL+F to repeat the filter. Deselect the back wheel.

Continued >

STUDENT ASSIGNMENTS

Extend Your Knowledge *continued*

7. To tint the windshield and side windows:

a. With the automobile layer still active, create a selection marquee around the windshield. Use the 'Add to selection' button to add the side windows to the selection.

b. Press CTRL+J or use the Layer via Copy command to create a new layer. Assign the layer an appropriate name and color.

c. Press CTRL+L to display the Levels dialog box.

d. Drag the white Output Levels slider to the left until the windows look tinted.

e. Click OK to close the dialog box.

8. Save the file again. Flatten the image.

9. Save the image as Extend 5-1 Auto Complete in the TIFF format. If Photoshop displays a dialog box, click the OK button.

10. Submit the assignment in the format specified by your instructor.

11. Quit Photoshop.

Make It Right

Analyze a project and correct all errors and/or improve the design.

Correcting a Photo

Instructions: Start Photoshop and perform the customization steps found on pages PS 6 through PS 10. Open the Make It Right 5-1 Girl file from the Chapter 05 folder of the Data Files for Students. Visit www.cengage.com/ct/studentdownload for detailed instructions or contact your instructor for information about accessing the required files.

A friend of yours would like you to correct the red-eye, brighten the blue dress, whiten the teeth, and use a blending mode to lighten the photo.

Perform the following tasks:

Using the techniques you learned in the chapter, make the following corrections.

1. Save the file with the name Make It Right 5-1 Girl Repaired, in the PSD format, on your storage device.

2. Create a Layer From Background, named corrections.

3. Correct the red-eye.

4. Use the Sponge tool to brighten the dress and bring out more of the blue color.

5. Select the teeth and then use the Dodge Tool to lighten the teeth.

6. Save the file again.

Figure 5–67

In the Lab

Design and/or create a document using the guidelines, concepts, and skills presented in this chapter. Labs are listed in order of increasing difficulty.

Lab 1: Enhancing an Old Photo

Problem: You would like to enhance a photo of your great-great-grandparents and print several copies. The repaired photo is shown in Figure 5–68.

Figure 5–68

Note: To complete this assignment, you will be required to use the Data Files for Students. Visit www.cengage.com/ct/studentdownload for detailed instructions or contact your instructor for information about accessing the required files.

Instructions: Perform the following tasks:

1. Start Photoshop. Set the Default Workspace and then reset the workspace, all tools, and colors.

2. Open the file Lab 5-1 Couple from the Chapter 05 folder of the Data Files for Students.

3. Click the Save As command on the File menu. Type `Lab 5-1 Couple Repaired` as the file name. Save the file in the PSD format on your USB flash drive.

4. Click Image on the Application bar, point to Mode, and then click Grayscale to remove the yellowing in the photo.

5. Duplicate the Background layer and name it, corrections.

6. Zoom to the top of the photo.

7. Select the Spot Healing Brush Tool. On the options bar, click Content-Aware, if necessary. Using the BRACKET keys, change the size of the brush to be slightly larger than the hole punched in the picture. Click to repair the spot.

8. Fix the spots on the woman's face. If you make a bad correction, press CTRL+Z and then decrease your brush size before trying again.

Continued >

In the Lab *continued*

9. Zoom to the blackened spot on the leg of the man's overalls.

10. Select the Patch tool. To create a more believable correction, you will patch the spot twice. First, drag to create a selection around the upper half of the blackened area. Drag the patch upward, just above the blackened area. Second, drag to create a selection around the lower half of the blackened area. Drag the patch downward, just below the blackened area.

11. Click the Curves icon on the Adjustments panel. Drag the white point slider to the second grid mark on the left. Drag the black point slider to the first grid mark on the right. Adjust the pointers as needed to improve the brightness of the photograph.

12. Make any other repairs you feel are necessary. Turn off and on the visibility of the corrections and Background layers to notice the difference between the original and the corrections.

13. Save the image again. Flatten the layers. Save the image with the file name Lab 5-1 Couple Final in the TIFF format, and then print a copy for your instructor.

In the Lab

Lab 2: Creating a Vignette

Problem: The local historical society would like you to create a vignette around the picture of a sailor from World War II. After your edits, the photo should appear as shown in Figure 5–69.

Note: To complete this assignment, you will be required to use the Data Files for Students. Visit www.cengage.com/ct/studentdownload for detailed instructions or contact your instructor for information about accessing the required files.

Instructions: Perform the following tasks:

1. Start Photoshop. Set the Default Workspace and then reset all tools, colors, and the workspace.

2. Open the Lab 5-2 Sailor file from the Chapter 05 folder of the Data Files for Students. Save the file on your USB flash drive storage device as Lab 5-2 Sailor Repaired in the PSD format.

3. Use the Lens Correction dialog box to straighten the photo vertically. Use the line of the nose as a guide.

4. Create a corrections layer, and then choose the Spot Healing Brush Tool and repair any blemishes or damaged areas of the photo.

5. Create a Curves adjustment to bring out the features of the sailor's face.

6. Create a selection of the sailor's pupils, and then use the Burn tool to darken his eyes.

7. To create the vignette:

    a. Use the Elliptical Marquee Tool to draw selection oval around the sailor's face.

    b. Use the Dodge Tool to lighten the selection.

    c. On the Select menu click Inverse.

    d. Use the Burn Tool to darken the selection.

8. Experiment with different blending modes using Table 5-5 on page PS 320 as a guide. Apply the one you like best.

9. Save the file again. Submit the assignment in the format specified by your instructor.

Figure 5–69

In the Lab

Lab 3: Fixing Distortions

Problem: A local real estate agent wants you to fix a photo of a beach house, so she can use it on the vacation rental Web site. The photo has barrel distortion and is not straight. If possible, you should remove the construction at the left side of the home. The details of the home also might be improved with sharpening and lightening. After your repairs, the photo should appear as shown in Figure 5–70.

Figure 5–70

Note: To complete this assignment, you will be required to use the Data Files for Students. Visit www.cengage.com/ct/studentdownload for detailed instructions or contact your instructor for information about accessing the required files.

Instructions: Perform the following tasks:
Start Photoshop and perform the customization steps found on pages PS 6 through PS 10. Open the file Lab 5-3 Beach House from the Data Files for Students. Save the file as Lab 5-3 Beach House Repaired.psd on your USB flash drive storage device.

Create a corrections layer. Open the Lens Correction dialog box and adjust the angles. Adjust the Geometric Distortion (*Hint:* Because the picture was taken at a significant angle, with the wrong lens, the correction will not make the building perfect.) Use the Straighten Tool button to straighten the photo, using the water as a guide. Change the edge to Edge Extension. Make any other adjustments you feel necessary. Save the image again.

Cases and Places

Apply your creative thinking and problem solving skills to design and implement a solution.

To complete these assignments, you may be required to use the Data Files for Students. Visit www.cengage.com/ct/studentdownload for detailed instructions or contact your instructor for information about accessing the required files.

Create a Clean Photo for a Slide Show

Academic

On a recent vacation, you took pictures of several monuments along the Lewis and Clark trail. You want to use a photo of a memorial in a slide show for your history class, but the picture you took has a trash can and light pole in the background. It also is a bit crooked. Open the Case 5-1 Memorial file that is located in the Chapter 05 folder of the Data Files for Students. Use the Lens Correction tool to straighten the photo. Use the Content-Aware Move Tool in Extend mode to fill in any resulting transparent edges. Use Content-Aware techniques to remove the unwanted background objects from the image. Save the file as Case 5-1 Memorial Repaired in the PSD format.

Repair a Favorite Photo

Personal

Your grandmother's favorite photo of your uncle has many issues. You decide to fix it for her. Start Photoshop and then reset all the defaults. Open the Case 5-2 Uncle photo that is located in the Chapter 05 folder of the Data Files for Students. Save the photo with the name Case 5-2 Uncle Edited, in the PSD format. Convert the photo to Grayscale. Create a corrections layer. Use the lens correction tool to straight the photo. Crop the photo to remove the border. Use the Content-Aware Move Tool and the Extend mode to fill in any white areas left around the edge of the crop. Use the Spot Healing Brush Tool to repair blemishes and spots. Use the Burn Tool to darken the faded area. Use the Sharpen Tool to bring out the features in the boy's face. Flatten the image. Save the photo again and submit an electronic copy to your instructor.

Creating a Signature File

Professional

You need to create a signature that you can place on various electronic documents, including PDF files. Sign your name on a piece of paper and scan it using a high resolution of black and white (or use the Case 5-3 Signature file included in the Chapter 05 folder of the Data Files for Students). Create a Layer From Background. Remove all of the white and extraneous marks. Lock the layer for transparency. Use the Burn Tool to darken the signature. Save the file with the name, Case 5-3 Signature Transparent as a PSD file.

6 | Applying Filters and Patterns

Adobe product screenshot(s) reprinted with permission from Adobe Systems Incorporated

Objectives

You will have mastered the material in this chapter when you can:

- Adjust the Color Panel
- Fill with the Paint Bucket Tool
- Describe the categories of filters in Photoshop
- Use the Filter Gallery to create special effects
- Apply Plastic Wrap, Glowing Edges, and Craquelure filters
- Create a shape clipping mask

- Apply a pattern
- Describe and use Blur filters
- Create dynamic text with effects
- Set text tracking, leading, and kerning
- Explain the terms knockout, trapping, surprinting, and misregistration
- Print a hard proof

6 | Applying Filters and Patterns

Introduction

Special effects or visual effects are commonplace, and because computers facilitate nearly all commercial graphics and animation, many clients and customers expect to see effects in their creative designs. Effects that seemed rare and unusual 10 years ago are now the norm. Special effects visually spice up static graphics with distortions, blurs, contour alterations, color manipulations, and applied overlays. Imaginative visual effects create a customized, attention-grabbing appearance, and are used in everything from DVD liners to billboards. It is not unusual for people to design branding logos with advanced visual effects for use in business and social media. Most people subconsciously expect to see fancy, stimulating graphics in every advertisement; indeed, when no special effects are included, some may interpret the graphic as retro or even boring.

The entertainment industry has led the way with artistic rendering and advanced animation techniques. Specialized graphic manipulations are saved and sold as downloadable filters for most popular graphic-editing software packages. Filters are the most common way to create special effects in Photoshop. In fact, entire books have been written about the vast number of filters included in the Photoshop installation, along with the thousands of third-party filters that can be added. Filters have the capability to mimic many traditional forms of art, such as pastels, line drawings, and watercolors. You can blend, blur, brush, or warp graphics in every way imaginable, allowing you to enliven commercial artwork in-house with relative ease.

In this chapter, as you learn about filters and patterns, you might find the many options and settings to be overwhelming at first. It is easy to become carried away when applying filters. Your goal should be a subtle, judicious, and purposeful use of filters to enhance the meaning of the digital image.

Project — Creating a Magazine Cover

Chapter 6 uses Photoshop to create a cover for an extreme sports magazine. The magazine cover incorporates graphics, color, shapes, and patterns. Photoshop filters are applied to the various images on the cover. The large image employs a blur filter. From top to bottom, the smaller, pentagon-shaped images use a Plastic Wrap, Glowing Edges, and Craquelure filter. A pattern adds visual interest to the background area of the smaller images. Advanced font and character techniques customize the headings and description text. The completed image is displayed in Figure 6–1.

☐ ☐ ☐ ☐   Feather: 0 px   Anti-alias   Style: Normal ⬦   Adobe **Photoshop CS6**

INSIDE THIS ISSUE:

WAKEBOARDING AT ITS BEST!

SCREAM EXTREME

THE MAGAZINE FOR EXTREME SPORTERS
SUMMER 2014 EDITION

Figure 6–1

Overview

As you read this chapter, you will learn how to create the magazine cover shown in Figure 6–1 by performing these general tasks:

- Create a background and add images.
- Apply filters.
- Use a pattern.
- Place pictures in a pentagon shape and stroke.
- Stroke and fill selections with color.
- Create and adjust text with special effects.
- Print a hard proof.

General Project Guidelines

When editing a photo, the actions you perform and decisions you make will affect the appearance and characteristics of the finished product. As you edit a photo, such as the one shown in Figure 6-1 on the previous page, you should follow these general guidelines:

1. **Plan your use of filters.** Think about your purpose in using filters. Is it for correction or decoration? Are you trying to create a special effect or does the filter enhance the purpose of the image? Decide if a filter is appropriate for the entire image or just a part. If you are working on a business photo, consult with the client, and offer him or her many examples or layer comps. After creating a new layer so the filter will be nondestructive, make sure you label the filter layer with the type and settings, so you can remember what you did.

2. **Use type wisely.** When using large text, pay close attention to formatting type styles, spacing, and character effects such as kerning, tracking, leading, and baseline shift. Use a stroke of color around the text for a more distinctive look that stands out. Apply overlays to prevent misregistration.

3. **Avoid color printing problems.** In commercial printing, the speed of the printer and possible shifts in the paper may make some colors run together, creating spreads of blended color, or the printer may leave small missed areas between very close objects or layers. Use knockout techniques and correct alignment to avoid color printing problems.

4. **Consult with printing professionals.** As design specialists create and modify artwork, they routinely consult with printing professionals to help plan the best method to produce projects. Print professionals have information on paper, color management systems, file transfer, output devices, and the way those devices interpret and process color and type information.

Starting and Customizing Photoshop

The following steps start Photoshop and reset the default workspace, tools, colors, and Layer panel options.

To Start Photoshop

The following steps, which assume Windows 7 is running, start Photoshop based on a typical installation. You may need to ask your instructor how to start Photoshop for your system.

1 Click the Start button on the Windows 7 taskbar to display the Start menu, and then type `Photoshop CS6` in the 'Search programs and files' box.

2 Click Adobe Photoshop CS6 in the list to start Photoshop.

3 If the Photoshop window is not maximized, click the Maximize button next to the Close button on the Application bar to maximize the window.

To Reset the Tools and the Options Bar

The following steps select the Rectangular Marquee Tool and reset all tool settings on the options bar.

1 If the tools in the Tools panel appear in two columns, click the double arrow at the top of the Tools panel.

2 If necessary, click the Rectangular Marquee Tool button on the Tools panel to select it.

3 Right-click the Rectangular Marquee Tool icon on the options bar to display the context menu, and then click Reset All Tools. When Photoshop displays a confirmation dialog box, click the OK button to restore the tools to their default settings.

To Set the Interface and Default Colors

The following steps set the interface to Medium Gray and the foreground and background colors to black over white.

1 Click Edit on the Application bar to display the Edit menu. Point to Preferences and then click Interface on the Preferences submenu to display the Preferences dialog box.

2 Click the third button, Medium Gray, to change the interface color scheme.

3 Click the OK button to close the Preferences dialog box.

4 Press the D key to reset the default foreground and background colors. If black is not over white on the Tools panel, press the X key.

To Select the Default Workspace

The following steps select the Default workspace.

1 Click Window on the Application bar, and then point to Workspace to display the Workspace submenu. Click Essentials (Default) on the Workspace submenu to select the workspace.

2 Click Window on the Application bar, and then point to Workspace to display the Workspace submenu again. Click Reset Essentials to reset the workspace.

To Create a Blank Canvas

Because you are working with a magazine medium that prints to the edge of the paper, you will create a blank canvas 8.5 inches wide x 10.75 inches high, which is a common magazine size. Nearly all magazines on the market today are full-color magazines, and they are printed using a four-color process (CMYK), providing bright color shades and an eye-catching look. However, more filter effects are available for RGB images, so you will create the image in RGB and later convert it to CMYK. The following steps create a blank canvas.

1 Press CTRL+N to open the New dialog box. Type `Magazine Cover` in the Name box.

2 Click the Width unit box arrow, and then click Inches, if necessary.

3 Set the width to 8.5 and the height to 10.75 to apply standard magazine measurements.

4 Set the resolution to 300, and set the Color Mode to RGB, 8 bit.

5 If necessary, click the Background Contents box arrow, and then click Transparent in the list (Figure 6–2 on the next page).

6 Click the OK button to create the transparent canvas.

7 If the rulers do not appear in the document window, press CTRL+R. Press CTRL+0 [zero] to fit the canvas on the screen.

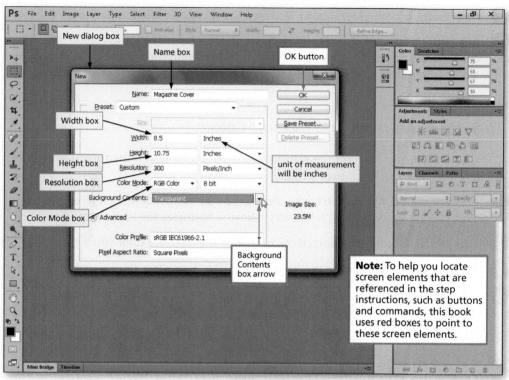

Figure 6–2

To Save the File

The following steps save the file in the PSD format using the Save As command.

1 With your USB flash drive connected to one of the computer's USB ports, press SHIFT+CTRL+S to display the Save As dialog box.

2 Click the Save in box arrow and then click Removable Disk (F:), or the location associated with your USB flash drive, in the list. If you want to create a folder for the photos in Chapter 6, click the Create New Folder button. Then, when the new folder is displayed, type a chapter name, such as Chapter 06, and press the ENTER key. Double-click the new folder to open it.

3 If necessary, click the Format button and then choose the Photoshop format.

4 Click the Save button in the Save As dialog box to save the file. If Photoshop displays a dialog box, click the OK button.

To Edit Layers

The following steps assign a name and an identification color to the existing layer and then create a new layer in preparation for the first image.

1 Double-click the name, Layer 1, on the Layers panel, type background, and then press the ENTER key to rename the layer.

2 Right-click the layer and choose an orange identification color.

3 Press SHIFT+CTRL+N to create a new layer. Name it wakeboarding and use a violet identification color (Figure 6–3).

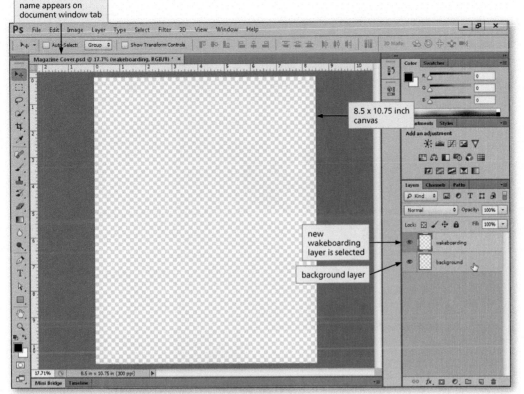

Figure 6–3

To Insert the Wakeboarding Graphic

The first graphic to insert is the main graphic on the magazine cover. To complete this assignment, you will be required to use the Data Files for Students. Visit www.cengage.com/ct/studentdownload for detailed instructions or contact your instructor for information about accessing the required files. The following steps copy and paste the image into the Magazine Cover.

1. Open the file named Wakeboarding from the Chapter 06 folder of the Data Files for Students.

2. Press CTRL+A to select the entire image, and then press CTRL+C to copy the selection.

3. Close the Wakeboarding window to return to the Magazine Cover file.

4. Press CTRL+V to paste the copy into the Magazine Cover file.

5. Activate the Move Tool and drag the pasted image to the upper-right corner of the magazine cover.

6. Press CTRL+T to display the transformation handles.

7. SHIFT+drag the lower-left sizing handle to leave a 2-inch margin on the left side, as shown in Figure 6–4 on the next page.

8. On the options bar, click the Commit transform (Enter) button to finish placing the image.

BTW

Layer Transparency
On the Layers panel, if your layers display a solid background, the Transparency Grid setting has been set to None. To display a checkerboard instead of a solid background, click Edit on the Application bar, point to Preferences, and then click Transparency & Gamut in the Preferences dialog box. Then adjust the Grid Size and Grid Colors.

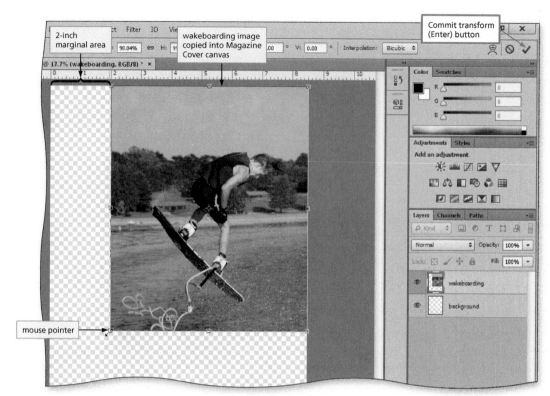

Figure 6–4

The Color Panel

Photoshop has many different ways to select or specify colors for use in the document window. You specify colors when you use paint, gradient, or fill tools. Previously you used the Color picker dialog box to choose colors. Some other ways include using the Color panel, the Swatches panel, the Eyedropper tool, the Color Sampler tool, and the Info panel.

A convenient way to select and edit colors is to use the Color panel (Figure 6–5), which displays numeric color values for the current foreground and background colors. Using the sliders or number boxes on the Color panel, you can edit the foreground and background colors using different color modes. At the bottom of the panel, you can choose a color from the entire color spectrum, by clicking the color bar. The Color panel menu allows you to change the color mode, change the displayed sliders, copy the color, or close the panel.

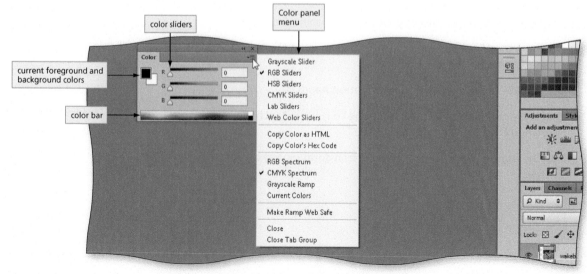

Figure 6–5

To Change the Sliders on the Color Panel

Because the ultimate version of the magazine cover will be saved in CMYK color mode, changing the sliders on the Color panel will help you determine whether your chosen colors adhere to the color mode. The following steps change the Color panel to reflect CMYK colors in the sliders and on the color bar.

①

- Click the Color panel menu button to display its menu (Figure 6–6).

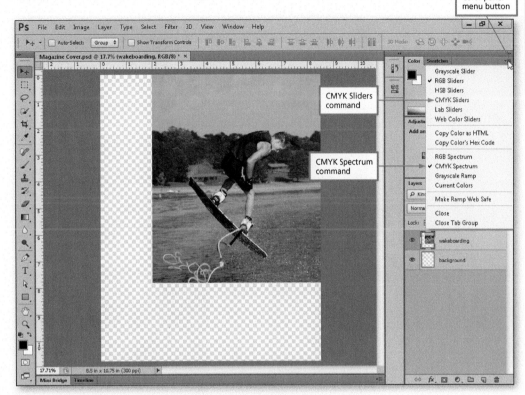

Figure 6–6

②

- Click CMYK Sliders to change the sliders in the Color panel.

- Click the menu button again, and then click CMYK Spectrum to change the color bar, if necessary (Figure 6–7).

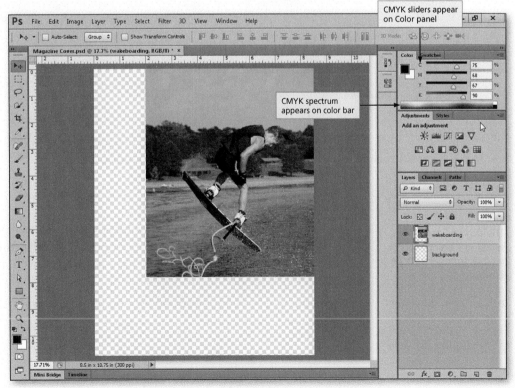

Figure 6–7

To Choose a Color with the Eyedropper Tool

When designing graphics around a main image, it is a good practice to use that image as a source for colors when possible. Recall that the Eyedropper Tool samples an existing color in a graphic or panel to assign a new foreground or background color. The following steps choose an orange color from the wakeboarding image to use as a background fill for the magazine cover.

1 Press the I key to select the Eyedropper Tool.

2 In the wakeboarding image, click the orange color on the wakeboarder's shorts to choose a new color (Figure 6–8).

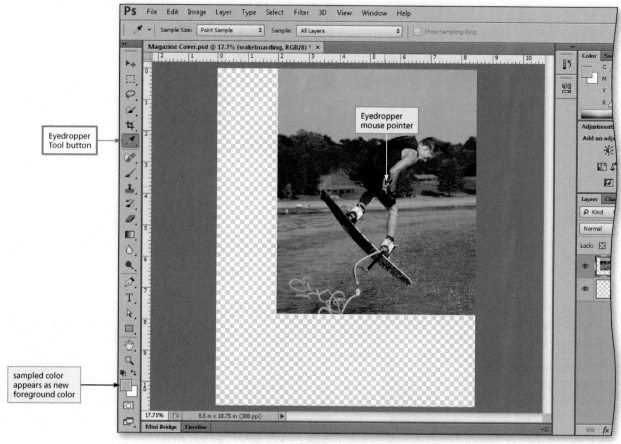

Figure 6–8

Out of Gamut Warning Icon
The Out of Gamut warning icon appears as a black triangle with an enclosed gray exclamation point. If the color cannot be created in the current color mode, the icon will appear on the Color panel, just above the color bar.

TO CORRECT AN OUT OF GAMUT COLOR

Recall that the gamut of reproducible ink colors is smaller than the colors we see with our eyes. In Photoshop, you will see an out of gamut warning if you select colors that have to be converted, because they have no equivalents in the CMYK model. If you see an out of gamut alert on the Color panel, perform the following step to correct it.

1. Click the Out of Gamut warning icon on the Color panel to convert the color to an acceptable CMYK color.

The Paint Bucket Tool

The Paint Bucket Tool fills similar pixels with a chosen color or pattern. To use the Paint Bucket Tool, you select it on the Tools panel and then click in the document window in the area you wish to replace. Recall that the Paint Bucket Tool appears on the same context menu as the Gradient tool. The Paint Bucket options bar displays choices for fine-tuning the use of the Paint Bucket tool (Figure 6–9). By default, the Paint Bucket tool uses the foreground color as its fill color, but you also can choose from a predefined pattern when filling. The Opacity and Tolerance boxes work the same way as they do for the Magic Wand Tool and the eraser tools. Recall that higher tolerance values fill a wider range of colors. The Contiguous check box allows you to fill only adjacent pixels of the same color within the tolerance. To fill pixels based on the merged color data from all visible layers, select the All Layers check box.

The Paint Bucket tool mouse pointer displays a paint bucket. The tip of the paint coming out of the bucket is the fill location.

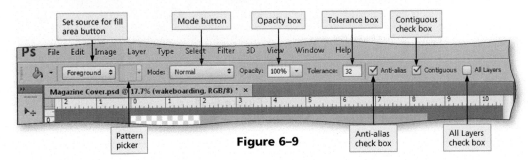

Figure 6–9

To Use the Paint Bucket Tool

The following steps use the Paint Bucket Tool to color the Background layer.

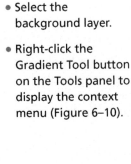

- Select the background layer.

- Right-click the Gradient Tool button on the Tools panel to display the context menu (Figure 6–10).

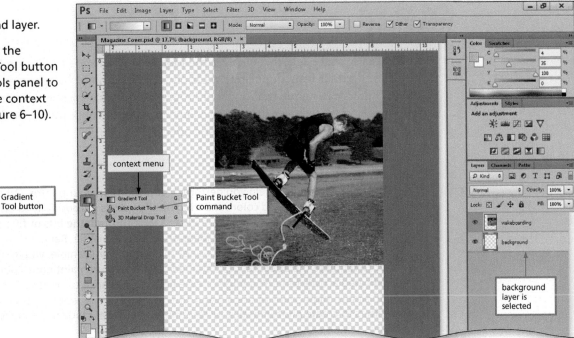

Figure 6–10

2

- Click the Paint Bucket Tool button to select it.

- Click the canvas to color the background layer with the color from the Color panel (Figure 6–11).

How does the Paint Bucket Tool determine which part of the image to color?

If the Contiguous check box is selected, the Paint Bucket Tool fills all pixels of the same color that are connected to the position of the click. If the Contiguous check box is not selected, all pixels of the same color are filled in.

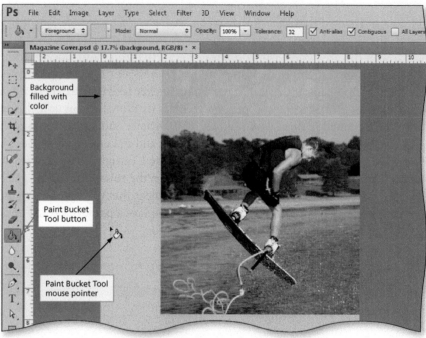

Figure 6–11

Other Ways

1. Press SHIFT+G, click document window

To Save the File

The following step saves the file.

1 Press CTRL+S to save the file.

Filters

A **filter** is a special effect that changes the look of your image or selection by altering the pixels — either by manipulating their physical location or by applying a color change. Filters can mimic traditional photographic filters, which are pieces of colored glass or gelatin placed over the lens to change the photo's appearance, or they can be more complex, creating advanced artistic effects.

Plan Ahead

Plan your use of filters.
Some filters in Photoshop help you perform restorations on your photos. Others alter color to create sophisticated color rendering or alter pixels purposefully to distort. The possibilities are endless. It is a good idea to look through the lists of filters in this chapter or use Photoshop Help to get ideas on what is available. Remember: your usage of filters should be driven by the purpose of the photo. For example, you might use a filter to simulate the appearance of stained glass or texture paintings to portray a sophisticated artistic tone. You might create lighting scenarios to create what-if images. Or, you simply might want to use a water filter on a picture of water. A popular trend uses filters to create **photomosaics**, or recognizable pictures made up of many smaller pictures.

Most filters can be applied either to the entire image or to a specific layer, channel, or selection. Filters can be used for correction or decoration, but they should always be applied to a nondestructive layer with correct labeling.

You used a Lens Correction filter in a previous chapter when you corrected perspective and straightened a photo. In this chapter, you will use additional filters to change the appearance of the graphics on the magazine cover. Filters are displayed in three ways on the Filter menu, as follows:

- Five specialized filters have their own commands on the Filter menu and display their own dialog box interface and buttons. These include the Adaptive Wide Angle, Lens Correction, Liquify, Oil Paint, and Vanishing Point filters. In CS6, some of these specialized filters require a video card that can perform graphic processor acceleration.

- The Filter Gallery command on the Filter menu categorizes standard filters into six groups: Artistic, Brush Strokes, Distort, Sketch, Stylize, and Texture. As you will learn later in this chapter, the Filter Gallery has its own interface and settings.

- Other filter commands appear only in submenus on the Filter menu. Rather than using the Filter Gallery interface, these filters open individual dialog boxes in the following categories: Blur, Distort, Noise, Pixelate, Render, Sharpen, Stylize, Video, and Other.

Some filters alter color or texture, while others actually rearrange the pixels themselves or recreate the image with new brush strokes. Although you will not use all of the filter categories in the magazine cover for this chapter, the following sections provide a general description of each category, along with a table of specific filters and their adjustable settings.

Artistic Filters

The Artistic filters (Table 6–1) create painting and artistic effects, adding a certain amount of texture, dimension, and abstraction to an image. The Artistic filters replicate traditional media effects such as grain patterns, oils, watercolors, charcoals, pastels, line drawings, neon shading, and sponges. Artistic filters are used in typography, commercial art, and personal art expression.

BTW

Installing Filters
To install a filter, you simply copy it into the Filters folder, usually located in C:\Program Files]Adobe\Adobe PhotoshopCS6\Required\ Plug-ins\Filters.

Table 6–1 Artistic Filters		
Artistic Filter	**Description**	**Adjustable Settings**
Colored Pencil	Redraws to simulate colored pencils on a solid background to create a crosshatched effect	Pencil Width, Stroke Pressure, Paper Brightness
Cutout	Redraws to simulate roughly cut pieces of colored paper, such as a collage or a screen print	Number of Levels, Edge Simplicity, Edge Fidelity
Dry Brush	Uses a dry brush technique on all edges and reduces the range of color	Brush Size, Brush Detail, Texture
Film Grain	Applies a film grain pattern to shadow tones and midtones with a smoother pattern to lighter areas; helps to unify diverse elements in an image	Grain, Highlight Area, Intensity
Fresco	Repaints using coarse, short, and rounded daubs	Brush Size, Brush Detail, Texture
Neon Glow	Inserts various types of glows to objects in the image	Glow Size, Glow Brightness, Glow Color
Paint Daubs	Redraws to simulate an oil painting	Brush Size, Sharpness, Brush Type
Palette Knife	Reduces detail to simulate a thinly painted canvas, revealing underlying textures	Stroke Size, Stroke Detail, Softness
Plastic Wrap	Redraws the image as if it were coated in shiny plastic	Highlight Strength, Detail, Smoothness

Continued

Table 6–1 Artistic Filters *(continued)*

Poster Edges	Reduces the number of colors in an image and draws black lines on edges	Edge Thickness, Edge Intensity, Posterization
Rough Pastels	Applies strokes of chalk, pastel-like color on a textured background; appears thicker in brighter colors	Stroke Length, Stroke Detail, Texture, Scaling, Relief, Light, Invert
Smudge Stick	Uses short diagonal strokes to smudge or smear darker parts of the image; lighter areas become brighter with a spotty texture and less detail	Stroke Length, Highlight Area, Intensity
Sponge	Creates textured areas of contrasting color that simulate the effect of sponge painting	Brush Size, Definition, Smoothness
Underpainting	Creates a textured background, and then paints the image over the background to create a paler, softer version; commonly used in conjunction with other filters	Brush Size, Texture Coverage, Texture, Scaling, Relief, Light, Invert
Watercolor	Creates a watercolor style that flattens yet brightens color; the greater the detail, the more realistic the image will appear	Brush Detail, Shadow Intensity, Texture

BTW

Filer Gallery Settings
Filter Gallery settings carry over each time you use the Filter Gallery. When you choose a new filter, he previous one is replaced. However if more than one filter appears in the list of filter effects, and you do not to use a filter, click the 'Delete effect layer' button.

Blur Filters

The Blur filters (Table 6–2) soften or smooth an image by locating defined edges, lines, and shadows, adding together the color values, and then averaging the pixels to create a new value. Commonly used for retouching, most of the Blur filters allow you to specify the radius of affected pixels. You can blur the background to draw attention to foreground objects, create dreamlike scenes and portraits, or add visual movement to an image.

Table 6–2 Blur Filters

Blur Filter	Description	Adjustable Settings
Field	Creates one or more areas of focus in the image, blurring the background by changing pixels	Blur
Iris	Adds focus points to simulate depth of field, allowing you to alter the size, shape, transition, and amount of blur using on-screen graphic controls	Blur
Tilt-Shift	Blurs with a gradient effect by placing multiple pins with different blur amounts, or by aligning one or more planes	Blur, Distortion, Symmetric Distortion
Average	Creates a smooth look by averaging the pixels in the entire selection or image to create a new replacement color	None
Blur, Blur More	Eliminates extraneous noise in areas with strong color transitions by averaging pixels	None
Box Blur	Averages the pixel color values of all neighboring pixels to create special effects; the larger the radius setting, the greater the blur	Radius
Gaussian Blur	Blurs using a weighted average to add low-frequency detail that produces a hazy effect	Radius
Lens Blur	Applies a blur with a narrower depth of field so that some objects in the image stay in focus and others are blurred	Depth Map, Iris, Specular Highlights, Noise
Motion Blur	Blurs in a specified direction and at a specified intensity or distance	Angle, Distance
Radial Blur	Simulates the blur of a zooming or rotating camera	Amount, Blur Method, Quality
Shape Blur	Blurs in a specified pattern or shape	Radius, Shape
Smart Blur	Blurs with precise settings	Radius, Threshold, Quality, Mode
Surface Blur	Blurs an image while preserving edges	Radius, Threshold

Brush Stroke Filters

The Brush Stroke filters (Table 6–3) paint with an artistic impression using different brush and ink stroke effects. Many of the filters allow you to set smoothness, sharpness, and intensity. Graphic artists use the Brush Stroke filters to achieve natural or traditional media effects.

Table 6–3 Brush Stroke Filters

Brush Stroke Filter	Description	Adjustable Settings
Accented Edges	Accentuates edges based on a brightness control	Edge Width, Edge Brightness, Smoothness
Angled Strokes	Creates brush strokes at opposite angles	Direction Balance, Stroke Length, Sharpness
Crosshatch	Preserves details while adding pencil hatching texture	Stroke Length, Sharpness, Strength
Dark Strokes	Paints dark areas with short, dark strokes, and light areas with long, white strokes	Balance, Black Intensity, White Intensity
Ink Outlines	Redraws with fine narrow lines creating a strong edge effect similar to an ink outline	Stroke Length, Dark Intensity, Light Intensity
Spatter	Simulates an airbrush, creating an exaggerated spatter and ripple effect	Spray Radius, Smoothness
Sprayed Strokes	Repaints using dominant colors, with angled, sprayed strokes in specific directions	Stroke Length, Spray Radius, Stroke Direction
Sumi-e	Creates soft, blurred edges with full ink blacks and uses a saturated brush style similar to Japanese rice paper painting	Stroke Width, Stroke Pressure, Contrast

Distort Filters

The Distort filters (Table 6–4) reshape images not by recoloring pixels, but by moving pixels in a geometric fashion to create 3-D effects and reshaping effects. Some of the distort filters purposefully add noise or altering effects to the image, while others correct the same kinds of problems. Distortion is used in advertising to give an emotional, comical, or exaggerated dimension for product recognition, or to express shape, size, and spatial relations. Some of the Distort filters are in the Filter Gallery; others open in their own dialog boxes from the Distort submenu.

BTW

Add-On Filters
A large number of filter plug-ins are available to add to your installation of Photoshop. These aftermarket filters add more power and features to Photoshop. Add-on filters can be purchased or downloaded as shareware from reputable Web sites.

Table 6–4 Distort Filters

Distort Filter	Description	Adjustable Settings
Diffuse Glow (Filter Gallery)	A soft diffusion filter that adds see-through white noise; glow fades from the center	Graininess, Glow Amount, Clear Amount
Displace	Distorts using a displacement map	Horizontal Scale, Vertical Scale, Displacement Map, Undefined Areas
Glass (Filter Gallery)	Distorts as if viewed through glass	Distortion, Smoothness, Texture Scaling, Invert
Ocean Ripple (Filter Gallery)	Ripples the surface randomly as if underwater	Ripple Size, Ripple Magnitude
Pinch	Squeezes from the center	Amount
Polar Coordinates	Toggles between rectangular and polar coordinates simulating a mirrored cylinder	Rectangular to Polar, Polar to Rectangular

Continued

Table 6–4 Distort Filters *(continued)*		
Ripple	Redraws with ripples	Amount, Size
Shear	Distorts or warps along a line	Undefined Areas
Spherize	Creates a spherical distortion	Amount, Mode
Twirl	Rotates, creating a twirl pattern	Angle
Wave	Precisely redraws with ripples	Number of Generators, Wavelength Amplitude, Scale, Type, Undefined Areas
ZigZag	Distorts radially, with reversals from center	Amount, Ridges, Style

Noise Filters

Noise is a term that refers to hazy, grainy, or extraneous pixels as well as flecks of random color distributed through a background. Noise also can refer to variation in brightness or color information. The Noise filters (Table 6–5) add or remove noise and help blend a selection into the surrounding pixels. Noise filters can create unusual textures or remove problem areas, such as dust and scratches.

Table 6–5 Noise Filters		
Noise Filter	**Description**	**Adjustable Settings**
Add Noise	Applies random pixels to an image, simulating the effect of high-speed film photography	Amount, Distribution, Monochromatic
Despeckle	Detects edges of color in an image and blurs all of the selection except those edges	None
Dust & Scratches	Reduces noise by changing dissimilar pixels	Radius, Threshold
Median	Reduces noise by blending the brightness of pixels within a selection, useful for eliminating or reducing the effect of motion on an image	Radius
Reduce Noise	Reduces noise while preserving edges based on user settings	Strength, Preserve Details, Reduce Color Noise, Sharpen Details, Remove JPEG Artifact

Pixelate Filters

The Pixelate filters (Table 6–6) redraw an image or selection by joining, grouping, or clustering pixels of similar color values into cells defined by the tolerance settings. The cells become blocks, rectangles, circles, or dots of color, creating an impression of looking at an image through a powerful magnifying glass. Many of the Pixelate filters replicate artistic movement styles such as pointillism, divisionism, or stippling.

Table 6–6 Pixelate Filters		
Pixelate Filter	**Description**	**Adjustable Settings**
Color Halftone	Replaces rectangular areas with circles of halftone screening on each color channel	Max. Radius, Screen Angles (Degrees)
Crystallize	Creates a solid color polygon shape by clustering pixels	Cell Size
Facet	Creates solid color by clustering similarly colored pixels; commonly used to remove color noise and specks	None
Fragment	Draws four copies of pixels and then averages the values and offsets them, creating a hazy blur	None
Mezzotint	Randomizes black-and-white areas or color areas, creating pixilation according to the chosen type	Type
Mosaic	Creates solid-colored, square blocks based on original pixel colors	Cell Size
Pointillize	Randomizes foreground colors and creates dots similar to pointillism; background simulates a canvas texture	Cell Size

BTW

Combining Filters
Many interesting effects can be created when combining filters as well as applying them more than once. The only restrictions are that filters cannot be applied to Bitmap or Index color images. Some filters will only work on 8-bit or RGB images.

BTW

Crystallize Filter Settings
The Crystallize filter combines pixels of the same color in rectangle-shaped cells. Its only adjustable setting is the Cell Size, used to create either a more detailed or a more blurred image.

Render Filters

In publishing, graphic design, and image editing, the term **render** simply means to create an artistic change. In Photoshop, rendering is used as a means to create a drawing or painting that is represented by discrete pixels, especially in perspective. The Render filters (Table 6–7) create cloud patterns, texture fills, 3-D shapes, refraction patterns, and simulated light reflections in an image. The Render effects are on the Filter menu. During rendering, image data on the active layer is replaced, so it is best to use the commands on layer copies rather than on the original.

Table 6–7 Render Filters		
Render Filter	**Description**	**Adjustable Settings**
Clouds	Creates a soft cloud pattern using random values that vary between the foreground and the background colors	None
Difference Clouds	Same as Clouds filter except the filter blends with existing pixels	None
Fibers	Generates the look of woven fibers using the foreground and background colors	Variance, Strength, Randomize
Lens Flare	Simulates camera lens refraction caused from bright lights	Brightness, Lens Type
Lighting Effects	Produces various lighting effects using settings	Style, Light Type, Properties, Texture Channel

Sharpen Filters

Sharpening means to emphasize the transitions between light and dark objects in an image. The Sharpen filters (Table 6–8) focus blurred images by increasing the contrast of adjacent pixels.

BTW

Filters and Printing
If you plan to print to a grayscale printer, convert a copy of the image to grayscale before applying filters to increase performance of Photoshop. Applying a filter to a color image, and then converting to grayscale, may not have the same effect as applying the filter to a grayscale version of the image.

Table 6–8 Sharpen Filters		
Sharpen Filter	**Description**	**Adjustable Settings**
Sharpen	Focuses a selection to improve its clarity	None
Sharpen Edges	Sharpens edges but preserves smoothness of the image	None
Sharpen More	Applies a stronger sharpening effect than the Sharpen filter	None
Smart Sharpen	Sharpens the parts of the image where significant color changes occur, with more control using the settings	Amount, Radius
Unsharp Mask	Adjusts the contrast of edge detail, producing lighter and darker edges	Amount, Radius, Threshold

Sketch Filters

The Sketch filters (Table 6–9 on the next page) add texture and changes in color, creating artistic 3-D effects and hand-drawn looks. Many of the filters mimic sketch media used for loosely executed freehand drawing, not intended as a finished work. The Sketch filters use many techniques, including overlapping lines, dry media imitation, pencil, pen, and watercolor simulations. Most of the Sketch filters convert the image to black and white; however, they can be applied to individual channels to create interesting color combinations in the composite.

Chalk and Charcoal Filter Settings
The Charcoal Area and Chalk Area settings allow you to balance the portion of the image that is redrawn using each of the mediums. The Stroke Pressure setting controls the contrast between the two.

Table 6–9 Sketch Filters

Sketch Filter	Description	Adjustable Settings
Bas Relief	Accents surface variations with carving-like strokes; dark areas use the foreground color, and light areas use the background color	Detail, Smoothness, Light
Chalk & Charcoal	Simulates a coarse chalk sketch with black diagonal charcoal lines in the foreground	Charcoal Area, Chalk Area, Stroke Pressure
Charcoal	Redraws with a smudged, posterized effect using diagonal strokes; a charcoal color is used on the foreground, while the background simulates paper	Charcoal Thickness, Detail, Light/Dark Balance
Chrome	Creates a polished chrome surface	Detail, Smoothness
Conté Crayon	Simulates the Conté style with textured crayon-like, chalk strokes	Foreground Level, Background Level, Texture, Scaling, Relief, Light
Graphic Pen	Redraws using thin, linear ink strokes for the foreground color, and uses background color to simulate paper	Stroke Length, Light/Dark Balance, Stroke Direction
Halftone Pattern	A halftone screen effect that maintains a continuous range of tones, consisting of dots that control how much ink is deposited at a specific location	Size, Contrast, Pattern Type
Note Paper	Replicates handmade paper with dark areas masked out to reveal background colors	Image Balance, Graininess, Relief
Photocopy	Creates a photocopy effect	Detail, Darkness
Plaster	Simulates molded plaster, with dark areas raised, and light areas recessed	Image Balance, Smoothness, Light
Reticulation	Distorts similar to film emulsion patterns in negatives caused by extreme changes of temperature or acidity and alkalinity during processing	Density, Foreground Level, Background Level
Stamp	Simulates a rubber or wooden stamp version	Light/Dark Balance, Smoothness
Torn Edges	Redraws to look like ragged, torn pieces of paper	Image Balance, Smoothness, Contrast
Water Paper	Daubs with color imitating fibrous, damp paper	Fiber Length, Brightness, Contrast

Stylize Filters

The Stylize filters (Table 6–10) displace pixels and heighten contrast in an image or selection, producing an impressionistic, painting-like effect. Graphic artists use the Stylize filters to create unique and interesting effects and accents on artwork. Several of the Stylize filters accent edges of contrast in the image, which then can be inverted to highlight the image inside the outlines. Some of the Stylize filters are in the Filter Gallery; others open in their own dialog boxes from the Stylize submenu.

Table 6–10 Stylize Filters

Stylize Filter	Description	Adjustable Settings
Diffuse	Softens focus by rearranging pixels randomly or by dark and light settings	Mode
Emboss	Converts fill color to gray and traces the edges to create raised or stamped effects	Angle, Height, Amount
Extrude	Adds a 3-D texture based on specific settings	Type, Size, Depth
Find Edges	Outlines edges with dark lines against a white background for a thickly outlined, coloring book effect	None
Glowing Edges (Filter Gallery)	Adds a neon glow to edges	Edge Width, Edge Brightness, Smoothness
Solarize	Creates a photographic light exposure tint	None
Tiles	Creates a series of offset blocks with tiled edges	Number Of Tiles, Maximum Offset, Fill Empty Area With
Trace Contour	Outlines transition areas in each channel, creating a contour map effect	Level, Edge
Wind	Redraws using small horizontal lines to create a windblown effect	Method, Direction

Texture Filters

The Texture filters (Table 6–11) add substance or depth to an image by simulating a texture or organic representation. Graphic artists use the Texture filters to add a 3-D effect or to apply a segmented style to photos.

Table 6–11 Texture Filters

Texture Filter	Description	Adjustable Settings
Craquelure	Creates an embossing effect with a network of cracks on a plaster-like background	Crack Spacing, Crack Depth, Crack Brightness
Grain	Simulates different types of graininess	Intensity, Contrast, Grain Type
Mosaic Tiles	Creates small tiles with grout	Tile Size, Grout Width, Lighten Grout
Patchwork	Redraws with randomly filled squares replicating highlights and shadows	Square Size, Relief
Stained Glass	Repaints using random, five-sided, polygonal shapes to emulate stained glass	Cell Size, Border Thickness Light Intensity
Texturizer	Applies selected texture with settings	Texture, Scaling, Relief, Light

BTW

Stained Glass Filter Settings
The Stained Glass filter repaints the image as single-colored adjacent pentagon and hexagon cells outlined in the foreground color. The Cell Size and Border Thickness settings adjust the sizes of the cells (panes of glass) and the border (grout) between panes. The Light Intensity setting measures how much light seems to shine through from the back of the image (through the window).

Break Point: If you wish to take a break, this is a good place to do so. To resume at a later time, start Photoshop, open the file called Magazine Cover, and continue following the steps from this location forward.

Specialized Filters

Photoshop CS6 now includes five specialized filters on the Filter menu: the Adaptive Wide Angle filter, the Oil Paint filter, the Lens Correction filter, the Vanishing Point filter, and the Liquify filter. The Adaptive Wide Angle filter is new to CS6. It allows you to correct perspective errors and straighten curves and lines in photos taken with a fisheye or wide-angle lens, with settings for scale. In many cases, the filter will recognize the kind of lens used to take the photo and correct the distortion automatically. You also can make manual corrections for the Adaptive Wide Angle filter such as changing the scale, focal length, or calibration.

Also new to CS6 is the Oil Paint filter, which makes a photo look like a painted image. Its dialog box contains specific settings related to the brush, such as stylization, cleanliness, scale, and bristle, as well as settings related to lighting, such as angular direction and shine.

You previously learned about the Lens Corrections filter that fixes common lens flaws such as keystone, barrel, and pincushion distortion; and corrects chromatic aberration and vignetting.

The Vanishing Point filter also corrects perspective errors but in a different way. The Vanishing Point filter allows you to specify a visual or conceptual plane, such as a road, building, wall, or other rectangular portion of the image. Then, the edits you make, such as painting, healing, copying, and transforming, are performed in the perspective of the plane. The results are more realistic because the edits are properly oriented and scaled to the perspective planes.

The fifth specialized filter, the Liquify filter, is explained in the following section.

Some of the specialized filters require a video card that can perform graphics processor acceleration. **Graphics processor acceleration** is a feature of your computer's video card that contains its own processor to boost performance. Also called GPU-accelerated features, these filters use the graphic card's processor to free up the computer's processor to execute other commands. If your video card cannot process the filter, Photoshop will display an error message. In that case, you may have to upgrade your video card. You can check your graphic processor acceleration by pressing CTRL+K to open Photoshop preferences and navigate to the Performance settings. If your video card cannot handle graphics processor acceleration, the Use Graphics Processor check box will be grayed out. See Appendix F for more information.

BTW

Filters and RAM
Some filter effects can be memory-intensive, especially when applied to a high-resolution image. To improve performance, try one of the following: apply filters on a smaller portion of the image, apply the filter in an individual channel, turn off the thumbnail display on the Layers panel, allocate more RAM to Photoshop, exit other applications to make more memory available to Photoshop, or try changing settings to improve the speed of memory-intensive filters.

The Liquify Filter

The Liquify filter lets you distort an image by pushing, pulling, or rotating any area of an image. The Liquify filter is a powerful tool for retouching images as well as for creating artistic effects. Like the Lens Correction filter that you used in Chapter 5, the Liquify filter has its own dialog box and tools panel. Table 6–12 displays some of the Liquify dialog box distortion tools. Other settings edit the brush, reconstruct the image, set the mask, and change the view.

Table 6–12 Liquify Filter Tools			
Name	**Description**	**Shortcut Key**	**Button**
Forward Warp	Pushes the pixels of the image forward as you drag	W	
Reconstruct	Reconstructs areas of the previously distorted image as you drag	R	
Twirl	Rotates pixels clockwise as you click or drag, or counterclockwise, as you ALT+click or ALT+drag	C	
Pucker	Moves pixels toward the center of the brush area as you click or drag	S	
Bloat	Moves pixels away from the center of the brush area as you click or drag	B	
Push Left	Moves pixels to the left as you drag up, to the right as you drag down, increases size as you drag clockwise, or decreases size as you drag counterclockwise	O	
Freeze Mask	Drag to protect the area from any change as you work with other filters	F	
Thaw Mask	Drag to unprotect the area, so other filters can be applied	D	
Hand	Drag to move preview area	H	
Zoom	Zooms in as you click, zooms out as you ALT+click	Z	

To Duplicate a Layer

The following steps create a copy of the wakeboarding layer on which to make edits.

1 On the Layers panel, right-click the wakeboarding layer, and then click Duplicate Layer on the context menu.

2 When Photoshop displays the Duplicate Layer dialog box, type `wakeboarding edits` as the new name. Click the OK button to close the dialog box.

3 Hide the original wakeboarding layer by clicking its 'Indicates layer visibility' icon.

4 Select the wakeboarding edits layer (Figure 6–12).

Figure 6–12

To Apply the Liquify Filter

The following steps use the Liquify filter to retouch the wakeboarding edits layer.

1

- With the wakeboarding edits layer still selected, click Filter on the Application bar to display the Filter menu (Figure 6–13).

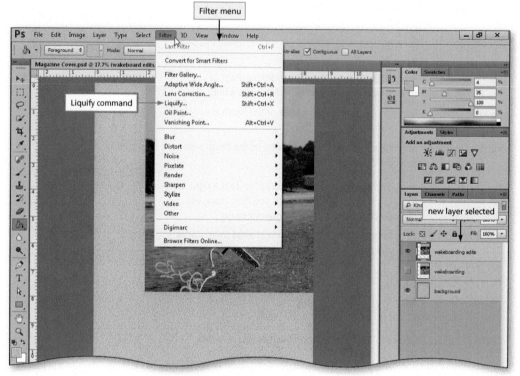

Figure 6–13

2

- Click Liquify to display the Liquify dialog box. If Photoshop displays a dialog box, click the OK button (Figure 6–14).

Experiment

- Select the Advanced Mode check box to see other Liquify tools.

Experiment

- Click the Mask All button to view the mask that covers the entire layer to protect it from editing. Click the None button to remove the mask.

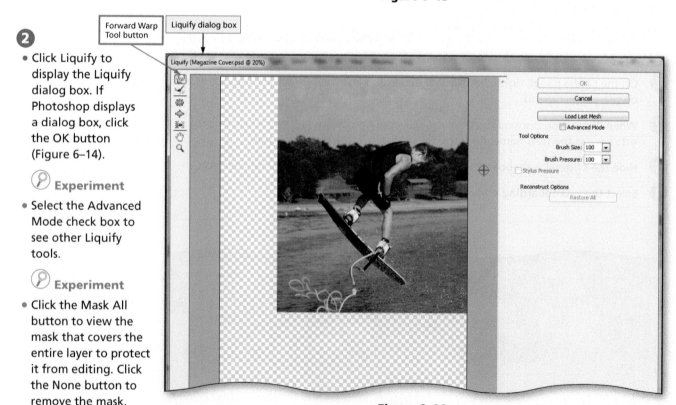

Figure 6–14

3

- If necessary, click the Forward Warp Tool button to select it.

- Position the crosshair mouse pointer near the lower-left corner of the image. Drag clockwise and down below the image to create a wavy effect.

- Move the mouse pointer to view the change (Figure 6–15).

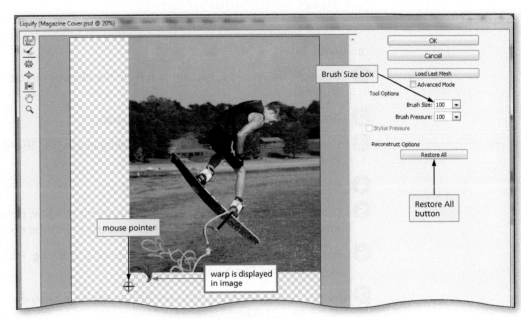

Figure 6–15

 Can I undo the changes if I do not like the outcome?

Yes. Press CTRL+ALT+Z to move backward through your keystrokes, or you can click the Restore All button in the Liquify Filter dialog box to start over.

Q&A Can I change the size of the mouse pointer?

Yes, as with other brushes, you can change the Forward Warp mouse pointer by using the LEFT BRACKET ([) or RIGHT BRACKET (]) keys. You also can use the Brush Size box on the right side of the dialog box to adjust the size of the brush.

4

- Create similar distortions randomly across the bottom of the image.

- Move the mouse pointer to view the change (Figure 6–16).

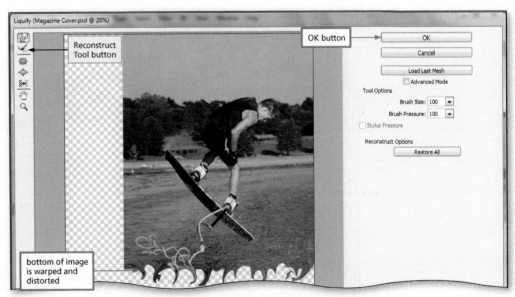

Figure 6–16

Q&A What does the Reconstruct Tool do?

After you make an edit to the preview, click the Reconstruct Tool button to reconstruct the most recent change, or click the Restore All button to return the image to its original state.

5

- Click the OK button to apply the filter.

Other Ways

1. Press SHIFT+CTRL+X, adjust settings, click OK button

To Insert Additional Graphics

The following steps insert three additional images for the left side of the magazine cover.

1 Open the file named Rock Climbing from the Chapter 06 folder of the Data Files for Students.

2 Arrange the document windows side by side.

3 Use the Move tool to drag the rock climbing image into the Magazine Cover document window.

4 Close the Rock Climbing document window.

5 Drag the image to the left side of the document window, positioning the top of the small image approximately 5.5 inches from the top of the document window.

6 Repeat Steps 1 through 5 with the file named Dirt Biking. Position the graphic slightly above the Rock Climbing layer.

7 Repeat Steps 1 through 5 with the file named Parasailing. Position the graphic slightly above the Dirt Biking layer.

8 Rename the layers as rock climbing, dirt biking, and parasailing. Assign a green identification color to each (Figure 6–17).

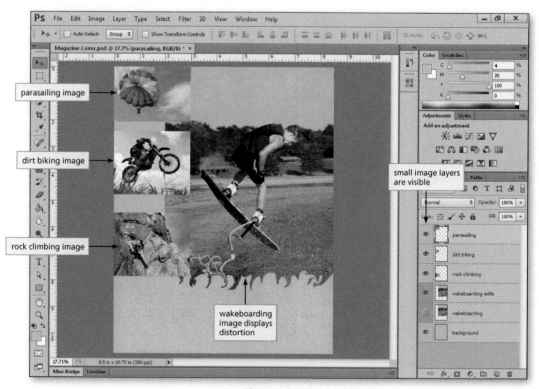

Figure 6–17

To Align and Distribute Layers

When you **align** shapes, you make the edges or the centers line up with one another. When you **distribute** shapes, you create equal distances between the edges or centers. The following steps use the Move Tool options bar to align and distribute the three layers.

1

- On the Layers panel, SHIFT+click each of the three small image layers to select them (Figure 6–18).

Figure 6–18

2

- On the Tools panel, select the Move Tool to display the Move Tool options bar.

- On the options bar, click the 'Align left edges' button to align the left side of the layers.

- Click the 'Distribute vertical centers' button to distribute the layers vertically (Figure 6–19).

Experiment

- One at a time, click other align and distribute buttons on the options bar to view other alignments. After each one, press CTRL+Z to undo the change. When you are finished, repeat Step 2.

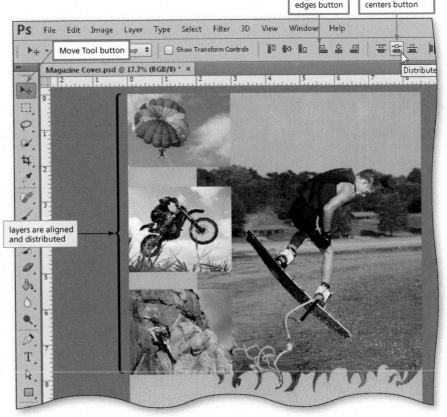

Figure 6–19

The Filter Gallery

New Effect Layer Button
In the lower-right corner of the Filter Gallery dialog box, the 'New effect layer' button gives you the capability of adding multiple filters at the same time. Use multiple filters judiciously to create specific effects.

The **Filter Gallery** lets you apply filters individually, cumulatively, or apply individual filters more than once. With thumbnail examples organized into folders, the Filter Gallery previews the effect that the filter will have on your image. You can use the Filter Gallery to make appropriate choices, rearrange filters, and change individual settings to achieve the desired special effect.

By default, filters change the pixels in a layer and, therefore, are considered destructive; however, you can use the Convert to Smart Filters command to convert your layers into smart objects that make the filter adjustable. Recall that smart objects are layers that preserve the source content of an image with all its original characteristics separately from any filters, edits, or styles. Smart Objects enable you to perform nondestructive editing to the layer. A filter added to a smart object is called a **smart filter**. Smart filters add to the size of the file on your storage device, but offer the luxury of keeping the pixels in the original layer — in case you want to make further edits, Smart filters also allow you to adjust or delete filter settings. Smart filters retain the name of the filter used and its filter settings, even when those may have been reset by you or another user. A smart filter, therefore, is a substitute for creating a copy of the layer on which to apply filters, and renaming it to include the filter name and settings.

Not all filters are included in the Filter Gallery. Those filters with adjustable settings that are not in the Filter Gallery present their own preview when selected from the menu system. Photoshop Help also has many visual examples of the various filters.

To Create a Smart Filter

In the following steps, you will use the Convert to Smart Filters command, to make layer changes editable.

1
- On the Layers panel, select the parasailing layer.

- Click Filter on the Application bar to display the Filter menu (Figure 6–20).

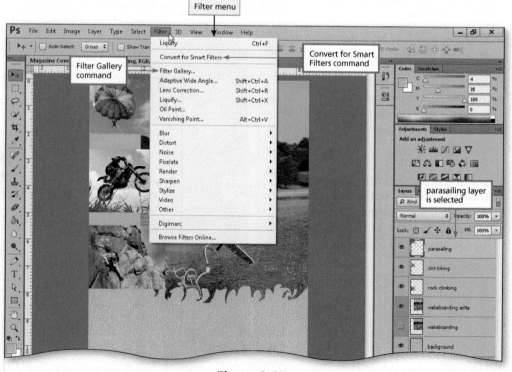

Figure 6–20

2

- Click Convert for Smart Filters to create an adjustable smart filter. If Photoshop displays a dialog box, click the OK button to create the smart filter (Figure 6–21).

Q&A

Should I see any difference?

Yes. The smart object icon is added to the layer on the layer's panel.

Figure 6–21

Other Ways
1. Right-click layer, click Convert to Smart Object

To Apply a Plastic Wrap Smart Filter

Using the Filter Gallery, you will apply the Plastic Wrap filter, which is an Artistic filter, to the parasailing layer in the following steps.

1

- Select the parasailing smart filter layer, if necessary.

- Click Filter on the Application bar, and then click Filter Gallery to display the Filter Gallery dialog box.

- Click the Zoom in or Zoom out button until the entire parasail is displayed in the preview.

- If more than one filter is displayed in the list of filter effects, click the 'Delete effect layer' button (Figure 6–22).

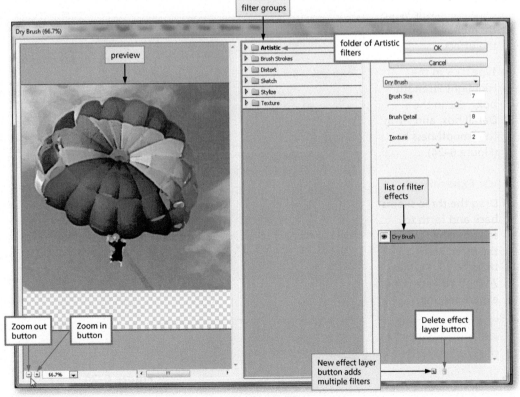

Figure 6–22

• Click Artistic in the list of filter groups to open the folder. Click any other open folders to close them (Figure 6–23).

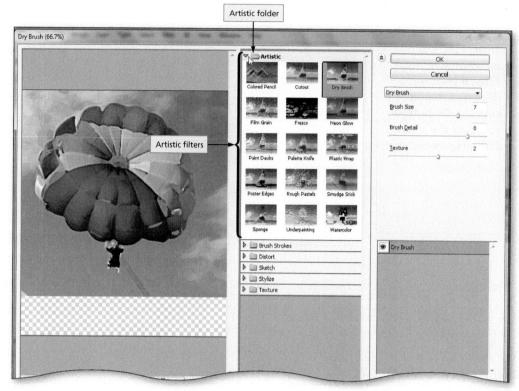

Figure 6–23

• Click the Plastic Wrap thumbnail to preview the effect.

• Type 15 in the Highlight Strength box, 11 in the Detail box, and 7 in the Smoothness box (Figure 6–24).

Experiment

• Drag the three sliders back and forth to see how they change the layer. Reset them to 15, 11, and 7 when you are done experimenting.

How do the settings affect the bubbles of the plastic wrap?

The Highlights Strength setting controls the brightness of the highlights in the plastic wrap. The Detail setting changes the frequency of the bubbles in the plastic wrap – larger numbers create more bubbles. The Smoothness setting changes the contrast between the top of the bubble and the bottom of the bubble. The larger the value, the more the highlights and contrast are blurred.

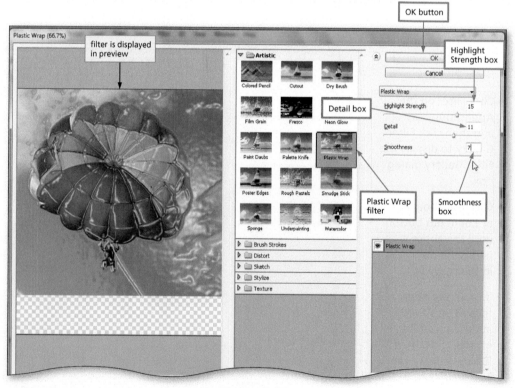

Figure 6–24

4

- Click the OK button to apply the Plastic Wrap filter to the parasailing layer (Figure 6–25).

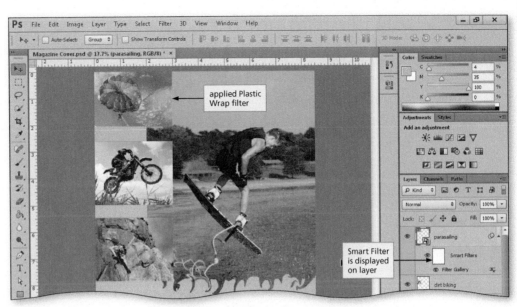

Figure 6–25

To Apply a Glowing Edges Smart Filter

You will apply the Glowing Edges filter to the dirt biking layer in the following steps. Upon opening the dirt biking layer in the Filter Gallery, the gallery will display the previously used filter, in this case, Plastic Wrap. The previous settings in the Filter Gallery will be replaced when you choose the Glowing Edges filter.

1

- On the Layers panel, select the dirt biking layer.

- Click Filter on the Application bar and then click Convert for Smart Filters. If Photoshop displays a dialog box, click the OK button to create the smart filter.

- Click Filter on the Application bar, and then click Filter Gallery to display the Filter Gallery dialog box. Adjust the size of the preview using the zoom buttons.

- If more than one filter is displayed in the list of filter effects, click the 'Delete effect layer' button.

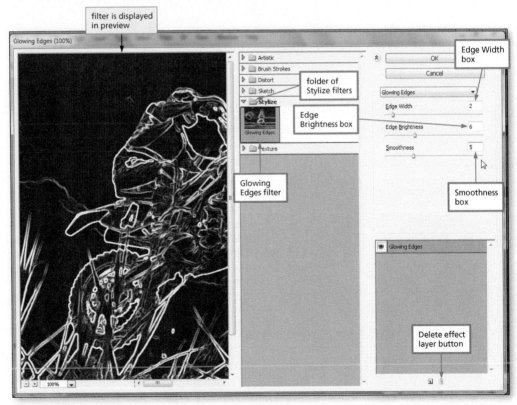

Figure 6–26

- Click Artistic in the filter list to close the Artistic folder.

- Click Stylize in the filter list to open the Stylize folder, and then click the Glowing Edges thumbnail.

- Type 2 in the Edge Width box, 6 in the Edge Brightness box, and 5 in the Smoothness box (Figure 6–26 on the previous page).

Q&A

I could not get the 'Delete effect layer' button to work. What did I do wrong?

The 'Delete effect layer' button only works when there is more than one filter in the list. You cannot delete the existing filter — you either can change the filter or cancel the operation.

2

- Click the OK button to apply the Glowing Edges filter to the dirt biking layer (Figure 6–27).

Q&A

What if I decide not to apply a filter?

If the Filter Gallery dialog box is still open, as shown in Figure 6-26, you can click the Cancel button. If you already have closed the Filter Gallery, you can press CTRL+Z to undo the filter. If you change your mind at a later date, you can right-click the Filter Gallery notation on the Layers panel, and then click Delete Smart Filter.

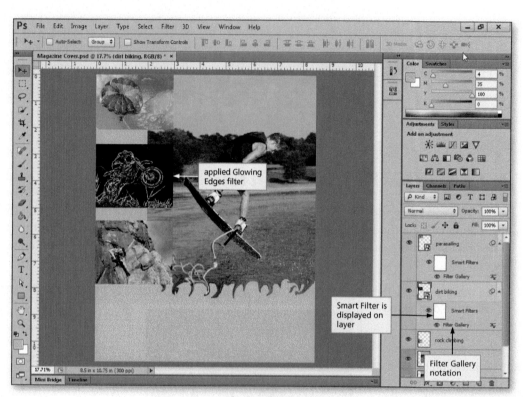

Figure 6–27

BTW

Glowing Edges Filter Settings
When using the Glowing Edges filter, Photoshop looks for strong color change to define an edges. The Edge Width setting increases or decreases the thickness of the edge lines. The Edge Brightness setting adjust the contrast between the edges and the background. Finally, the Smoothness setting softens the color change between the edges and the background.

To Apply a Craquelure Smart Filter

You will apply the Craquelure filter, a Texture filter, to the rock climbing layer in the following steps.

● Select the rock
climbing layer and
convert the layer to a
smart filter.

● Display the Filter
Gallery and adjust
the size of the
preview using the
zoom buttons.

● Delete multiple
filters, if they exist.

● Open the Texture
folder and then
click the Craquelure
thumbnail.

● Type 15 in the
Crack Spacing, 6
in the Crack Depth
box, and 9 in the
Crack Brightness box
(Figure 6–28).

● Click the OK button
to apply the filter.

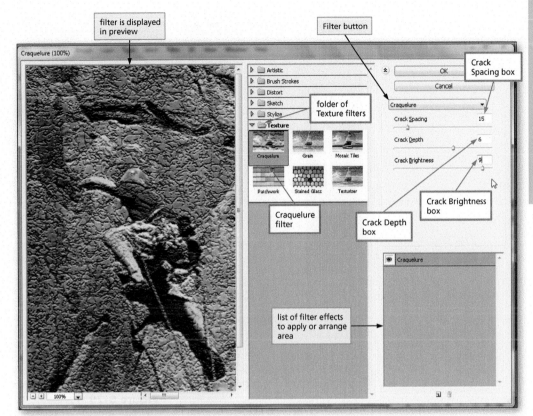

Figure 6–28

The Blur Filters

Three new filters appear at the top of the Blur filter submenu: Field, Iris, and
Tilt-Shift. The filters selectively blur portions of an image to create a stronger focus
on the nonblurred portions. Selective blurring is common in movies and television,
when the figure in the foreground slowly blurs to shift the focus to an object in the
background. Each of the filters uses bulleted center points to position the focus, as well
as a wheel and slider controls to increase or decrease the blur.

The Field blur option allows you to designate one or more center points and
adjust the blur using the wheel or a slider. The Iris blur has a center point, blur wheel,
pins to designate the transitional area, and an adjustable diameter circle. You can rotate
the blur by dragging rotation handles in the interface. The Tilt-Shift blur option
designates three adjustable areas around a center point: unaffected, transitional, and
blurred, with controls to adjust the blur, distortion, and Bokeh effect (Figure 6–29 on
the next page). In photography, the **Bokeh effect** refers to the way the camera lens
renders out-of-focus points of light, generated by differences in lens aberrations and
aperture shapes.

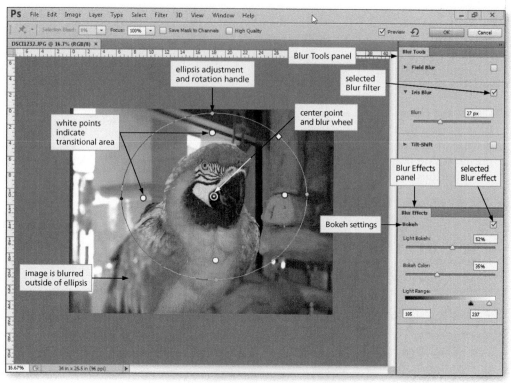

Figure 6–29

To Apply an Iris Blur Filter

The following steps apply an Iris Blur filter to a portion of the wakeboarding edits layer to focus on the wakeboarder.

- On the Layers panel, hide the three small image layers.

- Scroll as necessary to select the wakeboarding edits layer.

- Click Filter on the Application bar and then point to Blur to display the submenu (Figure 6–30).

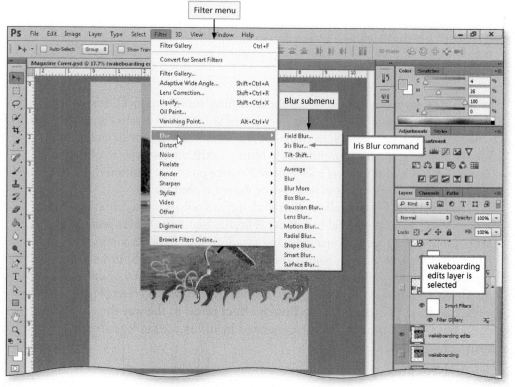

Figure 6–30

2

- Click Iris Blur to display the Blur Tools panel and options bar (Figure 6–31).

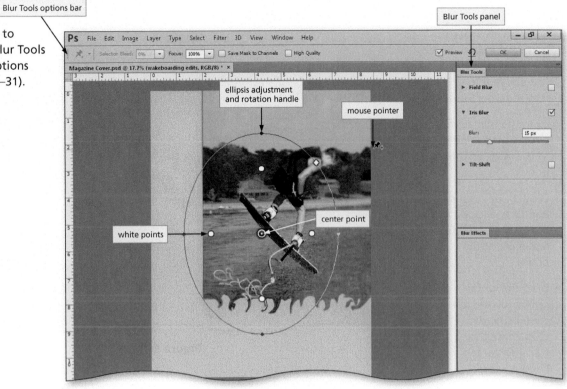

Figure 6–31

3

- On the Blur Tools panel, drag the Blur Slider to 40 px to increase the blur (Figure 6–32).

Experiment

- If your graphics card supports it, drag the wheel around the center point to adjust the blur.

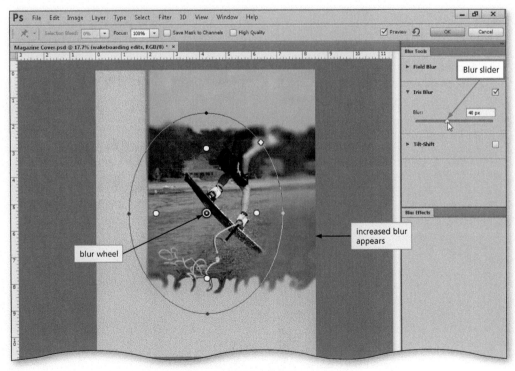

Figure 6–32

- Drag the top rotation handle clockwise and right to a position just above the wakeboarder's head.

- Drag the blur center point to the middle of the wakeboarder's body.

- Drag a side rotation handle to include all of the wakeboarder and most of the board.

- Drag the white points toward the center slightly to increase the transition area (Figure 6–33).

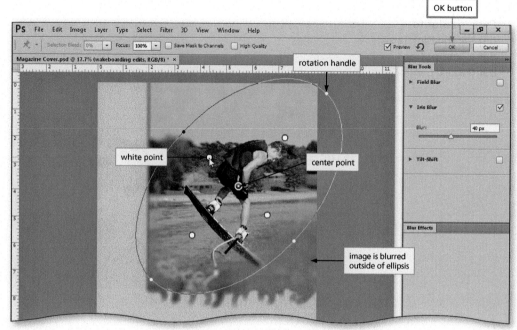

Figure 6–33

 **Experiment**

- Experiment by dragging the white points to increase and decrease the transitional area of the blur.

5

- On the options bar, click the OK button to apply the filter (Figure 6–34).

Q&A

Is it common for the blur to take a long time to appear?

Yes, as Photoshop has to change every pixel in the layer, it may take 15 seconds or longer for the image to appear blurred.

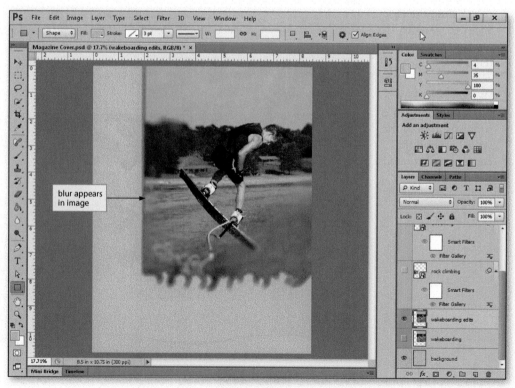

Figure 6–34

To Save the File

After adding many layers and applied filters, it is a good time to save the file again in the following step.

 Press CTRL+S. If Photoshop displays a dialog box, click the OK button.

Break Point: If you wish to take a break, this is a good place to do so. To resume at a later time, start Photoshop, open the file called Magazine Cover, and continue following the steps from this location forward.

Specialized Effects

Other specialized effects can be added to photos, original drawings, or artwork. You have learned about filters, strokes, and shapes, but additionally you can include masks, patterns, lines, and renderings, to add variety, attraction, and appeal to your publications.

Each of the small photos on the left side of the magazine cover will be masked in a pentagonal pattern using a dark green color. This will add another color to the magazine cover and draw attention to the three sports. The following sections create a pentagonal mask and a patterned background.

To Create a Pentagon

The following steps create a pentagon shape using the Polygon Tool. The Polygon Tool options bar allows you to fill, stroke, set the width, choose the number of sides, and select other tools to work with paths. You will learn about paths in a later chapter.

- On the Layers panel, display the three small image layers.

- Select the wakeboarding edits layer so that the pentagon will appear in front of the wakeboarding image. Increase the magnification setting to 50% and scroll as necessary to view the rock climbing image.

- On the Tools panel, right-click the current Shape Tool button (Figure 6–35).

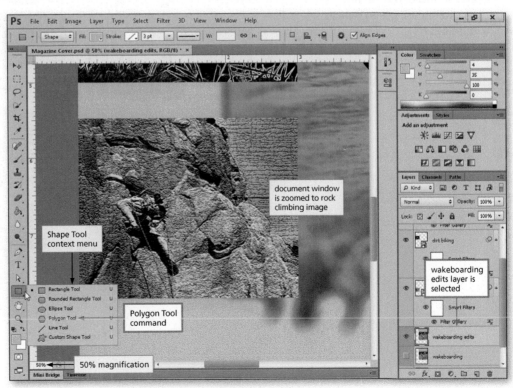

Figure 6–35

2

- Click Polygon Tool in the list.

- On the options bar, click the Fill button to display the Fill panel (Figure 6–36).

🔍 **Experiment**

- One at a time, click each of the four buttons across the top of the Fill panel to see the choices for No Fill, Color, Gradient, and Pattern.

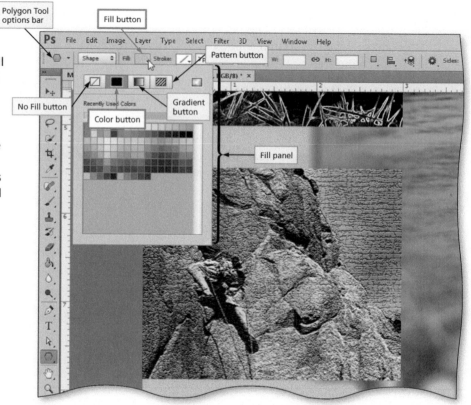

Figure 6–36

3

- Click the Color button on the Fill panel.

- Click the Stroke button and then click a dark green swatch (Figure 6–37).

Figure 6–37

4

- On the options bar, type   5 in the Sides box to create a pentagon.

- Select the Align Edges check box, if necessary.

- In the document window, slowly drag a pentagon that encompasses the rock climber. As you drag, if you need to adjust the placement of the pentagon, press and hold the SPACEBAR key. Use the Transformation Indicator box to help you draw a pentagon approximately 2.5 inches by 2.5 inches. Before releasing the mouse button, drag to straighten the pentagon (Figure 6–38).

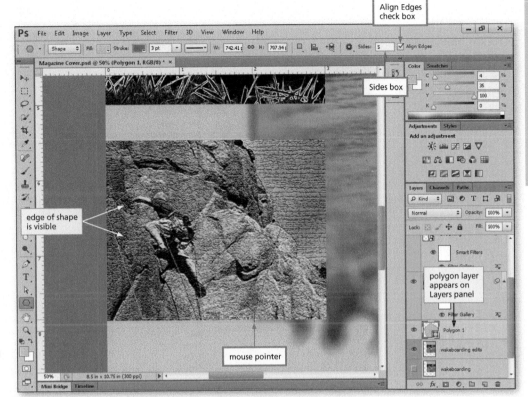

Figure 6–38

Q&A

I cannot see my pentagon. Did I do something wrong?

The pentagon may be difficult to see because it lies behind the rock climbing layer; however, you should be able to see its outline. It will become more evident in the next series of steps.

5

- Release the mouse button if necessary.

To Create a Clipping Mask

In a previous chapter, you created a layer mask that eclipsed a portion of an image without destroying pixels. Those layer masks resided on the same layer as the image; you used a brush to create or remove the mask. A clipping mask is similar; however, it uses its own layer and can employ a variety of shapes or other images as the mask. You do not have to use a brush stroke.

Clipping masks are a good way to create a picture inside a shape. Just make sure that the picture resides above the shape on the Layers panel, and that you apply a clipping mask to the picture layer, as you do in the steps on the next page.

1

- Right-click the rock climbing layer on the Layers panel to display the context menu (Figure 6–39).

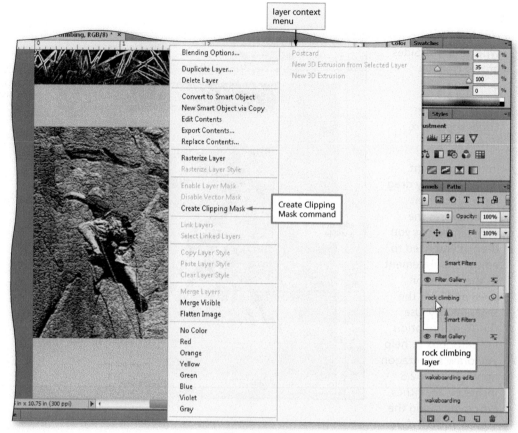

Figure 6–39

2

- Click Create Clipping Mask to clip the picture in the shape of the layer below it (Figure 6–40).

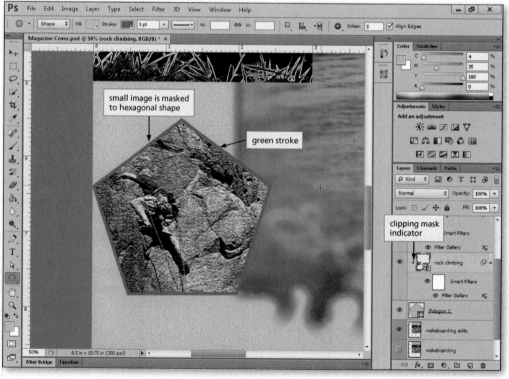

Figure 6–40

To Create More Clipping Masks

To apply identical clipping masks for the other two images, you will duplicate the shape layer twice, and then create a clipping mask for each one. The following steps create more clipping masks.

1 Press CTRL+0 (zero) to fit the document window on the screen.

2 ALT+drag the Polygon1 layer to a location just below the dirt biking layer to create a copy.

3 Press the V key to activate the Move Tool. Drag the copied polygon to a location around the dirt biking image.

4 On the Layers panel, right-click the dirt biking layer, and then click Create Clipping Mask on the context menu.

5 Repeat Steps 2 through 4 to create a clipping mask for the parasailing layer (Figure 6–41).

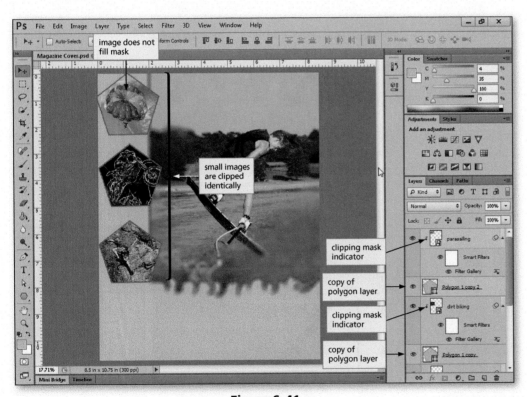

Figure 6–41

To Nudge

The steps on the next page reposition the images within the clipping masks. When you use arrow keys to move very small distances, it is called **nudging**.

1

- On the Layers panel, select the parasailing layer.

- Select the Move Tool, if necessary.

- Press the appropriate ARROW key, as necessary, to move the parasail to a centered position within the clipping mask (Figure 6–42).

 My parasail was already centered. Did I do something wrong?

Your images may have been centered well to begin with. You might need to nudge very little or not at all.

Figure 6–42

2

- Repeat Step 1 for the dirt biking layer and the rock climbing layer (Figure 6–43).

My pentagon is crooked. How can I fix that?

Select the shape layer on the Layers panel. Press CTRL+T and then drag outside of the bounding box. When your pentagon is straight, press the ENTER key. Repeat Step 1 if necessary.

Figure 6–43

Patterns

A **pattern** is an image that is tiled, or repeated, to fill a selection or a layer. Photoshop has libraries of preset patterns that can be loaded and used in any document, but by default, two patterns are loaded into the Pattern Picker box, including Bubbles and Tie Dye. You can access the Pattern Picker box from the Layer Style dialog box or from the options bar associated with the Paint Bucket tool, the Pattern Stamp tool, the

Healing Brush tool, and the Patch tool. Commands on the Pattern Picker menu allow users to load, save, and manage pattern libraries. Recall that libraries associated with many kinds of presets — including gradients, brushes, styles, and custom shapes — also can be managed using the Preset Manager command on the Edit menu.

In Photoshop, you can use one of the preset patterns or you can create your own patterns and save them for use with different tools and commands. Photoshop gives you the ability to create a specific pattern, either from scratch or from another image. Alternatively, you can use the Pattern Maker Filter that generates a random pattern based on a selection or image.

TO DEFINE A PATTERN

If you have an image you would like to use as a pattern, you would perform the following steps:

1. Open the file you want to use as a pattern.

2. Use the Rectangular Marquee Tool to draw a selection around the area of the image to use for the pattern.

3. Click Edit on the Application bar to display the menu, and then click Define Pattern to display the Pattern Name dialog box.

4. Type a name for your pattern in the Name box.

5. Click the OK button to close the Pattern Name dialog box.

6. Click the Close button on the file's document window tab. If Photoshop asks if you want to save the changes, click the No button.

To Use a Pattern

The next steps create a pattern along the left side of the wakeboarding image.

1

- On the Layers panel, hide all of the layers except the background and the wakeboarding edits layers. Select the background layer.

- Press SHIFT+CTRL+N to create a new layer above the wakeboarding edits layer.

- In the New Layer dialog box, type pattern in the Name box and use a gray identification color (Figure 6–44).

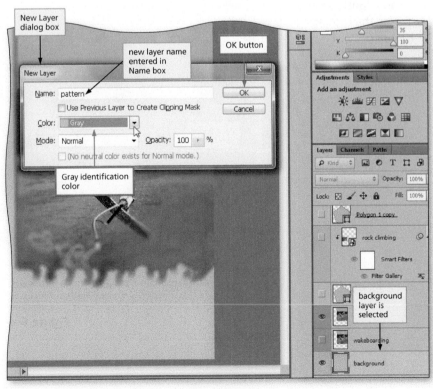

Figure 6–44

2

• Click the OK button to close the New Layer dialog box, creating a new pattern layer.

• Select the Rectangular Marquee Tool.

• Draw a rectangle, from the upper-left corner of the canvas down and to the right, to fill the orange area left of the wakeboarding image as shown in Figure 6–45.

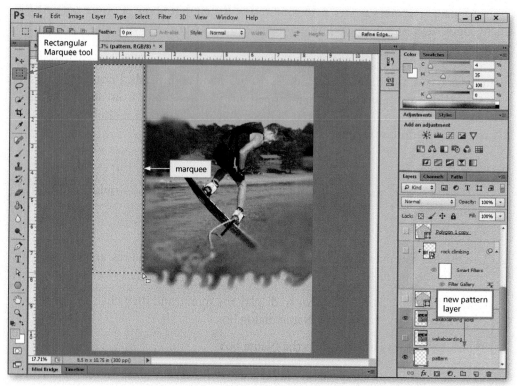

Figure 6–45

3

• Select the Paint Bucket Tool. On the options bar, click the 'Set source for fill area' button to display the choices (Figure 6–46).

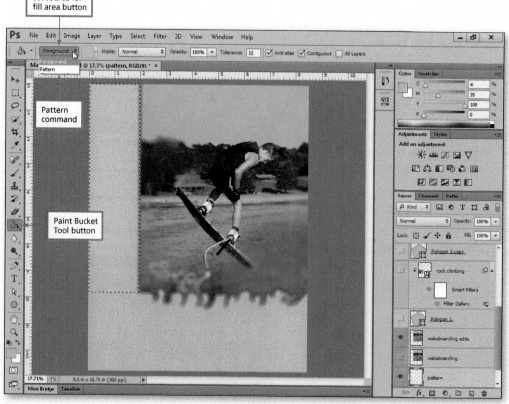

Figure 6–46

④
- Click Pattern in the list to select it.

- Click the Pattern picker to display its panel, and then click the panel menu button to display the menu (Figure 6–47).

Q&A
Should I click the Pattern picker button or the box arrow.

With this picker, you can click either one. The result is the same.

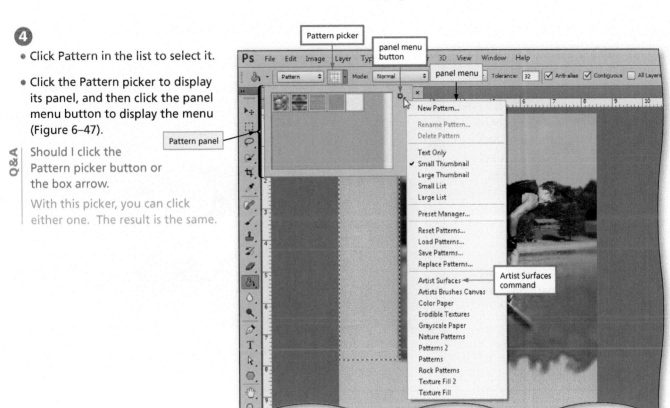

Figure 6–47

⑤
- Click Artist Surfaces to choose the pattern library.

- When Photoshop displays a dialog box, choose to Append the patterns to the current set.

- Click the Gauze pattern to select it (Figure 6–48).

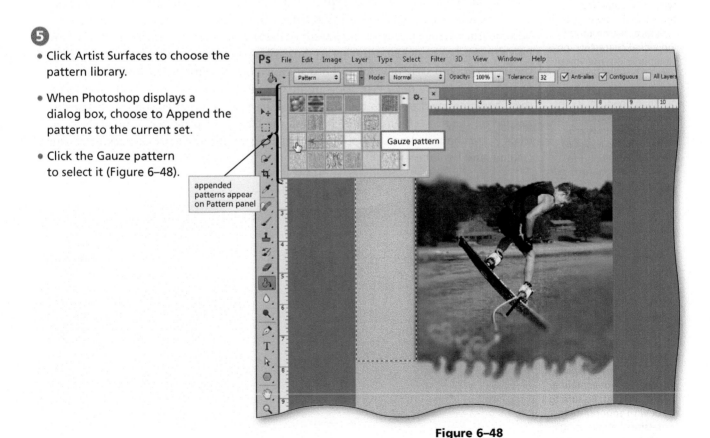

Figure 6–48

6

- Click inside the selection marquee to apply the pattern to the selection (Figure 6–49).

Q&A

My marquee is too narrow — I can see some orange on the right of the pattern. What should I do?

Press CTRL+ALT+Z twice, to undo the both the paint bucket and the marquee, then redraw the marquee and apply the pattern again.

7

- Deselect and show all the layers except the wakeboarding layer.

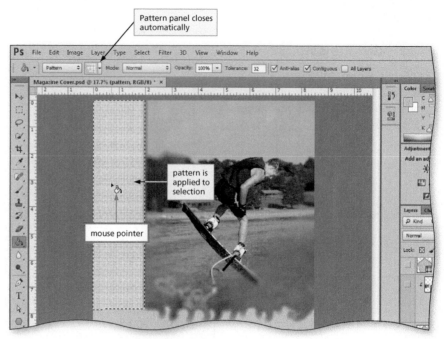

Figure 6–49

BTW

Typeface
Many of the terms used when working with type tools come from the field of typesetting. Typeface, the design of individual characters, now commonly is synonymous with the word, font. Typefaces are available in ore than one format. The most common formats are TrueType, Postscript, OpenType and New CID, a format developed to support non-English characters.

Formatting Type

Graphic designers use the term, **type**, to refer to the mathematically defined shapes of letters, numbers, and symbols in a typeface. The terms, type, text, and copy, have become interchangeable with the advent of desktop publishing; however, Photoshop uses the word, type, when referring to the various tools that manipulate text. Besides the basic text and style buttons and boxes shown on the options bar, Photoshop provides a set of extended type tools in the Character panel (Figure 6–50). You access the Character panel through the Toggle the Character and Paragraph panels button, located on the text options bar. Included in the Character panel are some of the same tools as are contained on the options bar with the addition of scaling, tracking, kerning, leading, and baseline shift.

BTW

Faux Bold
The second button in the font style buttons on the Character panel is Faux Bold. Faux Bold creates a heavier character when the font you have chosen does not contain a bold stylistic set. Be sure to check with your printing professional about using Faux Bold characters. You cannot warp text that has the Faux Bold attributed.

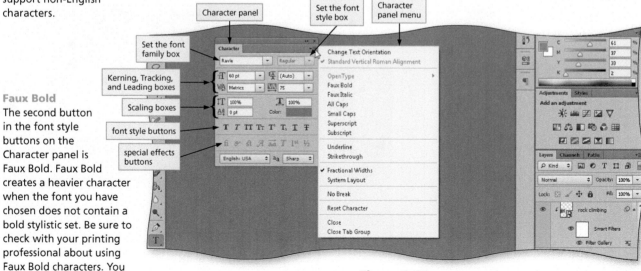

Figure 6–50

Use type wisely.
Make purposeful decisions about your type styles and typefaces, including the font family, font size, font style, direction, color, spacing, and stroking.

- When combining font families on the same page, choose fonts that strongly contrast in style, weight, and form. For example, if one typeface is tall and thin, choose a contrasting one that is short and thick — and vice versa.
- Be consistent about using the same font style for similar purposes, such as bold for emphasis.
- Look for the stress or slant of where the typeface displays wider vs. thinner lines within the same letter, or serifs on lowercase letters.
- Examine text for places where kerning, tracking, or leading might lead to increased legibility or contrast.
- Use a stroke of color around the text for a more distinctive look that stands out.
- Apply overlays to prevent misregistration.

Plan Ahead

Scaling, the process of shrinking or stretching text, changes the width of individual characters. **Tracking**, on the other hand, refers to the adjustment of the general spacing between characters. Tracking text compensates for the spacing irregularities caused when you make text much bigger or much smaller. For example, smaller type is easier to read when it has been tracked loosely. Tracking both maintains the original height and width of the characters and overrides adjustments made by justification or bounding box changes.

Kerning is a special form of tracking related to pairs of adjacent characters that can appear too far apart. For instance, certain letters such as T, V, W, and Y, often need kerning when they are preceded or followed by a, e, i, o, or u. For example, the word, Tom, typed in a large font might create too much space between the letters T and o. Selecting the letters and then adjusting the kerning would make the word more readable.

Leading, also called line spacing, refers to the amount of vertical spacing between lines of type; the term originates from the pre-computer practice of adding lead to create space between lines of metal type characters.

Baseline shift controls the distance of type from its original baseline, either raising or lowering the selected type. Shifting the baseline is especially useful when using superscripts, subscripts, and fractions. Below the Color box are the special effects buttons, and below that is the Language list box. The Character panel menu button displays many of the same commands and provides the capability to reset all value boxes so fractional settings can be used.

The Paragraph panel (Figure 6–51) contains buttons to change the formatting of columns and paragraphs, also called text blocks. Unique to the Paragraph panel are settings to change the justification for paragraphs, indenting margins and first lines, and changing the spacing above and below paragraphs. The panel's menu button displays other commands to change settings, including access to the Hyphenation dialog box where you can specify how and when hyphenation occurs.

BTW

Kerning
The term, kerning, comes from the pre-computer era, when individual type characters were made from metals, including lead. Bits of lead were shaved off wider characters, thus allowing the smaller character to be moved underneath the larger one. The resulting overhand was called a kern.

BTW

Tracking
A negative entry in the tracking box moves the selected letters closer together. A positive number moves the selected letters further apart.

BTW

Typography
Recall from Appendix B that font family, style, classification, and color all play important roles in typography. These choices set the tone for a layout. Readability is determined by font, point size, line space, line length, and style, such as italics or all caps.

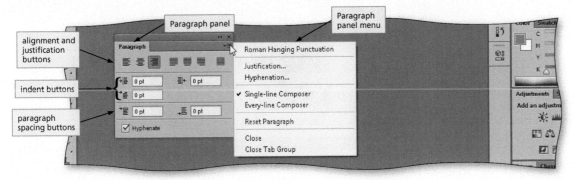

Figure 6–51

To Insert HeadlineText

Two headlines appear on the magazine cover. The first is the title of the magazine, and the second is the subtitle and information about the special issue. The first headline text will use the Ravie font, which looks energetic, bouncy, and fun for a sports magazine headline.

1 On the Layers panel, select the wakeboarding edits layer.

2 Press the T key to access the type tools. If the Horizontal Type tool is not displayed on the Tools panel, right-click the current type tool button, and then click Horizontal Type Tool in the list.

3 On the options bar, click the 'Set the font family' box arrow, and then choose the Ravie font. If you do not have that particular font, choose a similar font. Set the font size to 60. Set the anti-aliasing to Sharp. Click the 'Right align text' button.

4 Click the 'Set the text color' box. When Photoshop displays the Color Picker (Text color) dialog box, move the mouse pointer into the wakeboarding image and click a blue color in the water to select a new foreground color. Click the OK button.

5 Drag a box in the lower portion of the magazine cover, below the wakeboarding image, approximately 6.5 inches wide and 1.75 inches tall.

6 Type SCREAM and then press the ENTER key. Type EXTREME to complete the text (Figure 6–52).

7 On the options bar, click the 'Commit any current edits' button.

8 Click the 'Add a layer style' button on the Layers panel status bar, and then click Stroke. Accept the default settings and click the OK button.

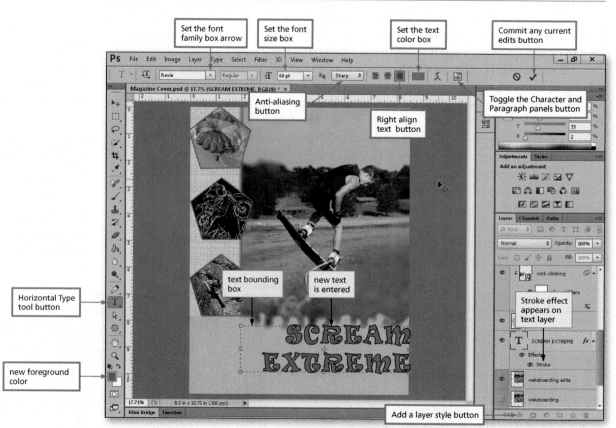

Figure 6–52

To Set the Tracking

The following steps increase the tracking of the characters in the headline to create more space between the letters.

1
- Click the text again, and then drag to select all of the text.

- On the options bar, click the Toggle the Character and Paragraph panels button to show the panels.

- Click the 'Set the tracking' box arrow (Figure 6–53).

2
- Click 75 in the list to display the characters further apart.

- On the options bar, click the 'Commit any current edits' button.

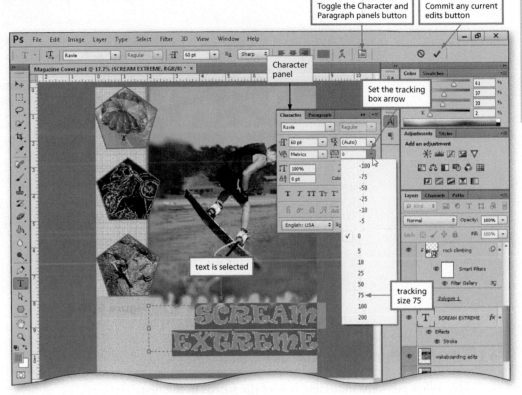

Figure 6–53

To Insert Subtitle Text

In the subtitle, or secondary headline, the text will use the Stencil font in black. Fonts such as Stencil work well in conjunction with decorative, slab fonts like Ravie, because the Stencil font is less distracting visually. It is good practice to either use the same font as the heading, perhaps in a different size, or a font that is noticeably opposite in its style, serifs, vertical stress, and stroke transitions.

The following steps insert the two lines of subtitle text with a complementary font.

1 Press the T key to activate the Horizontal Type Tool. Drag a box below the previous text that fills the bottom of the image.

2 Use the Character panel to select the Stencil font. Enter 24 pt in the 'Set the font size' box.

3 Click the 'Right align text' button.

4 Click the 'Set the text color' box. When the Select Color (Text Color) box is displayed, select a black color, and then click the OK button to close the color box.

5 Type The Magazine for Extreme Sporters and then press the ENTER key. Type Summer 2014 Edition to complete the text (Figure 6–54 on the next page).

BTW

Type Professions
The art of designing typefaces is called type design. **Type designers** work for software companies and graphic design firms, and sometimes freelance as calligraphers and artists. **Typographers** are responsible for designing the layout of the printed word and blocks of text on a page. Because the chosen font contributes significantly to an overall layout, typographers have in-depth knowledge and understanding about the intricacies in which typefaces are utilized to convey particular messages.

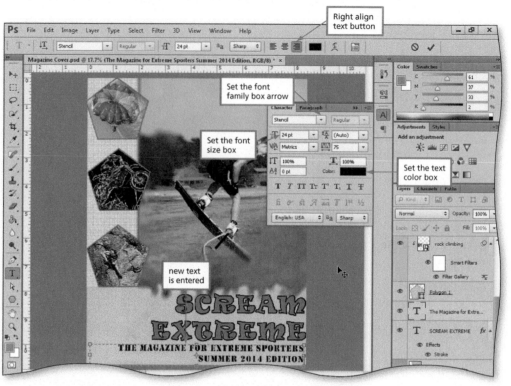

Figure 6–54

To Underline Text

The following steps underline one of the words in the text.

1

- In the text bounding box, drag to highlight the first word, The.

- On the Character panel, click the Underline button (Figure 6–55).

Figure 6–55

2

- On the options bar, click the 'Commit any current edits' button.

- Click the Toggle the Character and Paragraph panels button on the options bar to hide the panels (Figure 6–56).

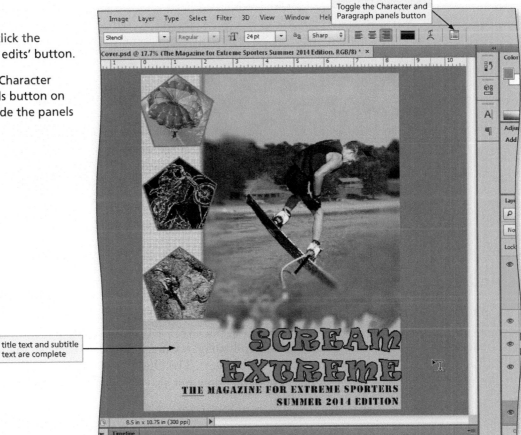

Toggle the Character and Paragraph panels button

title text and subtitle text are complete

Figure 6–56

To Insert Description Text

At the top of the magazine, you will create green text, describing the issue. For consistency, the text will repeat the same font as the subtitle and the green color from the pentagon strokes.

1 Select the Horizontal Type Tool, if necessary.

2 Drag a box that encompasses the sky area in the wakeboarding image.

3 On the options bar, select the Stencil Font, if necessary. Select a 30 pt font, and then click the 'Left align text' button to left-justify the text.

4 Click the 'Set the text color' box. When Photoshop displays the Color Picker (Text color) dialog box, move the mouse pointer into the image, and click the green color that strokes the pentagons. Click the OK button to close the dialog box.

5 Click to deselect the Underline button, if necessary, type Inside this issue:, press the ENTER key, and then click the Center text button on the options bar.

6 Type Wakeboarding at and then press the ENTER key. Type its best! to complete the text (Figure 6–57 on the next page).

7 Click the 'Commit any current edits' button on the options bar.

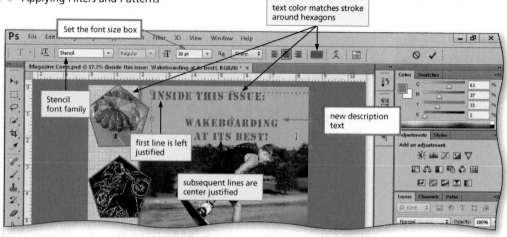

Figure 6–57

To Add an Outer Glow

Another way to differentiate text, without changing the font family, is to add a layer style. Recall that layer styles are applied to a layer, rather than by changing the layer's actual pixels with a filter. Layer styles alter the appearance of the layer by adding depth, shadow, shading, texture, or overlay. To make the text stand out, you will add an Outer Glow layer style to the description text. The Outer Glow layer style has some unique settings to tailor not only the color, opacity, and noise of the glow, but also to change the contour of the glow.

1

- With the type layer still selected on the Layers panel, click the 'Add a layer style' button on the Layers panel status bar. When Photoshop displays the context menu, click Outer Glow to open the Layer Style dialog box.

- Drag the title bar of the dialog box down so you can view the text changes in the document window.

- In the Structure area, click the Blend Mode box arrow to display the list (Figure 6–58).

How will changing the blending mode affect the characters in the text?

Because you chose Outer Glow, the blending mode will be applied around the edges of the characters, rather than to the characters themselves.

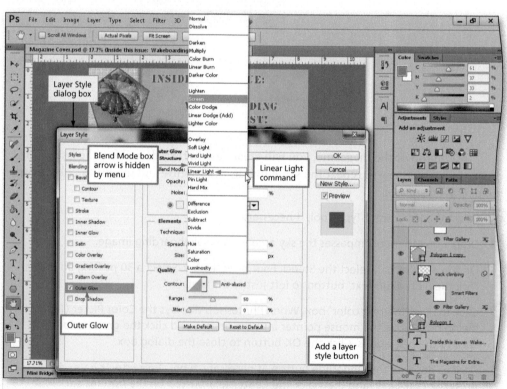

Figure 6–58

2

- Click Linear Light to select the blending mode.

- Drag the Opacity slider to 50%.

- Drag the Noise slider to 0% (Figure 6–59).

 Q&A

What is the effect of the Linear Light blending mode?

Linear Light dodges light colors by increasing the brightness of the selected color — in this case the yellow color of the glow.

Experiment

- Drag the Noise slider all the way to the right and notice the difference in the text. Drag the slider back to 0%.

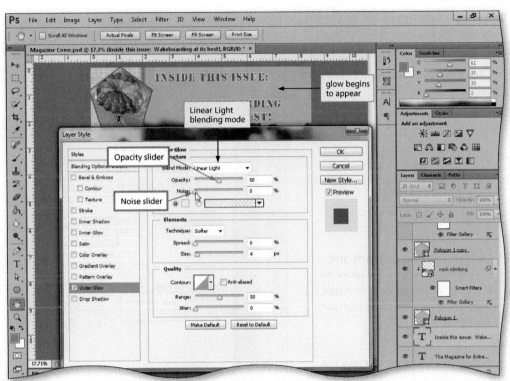

Figure 6–59

3

- In the Elements area, drag the Spread slider to 15% to expand the glow (Figure 6–60).

Q&A

What is the difference between Spread and Size?

Size changes the diameter of the setting, in this case the outer glow. Spread changes the diameter and blurs slightly.

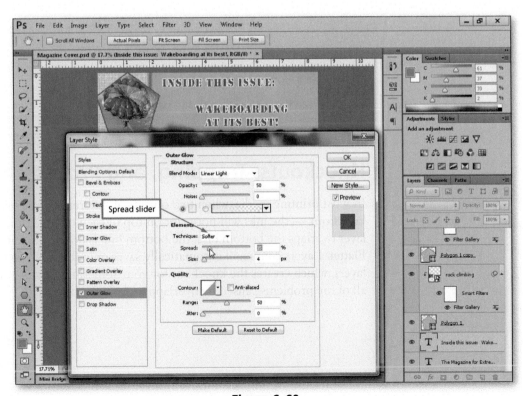

Figure 6–60

- Click the Contour picker box arrow to display the available contours for the glow.

- Click the Cove – Shallow contour to select it (Figure 6–61).

Can I create my own contour?

Yes, if you click the Contour picker box itself, Photoshop displays a Contour Editor dialog box, where you can drag to edit the line of the contour.

 Experiment

- Click each of the contours and notice the effect of the glow on the text. When you are finished, click the Cove - Shallow contour again.

❺

- Click the OK button to close the dialog box and apply the glow.

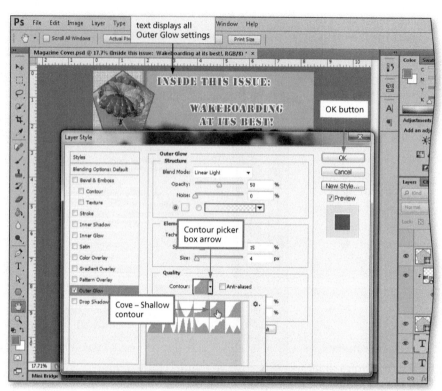

Figure 6–61

To Save the File with the Text Layers

The following step saves the file again.

❶ Save the file with the same file name.

Knockouts, Trapping, and Proofs

In most printing media, when two objects of different colors overlap they create a **knockout** — the inks will not print on top of each other. At the point where the top layer overlaps the bottom one, the bottom one is not printed at all. In Photoshop, the Flatten Layers command automatically saves only the topmost color in overlapped layers, which creates the knockout for you. Sometimes that is not enough to prevent all of the problems caused by overlapping colors, however.

Avoid color printing problems.

As you plan your graphic designs, consider the following ways to avoid color printing problems.

- Avoid putting colored objects too close together. Leave some white space between objects in your design or use black to stroke objects that overlap, or meet, with black outlines.

- Use common process colors when colors need to touch each other.

- For contiguous colors, use colors within 20% of each other in the CMYK color spectrum.

- Overprint black text using an overlay blending mode on type layers to cancel the knockout and force black ink to print on the background color.

When you print a hard copy using a desktop printer, the color is applied all at once; each color normally is printed where you expect it to be. In commercial printing, the printing device makes multiple passes over the paper. The speed of the printer and possible shifts in the paper may make some colors run together, creating spreads of blended color, or the printer may leave small missed areas between very close objects or layers (Figure 6–62). Service bureaus use the term **misregistration** to describe those gaps in printing that are out of the printer's register or alignment. **Trapping** is a prepress activity of calculating an intentional compensation for the misregistration. Chokes and spreads are both methods of trapping. **Chokes** intentionally shrink an image to eliminate overprinting, and **spreads** intentionally overlap images to avoid gaps in the ink coverage where the base paper might show through.

Figure 6–62

When you cannot avoid placing colors close together, intentionally printing one layer of ink on top of another is called **overprinting**, or **surprinting**. Most service bureaus determine if trapping is needed in the overprinting process and can perform that prepress activity for you. It is not recommended you do this yourself, but if you need or want to do it, you will have to enter values in the Trap dialog box. The Trap command is located on the Image menu. The service bureau, which understands its printing process best, is the ideal source for correctly gauging these values.

Photoshop's automatic settings use industry standard rules when applying a trap:

- White is knocked out automatically.
- All colors spread under black.
- Lighter colors spread under darker colors.
- Yellow spreads under cyan, magenta, and black.
- Pure cyan and pure magenta spread under each other equally. White graphics and text will not cause a problem because it will be knocked out to the paper color.

To Convert to the CMYK Color Mode

The next step is to convert the image to CMYK and merge the layers. Recall that the color mode is changed using the Image menu. CMYK is the correct color mode for professional print jobs.

1 Click Image on the Application bar, point to Mode, and then click CMYK Color.

2 When Photoshop displays a warning message about rasterizing the image, click the Rasterize button. If Photoshop displays a warning message about merging layers, click the Merge button. If Photoshop displays a dialog box about conversion profiles, click the OK button.

Proofs

A **proof** is a copy of a document that you can examine to check color, layout, spelling, and other details before printing the final copy. A hard proof simulates what your final output will look like on a printing press. Sometimes called a proof print, or a match print, a **hard proof** is produced on an output device that is less expensive to operate than a printing press. Some ink-jet printers have the resolution necessary to produce inexpensive prints that can be used as hard proofs. Hard proofs need to fit on the page of the proof printer, so it sometimes is necessary to scale the proof. Alternatively, if you need to see a full-size proof, you may be able to tile or poster print the image, printing smaller portions of the image, each on its own sheet of paper, but at actual size. Be careful about judging color with a desktop printer. Less-expensive printers sometimes produce output that does not represent the screen color accurately. For example, lower-quality printers can produce a blue hue that appears slightly purple; red hues sometimes appear orange. Users should be aware that the use of inferior printers could result in somewhat false or misleading output— sometimes indicating problems where none exists. Ask your service bureau about color matching.

Plan
Ahead

Consult with printing professionals.
Printing professionals can help you make decisions about paper, color, type, and
surprinting, trapping, knockouts, and misregistration. Some print shops do professional
proofreading, prepress activities, digital proofing, die-cutting, typesetting, binding, and
a variety of other services. Digital typesetters, lithographers, and machine operators are
the best source of information because they know the machinery, color management
systems, and font libraries.

While a hard proof is a printed copy, a **soft proof** is a copy you look at on
the screen. Soft proofs can be as simple as a preview or more complex when color
adjustments and monitor calibrations take place.

To Print a Hard Proof

The following steps print a hard proof that resembles what a final copy of the magazine cover should
look like. Settings in the Print Preview dialog box are adjusted to match professional print settings. The quality
of your hard proof will depend on your printer. Some printers handle color matching and overlays better than
others do. See your instructor for exact settings.

1

- Click View on the
Application bar,
and then point
to Proof Setup to
display the submenu
(Figure 6–63).

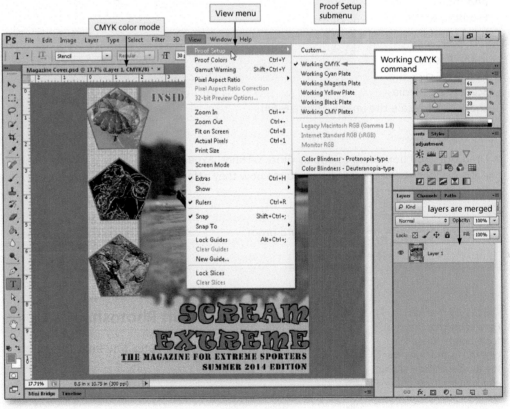

Figure 6–63

2

- If the Working CMYK command does not display a check mark, click it.

- Click File on the Application bar, and then click Print to display the Photoshop Print Settings dialog box.

- In the Color Management area, click the Color Handling box arrow and then click Photoshop Manages Colors. Click the Normal box arrow, and then click Hard Proofing to print a hard proof.

- In the Position and Size area, click the Scale to Fit Media check box to scale the image (Figure 6–64).

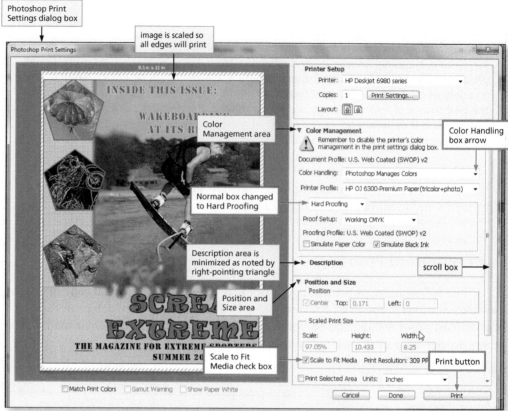

Figure 6–64

 **Experiment**

- Drag the scroll box down to display other settings. Expand the Printing Marks area and click the check boxes one at a time to see how they affect the preview. When you are finished, remove the check marks.

3

- Click the Print button to print the hard proof.

To Save the File and Quit Photoshop

The magazine cover is complete. The final steps are to save the file and quit Photoshop.

1 Press SHIFT+CTRL+S to open the Save As dialog box.

2 Type `Magazine Cover CMYK` in the File name text box.

3 Click the Save button. If Photoshop displays an options dialog box, click the OK button.

4 Click the Close button on the Photoshop application bar.

Chapter Summary

In this chapter, you created a magazine cover from scratch. After choosing CMYK sliders on the Color panel, you used the Paint Bucket Tool to fill in a background. You learned that Photoshop contains a large number of filters that can be combined and edited to produce an endless number of special effects. Some of the filters manipulate the pixels geometrically, while others change the color. Filters that specialize in strokes and edges analyze the image to produce effects only in certain areas. You used the Liquify filter to push and distort parts of an image. You created smart filters and applied the Plastic Wrap, Glowing Edges, and Craquelure filters. You used the new Blur filters to focus certain positions of the image. By creating a clipping mask, you put a picture inside a shape. After creating a pattern, you used advanced text-editing techniques to create dynamic text that provided both consistency and contrast. Finally, you learned about misregistration, potential printing problems associated with objects being close to one another, and the value of consulting with a print service bureau to obtain information about printing details. With the magazine cover complete, you converted it to CMYK and printed a hard proof.

The items listed below include all the new Photoshop skills you have learned in this chapter:

1. Change the Sliders on the Color Panel (PS 343)
2. To Correct an Out of Gamut Color (PS 344)
3. Use the Paint Bucket Tool (PS 345)
4. Apply the Liquify Filter (PS 356)
5. Align and Distribute Layers (PS 359)
6. Create a Smart Filter (PS 360)
7. Apply a Plastic Wrap Smart Filter (PS 361)
8. Apply a Glowing Edges Smart Filter (PS 363)
9. Apply a Craquelure Smart Filter (PS 364)
10. Apply an Iris Blur Filter (PS 366)
11. Create a Pentagon (PS 369)
12. Create a Clipping Mask (PS 371)
13. Nudge (PS 373)
14. Define a Pattern (PS 375)
15. Use a Pattern (PS 375)
16. Set the Tracking (PS 381)
17. Underline Text (PS 382)
18. Add an Outer Glow (PS 384)
19. Print a Hard Proof (PS 389)

Apply Your Knowledge

Reinforce the skills and apply the concepts you learned in this chapter.

Creating a Digital Painting by Applying Multiple Filters

Instructions: Start Photoshop and perform the customization steps found on pages PS 6 through PS 10. Open the Apply 6-1 Garden file from the Chapter 06 folder of the Data Files for Students. Visit www.cengage.com/ct/studentdownload for detailed instructions or contact your instructor for information about accessing the required files. You will edit the file to create a digital painting from a digital photograph of a garden by increasing the saturation of color, adjusting the lighting, and then adding filters to create the painting shown in Figure 6–65 on the next page.

Perform the following tasks:
1. Save the image on your USB flash drive as a PSD file, with the file name Apply 6-1 Garden Painting.
2. On the Layers panel, right-click the Background layer and then click Duplicate Layer. Name the new layer, edits. Select only the edits layer, and hide the Background layer by clicking its visibility icon.
3. To increase the saturation of the colors, click Layer on the Application bar, point to New Adjustment Layer, and then click Hue/Saturation. When Photoshop displays the New Layer dialog box, click the OK button. On the Properties panel, click the Master box arrow, and then select Reds. Enter a saturation of 50. Similarly, select Yellows and enter a saturation of 60. Select Blues and enter a saturation of 73. On the Properties panel status bar, click the 'Clip to layer' button. Collapse the Properties panel.

Continued >

Apply Your Knowledge *continued*

4. On the Layers panel, select the edits layer. On the Filter menu, click Convert for Smart Filters to convert the layer. If Photoshop displays a dialog box, click the OK button.

5. On the Filter menu, click Filter Gallery. If more than one filter appears on the filter list, click the 'Delete effect layer' button until only one filter is displayed in the list.

6. Click the Zoom box arrow and then click Fit in View. If the Artistic filters are not displayed, click Artistic.

7. Click the Poster Edges thumbnail. Set the Edge Thickness to 6, the Edge Intensity to 0, and the Posterization to 5.

8. In the lower-right portion of the Filter Gallery, click the 'New effect layer' button to add another filter to the list.

9. Click the Cutout thumbnail. Set the Number of Levels to 6, the Edge Simplicity to 1, and the Edge Fidelity to 2.

10. Click the 'New effect layer' button to add another filter to the list.

11. Click the Rough Pastels thumbnail. Set the Stroke Length to 22, the Stroke Detail to 1, the Texture to Canvas, the Scaling to 136, the Relief to 3, and the Light to Bottom.

12. Click the OK button to close the Filter Gallery.

13. On the Layers panel, select all three layers. On the Image menu, point to Mode, and then click CMYK Color. If Photoshop displays a dialog box about rasterizing, click the Rasterize button. When Photoshop displays a dialog box, click the Merge button, and then click the OK button. On the View menu, point to Proof Setup. If the Working CMYK command does not display a check mark, click it.

14. On the File menu, click Print to display the Photoshop Print Settings dialog box. In the Color Management area, click the Color Handling box arrow, and then click Photoshop Manages Colors. Click the Normal Printing box arrow, and then click Hard Proofing to print a hard proof. In the Position and Size area, click the Scale to Fit Media check box to scale the image (Figure 6–65).

15. Ready the printer. Click the Print button and then when your printer's Print dialog box is displayed, click its Print button. Turn in the printout to your instructor. Save the file again and then quit Photoshop.

Figure 6–65

Extend Your Knowledge

Extend the skills you learned in this chapter and experiment with new skills. You may need to use Help to complete the assignment.

Creating the Illusion of Flowing Water

Instructions: Start Photoshop and perform the customization steps found on pages PS 6 through PS 10. Open the Extend 6-1 Faucet file from the Chapter 06 folder of the Data Files for Students. Visit www.cengage.com/ct/studentdownload for detailed instructions or contact your instructor for information about accessing the required files.

The Beta Faucet Company needs you to finish an ad for a new line of faucets. You are to add the appearance of water flowing from the end of the faucet, as shown in Figure 6–66.

Figure 6–66

Perform the following tasks:

1. On the File menu, click Save As. Save the image on your USB flash drive as a PSD file, with the file name Extend 6-1 Faucet Edited. You will notice that several layers are not visible.

2. Click the visibility icons next to the light blue and dark blue layers.

3. On the Tools panel, click the 'Set foreground color' button to display the Color Picker (Foreground Color) dialog box. In the document window, click the light blue color to select it. Click the OK button to close the Color Picker dialog box.

4. Repeat Step 3 to assign the background color to the dark blue color in the document window.

5. Select the background layer. On the Tools panel, select the Gradient Tool and create a radial gradient from left to right across the middle of the document window. Press SHIFT+CTRL+N to create a new layer above the background layer and name it, dark rectangle.

6. If a green ruler guide does not appear in the document window, click View on the Application bar to display the View menu, point to Show, and then click Guides. Use the Rectangular Marquee Tool to draw a rectangle enclosing the right side of the document window.

Continued >

Extend Your Knowledge *continued*

7. Change the foreground color to black and fill this new selection by using the Fill shortcut keys, ALT+BACKSPACE.

8. Deselect the marquee by clicking CTRL+D.

9. On the Layers panel, change the opacity of the dark rectangle layer to 60%, creating a navy blue color.

10. Open the Extend 6-1 Single Faucet file from the Chapter 06 folder of the Data Files for Students.

11. Arrange the document windows side by side, and then move the faucet image into the Extend 6-1 Faucet Edited document window. Close the Extend 6-1 Single Faucet document window.

12. Press the D key to reset the default colors.

13. Create a new layer below the faucet layer with the name, water, and select the layer.

14. On the Filter menu, point to Render, and then click Clouds.

15. On the Filter menu, point to Blur, and then click Gaussian Blur. Set the radius to 6, and then close the Gaussian Blur dialog box.

16. On the Filter menu, point to Blur, and then click Motion Blur. Enter the following settings, and then click the OK button:

    a. Angle 90

    b. Distance 80

17. On the Edit menu, point to Transform, and then click Scale. When Photoshop displays a dialog box, click the OK button.

18. On the options bar, set the width to 50% while leaving the height at 100%. Press the ENTER key to commit the transformation.

19. Open the Filter Gallery. Click the Artistic folder and then click Plastic Wrap. Apply the filter with the following settings:

    a. Highlight Strength: 15

    b. Detail: 10

    c. Smoothness: 10

20. Open the Filter Gallery. Click the Sketch folder and then click Chrome. Apply the filter with the following settings:

    a. Detail: 0

    b. Smoothness: 8

21. On the Edit menu, click Fade Filter Gallery. Set the Opacity to 100% and the Mode to Hard Light.

22. Press CTRL+T to display the transformation handles. Resize and move the selection to fit under the faucet. Press the ENTER key to commit the transformation.

23. On the Edit menu, point to Transform, and then click Warp. Adjust the anchor points to simulate a stream of running water below the faucet in the document window, as shown in Figure 6-66 on the previous page. Press the ENTER key to commit the transformation.

24. On the Layers panel, change the blending mode to Hard Light.

25. Click the visibility icons for the rest of the layers to view the completed image.

26. Save the file as Extend 6-1 Faucet Complete, and submit the assignment to your instructor in the specified format.

Make It Right

Analyze a document and correct all errors and/or improve the design.

Correcting Bokeh Errors

Instructions: Start Photoshop and perform the customization steps found on pages PS 6 through PS 10. Open the Make It Right 6-1 Butterfly file from the Chapter 06 folder of the Data Files for Students. Visit www.cengage.com/ct/studentdownload for detailed instructions or contact your instructor for information about accessing the required files.

The file contains an edits layer whose settings caused too high a distortion, as shown in Figure 6–67.

Figure 6–67

Perform the following tasks:

Delete the edits layer. Duplicate the background layer and name it corrections. With the corrections layer selected, use the Filter menu and the Blur submenu to access the Iris Blur. Adjust the focus ring to be a circle around the butterfly. Drag the center point as necessary. Use the following settings on the Blur Tools and Blur Effects panels:

a. Set the Blur to 35 px
b. Set the Light Bokeh to 30%
c. Set the Bokeh Color to 0%
d. Drag the black Light Range slider to 150
e. Drag the white Light Range slider to 250

Save the image as a PSD file on your storage device with the name, Make It Right 6-1 Butterfly Corrected.

In the Lab

Design and/or create a document using the guidelines, concepts, and skills presented in this chapter. Labs are listed in order of increasing difficulty.

Lab 1: Using the Liquify Filter

Problem: You are to enhance a music graphic on a poster by using the Liquify filter. The completed poster is displayed in Figure 6–68.

Note: This assignment requires the Data Files for Students. Visit www.cengage.com/ct/student-download for detailed instructions or contact your instructor for information about accessing the required files.

Instructions: Perform the following tasks:

1. Start Photoshop. Perform the customization steps found on pages PS 6 through PS 10.

2. Open the file Lab 6-1 Recital Graphic from the Chapter 06 folder of the Data Files for Students.

3. Click the Save As command on the File menu. Type `Lab 6-1 Recital Graphic Solution` as the file name. Choose the Photoshop PSD format. Browse to your USB flash drive storage device. Click the Save button. If Photoshop displays a dialog box, click the OK button.

4. Using the Layers panel menu, create a duplicate layer of the music layer and name it, edits. Hide the Background layer and music layer.

5. On the Filter menu, click Liquify. If Photoshop displays a message about the graphic processor, click the OK button. When the Liquify dialog box is displayed, use the Zoom Tool and Hand Tool to position the music layer in the preview area, if necessary.

6. Set the Brush Size to 150.

7. Click the Bloat Tool, and then click at the beginning of the musical staff to inflate the area. Click in several other areas. Experiment with clicking several times in the same place.

8. Click the OK button to close the Liquify dialog box.

9. Click the visibility icon beside the Background layer to make it visible.

10. Flatten the image, discarding hidden layers, and then save the file with the name Lab 6-1 Recital Graphic Complete in the TIFF format.

11. See your instructor for ways to print this poster-size image, if that service is available at your school. Otherwise, use the Image Size command on the Image menu to reduce the photo to fit on available printer paper. Print a hard proof using the directions from the chapter.

Figure 6–68

In the Lab

Lab 2: Creating a Flyer from Scratch

Problem: You work for a local auction house. Your supervisor has asked you to create a public auction flyer with text that stands out to attract attention. The flyer is displayed in Figure 6–69.

PUBLIC AUCTION

Baker Estate Auction
2750 Cliff Rd, Midland, TN

Saturday, May 30 at 9:30 AM

◆   Tractors & trailers
◆   Small farm equipment
◆   Log splitter
◆   Camping & fishing equipment
◆   Shop tools
◆   Outdoor equipment
◆   Furniture & household
◆   Antiques & collectibles

Able Auctioneers (931) 555-8689
www.ableauctioneers.biz

Auctioneer's Note: This auction presents the well-kept personal property of the Dale Baker Estate.

Figure 6–69

Instructions: Perform the following tasks:

1. Start Photoshop. Perform the customization steps found on pages PS 6 through PS 10.

2. Create a new file 8.5 by 11 inches in the RGB format. Use a resolution of 300 and a white background.

3. Save the file in the PSD format, with the name, Lab 6-2 Auction Flyer.

4. Place the graphic file named, Lab 6-2 Gavel, in the Lab 6-2 Auction Flyer image, and then drag the gavel graphic to the upper-left corner.

5. To create the heading text:

   a. Using the Horizontal Type Tool, create a text bounding box in the upper-right corner of the flyer. On the options bar click the 'Toggle the Character and Paragraph panels' button to display the Character panel. (*Hint:* Use the Character panel tool tips and Figure 6–50 on page PS 378 to help you locate the various settings.)

   b. Set the font family to Cooper Black and set the anti-aliasing method to Sharp.

   c. Set the font size to 60 and set the font color to black.

Continued >

   d. Set the tracking to 25 and set the leading to Auto.

   e. On the Character panel, click the Faux Bold, Faux Italic, and All Caps buttons.

   f. Use the options bar to set the justification to right aligned.

   g. Type PUBLIC and then press the ENTER key. Type AUCTION and then click the 'Commit any current edits' button on the options bar to close the bounding box.

6. To prepare for the body text:

   a. Create a second text box that fills the rest of the page.

   b. Set the font family to Arial, and set the font style to Regular.

   c. Set the font size to 24, and set the font color to black.

   d. Set the leading to Auto.

   e. Set the tracking to 10. Click the Faux Bold button.

   f. Use the options bar to set the justification to left aligned.

7. Type the body text as shown in Figure 6–69 on the previous page with the following changes:

   a. After the first line, click the Faux Bold button to turn it off.

   b. When you get to the bulleted text, type the letter t as a placeholder for the bullet on each line.

   c. When you get to the last three lines, change the justification to center-justified.

   d. Highlight the text, Auctioneer's Note, and then click the Faux Italic button on the Character panel.

   e. Highlight the t placeholder for the first bullet, and change the font to Wingdings so the bullet will appear. Repeat for the other bullets.

   f. Click the 'Commit any current edits' button on the options bar to close the bounding box.

8. Save the image again and submit the file as directed by your instructor.

In the Lab

Lab 3: Fizzy Root Beer Advertisement

Problem: The Fizzy Root Beer Company has a new label and needs you to finish the design for their latest advertisement. They want the background to look like bubbles, but they do not have any close-ups of root beer bubbles for you to use. By combining several filters, you will create a bubbly background and add a spotlight effect as shown in Figure 6–70.

Note: This assignment requires the Data Files for Students. Visit www.cengage.com/ct/studentdownload for detailed instructions, or contact your instructor for information about accessing the required files.

Instructions: Perform the following tasks:

Start Photoshop and perform the customization steps found on pages PS 6 through PS 10. Open the Lab 6-3 Fizzy file from the Data Files for Students. Save the image on your USB flash drive as a PSD file with the file name Lab 6-3 Fizzy Edited.

Hide the label layer. Select the background layer. Click the D key to reset the default colors. On the Filter menu, click Convert for Smart Filters. To simulate bubbles, apply the Render filter named Clouds. Apply the Stylize filter named Glowing Edges, setting the Edge width to 3, the Edge Brightness to 19, and the Smoothness to 15. Apply the Sketch filter named Plaster, setting the Image Balance to 16 and the Smoothness to 2.

Figure 6–70

To make the bubbles look like they are in liquid, add a lighting effect. On the Filter menu, point to Render, and then click Lighting Effects. Choose Blue Omni for the style. In the preview, drag the ellipse handles to create a circle that encompasses the entire preview. Drag the center point to the lower-left corner of the preview. Click the OK button to close the Lighting Effects dialog box.

Apply the Sketch filter named Chrome, setting the Detail to 8 and the Smoothness to 10.

To make the bubbles brown, click Hue/Saturation on the Adjustments panel to open the Properties panel. Select the Colorize check box so that it displays a check mark, set the Hue to 22, the Saturation to 70, and the Lightness to –25. Click the 'Clip to layer' button on the Properties panel status bar.

On the Layers panel, display the label layer. Add a spotlight filter to the label layer by clicking Render from the Filter menu, then clicking Lighting Effects. Select Flashlight as the Style and scale the light so that it covers the top and bottom of the label. Save the file again and submit it to your instructor in the specified format.

Cases and Places

Apply your creative thinking and problem solving skills to design and implement a solution.

Note: To complete these assignments, you may be required to use the Data Files for Students. Visit www.cengage.com/ct/studentdownload for detailed instructions or contact your instructor for information about accessing the required files.

1: Create a Surface Blur

Academic

A photo of your campus, taken from the roof of its tallest building, was taken on a very cloudy day. The school would like to use the picture on its Web site, but would prefer a brighter sky. Open the file named Case 6-1 Cityscape from the Chapter 06 folder of the Data Files for Students. Select the sky and create a layer via cut. Use the Color panel to select a very light blue foreground color. Use the Render Filter named Clouds to create clouds in the sky. Flatten the file and save it for Web & Devices in the .gif format.

2: Create a Coloring Book

Personal

You decide to make a coloring book for your nephew. Use pets or go to the local zoo and take several digital pictures. Open the first photo. Use the Find Edges filter in the Stylize category. Save the file with a name such as Monkey Find Edges. Open the second photo and use the Trace Contour filter in the Stylize category. Adjust the level to 50 or a suitable value for your photo. Save the file with a name such as Tiger Trace Contour 50. Open the third photo and convert it to grayscale. Use the Photocopy filter in the Sketch category and adjust the settings to 8 and 11, or suitable values for your photo. Save the file with a name such as Zebra Photocopy 8 11. Open each of your other animal photos and experiment with different filters and settings to create areas that could be colored. Save each file with a name indicative of the filter and settings. Print a copy of each edited photo, and staple them together in book form.

3: Using a Filter for Corrections

Professional

A professional photographer would like you to enhance a picture of a sunset with a filter. He plans to upload the picture to several social media sites. Specifically, he would like to reduce the JPG artifacts produced by his camera. Open the file named Case 6-3 Sunset from the Chapter 06 folder of the Data Files for Students. Duplicate the background and convert the layer into a smart filter. On the Filter menu, choose the Noise filter named Reduce Noise. Drag the Preserve Details slider and the Sharpen Details slider to the right. Slow drag the Reduce Color Noise slider to the left until you are happy with the result. Click the OK button in the Reduce Noise dialog box and then save the file with the name, Case 6-3 Sunset Edited in the PSD format.

7 | Creating Color Channels and Actions

Objectives

You will have mastered the material in this chapter when you can:

- Create a master image
- View channel color separations
- Use the Channels panel to create alpha channels
- Use a brush in overlay mode to help define a selection
- Use a brush in color mode to recolor a selection
- Convert an image to black and white using different methods
- Create black-and-white, sepia, and duotone versions of an image

- Create an advertisement with warped text
- Create a new action set
- Record, save, edit, and play back an action
- Convert an RGB image to LAB color and then to CMYK
- List prepress activities
- Resize and resample images
- Print color separations

7 | Creating Color Channels and Actions

Introduction

Photographers and graphic artists routinely create multiple versions of the same image. Creating a master version, along with versions for the Web, for black-and-white advertising media, for color separations and tints, and for various color modes and sizes, enables maximum repurposing. Multiple versions of photos are used commonly in advertising, photo cataloging, and on photo Web sites. Portrait studios produce and sell a wide assortment of special effect portraits, which require a variety of image versions. Creating a reusable logo adds flexibility for business publications.

Another timesaving tool is the ability to record your steps as you work in Photoshop and play them back when needed. The saved recording, called a Photoshop action, is a powerful automation device. Tasks that you perform repeatedly, such as adding a logo to each publication, can be recorded and then played back with a single keystroke.

You will learn about channels, color changes, actions, resizing, and resampling as you work through this chapter.

Project — Animal Adoption Advertising

Chapter 7 uses Photoshop to edit photographs for an animal adoption event advertisement. First, you will hide the background and create a masked piece of artwork that can be dropped into other backgrounds and page layout applications. Second, you will create warped text featuring event details. A black-and-white version of the photo will be created for newspaper placement. Sepia and tinted versions will provide visual variety and styling, such as retro or filtered special effects. You will style the advertisement with a special effect and resize it with an automated action. Finally, an image with exact size and resolution requirements will be created for an advertisement insert. The ad, complete with graphics and text, will be converted to the CMYK color model and printed with color separations. The images are shown in Figure 7–1.

Figure 7–1

Overview

As you read this chapter, you will learn how to create the images shown in Figure 7–1 by performing these general tasks:

- Add an alpha channel.
- Hide the background to create a floating image.
- Insert and warp text.
- Recolor images to produce black and white, sepia, and duotones.
- Use action sets.
- Record and play back an action.
- Resample and resize an image.
- Print color separations.

Plan Ahead

> **General Project Guidelines**
>
> When editing a photo, the actions you perform and decisions you make will affect the appearance and characteristics of the finished product. As you edit photos, such as the ones shown in Figure 7–1 on the previous page, you should follow these general guidelines:
>
> 1. **Plan your versions.** Always start with a high-quality photo and create a master image. Anticipate all the ways the image might be used or repurposed. Consider client needs as you create versions, such as color, masked images, black and white, tints, and color modes.
>
> 2. **Choose the best tool for the job.** As you make decisions about how to edit your image, look at various ways to accomplish the same task. For example, compare using a simple delete command versus an alpha channel mask. Ask yourself if you will need to use the selection again. Is the background complicated? If you are considering a black-and-white version, decide whether a simple grayscale will be as effective as an adjustment layer where you can fine-tune the contrast.
>
> 3. **Record actions for repetitive tasks.** If you or your client have specialized, repetitive tasks that you perform on a regular basis, consider recording an action. This playback feature will not only save time, it will create consistency by applying revisions in the same way each time. Actions can give users flexibility by pausing for user decisions at critical points or by waiting for dialog box responses.
>
> 4. **Create print versions of artwork.** If you plan to print your artwork, convert and save a copy of it in the CMYK color mode. The RGB color mode, used for display on electronic devices such as computers and smart phones, is not suitable for printing. Converting to CMYK gives a better representation on the computer screen of how the image will look when printed. You can then make adjustments to the CMYK version before printing, if necessary.
>
> When necessary, more specific details concerning the above guidelines are presented at appropriate points in the chapter. The chapter also will identify the actions performed and decisions made regarding these guidelines during the creation of the edited photos shown in Figure 7–1.

To Start Photoshop

If you are stepping through this project on a computer and you want your screen to match the figures in this book, then you should change your computer's resolution to 1024 × 768 and reset the panels, tools, and colors. For more information about how to change the resolution on your computer, and other advanced Photoshop settings, read the Changing Screen Resolution appendix.

The following steps, which assume Windows 7 is running, start Photoshop based on a typical installation. You may need to ask your instructor how to start Photoshop for your system.

1 Click the Start button on the Windows 7 taskbar to display the Start menu and then type `Photoshop CS6` in the 'Search programs and files' box.

2 Click Adobe Photoshop CS6 in the list to start Photoshop.

3 If the Photoshop window is not maximized, click the Maximize button next to the Close button on the Application bar to maximize the window.

To Reset the Workspace

As discussed in Chapter 1, it is helpful to reset the workspace so that the tools and panels appear in their default positions. The following steps select the Essentials workspace.

① Click Window on the Application bar to display the Window menu, and then point to Workspace to display the Workspace submenu.

② Click Essentials (Default) on the Workspace submenu to select the default workspace panels.

③ Click Window on the Application bar, and then point to Workspace again to display the list.

④ Click Reset Essentials to restore the workspace to its default settings and reposition any panels that may have been moved.

To Reset the Tools and the Options Bar

Recall that the Tools panel and the options bar retain their settings from previous Photoshop sessions. The following steps select the Rectangular Marquee Tool and reset all tool settings in the options bar.

① If the tools in the Tools panel appear in two columns, click the double arrow at the top of the Tools panel.

② If necessary, click the Rectangular Marquee Tool button on the Tools panel to select it.

③ Right-click the Rectangular Marquee Tool icon on the options bar to display the context menu, and then click Reset All Tools. When Photoshop displays a confirmation dialog box, click the OK button to restore the tools to their default settings.

To Set the Interface and Default Colors

Recall that Photoshop retains the interface color scheme, as well as the foreground and background colors, from session to session. The following steps set the interface to Medium Gray and the foreground and background colors to black over white.

① Click Edit on the Application bar to display the Edit menu. Point to Preferences and then click Interface on the Preferences submenu to display the Preferences dialog box.

② Click the third button, Medium Gray, to change the interface color scheme.

③ Click the OK button to close the Preferences dialog box.

④ Press the D key to reset the default foreground and background colors. If black is not over white on the Tools panel, press the X key.

To Open a File

To open a file in Photoshop, it must be stored as a digital file on your computer system or on an external storage device. The photos used in this book are stored in the Data Files for Students. To complete this assignment, you will be required to use the Data Files for Students. Visit www.cengage.com/ct/studentdownload for detailed instructions or contact your instructor for information about accessing the required files. The steps on the next page open the Supplies file from the Data Files for Students.

1 Open the Supplies file from the Chapter 07 folder of the Data Files for Students.

2 When Photoshop displays the image in the document window, if the magnification shown on the status bar is not 33.33%, double-click the magnification box on the document window status bar, type `33.33`, and then press the ENTER key to change the magnification.

To View Rulers

The following steps display the rulers in the document window to facilitate making precise measurements.

1 If the rulers are not shown on the top and left sides of the document window, press CTRL+R to display the rulers in the workspace.

2 If necessary, right-click the horizontal ruler and then click Inches on the context menu to display the rulers in inches.

Using Channels

The first version of the photo will be a floating image without a background. **Floating images** have a transparent background so they can be placed in front of other elements. There are many ways to remove a background, including methods you have used before, such as using the Eraser Tool, layer masks, or editing selections. Another way to isolate and remove the background is to use Photoshop channels.

As you learned in previous chapters, digital images are made of many pixels, or tiny dots, each of which represents an abstract sample of color. Pixels use combinations of primary colors, or pigments. Recall that additive colors involve light emitted directly from a source. Subtractive colors absorb some wavelengths of light and reflect others. The two color modes RGB and CMYK are based respectively on the additive and subtractive primary colors.

Each of the primary colors creates a channel in Photoshop. In an image, a **channel** consists of all the pixels of the same color, identified using the color modes. An image from a digital camera will have a red, green, and blue channel, whereas a printed image will have a cyan, magenta, yellow, and black channel. Channels are used in Photoshop to separate and store information about an image's colors so that users can manipulate them. Traditionally, the term **color separations** refers to the process of separating image colors into individual films or pattern plates of cyan, magenta, yellow, and black in preparation for printing. Photoshop takes that process one step further by automatically creating the color separation anytime you convert a file to the CMYK color mode.

Channels are created automatically when you open a new image. The color mode you are using determines the number of color channels created. By default, bitmap, grayscale, duotone, and indexed-color images have one channel; RGB and LAB images have three, plus a composite; and CMYK images have four, plus a composite. You can add specialized channels to all image types except bitmap images.

In addition to the default color channels, extra channels — called alpha channels — are used for storing and editing selections as masks; spot color channels

BTW

Primary Colors
A primary color is one that cannot be created by mixing other colors in the gamut of a given color space. Traditionally, the colors red, yellow, and blue are considered primary colors. Those colors, however, are not the same hues as the red, yellow, and blue used on most computer monitors. Many modern computer applications and hardware devices use the primary additive colors of red, green, and blue, and the primary subtractive colors of magenta, yellow, and cyan.

can be added to incorporate spot color plates for printing. A **spot color plate** is an extra part of the separation printing process that applies a single color to areas of the artwork. Alpha channels are described in detail later in this chapter.

Plan your versions.

Once you create a master image, plan for possible uses and versions. If you are creating a photo for a client or business, consider all the ways the image could be repurposed. **Repurposing** is using all or part of a photo for something other than its original purpose. Ask yourself these questions and create versions based on your needs:

- Might the image need to be used with and without its background?

- Will the image be used in more than one medium, such as Web, newspaper, posters, flyers, and so on?

- Might you need both a color and black-and-white version?

- Would special tints, such as sepia or duotones, extend the possibilities for the image?

- Could you use all or part of the photo in another composite image?

- Can you save money by performing some prepress activities yourself?

- How will you organize your versions for maximum shelf life?

**Plan
Ahead**

The Channels Panel

The Channels panel (Figure 7–2) is used to create and manage channels. The panel lists all channels in the image — the composite channel first, then each individual color channel, followed by any spot color channels, and finally any alpha channels. As in the Layers panel, the Channels panel displays a visibility icon and a thumbnail of each channel's contents. The visibility icon is useful for viewing specific colors in the document window or to see how edits might affect a specific color.

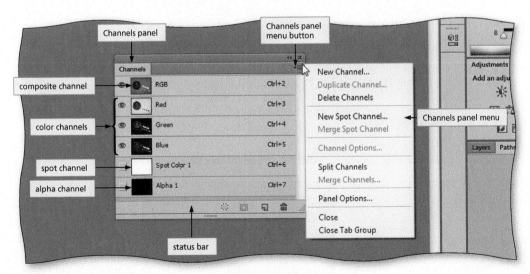

Figure 7–2

When you select one specific channel, it is displayed in grayscale in the document window by default. If more than one channel is selected, the document window displays the color combinations.

The Channels panel menu displays commands to create new channels, change the color overlay, or set other channel options.

RGB Channels

When you view a single RGB channel, pixels with a high concentration of the color indicated by the channel appear light, while pixels with a low concentration appear dark. For example, when viewing the red channel, areas of the original image that are red appear almost white, and areas that do not contain red appear almost black.

Recall that the RGB color mode is an additive color mode. When the maximum amounts of red, green, and blue are combined, white is produced, which means that white areas of an image contain a high concentration of red, green, and blue. When minimal amounts of red, green, and blue are combined, black is produced. Therefore, black areas of an image contain very little red, green, or blue. For this reason, white areas of the original image will appear as white no matter which channel is viewed because those white pixels are produced by combining large amounts of red, green, and blue. Black areas of the original image will appear as black no matter which channel is viewed because those black pixels are produced by removing red, green, and blue and therefore have very little of any of the colors represented by the channels.

For example, when viewing in the green channel a picture of a white golf ball and a black hole on green grass, both the green grass and white ball appear as white because they have a high concentration of green. The black hole will appear as black because it has a low concentration of green. However, the same image when viewed in the red channel will look completely different. In the red and blue channels, only the white ball will be displayed as white. The green grass and black hole, which both lack red and blue, will appear as dark gray (Figure 7–3).

all channels are visible

Source: LotusHead, www.pixelpusher.co.za

grass appears dark in the red channel because it has very little red color information

grass appears light in the green channel because it has a lot of green color information

Figure 7–3

To View Channels

The following steps open the Channels panel and allow you to view individual channels. As you view each channel, the channel color will appear almost white; other colors will appear in shades of gray.

1

• Click the Channels panel tab to access the Channels panel (Figure 7–4).

Experiment

• One at a time, click each of the channels. Be sure to click the channel thumbnail or name — do not click the visibility icons. As you view each channel, look for strong contrast between the lightest and darkest colors in the image, which will make it easier to isolate parts of the image.

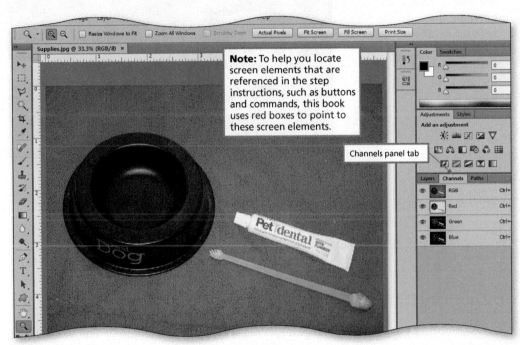

Figure 7–4

2

• Click the Red channel, not the visibility icon, to display the channel (Figure 7–5).

Q&A

Why can I not see all of the words on the toothpaste tube?

The red word, dental, on the toothpaste tube appears almost white while the green toothbrush and black bowl, which have virtually no red, appear almost black. Remember that in the RGB color mode, white is created by adding the maximum amounts of red, green, and blue. Therefore, the white toothpaste tube contains a high red content, which is why it appears nearly white in the channel.

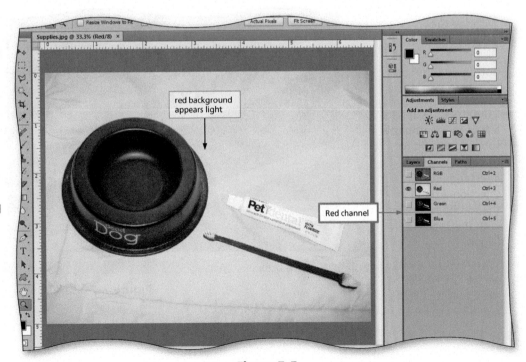

Figure 7–5

• Click the Green channel to view the channel displaying the most contrast between the toothbrush and toothpaste and the background (Figure 7–6).

red background appears dark

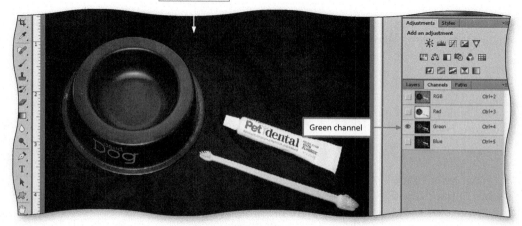

Green channel

Figure 7–6

Other Ways

1. To display composite, press CTRL+2

2. To display first channel, press CTRL+3

3. To display second channel, press CTRL+4

4. To display third channel, press CTRL+5

To Zoom by Dragging

Sometimes you need to enlarge a specific area of the document as you work. Dragging with the Zoom Tool allows you to target a specific area of your document for zooming. The following steps zoom in on the toothpaste tube.

• With the Green channel still selected, click the Zoom Tool button on the Tools panel to select it.

• Drag from the upper-left of the toothpaste tube, down and to the right to create a rectangular selection around the toothpaste tube with the Zoom Tool (Figure 7–7).

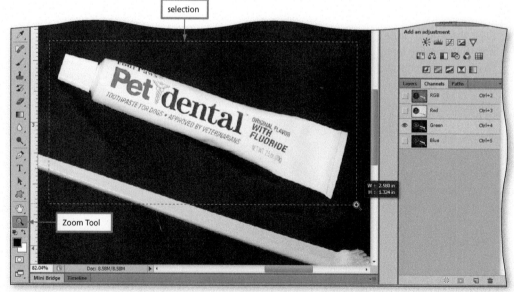

selection

Zoom Tool

W: 2.580 in
H: 1.324 in

Figure 7–7

Q&A My screen zoomed to where I clicked with the Zoom Tool, not to the area around that I dragged. What happened?

Your version of Photoshop might be configured to use the Scrubby Zoom option, available only on computers with a high-end video card. Double-click the Hand Tool to fit the canvas to your screen, click the Zoom Tool, uncheck the Scrubby Zoom option in the options bar, and drag again with the Zoom Tool to zoom without Scrubby Zoom.

• Release the mouse button to apply the zoom.

To Select using a Channel

The first goal in editing the Supplies image is to isolate the toothpaste tube and remove its background to create a floating image that can be repurposed. Recall that removing the background in an image involves isolating it in a selection area and then deleting or masking it. When you have a solid background, it is easy to select and delete. But often, the background is busy or shaded, requiring more creative steps to remove it. Variegated colors, such as shades of green in grassy areas or blue in sky areas, may be hard to delete because they appear behind, between, and around other objects. In a channel, those kinds of backgrounds appear as a single color; thus, they are isolated and selected easily.

The following step uses the Magnetic Lasso Tool to select as much of the toothpaste tube as possible in the Green channel.

1

- Right-click the Lasso Tool button on the Tools panel to display a context menu, and then click Magnetic Lasso Tool.

- Click the edge of the toothpaste tube and then drag around it, staying close to the edges, to create a selection.

- Click the starting point as you finish to close the selection (Figure 7–8).

Q&A

Could I have used the Magic Wand Tool to select the toothpaste tube?

Yes, you could have, but it would have been tedious to get the tolerance setting correct.

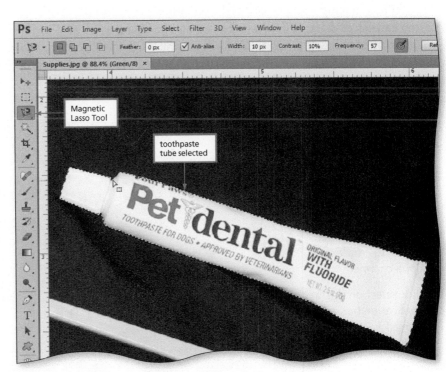

Figure 7–8

Alpha Channels

When you create a new channel, by default it becomes an alpha channel. An **alpha channel,** or **alpha channel mask,** is a special channel that saves and loads selection marquees. It is similar to a new layer or layer mask in that it is used to edit or mask parts of an image. Alpha channel masking can be performed on the background layer, whereas masks created using the Layers panel cannot. Alpha channels represent selections and exist independently of any particular layer — for that reason, storing selections as alpha channels creates more permanent masks than saving as layer masks. You can reuse the stored selections or even load them into another image. The Channel Options command on the Channels panel menu allows you to name the alpha channel and adjust settings related to editing.

Most commonly, alpha channels are used to isolate and protect areas of an image as you apply color changes, filters, or other effects to the rest of the image. Additionally, alpha channels are used for complex image editing, such as gradually applying color or filter effects to an image. For instance, viewing an alpha channel and the composite channel together allows you to see how changes made in the alpha channel relate to the entire image. When you display an alpha channel at the same time as a color channel, the alpha channel appears as a transparent color overlay in the document window.

To Create an Alpha Channel from a Selection

When making an alpha channel, you either can create the channel first and then paint the selected area, or you can select the area first and then create the channel. The following step creates an alpha channel when a selection already has been made. You will use the 'Save selection as channel' button on the Channels panel status bar to create an alpha channel with colored overlay and adjustable opacity. You can edit the channel using any painting tool, or modify it with a filter.

- With the Green channel still selected in the Channels panel and the selection around the toothpaste tube still active, click the 'Save selection as channel' button to create an alpha channel.

- Click Select on the Application bar, and then click Deselect to deselect your selection.

- Click the 'Indicates channel visibility' button to the left of the Alpha 1 channel to display its color overlay (Figure 7–9).

 **Experiment**

- Double-click the Alpha 1 channel thumbnail and view the name, color, and opacity settings. Click the OK button to close the dialog box.

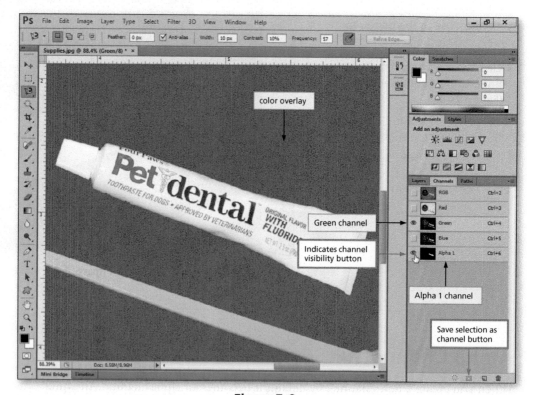

Figure 7–9

Other Ways
1. On Channels panel status bar, ALT+click 'Create new channel' button
2. On Channel panel menu, click New Channel, edit settings

To Edit an Alpha Channel

It is likely that after creating an initial selection and creating an alpha channel, you will need to edit the channel to modify the selection. It often is easiest to do this using the Brush Tool and painting with black or white, which are the colors used with masks. Painting with white adds to the selection while painting with black subtracts from the selection. You can use any selection tool to make new selections on a channel and then fill them with black or white. The following steps edit the toothpaste tube selection to create what will become a good starting point for a mask. As you paint with black, the area you paint will turn red to match the red overlay.

1

- Click the Alpha 1 channel to select it, if necessary. Be sure only the Green and Alpha 1 channels are visible.

- Click the Brush Tool button to make it the active tool.

- Click the Brush Preset picker button on the options bar to display the Brush Preset picker, double-click the value in the Size box, and then type 5 to set the brush size to 5 px.

- Double-click the value in the Hardness box, and type 100 to set the hardness to 100% (Figure 7–10).

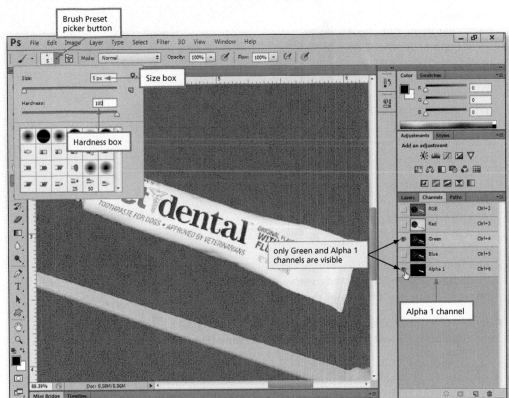

Figure 7–10

Why am I setting the Hardness to 100%?

The high Hardness setting lets you paint with crisp edges rather than with feathered edges that create a fade.

2

- Click the Brush Preset picker button again to close it.

- Drag the mouse pointer over any gray areas in the document window close to the toothpaste tube to paint over them, but do not paint over the toothpaste tube itself. Adjust the brush size as you paint to get in to the smaller spaces and corners around the cap of the toothpaste tube.

- If necessary, switch the foreground color to white and paint in any parts of the toothpaste tube that have been accidentally covered by the red overlay, such as the letters in the upper-left area of the tube.

- Double-click the channel name Alpha 1, type `Toothpaste` to rename the channel, and then press the ENTER key to save the new name (Figure 7–11).

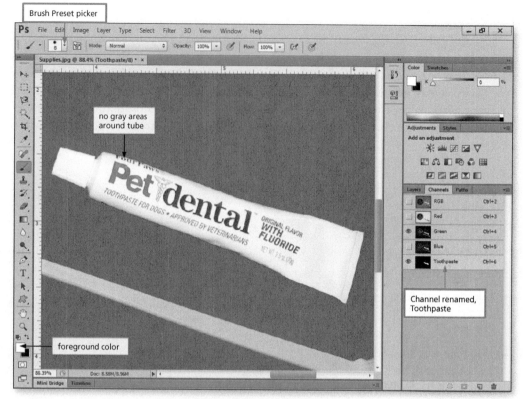

Figure 7–11

To Save a Photo

Now that you have edited channels and saved selections, it is a good practice to save the file on your personal storage device. Selections and additional alpha channels cannot be saved using the JPG format. The following steps save the photo with the name Supplies Selections in the Photoshop format in a new folder named Chapter 07.

1 With your USB flash drive connected to one of the computer's USB ports, click File on the Application bar to display the File menu and then click Save As to display the Save As dialog box.

2 In the File name text box, type `Supplies Selections` to rename the file. Do not press the ENTER key after typing the file name.

3 In the Format box beneath the file name, ensure the format is set to Photoshop (*.PSD, *.PDD).

4 Click the Save in box arrow and then click Removable Disk (F:), or the location associated with your USB flash drive, in the list, if necessary.

5 On the Save As dialog box toolbar, click the New Folder button to create a new folder on the selected storage device.

6 When the new folder appears, type Chapter 07 to change the name of the folder, and then press the ENTER key. Double-click the new folder to open it.

7 Click the Save button in the Save As dialog box to save the file in the new folder.

To Create a Second Alpha Channel

Photoshop allows you to create and save multiple alpha channels. This is helpful because it lets you store multiple selections for later use. The following steps create a second alpha channel to store a mask or selection for the toothbrush.

1 Click the Zoom Tool button on the Tools panel to select it.

2 ALT+click the toothbrush twice to zoom out.

3 In the Supplies document window, scroll to view the entire toothbrush.

4 Click the 'Indicates channel visibility' button beside the Toothpaste channel to hide it.

5 Click the Green channel to select it because it offers the greatest contrast between the toothbrush and the background.

6 Use the Magnetic Lasso Tool to create a rough selection around the toothbrush.

7 Click the 'Save selection as channel' button.

8 Rename the new channel, Toothbrush.

9 Press CTRL+D to deselect.

10 If necessary, click the 'Indicates channel visibility' buttons for both the Toothbrush and Green channels so they both are visible (Figure 7–12).

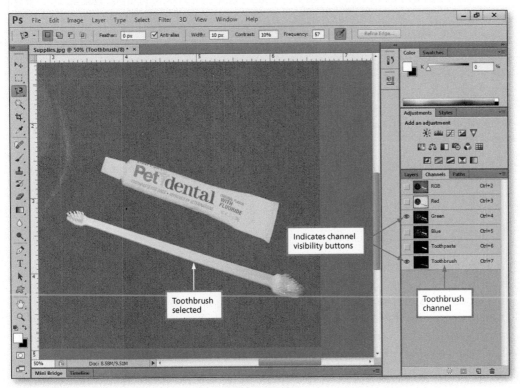

Figure 7–12

To Fine-Tune the Second Alpha Channel

The following steps fine-tune the rough selection around the toothbrush to remove the portions of the gray background that still show through.

1 With the Toothbrush channel selected, select the Brush Tool.

2 Press the D key to reset the default colors.

3 Drag to paint any gray areas surrounding the toothbrush to mask them.

4 If necessary, switch the foreground color to white and paint any parts of the toothbrush that have been covered accidentally by the red overlay. Zoom as necessary to access the areas between the bristles (Figure 7–13).

5 Press CTRL+S to save your changes.

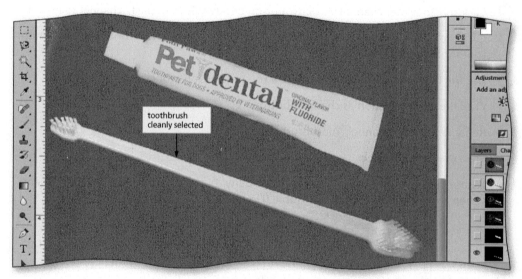

Figure 7–13

To Close a Photo

You will use the selections you have saved in the Supplies Selections file later when you copy the toothpaste tube and toothbrush to another document. For now, you are finished with the Supplies Selections file.

1 Click the Close button in the document tab to close the file but leave Photoshop open.

Brush Modes

You can use the Brush Tool in a variety of brush or blending modes. Recall that you have used the Normal brush or blending mode in previous chapters, which is the default mode. A brush's mode determines how the pixels you create with the Brush Tool interact with the layers below the current layer. You set the brush mode on the options bar for the currently selected tool. Table 7–1 lists a few common brush modes. The best way to learn the capabilities and effect of the brush modes is to experiment with them.

Table 7–1 Brush Modes

Mode	Use
Normal	The default mode. Use when you want to paint normally.
Darken	Pixels combine to form a darker color than the painted colors or the original pixels. The texture of the original pixels is retained.
Lighten	Pixels combine to form a lighter color than the painted colors or the original pixels. The texture of the original pixels is retained.
Overlay	When used on a mask, light areas can be made lighter without affecting dark areas. Dark areas can be made darker without affecting light areas.
Color	The painted pixels resemble the Paint Brush color while retaining the texture of the original pixels.

Brush Overlay Mode

Using channels to create and fine-tune selections is an ideal way to isolate challenging selections, such as masking around hair, tree branches, or other small and thin objects that would be difficult to select with other tools. You have learned how to paint on an existing alpha channel with black and white to fine-tune a selection using the brush in its default normal mode. Using a brush in overlay mode allows you to make finer selections.

When painting in overlay mode, painting with black makes dark areas darker without affecting light areas. Similarly, painting with white in overlay mode makes light areas lighter without affecting dark areas. This approach is ideal when working with the grayscale pixels in an alpha channel.

To Open the Dog File

The following steps open the file, Dog, from the Data Files for Students.

1 Open the file, Dog, from the Chapter 07 folder of the Data Files for Students.

2 When Photoshop displays the image in the document window, change the magnification to 33.33%, if necessary.

To Create an Alpha Channel from Scratch

Sometimes it is easier to create a selection by painting with the Brush Tool rather than creating a rough selection first with a selection tool. To paint a selection, you should start with a new alpha channel to avoid painting directly on an existing color channel, which would permanently change the image's color information. The steps on the next page create a new alpha channel that will contain information for the dog image.

1

• Click the Blue channel thumbnail to select the Blue channel, because it provides the most contrast between the dog and its background.

• Right-click the Blue channel and choose Duplicate Channel on the context menu to display the Duplicate Channel dialog box.

• In the As text box, type Dog as the channel name (Figure 7–14).

Q&A Why do I need to choose the channel with the strongest contrast?

The strong contrast helps in selecting objects. For example, selecting a gray dog on a gray background would be difficult, but selecting a white dog on a black background would be easy.

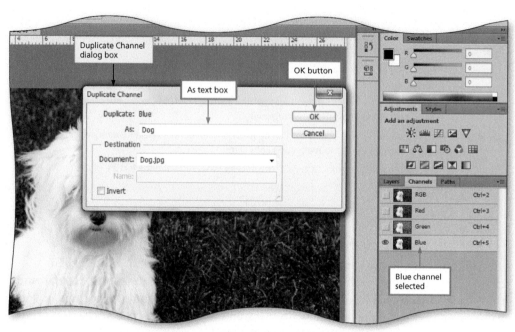

Figure 7–14

2

• Click the OK button to close the Duplicate Channel dialog box.

• Display the Dog channel and click the Indicates channel visibility button for the Blue channel to hide the channel (Figure 7–15).

Figure 7–15

Source: stock.xchng

To Make a Selection in Brush Overlay Mode

The following steps use the Brush Tool's overlay mode to isolate the dog, mask out the background, and retain the fine wisps of hair.

1

- Select the Zoom Tool and then drag from upper-left to lower-right of the dog to zoom in on it.

- Click the Brush Tool button.

- On the options bar, click the Mode button and then select Overlay.

- Click the Brush Preset picker button to open the Brush Preset picker.

- Double-click the value in the Size box and type   7 0 to set the brush size to 70 px, then double-click the value in the Hardness box and type   0, if necessary, to create a brush tip with a feathered edge (Figure 7–16).

Why do I need to set the Hardness to 0?

Using a soft-edged brush helps to retain the details of the wisps of hair.

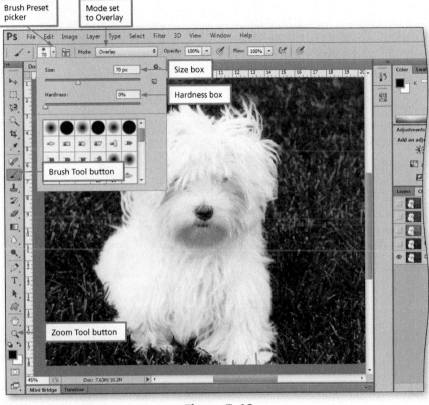

Figure 7–16

2

- Click the Brush Preset picker button again to close the Brush Preset picker.

- If necessary, press the D key to reset the foreground/background colors, then press the X key so white is the foreground color.

- Point to the lower-left edge of the dog, then drag to begin to paint the body white. As you paint, drag slightly outside the body so the brush paints a little on the grass background. Continue until the lower-left area of the body is completely white (Figure 7–17).

Why is the grass not turning white like the body?

In overlay mode, light areas (like the ear) turn white when painted with white, but darker areas (like the grass) remain relatively unaffected.

Figure 7–17

• Continue painting with white on the dog, leaving the wisps of hair for later. Be very careful not to paint too far outside the edges of the dog. Do not worry about making the entire inside of the dog white as there are some dark areas inside the dog that will require a different technique.

• Press the X key to reverse the colors, and set the foreground color to black.

• Drag the mouse pointer over the grassy background around the dog to paint a wide black area. Because you are in overlay mode, painting on the white parts will not affect them (Figure 7–18).

Figure 7–18

• Press the X key to reverse the colors and set the foreground color to white.

• Drag the the wispy edges of the hair. Drag only once over the wisps, without dragging back and forth, to lightly paint them with white. It is OK if some of the edges remain gray instead of pure black or white (Figure 7–19).

BTW

Inverting Channels
If you need to swap the colors of a channel, you can press CTRL+I to invert the colors of the channel.

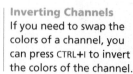

Figure 7–19

To Fine-Tune the Selection

Because you are creating a channel that can be used as a mask, the areas you want to hide must be completely black and the areas you want to keep visible must be completely white. Brush overlay mode helps you define the edges of a difficult selection. For larger selections, such as the dog's face and the rest of the grassy background, you can use selection tools and the Fill command to complete the rest of the channel. The next steps fill the rest of the channel, creating a black and white channel that can be used as a mask.

1

- Select the Lasso Tool and draw a selection around the inside of the dog's face. Be sure to stay within the solid white areas you defined in the previous steps (Figure 7–20).

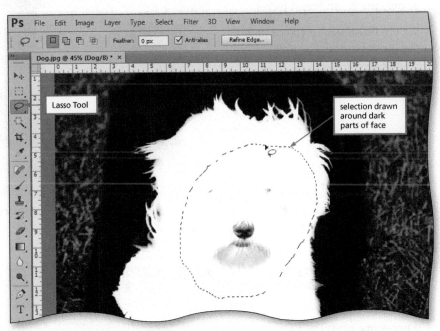

Figure 7–20

2

- Click Edit on the Application bar, and then click Fill to display the Fill dialog box.

- Click the Use box arrow to display the Use list. Click White to select the fill color, and then click the OK button to fill the selection with white.

- Press CTRL+D to deselect the selection.

- Double-click the Hand Tool button on the Tools panel to zoom out and view the entire image (Figure 7–21).

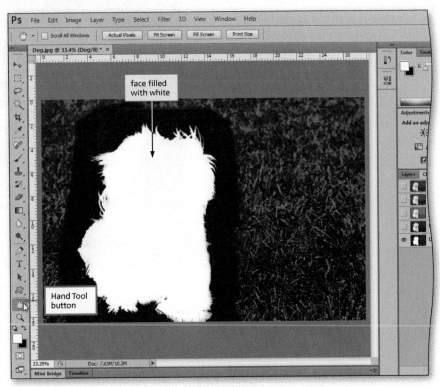

Figure 7–21

● Select the Brush Tool.

● On the Options bar, click the Mode button and set the mode to Normal.

● Click the Brush Preset picker button on the Options bar to display the Brush Preset picker.

● Set the brush size to 400 px and the brush hardness to 100% (Figure 7–22).

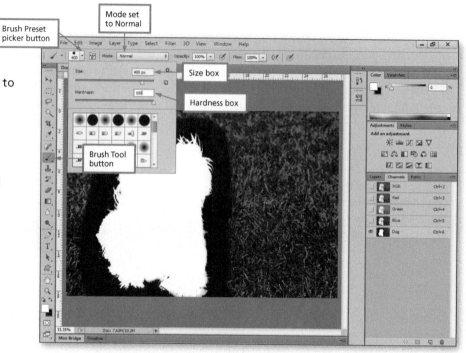

Figure 7–22

● Click the Brush Preset picker button to close the Brush Preset picker.

● If necessary, press the X key to change the foreground color to black.

● Paint the rest of the background black, avoiding the white dog. Increase the brush size as necessary (Figure 7–23).

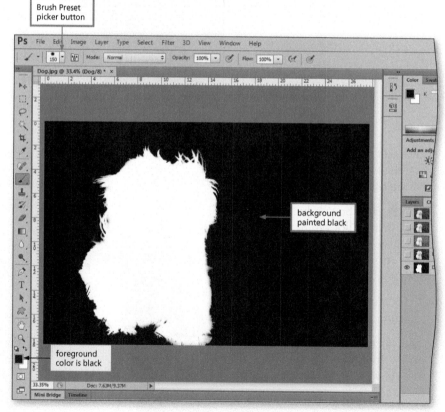

Figure 7–23

To Save the File with Channels

The following steps save the file with the name Pet Adoption Complete in the Photoshop format in the Chapter 07 folder. Because you have created a new channel and made a selection around the dog in preparation to mask out the background, the Dog.jpg file must be saved as a Photoshop PSD file.

1 With your USB flash drive connected to one of the computer's USB ports, click File on the Application bar to display the File menu, and then click Save As to display the Save As dialog box.

2 In the File name text box, type `Pet Adoption Complete` to rename the file. Do not press the ENTER key after typing the file name.

3 Click the Format box arrow and then click Photoshop (*.PSD, *.PDD) in the list, if necessary.

4 Click the Save in box arrow and then click Removable Disk (F:), or the location associated with your USB flash drive, in the list, if necessary.

5 Double-click the Chapter 07 folder to open it.

6 Click the Save button in the Save As dialog box to save the file in the Chapter 07 folder.

To Create a Composite

Recall that a composite image is a Photoshop document that contains layers or images from other documents. The following steps copy a sky background from a second image to the Dog document and position the background so the dog's body extends off the left edge of the document.

1 Click the RGB channel on the Channels panel to show the Red, Green, and Blue channels and hide the Dog channel.

2 Click the Layers tab to display the Layers panel.

3 Double-click the Background layer name and rename it, Dog.

4 Open the Sky Background file from the Chapter 07 folder of the Data Files for Students, or a location specified by your instructor.

5 Arrange the document windows side by side.

6 Using the Move Tool, drag the sky image from the Sky Background window to the Pet Adoption Complete document.

7 Close the Sky Background document window.

8 Use the Move Tool to position the sky so it fills the document window.

9 Rename the sky layer, Sky.

To Reorder Layers

The following step moves the Sky layer behind the Dog layer.

1 In the Layers panel, drag the Sky layer below the Dog layer so that the dog is visible.

To Create a Layer Mask from an Alpha Channel

The following steps create a layer mask from a channel. The mask is used to hide the grass background so only the dog shows on the Dog layer and the sky is visible behind.

1

- Click Select on the Application bar, and then click Load Selection to display the Load Selection dialog box.

- Click the Channel box arrow to display the list, select Dog to select the Dog channel you created previously (Figure 7–24).

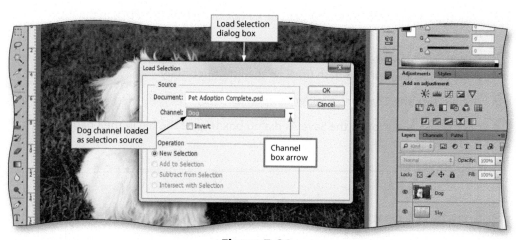

Figure 7–24

2

- Click the OK button to load the selection.

- Click the Dog layer on the Layers panel to make it the active layer.

- Click the Add layer mask button to create a mask from the selection (Figure 7–25).

 Q&A

What does the Load Selection dialog box do?

Loading a selection is the same process as making a selection. Loading the channel as a selection selects the channel, displaying the dashed border visible around the dog just as if you made a selection with a lasso tool.

Figure 7–25

Refine Mask

It is unlikely that a mask selection in a difficult image, like an object with hair or fur, will be perfect the first time. You can use Photoshop's Refine Mask tool to adjust the edges of the mask to achieve better results (Figure 7–26). The Refine Mask tool is available from the Select menu, but only when a mask thumbnail on the Layers panel is selected. Table 7–2 describes the options in the Refine Mask tool and their uses.

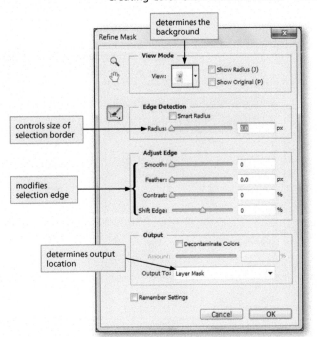

Figure 7–26

Table 7–2 Refine Mask Options	
Option	**Use**
View	Determines the background. For example, the masked layer can be shown on a white background, a black background, the underlying layers, or other choices. Set View to On Layers to see how your masked layer interacts with the rest of the layers in the document.
Radius	Controls the size of the selection border where the edge refinement occurs.
Smooth	Smoothes the selection border, eliminating hills and valleys.
Feather	Blurs the transition between the selection and its surrounding pixels.
Contrast	Increase to make soft-edged transitions more abrupt.
Shift Edge	Removes unwanted background colors from soft selection edges. Negative values move the selection edges inward while positive values move the selection edges outward.
Decontaminate Colors	Replaces the color of the outermost pixels within a selection with fully selected pixels nearby. This helps reduce unwanted outlines around a selection.
Output	Determines whether the refined selection becomes a new mask on the current layer or a new layer with the mask applied.

To Use the Refine Mask Tool

The steps on the next page use the Refine Mask tool to remove the dark outline around the masked dog, decontaminating the mask colors. You will export the refinement to a new layer that has the refined mask applied so that the original mask remains unaltered in case you need to start over.

1

- Click the mask thumbnail on the Dog layer to select it.

- Click Select on the Application bar, and then click Refine Mask to display the Refine Mask dialog box (Figure 7–27).

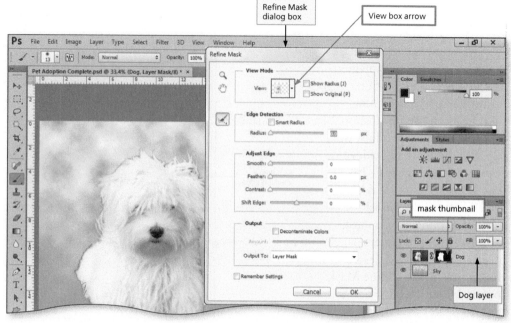

Figure 7–27

2

- Click the View box arrow and then click On Layers to select it. Click the View box arrow again to close it.

- Drag the Shift Edge slider to the left until the value is at approximately -50. If gaps or holes appear in the dog's body, drag the Shift Edge slider to the right to increase the value.

- Select the Decontaminate Colors check box to enable that option.

- Drag the Amount slider to the right until the value reaches 100, so that the maximum amount of colors are decontaminated.

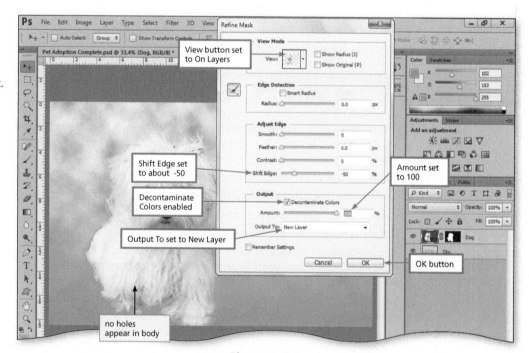

Figure 7–28

- Click the Output To box arrow and then click New Layer so that Photoshop creates a new layer with the refined mask applied (Figure 7–28).

Q&A Why would there be holes in the dog body?

Holes or gaps are caused by changing the black and white pixels in a mask. When white pixels turn black, they create a transparency which results in portions of an image turning invisible. These area look like holes.

Experiment

- Drag the Shift Edge slider all the way to the left, and notice areas of the dog turn invisible, looking like holes in the dog. Try different values for the Shift Edge to see how the mask is affected. When you are finished, return the Sift Edge value to about -50.

3

• Click the OK button to apply the refinement.

• Rename the new layer, Dog Refined.

Q&A   Should I delete the original Dog layer because it has been hidden and is no longer being used?

No. It is best to leave the original Dog layer in the document because you have spent a lot of time creating the initial mask. This layer now acts as a backup in case you need start over and refine the mask again.

Other Ways
1. ALT+CTRL+R

To Move the Dog into Position

The following steps move the dog into position.

1 Click the Move Tool to select it.

2 If necessary, click the Dog Refined layer on the Layers panel to select it.

3 Drag the dog in the document window down and to the left.

4 Press CTRL+S to save the changes.

BTW

Photoshop Help
The best way to become familiar with Photoshop Help is to use it. Appendix D includes detailed information about Photoshop Help and exercises that will help you gain confidence in using it.

Loading Channels

Once you create an alpha channel, you can select it and use it to delete pixels, apply special effects, protect areas of a layer, or act as a mask. Loading a channel as a selection and then creating a layer mask from the selection allows you to edit and fine-tune the layer mask without affecting the original channel. This means you can experiment with the layer mask, and if you are not happy with the results, you simply can delete and load a fresh selection from the original channel.

To Open and Arrange the Supplies Selections File

The following steps open the Supplies Selections file from your USB drive and arrange the Pet Adoption Complete and Supplies Selections documents side by side so that layers can be easily copied between them.

1 Open the Supplies Selections file from the Chapter 07 folder on your USB drive.

2 Arrange the document windows side by side.

3 Drag the scrollbar at the bottom of the Supplies Selections window to the right until you can see both the toothbrush and toothpaste.

To Duplicate a Layer

The following steps duplicate the Background layer of the Supplies Selections document twice, so that the toothbrush and toothpaste can reside on their own layers.

1 Right-click the Background layer on the Layers panel of the Supplies Selections document.

2 Click Duplicate Layer in the context menu.

3 In the As box, type `Toothpaste` and then click the OK button.

4 Repeat Steps 1 and 2, and in the As box, type `Toothbrush` and then click the OK button (Figure 7–29).

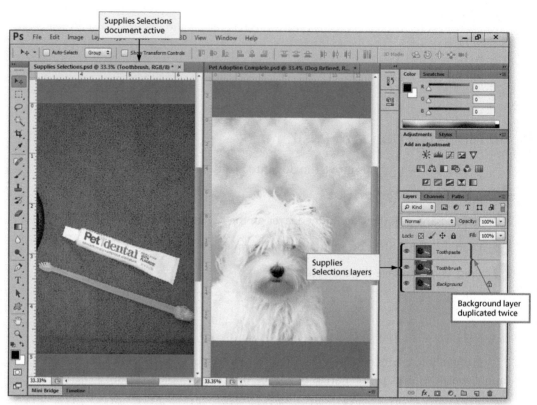

Figure 7–29

To Add a Layer Mask from an Alpha Channel

The following steps add a layer mask based on a transparency from a channel. The mask is used to hide the background so only the toothpaste shows.

- With the Supplies Selections document as the active document, click the Toothpaste layer on the Layers panel to select it.

- Click Select on the Application bar, and then click Load Selection to display the Load Selection dialog box (Figure 7–30).

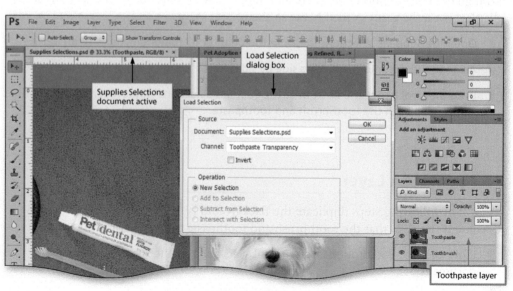

Figure 7–30

- From the Channel menu, select Toothpaste (Figure 7–31).

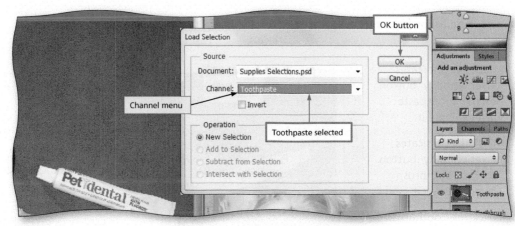

Figure 7–31

- Click the OK button to load the alpha channel as a selection.

- Click the 'Add layer mask' button on the Layers panel status bar to turn the selection into a mask (Figure 7–32).

Figure 7–32

- Click the 'Indicates layer visibility' button on the Toothbrush layer to hide it.

- Click the 'Indicates layer visibility' button on the Background layer to hide it (Figure 7–33).

Figure 7–33

To Mask using an Existing Alpha Channel

The following steps mask the toothbrush, using the existing alpha channel.

1

- Click the 'Indicates layer visibility' button on the Toothpaste layer to hide it.

- Click the 'Indicates layer visibility' button on the Toothbrush layer to show it.

- Click the Toothbrush layer to select it (Figure 7–34).

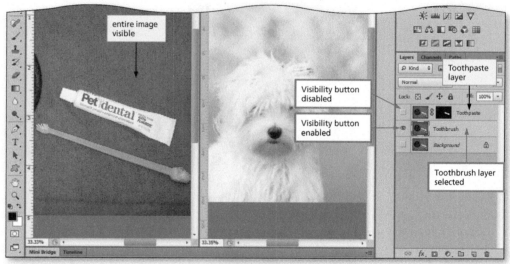

Figure 7–34

 2

- Click Select on the Application bar, and then click Load Selection to display the Load Selection dialog box.

- From the Channel menu, select Toothbrush (Figure 7–35).

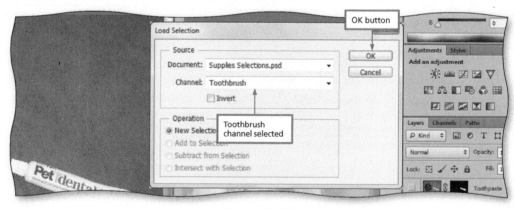

Figure 7–35

 4

- Click the OK button to load the alpha channel as a selection.

- Click the 'Add layer mask' button on the Layers panel status bar to turn the selection into a mask.

- Press CTRL+S to save the changes (Figure 7–36).

Figure 7–36

To Copy the Toothbrush and Toothpaste to the Final Document

The following steps copy the toothbrush and toothpaste to the Pet Adoption Complete document.

1 Drag the Toothbrush layer from the Layers panel onto the Pet Adoption Complete window to copy the toothbrush to it. Be sure to drag from the layer's name, Toothbrush.

2 Click the Supplies Selections window to make it active and display its layers in the Layers panel.

3 Drag the Toothpaste layer from the Layers panel onto the Pet Adoption Complete window to copy the toothpaste to it. Be sure to drag from the layer's name, Toothpaste.

4 Click the Close button in the document tab of the Supplies Selections window to close it. Click No if prompted to save it.

5 Drag the Toothpaste into position so that your screen roughly matches Figure 7–37.

6 Click the Toothbrush layer in the Layers panel to select it, and then drag the toothbrush into position so that your screen roughly matches Figure 7–37.

Figure 7–37

To Refine a Mask

The following steps use the Refine Mask tool to remove the red edges of the toothbrush left over from the original red background.

1

- Click the mask thumbnail on the Toothbrush layer in the Layers panel to select it.

- Click Select on the Application bar, and then click Refine Mask to display the Refine Mask dialog box.

- Drag the Shift Edge slide to the left until its value shows -50.

- Click the Decontaminate Colors check box to enable that option.

- Drag the Amount slider to the right until its value shows 100.

- Set the Output To menu to New Layer (Figure 7–38).

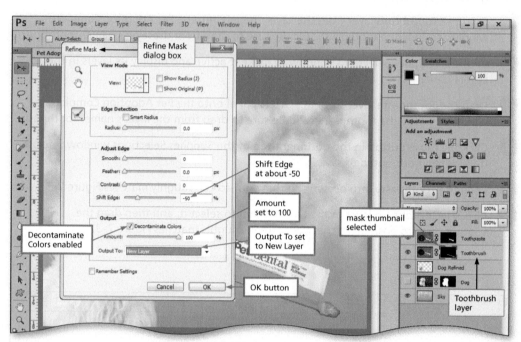

Figure 7–38

2

- Click the OK button to apply the refinement.

- Rename the new layer, Toothbrush Refined (Figure 7–39).

Q&A

The green handle of the toothbrush looks good, but the bristles still show some red.

Some masked pixels are more difficult to decontaminate than others. Not all techniques work in all situations. You will apply a different technique later to remove the red from the bristles.

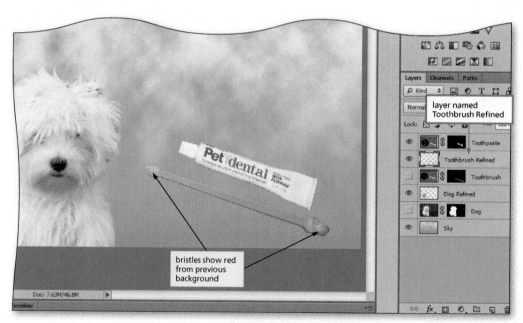

Figure 7–39

To Decontaminate Colors

The Color brush mode allows you to change the color of pixels in an image while retaining the original texture. For example, you can use a foreground color of red with a brush in Color mode to paint a green bush. The bush will appear red but maintain its texture, essentially turning the leaves red. This mode is helpful when you need to re-color part of a photograph.

The following steps remove the red in the toothbrush bristles using the Brush Tool in Color mode.

1

- Click the Brush Tool button to select it.

- Set the brush size to about 50.

- Press the D key to reset the colors to the default setting.

- Press the X key to reverse the colors so that white is the foreground color.

- Click the 'Lock transparent pixels' button at the top of the Layers panel so that the transparency of the Toothbrush Refined layer is protected.

- Click the Mode button on the options bar to display the brush modes (Figure 7–40).

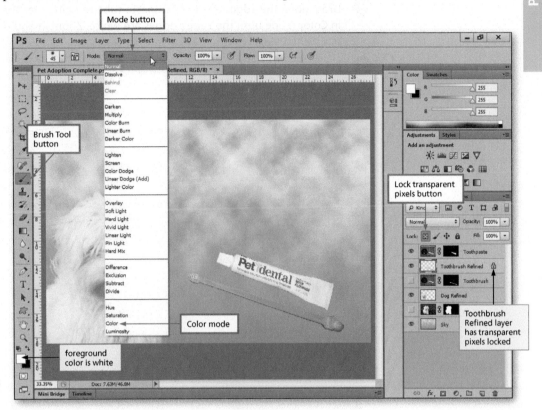

Figure 7–40

2

- Click Color at the bottom of the Mode menu to set the brush mode.

- Drag back and forth across the left bristles of the toothbrush until the red is removed and the bristles are mostly white. Be careful not to paint over the green handle.

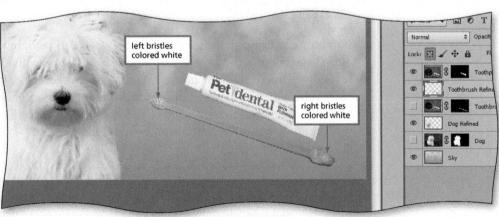

Figure 7–41

- Drag back and forth across the larger right bristles of the toothbrush until the red is removed and the bristles are mostly white. Be careful not to paint over the green handle (Figure 7–41).

Q&A The toothbrush's bristles are too small and my brush is too large.

Change the brush size as necessary, using the Brush Preset Picker or the [and] keys. Use the Zoom Tool to change the magnification of the document as needed.

To Decontaminate the Toothpaste Tube

The following steps remove the red along the sides of the toothpaste tube using the Brush Tool in Color mode.

1 Click the pixels thumbnail of the Toothpaste layer on the Layers panel to select it. Be sure to click the pixels thumbnail and not the mask thumbnail.

2 Drag along the edges of the toothpaste tube to paint over the red edges with white in Color mode until the tube's edges are white. Zoom in and out and adjust your brush size as necessary.

3 Press CTRL+S to save your changes (Figure 7–42).

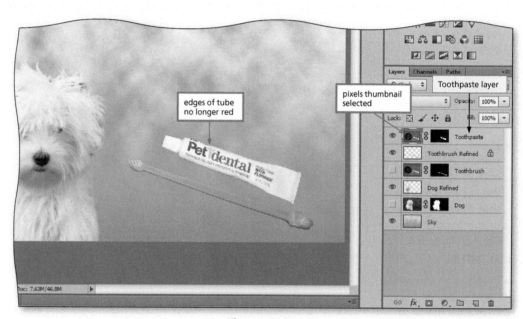

Figure 7–42

Warped Text

Not only can text provide information for people to read, but it also can provide visual appeal and add interest to a design. Photoshop has tools that let you bend and warp text nondestructively. This means the text remains editable after it has been warped.

The advertisement for the pet adoption needs the event name added at the top so that it is easy to read. It also needs additional text advertising a free giveaway in a way that provides information along with visual interest.

Plan Ahead

Choose the best tool for the job.
With so many ways to accomplish the same or similar tasks (such as making a selection), sometimes it is hard to decide which tool to use. While using the tool with which you are most familiar may save you time, the result might not be as satisfactory as you could achieve with a different tool. Look through the various tools related to your task and experiment with the settings. For example, there are five Healing Brush tools, more than 20 adjustments on the Adjustments panel, two menus with adjustment commands, countless ways to select, copy, move, and delete. Unless your image is just a quick mock-up or sketch, choose the tool that gives you the most flexibility and settings. Also, do not forget the detail edits. Adjustments and color toning are among the most important edits you can perform.

To Add Heading Text

The following steps add the event name and the date and time to the top of the advertisement.

1 Press the T key to access the Horizontal Type Tool.

2 In the options bar, set the font to Impact, type 375 in the font size box, and set the text color to white.

3 Click anywhere on the canvas and type Pet Adoption.

4 Click the Move Tool button and drag the text into position so that it roughly matches Figure 7–43.

5 Press the T key to access the Horizontal Type Tool again.

6 Click anywhere on the canvas below the existing text to position the new text.

7 In the options bar, type 100 in the font size box.

8 Type Saturday, 9am - 3pm.

9 Use the Move Tool button to drag the text into position so that it roughly matches Figure 7–43.

Figure 7–43

To Select a Text Color from the Image

The following steps sample a green color from the toothbrush to use as the text color for text you will type later.

1 Click the Sky layer on the Layers panel so you do not accidentally change the color of existing text.

2 Press the T key to access the Horizontal Type Tool.

3 On the options bar, click the 'Set the text color' button to display the Color Picker (Text Color) dialog box.

4 If necessary, drag the dialog box out of the way so you can see the green handle of the toothbrush.

5 Click the green color in the middle of the toothbrush handle to set the text color to match the toothbrush (Figure 7–44).

6 Click the OK button to close the dialog box.

Figure 7–44

To Warp Text

One way to make your text eye-catching is to use the Warp Text dialog box. Photoshop has 15 different warp styles, each with adjustable settings, to create an endless number of possibilities for warped text. The following steps create warped text for the advertisement. Your text will use the color set in the previous exercise. This color, while it matches the toothbrush and helps to tie the design together, is difficult to read against the blue background. You will add a layer style in a later exercise to make the text easier to read.

1

- On the options bar, set the font size to 90 and click the Center text button, if necessary. (Figure 7–45)

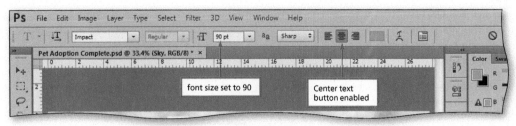

Figure 7–45

2

- Click at the bottom of the document to the right of the dog and above the toothpaste to set the starting point for the text.

- Type Free Pet Care Kit, press the ENTER key, and type with each adoption!.

- Click the Move Tool on the Tools panel and drag the new text to the space above the toothpaste tube.

- Press the T key to access the Horizontal Type Tool.

- On the options bar, click the 'Create warped text' button to display the Warp Text dialog box.

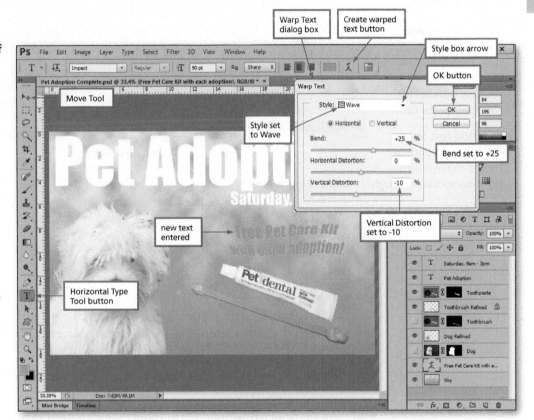

Figure 7–46

- Drag the dialog box title bar to move the dialog box to the side if necessary, so the text is fully visible.

- Click the Style box arrow (Warp Text dialog box) to display its list, and then click Wave to select that style.

- Drag the Bend slider to +25 to warp the text.

- Drag the Vertical Distortion slider to -10 to further warp the text (Figure 7–46).

 **Experiment**

- Drag the Bend, Horizontal Distortion, and Vertical Distortion sliders to both the right and left, watching how they affect the text box. When finished, return Bend to +25, Horizontal Distortion to 0 and Vertical Distortion to –10.

3

- Click the OK button in the Warp Text dialog box to commit the changes.

- Press CTRL+T to freely transform the text.

- Point to the outside of the bounding box until your mouse pointer displays a curved arrow, and then drag up or down to rotate the text box so that it is roughly parallel with the toothpaste tube.

- Drag the text from inside the bounding box to move it into position so that it roughly matches Figure 7–47.

- Press the ENTER key to apply the transformation.

Figure 7–47

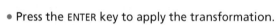

To Enhance the Text

The following steps rearrange the layers so that the type layers are grouped together. You then add a drop shadow to each type layer to make the text stand out from the background and increase readability.

1 On the Layers panel, drag the Free Pet Care Kit layer up so that it is below the Pet Adoption type layer.

2 Click the 'Add a layer style' button, and then click Drop Shadow at the bottom of the menu.

3 Click the OK button to apply the default drop shadow.

4 Click the Pet Adoption layer on the Layers panel, and repeat Steps 2 and 3 to apply a drop shadow.

5 Apply a drop shadow to the Saturday, 9am – 3pm type layer so that all three type layers display the same drop shadow effect.

6 Press CTRL+S to save your changes (Figure 7–48).

Figure 7–48

To Merge and Save

The following steps merge the visible layers and then save the document with a new file name. Photoshop uses the name of the layer that was selected when the merge command was executed. Because the Saturday, 9am – 3pm type layer was selected when the merge command was executed, the new merged layer is named Saturday, 9am – 3pm.

1 Press SHIFT+CTRL+E to merge the visible layers into a single layer.

2 Click File on the Application bar, and then click Save As to display the Save As dialog box.

3 Type `Pet Adoption Merged` in the File name box and ensure the Format is set to Photoshop (*.PSD, *.PDD).

4 If necessary, browse to your storage location. Click the Save button to save the merged file.

5 If Photoshop displays a Photoshop Format Options dialog box, click the OK button.

Break Point: If you wish to take a break, this is a good place to do so. You can quit Photoshop now. To resume at a later time, start Photoshop, open the file called Pet Adoption Merged, and continue following the steps from this location forward.

Actions

An **action** is an automation task that stores a series of commands and keystrokes for repeated use later. For example, because of the large number of pixels generated by digital cameras, Photoshop typically imports those photos with very large document dimensions. If you often use a digital camera to generate the images you use in Photoshop, you could save the resize process as an action. Then, each time you edit a photo from your camera, you could use a single command to play the action and perform the steps again. You can create your own actions, download sample actions from the Web, or use predefined actions that come with Photoshop.

The process of creating an action involves recording the steps as they occur and then saving the recorded steps as a file in a location on your system. The next time you need the action, you can load it and play it — effectively performing the steps automatically. Action recording and playback steps are not recorded as states on the History panel. Actions are comparable to macros or functions in other software applications. Photoshop records nearly all commands and tools used in the Photoshop window; it will not record steps performed in other windows.

Actions might include **stops** or pauses that occur during playback. Stops typically require user input, such as choosing a brush size. Actions also might include **modal** controls that stop to let you enter values in a dialog box while playing an action. If there are modal controls in an action, you can choose not to display the various dialog boxes and instead automatically accept the values that were used when the action was created. When you toggle modal controls off, the playback runs through the steps seamlessly, without any visible dialog boxes.

Plan Ahead

> **Record actions for repetitive tasks.**
> If you perform the same Photoshop tasks repeatedly, record the keystrokes for quick playback using an action. When creating and saving an action, the general workflow is as follows:
>
> 1. Practice the action and write down the steps.
>
> 2. Create a new action set, or select one you have previously created.
>
> 3. Create a new action, giving it a name and keyboard shortcut.
>
> 4. Click the Record button.
>
> 5. Carefully proceed through the steps of your task.
>
> 6. Click the Stop button.
>
> 7. Turn on dialog boxes and then edit stop points as necessary.
>
> 8. Save the set as an atn file for use in other documents.
>
> If you make a mistake while recording the action, the best solution may be to stop the recording and begin again. If you decide to edit an action, you can double-click an individual step in the Actions panel and then change its settings. To omit a recorded step during playback, click the Toggle item on/off box in the left column of the Actions panel.

The Actions Panel

The Actions panel helps you manage actions you have created and those predefined actions that come with Photoshop (Figure 7–49). Each time you create a new action, it is added to the panel. An **action set** is an organizational folder that includes multiple actions, and can be opened or expanded by clicking the triangle to the left of the action set.

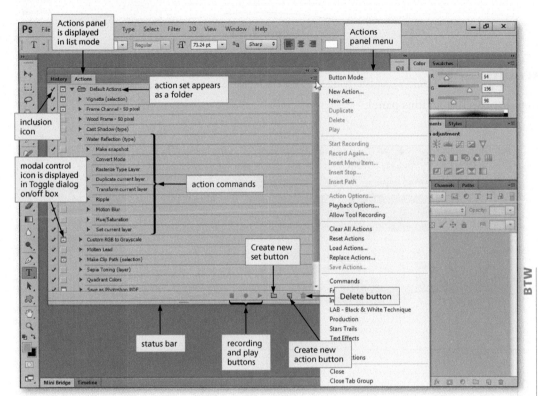

Figure 7–49

In Figure 7–49, the Default Actions set is expanded to display the predefined actions. The Water Reflection action is expanded to display the individual commands. On the left, a column of check marks indicates each command's inclusion in the action. Photoshop allows you to exclude specific commands during playback if you wish. The second column indicates whether the action is modal. To enable modal controls so that you can enter your own values in dialog boxes used in the action, click the Toggle dialog on/off box on the Actions panel. On the panel's status bar are tape recorder-style buttons for stop, record, and play, as well as buttons to create sets and actions. The Actions panel menu displays commands to manage actions, set options, and load new sets of predefined actions. Action sets can be saved independently for use in other images. A saved action displays a file extension of atn. In the Save Action dialog box, Photoshop opens the folder where it stores other atn files by default.

The Actions panel can be displayed in two modes. The list mode, shown in Figure 7–49, allows you to make more choices about selecting, editing, playing, and managing your actions. The Button Mode, shown in Figure 7–50 on the next page, is used for quick playbacks. To switch modes, choose the desired mode from the Actions panel menu.

BTW

Modal Icons
Each step in an action can have its own modality, which means that the action will stop at every dialog box. You might want the playback to stop at certain points to allow user decisions, while at other steps, you might want to mandate settings. If an action set contains steps with mixed modalities, the modal icon beside the action set is displayed in red. If all steps are modal, the modal icon will be displayed in black.

BTW

Actions with Prerequisites
If you see parentheses around the action name, the action will only work at certain times. For example, if the word, Type, is in parentheses, you must have a text box selected. If the word, Selection, is in parentheses, the action will work only if you have a current selection marquee.

Figure 7–50

To Display the Actions Panel

The following step displays the Actions panel.

- Click Window on the Application bar, and then click Actions to display the Actions panel (Figure 7–51).

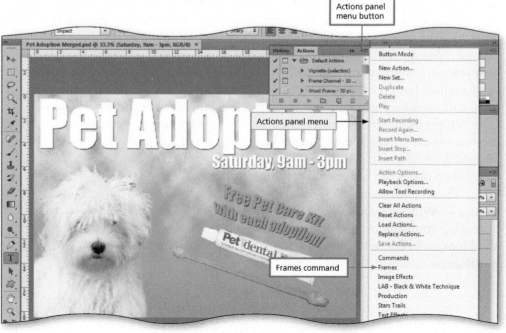

Figure 7–51

To Append Action Sets

The Actions panel menu contains a Default Actions set that provides 13 different actions. In addition to the Default Actions set, nine other sets are available on the Actions panel menu. In the following steps, you will append one of those sets to the list of default actions in the Actions panel.

- Click the Actions panel menu button to display the Actions panel menu (Figure 7–52).

What does the Load Actions command do?

It opens a dialog box so you can navigate to the location of an action set. Any actions or action sets not saved previously with the image must be loaded into the current file.

Figure 7–52

2

- Click Frames to select the action set.

- Drag the bottom-right corner of the Actions panel down to make the Actions panel taller and display more items.

- Scroll in the panel to display the Frames set, and then click the Brushed Aluminum Frame action to select it (Figure 7–53).

Figure 7–53

To Play an Action

To play an action, you click the Play selection button on the Actions panel status bar. In the steps that follow, the Brushed Aluminum Frame action is played to create a picture frame around the advertisement. Later in this chapter, you will create a custom action.

- Point to the Play selection button on the Actions panel status bar (Figure 7–54).

Figure 7–54

2

- Click the Play selection button to play the action (Figure 7–55).

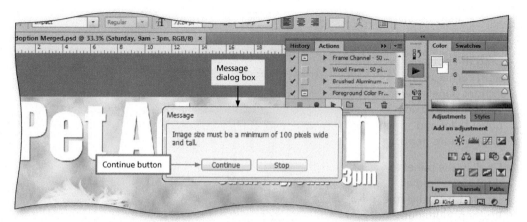

Figure 7–55

3

- Click the Continue button (Message dialog box) to apply the action (Figure 7–56).

Q&A

What are the right-pointing triangles on the Actions panel?

If you click a right-pointing triangle, Photoshop displays the steps taken in the action.

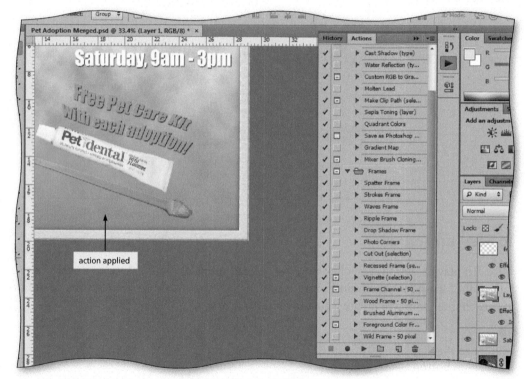

Figure 7–56

BTW

Organizing Actions
You can organize sets of actions for different types of work, such as online publishing or print publishing, and then transfer sets to other computers. Normally, user-defined action sets are stored with the file in which they are created. You can save your sets and actions to a separate actions file, however, so you can recover them if the file in which they were created in is destroyed.

To Merge and Save the Document Again

The advertisement is complete. The next steps merge layers and save the file.

1 Double-click the Hand Tool button to fit the document to your screen.

2 Press CTRL+SHIFT+E to merge the visible layers.

3 In the Layers panel, double-click the new merged layer's name, type Pet Adoption Merged to rename the layer, and then press the ENTER key to apply the name change.

4 Press CTRL+S to save the file again. If Photoshop displays a dialog box, click the OK button.

To Create a New Action Set

The following steps create a new action set named Pet Adoption Actions in the Pet Adoption Merged file. Saving your actions in a new action set keeps them separate from the built-in actions included in Photoshop.

- On the Actions panel status bar, click the 'Create new set' button to display the New Set dialog box.

- Type Pet Adoption Actions in the Name text box to name the action set (Figure 7–57).

Figure 7–57

- Click the OK button to create the action set and add it to the Actions panel (Figure 7–58).

Figure 7–58

Other Ways

1. On Actions panel menu, click New Set

To Create a New Action

When you click the 'Create new action' button, the New Action dialog box is displayed. The New Action dialog box allows you to name the action, position it within a set, assign a function key, and choose a display color for the action in the panel. After you edit the settings, you use the Record button to begin the process. The following step creates a new action called Poster Thumbnail and assigns an identification color. You add the functionality to the action in a later set of steps.

- On the Actions panel status bar, click the 'Create new action' button to display the New Action dialog box.

- Type Poster Thumbnail in the Name text box to name the action.

- Click the Function Key box arrow, and then click F11 in the list to assign a function key to the action.

- Click the Color box arrow and then click Red in the list to assign a color to the new action (Figure 7–59).

Figure 7–59

To Record an Action

The next steps record an action that applies the Poster Edges artistic filter and reduces the size of the document to 300 pixels wide. This is an appropriate size to include on a Web page or to use for e-mailing a client a sample of the artwork.

1

- In the New Action dialog box, click the Record button (shown in Figure 7–59) to close the dialog box and begin recording keystrokes (Figure 7–60).

Figure 7–60

2

- Press the D key to reset the default colors in preparation for the filter.

- Click Filter on the Application bar to display the Filter menu (Figure 7–61).

Figure 7–61

3

● Click Filter Gallery to display the Filter Gallery window.

● Click the Artistic category, and then click Poster Edges to record the first step of the action.

● Click the Zoom Out button at the bottom-left corner of the Poster Edges dialog box four times so that you can see most of the image.

● Slide the Edge Thickness slider so the value reads 5.

● Slide the Edge Intensity slider so the value reads 5.

● Slide the Posterization slider so the value reads 1 (Figure 7–62).

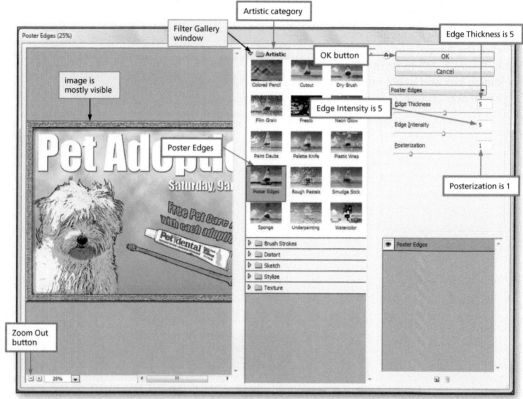

Figure 7–62

4

● Click the OK button (Poster Edges dialog box) to accept the new settings of the filter and apply the Poster Edges filter.

● Click Image on the Application bar to display the Image menu, and then click Image Size to display the Image Size dialog box.

● Confirm that the Scale Styles, Constrain Proportions, and Resample Image check boxes are all checked.

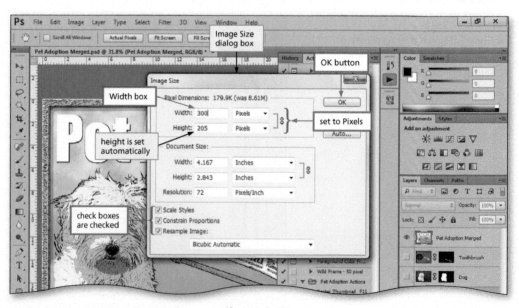

Figure 7–63

● Confirm that the Pixel Dimensions units are set to pixels.

● Type 300 in the Width box to set the new width to 300 pixels (Figure 7–63).

● Click the OK button to resize the image and close the Image Size dialog box.

Q&A Why did the image get so small? It looks much smaller than 300 pixels.

The Image was resized to 300 pixels wide, but probably looks a lot smaller on your screen because you are not viewing it at 100 percent.

5

- Double-click the Zoom Tool button to display the document at 100 percent.

Q&A What if I make a mistake while recording an action?

If you click inadvertently while creating an action, you can press CTRL+Z to cancel the recording and then start over.

- Click the 'Stop playing/recording' button to stop the recording (Figure 7–64).

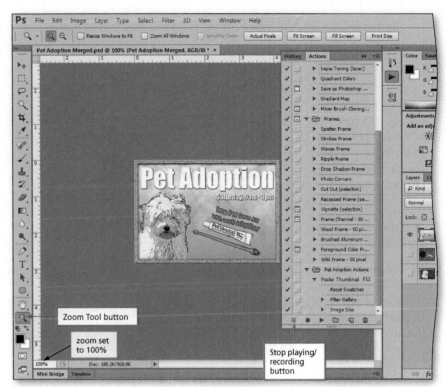

Figure 7–64

To Save the File in the JPEG Format

The following steps save a copy of the altered file in a format appropriate for sharing with a client by e-mail. You then revert the file back to its original state.

1 With your USB flash drive connected to one of the computer's USB ports, click File on the Application bar to display the File menu.

2 Click Save As to display the Save As dialog box.

3 When the Save As dialog box is displayed, click the Save in box arrow and then click Removable Disk (F:), or the location associated with your USB flash drive, in the list.

4 Double-click the Chapter 07 folder to open it.

5 Type `Pet Adoption Sample` in the File name text box.

6 Click the Format button and select JPEG (*.JPG, *.JPEG, *.JPE) from the list of options.

7 Click the Save button to save the document as a JPEG file.

8 Click the OK button to accept the default settings in the JPEG Options dialog box.

9 Press the F12 key to revert the document to its last saved state and undo all the changes made by the action.

10 Double-click the Hand Tool button to zoom out so you can see the entire document.

BTW

Creating Actions
You must be careful when you record actions that involve selecting a named layer. When you play back the action in a different file, Photoshop will look for that layer. If the named layer does not exist in the file, the action will not function correctly.

BTW

Editing Actions
Other edits that you can perform on the recorded steps include deselecting some check boxes, dragging a command to the Delete button on the status bar to remove it permanently, and setting playback options on the Actions panel menu.

To Test the Action

To test the action, the following steps open a new file and then play back the action using the function key to confirm that it works.

- Open the file called Test Action from the Chapter 07 folder of the Data Files for Students, or a location specified by your instructor.

- Press the F11 key to play the action and apply the effect.

- Double-click the Zoom Tool button to zoom to 100% to view the effect (Figure 7–65).

Figure 7–65

- Close the Test Action file.

- Click the No button to confirm closing the file without saving any changes.

To Save an Action Set

The following steps save a new action set using the Actions panel menu.

- On the Actions panel, click the Pet Adoption Actions set.

- Click the Actions panel menu button to display the menu (Figure 7–66).

Figure 7–66

2

- With your USB flash drive connected to one of the computer's USB ports, click Save Actions to display the Save dialog box.

- Click the Save in box arrow and then click Removable Disk (F:), or the location associated with your USB flash drive, in the list and then double-click the Chapter 07 folder to open it (Figure 7– 67).

 Could I save the action set in the Actions folder with the installed Photoshop actions?

Yes; however, saving on a personal storage device keeps lab installation actions unchanged for other students.

3

- Click the Save button to save the Action Set.

- Click the Collapse Panel button to collapse the Actions panel.

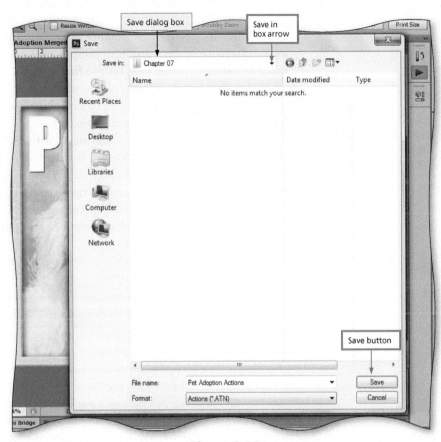

Figure 7–67

Color Toning and Conversions

Color toning is the process of changing or intensifying the color of a photograph after it has been processed by the camera. In traditional photography, toning was a darkroom technique that changed the black colors in a black-and-white photograph to a chosen color, such as sepia or blue. In digital photography, toning includes a variety of techniques, including converting to black and white, creating duotones or split tones, and adding tints.

Create print versions.
Consider where your artwork will be used. If it will be used on a Web site, mobile application, computer game, or for another purpose in electronic format, the RGB color mode is the best choice because all colors in the image are created by a combination of red, green, and blue pixels. This matches how computer screens generate color images. If your artwork will be printed, then cyan, magenta, yellow, and black inks will be used to create the color print. Images in the RGB color mode often print darker than expected or suffer significant changes in color when printed. Converting the image from RGB to CMYK allows you to see more precisely how the image will print and allows you to make adjustments in the overall color before sending the image to a printer.

Plan Ahead

Many of the color toning adjustments are located on the Adjustments panel, but some are available only through the menu system. Most of the tools work in the same way — they map or plot an existing range of pixel values to a new range of values. The main difference is the amount of control each tool provides. For example, the various color adjustment commands on the Image menu alter the pixels in the current layer.

Another way to adjust color is to use an adjustment layer created using the Layer menu. This approach allows you to experiment with color and tonal adjustments first, before committing them to the image.

Another way to access adjustments is to use the New Adjustment Layer submenu on the Layer menu. The difference is that when you access the settings using the menu system, Photoshop opens a dialog box allowing you to name and color the layer as you create it. You fine-tune the settings using the Adjustments panel either way.

Table 7–3 displays color adjustment commands that are not located on the Adjustments panel and therefore must be accessed through the menu system.

BTW

Layers and File Size
Using an adjustment layer adds to the file size of the image, however; it also demands more random access memory (RAM) from your computer.

Table 7–3 Menu-Only Adjustment Controls

Option	Use	Menu Access
Desaturate	Produces a grayscale image but leaves the image in the same color mode	Image | Adjustments
Equalize	Redistributes the brightness values of all pixels so they represent the entire range of brightness levels more evenly	Image | Adjustments
Match Color	Matches the color across selections, layers, or photos as well as adjusts luminance, color range, and color casts in an image	Image | Adjustments
Replace Color	Replaces specified colors in an image with new color values	Image | Adjustments
Shadows/Highlights	Lightens or darkens based on surrounding pixels to correct photos with strong backlighting or other lighting errors	Image | Adjustments
Variations	Adjusts the color balance, contrast, and saturation of an image using thumbnail samples	Image | Adjustments

Black and White

Recall that converting a color image to the Grayscale mode on the Image Mode submenu is one way to discard color information from the pixels in the image. If you change the color mode to LAB Color, a Lightness channel also creates a black-and-white image. The Adjustments panel contains several settings that you can use to create a black-and-white or grayscale image. Additionally, some graphic artists create two adjustments layers, one for black and one for white, to emulate the film and filter process of traditional photography.

First, you will use the Desaturate command to view the image in grayscale, then you will undo and use the Black & White settings on the Adjustments panel.

To Desaturate

The following steps use the Desaturate command on the Adjustments submenu to produce a grayscale image for use in black and white advertising or for use as on letterhead printed on a black-and-white printer.

- Click the top layer, Pet Adoption Merged, to select it in the Layers panel, if necessary.

- On the Application bar, click Image and then point to Adjustments to display the Adjustments submenu (Figure 7–68).

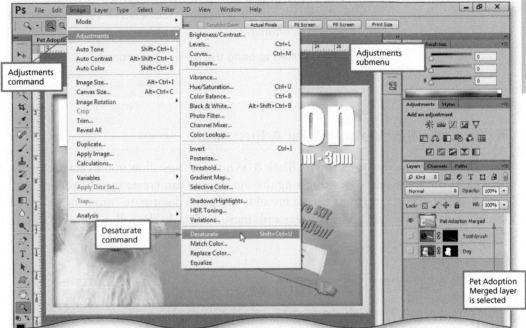

Figure 7–68

- Click Desaturate to produce a grayscale image (Figure 7–69).

Figure 7–69

Other Ways
1. Press SHIFT+CTRL+U

To Undo the Desaturate Command and Save the File

While the Desaturate command is appropriate for technical illustrations or when you want to neutralize or de-emphasize a background, it leaves the image in the same color mode, usually rendering a flat, lifeless version compared to other methods. Additionally, it sometimes reduces the contrast between foreground and background objects, making them difficult to see. Therefore, the following step undoes the Desaturate command.

 Press CTRL+Z to undo the previous command.

To Create a Black-and-White Adjustment

The Adjustments panel and its Black & White settings allow you to customize the shades of gray in the document window itself. By customizing the shades, you can create more diversity among the various shaded toys. For example, the text was almost invisible when the desaturate command was used. By adjusting a channel, the black-and-white version will appear with more variety. In the following steps, the text will be made a darker shade of gray.

- Click the Adjustments tab to display the Adjustments panel, if necessary (Figure 7–70).

Figure 7–70

2

- Click the Black & White icon on the Adjustments panel to display the black and white settings.

- On the Adjustments panel status bar, click the 'Clip to layer' button so that the changes affect only the Pet Adoption Merged layer.

- Click the 'Modify a slider' button to enable color changes in the document itself, and then move the mouse pointer into the document window and position it over an area of the toothbrush, as shown in Figure 7–71.

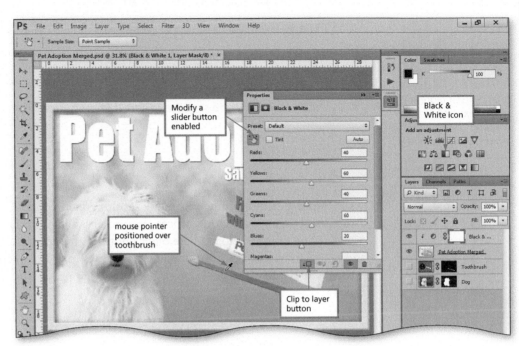

Figure 7–71

3

- In the document window, drag to the left to darken the toothbrush and the text above the toothpaste (Figure 7–72).

Q&A

Could I have used the sliders on the Adjustments panel to make the changes?

Yes, the sliders work the same way on the panel as they do in the document window.

Experiment

- Try dragging from other areas of the document to darken or lighten it. Continue dragging until you are satisfied with the changes.

Figure 7–72

4

- At the top of the Adjustments panel, click the Collapse Panel button to close the Black & White settings on the Adjustments panel.

To Save the Black-and-White Image

BTW

The Channel Mixer
The Channel Mixer creates high-quality images by choosing the percentages from each color channel. It lends itself more toward artistic expression than for tasks related to simple restoration or technical graphics. Artists use the Channel Mixer to create a variety of tints, pastels, infrareds, and sepia tones.

The black-and-white image is complete. The next steps save the file.

1 Press SHIFT+CTRL+S to open the Save As dialog box.

2 Type Pet Adoption Black and White to enter the file name.

3 Click the Save button to save the image. If Photoshop displays a dialog box, click the OK button.

Sepia

Sepia is a color toning technique resulting in a reddish-brown tint. Originally created through a pigmenting process for preservation of photos, it has become a popular kind of tinting to emulate older photos or for special effects. As with black-and-white conversions, Photoshop has many ways to create a sepia tone, including tints, channel mixing, selective coloring, filters, and processing raw data from a digital camera.

To Create a Sepia Image using Selective Color

The following steps create a sepia version of the Pet Adoption ad using the Selective Color settings on the Adjustments panel.

1
• On the Adjustments panel, click the Selective Color icon to display its settings (Figure 7–73).

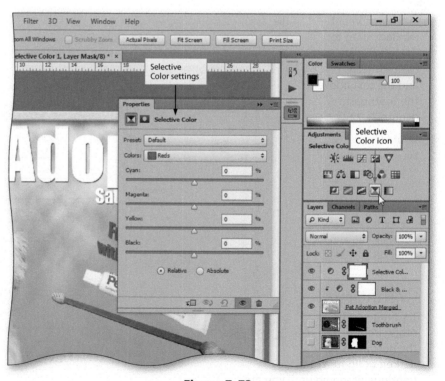

Figure 7–73

- Click the 'Clip to layer' button on the status bar so that only the Pet Adoption Merged layer is affected.

- Click the Colors box arrow to display its list (Figure 7–74).

Figure 7–74

- Click Neutrals to adjust the neutral colors in the image.

- Drag the Cyan slider to –53, drag the Magenta slider to –31, drag the Yellow slider to –18, and drag the Black slider to 49 until a warm brown color is attained (Figure 7–75).

Q&A What do the Relative and Absolute option buttons do?

If you select the Relative option button, the percentage of change is multiplied by the current color. If you select the Absolute option button, the percentage of change is added to the current color.

Figure 7–75

- At the top of the Adjustments panel, click the Collapse to Panel button.

To Save the Sepia Image

The sepia image is complete. The next steps save the file.

1 Press SHIFT+CTRL+S to open the Save As dialog box.

2 Type Pet Adoption Sepia as the file name.

3 Click the Save button to save the image. If Photoshop displays a dialog box, click the OK button.

Duotone

Duotone is a generic term for a variety of grayscale images printed with the addition of one, two, three, or four inks. In these images, colored inks, rather than different shades of gray, are used to reproduce tinted grays, increasing the tonal range of a grayscale image. Although a grayscale image displays up to 256 shades of gray, a printing press can reproduce only about 50 shades. For this reason, a grayscale image printed with only black ink can look significantly coarser than the same image on the screen. Printing with two, three, or four inks, each reproducing up to 50 levels of gray, produces an image with a slight tint and a wider dynamic range.

Because duotones affect only the gray levels, they contain only one channel; however, you can manipulate a wide range of tints using the Duotone Options dialog box. Creating a duotone version of an image is useful when the image will be printed in a single color, such as in a black and white newspaper, grayscale newsletter, or for a color special effect.

To Convert an Image to Duotone

Because duotone requires a completely grayscale image, you will convert the current image to grayscale and then to duotone.

1

- On the Image menu, point to Mode and then click Grayscale.

- When Photoshop asks to discard adjustment layers, click the OK button.

- When Photoshop asks to discard color information, click the Discard button to accept the change (Figure 7–76).

Figure 7–76

2

- On the Image menu, point to Mode and then click Duotone to display the Duotone Options dialog box. Click the Preview check box to preview the image, if necessary.

- Drag the title bar of the dialog box up and to the right to display more of the image (Figure 7–77).

Figure 7–77

3

- Click the Type box arrow to display its list (Figure 7–78).

Q&A

What do the two boxes in front of the Black tone represent?

The first box indicates how the color is spread across the image. The second box is the color itself. Clicking either box allows you to adjust the settings.

Figure 7–78

● Click Duotone to add one color to the original black (Figure 7–79).

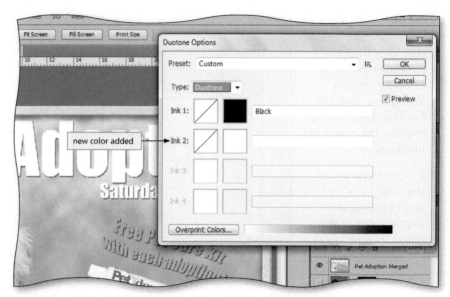

Figure 7–79

● To specify the second color, click the Preset box arrow to display its list (Figure 7–80).

Q&A Could I just choose the color using the 'Select an ink' color box?

Yes, but the Preset box list includes standard colors that print shops and service bureaus can match easily.

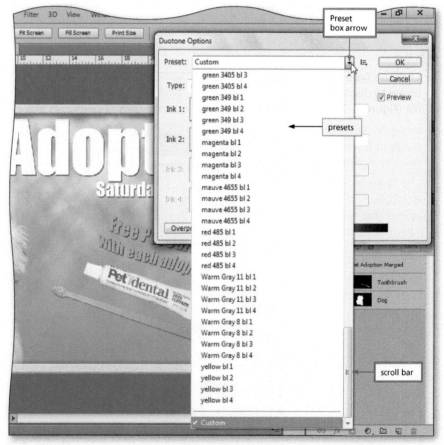

Figure 7–80

6

• Scroll as necessary and then click cyan bl 1 to select a blue duotone (Figure 7–81).

7

• Click the OK button to choose the blue duotone.

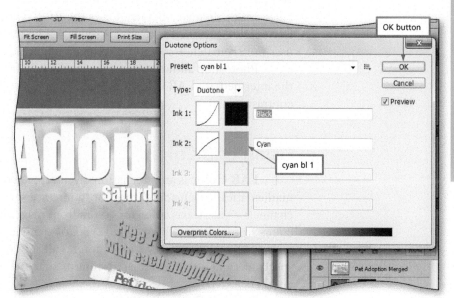

Figure 7–81

To Save the Duotone Image

The duotone image is complete. The next steps save the file.

1 Press SHIFT+CTRL+S to open the Save As dialog box.

2 Type `Pet Adoption Duotone` to enter the file name.

3 Click the Save button to save the image. If Photoshop displays a dialog box, click the OK button.

To Close the Converted File and Reopen the Merged File

You now have created color, black-and-white, sepia, and duotone versions of the Pet Adoption ad. Because you are finished with the color conversions, you will close the duotone file and open the merged file in the following steps.

1 Click the Close button on the Pet Adoption Duotone document window tab.

2 Open the Pet Adoption Merged file from the Chapter 07 folder of your storage location.

3 Double-click the Hand Tool button to fit the document to your screen.

BTW

Layer vs. Channel Versions
Many of the adjustments you make when working with color channels are destructive and thus cannot be saved as a layer in a single document. For example, you cannot save a document as full color and duotone. You have to save different copies. Also if layers are merged, you lose the layers — so merged documents should be saved as a copy.

Preparing for Four-Color Processing

Most digital cameras create an RGB file. While that is fine for online viewing and Web graphics, many traditional full-color printing presses can print only four colors: cyan, magenta, yellow, and black (CMYK). Other colors in the spectrum are simulated using various combinations of those colors. When you plan to print a photo professionally, you may have to convert it from one color model to the other. The dog image was taken with a digital camera and uses the RGB color model. The pet store wants a professional color print of the advertisement. The service bureau that will print the ad uses the Trumatch 4-color matching system, which requires the CMYK color model.

Photoshop allows you to convert directly from RGB to CMYK; however, using the intermediary LAB color mode gives you more flexibility in color changes and contrast.

Using LAB Color

LAB Color is an internationally accepted color mode that defines colors mathematically using a lightness or luminance setting, and two color or chromatic channels — an A-axis color for colors from magenta to green, and a B-axis color for colors from yellow to blue. The LAB Color mode, which tries to emulate the colors viewable by the human eye, incorporates all the colors in the RGB and CMYK color spectrums and often is used as an intermediary when converting from one format to another.

In Figure 7–82, the LAB color space is represented by the color spectrum. The black outline represents RGB's color space. The white outline represents CMYK's color space. RGB and CMYK are subsets, but they also are slanted in the color spectrum. For example, when converting from RGB to CMYK, you lose some of the blue's intensity but gain yellow. Reds and greens are better in RGB; cyans (blues) and magentas are better in CMYK, as you would expect. Contrast, a result of how bright the white is and how dark the black is, is represented poorly in CMYK. The printer cannot make white any brighter than the paper on which it is printed. A solid black does not exist in CMYK on a display monitor. Therefore, when adjusting color and contrast during a conversion, it is appropriate to convert it to LAB Color first, make your adjustments, and then convert it to CMYK.

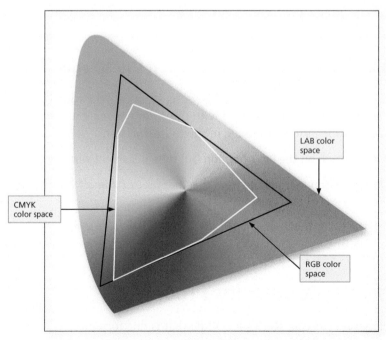

LAB color space

CMYK color space

RGB color space

Figure 7–82

The LAB Color mode calculates each color description, rather than generating it from a combination, as is the case for RGB. Because RGB colors are combinations of colors, they may look different on different devices. For example, a row of televisions in a department store displaying the same program will look different because different television manufacturers combine red, green, and blue in slightly different ways. Working with LAB colors usually provides colors that are more consistent across platforms.

The LAB Color mode is independent of the type of device or media, and may be used for either display or printing. Many photo CD images use LAB colors where the luminance and color values are edited independently.

To Convert to LAB Color

The LAB Color mode will be used in the conversion process for the advertisement. Converting to LAB color rasterizes or changes vector-based text layers to pixel-based images. The conversion process also merges the layers. The following step converts to LAB color.

- Click Image on the Application bar, point to Mode, and then click Lab Color to begin the conversion (Figure 7–83).

- When Photoshop displays a message about merging layers, click the Merge button.

Figure 7–83

To Convert to CMYK

Converting the file to CMYK allows you to make size, color, and tonal changes before printing. The following step converts to CMYK.

1. Click Image on the Application bar, point to Mode, and then click CMYK Color to convert the image to CMYK. If Photoshop displays a dialog box, click the OK button.

To Save the Advertisement

After the conversion to LAB and the conversion to CMYK, it is a good idea to save the file again.

1 Press CTRL+SHIFT+S to save the file.

2 Type Pet Adoption CMYK to enter the file name.

3 Click the Save button to save the image. If Photoshop displays a dialog box, click the OK button.

BTW

Resampling
In the General Preferences dialog box, you can specify which default interpolation method to use whenever you resample images using the Image Size or transformation commands. The Image Size command also lets you specify an interpolation method other than the default.

Resizing, Resampling, and Interpolation

Recall that you used the Image Size dialog box to resize an image earlier in this chapter. Resizing an image can reduce the image quality. For example, when you resize an image to larger dimensions, the image may lose some detail and sharpness because Photoshop has to add or stretch pixels. When you make an image smaller, some pixels must be reduced or discarded and cannot be recovered once the image is saved. That is why you should always work with a copy of the original image, in case you do not like the changes.

Changing the document size, or physical size, of photos is one of the most common tasks in digital imagery, as is changing the file size, or number of required bytes to store the image.

Photoshop allows you to make the interpolation, resampling, and sizing changes yourself. Interpolation is the mathematical process of adding or subtracting pixels in an image, either to enlarge or to reduce the size. Once the location of the interpolated pixels is determined, Photoshop uses a **resampling method** that assigns a new color value to pixels by taking a sample of the surrounding ones. Before you resample, however, it is important to check with your lab or service bureau, as some services automatically resample and resize at the time of printing. In those cases, retaining as much digital data as possible is the best choice. On the other hand, if a digital image must have a specific resolution and a specific size, then resampling may be warranted.

If you **downsample**, or decrease the number of pixels, information is deleted from the image. Downsampling reduces image data by representing a group of pixels with a single pixel. For instance, if an image needs to be reduced by 50 percent, Photoshop will have to destroy half of the pixels. If during the destruction, black-and-white pixels come next to each other, both pixels are changed using a complex calculation to produce a smoother tonal gradation of gray. The disadvantage of downsampling is the loss of data, or **lossiness**.

If you **upsample**, or increase the number of pixels, Photoshop assigns a new color to the added pixels based on an average interpolation. For example, if an image needs to be enlarged, the interpolation notes where a new pixel should be added. If that new pixel falls at the edge of a yellow insignia on a red sweater, the new pixel would be orange. Photoshop samples the two colors and averages the color values. At the pixel level, it would be hard to notice orange in the finished product, but it is something to keep in mind when upsampling. Remember that Photoshop cannot insert detailed information that was not captured from the original image. Photos will start to look softer, with less detail, as they are enlarged.

Table 7–4 lists the five interpolation methods offered by Photoshop; however, other interpolation methods can be downloaded from the Web.

Table 7–4 Photoshop Interpolation Methods

Interpolation Method	Description
Bicubic (best for smooth gradients)	A slow, but precise, interpolation method based on an examination of the values of surrounding pixels — applies more complex calculations to produce smoother tonal gradations
Bicubic Sharper (best for reduction)	A bicubic interpolation method that works well for reducing images with enhanced sharpening while maintaining details
Bicubic Smoother (best for enlargement)	An interpolation method that works well for enlarging images with smoother results than bicubic alone
Bicubic Automatic	Photoshop automatically chooses the best Bicubic method for the image resize being performed
Bilinear	An interpolation method that produces medium-quality results by averaging the color values to produce new pixels
Nearest Neighbor (preserve hard edges)	A fast interpolation method that produces a smaller file size but may become jagged when scaling as it tries to preserve hard edges

No matter what resampling method you choose, it may introduce artifacts, or changed pixels, that do not look good and were not in the original image. Blurs or halos may be introduced. Jagged edges may appear when upsampling, and moiré patterns may appear when downsampling. A **moiré pattern** is an alternating of blurred and clear areas, forming thin stripes or dots on the screen. Table 7–5 describes some of the problems related to resampling.

Table 7–5 Resampling Problems

Problem	Description	Possible Solution	Sample
Aliasing	Jagged edges or moiré patterns	Set anti-aliasing options (during down-scaling)	
Blur	A loss of image sharpness, more visible at higher magnifications	Use the Unsharp Mask filter	
Halos	Appears as a halo around edges — while a small amount may improve the perceived sharpness, a high amount does not look good	Use Defringe matting	

The Image Size Dialog Box

Recall that Photoshop uses the Image Size dialog box to specify choices about the number of pixels, the document size, and the resampling method. Each setting in the Image Size dialog box makes a difference in the resulting type of file and document. Table 7–6 on the next page displays the settings and their effects. When resampling, pixels are added or subtracted during resizing. Without resampling, you are stretching or compressing the existing pixels by changing the resolution.

BTW

JPEG Artifacts
Sometimes, when converting from RGB to LAB color, a JPEG image will leave behind some small blotches of irregular color, called **artifacts,** because of the compression method involved. Sharpening the image will remove those kinds of artifacts.

Table 7–6 Image Size Dialog Box Settings			
Setting	Unit of Measurement	Effect With Resampling	Effect Without Resampling
Pixel Dimensions	Percent or pixels	The document size is adjusted in proportion to pixel dimensions, but the resolution does not change.	The pixel dimensions remain the same, but the resolution value changes to represent what the image can provide at that size.
Document Size	Percent, inches, centimeters, millimeters, points, picas, or columns	The pixels are adjusted in proportion to document size, but the resolution does not change.	The pixel dimensions remain the same, but the resolution value changes to represent what the image can provide at that size.
Resolution	Pixels per inch or pixels per centimeter	The pixel dimensions change and the document size remains the same.	The document size changes and the pixel dimensions remain the same.

If you make changes in the Image Size dialog box and want to go back to the original dimensions or resolution, press and hold the ALT key before closing the dialog box. The Cancel button will change to a Reset button.

To Resize a File with Resampling

The current dimensions of the Pet Adoption CMYK image are approximately 29.2 inches wide by 19.9 inches tall. The advertisement for the insert should be a half-page ad measuring approximately 5.5 inches wide. In addition, the printing service has specified a file resolution of 300 pixels per inch for best print results. The steps on the next page resize the file with resampling, which means the pixels will be downsampled using the Bicubic Sharper method because it works well for reducing images while maintaining details.

- Click Image on the Application bar, and then click Image Size to display the Image Size dialog box.

- Click the Resample Image check box to select it, if necessary.

- Click the Constrain Proportions check box to select it, if necessary.

- Click the Resample Image box arrow to display the interpolation methods (Figure 7–84).

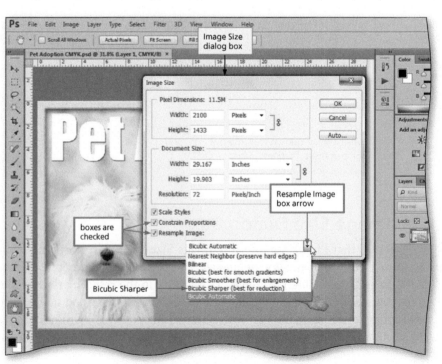

Figure 7–84

2

- Click Bicubic Sharper (best for reduction).

- If necessary, click the Width unit box arrow in the Document Size area and then click Inches in the list.

- Type 5 . 5 in the Width box.

- Type 3 0 0 in the Resolution box (Figure 7–85).

Q&A

Should I enter a height value?

No, Photoshop supplies the Height value automatically because Constrain Proportions is selected. Your document height might differ. The Pixel Dimensions settings also are adjusted.

3

- Click the OK button to close the dialog box and apply the settings.

- Double-click the Hand Tool button to fit the document to your screen.

Figure 7–85

Printing Color Separations

Graphic professionals sometimes use print shops, labs, or service bureaus for their advanced printing needs. Service bureaus typically use image setters to create high-quality prints. An **image setter** is a high-resolution output device that can transfer electronic files directly to photosensitive paper, plates, or film. While many service bureaus can resize and edit color at the time of printing, you save both time and money by performing these prepress tasks ahead of time in Photoshop. **Prepress tasks** are the various printing-related services performed before ink actually is put on the printed page.

When preparing your image for prepress, and working with CMYK images or images with spot color, you can print each color channel as a separate page. Photoshop also has a Split Channels command on the Channels panel menu that will split the channels into separate document windows for view and adjusting, if desired. Different service bureaus and labs require different kinds of submissions that are highly printer-dependent. Even when supplying a composite for reference by the service bureau, you might want to print color separations for proofing purposes. Separations help you see if your composite file will separate correctly and help you catch other problems that might not be apparent by looking at the composite.

To Print Color Separations

Printing the project in color separations allows you to determine whether your composite will separate properly and helps you spot problems before going to press. The following steps print the Pet Adoption CMYK document as color separations.

- Ready the printer attached to your computer.

- Click File on the Application bar, and then click Print to display the Photoshop Print Settings dialog box.

- Click the Color Handling box arrow to display its list (Figure 7–86).

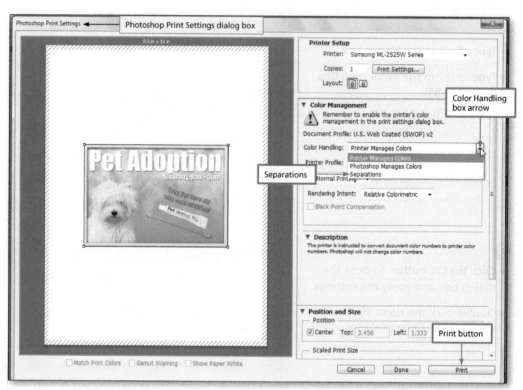

Figure 7–86

- Click Separations in the list.

- Click the Print button to display your printer-dependent Print dialog box.

- Click the Print button or the appropriate button for your printer to print the image.

- Retrieve your four printouts from the printer.

Q&A Why do I have four different printouts?

You printed separations. Just as the RGB channels you examined earlier in this chapter showed different grayscale versions of an image depending on how much red, green, or blue was present, the printed color separations show the same thing — but for the cyan, magenta, yellow, and black channels.

BTW
Quick Reference
For a table that lists how to complete the tasks covered in this book using the mouse, context menu, and keyboard, see the Quick Reference summary at the back of this book.

To Save and Close the Four-Color Version

The following steps save and close the CMYK four-color version of the Pet Adoption document.

1. Press CTRL+S to save the file with the same name.

2. Click the Close button on the document window title bar to close the image.

To Quit Photoshop

The chapter is complete. The final step is to quit Photoshop.

1 Click the Close button on the right side of the Photoshop title bar to quit Photoshop.

Chapter Summary

In this chapter, you used a master copy of an image as the basis for creating several new versions. First, you used channels to aid in the creation of complex selections, which were later used as masks. You added warped text and used an action to embellish the image. You recorded an action to apply an artistic filter and resize a thumbnail version of the image. You learned various ways to create black-and-white, sepia, and duotone images. Finally, you converted the image to LAB Color mode, then converted it to CMYK color. Among the prepress activities, you resized and resampled the image, and then printed color separations.

The items listed below include all the new Photoshop skills you have learned in this chapter:

1. View Channels (PS 409)
2. Zoom by Dragging (PS 410)
3. Select using a Channel (PS 411)
4. Create an Alpha Channel from a Selection (PS 412)
5. Edit an Alpha Channel (PS 413)
6. Create an Alpha Channel from Scratch (PS 417)
7. Make a Selection in Brush Overlay Mode (PS 419)
8. Fine-Tune the Selection (PS 421)
9. Create a Layer Mask from an Alpha Channel (PS 424)
10. Use the Refine Mask Tool (PS 425)
11. Add a Layer Mask from an Alpha Channel (PS 428)
12. Mask using an Existing Alpha Channel (PS 430)
13. Refine a Mask (PS 432)
14. Decontaminate Colors (PS 433)
15. Warp Text (PS 436)
16. Display the Actions Panel (PS 442)
17. Append Action Sets (PS 442)
18. Play an Action (PS 443)
19. Create a New Action Set (PS 445)
20. Create a New Action (PS 446)
21. Record an Action (PS 446)
22. Test the Action (PS 450)
23. Save an Action Set (PS 450)
24. Desaturate (PS 453)
25. Create a Black-and-White Adjustment (PS 454)
26. Create a Sepia Image using Selective Color (PS 456)
27. Convert an Image to Duotone (PS 458)
28. Convert to LAB Color (PS 463)
29. Resize a File with Resampling (PS 466)
30. Print Color Separations (PS 468)

Apply Your Knowledge

Reinforce the skills and apply the concepts you learned in this chapter.

Creating an Alpha Channel

Instructions: Start Photoshop and perform the customization steps found on pages PS 6 through PS 10. Open the Apply 7-1 Dark Sky file from the Chapter 07 folder of the Data Files for Students. Visit www.cengage.com/ct/studentdownload for detailed instructions or contact your instructor for information about accessing the required files.

You will edit the file to create an alpha channel, hide the dark sky background, and insert a new sky background to create the photo shown in Figure 7–87 on the next page.

Continued >

STUDENT ASSIGNMENTS

Apply Your Knowledge *continued*

Source: Syed Reza Saeedzadeh, stock.xchng; Nicolas Raymond, stock.xchng

Figure 7–87

Perform the following tasks:

1. On the File menu, click Save As. Save the image on your USB flash drive as a PSD file, with the file name Apply 7 - 1 Sky Complete.

2. On the Layers panel, right-click the Background layer and then click Duplicate Layer. Name the new layer, Foreground. Select only the Foreground layer, and hide the Background layer by clicking its visibility icon.

3. Click the Channels panel and then, one at a time, view each channel independent of the others. Decide which channel has the most contrast to facilitate removing the sky background.

4. Right-click the Blue channel and then click Duplicate Channel. Name the new channel Old Background.

5. If necessary, click the Old Background channel to select it and ensure it is the only visible channel. All other channels should have their visibility icons toggled off.

6. To define the foreground:

   a. Use the Brush Tool set to Overlay mode and black as the foreground color. Drag across the top of the trees and grass where they meet the sky to paint them black. Be sure to drag across them only once or you may make them too dark.

   b. Drag a second time across the trees and grass below the initial swatch of black to paint more of the trees and grass black.

   c. Change the brush to Normal mode and paint the rest of the bottom portion of the image black.

7. To define the background:

   a. Change the brush back to Overlay mode and change the foreground color to white.

   b. Drag just above the trees to paint the bottom portion of the sky white. You may need to click any trouble spots to turn them white.

c. Continue painting the sky white where it is close to the trees.

d. Change the brush to Normal mode and paint the remaining top portion of the image and the rest of the sky white.

e. Continue to switch between black and white and Normal and Overlay modes until the top portion of the Image (sky) is completely white, and the foreground (trees and grass) is black.

8. Because the black areas will hide pixels when used as a mask while the white areas will allow the pixels to show through, you must reverse the colors within the channel. Black needs to become white, and white needs to become black. Press CTRL+I to invert the colors of the channel.

9. To view all channels and return to the Layers panel:

a. Click the RGB channel.

b. Click the Layers panel.

c. Click the Foreground layer to select it, if necessary.

10. To load the channel as a selection and create a mask:

a. Click Select on the Application bar.

b. Click Load Selection.

c. From the Channel menu, choose Old Background and click OK.

d. Click the 'Add layer mask' button on the Layers panel status bar.

11. To insert the new background file:

a. Open the Apply 7 - 1 Good Sky file from the Chapter 07 folder of the Data Files for Students.

b. Position the two open documents side by side.

c. Use the Move Tool to drag the good sky image to the Apply 7-1 Sky Complete document.

d. Close the Apply 7 - 1 Good Sky document.

e. Rename the new layer, Layer 1, to New Sky.

12. To position the new background:

a. Drag the layers in the Layers panel to restack them, if necessary, so the Foreground layer is the top layer and the New Sky layer is beneath it.

b. Use the Move Tool to position the New Sky layer as necessary.

13. Save the image.

14. To resize the image for printing on a desktop printer:

a. On the Image menu, click Image Size.

b. Click the Resample Image check box to deselect it.

c. Type 9 in the Document Size Width box.

d. Click the OK button.

15. Ready your printer. Print color separations in Landscape mode and turn them in to your instructor.

16. Quit Photoshop without saving the resized file.

Extend Your Knowledge

Extend the skills you learned in this chapter and experiment with new skills. You may need to use Help to complete the assignment.

Adding Spot Colors to a Print

Instructions: Start Photoshop and perform the customization steps found on pages PS 6 through PS 10. Open the Extend 7-1 Spot Color file from the Chapter 07 folder of the Data Files for Students. Visit www.cengage.com/ct/studentdownload for detailed instructions or contact your instructor for information about accessing the required files. The purpose of this exercise is to add two spot colors to a four-color travel flyer. The two inks are PANTONE shades, not contained in the standard CMYK range. The file contains two extra channels with saved text selections that will be loaded and recolored. The final edited photo is displayed in Figure 7–88.

Source: Nina Brisk, stock.xchng

Figure 7–88

Perform the following tasks:
1. Press SHIFT+CTRL+S to save the image on your USB flash drive as a PSD file, with the file name Extend 7–1 Spot Color Complete.
2. To convert the image from RGB mode to CMYK mode:
   a. Point to Mode on the Image menu, and then click CMYK Color.
   b. If Photoshop displays a dialog box warning you about converting to CMYK, click the OK button.
3. Click the Channels panel tab to activate the panel.
4. Click Select on the Application bar, and then click Load Selection to open the Load Selection dialog box.
5. Click the Channel box arrow, click the Stonehenge channel, and then click the OK button to load the first text channel and display the selection marquee in the document window.

6. Click the Channels panel menu button, and then click New Spot Channel to open the New Spot Channel dialog box.

7. Type 100 in the Solidity box, and click the color box to access a color selection dialog box. If the Color Picker (Spot Color) dialog box appears, click the Color Libraries button to display the Color Libraries dialog box.

8. Click the Book box arrow and then click PANTONE+ Pastels & Neons Uncoated in the list. Scroll in the color bar and select an appropriate color.

9. Click the OK button to close the Color Libraries dialog box. Click the OK button again to close the New Spot Channel dialog box.

10. Repeat Steps 4 through 9 for the Legendary Travel channel. Choose a color from the PANTONE+ Metallic Coated colors.

11. Save the image again.

12. Use the Save As command to save a copy of the file as Extend 7-1 Spot Color Complete in the Photoshop DCS 2.0 (*.EPS) in the format, which saves the file in a format that contains the extra spot channels.

13. Submit the assignment in the format specified by your instructor.

Make It Right

Analyze a project and correct all errors and/or improve the design.

Fixing a Grainy Photo Using Channels

Instructions: Start Photoshop and perform the customization steps found on pages PS 6 through PS 10. Open the Make It Right 7-1 Grainy file from the Data Files for Students and save it as Make It Right 7-1 Grainy Complete in the PSD file format. Visit www.cengage.com/ct/student-download for detailed instructions or contact your instructor for information about accessing the required files. You have a poor quality photo of an image (Figure 7–89) that you need for a brochure. Because the ISO settings on your camera were set too high, there is a lot of visual noise in the pixels, which makes the image appear grainy. You will use channels to fix the problem.

Perform the following tasks:

Access the Channels panel and click each color channel one at a time. Notice that the Red and Blue channels appear fine but the Green channel is full of noise and pixilation. With the Green channel selected, click the visibility icon next to the RGB master channel. On the Application bar, click Filter, point to Blur, and then click Gaussian Blur to open the Gaussian Blur dialog box. Adjust the Radius, blurring the Green channel to reduce some of the noise in the photo. On the Application bar, click Filter, point to Noise, and then click Reduce Noise. Adjust the settings to reduce the noise and pixilation further. When you are happy with the outcome, save the file with the name, Make It Right 7–1 Grainy Fixed, and turn it in to your instructor.

Continued >

Make It Right *continued*

Figure 7–89

In the Lab

Design and/or create a project using the guidelines, concepts, and skills presented in this chapter. Labs are listed in order of increasing difficulty.

Lab 1: Creating a Frost Effect Using Channels

Problem: You need a photo of a field with an early frost on the ground for a collage, but it is the middle of the summer and everything is green. You will use your knowledge of channels to make the grass and trees look as though they have frost on them. The finished product is displayed in Figure 7–90.

Figure 7–90

Note: To complete this assignment, you will be required to use the Data Files for Students. Visit www.cengage.com/ct/studentdownload for detailed instructions or contact your instructor for information about accessing the required files.

Instructions: Perform the following tasks:

1. Start Photoshop. Perform the customization steps found on pages PS 6 through PS 10.

2. Open the file Lab 7 - 1 Green Grass from the Chapter 07 folder of the Data Files for Students.

3. Save the file as Lab 7 - 1 White Frost. Browse to your USB flash drive storage device. Click the Save button. If Photoshop displays a dialog box, click the OK button.

4. If necessary, click the Layers panel tab to display the layers. Right-click the Background layer and then click Duplicate Layer on the context menu. Name the new layer, Frost.

5. At the top of the Layers panel, click the Blending Mode box arrow and then click Lighten.

6. Click the Adjustments panel tab to access the Adjustments panel. Click the Channel Mixer icon to display its settings. (*Hint:* The Channel Mixer icon is the next-to-last one in the second row.)

   a. Click the Monochrome check box to select it.

   b. Type 200 in the Red box.

   c. Type 150 in the Green box.

   d. Type -150 in the Blue box.

   e. Type 0 in the Contrast box, if necessary.

   f. Collapse the Channel Mixer panel.

7. In the Layers tab select the Background layer.

8. To select the sky:

   a. Click the Channels panel tab to access the Channels panel.

   b. Notice that an alpha channel has been created previously and was named, sky.

   c. Click the Layers panel tab.

   d. On the Application bar, click Select and then click Load Selection to display the Load Selection dialog box.

   e. Click the Channel box arrow and then click sky in the list, if necessary.

   f. Click the OK button to close the Load Selection dialog box and to display the selection marquee in the document window.

   g. Press CTRL+J to create a new layer. Name the layer, Sky.

   h. On the Layers panel, drag the new Sky layer above the others.

9. Save the file again.

10. To adjust the amount of frost:

    a. On the Layers panel, click the Channel Mixer layer.

    b. At the top of the Layers panel, change the opacity to 70%.

    c. Save your changes.

11. Flatten the image and then save the file in the JPEG format and submit it to your instructor as directed.

In the Lab

Lab 2: Using Predefined Actions

Problem: Your neighbor wants you to use her photo of homegrown berries to create flyer for a farmer's market. You decide to investigate Photoshop's predefined actions to look for a specialized frame that you can apply to the photo. The finished product is displayed in Figure 7–91.

Note: To complete this assignment, you will be required to use the Data Files for Students. Visit www.cengage.com/ct/studentdownload for detailed instructions or contact your instructor for information about accessing the required files.

Source: William Stadler, stock.xchng

Figure 7–91

Instructions: Perform the following tasks:

1. Start Photoshop. Perform the customization steps found on pages PS 6 through PS 10.

2. Open the file Lab 7-2 Berries from the Chapter 07 folder of the Data Files for Students.

3. Click the Save As command on the File menu. Type `Lab 7-2 Flyer` as the file name and set the format to the Photoshop PSD format, if necessary. Browse to your USB flash drive storage device. Click the Save button. If Photoshop displays a dialog box, click the OK button.

4. Press ALT+F9 to display the Actions panel. If the Frames action set is not listed, click the panel menu button, and then click Frames. If necessary, click the right-pointing triangle of the Frames action set to display the actions stored in the set. Scroll down and click the Photo Corners action.

5. Click the Play selection button on the Actions panel status bar. When the action is complete, close the Actions panel.

6. On the Layers panel, select the photo corners layer, if necessary.

7. To size and rotate the berries:

   a. Press CTRL+T to freely transform the layer.

   b. SHIFT+drag the lower-left corner of the selection border up and to the right until the mouse pointer is positioned approximately in the center of the document.

    c. Point to the outside of the selection border until the mouse pointer appears as a curved arrow and then drag up to rotate the selection.

    d. Point to the inside of the selection border and drag the berries into position.

    e. Press the ENTER key to apply the transformation.

8. To change the background color:

    a. Click the Set foreground color button at the bottom of the Tools panel to display the Color Picker.

    b. In the R box, type 250. In the G box, type 131. In the B box, type 4. Alternatively, choose a color of your liking.

    c. Click the OK button to set the foreground color.

    d. Click the new background layer in the Layers panel to select it.

    e. Press SHIFT+G repeatedly until the Paint Bucket Tool is selected.

    f. Click in the document window to fill the new background layer with the new color.

9. Click the Horizontal Type Tool button on the Tools panel.

10. To adjust the text settings:

    a. On the options bar, select the Cooper Std font family or a similar font.

    b. Set the font size to 12.

    c. Set the anti-aliasing method to Smooth.

    d. Click the Center text button.

    e. Choose a white font color.

11. Drag a text box that fills the left side of the image. In the text box, type Farmer's Market every Saturday 7am – noon Community Center parking lot, pressing the ENTER key as necessary to create the lines shown in Figure 7–96. When you are finished, click the 'Commit any current edits' button on the options bar. Use the Move Tool to adjust the placement of the text box if needed. Save your changes.

12. When you are finished, press CTRL+SHIFT+S to display the Save As dialog box. Save the file with the name, Lab 7-2 Flyer Complete, in the JPG format.

13. E-mail your instructor with the Lab 7-2 Flyer Complete file as an attachment, or see your instructor for another way to submit this assignment.

In the Lab

Lab 3: Changing Band membership

Problem: A local band has contracted you to alter a concert photo to include their new bass player. They have provided you with a photo of their band in concert and a separate photo of the bass player. You are to edit the bass player photo and place him on the concert stage, creating a picture the band can use for promotional purposes. The edited photo is shown Figure 7–92.

Note: To complete this assignment, you will be required to use the Data Files for Students. Visit www.cengage.com/ct/studentdownload for detailed instructions or contact your instructor for information about accessing the required files.

Continued >

In the Lab continued

Figure 7–92

Instructions: Perform the following tasks:
Start Photoshop. Perform the customization steps found on pages PS 6 through PS 10. Open the Lab 7 - 3 Bassist photo from the Chapter 07 folder of the Data Files for Students. Select the background and create an alpha channel. Hide or delete the background and edit as necessary to display only the bassist. Open the file named Lab 7 - 3 Concert. Arrange the documents side by side and then use the Move Tool to drag the bassist image into the Lab 7 - 3 Concert document window. Adjust and scale the layers as necessary. Refine the bass player's mask to decontaminate the edge colors. Use the Adjustments panel to adjust the levels and contrast so the bassist matches the concert scene. Delete portions of the bass player or create a mask so he appears behind the stage speakers and other band members. Create a Warped text box with the band name, as shown in Figure 7–92. Sample the blue in the guitar strap for the color of the text and apply a layer style to emphasize the text. Save the file as Lab 7 - 3 New Bass Player in the PSD format.

Cases and Places

Apply your creative thinking and problem-solving skills to design and implement a solution.

1: Converting to Black and White

Academic

Your school prints a monthly newsletter in black and white. Open the Case 7 - 1 School image that is located in the Chapter 07 folder of the Data Files for Students. Use the Adjustments panel and the Black & White adjustment to create a black-and-white version of the image that maintains good contrast and is not washed out. Write down the settings you used, and then revert the image to its original state. Using the Case 7 - 1 School image, record a new action named Convert to B&W and apply the settings you wrote down earlier as you record the action. Apply the saved action to the Case 7 - 1 Football and Case 7 - 1 Graduation images located in the Chapter 07 folder. Save the three black-and-white images with the description, B&W, appended to the end of the default file name.

2: Changing a Background

Personal

You are volunteering your graphic design skills to help a local ranch advertise horseback riding lessons. As part of the brochure, management wants to use an image of a horse on their own background. Open the Case 7-2 Horse image that is located in the Chapter 07 folder of the Data Files for Students. Determine the channel that offers the best contrast between the horse and its background and then duplicate the channel, naming it Horse. Paint in the Horse channel to make the background black and the horse white. (*Hint*: You might begin by making the horse black and the background white, then press CTRL+I to invert the colors.) Use any selection tool you believe is appropriate. (*Hint*: Try using the Brush in overlay mode to help mask around the hair.) Load the channel as a selection and then apply the selection as a layer mask, hiding the background and leaving only the horse visible. Save the file as Case 7-2 Horse Masked.psd. Copy the masked horse to the Case 7-2 Trees file (also in the Chapter 07 folder) and resize and position as necessary. Add text in an appropriate font with the ranch's name, Fairview Ranch, and warp the text artistically. Save the file as Case 7-2 Trees Horse.psd and submit it to your instructor.

3: Converting to Duotone

Professional

A wedding planner wants to use a picture of a tulip on her business cards. The tulip is in full color, but her business cards are going to use brown spot color on ivory paper. Open the Case 7-3 Tulip image that is located in the Chapter 07 folder of the Data Files for Students. Save the image on your storage device with the name Case 7-3 Tulip Edited. Use an alpha channel to remove the background. Flatten the image. Convert the image to grayscale and then convert the image to duotone. When the Duotone dialog box is displayed, double-click the Color Picker and choose a sepia color. Type sepia in the Name text box. Click the OK button. Convert the image to CMYK color. Save the image again, and then print a copy.

8 | Working with Vector Graphics

Adobe product screenshot(s) reprinted with permission from Adobe Systems Incorporated

Objectives

You will have mastered the material in this chapter when you can:

- Describe the characteristics of clip art and vector graphics
- Create and manage layer groups using the Layers panel
- Differentiate between vector and raster graphic images
- Create shape layers and paths with the Pen Tool
- Draw line segments and curved paths
- Add and convert anchor points

- Move and modify paths using the Path Selection and Direct Selection Tools
- Use the Freeform Pen Tool with the magnetic pen option
- Add detail to clip art images
- Use the Note Tool
- Enter text in a custom shape
- Apply effects to optimize clip art

8 | Working with Vector Graphics

Introduction

With the advent of page layout and word processing software, images have become common in all kinds of documents. Web sites without graphics are passé. Business stationery now includes artwork and logos in addition to the standard address and content data, lectures and oral presentations are considered uninteresting without graphics and multimedia effects, and textbooks are loaded with graphics to help improve students' focus and comprehension. Today, students routinely insert clip art into papers and presentations.

The term **clip art** refers to individual images or groups of graphics that can be transferred across computer applications and platforms. Clip art commonly is an illustrative, vibrant drawing that features solid blocks of color, rather than a photo, but the term is applied loosely to any image that accompanies or decorates text, including black-and-white images. The term clip art also is applied to visual elements such as bullets, lines, shapes, and callouts. Photos, typically with full-color backgrounds, are not considered clip art.

Project — Creating a Clip Art Image

A local ceramics studio needs a graphic for a flyer and Web site. You will begin by drawing an awning, then use a photograph of a mug to create an outline or tracing as the basis for a vector graphic of the same image. Additionally, you will insert text, convert the letters to shapes, and then reshape the letters to create a custom lettering style. Using paths, opacity changes, and layer styles, portions of the image are recolored to create a cartoon look and feel. Text also is wrapped to fit within a shape. The before and after images are displayed in Figure 8–1.

Overview

As you read this chapter, you will learn how to create the clip art image shown in Figure 8–1 by performing these general tasks:

- Create layer groups on a transparent background.
- Use paths to create vector graphics.
- Save paths using the Paths panel.
- Use the Path and Pen Tools to create shapes.
- Add detail to clip art.
- Annotate a clip art image using the Note Tool.
- Optimize clip art files for the Web.

Figure 8−1

Plan
Ahead

General Project Guidelines
When editing a photo, the actions you perform and decisions you make will affect the appearance and characteristics of the finished product. As you edit photos, such as the one shown in Figure 8−1, you should follow these general guidelines:

1. **Plan and organize layers.** Organize your clip art from the back to the front in the document window, and from the bottom up on the Layers panel. Layer groups reduce clutter on the Layers panel and logically order the various parts of an image. Layer groups also can be used to apply attributes and masks to multiple layers simultaneously, which saves time and effort.

2. **Use vector graphics for clip art.** When creating clip art, use vector graphics. Vector graphics are high-quality graphics used in illustrations, typography, logos, and advertisements. They retain their crisp edges when resized, moved, or recolored. Vector graphics do not pixelate when transferred to other applications.

3. **Add detail to enhance clip art.** Good clip art uses strong lines and colors with enough detail to highlight the image's purpose. Keep the purpose, context, and audience in mind as you add detail to create movement, depth, and light to the clip art.

4. **Annotate graphics within the file.** Consider adding notes within the file itself, rather than using e-mail with an attached photo, to provide documentation and explanations. That way, the information stays with the graphic and can be accessed by others.

When necessary, more specific details concerning the preceding guidelines are presented at appropriate points in the chapter. The chapter also will identify the actions performed and decisions made regarding these guidelines during the creation of the edited photos shown in Figure 8−1.

Clip Art

Clip art images can be created from scratch, produced from a photo, copied and pasted from another source, or imported directly as a file into some applications. The use of clip art can save artists time and money, and in some cases, using clip art in a project allows artwork to be included when it would otherwise not be possible to do so. Clip art galleries that come with some page layout and word processing applications often contain hundreds of images.

Clip art comes in a variety of file formats. **Bitmap images** work best in the size and orientation at which they are created, and typically are stored in the GIF, JPG, BMP, TIF, or PNG formats. **Vector images** are resolution-independent and do not pixelate when resized. They commonly are stored as EPS, SVG, WMF, SWF, or PDF files. Choosing the appropriate file format often depends on the purpose of the graphic — print, Web, or file transfer — as well as the scalability and resolution.

For print publications, vector images can be resized, rotated, and stretched easily. The disadvantage is that many vector formats are specific to the software in which the image was created. For example, Windows Metafile is a format used with Microsoft products and associated clip art. It is saved with the extension WMF. A graphic created with Adobe Flash has the extension SWF. While you can copy and import those types of vector images between applications, you might not be able to edit them without using the original software.

Clip art is not always free. Application software companies provide a license for registered users to import and distribute the clip art provided with the package without charge. Some Web clip art galleries might specify royalty-free images for one-time use, but not for commercial use intended to generate profit. For other uses, you must purchase clip art packages on CD or for download. It is important to read all licensing agreements carefully. The usage of some artwork requires written permission. Copyright laws apply to all images equally — the right of legal use depends on the intended use and conditions of the copyright owner. All images are copyrighted, regardless of whether they are marked as copyrighted.

Table 8–1 displays some of the categories, descriptions, and usages of clip art sources.

In this chapter, you will create your own clip art — clip art that has no legal restrictions because you are designing it yourself. Artists, graphic design professionals, typographers, and casual users all use Photoshop to create specialized graphics such as clip art to avoid potential copyright problems.

Table 8–1 Clip Art		
Clip Art Category	**Warnings**	**Use**
Free — An image that is given or provided free of charge	It is important to check the Web site owner's motive for giving away clip art. Some free graphics are unlabeled, copyrighted images. Images might contain spyware or viruses.	Appropriate for personal use and sometimes for educational purposes, but because the original source might be obscure, free clip art is not recommended for business use.
Published clip art — images in print or online	Ask for written permission to use the image. Do not use the image unless you can track it to its original source.	Published clip art is appropriate for personal use, educational purposes, and one-time use on a Web site. With permission, it may be used commercially.

Table 8–1 Clip Art (*continued*)		
Clip Art Category	**Warnings**	**Use**
Copyrighted — trademarked images that have legal owners	Do not use unless you have a written agreement with the copyright holder.	Copyrighted clip art has limited legal use. Only fully licensed resellers may use copyrighted clip art. It is not appropriate for any personal or educational use.
Royalty-free — images provided at little or no cost by the owner	Carefully read the rights and usages. Trading post Web sites require the permission of the artist or photographer. Even legitimate images might contain spyware or viruses.	With written permission from the owner, royalty-free clip art and stock images normally can be used by anyone — even for commercial use such as on Web sites and business stationery — but without redistribution rights.
Rights-protected — images created and sold for a specific use	You must buy the right to use the image exclusively. You may not use the image for any use other than its intended purpose.	Written businesses contract with artists to design rights-protected logos and artwork. The seller promises not to sell that image to anyone else for that purpose.
Editorial rights — photos used in public interest	Some editorial-use images also are copyrighted. Read the agreement carefully.	Editorial-rights images are used with written permission for news, sports, entertainment, and other public purposes with appropriate citation. These images are usually less restrictive and less expensive than rights-protected images.

Starting and Customizing Photoshop

The following steps start Photoshop and reset the default workspace, tools, colors, and Layers panel options.

To Start Photoshop

If you are stepping through this project on a computer and you want your screen to match the figures in this book, then you should change your computer's resolution to 1024 × 768 and reset the panels, tools, and colors. For more information about how to change the resolution on your computer, and other advanced Photoshop settings, read the Changing Screen Resolution appendix.

The following steps, which assume Windows 7 is running, start Photoshop based on a typical installation. You may need to ask your instructor how to start Photoshop for your system.

1 Click the Start button on the Windows 7 taskbar to display the Start menu and then type `Photoshop CS6` in the 'Search programs and files' box.

2 Click Adobe Photoshop CS6 in the list to start Photoshop.

3 If the Photoshop window is not maximized, click the Maximize button next to the Close button on the Application bar to maximize the window.

To Reset the Workspace

As discussed in Chapter 1, it is helpful to reset the workspace so that the tools and panels appear in their default positions. The following steps select the Essentials workspace.

1 Click Window on the Application bar to display the Window menu and then point to Workspace to display the Workspace submenu.

2 Click Essentials (Default) on the Workspace submenu to select the default workspace panels.

3 Click Window on the Application bar, and then point to Workspace again to display the list.

4 Click Reset Essentials to restore the workspace to its default settings, and reposition any panels that may have been moved.

To Reset the Tools and the Options Bar

Recall that the Tools panel and the options bar retain their settings from previous Photoshop sessions. The following steps select the Rectangular Marquee Tool and reset all tool settings in the options bar.

1 If the tools in the Tools panel appear in two columns, click the double arrow at the top of the Tools panel.

2 If necessary, click the Rectangular Marquee Tool button on the Tools panel to select it.

3 Right-click the Rectangular Marquee Tool icon on the options bar to display the context menu, and then click Reset All Tools. When Photoshop displays a confirmation dialog box, click the OK button to restore the tools to their default settings.

To Set the Interface and Default Colors

Recall that Photoshop retains the interface color scheme, as well as the foreground and background colors, from session to session. The following steps set the interface to Medium Gray and the foreground and background colors to black over white.

1 Click Edit on the Application bar to display the Edit menu. Point to Preferences and then click Interface on the Preferences submenu to display the Preferences dialog box.

2 Click the third button, Medium Gray, to change the interface color scheme.

3 Click the OK button to close the Preferences dialog box.

4 Press the D key to reset the default foreground and background colors. If black is not over white on the Tools panel, press the X key.

To Reset the Layers Panel

The following steps reset the Layers panel to make the thumbnails match the figures shown in this book.

1 Click the Layers panel menu button, and then click Panel Options on the list to display the Layers Panel Options dialog box.

2 Click the option button for the smallest of the thumbnail sizes.

3 If necessary, click the Layer Bounds option button to select it.

4 If necessary, place a check mark next to each of the three check boxes at the bottom of the Layers Panel Options dialog box.

5 Click the OK button (Layers Panel Options dialog box) to close the dialog box, resetting the Layers panel.

Creating a New File with a Transparent Background

A desirable attribute of clip art is the transparent background. A clip art with **transparency** can be placed closer to text and other graphics when inserted into Web pages, slide presentations, and print publications. The graphic will appear without a white, cornered background obstructing the view. In Photoshop, when you create an image with transparent content, the image does not have a traditional Background layer. Each layer neither is drawn on, nor constrained by, the background; you can add layers anywhere in the document window.

To Create a File with a Transparent Background

The following steps use a shortcut key to display the New dialog box and then set the attributes for an image with a transparent background.

1 Press CTRL+N to display the New dialog box.

2 Type `Creative Ceramics` in the Name box to name the graphic.

3 Click the Width unit box arrow, and then click inches in the list, if necessary.

4 Set the Width to 7 inches and the Height to 5 inches.

5 Set the Resolution to 300 Pixels/Inch.

6 Set the Color Mode to RGB Color, 8 bit.

7 Set the Background Contents to Transparent (Figure 8–2 on the next page).

8 Click the OK button to create the document.

9 Double-click the Hand tool on the Tools panel to fit the canvas to your screen. If the rulers do not appear in the document window, press CTRL+R.

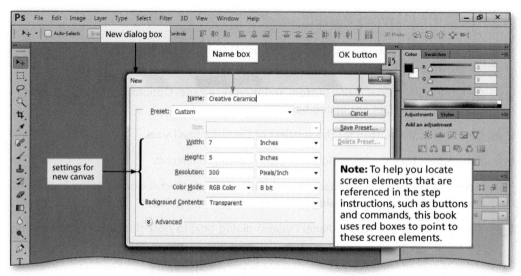

Figure 8–2

Managing the Layers Panel

Converting a photo into clip art requires many steps with many layers. First, you must import the original photo onto your transparent background to use as a basis for drawing the clip art. Locking or partially locking the original photo is a good way to prevent accidental deletion of the image.

Each color you create in the clip art becomes a new path or shape, at least temporarily until the image is flattened and prepared for distribution. To manage the many layers, users find it easier to group multiple shapes and their special effects by style, category, or object.

Plan Ahead

Plan and organize layers.

As you build your clip art from the back to the front, keep the layers in order from bottom (back) to top (front) on the Layers panel. Always use a locked background and then organize other parts of the clip art in layer groups. Advantages of using layer groups include the ability to:

- Create a new document from a layer group.
- Move layer groups from one image to another.
- Nest layer groups within one another.
- Align and merge layer groups.
- Apply attributes and masks to multiple layers simultaneously.

The sections that follow rename the transparent layer, import the photo, create layer groups, and save the file.

To Rename the Transparent Layer

The first step is to rename the transparent background layer that you created. Later in this chapter, you will create a gradient background on this transparent layer.

1 If necessary, click the Layers panel tab to display the Layers panel.

2 On the Layers panel, double-click the name of the layer, Layer 1. Type `Background`, and then press the ENTER key to rename the layer.

To Insert the Mug Graphic

The next step in creating the clip art image is to import the original photo of a mug. The steps that follow open the Mug file and move the image into the Creative Ceramics document window, creating a new layer.

1 Open the file named Mug from the Chapter 08 folder of the Data Files for Students.

2 Arrange the documents side by side.

3 Activate the Move Tool and then drag the mug image into the Creative Ceramics document window. Close the Mug document window.

4 Position the image so the mug is roughly centered in the canvas.

5 Rename the layer, Original Mug (Figure 8–3).

Figure 8–3

Locking Layers

Layers can be locked fully to prevent further editing or locked partially to allow movement of the layer without disturbing the effects and settings. Table 8–2 displays information about the four locking buttons.

Table 8–2 Layers Panel Locking Buttons		
Type of Lock	**Description**	**Button**
Lock transparent pixels	Confines editing to the opaque portions of the layer	
Lock image pixels	Prevents painting tool modifications of the layer	
Lock position	Prevents the layer's pixels from being moved	
Lock all	Locks transparent pixels, image pixels, and position	

To Lock Layers

The following steps use the Lock all button to lock the transparent background fully and use the Lock position button to partially lock the Original Mug layer. You later will unlock the background when you are ready to work with it. Partially locking the Original Mug will protect it from accidental movement.

1

- On the Layers panel, select the Background layer.

- Click the Lock all button to lock the layer and to display the solid lock icon (Figure 8–4).

Q&A

When should I lock layers?

You might want to lock a layer fully when you finish working with it. You might want to lock a layer partially if it has the correct transparency and styles, but you still are deciding on the layer's position.

Figure 8–4

2

- Select the Original Mug layer.

- Click the Lock position button to lock the layer partially and to display a hollow lock icon (Figure 8–5).

Figure 8–5

To Save the File in the PSD Format

The following steps save the file in the PSD format for maximum editing flexibility.

1 With your USB flash drive connected to one of the computer's USB ports, click File on the Application bar to display the File menu, and then click Save As to display the Save As dialog box.

2 Click the Save in box arrow and then click Removable Disk (F:), or the location associated with your USB flash drive, in the list. If you want to create a folder for the photos in Chapter 8, click the Create New Folder button. Then, when the new folder is displayed, type a chapter name, such as Chapter 08, and press the ENTER key.

3 If necessary, click the Format box arrow and then click Photoshop (*.PSD;*.PDD) in the list.

4 Click the Save button. If Photoshop displays a Photoshop Format Options dialog box, click the OK button.

Vector Graphics

Vector and bitmap are the two image file types available in Photoshop. As you have learned, vectors — also called vector graphics — are made up of shapes, lines, and curves that are defined by mathematical objects, or vectors. **Vector graphics** are high-quality graphics used in illustrations, typography, logos, and advertisements. Vector graphics retain their crisp edges when resized, moved, or recolored because they are made up of individual, scalable lines and objects rather than bitmapped pixels. Therefore, vector graphics are not directly editable at the pixel level. You can change a vector graphic, but not in the same way as you can change a non-vector graphic. When you edit a vector graphic, you change its attributes such as color, fill, and outline. For example, if you create a circle as a shape layer, the vector graphic is generated using the current color scheme and style displayed on the options bar. You cannot edit a vector graphic with the brush or eraser tools, nor can you fill it with color using the Paint Bucket Tool. If you change your mind about the color, for instance, you must select the shape layer and then change the color using the options bar. Changing the attributes of a vector object does not affect the object itself; it merely applies the change as it shapes and transforms the layer along a path. In a previous chapter, you used the Shape layers button on the Shape options bar to create a vector graphic automatically. You might have seen or used vector graphics as clip art in page layout and word processing programs.

The other graphic file type is a bitmap image, also called a raster image. **Raster images** are made up of pixels of color and are resolution dependent; thus, they are appropriate for photographs and artwork with continuous color, such as paintings. Images from scanners and digital cameras are raster images because they need to use continuous color to form the image.

Because vector graphics are drawn instead of compiled from pixels, they are more difficult to edit. For example, before you modify text — changing the shape of type — you must convert it from a vector graphic to a flat raster image, in a process called **rasterizing**. When you rasterize, you might need to set the pixel dimensions, color mode, anti-aliasing, dithering, and resolution. The disadvantage of rasterizing is that the image becomes resolution dependent, making it difficult to resize without sacrificing a degree of image quality. While raster images are scaled quite successfully in page layout programs, a permanent change in size is harder to interpolate.

> **Use vector graphics for clip art.**
> Begin with a good photo of the subject to use as a pattern. Study the shapes, angles, lines, and lighting. Because composition is such an important factor in clip art, consider using the photo as your outline to create the vector graphic or vector art. As you use paths to draw the vectors, experiment with different colors for each part of the vector graphic to differentiate it. Create each shape before adding detail.
>
> By creating an original piece of vector art, you can express exactly what you or your client wants to convey through an image.

Path Lines and Anchor Points

Although you can use any of Photoshop's shape tools to create vector graphics, the most versatile are the Pen Tool and the Freeform Pen Tool, which create paths. A **path** is an outline that you can turn into a shape, turn into a selection, or fill and stroke with color. A path is different from a regular selection, not only in its vector graphic qualities, but also in the user's ability to use the Pen Tools for drawing and adjusting. When you use the pen tools to create path lines, each click in the document window becomes an anchor point, or node. An **anchor point** is a single handle created from a click along a path line or border. An anchor point is displayed as a small square. Press the BACKSPACE key to delete the current anchor point. The current or latest anchor point is always a solid square, indicating that it is selected. Non-selected anchor points are displayed as hollow squares and are used to alter the shape and angle of line segments at adjacent segments along the path. You will learn more about paths later in the chapter.

Not all paths have to be two-dimensional shapes; a path can be as simple as a line. To create a straight line path, you click the document window using the Pen Tool, creating an anchor point. When you click again, a second anchor point is displayed and a line connects the two in the document window.

When you want to create curved lines, you drag with the Pen Tool. Photoshop will display an anchor point and two direction lines with direction points (Figure 8–6). The direction lines move outward as you drag. The direction of the drag determines the eventual direction of the curve. For instance, if you drag to the right, the bump of the curve will be to the right. The length of the drag determines how much influence the anchor point will have over the curve — the longer the drag, the more exaggerated the curve. To create the other end of the curved line, simply click the desired end point and drag again. Dragging the end point in the opposite direction creates an arc; dragging in the same direction creates an S curve. Once the curve is completed, the direction lines no longer appear; the curve is the only thing that is displayed in the document window.

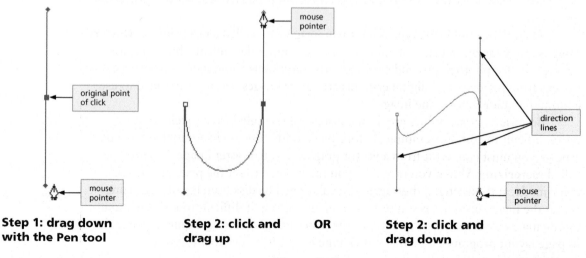

**Step 1: drag down
with the Pen tool**   **Step 2: click and
drag up**   **OR**   **Step 2: click and
drag down**

Figure 8–6

Whether straight or curved, when you are finished with a path, you have two choices: create an open path or a closed path. You can CTRL+click to create an open path. The ends of an **open path** do not connect, thus creating a line or curve, rather than a polygon or ellipse. Open paths can be used to create outlines or color strokes, or they can be used to place text such as words that appear contoured along a curve. If you finish a path by joining the ends, it is called a **closed path** and creates a two-dimensional shape such as a rectangle, triangle, or oval. When your mouse pointer gets close to the first anchor point, a small circle is displayed next to the tip of the mouse pointer. Clicking then connects the anchor points and closes the path.

Table 8–3 displays some of the possible tasks when creating path lines.

Table 8–3 Creating Path Lines

Task	Steps	Result
Create a straight line path.	Click a beginning point. Click an ending point.	
Add an anchor point.	Click along a path.	
Delete an existing anchor point.	If the Auto Add/Delete option is selected on the options bar, you can click an existing point to delete it. You can also press the BACKSPACE key to delete the current point or ALT+click a point to remove the direction handle and convert the point into an anchor point.	
Create an arc.	Drag the first anchor point in the direction of the bump of the curve. Drag the second anchor point in the opposite direction.	
Create an S curve.	Drag both anchor points in the same direction.	
Create a polygon.	Click at least three times to create anchor points, and then click the original anchor point again.	
Create an ellipse.	Create a line. Drag the beginning point. Drag the ending point in the opposite direction. Click the beginning point.	

As you will learn in the next section, you have three basic choices, or modes, when creating open and closed paths. You can create a path that is a shape layer, a path on the Paths panel, or a non-vector, filled shape.

Shape Layers and Modes

As you create paths, if you select the Shape layers button on the options bar, Photoshop creates a **shape layer** on the Layers panel. Two clicks create a line path that is displayed in gray in the document window; a path with more than two points creates a filled path using the current foreground color. A shape layer displays the fill that defines the shape color and also displays a linked vector mask that defines the path or shape outline. The outline of a shape appears as a path on the Paths panel as well, but the shape exists in its own layer on the Layers panel, making it easier to edit than other paths.

You can use the pen tools or other shape tools to create shape layer paths. Because they are easily moved, aligned, resized, and distributed, shape layers are ideal for making graphics for clip art and for Web pages. Additionally, you can create multiple shapes on a single layer.

The Shape options bar contains the 'Pick tool mode' button, which lets you choose a drawing mode. The three drawing modes are Shape, Path, and Pixels. If you use the Shape mode, Photoshop creates a new vector shape filled with the color visible on the options bar. If you choose the Path mode, a working shape appears as a path. If you use the Pixels mode, the shape will be filled with the current foreground color. The next sections use these different modes.

To Hide a Layer

The next few exercises create a closed path with the Pen Tool to simulate a store awning in a blue color as shown in Figure 8–1 on page PS 485. The path will become a shape layer on the Layers panel. Photoshop creates new shape layers above the selected layer on the Layers panel. Before you begin to draw the awning, you will hide the mug so it will not distract from your drawing. The following step hides the Original Mug layer so it does not distract from working with the other layers.

1 Click the Indicates layer visibility button for the Original Mug layer to hide the mug so it does not distract from your drawing.

To Select a Color from the Swatches Panel

The following step selects a color from the Swatches panel to use as the fill color for the awning you will create later.

1 Click the Swatches panel tab to display the Swatches panel, and then click Pastel Cyan to change the foreground color (Figure 8–7).

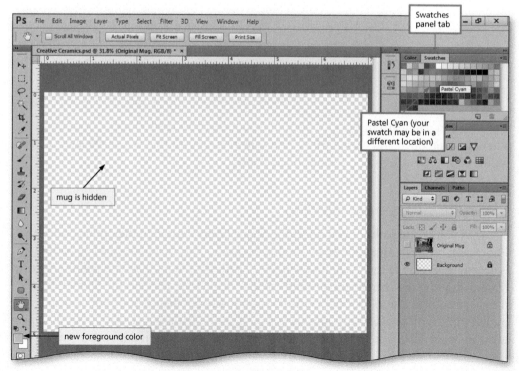

Figure 8–7

To Choose the Pen Tool

The following steps choose the Pen Tool in preparation for drawing the awning.

- On the Layers panel, select the Original Mug layer, if necessary, so that any new layers will be created above it.

- On the Tools panel, right-click the current Pen Tool button to display the context menu (Figure 8–8).

Q&A If I locked that layer earlier, and made it not visible, why am I selecting it?

Remember that layers — and paths — are created from the bottom up. The new path shape will appear above the layer in the Layers panel and in front of the original mug in the document window.

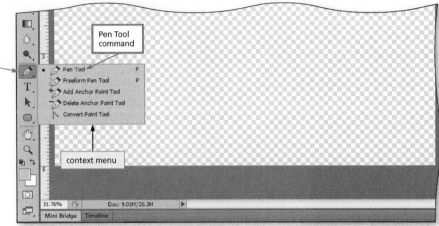

Figure 8–8

- Click Pen Tool to select it.

- On the options bar, click the 'Pick tool mode' button to display the mode options (Figure 8–9).

- Click Shape to set the Pen Tool to draw in Shape mode.

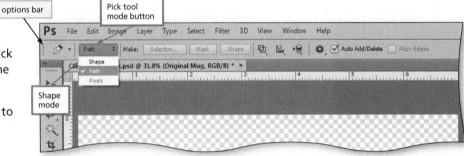

Figure 8–9

To Create a Shape Layer using the Pen Tool

The following steps begin to create the awning in the blue color selected in a previous exercise.

- In the document window, click just outside the canvas in the gray area to the left, about 2 inches down from the top of the canvas, to display the first anchor point (Figure 8–10).

Q&A Why must I click outside the canvas?

Doing so guarantees the shape will cover the edges of the canvas.

Q&A What if I do not have enough room to click outside the canvas?

Zoom out or use the scroll bars to view more of the area outside the canvas.

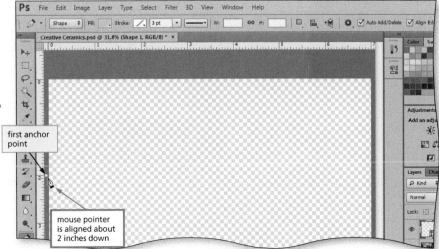

Figure 8–10

2

- Move the mouse pointer to the right to the 1-inch mark on the horizontal ruler, taking care to maintain the 2-inch position on the vertical ruler.

- Click the location and drag the mouse pointer up and to the right to display the second anchor point and create the first curve (Figure 8–11).

Q&A

Why did a blue shape appear?

When you create more than two anchor points, Photoshop begins to fill the shape layer with the selected color.

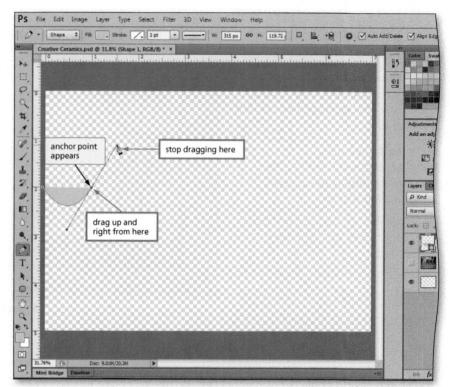

Figure 8–11

3

- Position the mouse pointer to align with 2 inches on the horizontal ruler and 2 inches on the vertical ruler.

- Click the location and drag the mouse pointer up and to the right to create another curve (Figure 8–12).

Q&A

Why did the new line first curve up and then down?

The path is following the direction line created by the previous anchor point, which was dragged up and to the right. The curve should have a sharp point at the top, so the second anchor point must be converted to a corner point.

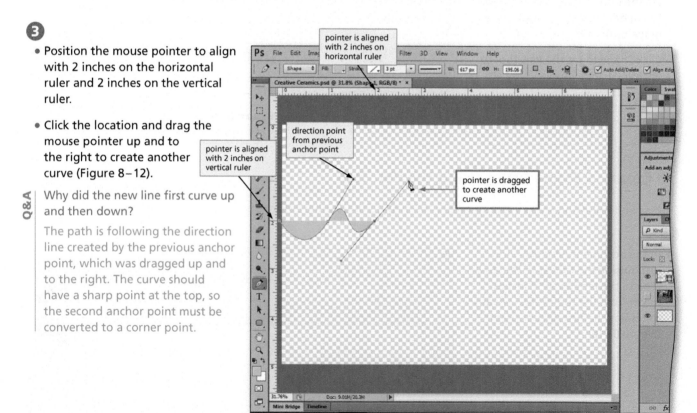

Figure 8–12

- Press the BACKSPACE key to delete the third anchor point.

- Click the second anchor point to reestablish the path (Figure 8–13).

Q&A Why did I have to click the second anchor point?

Clicking the last, or previous, anchor point selects the path so it can be continued.

Q&A How can I tell which anchor point is selected?

The selected anchor point displays a solid square. Other anchor points are hollow.

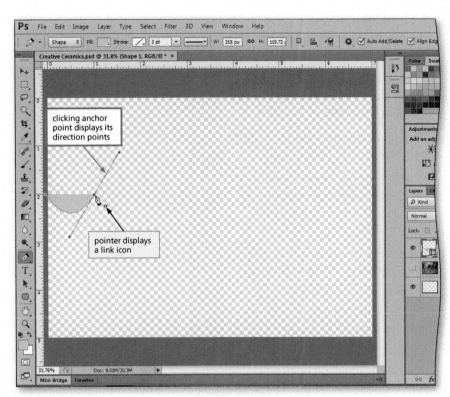

Figure 8–13

- ALT+click the second anchor point to remove the direction point and convert the point to a corner point.

- Position the mouse pointer to align with 2 inches on the horizontal ruler and 2 inches on the vertical ruler.

- Drag up and to the right to create a scalloped curve (Figure 8–14).

Q&A Why does the scallop now have a sharp point at the top instead of a curve?

By converting the second anchor point to a corner point, you removed the direction handles. Paths originating from a corner point do not begin with a curve, as there is no direction point to follow.

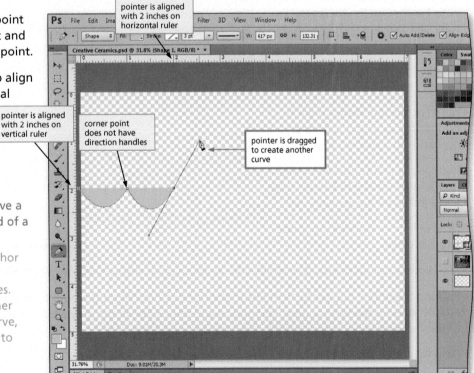

Figure 8–14

- ALT+click the last anchor point to remove the direction point and convert it to a corner point.

- Position the mouse pointer to align with 3 inches on the horizontal ruler and 2 inches on the vertical ruler.

- Drag up and to the right to create another curve.

- ALT+click the last anchor point to remove the direction point and convert it to a corner point (Figure 8–15).

- Position the mouse pointer to align with 4 inches on the horizontal ruler and 2 inches on the vertical ruler.

- Drag up and to the right to create another curve.

- ALT+click the last anchor point to remove the direction point and convert it to a corner point.

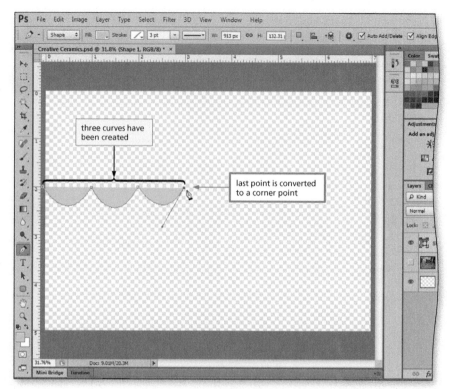

Figure 8–15

- Position the mouse pointer to align with 5 inches on the horizontal ruler and 2 inches on the vertical ruler.

- Drag up and to the right to create another curve.

- ALT+click the last anchor point to remove the direction point and convert it to a corner point.

- Position the mouse pointer to align with 6 inches on the horizontal ruler and 2 inches on the vertical ruler.

- Drag up and to the right to create another curve.

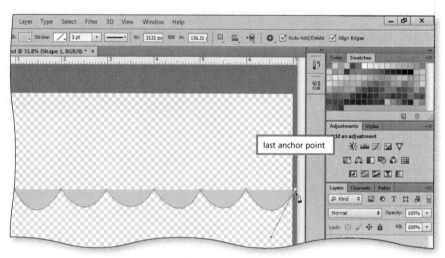

Figure 8–16

- ALT+click the last anchor point to remove the direction point and convert it to a corner point.

- Position the mouse pointer to align just to the right of 7 inches on the horizontal ruler and 2 inches on the vertical ruler. Your mouse pointer will be in the gray area to the right of the canvas.

- Drag up and to the right to create another curve.

- ALT+click the last anchor point to remove the direction point and convert it to a corner point (Figure 8–16).

Q&A What if I do not like the path or parts of it are wrong?

You can back up through your steps on the History panel or delete the path entirely and start again. Later in this chapter you will learn how to adjust path points by adding, deleting, converting, and moving them.

- Position the mouse pointer so that it is in the gray area just above and to the right of the upper-right corner of the canvas, then click once to add an anchor point without dragging.

- Point to the starting anchor point so the mouse pointer displays a small circle next to the pen icon, then click to close the path (Figure 8–17).

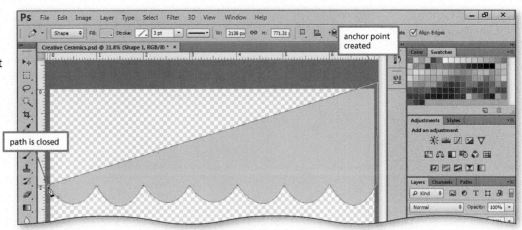

Figure 8–17

The upper-left area of the canvas is not filled with the shape. How can I fix this?

You will add points in the next steps to fix this.

To Add Anchor Points to a Shape

For precise adjustments along path segments, you sometimes need to insert additional anchor points. Photoshop creates direction lines automatically with each added anchor point to give you more flexibility in editing. The following steps add anchor points using the Add Anchor Point Tool.

- On the Tools panel, right-click the Pen Tool button to display the context menu (Figure 8–18).

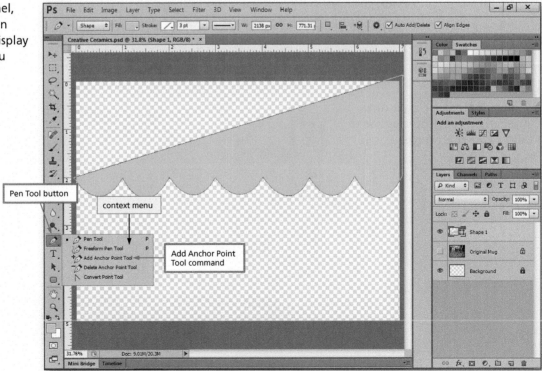

Figure 8–18

- Click Add Anchor Point Tool to select it.

- In the document window, click the middle of the top edge of the path to add an anchor point (Figure 8–19).

Q&A

Why did the mouse pointer display a plus sign?

The mouse pointer displays a plus sign (+) next to the tip of the pen when you add anchor points, and direction points appear.

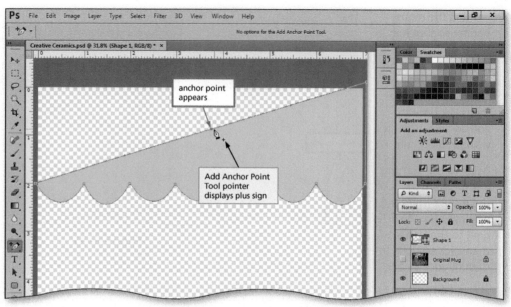

Figure 8–19

Other Ways

1. Right-click path, click Add Anchor Point
2. On the Pen Tool options bar, click Auto Add/ Delete, click Path

The Path Selection and Direct Selection Tools

Two tools are particularly useful to edit the shape and placement of paths by moving lines and anchor points. The Path Selection Tool moves the entire path. The Direct Selection Tool moves individual anchor points and direction points.

To Reposition an Anchor Point

The following steps select and move an anchor point with the Direct Selection Tool.

- On the Tools panel, right-click the Path Selection Tool button to display the context menu.

- Click Direct Selection Tool in the list (Figure 8–20).

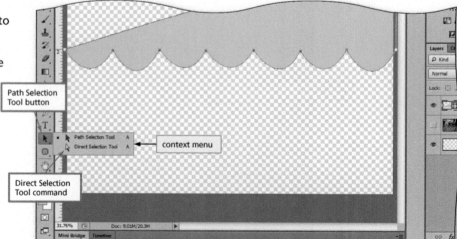

Figure 8–20

2

- Drag the new anchor point up and to the left to reposition the path so it fills the top portion of the canvas (Figure 8–21).

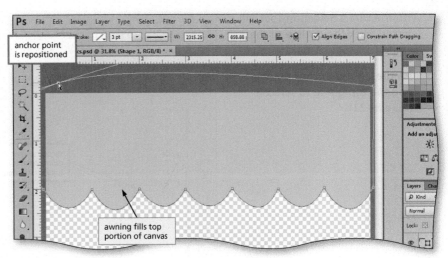

Figure 8–21

To Set Guides

The following steps create guides so that the curves of the awning can be altered to a uniform size.

1 Position the mouse pointer inside the horizontal ruler at the top of the screen.

2 Drag down until the pointer aligns with the 2-inch mark on the vertical ruler to place a horizontal guide across the canvas 2 inches from the top.

3 Drag down from the horizontal ruler at the top of the screen a second time until the pointer aligns with the 2.5-inch mark on the vertical ruler to create a second guide 2.5 inches down from the top.

To Use Direction Points

Recall that anchor points contain a direction line that extends in opposite directions out from the anchor point. The direction line contains a direction point on either end, as well as the center anchor point itself. Dragging a direction point alters the length and angle of the direction line, which in turn changes the shape of the path. Anchor points that have been converted to corner points contain a direction line that extends in a single direction on one side only of the anchor point. The following steps adjust the path using the direction points to tweak the shape of the awning.

1

- With the Direct Selection Tool still selected, click the outline of the awning to display its anchor points.

- Click the second anchor point along the top guide to select it (Figure 8–22).

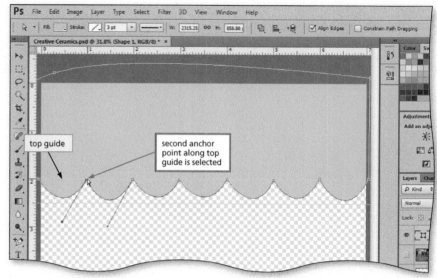

Figure 8–22

2

- Drag the anchor point until it aligns perfectly with 1 inch on the horizontal ruler and 2 inches on the vertical ruler (Figure 8–23).

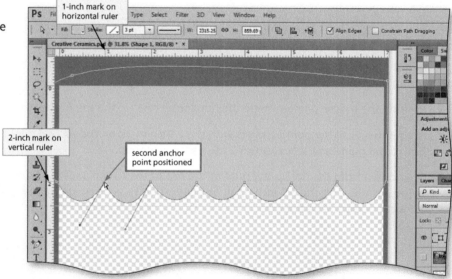

Figure 8–23

3

- Drag the endpoint of the second anchor point's direction line up or down until the bottom of the curve touches the bottom guide.

- Drag the endpoint of the direction line right or left until the curve is roughly symmetric (Figure 8–24).

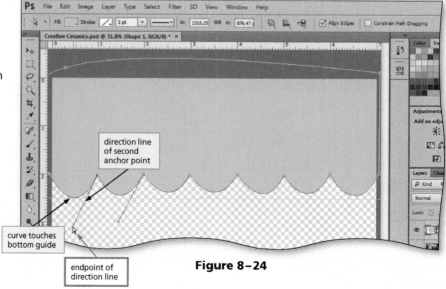

Figure 8–24

4

- Click the third anchor point along the top guide to display its direction line.

- Drag the anchor point until it aligns perfectly with 2 inches on the horizontal ruler and 2 inches on the vertical ruler.

- Drag the endpoint of the direction line until the curve is roughly symmetrical and the bottom of the curve touches the bottom guide (Figure 8–25).

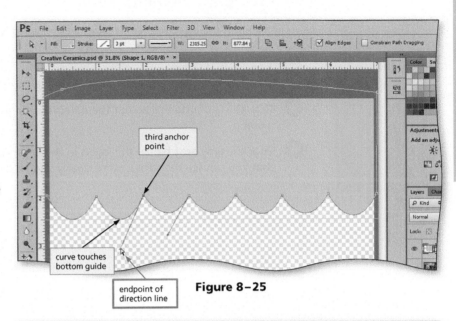

Figure 8–25

5

- Continue adjusting the remaining anchor points and curves along the top guide until the curves are uniformly shaped (Figure 8–26).

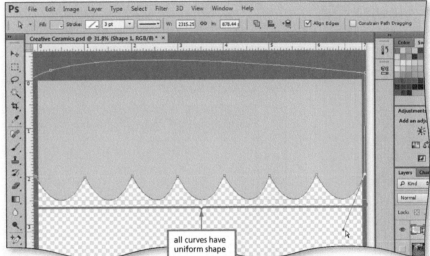

Figure 8–26

To Rename the Layer and Save the Document

The following steps rename the awning layer and save the document.

1 Double-click the Shape 1 layer name. Type `Awning` and then press the ENTER key to rename the layer.

2 Press CTRL+S to save the document.

To Create the Awning Outline

The following steps add a layer style to outline the awning using a stroke.

1 Click the 'Add a layer style' button on the Layers panel status bar to display its menu.

2 Click Stroke to display the Layer Style dialog box with the stroke settings.

3 Click the OK button to accept the default settings and add a 3-pixel black stroke to the awning.

4 Click the gray area below the layers in the Layers panel to deselect the Awning layer so that you can see the stroke more clearly (Figure 8–27).

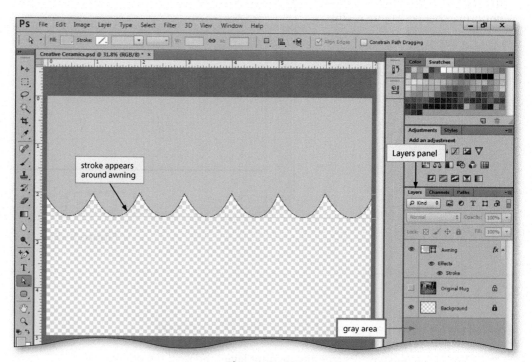

Figure 8–27

To Set the Foreground Color

The following step sets the foreground color for lines that will be drawn inside the awning.

1 Press the D key to reset the foreground and background colors to their default values.

To Create the Lines Layer

The following steps create a new layer above the Awning layer to hold the lines you will draw later.

1 Click the Awning layer on the Layers panel to select it.

2 Click the 'Create a new layer' button on the Layers panel status bar to create a new layer above the Awning layer.

3 Rename the new layer, Lines.

To Use a Shape Tool in Pixel Mode

The following steps use the Line Tool in pixel mode to draw straight lines on a new layer. The straight lines will add depth and dimension to the awning.

1

- On the Tools panel, right-click the current shape tool button to display the context menu and then click Line Tool to select it.

- On the options bar, click the 'Pick tool mode' button to display its menu.

- On the 'Pick tool mode' button, click Pixels to draw pixels rather than a shape.

- On the options bar, set the Weight to 3 px.

- Position the mouse pointer to the left of the canvas so that the horizontal line of the crosshair aligns with the top guide (Figure 8–28).

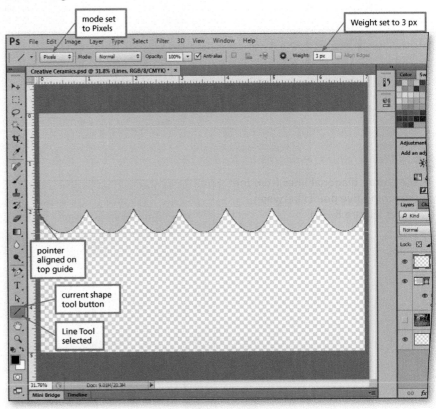

Figure 8–28

- SHIFT+drag to the right until the mouse pointer reaches the gray area beyond the right side of the canvas to draw a straight line along the top guide (Figure 8–29).

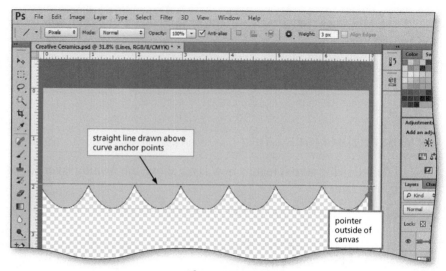

Figure 8–29

- Position the mouse pointer on the point where the first two curves meet.

- SHIFT+drag up and to the right to draw a diagonal line that extends off the top of the canvas (Figure 8–30).

Q&A Why do I need to hold the SHIFT key as I drag?

Holding the SHIFT key forces Photoshop to draw a horizontal, vertical, or 45-degree diagonal. This ensures that all the lines you draw will be parallel.

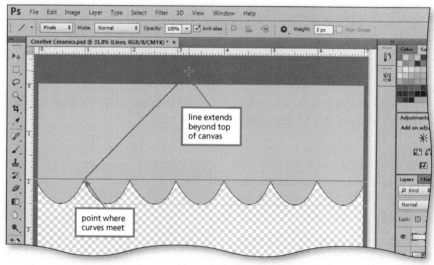

Figure 8–30

- SHIFT+drag diagonal lines from the remaining five points between curves (Figure 8–31).

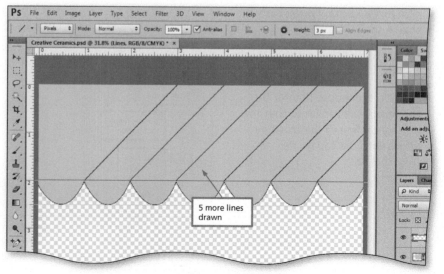

Figure 8–31

5

- Draw two more diagonal lines starting from outside the left edge of the canvas. You will have to estimate so that the lines are roughly evenly spaced (Figure 8–32).

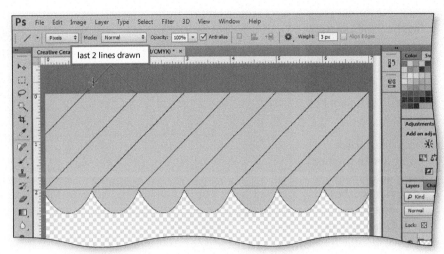

Figure 8–32

To Clear the Guides and Save the Document

The following steps clear the guides and save the document.

1 Click View on the Application bar, point to Show, and click Guides to hide the guides.

2 Press CTRL+S to save your changes.

To Fine-Tune a Shape

Sometimes, the shape outline is distracting and obscures details you need to see. To temporarily hide the outline, press CTRL+H. To show the outline again so that you can work with the anchor points and direction lines, press CTRL+H again. The following steps adjust the position of the anchor points between the curves to match the diagonal lines, hiding and showing the outline as necessary.

1

- Double-click the Zoom Tool on the Tools panel to zoom to 100%.

- Drag the horizontal scroll bar to the left to scroll to the left edge of the canvas.

- Examine the point where the first two curves meet. The one shown in Figure 8–33 does not touch the horizontal or diagonal line.

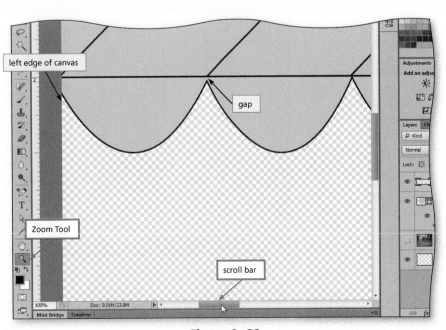

Figure 8–33

2

- Click the Awning layer on the Layers panel to select it.

- Click the Direct Selection Tool button on the Tools panel to select it.

- Drag the anchor point where the first two curves meet so that it touches the horizontal and diagonal lines (Figure 8–34).

 Experiment

- Press CTRL+H to hide the outline so that you can more clearly see the anchor point. Press CTRL+H again to make the outline visible and drag the anchor point as necessary.

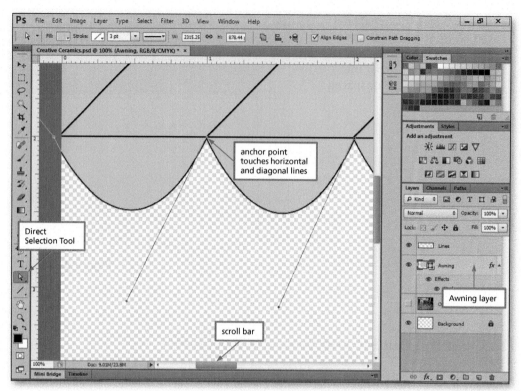

Figure 8–34

3

- Drag the horizontal scroll bar to the right until you can see the next curve.

- Drag the next anchor point into position so that it touches the horizontal and diagonal lines (Figure 8–35).

- Hide the outline to view the anchor point, make the outline visible, and then drag the anchor point as necessary.

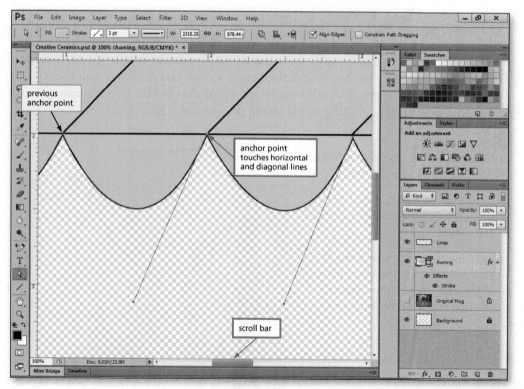

Figure 8–35

4

- Continue scrolling the canvas and dragging the anchor points between the curves until all the anchor points touch the horizontal and diagonal lines and there are no gaps, pressing CTRL+H as necessary to hide/show the outline.

- When you are finished repositioning the anchor points, double-click the Hand Tool to fit the canvas to your screen.

- If the shape outline is not visible, press CTRL+H to make it visible (Figure 8–36).

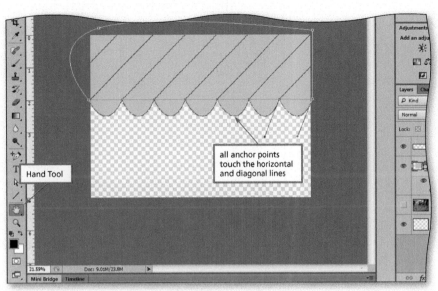

Figure 8–36

To Save the Document

The following step saves the document.

1 Press CTRL+S to save the document.

Break Point: If you wish to take a break, this is a good place to do so. You can quit Photoshop now. To resume at a later time, start Photoshop, open the file called Creative Ceramics, and continue following the steps from this location forward.

Paths

If you select the Paths menu option on the Shapes options bar, the path does not create a shape layer on the Layers panel; instead, it becomes a path or work path on the Paths panel. The Paths panel (Figure 8–37 on the next page) lists the name and a thumbnail image of each saved path, the current work path, and the current vector mask. Once created, you can use a path to make a selection, create a vector mask, or fill and stroke with color to create raster graphics. A **work path** is a temporary path that opens in the Paths panel and defines the outline of the shape until you save or rename it. If you need to create a complex shape, you can begin by creating multiple paths and then combine them into a single shape.

BTW

Viewing Anchor Points
If you want to see a line while you create new anchor points, you can click the Geometry options button on the options bar. One of the geometry options for the Pen Tool is a Rubber Band check box. The Rubber Band feature helps guide the next anchor point by displaying a stretch line between anchor points, even before you click.

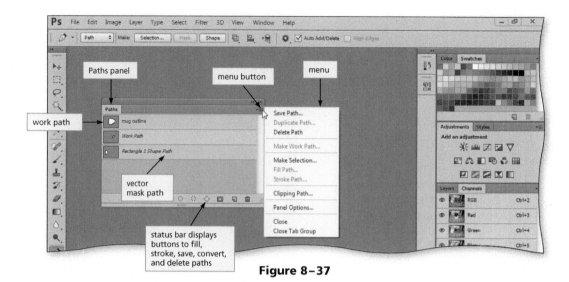

Figure 8–37

To Ready the Layers

The following steps toggle the visibility of the Lines, Awning, and Original Mug layers so that you can trace the mug.

 1 Click the 'Indicates layer visibility' button on the Lines layer on the Layers panel to hide it.

2 Click the 'Indicates layer visibility' button on the Awning layer to hide it.

3 Click the 'Indicates layer visibility' button on the Original Mug layer to show it.

To Create a Work Path using the Pen Tool

In the Creative Ceramics document window, you will use the Pen Tool to create two paths — one for a mug and one for the space inside the handle. You will then combine the two paths into a single shape. The following steps create a work path around the mug using the Pen Tool.

1

- On the Layers panel, click the Original Mug layer to select it.

- Select the Pen Tool.

- On the options bar, click the 'Pick tool mode' button and then click Path to select the mode that creates a path on the Paths panel (Figure 8–38).

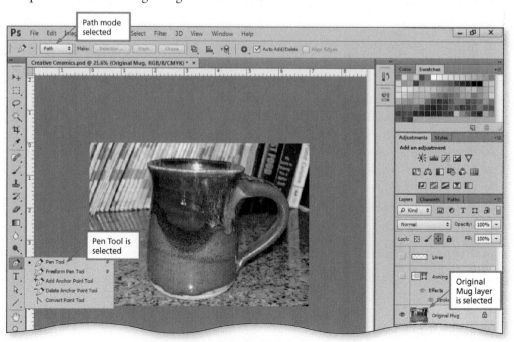

Figure 8–38

- Click the top-center of the mug to create the first anchor point.

- Click the top-left side of the mug, along the rim, to create the second anchor point and drag slightly down and left to follow the curve of the rim (Figure 8–39).

Figure 8–39

- ALT+click the second anchor point to convert it to a corner point.

- Click the left side of the mug where the blue changes to brown and drag slightly down and left to follow the curve (Figure 8–40).

Figure 8–40

- ALT+click the third anchor point to convert it to a corner point.

- Click the lower-left area of the mug where the side meets the base and drag slightly down and right to follow the curve of the mug.

- ALT+click the fourth anchor point to convert it to a corner point.

- Click the bottom-right area of the mug where the base meets the right side and drag slightly up and right to follow the curve.

- ALT+click the fifth anchor point to convert it to a corner point.

Figure 8–41

- Click the right side of the mug where the bottom of the handle meets the right edge and drag up and to the right to follow the curve.

- ALT+click the sixth anchor point to convert it to a corner point (Figure 8–41).

- Click the right-most edge of the handle to create the seventh anchor point and drag up and right. The bottom of this curve will not exactly match the curve of the handle.

- ALT+click the seventh anchor point to convert it to a corner point.

- Click the upper-right area where the top of the handle meets the mug to create the eighth anchor point and drag left to follow the curve of the handle.

- ALT+click the eighth anchor point to convert it to a corner point.

Figure 8–42

- Click the first anchor point to close the path and drag left to follow the curve of the rim (Figure 8–42).

Q&A

Why does the path not follow the handle exactly?

Because of where the anchor points were placed, the curve cannot be duplicated exactly. If it is important to you to follow the shape exactly, you can use the Direct Selection Tool to adjust the position of the anchor points and direction lines. However, when creating clip art, you rarely have to be concerned with getting an exact match.

To Display the Paths Panel

The following step displays the Paths panel and the work path that was created in the previous steps.

❶

- Click the Paths panel tab to display the Paths panel (Figure 8–43).

Figure 8–43

To Save a Work Path as a Named Path

Because work paths are temporary, the following step saves and names the path.

1

- On the Paths panel, double-click the Work Path name, type Mug Outline, and press the ENTER key to rename the path.

Q&A Why should I rename the path?

Renaming a Work Path saves the path. If you did not rename the Work Path, it would disappear as soon as the path was deselected.

- Click the gray area of the Paths panel below the Mug Outline path to deselect it (Figure 8–44).

path is renamed

clicking gray area deselects path

Figure 8–44

Other Ways

1. On Paths panel menu, click Save Path, enter name, deselect

To Create a Path using the Freeform Pen Tool

The following steps create a path around the space inside the handle, which is required to create the hole. You will use the magnetic option of the Freeform Pen Tool to draw around the inside of the handle. The magnetism is similar to the Magnetic Lasso Tool in that the marquee is attracted to the edge of the object around which you drag. As you move the mouse pointer using the magnetic option, work slowly. If the line goes astray, move the mouse backward. If several points become misaligned, press the ESC key and begin again.

1

- On the Tools panel, right-click the current Pen Tool button to display the context menu.

- Click Freeform Pen Tool to select it.

- On the options bar, click the Magnetic check box so that it displays a check mark (Figure 8–45).

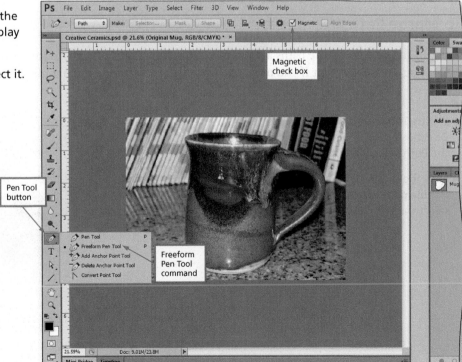

Magnetic check box

Pen Tool button

Freeform Pen Tool command

Figure 8–45

- Click the bottom corner of the inside of the handle where the handle meets the side of the mug, and then release the mouse button.

- Drag slowly around the inside of the handle, keeping the point of the pen icon on the inside edge of the handle.

- When you return to the starting point, point to the first anchor point so that the mouse pointer displays a small circle indicating the path will be closed (Figure 8–46).

- Click the first anchor point to close the path.

freehand path drawn inside handle

pointer displays circle when over first anchor point

Figure 8–46

To Save the Second Path

The following steps save the path and the document.

1 On the Paths panel, double-click the Work Path name, type `Inside Handle` to rename the path, and press the ENTER key to rename the path.

2 Press CTRL+S to save your changes.

To Merge Paths

In the next steps, the paths are merged. Merging makes the mug outline and the space inside the handle into a single shape, so that if you move the mug, the space inside the handle moves too.

- On the Tools panel, right-click the Direct Selection Tool and then click the Path Selection Tool to select it.

- Click the outline of the Inside Handle path on the canvas to select the path (Figure 8–47).

path displays anchor points when selected

Path Selection Tool

Figure 8–47

- Press CTRL+C to copy the path.

- On the Paths panel, click the Mug Outline path to select it.

- Press CTRL+V to paste the copied space path to the Mug Outline path (Figure 8–48).

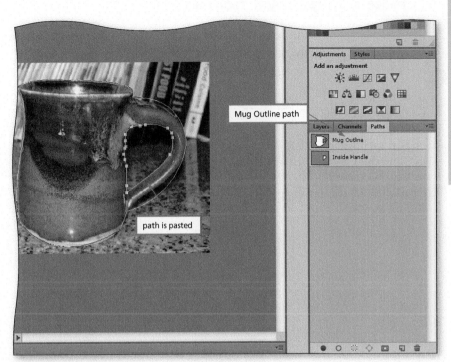

Figure 8–48

To Delete and Rename Paths

Because the two paths have been combined into a single path, the Inside Handle path is no longer needed. Additionally, the path name Mug Outline no longer describes the new merged path, because it now contains the hole inside the handle. In the following step, you will delete the Inside Handle path and rename the Mug Outline path.

- Click the Inside Handle path on the Paths panel to select it.

- Click the 'Delete current path' button on the Paths panel status bar to delete the Inside Handle path.

- Click the Yes button when prompted to confirm the deletion.

- Rename the Mug Outline path, `Mug Complete` (Figure 8–49).

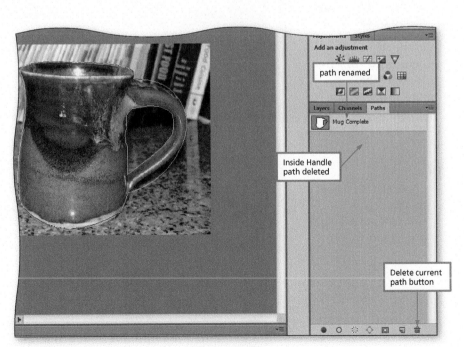

Figure 8–49

To Create a Shape Layer from a Path

The merged path now includes shapes that represent the mug. The following steps create a new shape layer, consisting of the merged path that can be colored.

1

- With the Mug Complete path still selected, click Layer on the application bar, and then point to New Fill Layer to display the fill choices (Figure 8–50).

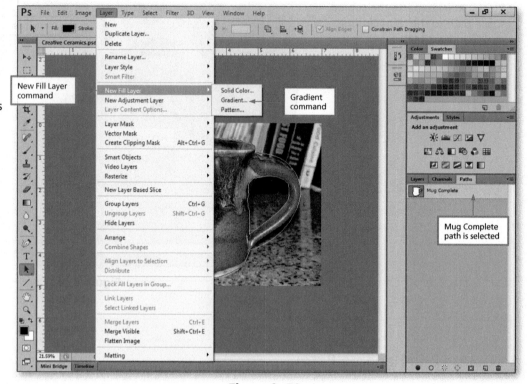

Figure 8–50

2

- Click Gradient to display the New Layer dialog box.

- In the Name box, type Mug Shape to name the new shape layer (Figure 8–51).

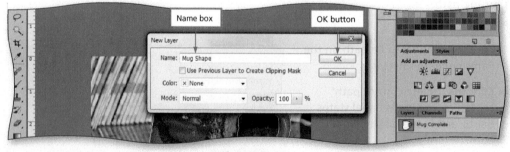

Figure 8–51

3

- Click the OK button to display the Gradient Fill dialog box (Figure 8–52).

Figure 8–52

4

- Click the 'Click to edit the gradient' color bar to display Gradient Editor dialog box.

- Click the left color stop button to select it (Figure 8–53).

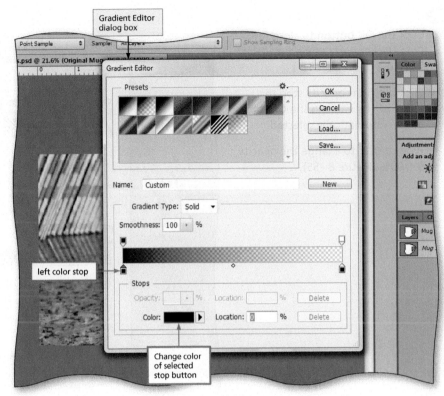

Gradient Editor dialog box

left color stop

Change color of selected stop button

Figure 8–53

5

- Click the 'Change color of selected stop' button to display the Color Picker (Stop Color) dialog box.

- Clear the Only Web Colors check box, if necessary, so it does not display a check mark.

- Click the lower-right area of the color box to select a dark red color (Figure 8–54).

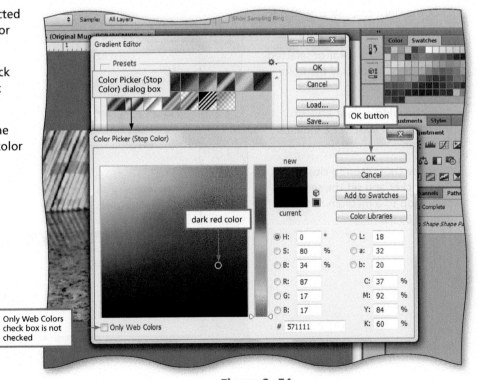

Color Picker (Stop Color) dialog box

OK button

dark red color

Only Web Colors check box is not checked

Figure 8–54

6

- Click the OK button to close the Color Picker and set the first color stop to a dark red.

- Click the right opacity stop to select it. The value in the Opacity box is automatically selected.

- Type 100 to change the opacity to 100% (Figure 8–55).

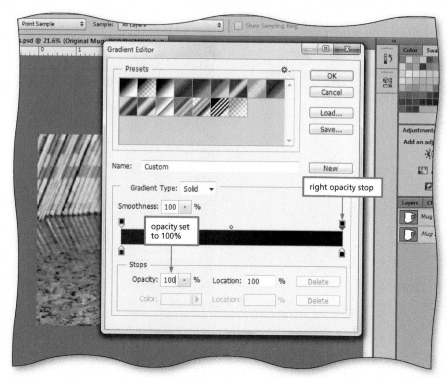

Figure 8–55

7

- Click the right color stop button to select it.

- Click the 'Change color of selected stop' button to display the Color Picker dialog box.

- Click the middle-right area of the color box to select a medium red color.

- Click the OK button to close the Color Picker and set the second color stop to a medium red (Figure 8–56).

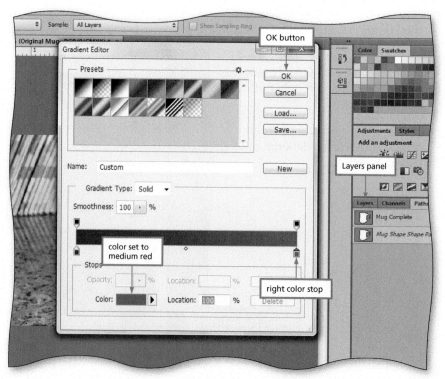

Figure 8–56

8

- Click the OK button to close the Gradient Editor dialog box.

- Click the OK button to close the Gradient Fill dialog box and apply the fill.

- Click the Layers panel to display the layers (Figure 8–57).

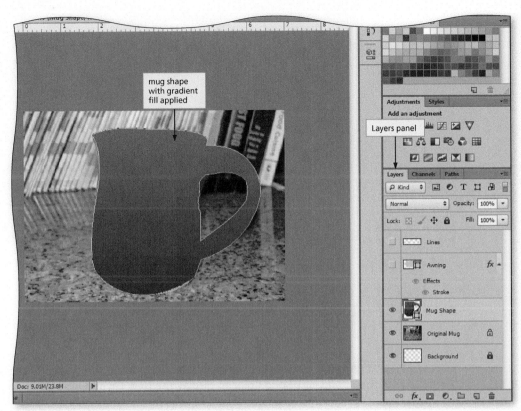

Figure 8–57

To Create a Path for a New Shape Layer

The following steps create a path that will be converted to a new shape layer to simulate coffee or hot chocolate in the mug.

1. Click the 'Indicates layer visibility' button of the Mug Shape layer on the Layers panel to hide it so you can see the original mug again.

2. Right-click the current Pen Tool button on the Tools panel and select the Pen Tool.

3. Click the top of the bright white highlight inside the top of the mug to create the first anchor point.

4. Click the edge of the lower lip of the mug's rim to create the second anchor point, and then drag right and down to curve the path along the left edge of the rim.

5. Click the first anchor point to close the path, then and drag slightly left and up to create a curve on the right side (Figure 8–58 on the next page).

Figure 8–58

To Create a Shape Layer

The following steps create a new shape layer.

1 Click Layer on the Application bar to display the Layer menu, point to New Fill Layer, and click Solid Color to display the New Layer dialog box.

2 Type `Liquid` in the Name box and click the OK button to create the new layer and display the Color Picker dialog box.

3 Click toward the bottom center of the color box to select dark grayish red, and then click the OK button to close the Color Picker.

4 Click the 'Indicates layer visibility' button on the Mug Shape layer to show the mug.

5 Click the Background layer so that the Liquid layer is deselected and the path outline no longer appears (Figure 8–59).

Figure 8–59

To Create Highlights

The following steps draw a shape to create highlights, adding depth and dimension to the mug.

1 Press the D key to reset the default foreground and background colors.

2 Press the X key to reverse the foreground and background colors so that white is on top.

3 Click the Lines layer to select it so that the new layer is created above it.

4 Set the 'Pick tool mode' button in the options bar to Shape (Figure 8–60) so that you create a shape rather than a path.

5 Position the mouse pointer at the 2-inch mark on the horizontal ruler and the 1-inch mark on the vertical ruler, and then click once to create the first anchor point.

6 Align your mouse pointer at the 4-inch mark on the horizontal ruler and the 1-inch mark on the vertical ruler, click to create the second anchor point, and drag slightly up and to the right to create a shallow curved path.

7 Align your mouse pointer at the 3.5-inch mark on the horizontal ruler and the 1.25-inch mark on the vertical ruler, click to create the third anchor point, and drag left until your mouse pointer is about even with the first anchor point.

8 Click the first anchor point to close the path and drag slightly up and to the right to create a curved end on the left side of the path.

9 Rename the new layer, Highlight Top.

10 Click the Path Selection Tool on the Tools panel and drag the highlight on the canvas into its final position. Use Figure 8–60 as a reference.

11 Set the Opacity at the top of the Layers panel to 20% to reduce the opacity of the Highlight Top layer.

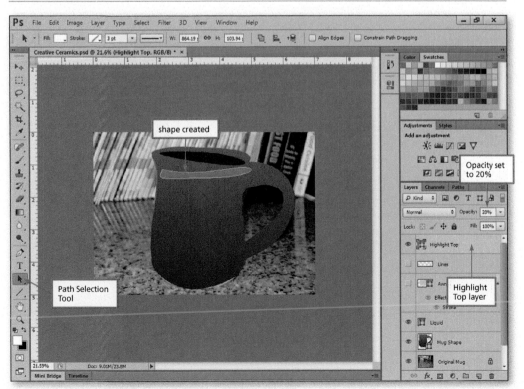

Figure 8–60

To Save the Document

The following step saves the document.

 Press CTRL+S to save the document.

Layer Groups

A **layer group** is a named folder on the Layers panel that is used to contain a collection of layers. Layers can be created within the folder or moved into the folder. The number of additional layers, layer effects, and layer groups is limited only by the computer's memory capacity. The New Group command creates an empty group. The New Group from Layers command creates a group and places the selected layers in it.

When you create a new layer group, you can specify its name, its identifying color on the Layers panel, a blending mode, and an opacity setting. The settings apply to all layers created in, or moved to, the group. A layer group is displayed on the panel with a folder icon and with a triangle, called a Hide/Show layers icon, that points down to reveal the individual layers in the group, or points right to hide them (Figure 8–61). The icon does not affect the document window, however. The visibility icon determines whether the layer group is hidden or is displayed in the document window. Just like layers, a hidden layer group does not print.

Layer groups can be nested. This is helpful when you need to subdivide a large group into several smaller related groups. To nest layer groups, drag a layer group on top of another layer group in the Layers panel. To undo the nesting, drag the nested group out. Pay close attention to the Layers panel; as you drag, Photoshop displays borders to help identify the drop zones.

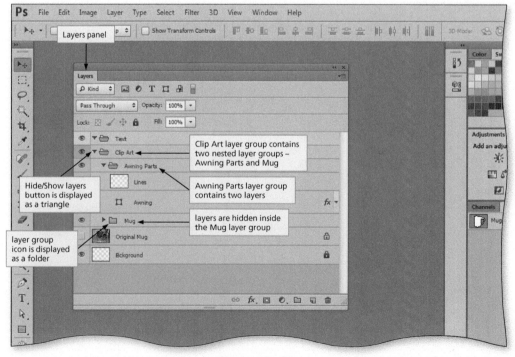

Figure 8–61

To Create a Layer Group from Layers

Four layer groups will eventually be created for the Creative Ceramics document: one to hold shapes related to the mug, one group holding the awning layers, one group to hold both the mug and awning as nested groups, and one final group for the text, which you create in a later exercise.

1

- Click the Highlight Top layer in the Layers panel to select it, if necessary.

- CTRL+click the Liquid layer and the the Mug Shape layer to add them to the selection (Figure 8–62).

Figure 8–62

2

- Click the Layers panel menu button to display the menu (Figure 8–63).

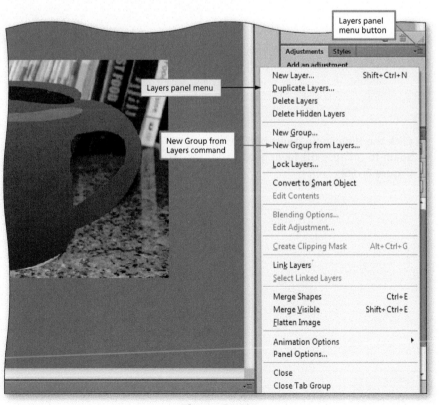

Figure 8–63

- Click New Group from Layers to display the New Group from Layers dialog box.

- Type Mug in the Name text box. Click the Color box arrow, and then click Green in the list to change the color for the new layer group (Figure 8–64).

Q&A
What does Pass Through mean in the Mode box?

Pass Through is the default blending mode for layer groups and means the group will have no blending properties of its own.

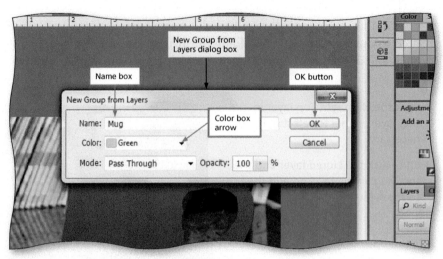

Figure 8–64

- Click the OK button to create the new layer group.

- Click the Hide/Show layers button on the Mug layer group to expand it and see its contents (Figure 8–65).

Q&A
How do I know that the Highlight Top, Liquid, and Mug Shape layers are inside the layer group?

On the Layers panel, layers within the layer group are indented.

Figure 8–65

- Click the Hide/Show layers button again to collapse the layer group (Figure 8–66).

Figure 8–66

Other Ways

1. On Layer menu, point to New, click Group from Layers
2. Click 'Create a new group' button
3. Select layers, press CTRL+G

To Create Another Group from Layers

The following steps create one more layer group.

1 Click the 'Indicates layer visibility' button on the Original Mug to hide it.

2 Click the 'Indicates layer visibility' button on the Lines layer to make it visible.

3 Click the 'Indicates layer visibility' button on the Awning layer to make it visible.

4 Click the Lines layer to select it.

5 CTRL+click the Awning layer to select it.

6 Click the Layers panel menu button to display the menu.

7 Click New Group from Layers to display the New Group from Layers dialog box.

8 Type `Awning Parts` in the Name box, select Orange as the layer group color, and click the OK button (New Group from Layers dialog box) to create the layer group.

9 Click the Hide/Show layers icon to the left of the Awning Parts layer group to view its contents.

10 Click the Hide/Show layers icon again to collapse the layer group.

To Create a New Empty Layer Group

The following step creates two new empty layer groups, rather than groups from layers. Later, you will add layers to them.

1

- Display the Layers panel menu and then click New Group.

- Name the group, Clip Art, assign Red as the color, and click the OK button to create the first new empty group.

- ALT+click the 'Create a new group' button on the Layers panel status bar to create a group named, Text, assign Yellow as the color, and click the OK button to create the second new empty group (Figure 8–67).

Figure 8–67

Q&A Why did I ALT+click the 'Create a new group' button rather than single click it?

When you ALT+click the 'Create a new group' button, the New Group dialog box appears, allowing you to name and set other options for the layer group.

To Nest Layer Groups

Nesting layer groups helps to organize your content. The following step nests the Mug and Awning Parts groups inside the Clip Art layer group.

①

- On the Layers panel, drag the Awning Parts layer group into the Clip Art layer group to move Awning Parts into the Clip Art group.

- Drag the Mug layer group into the Clip Art layer to nest it (Figure 8–68).

Q&A Why does the mug now appear behind the awning?

Contents are arranged in the order in which they are placed in a layer group. Because the Awning Parts layer group was added first, it is on top. If another layer or layer group were added to the Clip Art layer group, it would be placed under the Mug layer group. You always can drag the layers and layer groups to reposition them.

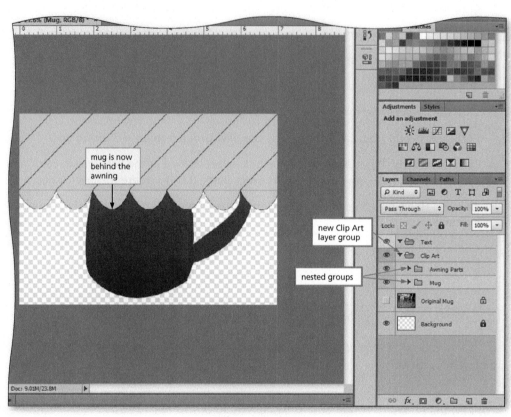

Figure 8–68

Q&A How do I know I am moving the Awning Parts group inside the Clip Art group rather than just changing the stacking order?

The Clip Art layer group displays a border around all four sides before you release the mouse button. This indicates that the dragged Awning Parts layer group will be placed inside the Clip Art layer group.

To Resize Layer Group Contents

When a layer group is scaled, rotated, or otherwise transformed, its contents are transformed as if they were a single object. The next steps resize the mug to fit beneath the awning.

① On the Layers panel, click the Mug layer group to select it.

② Press CTRL+T to display the free transform border around the Mug layer group.

3 SHIFT+drag the upper-right corner of the Mug's border toward the center of the mug until the entire mug is visible.

4 Drag the mug to the right until it is roughly centered below the last three awning curves.

5 Press the ENTER key to apply the transformation and the move.

6 Press CTRL+S to save the document.

Using Text with Vector Shapes

The gold seal that is displayed in Figure 8–1 on page PS 483 is made up of a custom shape and a text element. You will append the Banners and Awards library of shapes using the Shape Preset picker. Then you will add the text. Text created in a vector shape will automatically adjust to fit the shape. Both components will become layers within the Text layer group that you created earlier.

To Create the Seal using a Custom Shape

On page PS 525, you created a layer group named, Text. The following steps create the award shape in the Text layer group using the Shape Preset picker.

1

- On the Layers panel, click the Text layer group.

- On the Tools panel, right-click the current Shape Tool button, and then click Custom Shape Tool.

- On the options bar, click the 'Pick tool mode' button, and then click Shape if necessary, to select it.

- On the options bar, click the 'Set shape fill type' button and then click the Pure Yellow swatch to set the fill color of the shape.

- Click the Custom Shape picker button, and then click the Custom Shape picker menu button to display the Shapes menu (Figure 8–69).

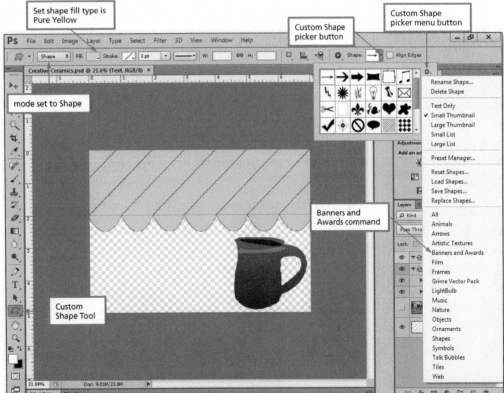

Figure 8–69

2

- Click Banners and Awards to load that library of shapes.

- Click the OK button when prompted to replace the current shapes.

- Click the Seal shape in the Custom Shape picker.

- In the document window, SHIFT+drag a shape that almost fills the space to the left of the mug.

- If necessary, use the Move Tool to reposition the shape.

- Rename the new shape layer, Seal (Figure 8–70).

Figure 8–70

To Reset the Custom Shapes

The following steps reset the default shapes.

1 Click the Custom Shape Tool on the Tools panel to select it, if necessary.

2 Click the Custom Shape picker button, and then click the Custom Shape picker menu button to display the Shapes menu.

3 Click Reset Shapes and then click the OK button to reset the custom shapes to the default settings.

4 Press the ESC key to close the Custom Shape picker.

Text within a Shape

The next step is to create a type element within the seal. Text created in a vector shape will automatically adjust to fit the shape. The type settings for the seal shape are shown in Table 8–4.

Table 8–4 Type Tool Settings	
Type Option	**Setting**
Set the font family	Bookman Old Style or a similar font
Set the font style	Regular
Set the font size	30 pt
Set the anti-aliasing method	Smooth
Set the text alignment	Centered
Set the text color	Black

To Create Text within a Shape

The following steps create text in the seal.

1

- Press the T key to access the current Type Tool.

- On the options bar, enter the settings from Table 8–4.

- In the document window, point to the seal (Figure 8–71).

Q&A Why did the mouse pointer change?

The dotted oval mouse pointer indicates that the text will be created inside the shape, rather than as a new text box where the mouse pointer would display a rectangular shape around the insertion point.

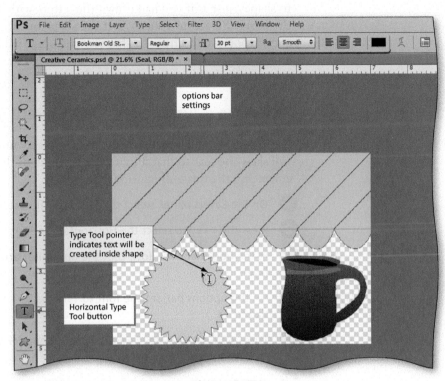

Figure 8–71

2

- Click the shape and then type `Grand Opening May 1st` to enter the text (Figure 8–72).

- On the options bar, click the 'Commit any current edits' button to close the text box.

- On the Tools panel, click the Move Tool and reposition the text as necessary.

Q&A What should I do if my text does not fit in the seal correctly?

Make the seal slightly larger by pressing CTRL+T to enter free transform mode. Drag the sizing handle of the bounding box to scale the shape, and then press the ENTER key to apply the change. Alternatively, you can change the font size by a few points.

Figure 8–72

Converting Text to a Shape

If you cannot find the exact font you want, you can start with a font that is similar and then convert the text to a shape. This converts the letters on the type layer to shapes, just as if you had drawn the letters with the Pen Tool. You then can use the Direct Selection Tool to alter the shape of each letter just as you would alter the anchor points and lines of a shape or path. You will create a type layer, skew the text, and finally convert it to a shape and manipulate it.

To Create a Type Layer and Convert Text to a Shape

You will add a regular type layer to the awning in the following steps. You then will skew the text so that it matches the angle of the lines on the awning, further enhancing the three-dimensional effect.

1. On the Layers panel, select the Seal layer if necessary.

2. Press the T key to select the Horizontal Type Tool, if necessary.

3. In the document window, click the upper-left area of the awning to create a new type layer.

4. On the options bar, set the font to Tahoma, the font style to Bold, and the font size to 48.

5. Type Creative Ceramics and then click the 'Commit any current edits' button to close the text box.

6. If necessary, use the Move Tool to reposition the text.

7. On the Application bar, click Edit, point to Transform, and then click Skew.

8. Drag the top-center handle of the text border to the right until the tip box indicates an angle of about -45 degrees so the skew matches the angle of the awning lines (Figure 8–73).

9. Press the ENTER key to apply the transformation.

10. Use the Move Tool, if necessary, to position the text so it is roughly centered horizontally in the awning.

tip box indicates approximately -45 degrees

Figure 8–73

To Convert Text to a Shape

The following step converts the Creative Ceramics text to a shape, which gives you the ability to manipulate the letters for visual interest.

- Click Type on the Application bar to display the Type menu.

- Click Convert to Shape to convert the text to a shape (Figure 8–74).

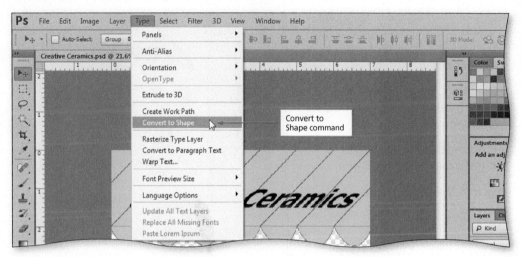

Figure 8–74

To Alter the Shape of Letters

The following steps alter the shape of the letters.

- Press the A key to select the Direct Selection Tool.

- Click the outline of the capital C in Creative to select it.

- Press CTRL+T to display the free transform border around the shape (Figure 8–75).

Q&A

What if the Path Selection Tool was selected instead?

Because both the Path Selection Tool and the Direct Selection Tool use the same keyboard shortcut, A, you can press SHIFT+A to switch between the tools. If the Path Selection Tool is selected, press SHIFT+A to switch to the Direct Selection Tool.

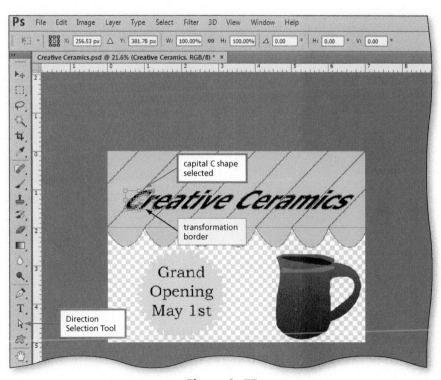

Figure 8–75

- Drag the bottom-center handle of the border down until it snaps to the horizontal line across the awning.

- CTRL+SHIFT+drag the bottom-center handle of the border to the left to skew it until the tip box indicates a skew of about -20 degrees.

- Drag the C shape up until it is roughly centered vertically next to the lowercase 'r'.

- Press the ENTER key to apply the transformation (Figure 8–76).

Figure 8–76

- Repeat steps 1 and 2 for the capital C in Ceramics.

- Click a transparent area of the canvas to deselect the C (Figure 8–77).

Figure 8–77

To Save the Document

The following step saves the document.

 Press CTRL+S to save the document.

Clip Art Detail

Good clip art uses strong lines and colors with enough detail to emphasize the purpose of the image. A clip art's purpose might be as simple as object identification requiring modest detail, or as complex as an idea within a context that might require intensive detail to get the point across. Movement, depth, and light play important roles in clip art, but without purpose, context, and visual detail, sometimes clip art is flat, static, and unsophisticated. In the following sections, you will add detail to the clip art, including overlays, layer styles, and shadows. Figure 8–78 displays examples of color overlays, shadows, and reflections.

Figure 8–78

Add detail to enhance clip art.
There are many ways to add detail to vector graphics and clip art, including overlays, layer styles, shadows, blending modes, and reflections. Make sure each of your edits is purposeful and not distracting. It is best to create a new layer for each enhancement.

Plan
Ahead

To Fill a Shape with a Pattern

Clip art sometimes is created using layer styles to add detail. Recall that layer styles affect the appearance of the layer by adding depth, shadow, shading, texture, or overlay. The following steps use a layer style to add texture to the awning.

1

- On the Tools panel, double-click the Hand Tool to fit the document to the screen.

- On the Layers panel, click the triangle to the left of the Text layer group to hide its contents, if necessary.

- On the Layers panel, click the triangle to the left of the Clip Art layer group to show its contents, if necessary.

- On the Layers panel, click the triangle to the left of the Awning Parts layer group to show its contents, if necessary.

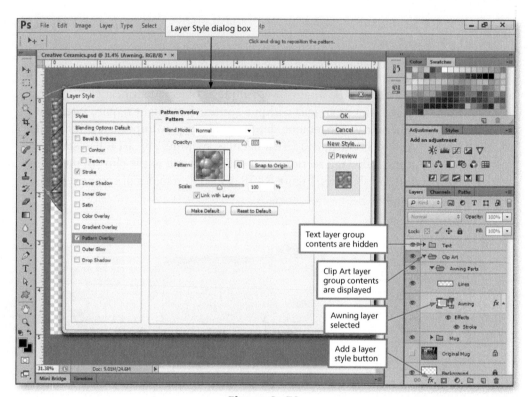

Figure 8–79

- Select the Awning layer.

- Click the 'Add a layer style' button on the Layers panel status bar to display the list of layer styles.

- Click Pattern Overlay to display the Layer Style dialog box (Figure 8–79).

2

- In the Layer Style dialog box, click the Pattern picker to display thumbnails of the current patterns.

- Click the third thumbnail, Laid-horizontal (256 by 256 pixels , RGB mode), to select it.

- Set the opacity to 20% (Figure 8–80).

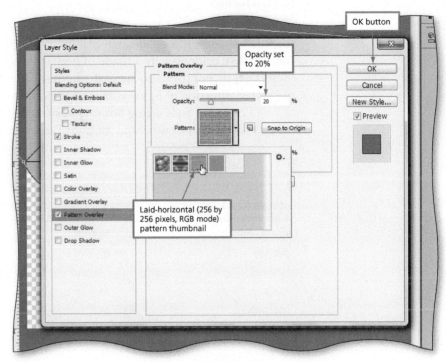

Figure 8–80

 3

- Click the OK button (Layer Style dialog box) to apply the pattern (Figure 8–81).

Figure 8–81

Shadows

Another typical way to add detail to a clip art is by using shadows to represent depth. A **shadow** is a small extension on one or two sides of a graphic with a different, unobtrusive color, usually a shade of gray with no visible border. Shadows not only depict depth, but they also suggest a light source. A shadow is displayed opposite the perceived direction of light, or behind the object.

The Layer Style dialog box is an easy way to add a shadow. You will use a layer style to create a drop shadow behind the award seal with the settings shown in Table 8–5.

Table 8–5 Drop Shadow Settings	
Drop Shadow Effect	**Setting**
Blend Mode	Multiply
Opacity	80
Use Global Light	Checked
Angle	150
Distance	15
Spread	20
Size	15
Noise	0
Contour	Linear
Anti-aliased	Unchecked
Layer Knocks Out Drop Shadow	Checked

To Add a Shadow using a Layer Style

The following steps add a shadow to the award seal.

1 On the Layers panel, expand the Text layer group and select the Seal layer.

2 On the Layers panel status bar, click the 'Add a layer style' button, and then click Drop Shadow on the list.

3 Enter the settings from Table 8–5 in the Layer Style dialog box.

4 Click the OK button (Layer Style dialog box) to apply the settings.

To Copy and Paste a Layer Style

You can copy a previously created layer style and apply it to other layers in the document. The following steps copy the shadow you applied to the Seal layer and paste it to the Awning layer and the Mug layer group.

1 On the Layers panel, right-click the layer name, Seal, to display the context menu. Do not right-click the layer thumbnail.

2 Click Copy Layer Style to copy the style to the Clipboard.

3 Scroll down in the Layers panel until you see the Awning layer.

④ Right-click the Awning shape layer to display the context menu.

⑤ Click Paste Layer Style to paste the style to the Awning layer.

⑥ Right-click the Mug layer group to display the context menu.

⑦ Click Paste Layer Style to paste the style to the Mug layer group (Figure 8–82).

Figure 8–82

Bevels

A **bevel** adds highlights and shadows to create a three-dimensional effect. An **inner bevel** adds the shading to the inside of a shape, while an **outer bevel** adds the shading to the outside of a shape. An inner bevel usually creates more of a three-dimensional look.

You will use a layer style to create an inner bevel on the mug.

To Add a Bevel using a Layer Style

The following steps add a three-dimensional bevel to the mug.

① On the Layers panel, click the Mug layer group to select it, if necessary, to apply the effect to the entire layer group.

② On the Layers panel status bar, click the 'Add a layer style' button, and then click Bevel & Emboss on the list.

③ Set the Size to 100 and the Highlight Mode's Opacity to 40. Leave all other settings at their default.

④ Click the OK button (Layer Style dialog box) to apply the settings.

To Rotate the Mug

The following steps rotate the mug to add visual interest.

1 Press CTRL+T to display the free transform border around the mug.

2 Point outside the mug's border so that the mouse pointer displays a curved arrow.

3 Drag left to rotate the mug slightly.

4 Drag the mug up until it almost reaches the awning.

5 Press the ENTER key to apply the transformation.

To Fade the Awning Lines

The following steps fade the awning lines by reducing the opacity, so they blend better with the awning and are less dominant.

1 On the Layers panel, click the Lines layer to select it.

2 At the top of the Layers panel, set the Opacity to 30%.

To Create a Background Gradient

The following steps complete the document by adding a gradient background.

1 On the Layers panel, collapse any open layer groups so the Layers panel appears less cluttered.

2 Click the bottom layer, Background, to select it.

Click the Lock all button to toggle the lock off.

4 Press the D key to reset the colors to their default settings of black and white.

5 On the Swatches panel, click Pale Cool Brown to set the foreground color.

6 Click Layer on the Application bar, point to New Fill Layer, and click Gradient to display the New Layer dialog box.

7 Click the OK button (New Layer dialog box) to accept the default settings and display the Gradient Fill dialog box.

8 Click the Gradient picker button (Gradient Fill dialog box) to display the Gradient picker.

9 Click the first gradient, Foreground to Background.

10 Click the Gradient picker button again to close the Gradient picker.

11 Click to display a check mark in the Reverse check box so the gradient goes from brown at the top to white at the bottom.

12 Click the OK button (Gradient Fill dialog box) to apply the gradient (Figure 8–83).

Figure 8–83

To Save the Document

The following step saves the document.

1 Press CTRL+S to save the document.

The Note Tool and Notes Panel

In Photoshop, an **annotation** is an explanatory note or comment included within the file itself. The Note Tool, included with the Eyedropper Tool on the Tools panel, opens the Notes panel, in which you can enter comments. Notes in the Notes panel have scrolling capabilities, standard editing functions, and a Close button in the corner. A yellow note icon appears in the document window when you click the Note Tool button and the Note options bar is displayed. The Note options bar contains choices for author, color, and font size. The name you enter in the Author box becomes the text on the Notes panel title bar. You can edit, delete, or reposition notes anywhere on the image for greater emphasis; they stay with the file until they are deleted. These notes are different from the metadata and keywords stored by Adobe Bridge. Annotations are more like the popular, small, yellow sticky notes that you might attach physically, a comment inserted in many Office programs, or a short phone message.

Once it is created, to read a note, double-click it — you do not have to click the Note Tool to read notes. Notes do not print, and they are unique to Photoshop; a note in a Photoshop document is not visible in other graphic-editing software packages.

Plan Ahead

Annotate graphics within the file.
Photoshop gives you the opportunity to save notes with any image file. You might want to write a note to another person on your team about the use of the graphic, or you might want to keep some notes for yourself about which filter you used, or which settings you changed on a blend mode. Still other times, you might want to list some special instructions.

To Create a Note

The next steps create a note in the Creative Ceramics image. The note will remind a coworker to add keywords to the clip art in Adobe Bridge.

1

- Right-click the Eyedropper Tool button to display its context menu (Figure 8–84).

Figure 8–84

2

- Click Note Tool in the menu.

- Click the upper-left corner of the canvas to place the note location and open the Notes panel.

- In the Notes panel window, type Anita, don't forget to add keywords to this image using Adobe Bridge before you upload it to the server. to complete the note (Figure 8–85).

Figure 8–85

3

- Click the Notes icon on the vertical docking to hide the panel.

To View a Note

The next steps view the note as a different user would.

1

- Double-click the note icon on the canvas to open the Notes panel and display the note (Figure 8–86).

2

- Click the Notes icon on the vertical docking to hide the panel.

Figure 8–86

To Save the Document

The following step saves the fully layered, PSD version of the image.

1 Press CTRL+S.

Preparing the Image for Page Layout Applications

Currently, the Creative Ceramics document features a gradient background. Oftentimes, clip art is created with a transparent background so the background of the page on which it is used shows through. For example, the clip art mug that you created in this chapter might be usable in a variety of projects. In preparation for using the image in page layout applications, you will create a transparent background and convert the image to the PDF format. The PDF, or Portable Document Format, format produces a file consisting of all the Photoshop layers and also supports transparency. It is a format suitable for import to a page layout application and is also a format often requested by printing companies.

To Create a Transparent Background

In the following step, you will hide the gradient background to create a transparency.

1 Click the 'Indicates layer visibility' button on the Background layer in the Layers panel to hide it (Figure 8–87).

Figure 8–87

To Save in the PDF Format

With the background now transparent, the next step is to save the file as a PDF suitable for import to a page layout program.

1 Press SHIFT+CTRL+S to display the Save As dialog box.

2 Type `Creative Ceramics Transparency` in the File name box. Do not press the ENTER key.

3 Click the Format box arrow, and then click Photoshop PDF (*.PDF, *.PDP) in the list.

4 In the Save Options section, ensure only the Layers and Notes boxes are checked.

5 Click the Save in box arrow and then click Removable Disk (F:), or the location associated with your USB flash drive, in the list and then double-click the Chapter 08 folder to open it.

6 Click the Save button (Save As dialog box) to begin the save process.

7 If an Adobe Photoshop CS6 Extended dialog box appears, click the OK button.

8 When the Save Adobe PDF dialog box appears, click the General category, if necessary.

9 Ensure only the first and third check boxes are checked (Figure 8–88).

10 Click the Save PDF button (Save Adobe PDF dialog box) to save the PDF.

11 If Photoshop displays a warning box about Photoshop editing capabilities, click the Yes button.

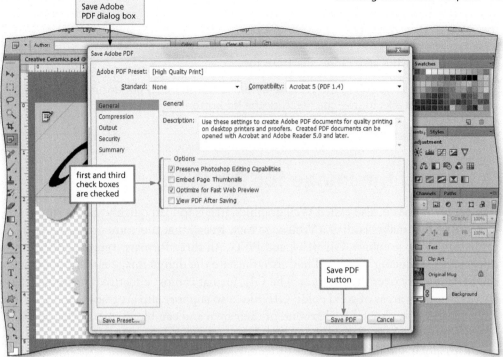

Figure 8–88

Displaying the Graphic in a Page Layout Program

The clip art now is ready to import to a page layout program. Figure 8–89 displays the PDF clip art file on a solid background in Adobe InDesign, a page layout program. As you can see, the graphic transparency is maintained, and it can be resized without any change in resolution.

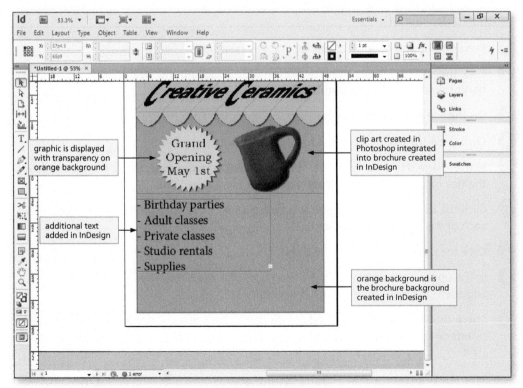

Figure 8–89

To Close the PDF Version

The following step closes the PDF file.

1 Click the Close button in the Creative Ceramics Transparency.pdf document window. If Photoshop asks to save the file, click the No button.

Preparing the Image for the Web

Clip art for the Web, also called Web graphics, needs to load quickly and be stored in a format that makes coding a Web page easy. Recall that there are three standard formats for Web graphics: GIF, JPG, and PNG. All three formats compress the picture information, reducing file size. They also translate the digital image into a code that can be sent easily over the Internet. The GIF format is most effective on graphics that have contiguous areas of solid color. GIF files also support clip art transparency, so the graphics appear without a background of their own and can blend into the background of the canvas to which they are imported. However, on graphics that contain transparencies along with shadows, GIFs often display an unwanted color border around the shadows. The PNG format also supports transparency but does not create the unwanted colored border. While PNG typically creates larger file sizes than GIF, the quality of the transparency is much higher and worth the additional file size.

You will open the PSD version of the graphic and create a PNG version for the Web. You then will preview it in a browser.

To Create a Version for the Web

Recall that the Save for Web command allows you to create a version of an image that is optimized for the Web. The following steps create a Web-optimized version of the clip art.

1 Press CTRL+O and open the Creative Ceramics.psd file.

2 Click the 'Indicates layer visibility' button of the Background layer to hide the background and create a transparency.

3 On the File menu, click Save for Web to display the Save for Web dialog box.

4 Click the 4-Up tab, if necessary, to display the preview options.

5 In the Image size area, type 15 in the Percent box and press the ENTER key to reduce the size of the image so it is appropriate for use on the Web.

6 Click the Zoom Level box arrow, and then click Fit in View to display the full graphic in each of the four preview panes.

7 Click the upper-right preview to select it.

8 In the upper-right portion of the dialog box, click the 'Optimized file format' button, and then click PNG-24 in the list, if necessary.

9 Check the Transparency check box to display a check mark, if necessary, for best display results on the Web (Figure 8–90).

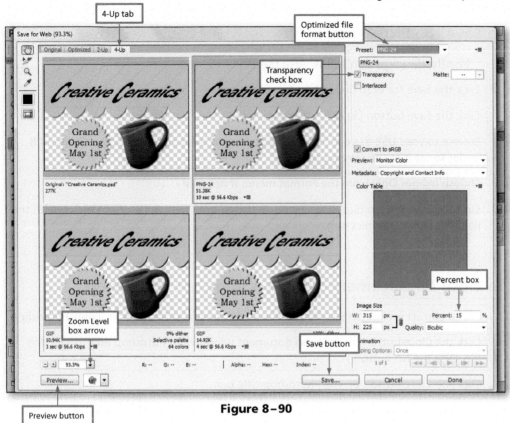

Figure 8–90

To Preview the Image

The steps that follow preview the PNG version of the clip art.

1 In the Save for Web dialog box, click the Preview button to view the image in a browser (Figure 8–91).

2 Close the browser window.

Figure 8–91

To Save the PNG Version

BTW

Quick Reference
For a table that lists how to complete the tasks covered in this book using the mouse, context menu, and keyboard, see the Quick Reference summary at the back of this book.

Finally, the steps that follow save the PNG version.

1 Click the Save for Web dialog box to make it active.

2 Click the Save button (Save for Web dialog box).

3 Browse to your USB drive or storage location, and then double-click the **Chapter 08** folder to set it as the save location.

4 Choose Images Only from the Format menu, if necessary.

5 Click the Save button (Save Optimized As dialog box) to save the Web version with the name Creative-Ceramics.png.

To Close All Document Windows and Quit Photoshop

The clip art is complete, so you can close the document window and quit Photoshop.

1 Click the Close button in any open document window. If Photoshop asks to save the file, click the No button.

2 Click the Close button on the Photoshop title bar.

Chapter Summary

In this chapter, you converted a photo into clip art for a ceramics studio brochure and Web site. You added details to give depth to the clip art. You learned about the general characteristics of clip art and transparency-based files destined for page layout applications and the difference between vector and raster graphics.

As you created layer groups and organized your objects, you created both paths and shape layers. You used the Pen and Freeform Pen Tools to draw line segments and anchor points. You added and converted anchor points to create straight lines and curves. The Path Selection and Direct Selection Tools helped position paths and shapes. You added detail to the clip art image, including background shape and color, shadows, blends, and impact lines. You used the Note Tool to annotate your file. Finally, you readied the clip art for use in a page layout application by converting it to the PDF format, and prepared the file for Web usage by saving it as a PNG file.

The items listed below include all the new Photoshop skills you have learned in this chapter:

1. Lock Layers (PS 490)
2. Choose the Pen Tool (PS 495)
3. Create a Shape Layer using the Pen Tool (PS 495)
4. Add Anchor Points to a Shape (PS 499)
5. Reposition an Anchor Point (PS 500)
6. Use Direction Points (PS 501)
7. Use a Shape Tool in Pixel Mode (PS 505)
8. Fine-Tune a Shape (PS 507)
9. Create a Work Path using the Pen Tool (PS 510)
10. Display the Paths Panel (PS 512)
11. Save a Work Path as a Named Path (PS 513)
12. Create a Path using the Freeform Pen Tool (PS 513)
13. Merge Paths (PS 514)
14. Delete and Rename Paths (PS 515)
15. Create a Shape Layer from a Path (PS 516)
16. Create a Layer Group from Layers (PS 523)
17. Create a New Empty Layer Group (PS 525)
18. Nest Layer Groups (PS 526)
19. Create the Seal using a Custom Shape (PS 527)
20. Create Text within a Shape (PS 529)
21. Convert Text to a Shape (PS 531)
22. Alter the Shape of Letters (PS 531)
23. Fill a Shape with a Pattern (PS 534)
24. Create a Note (PS 540)
25. View a Note (PS 541)

Apply Your Knowledge

Reinforce the skills and apply the concepts you learned in this chapter.

Converting a Photo to Clip Art

Instructions: Start Photoshop and perform the customization steps found on pages PS 6 through PS 10. Open the Apply 8-1 Mailbox file from the Chapter 08 folder of the Data Files for Students. Visit www.cengage.com/ct/studentdownload for detailed instructions or contact your instructor for information about accessing the required files. The purpose of this exercise is to create a clip art image from a digital photograph. The photo you open is a picture of a mailbox, shown on the left in Figure 8–92. You will convert the image to a clip art image as shown on the right.

Figure 8–92

Perform the following tasks:

1. On the File menu, click Save As. Save the image on your USB flash drive as a PSD file, with the file name Apply 8-1 Mailbox Clip Art. If the Photoshop Format options dialog box is displayed, click the OK button.

2. On the Tools panel, click the Eyedropper Tool button. Click a light brown color at the bottom of the mailbox post to use it as the foreground color.

3. Select the Pen Tool on the Tools panel. On the options bar, click the Mode button and select Shape for the drawing mode. Click the lower-left corner of the mailbox post. Click again toward the upper-left of the mailbox post below where the post curves inward. Click higher up on the post above where the post curves inward and drag slightly up and left to roughly follow the curve. ALT+click the new anchor point to convert it to a corner point. Click the top of the post and drag slightly up and to the right to follow the curve of the top of the post.

Continued >

4. ALT+click the anchor point at the top of the post to convert it to a corner point. Click the post in the upper-right area above where the post curves inward, and drag slightly down and left to follow the curve of the post's top. ALT+click the new anchor point to convert it to a corner point. Click the spot just below the inward curve toward the top of the post and drag slightly down and to the right to follow the curve. ALT+click the new anchor point to convert it to a corner point. Click the lower-right corner of the post. Click the first anchor point at the lower-left corner of the post to close the shape.

5. Rename the layer, Post, and then click the 'Indicates layer visibility' button to hide it.

6. Select the Pen Tool on the Tools panel. Click the upper-right corner of the mailbox's horizontal wood post. Click the corner of the horizontal post below the first anchor point. Click the lower-right corner of the horizontal wood post and drag slightly down to follow the small curve on the right of the horizontal post. ALT+click the new anchor point to convert it to a corner point. Click where you estimate the lower-left corner of the horizontal post to be (about 0.5 on the horizontal ruler and about 3.25 on the vertical ruler). Click the upper-left corner of the horizontal post. Click the first anchor point at the upper-right of the horizontal post to close the path. Name the layer, Post Horizontal, and then hide the layer.

7. On the options bar, click the Fill button. Click a light gray color swatch to use it as the shape fill color.

8. Click on the left edge of the newspaper box just above its lower-left corner to place the first anchor point. Click on the bottom edge of the newspaper box just to the right of its lower-left corner and drag slightly to the right to create the lower-left curve. Continue placing anchor points, ALT+clicking points as necessary to convert them to corner points, until you have traced the outline of the newspaper box and have returned to the first anchor point. Click the first anchor point to close the path. Rename the layer, Newspaper Box, and then hide the layer.

9. On the options bar, click the Fill button. Click a black color swatch to use as the shape fill color.

10. Starting at the lower-left corner of the black mailbox, trace around the mailbox, trying to create a curve in the top-right corner. Close the path. Rename the layer, Mailbox.

11. Click the 'Indicates layer visibility' buttons on the Layers panel to hide the Background layer and show all the other layers. If one of your shapes has the wrong color, double-click the icon next to the layer name in the Layers panel to display the Color Picker, choose a new color, and then click the OK button to close the Color Picker.

12. Press the T key to select the Horizontal Type Tool. In the options bar, set the font to Impact, size 72, color white. Click a transparent area of the canvas and type 40. In the Layers panel, drag the new type layer to the top of the layer stack and use the Move Tool to position the number on the black mailbox.

13. Click the Background layer to select it. On the Application bar, click Layer, point to New Fill Layer, and then click Solid Color. Click the OK button in the New Layer dialog box to create the new layer and display the Color Picker. Choose a light blue from the Color Picker, and then click the OK button to add the background to the mailbox.

14. Save the image again.

Extend Your Knowledge

Extend the skills you learned in this chapter and experiment with new skills. You may need to use Help to complete the assignment.

Create an Ant Anatomy Illustration

Instructions: Start Photoshop and perform the customization steps found on pages PS 6 through PS 10. Open the Extend 8-1 Anatomy file from the Chapter 08 folder of the Data Files for Students. Visit www.cengage.com/ct/studentdownload for detailed instructions, or contact your instructor for information about accessing the required files. You have been asked to create a scientific illustration of an ant, such as the one shown in Figure 8–93 on the next page. This illustration will teach students the basic body parts of an ant. The client has provided you with a photo of an ant but wants it to look more like an illustration than a photograph.

Perform the following tasks:

1. On the File menu, click Save As. Save the image on your USB flash drive as a PSD file, with the file name, Extend 8-1 Anatomy Edited.

2. Look at the organization of the layers on the Layers panel. Click the 'Indicates layer visibility' button for the ant photo layer to display it.

3. Start with small items such as the eye. Use the Eyedropper Tool to sample the eye color, zooming as necessary.

4. Activate the Pen Tool. Click the Mode button on the options bar, and select Shape as the drawing mode.

5. Click around the eye to create a path that covers the ant's eye. Close the path.

6. On the Layers panel, rename the layer, Eye.

7. Create two more paths, one around each antenna. (*Hint:* As you click narrow images, such as the antenna, your path may fill temporarily at awkward-looking intersecting triangles. Just keep clicking close to the antennae.) Rename each layer.

8. Select the ant photo layer again. Use the Eyedropper Tool to select a lighter gray color from the head of the ant. Activate the Pen Tool again and click to create a closed path around the head.

9. Create additional paths for the legs, middle, and end of the ant. Rename each layer.

10. Hide and show the ant photo layer to view your work. Use the Direct Selection Tool to adjust any lines that are not smooth.

11. Create a different layer style for each part of the ant's body by selecting the layer and then clicking the 'Add a layer style' button on the Layers panel status bar. For information on using layer styles effectively, refer to Photoshop Help as necessary.

12. Create layer groups to organize the layers. Group the leg layers into one group; the head, antenna, and eye layers into another group; and finally the middle and end body parts into another group.

13. To create a label for the diagram, activate the Custom Shape Tool. Click the Shape picker button on the options bar to display its panel, and then click the panel menu button. Select Talk Bubbles and append the shape to the Shape picker panel. Select one of the Talk Bubble shapes. Choose a gray color. Drag in the document window to create a shape above the ant's head.

14. Activate the Horizontal Type Tool. Choose a sans serif font, such as Impact, with a font size of 36 points and a color of white. Click the shape and type head to create text within the shape.

15. Create additional labels for mesosoma, gaster, compound eyes, antennae, and legs, as shown in Figure 8–93.

16. Use the Direct Selection Tool to alter the shape of the talk bubbles as necessary so they point to the correct location on the ant. Hide the ant photo layer, if necessary.

17. Save the file again and turn it in to your instructor.

Continued >

Extend Your Knowledge *continued*

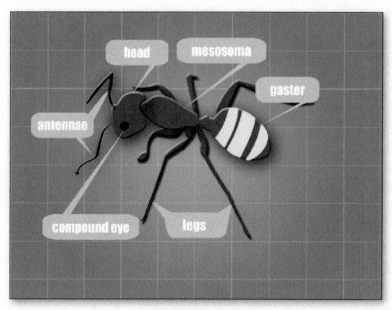

Figure 8-93

Make It Right

Analyze a project and correct all errors and/or improve the design.

Music Store Rock Camp

Problem: The music store needs help completing a new logo for its summer camp. A previous graphic designer started the project but did not finish it. A photo of a young guitarist needs to be converted to a silhouette.

Instructions: *Perform the following tasks:*

1. Start Photoshop and perform the customization steps found on pages PS 6 through PS 10. Open the file Make It Right 8-1 Rock Camp file from the Data Files for Students and save it as Make It Right 8-1 Rock Camp Edited in the PSD file format. Visit www.cengage.com/ct/ studentdownload for detailed instructions or contact your instructor for information about accessing the required files.

2. Look through the layers on the Layers panel (Figure 8-94). Select the Guitarist layer, if necessary. Use the Pen Tool in Path mode to trace slowly around the entire outline of the guitarist and the guitar, stopping at her knees. Do not be concerned with tracing her perfectly. Details such as the curly hair, bracelet, and spaces between the guitar's tuning pegs can be ignored. If necessary, use the Direct Selection Tool to make adjustments.

3. Create a new layer and name it, Silhouette. Click the Paths panel tab and notice that the guitarist outline is named Work Path in the panel. Rename the path, Guitarist Path. On the status bar, click the 'Load path as a selection' button. Click the Paths panel in the gray area below the paths to deselect the current path. Use the Eyedropper Tool to sample the gold color from the text surrounding the logo. Press ALT+BACKSPACE to fill the selection with gold. Click the Layers panel tab to switch to the Layers panel. Press CTRL+D to deselect the selection. Click the Guitarist layer 'Indicates layer visibility' icon to hide the layer, and then select the Silhouette layer. Move the silhouette layer so the knees slightly overlap the gold ring at the bottom and the guitarist appears to be rising inside the logo. In the Layers panel, drag the Silhouette layer down below the Gold Ring layer.

4. Add an inner shadow to the silhouette. Add a drop shadow to the gold ring layer. Save the file and turn it in to your instructor when you are happy with the results.

Figure 8–94

In the Lab

Design and/or create a project using the guidelines, concepts, and skills presented in this chapter. Labs are listed in order of increasing difficulty.

Lab 1: Creating a Sign

Problem: Your summer job is interning at a children's dentist's office. Your supervisor has asked you to make a sign for the waiting room. She would like the same image in a scalable format for use with desktop publishing products and in the newsletters the dentist's office sends out. You have taken a picture of a toothbrush and will convert it to a clip art character, as shown in Figure 8–95 on the next page. You will save it in both the PSD and PNG formats to preserve the transparency.

Note: To complete this assignment, you will be required to use the Data Files for Students. Visit www.cengage.com/ct/studentdownload for detailed instructions or contact you instructor for information about accessing the required files.

Instructions: *Perform the following tasks:*
1. Start Photoshop. Perform the customization steps found on pages PS 6 through PS 10.
2. Open the file Lab 8-1 Toothbrush from the Chapter 08 folder of the Data Files for Students.
3. Save the file on your storage device in the PSD format with the name, Lab 8-1 Dentist Clip Art.
4. To create the bottom portion:
    a. Use the Eyedropper Tool to sample some green from the bottom of the toothbrush.
    b. Use the Pen Tool in Shape mode to trace a shape around the green portion of the toothbrush.
    c. Name the new layer, Brush Bottom.
    d. Hide the Brush Bottom layer.
    e. Select the Background layer.

Continued >

5. To create the middle portion:

a. Use the Eyedropper Tool to sample some gray from the background.

b. Use the Pen Tool in Shape mode to trace a shape around the rest of the toothbrush.

c. Name the new layer, Brush Top.

d. Hide the Brush Top layer.

e. Select the Background layer.

6. To create the bristles:

a. Use the Eyedropper Tool to sample some white from the bristles.

b. Use the Pen Tool in Shape mode to trace a shape around the bristles of the toothbrush.

c. Name the new layer, Bristles.

d. Move the Bristles layer above the Brush Top layer in the Layers panel.

7. Hide the Background layer.

8. Show the Brush Bottom and Brush Top layers:

9. Use the Move Tool to reposition the shapes as necessary so that the green bottom of the toothbrush covers any raw edges of the gray portion and the bristles are centered at the top of the toothbrush.

10. To create the eyes:

a. On the Tools panel, select the Ellipse Tool.

b. SHIFT+drag to create a circular eye. Refer to Figure 8–95 for the size.

c. Use the Move Tool to position the eye to the upper-left of the toothbrush.

d. Name the layer, Left Eye.

e. Right-click the Left Eye layer on the Layers panel, and click Duplicate Layer.

f. Type Right Eye for the new layer name and click the OK button.

g. Use the Move Tool to position the right eye so that it slightly overlaps the left eye.

Figure 8–95

11. To create the pupils of the eyeballs:

   a. Select the Ellipse Tool.

   b. Click the Background layer to select it, and then set the foreground color to black.

   c. SHIFT+drag on a transparent area of the canvas to draw a much smaller circle for the pupil.

   d. Rename the new layer, Left Eyeball, drag it to the top of the layer stack in the Layers panel, and then use the Move Tool to drag it into position on the canvas inside the left eye.

   e. Right-click the Left Eyeball layer on the Layers panel, and then click Duplicate Layer.

   f. Type Right Eyeball for the new layer name, and then click the OK button.

   g. Use the Move Tool to move the right eyeball into position over the right eye.

12. To create the mouth:

   a. Click the Background layer to select it.

   b. Set the foreground color to a bright red.

   c. Select the Pen Tool and click once to create an anchor point.

   d. Click about 2 inches to the right of the first anchor point, and then drag up and to the left to create a deep symmetrical curve.

   e. ALT+click the new anchor point to convert it to an anchor point.

   f. Click the first anchor point and drag up and to the left to create the bottom curve of the mouth.

   g. Name the new layer, Mouth, drag it to the top of the layer stack in the Layers panel, and use the Move Tool to position it over the toothbrush.

13. Select all layers except the Background layer in the Layers panel, and create a new layer group named Toothbrush that holds all but the Background layer.

14. To create the arms and legs:

   a. Click the Background layer on the Layers panel to select it.

   b. Press the D key to reset the default colors.

   c. Select the Line Tool and set its weight in the options bar to 5 pt (*Hint:* The Weight setting is on the far right side of the options bar.), and then drag on the canvas to draw arms and legs resembling those shown in Figure 8–95.

   d. Select all of the arms and legs layers on the Layers panel and create a new layer group from them with the name, Arms and Legs.

15. To create the text:

   a. Press the T key to activate the Horizontal Type Tool.

   b. Choose a child-friendly font of your choice with an initial size of 60 pt.

   c. Set the text color to black and center-align the text.

   d. Click a transparent area of the canvas and type Do you brush every day?, pressing the ENTER key after each word.

   e. Select the Move Tool and move the text into position.

16. To create the background:

   a. Select the Background layer.

   b. Click Layer on the Application bar, point to New Fill Layer, and click Solid Color.

   c. Type New Background as the layer name and click the OK button to create the new layer.

   d. Select a bright yellow from the Color Picker and click the OK button to apply the color.

17. To save the file in the required formats:

   a. Press CTRL+S to save the file in the Photoshop PSD format. Click the OK button if prompted to maximize compatibility.

   b. Hide the New Background layer.

   c. Click File on the Application bar and then click Save for Web.

Continued >

STUDENT ASSIGNMENTS

d. Type 10 in the Percent box and press the ENTER key to reduce the size of the image.

e. Save the file in the PNG-24 format with transparency enabled to your Chapter 08 folder with the default name, Lab-8-1-Dentist-Clip-Art.png.

In the Lab

Lab 2: Using Saved Paths

Problem: The Bow-Wow dog treat company needs help in finishing the packaging for its newest variety of dog treats. Most of the artwork has been created in Adobe Illustrator and saved as paths in the main document. The art director has provided instructions for you to complete the layout. The final version is shown in Figure 8–96.

Note: To complete this assignment, you will be required to use the Data Files for Students. Visit www.cengage.com/ct/studentdownload for detailed instructions or contact you instructor for information about accessing the required files.

Instructions: *Perform the following tasks:*

1. Start Photoshop. Perform the customization steps found on pages PS 6 through PS 10. Open the file Lab 8-2 Bow-Wow from the Chapter 08 folder of the Data Files for Students. Save the file as Lab 8-2 Bow-Wow Edited on your USB drive.

2. The file contains a layer named Color Swatches. The swatch colors were provided for your use as you create the various packaging elements. Select the Color Swatches layer. Press SHIFT+CTRL+N to create a new layer above the color swatches layer and name it, Package.

3. Click the Paths tab to display the Paths panel.

4. To create the package background:

   a. Click the Package path to select it, if necessary.

   b. To convert the path into a selection, right-click the Package path on the Paths panel to display the context menu. Click Make Selection to display the Make Selection dialog box, and then click the OK button.

   c. Press the D key to reset the foreground and background colors to their default settings. Verify that the foreground color is black. Use the Eyedropper Tool to sample the tan color in the document window. Depending on your monitor, the swatch might look more yellow than tan. You want to use the second-to-last sample color.

   d. Activate the Gradient Tool. On the options bar, click the Radial Gradient button. If necessary, click the Gradient picker and then double-click the Foreground to Background preset. Check the Reverse button to reverse the colors.

   e. Create a radial gradient from the bottom of the selection to the top. Deselect the selection. On the Layers panel, click the 'Add a layer style' button, and then click Stroke. Use a black 3-px wide stroke around the Package layer. Keep all other default settings.

Figure 8–96

5. To create a bone-shaped background:

   a. On the Paths panel, select the Bone path, and then click the Load path as a selection button to create a selection marquee of the bone.

   b. On the Layers panel create a new layer named, Bone.

   c. Press ALT+BACKSPACE to fill the selection. Deselect the bone selection. Add a stroke layer style to the Bone layer using a size of 3 and the color black.

   d. Activate the Move Tool. ALT+drag to create a few copies of the bone, and then rotate the copies in various angles by pressing CTRL+T and dragging outside of the transform handles. Press the ENTER key to confirm each transformation.

6. To create a title banner:

   a. Create a new layer above the bone copy layers named, Banner Caps.

   b. On the Paths panel, select the Banner Caps path and then click the Load path as a selection button.

   c. Use the Eyedropper Tool to sample the dark blue color in the document window. Press ALT+BACKSPACE to fill the selection. Deselect the Banner Caps path.

   d. On the Layers panel, create a new layer above the Banner Caps layer named, Banner.

   e. On the Paths panel, select the Banner path and create a selection.

   f. Press the x key to reverse the foreground and background colors so the dark blue is the background color.

   g. Sample from the light blue color in the document window to make it the foreground color, using the Eyedropper Tool.

   h. Activate the Gradient Tool and drag from the middle of the banner selection outward. Deselect the banner.

   i. Add a Drop Shadow layer style to the Banner layer using the default values for the Drop Shadow.

   j. Create a new layer above the Banner layer, and name the new layer, Bow-wow.

   k. On the Paths panel, load the Bow-wow path as a selection.

   l. Sample the yellow/tan color, press ALT+BACKSPACE to fill the path, and then deselect.

7. To create the dog layer:

   a. On the Layers panel, click the visibility icon to show the Dog layer. Drag the layer to the top of the Layers panel.

   b. Activate the Freeform Pen Tool. On the options bar, click the Mode button, select Path as the drawing mode, and turn on the Magnetic option.

   c. Carefully trace around the dog's head and neck.

   d. To remove the background around the dog, click Layer on the Application bar, point to Vector Mask, and then click Current Path.

   e. Use the Move Tool to position the dog at the bottom of the package outline.

   f. Create a new layer named, Package Bottom.

8. Activate the Horizontal Type Tool. Drag a type box under the Bow-Wow banner, approximately 3 inches wide and .5 inches tall. Type Dog Treats, using Impact or a similar font, a size of 48, and a color sampled from the document window.

9. Hide the Color Swatches layer. Save the file again. Flatten the image and save it as Lab 8-2 Bow-Wow Complete in the TIF format. If Photoshop displays a warning about discarding hidden layers, click the OK button.

In the Lab

Lab 3: Creating a Promotional Flyer

Problem: A local bakery is hosting their annual "cupcake day" when they will sell their gourmet cupcakes (normally $3 each) for only 50¢. They have asked you to create a promotional flyer for the event in the style of a postage stamp (Figure 8–97).

Note: To complete this assignment, you will be required to use the Data Files for Students. Visit www.cengage.com/ct/studentdownload for detailed instructions or contact you instructor for information about accessing the required files.

Instructions: *Perform the following tasks:*

Start Photoshop. Perform the customization steps found on pages PS 6 through PS 10. Create a new document with a white background, 3 inches wide and 4 inches tall, and save the file in the Photoshop PSD format as Lab 8-3 Cupcake Flyer on your USB drive.

Use the Custom Shape Tool to create a stamp shape. (*Hint:* Load the Objects category of shapes from the Custom Shape Picker and use the Stamp 1 shape.) Name the layer, Stamp. Apply a 3-pixel black Stroke layer style to define the border of the stamp. Apply a Gradient Overlay layer style with the colors of your choice to add texture to the background of the stamp shape. Add text similar to that shown in Figure 8–97. Create a layer group named, Type, and drag the type layers into it.

Open the Lab 8-3 Cupcake file from the Chapter 08 folder of the Data Files for Students. Drag the cupcake photo into the Lab 8-3 Cupcake Flyer document. Hide the Stamp layer and Type layer group so you can focus on the cupcake. Use the Pen Tool and Freeform Pen Tool to trace the different parts of the cupcake. It may be helpful to zoom in so the cupcake is enlarged. Color the shapes appropriately and add layer styles, such as a Pattern Overlay, to add texture. Create a new layer group named, Cupcake, to store all the cupcake layers. Delete the original cupcake photo layer and resize the Cupcake layer group to enlarge your clip art cupcake. Rearrange the stacking order of the layer groups to your liking.

Rotate, resize, and reposition any layers to your liking. Apply any additional layer styles you think benefit the design. Save the file.

Figure 8–97

Cases and Places

Apply your creative thinking and problem-solving skills to design and implement a solution.

Note: To complete these assignments, you may be required to use the Data Files for Students. Visit www.cengage.com/ct/studentdownload for detailed instructions or contact you instructor for information about accessing the required files.

1: Map Demographics

Academic

Your political science professor has given you the assignment of creating an electoral map for your state from the last presidential election. Find a free graphic of your state map that shows county outlines. Research county election results using your state government's Web site. With the Freeform Pen Tool and the Shape layers button, draw around each county, filling it with either red for Republican or blue for Democrat. Save and print the file.

2: Create an Invitation

Personal

You are throwing a birthday party for a friend and need to make invitations. Create a new document in Photoshop with a solid, bright background. Take a digital picture of some gift boxes and another digital picture of a location, such as a swimming pool, roller rink, or bowling alley. If you do not have access to a digital camera or cannot find gift boxes or a location, download gift box or location photos from the Internet. Copy the location image into your new document, and then convert it into a vector graphic using the various Pen Tools. Convert just enough of the photograph so that the location is recognizable. You do not need to convert every detail. Add the gift box photo to your new document and convert the gift box to a vector graphic. Delete the layers containing the original photos. Use the Horizontal Type Tool to insert invitation text, such as the name of your friend and the location and date/time of the party. Add layer effects to enhance the invitation. Save the file in the format specified by your instructor.

3: Creating a Game Graphic

Professional

You recently took a job with a company that produces graphical adventure games for computers. Your assignment is to convert an image of a historical ruin into a clip art type of graphic to display on the CD liner. The photo, Archway, is located in the Chapter 08 folder of the Data Files for Students. Open the photo and create a layer group named Columns. Use the Pen Tool to create shape layers with the group for each column. Fill the area with a dark tan color. Use the Shape layers button along with the Pen Tool, Freeform Pen Tool, and anchor point tools to draw around other parts of the archway with darker and lighter shades. Do not recolor the blue sky. Save the file as a PDF format and submit a copy to your instructor.

9 | Creating Web Pages and Animations

Adobe product screenshot(s) reprinted with permission from Adobe Systems Incorporated

Ps

Objectives

You will have mastered the material in this chapter when you can:

- Explain why planning is the most important step in Web design
- Organize photos for inclusion in a Web gallery
- Generate a Web gallery
- Differentiate between a Web page and a Web site
- Slice an image
- Apply slice settings

- Create animation frames
- Describe the process of creating an animation and optimization
- Tween an animation
- Loop an animation
- Optimize an animation
- Preview an animation

9 | Creating Web Pages and Animations

Introduction

Photoshop has several tools to help you design Web pages. While Photoshop is not Web page creation software, it can be used to create a mock up of a Web page as a sample or prototype in advance of creating a fully featured site. In a typical Web page design workflow, you create individual files and then combine them into a single unified design using Photoshop. In the project for this chapter, you will use Adobe Bridge to organize images in addition to creating a Web gallery, which is a Web page (or set of Web pages within a Web site) that features a thumbnail page with small preview versions of your photos. After organizing the images and creating a Web Gallery, you will use Photoshop to create a Web site home page, which is the first page or starting point of a Web site. Photoshop optimizes Web pages using slices with hyperlinks or hot spots. Designers use the Timeline panel to animate graphics and then optimize them for display on the Web. In this chapter, you will create an interactive Web site for a fictitious photography studio, complete with animation and a working photo gallery.

Project — Web Site for Freeze Frame

This chapter examines some of the Web tools used by Photoshop and Bridge as you create a home page for a fictitious photography studio. A **home page** is a Web page designated as the first page and point of entry into a **Web site**, which is a collection of related Web pages. Also called the main page or index page, a home page typically welcomes the visitor by introducing the purpose of the site, indicating the business name or personal name of the Web site's owner, and providing links to the lower-level pages of the site.

The Freeze Frame home page uses a black-and-white color scheme. Many photography Web sites are designed in black and white so that the site does not distract from the colors in the photographs. A **masthead** is the top portion of a design and is usually the first thing people notice when looking at a Web page. Therefore, the masthead is the ideal place to locate the company name, exciting imagery, contact information, and anything else you want to be sure your visitors see. A set of links to other Web pages in the Freeze Frame site appears below the masthead. One of the links will take visitors to a Web gallery generated with a Bridge automation command. Finally, when the home page first appears, a picture and frame will rotate and move into the Web page in an animated special effect. The Web page is illustrated in Figure 9–1a. The area below the links is intentionally left blank at this stage of the design because it is reserved for content provided by the client. The Web gallery, opened from a link on the Web page, is illustrated in Figure 9–1b.

Source: www.istockphoto.com

Source: www.istockphoto.com

(a) Web page

(b) Web gallery

Figure 9–1

Overview

As you read this chapter, you will learn how to create the Web site shown in Figure 9–1 by performing these general tasks:

- Create a folder and copy files in the Bridge Output workspace.
- Set options and save a Web gallery.
- Create slices from text for navigation.
- Set slice options for hyperlinks.
- Create multiple layers and position them for animation.
- Create frames in the Timeline panel.
- Create new frames using tweening.
- Use the Timeline panel to set animation options.
- Preview the animation.
- Save the Web page, optimized for animation.

Plan
Ahead

General Project Guidelines

When creating a Web site design, the actions you perform and decisions you make will affect the appearance and characteristics of the finished product. As you create Web sites, such as the one shown in Figure 9–1 on the previous page, you should follow these general guidelines:

1. **Organize photos for a Web site and gallery pages.** Collect the photos you will need and store them in a Windows folder. Make sure each photo and the folder are named appropriately.

2. **Use standard Web design and planning principles.** As you develop the site, keep in mind the site's purpose, the audience, the elements you plan to include, the visual impact, and the placement of the pages within the Web site structure.

3. **Employ animation carefully.** Use animation to draw attention to or create interest in a Web site, but do not overdo it. Animations that loop continuously make it difficult for users to focus on content; scrolling marquees are difficult to read and distract from the purpose of the Web page. You should use animation to draw the viewer's attention to a specific element on the page, alert readers to updated information, or create hot spots. Animation always should have a purpose that is related to the content in the page. Weigh the value the animation adds against its disadvantages: animation reduces performance, uses more system resources, increases load time, and seldom runs optimally on both low-end and high-end computing systems. Research also suggests that animation is distracting and reduces the user's ability to seek information on the Web page. Resist the temptation to include special effects simply because you have the know-how.

Starting and Customizing Photoshop

The following steps start Photoshop and reset the default workspace, tools, colors, and Layers panel options.

To Start Photoshop

If you are stepping through this project on a computer and you want your screen to match the figures in this book, then you should change your computer's resolution to 1024 × 768 and reset the panels, tools, and colors. For more information about how to change the resolution on your computer, and other advanced Photoshop settings, read the Changing Screen Resolution appendix.

The following steps, which assume Windows 7 is running, start Photoshop based on a typical installation. You may need to ask your instructor how to start Photoshop for your system.

1 Click the Start button on the Windows 7 taskbar to display the Start menu, and then type `Photoshop CS6` in the 'Search programs and files' box.

2 Click Photoshop CS6 in the list to start Photoshop.

3 If the Photoshop window is not maximized, click the Maximize button next to the Close button on the Application bar to maximize the window.

To Reset the Workspace

As discussed in Chapter 1, it is helpful to reset the workspace so that the tools and panels appear in their default positions. The following steps select the Essentials workspace.

1 Click Window on the Application bar to display the Window menu, and then point to Workspace to display the Workspace submenu.

2 Click Essentials (Default) on the Workspace submenu to select the default workspace panels.

3 Click Window on the Application bar, and then point to Workspace again to display the list.

4 Click Reset Essentials to restore the workspace to its default settings and reposition any panels that may have been moved.

To Reset the Tools and the Options Bar

Recall that the Tools panel and the options bar retain their settings from previous Photoshop sessions. The following steps select the Rectangular Marquee Tool and reset all tool settings in the options bar.

1 If the tools in the Tools panel appear in two columns, click the double arrow at the top of the Tools panel.

2 If necessary, click the Rectangular Marquee Tool button on the Tools panel to select it.

3 Right-click the Rectangular Marquee Tool icon on the options bar to display the context menu, and then click Reset All Tools. When Photoshop displays a confirmation dialog box, click the OK button to restore the tools to their default settings.

To Set the Interface and Default Colors

Recall that Photoshop retains the interface color scheme, as well as the foreground and background colors from session to session. The following steps set the interface to Medium Gray and the foreground and background colors to black over white.

1 Click Edit on the Application bar to display the edit menu. Point to Preferences and then click Interface on the Preferences submenu to display the Preferences dialog box.

2 Click the third button, Medium Gray, to change the interface color scheme.

3 Click the OK button to close the Preferences dialog box.

4 Press the D key to reset the default foreground and background colors.

To Reset the Layers Panel

The following steps reset the Layers panel to make the thumbnails match the figures shown in this book.

1 Click the Layers panel menu button, and then click Panel Options on the list to display the Layers Panel Options dialog box.

2 Click the option button for the smallest of the thumbnail sizes.

3 If necessary, click the Layer Bounds option button to select it.

4 If necessary, place a check mark next to each of the three check boxes at the bottom of the Layers Panel Options dialog box.

5 Click the OK button (Layers Panel Options dialog box) to close the dialog box, resetting the Layers panel.

Web Galleries

Anyone who creates graphics or digital photos appreciates the opportunity to show them off. In today's technology-oriented world, distribution of your personal artwork and photographs commonly is done on the Web. In addition, clients often want collections of photographs on their Web site that feature their products, location, work samples, employees, or more. Adobe Bridge provides a set of tools to create a display of images on the Web. In a Web gallery, each thumbnail is linked to a gallery page that displays a full-size image. The home page and each gallery page contain links that allow visitors to navigate your gallery site.

Plan Ahead

Organize photos for a Web site and gallery pages.
You should organize the photos that you plan to use for the Web site, Web gallery, or animation into a Windows folder for more efficient manipulation. Put the photos in the order in which they will appear in the gallery or automation before you create the Web gallery. Use descriptive names for both the photos and the folder.

To Launch Bridge

The first step is to launch Adobe Bridge because you will use Bridge to organize your files. Additionally, the command to create a Web gallery is in Bridge.

1 With your USB flash drive connected to one of the computer's USB ports, click the Start button on the Windows 7 taskbar to display the Start menu, and then type `Bridge` in the 'Search programs and files' box.

2 Click Adobe Bridge CS6 in the list to start Bridge.

3 If the Bridge window is not maximized, click the Maximize button next to the Close button on the Application bar to maximize the window.

4 Click Essentials on the Bridge Application bar to set the workspace to Essentials.

5 Click the Favorites panel to display it, if necessary.

6 Click Computer in the Favorites panel to display the locations.

7 In the lower-right corner of the Adobe Bridge window, click the 'View content as thumbnails' button, if necessary (Figure 9–2).

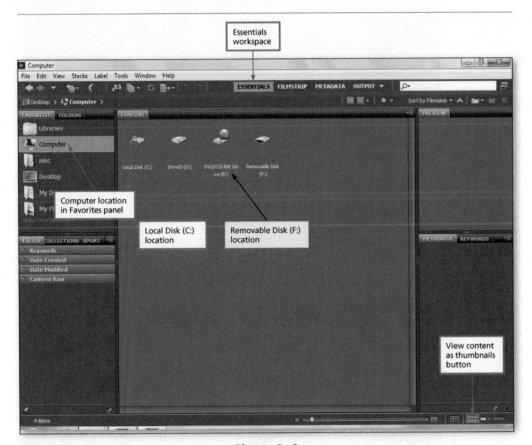

Figure 9–2

Organizing Photos

You should store the photos that you use for the Web gallery or for any of Photoshop's automation options in a dedicated folder for more efficient organization. Adobe Bridge offers an excellent way to copy files and folders between devices and organize files.

To Copy Files

It is important to keep Web site files and folders organized. The steps on the next page copy the Chapter 09 folder from the Data Files for Students to your storage device so that you can practice organizing the files without altering the original data files.

- Double-click Local Disk (C:) in the Content panel to view its contents.

- Double-click the Cengage folder to view its contents.

- Double-click the Photoshop folder to view its contents.

- Double-click the Data Files for Students folder to view its contents.

- Click the Chapter 09 folder to select it.

- Press CTRL+C to copy the folder and its contents to the Windows Clipboard (Figure 9–3).

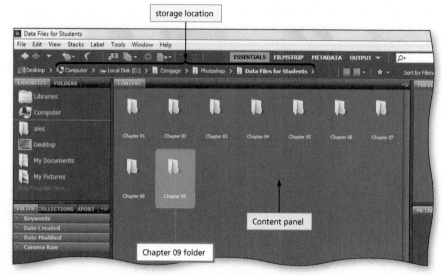

Figure 9–3

- In the Favorites panel, click Computer to display the locations (Figure 9–4).

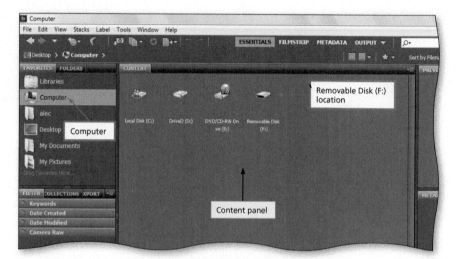

Figure 9–4

- In the Content panel, double-click Removable Disk (F:) to display its contents.

- Press CTRL+V to paste the copied folder to the USB drive (Figure 9–5).

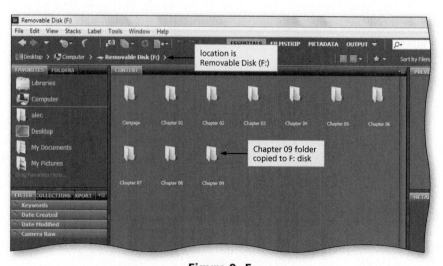

Figure 9–5

To Create a Folder in Bridge

The following steps create a folder for storing the gallery images and copy the five files into the new folder.

1

- In the Content panel, double-click the Chapter 09 folder to display its contents in Bridge.

- Right-click a blank area of the Content panel to display its context menu (Figure 9–6).

Q&A
Why do my Bridge window and context menu look different?

You might store your files in a different location, so the Bridge window will look different. Context menus are user dependent. You might have different files selected, your screen resolution might differ, or your system Clipboard might contain content, so the Paste command might be displayed.

Figure 9–6

2

- Click New Folder to create a new folder on your storage device.

- When the new folder is displayed, type My Web Site, and then press the ENTER key to rename the folder.

- Click away from the new folder icon for better viewing (Figure 9–7).

Q&A
How much storage space will I need for my Web site?

Because a Web gallery contains many pictures, and later in the chapter, you will create an animation, you will need approximately 65 MB of storage to save all the files. If you want to include different pictures in your Web gallery, your storage needs will change.

Figure 9–7

Other Ways

1. On Bridge File menu, click New Folder

2. In Windows Explorer window, right-click content pane, point to New, click Folder

To Copy and Paste Files in Bridge

The following steps use context menus to copy and paste files into the My Web Site folder. The location of your files might differ.

1

- Click the Family 1 file to select it.

- SHIFT+click the Family 5 file to add it to the selection, and all the Family files in between to the selection (Figure 9–8).

- Press CTRL+C to copy the files to the system Clipboard.

Figure 9–8

2

- Double-click the My Web Site folder to open it in Bridge.

- Press CTRL+V to paste the files into the folder (Figure 9–9).

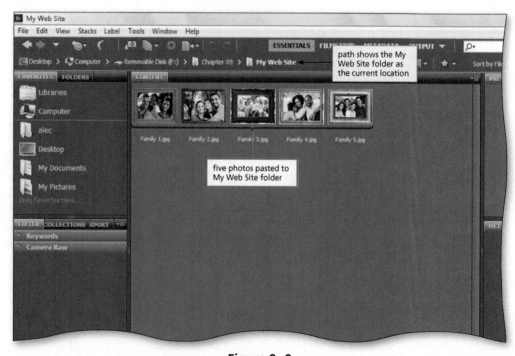

Figure 9–9

To Organize the Remaining Files

The following steps create additional folders and organize more files in the Chapter 09 folder from within Bridge.

1

• Click the Go back button on the Application bar to return to the previous folder.

• Right-click a blank area of the Content panel to display its context menu (Figure 9–10).

Figure 9–10

2

• Click New Folder to create a new folder in the Chapter 09 folder on your storage device.

• When the new folder is displayed, type `Extra Web Site Files`, and then press the ENTER key to rename the folder.

• Click away from the new folder icon for better viewing (Figure 9–11).

Figure 9–11

- Click the Content Frame.jpg file to select it.
- CTRL+click the five Family files to add them to the selection.
- CTRL+click Masthead. jpg, Oval Frame.jpg, Photo Shoot.png, Rectangular Frame. jpg, and Silhouette. png to add them to the selection (Figure 9–12).

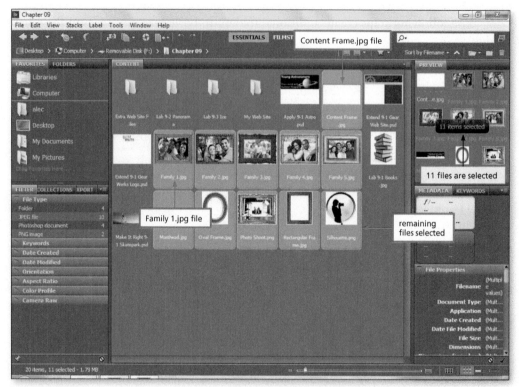

Figure 9–12

- Drag the Family 1.jpg file onto the Extra Web Site Files folder to move all 11 selected files into the Extra Web Site Files folder (Figure 9–13).

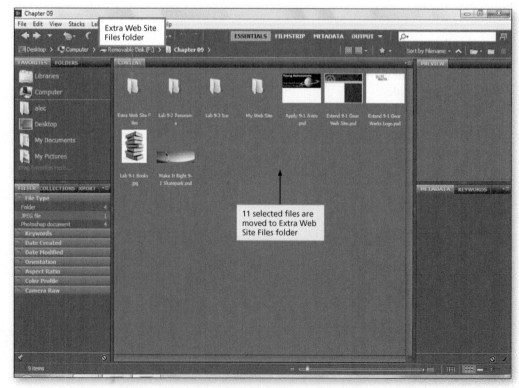

Figure 9–13

Creating a Web Gallery

The Output panel in Adobe Bridge contains settings and buttons to generate the Web pages that display your photos and graphic objects in a gallery format. Once you select the photos, you can choose one of Bridge's templates and styles for the layout and design of the Web gallery pages, specify the gallery title, edit colors, and change the appearance of the gallery before saving or uploading the site. A **template** determines the layout of the Web Gallery while the **style** determines the color scheme and fonts.

To Select Files

The following steps select the image files you will use to create a Web gallery.

1 Double-click the Extra Web Site Files folder to display its contents.

2 Click the Family 1.jpg file to select it.

3 SHIFT+click the Family 5.jpg file to add it, and all Family files in between, to the selection.

To Display the Bridge Output Panel

The following step displays the selected photos in the Bridge Output workspace and the Output panel, which is used to export selected objects as Web Galleries or as PDFs of thumbnails.

1

• On the Bridge Application bar, click Output to display the Output workspace (Figure 9–14).

Q&A

Where is the Output workspace link?

It is possible that another user has changed the default links. Press CTRL+F4 to display the Output workspace.

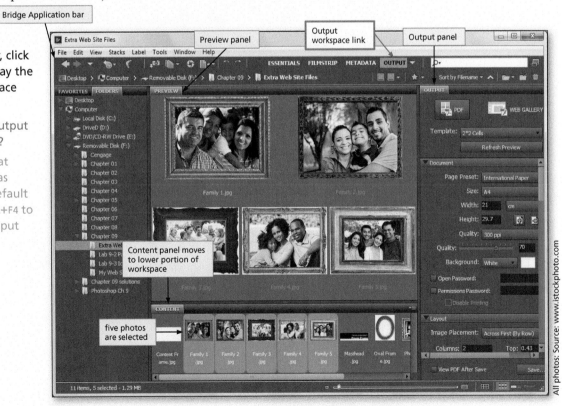

Figure 9–14

Other Ways

1. Press CTRL+F4
2. On Bridge Window menu, point to Workspace, click Output
3. On Bridge Application bar, click Workspace picker button, click Output

To Choose a Template and Style

You will choose the Lightroom Flash Gallery template and the Paper White style in the steps that follow. Bridge includes the template and style, in addition to others, to offer you quick formatting of a professional-looking Web gallery.

1

• On the Output panel, click the Web Gallery button, if necessary, to select it.

• Click the Template button to display the list of templates (Figure 9–15).

 Q&A

What does the PDF button do?

The PDF button displays options for placing a photo in a PDF layout, along with paper sizes, templates, a watermark, and the option to apply a password. A Save button then saves the layout in the PDF format.

Figure 9–15

2

• Click Lightroom Flash Gallery to select it as the template for the gallery.

• Click the Style button to display the list of styles (Figure 9–16).

Figure 9–16

3

- Click Paper White to apply the style (Figure 9–17).

How do I know what the styles look like?

Older versions of Bridge had a Refresh Preview button that allowed you to view the style directly in Bridge. Unfortunately, that option is no longer available in Bridge CS6. To preview a style, you must select it from the Style menu, click the Preview in Browser button, and then close the browser window to return to Bridge. You will preview the style in a later exercise.

Figure 9–17

To Edit Site Information

The site information fields allow Bridge to create headings, descriptions, and contact information that will appear in the Web gallery. The Site Title will appear across the top of the gallery. The Collection Title will appear as a subheading in the upper-right corner of the gallery. The Contact information will appear just below the Collection Title. The following step edits the site information fields.

1

- In the Site Info area, select the text in the Site Title box, and then type `Freeze Frame` to replace the text.

- Type `Web Gallery` in the Collection Title box.

- Type your name in the Contact Info box, and type your e-mail address in the E-mail or Web Address box (Figure 9–18).

What should I type in the Collection Description box?

You may leave the default text in the box, or you can add information about your work in Photoshop and your design skills. The Collection Description appears when accessing the About this Gallery command on the gallery's View menu.

Figure 9–18

To Preview the Web Gallery

It is a good idea to view the Web gallery in a browser to ensure that it appears as you expected. The following steps preview the Web gallery in a browser window.

1

- On the Output panel, click the Preview in Browser button (shown in Figure 9–18) to open a browser window.

- When the browser window opens, double-click the title bar to maximize the window, if necessary (Figure 9–19).

Experiment

- Click any of the links or navigation buttons to experiment with navigating the site.

2

- When you are finished, click the Close button in the browser window title bar to return to Bridge.

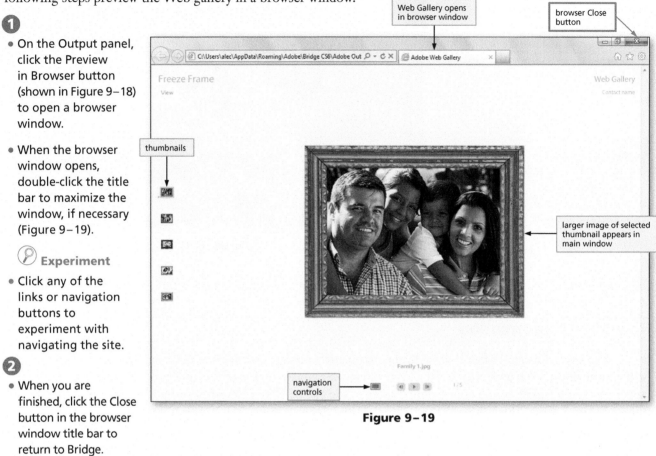

Figure 9–19

To Save the Web Gallery

In the steps that follow, you will save the gallery files to your USB storage device or a location specified by your instructor. Optionally, Bridge allows you to upload the files directly to a server if you have server space and uploading privileges.

1

- On the Output panel, scroll down to display the Create Gallery area (Figure 9–20).

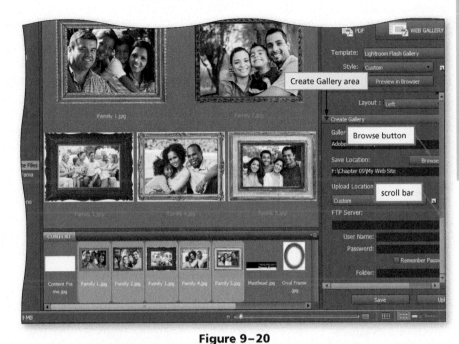

Figure 9–20

2

- Click the Browse button to display the Choose a Folder dialog box.

- Click Computer in the list, click Removable Disk (F:) or the location of your storage device, and then click the Chapter 09 folder to display its files and folders.

- Click the My Web Site folder to select it as the storage location (Figure 9–21).

- Click the OK button to accept the location.

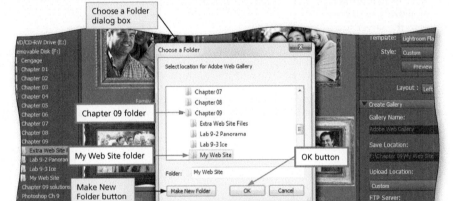

Figure 9–21

3

- In the Output panel, click the Save button to start the Save process (Figure 9–22).

Q&A

How do I adjust the width of the output panel to see more of the buttons and settings?

Drag the border between panels to adjust the width.

4

- Click the OK button in the Create Gallery dialog box to create the gallery.

Figure 9–22

BTW

Web Servers
A Web server is a computer that is responsible for providing Web space and hosting Web pages. Uploading or posting files to the server usually requires authentication with a password. Viewing files usually requires only a browser. Some schools and Internet service providers offer free Web space. Businesses commonly lease or purchase space on a Web server.

BTW

Posting Web Pages
If you want to post, or upload, your Web pages or Web site to the Web, you will need access to a Web server. Most Web servers have an easy-to-use software interface that allows you to copy files to the server space. For the Web site to work properly, you must post all of the HTML files and any supporting file folders.

Web Gallery Files

When a user views your Web gallery, he or she will see the files in the order in which they are displayed in the gallery folder in Bridge. If you prefer a different order, change the order of the files using Adobe Bridge by dragging them in the Content pane. By default, Bridge creates a start page for the gallery with the name, index.html, in a folder named Adobe Web Gallery (Figure 9–23). It also creates a set of accompanying files and folders in the Adobe Web Gallery folder. The Web Gallery, once complete, can be integrated into the rest of a Web site by the programmer.

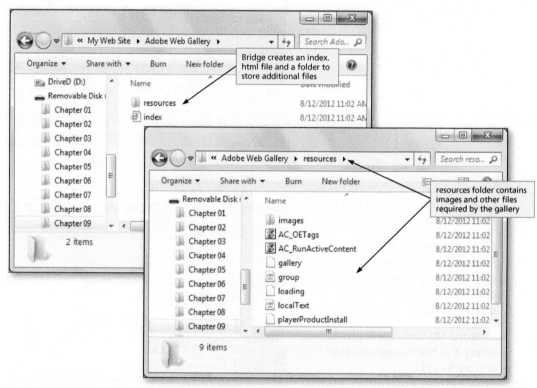

Figure 9–23

To Close Bridge

Because you are done with Adobe Bridge, the following step closes the application. You will then work in Photoshop to create the Web site.

1 Click the Close button on the Bridge title bar.

Designing a Web Page

Planning is the most important step when designing Web pages and Web sites. A Web page is a browser-accessible single page of graphics and information. A Web site is a collection of Web pages that are linked logically, and located together on a hosting computer. Web pages within Web sites typically share a common design and are navigated, or browsed, using some kind of graphic elements — buttons or images — that move the browser from page to page. To be an effective Web designer, you need to understand and apply principles of Web design and programming protocols, and become proficient with many planning and design tools, including Web programming languages and scripting tools. As a graphic designer, however, you may use Photoshop to prepare graphics for the Web page or to plan the site with galleries, graphics, color, links, and animation. Without the visual impact of color, shapes, and contrast, Web pages are neither interesting nor motivating.

You begin creating the Freeze Frame Web site by designing a home page, which serves as a starting place from which to access several other pages, including informational pages with contact information and frequently asked questions (FAQ) along with the Web gallery created in the previous steps. Therefore, a heading and links are important elements of the home page. For visual impact, an animation will attract attention when the page is loaded.

Plan Ahead

Use standard Web design and planning principles.

When planning Web pages, several important issues must be considered:

- **Purpose** — Decide on the site's intended use; for example, advertising, direct sales, business-to-business tasks, prospect generation, employee communications, customer support, information, or education.

- **Audience** — Take into account the target population and the characteristics, preferences, Web experience, and computer systems of the audience, and adapt the site design accordingly.

- **Viewer expectations** — Examine the Web page to see if links and other elements are located in common places, test the ease of navigation and form fields, check for usability issues, and so on. Navigation elements, such as buttons and tabs, typically are placed on the top or left side of a Web page.

- **Nature of planned elements or content** — Make sure that text, images, color, and animation are used judiciously and with purpose.

- **Viewer's visual impact** — Research shows that Web users form first impressions of Web pages in as little as 50 milliseconds, making nearly instantaneous judgments of a Web site's visual appeal, including the loading speed, perceived credibility, usability, and attraction.

- **Page's placement within the Web site structure** — Careful planning of the home page, secondary page(s), links, and accompanying folders involves standard naming conventions, file hierarchy, and structure.

Setting Web Page Dimensions

While Web pages come in a variety of sizes, most pages usually fall within certain height and width limits. It is important to choose a size for your Web page that will accommodate the majority of users' monitors and screen size settings. Oversized Web pages, designed on larger screens with resolutions of 1024 × 768 or higher, become unreadable when viewing the page using narrower browser widths. The graphics may be too wide to fit the browser window, and unwrapped text may create long, unreadable lines. Web designers constantly analyze and compare existing Web sites for usage guidelines related to screen colors, screen size, scrolling, graphics, and readability of text.

Another consideration is the possibility that the site visitor will want to print the Web page. Setting the dimensions of the Web page to 800 × 600 pixels will accommodate most users visually, but for Web pages destined for print on 8.5 × 11-inch paper, you should try to keep text and graphics within 760 pixels wide and 410 pixels high to account for margins when printed.

BTW

Scrolling Web Pages
Most Web users do not want to scroll from side to side; they also prefer limited vertical scrolling. Therefore, when designing Web pages, you should choose a page size used by a majority of users.

BTW

Using Pixels on the Rulers

Using pixels as the unit of measure on the rulers allows you to keep in mind the page layout, both for browsers and for printing of graphics and text. By using 1024 x 768, most visitors to the Web page will not have to scroll. Later, as part of a complete Web site solution, HTML and CSS code could be added to create more flexibility and to adjust the screen size further.

To Set Attributes for a New Document

The following steps use the New command on the File menu to set the attributes for a new Web document that will be used as the Freeze Frame home page. Recall that a common resolution for Web products is 72 pixels per inch (PPI).

Because this is a Web site for a photo studio, you will use the default white background to provide a neutral backdrop for the photography.

1 Click the Photoshop button on the Windows taskbar to switch to Photoshop, if necessary.

2 Click File on the Application bar and then click New. When the New dialog box is displayed, type Freeze Frame in the Name text box.

3 Click the Preset box arrow and then click Custom, if necessary.

4 Double-click the Width box and then type 800 as the width. Click the Width unit box arrow and then click Pixels in the list, if necessary.

5 Double-click the Height box and then type 600 as the height. If necessary, click the Height unit box arrow, and then click Pixels in the list.

6 Double-click the Resolution box and then type 72 as the entry. Click the Resolution unit box arrow and then click Pixels/Inch in the list, if necessary.

7 Click the Color Mode box arrow. If necessary, click RGB Color in the list. If necessary, click the Color Mode unit box arrow and then click 8 bit in the list.

8 If necessary, click the Background Contents box arrow and then click White in the list to finish setting the attributes for the new file (Figure 9–24).

9 Click the OK button to create the new document.

10 If the rulers are not displayed in the document window, press CTRL+R.

11 Right-click either of the rulers, and then click Pixels in the list to change the ruler units to pixels.

12 Double-click the Hand Tool to fit the canvas to your screen.

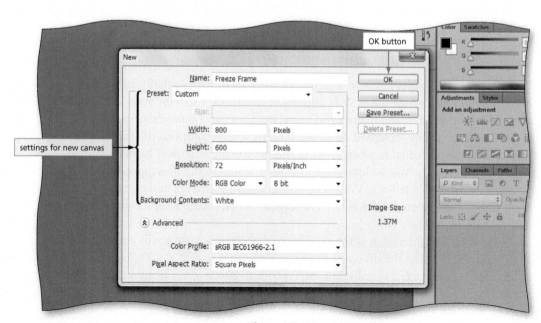

Figure 9–24

To Save the New Document

With the settings complete, it is a good practice to save the new blank document on a storage device as described in the following steps. You will save it in the PSD format for now; later in the chapter, you will save it in the HTML Web format.

1 With your USB flash drive connected to one of the computer's USB ports, click File on the Application bar, and then click Save As.

2 Click the Save in box arrow, and then click Removable Disk (F:), or the location associated with your USB flash drive, in the list. Navigate to the Chapter 09 folder.

3 Click the Format button to display the list of available file formats, and then click Photoshop (*.PSD; *.PDD) in the list.

4 Click the Save button.

To Add a Masthead Background Graphic

The following steps insert a graphic to use as a masthead for the Freeze Frame Web site.

1 Open the file named Masthead from the Extra Web Site Files folder in the Chapter 09 folder on your USB drive.

2 Arrange the documents side by side.

3 Activate the Move Tool, and then drag the Masthead image into the Freeze Frame document window. Close the Masthead document window.

4 Position the masthead image at the top of the Freeze Frame document window. It should span the full width of the canvas.

5 Double-click Layer 1 in the Layers panel, type `Masthead,` and press the ENTER key to rename the layer (Figure 9–25).

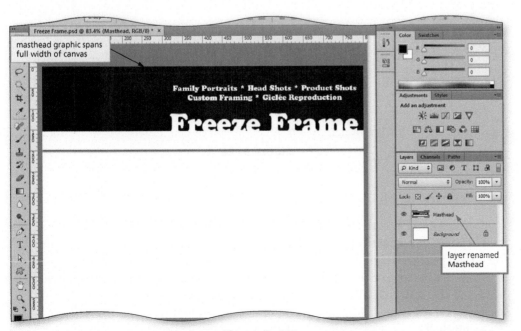

Figure 9–25

To Add Images to the Masthead

The next steps insert two graphics to enhance the masthead.

1 Open the file named Silhouette from the Extra Web Site Files folder in the Chapter 09 folder on your USB drive.

2 Arrange the documents side by side.

3 Activate the Move Tool and then drag the Silhouette image into the Freeze Frame document window. Close the Silhouette document window.

4 Position the Silhouette image at the upper-left corner of the Freeze Frame document window (Figure 9–26).

5 Open the file named Photo Shoot from the Extra Web Site Files folder in the Chapter 09 folder on your USB drive.

6 Arrange the documents side by side.

7 Activate the Move Tool and then drag the Photo Shoot image into the Freeze Frame document window. Close the Photo Shoot document window.

8 Position the Photo Shoot image at the upper-left corner of the Freeze Frame document window (Figure 9–26). You will reposition and animate the Photo Shoot image later in this chapter.

9 In the Layers panel, rename the two new layers, Silhouette and Photo Shoot.

Figure 9–26

Inserting Text

After looking at the masthead to identify the Web site, most users look for a text heading or **navigation bar** to identify site's content. A navigation bar is an area on a Web page that contains the links to other pages in the site. Navigation elements typically are buttons or text links, and they should be consistent in their appearance, with text characteristics that differentiate the navigational elements from other elements on the page. Using placement, font size, and font style appropriately and consistently for various text elements helps users identify the Web page heading, navigation bar links, and regular page content. Color is a secondary consideration for text because not all users will be able to distinguish colors. Choosing colors with high contrast is the best choice for accessibility and readability. In this chapter, you will use the Photoshop Horizontal Type Tool to create the navigation element, and then later add functionality using slices.

Web pages sometimes require **special characters**, such as letters with diacritical marks. These characters do not appear on the standard keyboard. Photoshop's type tools use the ALT key combined with a character code to create letters such as é, ñ, or ü, among others. You must type the character codes using the numeric keypad rather than the numbers on the standard keyboard. If you are a Windows user and use a laptop or a keyboard without a keypad, use the Character Map utility that comes free with Windows to insert special characters.

To Insert Text with Special Characters

When designing a Web site, your focus is typically on imagery and layout. The Web site programmer normally adds the actual text on a Web page with HTML code after receiving it from the client. Therefore, Web designers commonly insert placeholder text with the understanding that it will be replaced at a later time when the Web page is coded with HTML. Including the placeholder text in Photoshop allows the client to preview the design and offer feedback before the actual Web page is coded. Additionally, the coders find the placeholder text useful as a guide in formatting the text with the Web page code. The following steps insert placeholder text that includes a special character in the word giclée (a high-quality print of an original photograph or painting).

1

- Double-click the Zoom Tool at the bottom of the Tools panel to zoom the document view to 100%.

- If necessary, scroll the document window until you see the upper-left portion of the canvas.

- Press the T key. If the Horizontal Type Tool is not active, right-click the current type tool button, and then click Horizontal Type Tool in the list.

- Using the box arrows on the options bar, select Arial, Regular, 14 pt, None, Left align, and black text as the text characteristics.

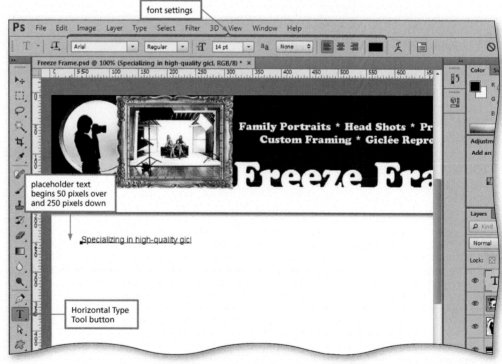

Figure 9–27

- In the document window, position the mouse pointer at 50 pixels on the horizontal ruler and 250 pixels on the vertical ruler, then click to place the insertion point.

- In the document window, click in the text box, and then type `Specializing in high-quality gicl` to begin entering the placeholder text (Figure 9–27).

2

- Using the numeric keypad, press ALT+0233 to create the special character, é, at the end of the word.

Q&A My laptop does not have a numeric keypad. How can I type the accented e?

You can use the Windows 7 Character map. Click the Start button, click All Programs, click Accessories, click System Tools, and then click Character Map. Click the é character, click the Select button, and then click the Copy button. Return to Photoshop, and then click CTRL+V to paste the character into the Photoshop text box. Return to Character Map, close the Character Map window, and then return to Photoshop.

3

- Type e , press the SPACEBAR and then type reproductions. to end the sentence (Figure 9–28).

Q&A Why am I leaving so much empty space at the bottom of the canvas?

You are typing placeholder text, which, in a professional setting, would give the Web page HTML programmer an idea of where to position the text. If necessary, the site owner or client would instruct the programmer to place any additional text here. The HTML coder will add the real (and complete) text when the Web site is coded with HTML.

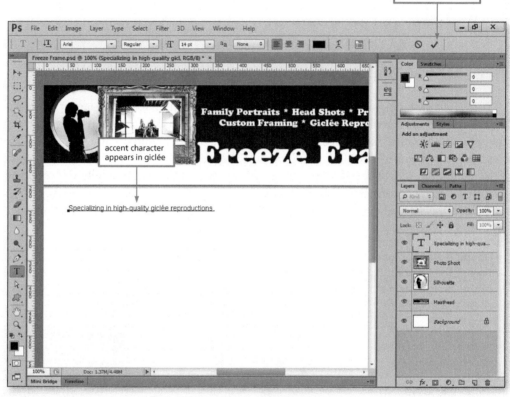

Figure 9–28

4

- On the options bar, click the 'Commit any current edits' button to finish entering the text.

BTW

Photoshop Help
The best way to become familiar with Photoshop Help is to use it. Appendix D includes detailed information about Photoshop Help and exercises that will help you gain confidence in using it.

To Create the Navigation Bar

The following steps create the text that will later become the navigation bar. The navigation bar will include the elements that allow a user to navigate around the site.

1

- Double-click the Hand Tool on the Tools panel to fit the canvas to the screen.

- Press the T key to activate the Horizontal Type Tool.

- Click in the document window at about 350 pixels on the vertical ruler and about 50 on the horizontal ruler. You will move the navigation bar into position after you type.

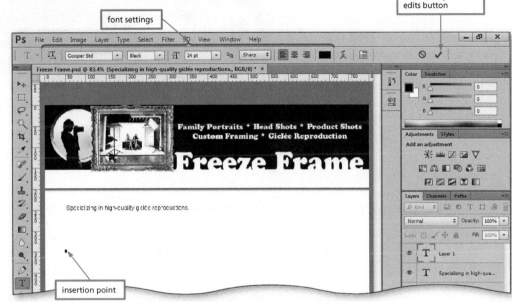

Figure 9–29

- Using the box arrows on the options bar, select Cooper Std, Black, 24 pt, Sharp, and Left align text. Choose a different appropriate font if your computer does not have Cooper Std (Figure 9–29).

2

- Click the canvas at the insertion point so that you can type on it.

- Type Home and then press the SPACEBAR five times.

- Type Gallery and then press the SPACEBAR five times.

- Type FAQ and then press the SPACEBAR five times.

- Type Contact to complete the navigation bar text.

- On the options bar, click the 'Commit any current edits' button to complete the creation of the navigation bar (Figure 9–30).

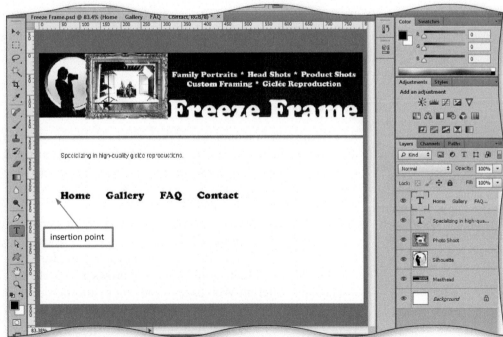

Figure 9–30

3

- Click the Move Tool on the Tools panel.

- Drag the navigation bar to the right side of the canvas below the masthead. Try to center the navigation bar below the text Freeze Frame. Try to balance the space around the top and bottom of the navigation bar so it is not cramped (Figure 9–31).

Q&A

Why does my text look jagged and distorted?

You are not viewing the document at 100% so the text is not clear. If you zoom to 100%, the text will be sharp and clear.

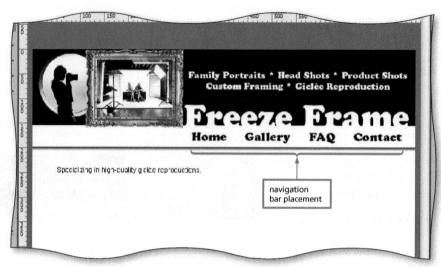

Figure 9–31

To Save the File Again

Because you have completed entering the text for the site, the following step saves the file.

1 Press CTRL+S. If Photoshop displays a dialog box, click the OK button.

Break Point: If you wish to take a break, this is a good place to do so. To resume at a later time, start Photoshop, open the file called Freeze Frame, and continue following the steps from this location forward.

Creating Slices

BTW

Hyperlinks
Most hyperlinks are created using HTML code, either written by a Web developer or created by application software. Slices more commonly are used for hot spots, areas, and images.

The navigation functionality — the visitor's ability to move from one Web page to another — will be assigned to the navigation bar you just created. You will convert each of the navigation text elements to a slice. A **slice** is a defined rectangular area in a document that performs a specific function, such as opening a different Web page, when the page is viewed in a Web browser. Another common application of slices is the creation of image maps. An **image map** is a graphic containing one or more invisible regions, called **hot spots**, which are hyperlinked. For example, you could slice a map of the United States into an image map by assigning hot spots to each state. Clicking an individual state then would cause the browser to perform a designated task such as displaying a different Web page or moving to another location on the current page. Slices give you better control over the function and file size of your image because you can optimize slices to load individually. An image may have many slices — all of which are reassembled when the Web page is displayed. When you save a sliced image for the Web, each slice is saved as an independent file with its own settings and color table; the slice preserves hyperlinks and special effects.

You create a slice by using the Slice Tool or by creating layer-based slices, which are slices that are created automatically from the contents of a layer. The Slice Tool is located with the Crop Tool on the Tools panel. Once you create a slice, you can select, move, resize, or align it. You can assign each slice an individual hyperlink.

When you create a slice, Photoshop displays a number and a badge. A **slice badge** is an icon that appears next to the slice number, indicating certain information about the slice. A slice badge indicates whether the slice is image based, layer based, or has no content. Photoshop displays a blue slice number and blue slice badge on user-defined slices; automatically created slices display gray slice numbers and gray slice badges.

Numbering of slices is from left to right and top to bottom, beginning in the upper-left corner of the image. If you change the arrangement or total number of slices, Photoshop updates the slice numbers to reflect the new order.

The Slice Tool options bar allows you to designate an exact size for the slice or use guides to create a slice.

BTW

Rollovers
A rollover is an image that appears when a user moves the pointer over the slice. Rollovers can be an animation, a separate image, or other effect. Photoshop does not support automating rollovers – users must write the JavaScript code or employ a program such as Dreamweaver or Fireworks.

To Create Slices

The following steps create slices in the Freeze Frame file that will serve as links to various parts of the Web site.

1

- On the Tools panel, right-click the Crop Tool button to display the context menu (Figure 9–32).

Figure 9–32

2

- Click Slice Tool to select it.

- In the document window, drag a rectangle around the word, Home (Figure 9–33), being sure to include the drop-shadow below the word. The size of your slices may differ from the figure.

Q&A What are all those symbols and lines?

After you create your custom slice, Photoshop slices the remaining areas of the page into numbered pieces above, below, and to either side of the Home slice. In the slice badge, a mountain icon indicates that the slice has image content.

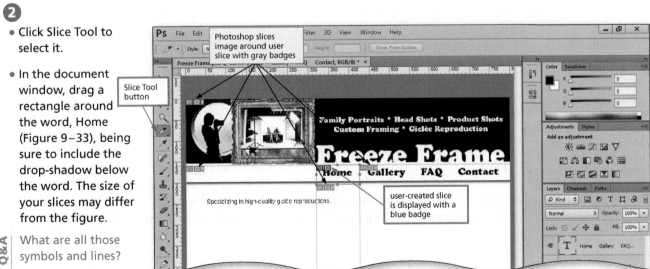

Figure 9–33

3

● In the document window, drag a rectangle around the word, Gallery, to create a slice. As you drag, allow Photoshop to snap the slice into position so it is the same height as the Home slice (Figure 9–34).

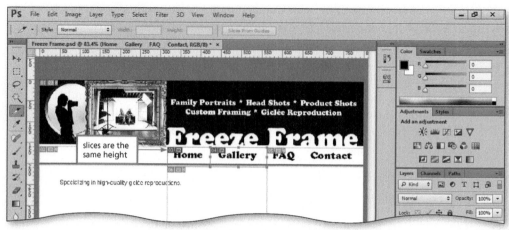

Figure 9–34

4

● Create slices for the FAQ and Contact words (Figure 9–35).

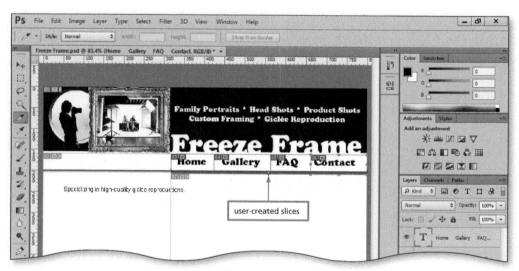

Figure 9–35

Other Ways

1. On Layer menu, click New Layer Based Slice

BTW

Relative vs. Absolute References
A URL without a full Web address, such as index. html, creates a relative reference, which is a link to a page within the same site. An absolute reference has a full path notation, such as C:\Program Files\ User\index.html or http:// www.cengage.com.

The Slice Select Tool

Once you create a slice, you can select, move, resize, align, distribute, and assign attributes using the Slice Select Tool. With the Slice Select Tool activated, you select a slice by clicking it. To move a slice, click within the slice and drag. To resize a slice, drag its border or drag a handle. The Slice Select Tool options bar displays many buttons to reorder, align, and distribute (Figure 9–36). Other Slice Select Tool options — including the ability to delete, divide, and reorder — are available by right-clicking the slice.

layering buttons

align and distribute buttons

set options for the current slice button

Promote button

Divide button

Figure 9–36

Show or hide auto slices button

The Slice Options dialog box (Figure 9–37) appears when you double-click a slice; you can use it to set values associated with a slice.

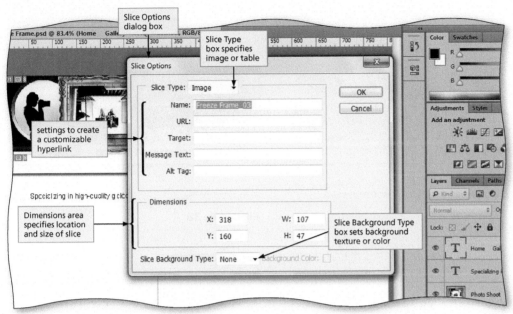

Figure 9–37

Each slice becomes a small image when converted to HTML. The Name box of the Slice Options dialog box automatically generates the name of that image, although you can change it. The URL box holds the Web page address of the hyperlink. The Target box allows you to specify how the link will open — in a new browser window (or browser tab) or as a replacement of the current page. For example, a target setting of _blank will cause the hyperlink to open the Web page in a new browser window or tab. The Message Text box allows you to specify text that will be displayed in the browser's status bar when a user points to the hyperlink. You can use the Alt Tag box to create alternative text used by screen readers. The alternative text also becomes a tool tip in most browsers; it appears as placeholder text if a user chooses not to download graphics. At the bottom of the Slice Options dialog box are dimension settings and the background type setting.

BTW

Target Attributes
HTML target attributes can be used in the Target box in the Slice Options dialog box. The _blank value displays the linked file in a new window or tab. The _self value displays the linked file in the same frame as the original file. The _parent value displays the linked file in its own original parent frameset. The _top value replaces the entire browser window with the linked file, removing all current frames.

To Enter Slice Settings

In the Freeze Frame image, you will select a slice with the Slice Select Tool and then enter hyperlink settings for the Gallery slice. The link will take Web page visitors to the index.html page of the Web gallery. The Message Text setting defines text that appears at the bottom of a Web browser window when a user points to a slice on the Web page. The Alt Tag setting provides alternative text that is displayed on the Web page if the Web browser cannot display the image. The Alt Tag text is also read aloud by some computers. This allows a visually impaired user to know where a hyperlinked slice will take them without physically seeing the Web page.

- Right-click the Slice Tool button to display the context menu (Figure 9–38).

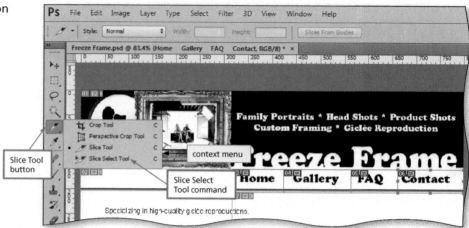

Figure 9–38

- Click Slice Select Tool to choose the tool.

- Double-click the Gallery slice to display the Slice Options dialog box.

- Type `Gallery` to replace the text in the Name box.

- Click the URL box and then type `Adobe Web Gallery/ index.html` as the entry. Recall that this is the name and location of the Web gallery start page, created earlier in Bridge.

- Click the Target box and then type `_blank` as the entry.

- Click the Message Text box and then type `Go to the Web gallery` as the entry.

- Click the Alt Tag box and then type `This link opens the Web gallery` as the entry (Figure 9–39).

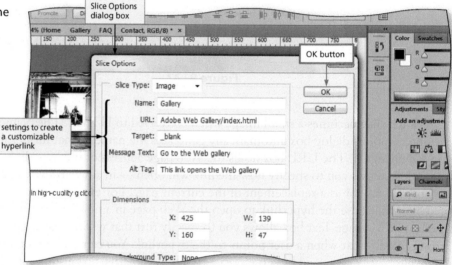

Figure 9–39

Q&A

What are the parts of the URL entry?

Adobe Web Gallery is the folder that Bridge created automatically. The file, index.html, is the name of the first page in the Web gallery. The / (slash) in the URL separates the name of the folder and the file name.

- Click the OK button to apply the settings and close the dialog box.

Other Ways

1. Right-click slice, click Edit Slice Options, enter settings, click OK

2. On options bar, click "Set options for current slice" button, enter settings, click OK

To Enter More Slice Settings

The following steps set the options for the remaining slices.

1 Double-click the Home slice to display the Slice Options dialog box, select any existing type in the Name text box, and then type Home.

2 Click the URL box, select any existing text, and then type index.html as the entry (Figure 9–40).

3 Click the OK button to apply the settings and close the dialog box.

4 Double-click the FAQ slice to display the Slice Options dialog box.

5 Type FAQ in the Name box, type faq.html in the URL box, and then click the OK button to apply the settings and close the dialog box.

6 Double-click the Contact slice to display the Slice Options dialog box, type Contact in the Name text box, type contact.html in the URL box, and then click the OK button to apply the settings and close the dialog box.

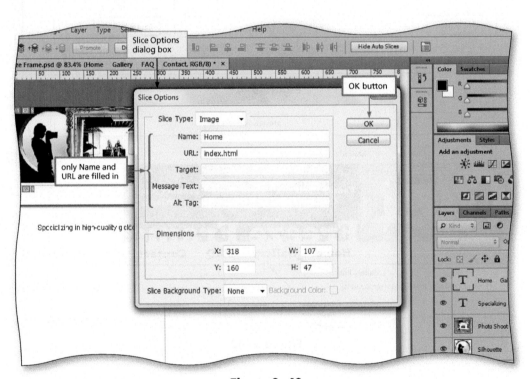

Figure 9–40

Previewing the Web Page

As you learned in a previous chapter, Photoshop uses the Save for Web dialog box to preview an image or Web page within a browser. This approach is fine for viewing the page and its settings, but it will not allow you to navigate the hyperlinks — move from one page to another — unless you are connected to the Web.

To Preview the Hyperlink

The steps on the next page preview the hyperlink settings.

1

- Click File on the Application bar, and then click Save for Web to display the Save for Web dialog box (Figure 9–41).

- Click the 4-Up tab, if necessary, to display four preview versions of the document.

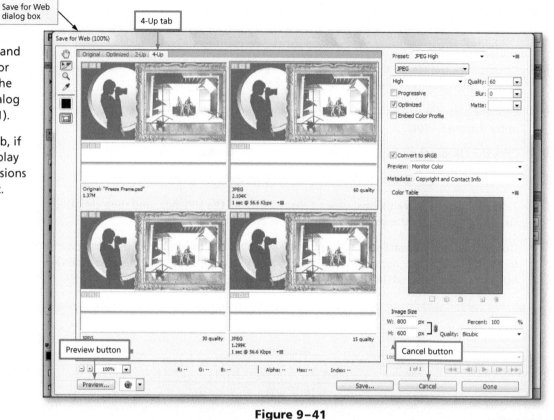

Figure 9–41

2

- Click the Preview button.

- When the browser window opens, if a yellow security bar appears across the bottom of the window, click it, and then click Allow blocked button.

- If Windows displays a security warning dialog box, click the Yes button.

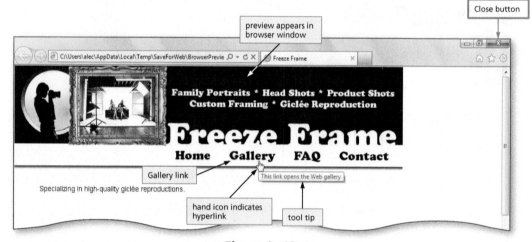

Figure 9–42

- If necessary, maximize the browser window.

- Point to the Gallery link to display the hand icon and tool tip (Figure 9–42).

Q&A

Can I click the Gallery link to display the Web gallery?

The preview is stored in a temporary location that cannot access the index.html page of the gallery. Later in the chapter, you will save the Web page and test the link.

3

- Close the browser window.

- Return to Photoshop, if necessary, and click the Cancel button in the Save for Web dialog box.

To Save the File

The following step saves the file again.

 Press CTRL+S.

Animation

The next step in developing the Freeze Frame Web site is to create an animation that moves an image across the home page. An **animation** is a sequence of frames or images, displayed over time to convey movement. A **frame** is a single view of the image within the sequence, which can be edited and optimized. Each frame in an animation varies slightly from the preceding frame; the variation is the result of changing effects, filters, or repositioning objects. This variation creates the illusion of movement when the frames are viewed or played in quick succession. Professional animators create hundreds or thousands of frames, each with a tiny change from frame to frame, to emulate smooth movement. In small animations that are used on the Web, such as **animated GIFs,** the number of frames varies, but commonly includes from 5 to 50 frames and can run several seconds or longer, depending on how the timing for the animation is set.

Designers create animations using a wide variety of application software. While Photoshop is a high-end graphic-editing tool, it is not intended for the creation of advanced animations with film or movie quality. You can create basic animations in Photoshop, however.

To learn all of the animation and optimization features in Photoshop takes time and practice. In this chapter, you will create a simple animation with approximately 30 frames. Building this animation presents you with an introduction to the basic techniques and tools used in animation and optimization. Further study will be required to master these tools and techniques.

BTW

Animations
Adobe Flash CS6 is an authoring environment for creating animations and interactivity. Flash animations are platform-independent and can be displayed on a variety of devices.

Plan Ahead

Employ animation carefully.
The judicious use of animation in a Web site can add impact and increase comprehension, but a little goes a long way. Animations that illustrate a dynamic process, enliven a logo, or pace the delivery of information are best. Keep in mind the following rules when creating animations:

• Animations should enhance content. All Web sites present information, so animated effects should support the content by delivering information, identifying key elements or purpose, or clarifying a complex process.

• Simple animations are more effective than complex ones. Animated effects should enhance, not distract from, content. Choose subtle effects, such as dissolves and fades.

• Keep your animations consistent; do not try to do too many different kinds of animations on a Web site.

Creating the Animation Graphic for the Freeze Frame Web Page

The animation in the Freeze Frame Web page creates a rotating picture frame that starts in the upper-right corner and finishes behind the silhouette on the left side of the masthead. First, you will temporarily hide the slices and layers that are not involved in the animation. Then, you will create a layer group, and open and copy it to multiple layers, placing them in different locations on the page. Relocation of the layer groups gives the illusion of motion when viewed in quick succession. You will align and distribute the layers evenly. Finally, you will place each layer as a frame in the animation and have Photoshop create additional frames for smooth transitions.

To Hide Layers and Slices

The following step temporarily hides layers that are not involved in the animation. You also will hide the slices.

- Display the Layers panel, if necessary.

- Hide the Background and the two type layers so they are not visible in the document window.

- Press CTRL+H to hide extras (such as guides, grids, bounding boxes, and selections) and hide the slices (Figure 9–43).

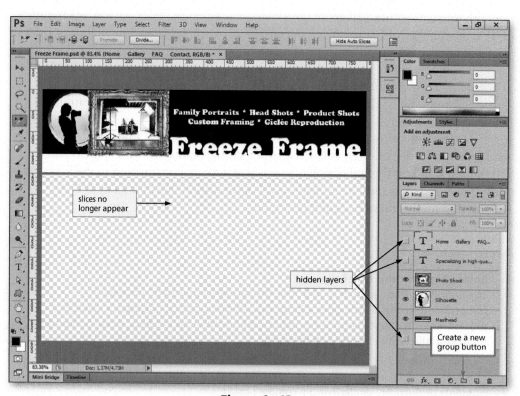

Figure 9–43

To Create a Layer Group

The steps that follow create a layer group named Rotation.

1 On the Layers panel, click the 'Create a new group' button.

2 Name the layer group, Rotation.

3 On the Layers panel, drag to move the new layer group to the location immediately above the Masthead layer.

To Move the Photo Shoot Layer

The following steps move the Photo Shoot layer into the Rotation group.

1 On the Layers panel, drag the Photo Shoot layer onto the Rotation group to move it into the group. The Photo Shoot layer should now appear indented below the Rotation group.

2 If necessary, click the Hide/Show layers icon to the left of the Rotation group to expand its contents (Figure 9–44).

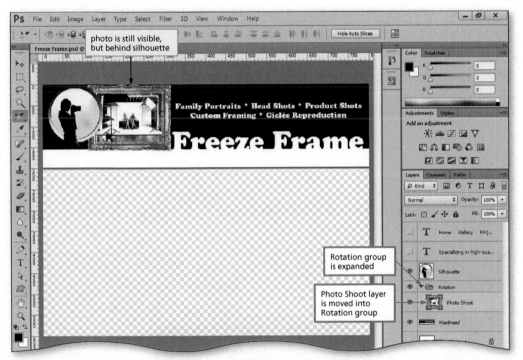

Figure 9–44

To Create Copies of the Photo Shoot Layer

The steps that follow create copies of the Photo Shoot layer, numbering them from 2 to 7; the layers will be used to create animation frames.

1 On the Layers panel, right-click the Photo Shoot layer, and then click Duplicate Layer on the context menu to display the Duplicate Layer dialog box.

2 Type `Photo Shoot 2` in the As text box, and then click the OK button to create the new layer.

3 Repeat Steps 1 and 2 to create a total of seven layers named Photo Shoot, and Photo Shoot 2 through Photo Shoot 7.

4 Drag the Photo Shoot layers within the Rotation group to rearrange them, if necessary, as shown in Figure 9–45 on the next page.

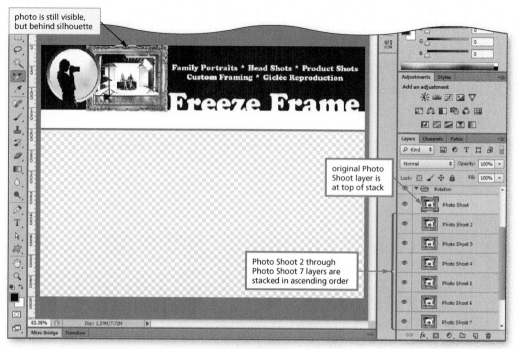

Figure 9–45

To Rotate the Layers

The following steps rotate and position the original Photo Shoot layer.

1

- Click the original Photo Shoot layer in the Layers panel to select it, if necessary.

- Press the V key to activate the Move Tool.

- Press CTRL+T to activate the transform controls and display the bounding box.

- Position the mouse pointer just outside the upper-right corner of the bounding box to display the rotation handle. (Figure 9–46).

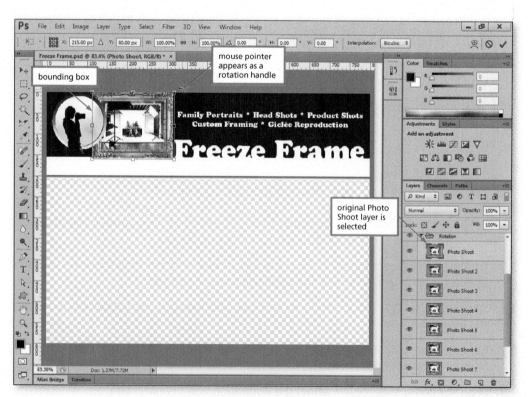

Figure 9–46

- Drag down to rotate the photo so that the right side angles down. Use Figure 9–47 as a reference.

- Use the arrow keys on the keyboard to nudge the photo into place so that the photo does not extend beyond the black of the masthead and none of the text in the masthead is obscured. This position of the photo represents the completed state of the animation.

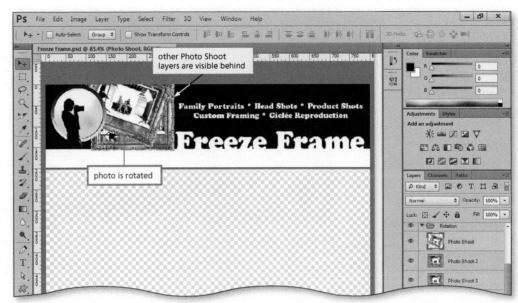

Figure 9–47

- Press the ENTER key to apply the transformation (Figure 9–47).

To Move the Layers

The following step moves the layers to locations diagonally across the document window.

- On the Layers panel, click the Photo Shoot 2 layer to select it.

- In the document window, drag it to a location slightly to the right of and above the Photo Shoot layer.

- Repeat the previous steps, moving Photo Shoot layers 3, 4, 5, 6, and 7 to locations to the right and slightly above each of the previous layers (Figure 9–48). Do not be concerned with spacing the photos evenly. You will use a Photoshop command to distribute the photos equally later in this chapter.

Figure 9–48

To Rotate the Remaining Layers

The following steps rotate each of the Photo Shoot layers approximately 20 degrees counterclockwise so the animated photo will appear to be rotating.

- On the Layers panel, select the Photo Shoot 3 layer.

- Press CTRL+T to display the bounding box.

- Position the mouse pointer just outside the lower-right corner of the bounding box to display the rotation handle (Figure 9–49).

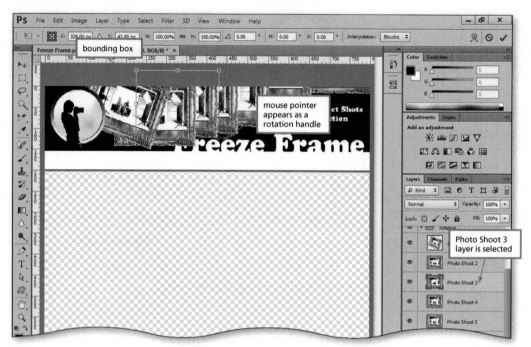

Figure 9–49

- Drag the layer approximately 20 degrees counterclockwise (Figure 9–50).

Q&A

How can I tell when I am close to 20 degrees?

As you drag, a tool tip will appear in the document window near the mouse pointer. The value in this tool tip changes in real time as you rotate the layer, giving you the exact degree measurement.

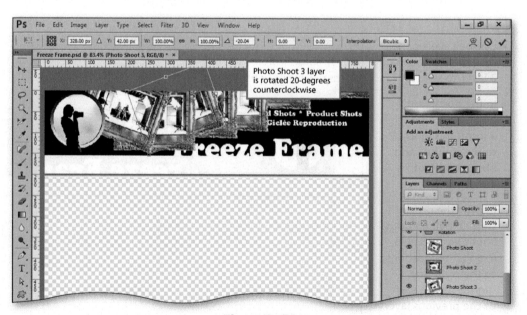

Figure 9–50

3

- Press the ENTER key to confirm the transformation

- Repeat Steps 1 and 2 for the layers named Photo Shoot 4, 5, 6, and 7, adding an additional 20 degrees to each successive rotation so that Photo Shoot 7 is rotated approximately 100 degrees counterclockwise (Figure 9–51).

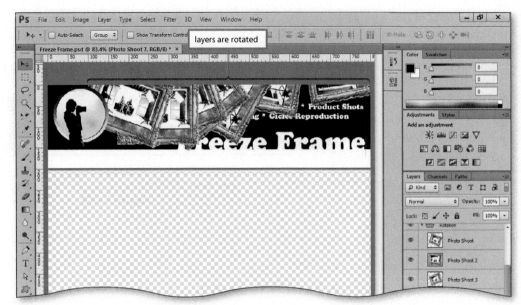

Figure 9–51

To Distribute the Layers

The following steps distribute the layers evenly across the image using buttons on the options bar. Distributing the layers improves the smoothness of the animation.

1

- CTRL+click each of the Photo Shoot layers on the Layers panel to select them all.

- On the options bar, click the 'Distribute vertical centers' button to evenly space the layers (Figure 9–52).

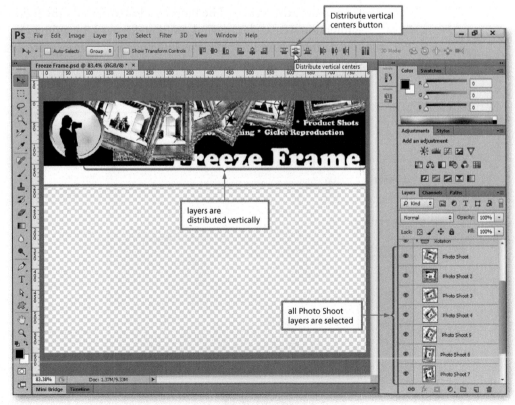

Figure 9–52

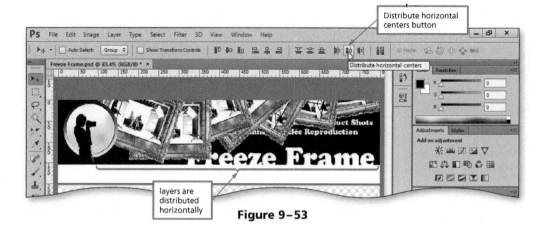

- On the options bar, click the 'Distribute horizontal centers' button to set the height of the layers (Figure 9–53).

- Press CTRL+S to save your changes.

Figure 9–53

The Timeline Panel

You will use the Timeline panel in conjunction with the Layers panel to create animation frames (Figure 9–54). The Timeline usually opens at the bottom of the Photoshop window, with one frame visible to start. To create an animation, you insert a new frame from the panel menu, and then edit the layers. Frames are added sequentially from left to right in the panel as you create them.

The Timeline panel menu displays commands to create, manipulate, and optimize the frames. Below each frame is a button used to set the timing or delay between the current frame and the next frame.

The Timeline panel displays buttons along the bottom that are used to manipulate the frames. The buttons allow you to do the following: edit how the animation loops; play, rewind, and fast-forward the animation; and tween, duplicate, and delete frames. Additionally, the Timeline panel can operate in a video mode that creates true video files — those shot with a camera — rather than graphic file animations.

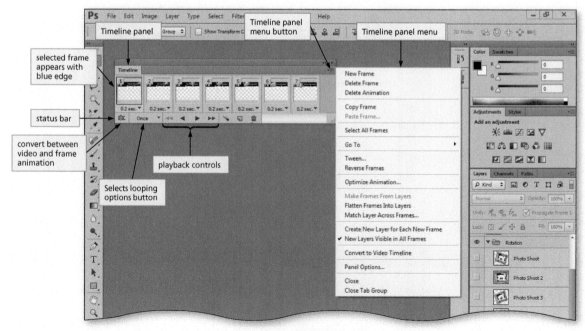

Figure 9–54

To Display the Timeline Panel

The following step uses the menu system to open the Timeline panel.

- Click Window on the Application bar to display the menu.

- Click Timeline to display the Timeline panel. If the Timeline panel does not resemble Figure 9–55, click the Create

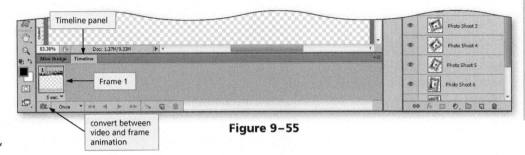

Figure 9–55

Frame Animation button in the center of the Timeline panel. If the button in the center reads Create Video Timeline instead, click the arrow next to the button, choose Create Frame Animation, and then click the Create Frame Animation button. If there is no button in the center of the Timeline panel, click the 'Convert to frame animation' button in the lower-left corner of the Timeline panel.

To Display Appropriate Layers

When the animation begins, you will want only the rightmost photo, Photo Shoot 7, to appear in the document window to display the starting state of the animation. The following step hides the other Photo Shoot layers so that only the Photo Shoot 7 layer is initially visible.

- Click the 'Indicates layer visibility' buttons for the Photo Shoot and Photo Shoot 2 through Photo Shoot 6 layers to hide them (Figure 9–56).

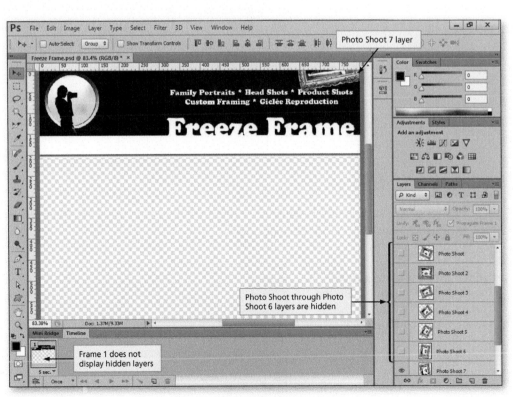

Figure 9–56

To Set the Timing

The amount of time that Photoshop takes to move from one frame to another during playback is called the **delay time**. In the following steps, you will set the time to .2 seconds so very little time elapses between frames. The delay time that you specify in Frame 1 automatically applies to subsequent frames as they are created.

- Click the 'Selects frame delay time' button to display the list of timings (Figure 9–57).

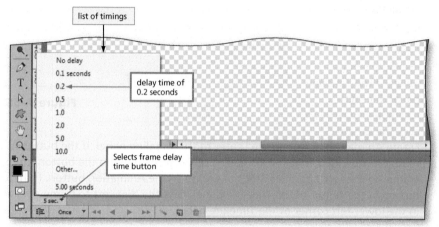

Figure 9–57

- Click 0.2 in the list to delay the next frame by two-tenths of a second (Figure 9–58).

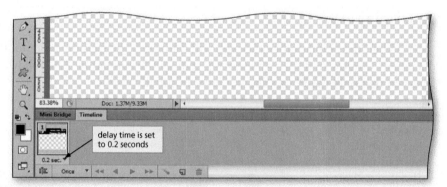

Figure 9–58

To Create New Frames

The following steps build the animation using the Timeline panel. As you duplicate each frame, you will hide the previous photo and display the next one.

- On the Timeline panel status bar, click the 'Duplicates selected frames' button to display the second frame (Figure 9–59).

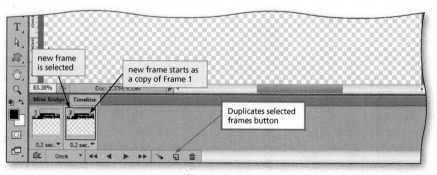

Figure 9–59

2

• Hide the visibility of the Photo Shoot 7 layer and turn on the visibility of the Photo Shoot 6 layer to display the Photo Shoot 6 image in Frame 2 (Figure 9–60).

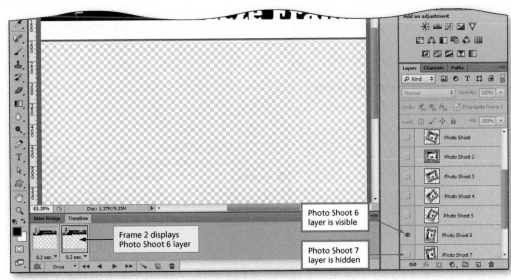

Frame 2 displays Photo Shoot 6 layer

Photo Shoot 6 layer is visible

Photo Shoot 7 layer is hidden

Figure 9–60

3

• Repeat Steps 1 and 2, hiding and showing each subsequent Photo Shoot layer until the original Photo Shoot layer is displayed in the seventh frame (Figure 9–61).

Q&A

How many frames should I have?

A total of seven frames should appear in the Timeline panel. Each frame will have a photo displayed at a different spot.

Family Portraits * Head Shots * Product Shots
Custom Framing * Giclée Reproduction

Freeze Frame

Photo Shoot layer

Photo Shoot layer is displayed in Frame 7

each frame displays a different Photo Shoot layer

Figure 9–61

Other Ways

1. On Animation panel menu, click Copy Frame, click Paste Frame

To Preview the Animation

The following steps preview the animation by clicking the Plays animation button on the Timeline status bar.

- On the Timeline panel, click Frame 1 to select it (Figure 9–62).

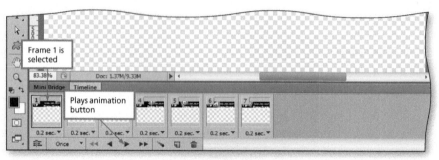

Figure 9–62

- On the Timeline panel status bar, click the Plays animation button to preview the animation (Figure 9–63). The Plays animation button becomes a Stop button after you click it and then becomes the Plays animation button at Frame 7.

Figure 9–63

Tweening

Tweening, a corruption of the phrase in-between, is a way to allow Photoshop to create new frames automatically between two existing frames. When you tween between two frames, Photoshop parses the data equally in the frames, creating graduated changes. Photoshop reduces the opacity of the layer evenly across the new frames and increments the layer position equally, and any special effects are interpolated across the new frames. For example, if two frames contain an opacity change from 50 percent to 100 percent, Photoshop creates a tween frame with 75 percent opacity. Similarly, if two frames display an object that has been moved, the tween frame will display the object placed halfway between the two. Tweening significantly reduces the time required to create animation effects, but is more effective with images that are simpler in composition; a highly complex animation does not generate a great result with tweening. Tweened frames are fully editable.

To Tween

The following steps create three new frames between each of the current frames, tweening the animation.

1

- In the Timeline panel, click Frame 7 to select it, if necessary.

- On the Animation status bar, click the 'Tweens animation frames' button to display the Tween dialog box (Figure 9–64).

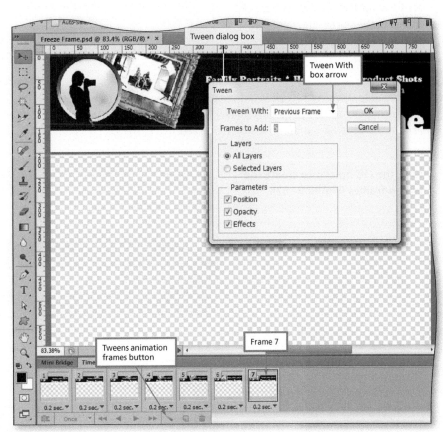

Figure 9–64

2

- Click the Tween With box arrow to display the list (Figure 9–65).

Q&A

How does Photoshop create the tween?

Photoshop adds a new frame, interpolating the layer properties evenly between the two surrounding frames.

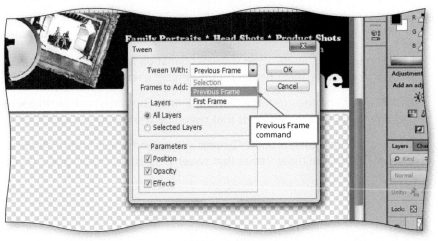

Figure 9–65

3

- Click Previous Frame to create tween frames between Frames 6 and 7.

- Type 3 in the Frames to Add box to create three frames between Frames 6 and 7.

- If necessary, click the All Layers option button to select it. Display a check mark in each of the check boxes in the Parameters area, as shown in Figure 9–66.

Q&A What does the All Layers option button do?

If the frame contains more than one layer with movement or opacity changes, the All Layers option will tween each layer. If you do not select the option, only the layer selected on the Layers panel will be tweened.

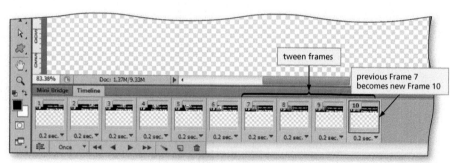

Figure 9–66

4

- Click the OK button to create the tween frames (Figure 9–67).

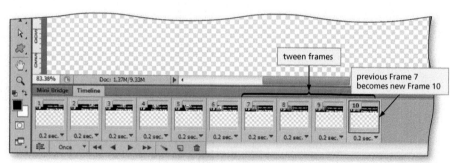

Figure 9–67

5

- Click Frame 6 and then click the 'Tweens animation frames' button. Repeat Steps 2 through 4 to create three frames that tween between Frames 5 and 6.

- Click Frame 5 and then click the 'Tweens animation frames' button. Repeat Steps 2 through 4 to create three frames that tween between Frames 4 and 5.

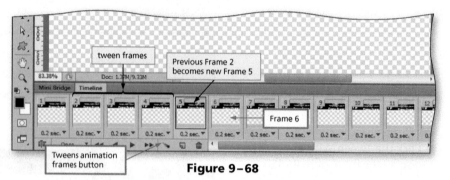

Figure 9–68

- Click Frame 4 and then click the 'Tweens animation frames' button. Repeat Steps 2 through 4 to create three frames that tween between Frames 3 and 4.

- Click Frame 3 and then click the 'Tweens animation frames' button. Repeat Steps 2 through 4 to create three frames that tween between Frames 2 and 3.

- Click Frame 2 and then click the 'Tweens animation frames' button. Repeat Steps 2 through 4 to create three frames that tween between Frames 1 and 2 (Figure 9–68).

Q&A How many total frames does the animation now contain?

You should have 25 frames: the original seven plus three between each one.

Other Ways

1. Select frames, on panel menu click Tween

To View Tween Frames

To look at the interpolation Photoshop creates in order to tween, the following step views a tween frame.

- Click Frame 2 to view how Photoshop tweens (Figure 9–69).

Experiment

- Continue clicking each frame, one at a time, and watch the opacity and movement changes.

Figure 9–69

To Preview the Animation Again

The following steps preview the animation again by clicking the Plays animation button at the bottom of the Timeline panel.

1. On the Timeline panel, scroll the frames to the left, and then click Frame 1 to select it (Figure 9–70 on the next page).

2. If necessary, click the 'Selects looping options' arrow and set the looping to Once.

3. On the Timeline panel status bar, click the Plays animation button to preview the animation.

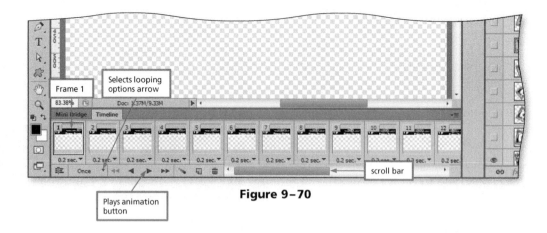

Figure 9–70

TO OFFSET FOR ANIMATION

If you want to create an animation that moves an object without any rotation, you can use a special filter in Photoshop to specify the exact movement in pixels. For example, if you wanted to create a ball that bounces across the screen, you would perform the following steps.

1. Duplicate the layer that contains the ball.

2. With the new layer selected, click Filter on the Application bar, point to Other, and then click Offset.

3. In the Offset dialog box, specify exactly how many pixels to move the object, both horizontally and vertically.

4. On the Timeline panel, in the first frame, make only the original layer visible.

5. Duplicate Frame 1 and make only the filtered frame visible.

6. Repeat Steps 1 through 5 for each new position of the bouncing ball.

Animation Settings

BTW

Disposing of Frames
The Dispose command, available on each frame's context menu, discards the current frame before displaying the next frame. When displayed on the Web, the disposal prevents flickering and provides a more consistent flow of animation.

You can choose to have an animation display just once, a specified number of times, or repeat continuously, which is called **looping**. The animation you created displayed once. The animation display choices are available through the 'Selects looping options' arrow, shown in Figure 9–70.

Additionally, you can optimize the animation for both performance and storage with two settings on the Timeline panel menu. Without optimizing, Photoshop includes the entire layer within each frame. Optimizing reduces file size by cropping each frame to include only the area that has changed from the preceding frame. Photoshop uses a bounding box that you access through the Timeline panel menu to automatically crop the frame. Optimizing can lessen the time needed to download the animation when viewed on a Web page. The Redundant Pixel Removal setting identifies the pixels in a frame that are unchanged from the preceding frame and makes them transparent. This can reduce the file size because unneeded pixels are removed. Later, when you save the file as a GIF or HTML file, you must select the Transparency option on the Optimize panel for the setting to work properly.

To Optimize the Animation

The following steps set the optimization for the animation.

1

- Click the Timeline panel menu button to display the menu (Figure 9–71).

What does the Match Layer Across Frames command do?

If you added an animation to an existing image, the Match command would make the contents of the selected layer visible throughout every frame of the animation.

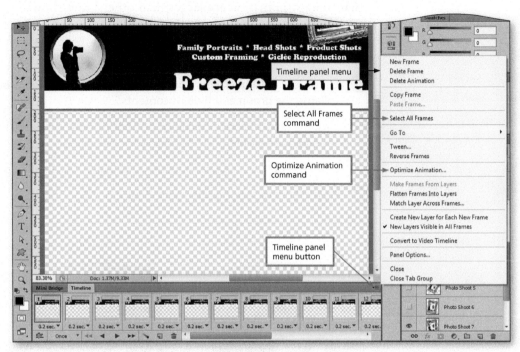

Figure 9–71

2

- Click Select All Frames to include all of the frames in the animation.

- Click the Timeline panel menu button, and then click Optimize Animation to display the Optimize Animation dialog box.

- If necessary, place a check mark in both the Bounding Box and Redundant Pixel Removal check boxes to select them (Figure 9–72).

3

- Click the OK button to close the dialog box.

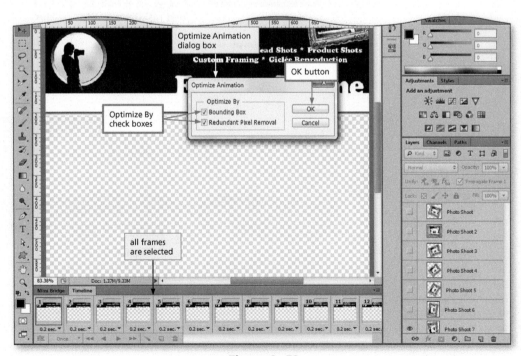

Figure 9–72

To Save the File with the Animation

Saving the file preserves the animation. Because you have used appropriate sizes and slices, you do not need to specify further optimization. Photoshop files that contain animation are larger than other Photoshop files. Make sure you have enough room on your storage device to hold the file, which is approximately 2.6 MB. If you do not have enough space, you will have to save your file in another location.

1 Click the Hide/Show layers icon to the left of the Rotation group on the Layers panel to collapse the group and hide its contents.

2 Click the 'Indicates layer visibility' buttons to show the three hidden layers so that all the layers are visible.

3 Double-click the Timeline panel tab to collapse the Timeline panel.

4 Press CTRL+S to save the file again (Figure 9–73).

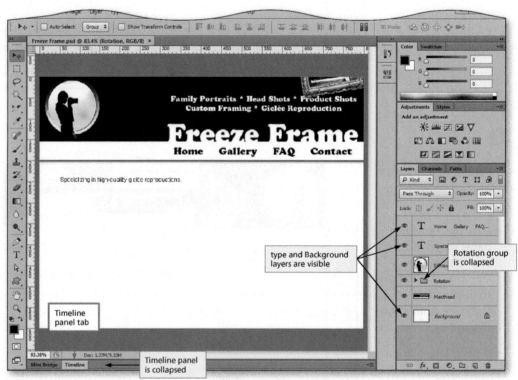

Figure 9–73

BTW

Quick Reference
For a table that lists how to complete the tasks covered in this book using the mouse, context menu, and keyboard, see the Quick Reference summary at the back of this book.

To Save the File as a Web Page

In the next steps, you will save the file in the HTML format that can be uploaded to a Web server. Because your document includes animation, you must save in the GIF format because only the GIF format supports animation.

1

- On the File menu, click Save for Web to display the Save for Web dialog box.

- Click the 4-Up tab, if necessary, to view the original image and three optimized previews.

- Click the upper-right preview to select it.

- Click the Preset box arrow to display the choices (Figure 9–74).

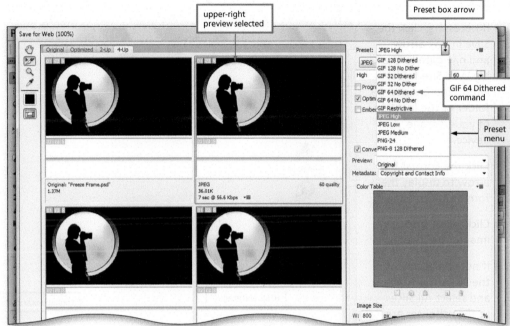

Figure 9–74

2

- Click GIF 64 Dithered in the Preset menu because that setting offers an acceptable balance between image quality and file size (Figure 9–75).

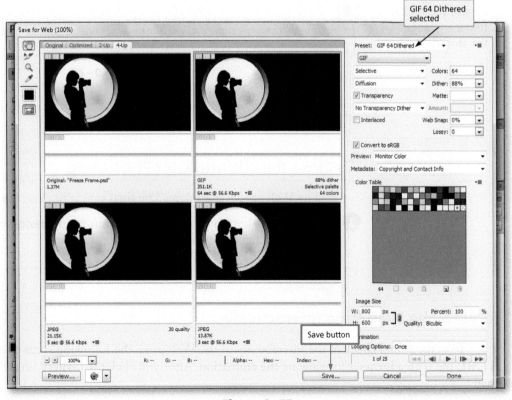

Figure 9–75

- Click the Save button to display the Save Optimized As dialog box.

- If necessary, click the Save in box arrow and navigate to the My Web Site folder within the Chapter 09 folder or the location of your storage device.

- Click the Format box arrow to display the format options.

- Click HTML and Images in the list.

- If necessary, click the Slices box arrow and select All Slices so that all slices are saved (Figure 9–76).

- Click the Save button to save the file and a folder of images on the storage device.

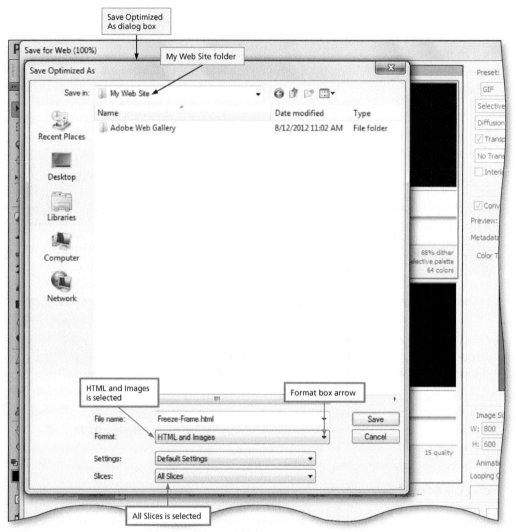

Figure 9–76

To Close the File and Quit Photoshop

The Web page is complete. The final step is to close the file and quit Photoshop.

① Click the Close button on the Photoshop title bar. If Photoshop displays a message about saving the file, click the No button.

To View the Web Page Interactively

To make a final check of the interactivity of the Web page, the following steps open the Freeze Frame HTML file with a browser for viewing the animation. After you click the Gallery link, the Web gallery will open.

1

- Click the Start button on the Windows 7 taskbar, and then click Computer on the Start menu.

- When the Computer window opens, navigate to your USB storage drive, open the folder named Chapter 09, and then open the My Web Site folder.

- If necessary, click More options on the toolbar and then click List to display a list of all the files (Figure 9–77).

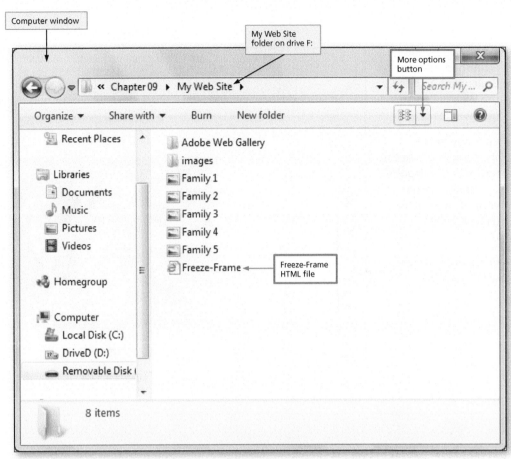

Figure 9–77

2

- Double-click the HTML file, Freeze-Frame, to launch your default Web browser, load the page, and view the animation (Figure 9–78).

- If a bar is displayed warning about running scripts, click the Allow blocked content button.

Q&A

My animation did not appear. Did I do something wrong?

If your animation does not play, your browser might not permit ActiveX controls. See your instructor for ways to play the animation in your browser.

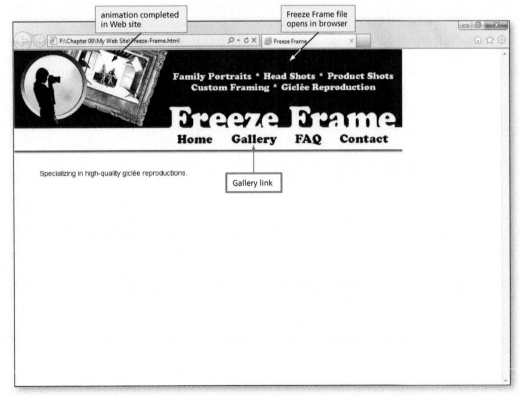

Figure 9–78

• When the animation is finished, click the Gallery link to open the Web gallery in a new window.

• Click any of the thumbnails or use the navigation buttons to display a larger view of each image (Figure 9–79).

• Close all of the open windows.

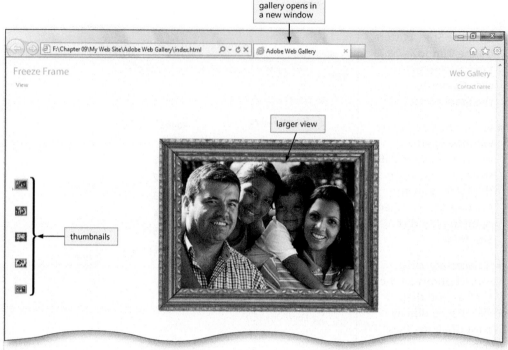

Figure 9–79

Chapter Summary

In this chapter, you created a Web site for the Freeze Frame photo studio. First, you organized images in a folder and created a Web gallery using an automation feature in Bridge. After inserting a masthead, you added placeholder text and a navigation bar. You entered text to serve as hyperlinks when the Web page is viewed in a browser. You sliced the image into multiple sections, one for each hyperlink. You used the Slice Options dialog box panel to enter specific settings for the hyperlink, such as the destination URL and Status bar message.

Finally, you created a series of frames that animated a graphic of a framed photo rotating across the screen. You created each part of the animation as a separate layer and then displayed each layer in its own animation frame. You learned about the Timeline panel and animation techniques such as looping, tweening, and optimizing. The completed animation was added to the home page of the Web site. With the Web site complete, you tested the animation and the hyperlink in a Web browser.

The items listed below include all the new Photoshop skills you have learned in this chapter:

1. Copy Files (PS 565)
2. Create a Folder in Bridge (PS 567)
3. Copy and Paste Files in Bridge (PS 568)
4. Organize the Remaining Files (PS 569)
5. Display the Bridge Output Panel (PS 571)
6. Choose a Template and Style (PS 572)
7. Edit Site Information (PS 573)
8. Preview the Web Gallery (PS 574)
9. Save the Web Gallery (PS 574)
10. Insert Text with Special Characters (PS 581)
11. Create the Navigation Bar (PS 583)
12. Create Slices (PS 585)
13. Enter Slice Settings (PS 587)
14. Preview the Hyperlink (PS 589)
15. Hide Layers and Slices (PS 592)
16. Rotate the Layers (PS 594)
17. Move the Layers (PS 595)
18. Rotate the Remaining Layers (PS 596)
19. Distribute the Layers (PS 597)
20. Display the Timeline Panel (PS 599)
21. Display Appropriate Layers (PS 599)
22. Set the Timing (PS 600)
23. Create New Frames (PS 600)
24. Preview the Animation (PS 602)
25. Tween (PS 603)
26. View Tween Frames (PS 605)
27. Offset for Animation (PS 606)
28. Optimize the Animation (PS 607)
29. Save the File as a Web Page (PS 609)
30. View the Web Page Interactively (PS 610)

Apply Your Knowledge

Reinforce the skills and apply the concepts you learned in this chapter.

Creating a Web Banner

Instructions: Start Photoshop and perform the customization steps found on pages PS 6 through PS 10. Open the Apply 9-1 Astro file from the Chapter 09 folder of the Data Files for Students. Visit www.cengage.com/ct/studentdownload for detailed instructions or contact your instructor for information about accessing the required files.

   The purpose of this exercise is to create a Web banner for an organization that offers astronomy programs for kids. The Apply 9-1 Astro file contains a banner with the name of the program, an image, and a short description. You are to create a folder to hold all of the associated files, add text slices, and animate the image in preparation for hyperlink entries. The final product is shown in Figure 9–80.

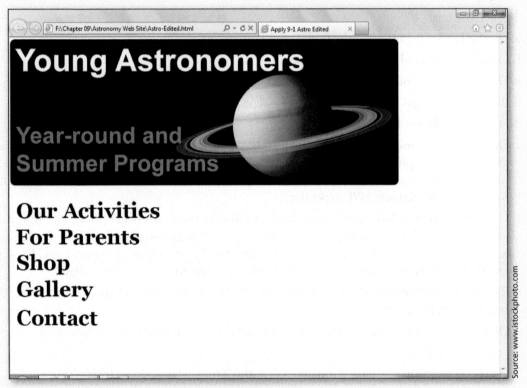

Source: www.istockphoto.com

Figure 9–80

Perform the following tasks:

1. On the File menu, click Save As. When the Save As dialog box is displayed, navigate to your storage device. If you created a Chapter 09 folder, double-click to open it, and then click the Create New Folder button on the toolbar. When the new folder is displayed, type `Astronomy Web Site` as the name, and then press the ENTER key to rename the folder. If necessary, double-click the Astronomy Web Site folder to open it. In the File name text box, type `Apply 9-1 Astro Edited` to name the file. If necessary, click the Format box arrow, and then click Photoshop (*.PSD;*.PDD) in the list. Click the Save button. If Photoshop displays an options dialog box, click the OK button.

Continued >

2. To create the text hyperlinks:

  a. On the Layers panel, click the Background layer to select it.

  b. On the Tools panel, click the Horizontal Type Tool button. On the options bar, set the font to Georgia, set the font style to Bold, set the size to 10, set the anti-aliasing to Sharp, set the alignment to Left, and set the color to black.

  c. Click on the left side of the document window, just below the black masthead shape. Type `Our Activities` and then click the 'Commit any current edits' button on the options bar.

  d. Press the v key to access the Move Tool. Drag the Our Activities text into position so that it resembles Figure 9–80 on the previous page. ALT+DRAG four copies of the text and position them along the left edge, below each other. One at a time, double-click the layer thumbnail of each new layer and type the words shown in Figure 9–80.

  e. Select the five type layers you added on the Layers panel. On the Tools panel, select the Move Tool. On the options bar, click the 'Distribute vertical centers' button and the 'Align left edges' button.

3. To slice the text:

  a. On the Layers panel, select the Our Activities text layer.

  b. On the Tools panel, click the Slice Tool button.

  c. Draw a slice around the Our Activities text element.

  d. Repeat the process for the remaining four type layers.

4. To create new layers for the animation:

  a. On the Layers panel, right-click the Saturn layer, click Duplicate Layer, and then click the OK button to duplicate the layer. Repeat the process until you have the Saturn layer and four copies. Rename the five Saturn layers from top to bottom Saturn 22, Saturn 44, Saturn 66, Saturn 88, and Saturn 100 respectively.

  b. Click the Saturn 22 layer and press CTRL+T to display the Transform options bar. In the Options bar, click the 'Maintain aspect ratio' button, if necessary, to select it. In the Set horizontal scale box, type `22` to resize the layer to 22 percent of its original size. Press the ENTER key to accept your entry, then press ENTER again to commit the change.

  c. Repeat Step 4b for the Saturn 44, Saturn 66, and Saturn 88 layers, resizing them to the 44, 66, and 88 percent, respectively.

  d. On the Layers panel, turn off the visibility of all the Saturn layers except Saturn 22.

5. To create animation frames:

  a. On the Window menu, click Timeline. Click the 'Duplicates selected frames' button.

  b. On the Layers panel, turn off the visibility of the Saturn 22 layer and turn on the visibility of the Saturn 44 layer.

  c. Create a third frame. On the Layers panel, turn off the visibility of the Saturn 44 layer and turn on the visibility of the Saturn 66 layer.

  d. Create a fourth frame. On the Layers panel, turn off the visibility of the Saturn 66 layer and turn on the visibility of the Saturn 88 layer.

  e. Create a fifth frame. On the Layers panel, turn off the visibility of the Saturn 88 layer and turn on the visibility of the Saturn 100 layer.

6. To create tweens:

  a. On the Timeline panel, click Frame 5 to select it, if necessary.

  b. Click the 'Tweens animation frames' button.

  c. Ensure the Tween With box is set to Previous Frame and set the Frames to Add box to 3.

d. Ensure the All Layers option is selected and all three Parameters check boxes are checked, then click the OK button.

e. Click Frame 4 and repeat Steps 6b through 6d to create tweened frames between Frames 3 and 4.

f. Click Frame 3 and repeat Steps 6b through 6d to create tweened frames between Frames 2 and 3.

g. Click Frame 2 and repeat Steps 6b through 6d to create tweened frames between Frames 1 and 2.

h. If desired, change the time delay by selecting all of the frames and then clicking the 'Selects frame time delay' button. When you are done, click Frame 1 to select it.

i. If necessary, set the Selects looping options menu to Once.

7. To save the file, press CTRL+S.

8. Click File on the Application bar and then click Save for Web. When the Save for Web dialog box appears, click the 4-Up tab, if necessary, set the Preset menu to GIF 64 Dithered, and then click the Preview button. Wait for the browser window to open; if necessary, click the Allow Blocked Content button. Watch the animation. Close the browser window.

9. Click the Save button. If necessary, navigate to the Astronomy Web Site folder. If necessary, type `Astro-Edited` in the File name box. If necessary, click the Format box, and then select HTML and Images in the list. Click the Save button.

10. Close the Apply 9-1 Astro Edited.psd document window. If Photoshop asks if you want to save the file again, click the No button. Quit Photoshop.

11. Submit the Astronomy Web Site folder in the format specified by your instructor.

Extend Your Knowledge

Extend the skills you learned in this chapter and experiment with new skills. You may need to use Help to complete the assignment.

Animating and Slicing a Web Page Header

Instructions: Start Photoshop and perform the customization steps found on pages PS 6 through PS 10. Open the Extend 9-1 Gear Web Site file from the Chapter 09 folder of the Data Files for Students. Visit www.cengage.com/ct/studentdownload for detailed instructions or contact your instructor for information about accessing the required files. You have just finished a mock-up of a new Web site for the company Gear Werks. After looking at the design of the header, you have decided to animate the main gear illustration. You also need to slice the design for production.

1. Press SHIFT+CTRL+S to save the image on your USB flash drive as a PSD file, with the file name Extend 9-1 Gear Web Site Edited.

2. Click Window on the Application bar, and then click Timeline to view the Timeline panel. If necessary, click the 'Create Frame Animation' button on the Timeline.

3. To create the animation:

a. On the Layers panel, click the Big Gear layer to make it active. Drag the layer down to the status bar and drop it on the 'Create a new layer' button to create a duplicate of the layer.

b. Rename the duplicate layer, Big Gear 2.

c. Press CTRL+T to transform the Big Gear 2 layer. On the options bar, enter `18` in the Set Rotation box. Click the Commit transformation (Enter) button to commit the transformation.

Continued >

d. On the Layers panel, drag the Big Gear 2 layer down to the 'Create a new layer' button to create another duplicate. Name the layer Big Gear 3. Repeat Step 3c to rotate this layer another 18 degrees.

e. Repeat to create two more rotated duplications. Name the layers Big Gear 4 and Big Gear 5.

f. Turn off the visibility for the Big Gear 2 through Big Gear 5 layers.

g. On the Timeline panel, click the 'Selects frame delay time' button in Frame 1 and set the timing to 1.0 seconds.

h. Duplicate the frame and turn off the visibility for the Big Gear layer. Turn on the visibility for the Big Gear 2 layer. Repeat the process for each of the Big Gear layers, creating a total of five frames.

i. Click the Play button to preview the animation.

4. On the layers panel, click the Big Gear 5 layer to select it, if necessary. Click File on the Application bar and then click Place. Navigate to the Chapter 09 folder of the Data Files for Students and then double-click the file named, Extend 9-1 Gear Werks Logo. Press the ENTER key to confirm the placement.

5. On the Timeline panel, click the Timeline panel menu button. Click Select All Frames. On the Layers panel, turn on the visibility of the Navigation and Content layer groups to add them to the animation.

6. To create the slices:

a. Select the Slice Tool on the Tools panel. Drag to create a slice over the top portion of the image, including the gear and the logo. Do not cover the navigation buttons. Right-click the slice and then click Edit Slice Options on the context menu to open the Slice Options dialog box. Type `Header` in the Name box, and then click the OK button to close the dialog box.

Figure 9–81

b. Create a slice over the about us button. Right-click the slice and then click Edit Slice Options. Enter the name, `btn about us`.

c. Create a slice over each of the remaining buttons and name them accordingly.

d. Create one last slice that covers the rest of the Web site mock-up. Right-click the slice and then click Edit Slice Options. Name this slice, content.

e. Save your changes.

7. On the File menu, click Save for Web. When the Save for Web dialog box opens, click the Optimized tab.

8. Click the Header slice and choose GIF 128 No Dither using the Preset box arrow. At the bottom of the dialog box, change the Animation Looping Options from Once to Forever. One at a time, click each remaining slice and change its preset to GIF 128 No Dither. Navigate in the preview as necessary.

9. Click the Save button. When the Saved Optimized As dialog box is displayed, navigate to your storage location and click the Create New Folder button and name the new folder, Gear Web Site. Double-click the Gear Web Site folder to open it. Name the file, Gear_Web_Site. Click the Format box arrow, and then click HTML and Images, if necessary. Click the Slices box arrow, and then click All Slices.

10. Click the Save button to create the images and HTML code.

11. Close the Extend 9-1 Gear Web Site Edited.psd document. Do not save changes if prompted.

12. Navigate to the Gear Web Site folder and double-click the file named Gear_Web_Site.html to view it in your Web browser (Figure 9–81).

Make It Right

Analyze a project and correct all errors and/or improve the design.

Improving a Skateboard Park Banner Advertisement

Problem: The Westville Skatepark has a Web banner that needs to grab the attention of visitors to their Web site. They have started work on an animated GIF banner using Photoshop's frame animation but it has several problems that you will need to fix: the background disappears and reappears, the animation is too fast, the phone number flashes, and the path of the skateboarder is incorrect.

Perform the following tasks:
Start Photoshop and perform the customization steps found on pages PS 6 through PS 10. Open the Make It Right 9-1 Skatepark file from the Chapter 09 folder of the Data Files for Students. Visit www.cengage.com/ct/studentdownload for detailed instructions or contact your instructor for information about accessing the required files. Press SHIFT+CTRL+S to save the image on your USB flash drive as a PSD file, with the file name Make It Right 9-1 Skatepark Edited.

1. Open the Timeline panel. Play the animation and notice how the background disappears and reappears, and the park name and phone number flash on and off. Notice also that the skateboarder's motion is haphazard. Finally, the animation is too fast (Figure 9–82 on the next page).

2. Click Frame 1 on the Timeline panel. Select the Background layer on the Layers panel. Click the Timeline panel menu button, and then click Match Layer Across Frames. When the dialog box appears, click the OK button.

Continued >

Make It Right *continued*

Source: www.istockphoto.com

Figure 9–82

3. Click the 'Indicates layer visibility' button to show all three layers of text (Westville, Skatepark, and 1-800-555-5555). Click the 1-800-555-5555 layer and then SHIFT+click the Westville layer to select all three layers. Click the Timeline panel menu button, and then click Match Layer Across Frames. When the Match Layer dialog box appears, click the OK button.

4. On the Layers panel, select the Skateboarder layer. Use the Move Tool to drag the Skateboarder layer to the far left side of the workspace, just off of the document window. Click Frame 2 and then use the Move Tool to position the skateboarder to the right of its location in the previous frame. Continue clicking the frames and moving the Skateboarder layer so the skateboarder's path moves from left to right. Frame 7 should display the skateboarder on the right side of the banner.

5. With Frame 7 selected, add four tween frames between Frames 7 and 6. Select Frame 6 and add two tween frames between Frames 6 and 5. Select all the frames and change their timings from 0.1 sec. to 0.2 sec.

6. Play the animation again and check for accuracy. Fix any other problems and adjust the timing as necessary. Save your changes. Use the Save for Web command to save the file in the GIF format with the name, Make-It-Right-9-1-Skatepark-Animated. Be sure to set the Format box to Images Only so only the GIF, and not the HTML files, is created. See your instructor for ways to submit this assignment.

In the Lab

Design and/or create a project using the guidelines, concepts, and skills presented in this chapter. Labs are listed in order of increasing difficulty.

Lab 1: Creating an Image Map

Problem: As an assignment for your economics class, you decide to make an image map, shown in Figure 9–83, that links books featuring specific languages to Web sites that offer English-language tourist guides for the country in which the language on the book spine is the native tongue. When users view the image map, clicking any book in the graphic will link them to a Web site featuring information about that country. Table 9–1 shows the URL of each Web site you will use for each country.

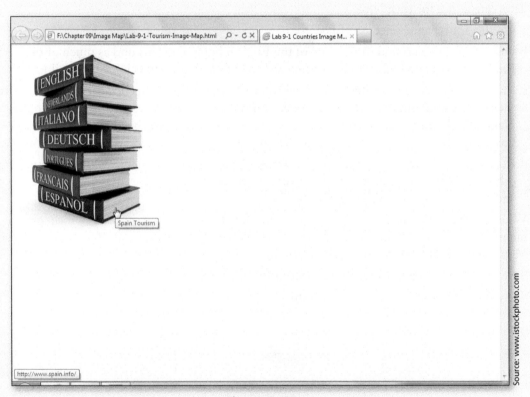

Source: www.istockphoto.com

Figure 9–83

Table 9–1	
Language	**URL**
English	http://www.usatourist.com
Nederlands	http://www.holland.com
Italiano	http://www.italia.it
Deutsch	http://www.germany.travel
Portugues	http://www.golisbon.com
Francais	http://us.franceguide.com
Espanol	http://www.spain.info

Continued >

In the Lab *continued*

Note: This assignment requires the Data Files for Students. Visit www.cengage.com/ct/ studentdownload for detailed instructions or contact your instructor for information about accessing the required files.

Instructions: Perform the following tasks:

1. Use Windows Explorer to open the Computer window, navigate to your storage device, and create a new folder named Image Map.

2. Start Photoshop. Perform the customization steps found on pages PS 6 through PS 10.

3. Open the file Lab 9-1 Books from the Chapter 09 folder of the Data Files for Students.

   Click the Save As command on the File menu. Type `Lab 9-1 Tourism Image Map` as the file name. Select the PSD format. Browse to the Image Map folder on your USB flash drive storage device and click the Save button. If Photoshop displays an options dialog box, click the OK button.

4. To create a slice for each book:

   a. On the Tools panel, select the Slice Tool.

   b. Drag a rectangle around the outline of the English book. Drag around as much of the English book as you can, while selecting as little of the Nederlands book as possible.

   c. Press SHIFT+C to activate the Select Slice Tool. On the options bar, click the 'Set options for the current slice' button to display the Slice Options dialog box. Type `English` in the Name box. Enter the URL from Table 9–1. Leave the Target box blank. In the Message Text box, type `USA` as the entry. In the Alt Tag box, type `USA Tourism`. Click the OK button.

   d. Repeat Steps 4b and 4c for each book. Draw as large a slice as possible, while overlapping other books as little as possible. (*Hint:* You can create multiple slices that cover a single book and point to the same Web site, if desired.)

5. When all the books are complete, click the Save for Web command on the Photoshop File menu. Choose the best optimization and save the file with the name, Lab-9-1-Tourism-Image-Map, using the HTML and Images format, in the Image Map folder.

6. Save the PSD file again and then quit Photoshop. Preview the Web site using a browser.

7. See your instructor for ways to submit this assignment.

In the Lab

Lab 2: Creating a Panoramic Photo

Problem: You have been asked to create a wide-screen, panoramic photo of a backyard view for a real estate Web site. Unfortunately, you do not have a camera that takes panoramic photographs, but you do have several photos that were taken from the same location at different angles from the back porch. Using Photoshop's Photomerge function, you can create a panoramic photo without the use of expensive cameras or lenses (Figure 9–84).

Figure 9–84

Note: This assignment requires the Data Files for Students. Visit www.cengage.com/ct/studentdownload for detailed instructions or contact your instructor for information about accessing the required files.

Instructions: Perform the following tasks:
1. Start Photoshop. Perform the customization steps found on pages PS 6 through PS 10.
2. On the File menu, point to Automate, and then click Photomerge.
3. When the Photomerge dialog box is displayed, click the Use box arrow, and then click Folder.
4. Click the Browse button and then navigate to the Chapter 09 folder of the Data Files for Students. Select the Lab 9-2 Panorama folder. Click the OK button to display the names of the four source files.
5. On the left side of the Photomerge window, click the Auto option button, if necessary. Click the OK button to start the automation process. The Photomerge process may take several minutes.
6. Select the Crop Tool on the Tools panel.
7. Drag a crop rectangle across the entire canvas. Press the CTRL key as you drag the top edge of the crop border down to eliminate the transparent pixels at the top. Repeat on the other three sides to exclude all transparent pixels. Press the ENTER key to crop the image.
8. Flatten the image and save the file with the file name, Lab 9-2 Panorama Complete, using the TIFF file format.
9. Submit the assignment as specified by your instructor.

In the Lab

Lab 3: Creating a Web Site Animation

Problem: As an intern for a Web design company, you have been assigned to create an animated GIF for an air conditioning service shop (Figure 9–85). The client has provided several photos of an ice cube melting, which are included with the Data Files for Students.

Note: This assignment requires the Data Files for Students. Visit www.cengage.com/ct/studentdownload for detailed instructions or contact your instructor for information about accessing the required files.

Instructions: Perform the following tasks:
Open the Lab 9-3 Ice Banner file from the folder named, Lab 9-3 Ice. Notice the dimensions of this file are 120 pixels wide × 240 pixels tall — standard dimensions for a vertical Web banner ad. Open each of the Ice photos in the Lab 9-3 Ice folder, and use the Move Tool to copy each photo into the Lab 9-3 Ice Banner document. Move the Blend layer to the top of the layer stack, and arrange the ice photos in order from solid to melted. Create a new text layer at the top of the document with the phrase, Air Conditioner Problems Burning You Up? Select an appropriate font and color so the phrase is readable against the black background. Create another new text layer at the bottom of the document with the company name and phone number, AirPros 1-800-555-5555. Select an appropriate font and color so the name and phone number are readable against the white background. Create a 10-frame animation that animates the ice melting. The text should be visible throughout all frames. Set the animation speed to 1 second for the first frame and 0.2 seconds for all remaining frames. Set the looping to repeat once. Save the file to the Lab 9-3 Ice folder with the name, Lab 9-3 Ice Banner Animated. Save the file for Web, in the HTML and Images format, to the Lab 9-3 Ice folder with the name, Ice-Animated. View it in a browser to watch the ice cube melt.

Figure 9–85

Cases and Places

Apply your creative thinking and problem-solving skills to design and implement a solution.

Note: To complete these assignments, you may be required to use the Data Files for Students. Visit www.cengage.com/ct/studentdownload for detailed instructions or contact your instructor for information about accessing the required files.

1: Create a Photoshop Resources Web Page

Academic

Your Web design instructor has given you an assignment to create a Web page that includes links to some useful Web sites. Create a folder in your storage location named Photoshop Resources. Use a light muted color and draw a large shape for the background. Use the Vertical Type Tool to create a text element down the left edge of the page. Use a contrasting color for the text. Type your name in the type bounding box. Using the same text color, create a horizontal text element heading that says, Photoshop Resources. Below the heading and to the right of your name, create four more horizontal text elements, using placeholder text such as 'replace this', in a complementary font, but use a smaller font size. Using your favorite search tool, find several Web sites that offer Photoshop tutorials or other Photoshop resources (such as custom brush or shape downloads). Type the name (not the URL) of one such Web site into the first of the five text elements. Type the names of four additional Web sites into the remaining text elements. Slice each text element. Use the Slice Options dialog box to insert a URL, a _blank target specification, an Alt tag, and a Status bar message for each slice. Save the file to your Photoshop Resources folder in the PSD format with the name, Case 9-1 My Photoshop Resources. Preview the Web page and make any necessary changes. Save the page as HTML and Images to the Photoshop Resources folder with the name, My_Photoshop_Resources. Exchange your Photoshop Resources folder with another student and explore their Photoshop resources Web pages.

2: Design a Personalized Web Banner

Personal

You have decided to put your name up in lights! Create a Web banner with a bold background color. Create a type bounding box using a large font in a contrasting color. Type your name. Add a layer effect to enhance the text. On the Layers panel, make sure the opacity is set to 100%. Duplicate the layer and set the opacity of the copy to 10%. Turn the visibility off on both text layers. Open the Timeline panel. In the first frame, turn on the visibility of the 10% layer. Create a second frame in which you turn off the 10% layer and turn on the 100% layer. Set the time delay on each frame to .5 seconds. Set the animation to play only once. Tween the two frames with 10 frames in between, applying only opacity changes. Create a folder in your storage location named Personalized Banner. Save the file in the PSD format to the Personalized Banner folder with the name Case 9-2 My Banner. Save the file optimized for the Web in HTML and Images format in the Personalized Banner folder with the name My-Banner. View your name up in lights using a browser window.

3: Customize Navigation Buttons

Professional

You need to make buttons for an upcoming slide show presentation and want something more than the traditional clip art buttons that come with your presentation software. Create a new file in Photoshop with a transparent background. Press the U key to access the Rectangle Tool. Draw four rectangles approximately 200 pixels square. The layers will be displayed on the Layers panel. Open the Styles panel and choose a different style for each rectangle. Press the T key to access the Type Tool. One at a time, click each button. On the options bar, choose a contrasting color for the text that complements the button. On the buttons, type Home, Back, Forward, and End, respectively. On the Layers panel, add a shadow effect on each text layer. For each button, point the shadow in a different direction. Order the layers so each text layer is displayed just above its button. One set at a time, click the button layer, and then SHIFT+click the button's text layer. On the panel menu, click Link Layers to link the button and its text together. Save the file to your storage location with the name, Case 9-3 Buttons. Have your instructor choose the best of the four buttons, and then copy and paste it into a presentation.

Appendix A

Project Planning Guidelines

Using Project Planning Guidelines

The process of communicating specific information to others is a learned, rational skill. Computers and software, especially Adobe Photoshop CS6, can help you develop ideas and present detailed information to a particular audience.

Using Adobe Photoshop CS6, you can edit photos and create original graphics. Computer hardware and image-editing software, such as Adobe Photoshop CS6, reduces much of the laborious work of drafting and revising projects. Some design professionals use sketch pads or storyboards, others compose directly on the computer, and others have developed unique strategies that work for their own particular thinking and artistic styles.

No matter what method you use to plan a project, follow specific guidelines to arrive at a final product that presents an image or images clearly and effectively (Figure A–1). Use some aspects of these guidelines every time you undertake a project and others as needed in specific instances. For example, in determining content for a project, you may decide an original graphic would communicate the idea more effectively than an existing photo. If so, you would create this graphical element from scratch.

Determine the Project's Purpose

Begin by clearly defining why you are undertaking this assignment. For example, you may want to correct camera errors and adjust image flaws. Or you might want to create a graphic for a specific publishing or marketing purpose. Once you clearly understand the purpose of your task, begin to draft ideas of how best to communicate this information.

Analyze Your Audience

Learn about the people who will use, analyze, or view your work. Where are they employed? What are their educational backgrounds? What are their expectations? What questions do they have? How will they interact with your product? What kind of computer system and Internet connection will they have? Design experts suggest drawing a

---

PROJECT PLANNING GUIDELINES

1. DETERMINE THE PROJECT'S PURPOSE
Why are you undertaking the project?

2. ANALYZE YOUR AUDIENCE
Who are the people who will use your work?

3. GATHER POSSIBLE CONTENT
What graphics exist, and in what forms?

4. DETERMINE WHAT CONTENT TO PRESENT TO YOUR AUDIENCE
What image will communicate the project's purpose to your audience in the most effective manner?

Figure A–1

mental picture of these people or finding photographs of people who fit this profile so that you can develop a project with the audience in mind.

By knowing your audience members, you can tailor a project to meet their interests and needs. You will not present them with information they already possess, and you will not omit the information they need to know.

Example: Your assignment is to raise the profile of your college's nursing program in the community. Your project should address questions such as the following: How much does the audience know about your college and the nursing curriculum? What are the admission requirements? How many of the applicants admitted complete the program? What percent of participants pass the state nursing boards?

Gather Possible Content

Rarely are you in a position to develop all the material for a project. Typically, you would begin by gathering existing images and photos, or designing new graphics based on information that may reside in spreadsheets or databases. Design work for clients often must align with and adhere to existing marketing campaigns or publicity materials. Web sites, pamphlets, magazine and newspaper articles, and books could provide insights of how others have approached your topic. Personal interviews often provide perspectives not available by any other means. Consider video and audio clips as potential sources for material that might complement or support the factual data you uncover. Make sure you have all legal rights to any photographs you plan to use.

Determine What Content to Present to Your Audience

Experienced designers recommend identifying three or four major ideas you want an audience member to remember after viewing your project. It also is helpful to envision your project's endpoint, the key fact or universal theme that you want to emphasize. All project elements should lead to this ending point.

As you make content decisions, you also need to think about other factors. Presentation of the project content is an important consideration. For example, will the content of your brochure look good when printed on thick, colored paper or transparencies? Will the format in which you save the content affect how your photo be viewed in a classroom with excellent lighting and a bright projector? How will the content look when viewed on a notebook computer monitor? Determine relevant time factors, such as the length of time to develop the project, how long editors will spend reviewing your project, or the amount of time allocated for presenting your designs to the customer. Your project will need to accommodate all of these constraints.

Decide whether a graphic, photograph, or artistic element can express or emphasize a particular concept. The right hemisphere of the brain processes images by attaching an emotion to them, so in the long run, audience members are more apt to recall themes from graphics rather than those from the text.

Finally, review your project to make sure the theme still easily is identifiable and has been emphasized successfully. Is the focal point clear and presented without distraction? Does the project satisfy the requirements?

Summary

When creating a project, it is beneficial to follow some basic guidelines from the outset. By taking some time at the beginning of the process to determine the project's purpose, analyze the audience, gather possible content, and determine what content to present to the audience, you can produce a project that is informative, relevant, and effective.

Appendix B

Graphic Design Overview

Understanding Design Principles

Understanding a few basic design principles can catapult you to the next level of digital artistry. Beyond knowing how to use software, a graphic designer must know how to create effective and readable layouts no matter what the product type. In this Appendix, you will learn the design principles, color theory, typography, and other technical knowledge required to create usable and successful graphic designs.

A major goal in graphic design work, whether for print or Web page layout, is to guide the viewer's eyes toward some key point. Another major goal of design work is to convey a certain emotion — a project can have the effect of making the viewer feel relaxed, energetic, hungry, hopeful, or even anxious. By implementing a few basic principles of design, you can control your viewers' physical focus so they look where you want them to look as you steer them toward a desired emotion. Design principles typically include the following:

- Balance
- Contrast
- Dominance
- Proximity
- Repetition
- Closure
- Continuance
- Negative space
- Unity

Balance

Visual elements can be **balanced** within a design, with visual elements distributed in a horizontal or vertical arrangement. Unbalanced designs can cause viewers to feel anxious or uncomfortable, or even as if they are falling sideways out of their seats. Balance may be achieved symmetrically or asymmetrically. Symmetrical balance mirrors a visual element to achieve equilibrium (Figure B–1). Asymmetrical balance can be achieved by balancing a small, dark element with a large, light element (Figure B–2) or balancing one large element with several smaller elements (Figure B–3).

with symmetrical balance, the left and right halves are mirror reflections, and the two trees, which are identical in size and shape, balance the composition

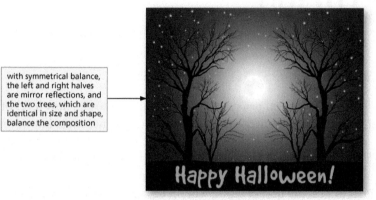

Figure B–1

left-heavy design with sparse right sidebar that is too white to add much weight

balanced design with a darker right sidebar adding weight to the right side

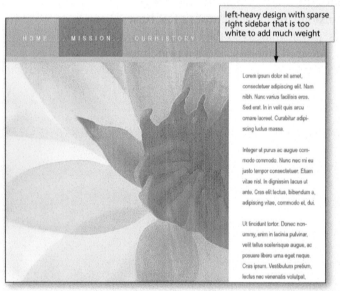
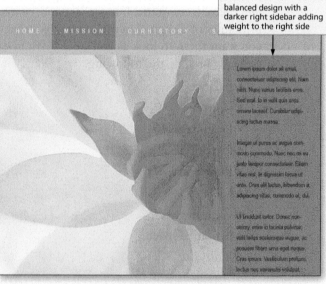

(a) Unbalanced design　　　**Figure B–2**　　　**(b) Balanced design**

large photo at right is asymmetrically balanced by the multiple small thumbnails on left

Figure B–3

Contrast

Contrast describes the visual differences between elements; it adds variety to a design and helps to draw the viewer's focus. Differences in color, scale, quantity, or other characteristics of visual elements help to achieve contrast. The element that is different from the others draws the viewer's attention. In Figure B–4, the words in white contrast against the other words on the page, and the viewer's eye is drawn to the contrasting sentence.

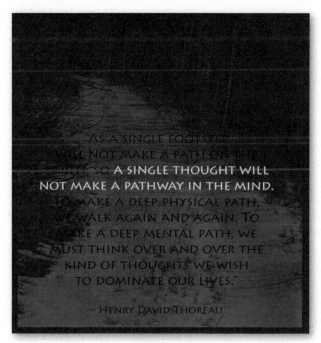

Figure B–4

Dominance

Dominance is a critical principle in controlling viewer focus. The dominant element in a design is the one to which a viewer's eyes and attention usually move first. An element's position within a design or its contrast to other elements can establish dominance. If you want your viewer to focus on a certain area of your design or on a specific design element, make it dominant, like the yellow V.I.P. banner in the discount card shown in Figure B–5, which grabs your attention with its contrasting color, even though it is not the largest element in the design.

Figure B–5

BTW

Dominant Object Placement
Placing an object at a certain location within a grid, such as the intersection of thirds or slightly above and to the right of center, helps to establish dominance.

Proximity

Proximity describes the relative space between elements. Related elements should be close to each other. Headings should be close to their related paragraph text, and product names should be close to their photos and prices. As shown in Figure B–6, when related items are not within close proximity of each other (Figure B–6a), the viewer might not know the items are related. When elements are too close, the design looks cluttered and text can become difficult to read. Strive for balance in your proximity, as in Figure B–6b.

(a) Items without proximity are not clearly related

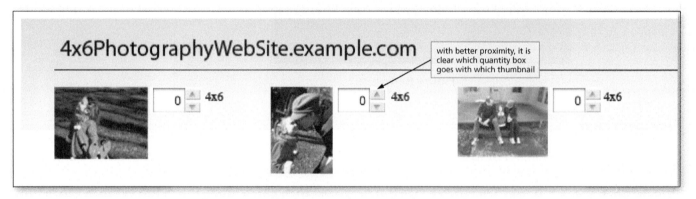

(b) Items with close proximity are clearly related

Figure B–6

Repetition

Repeating a visual element helps to tie a design together. **Repetition** of color, shape, texture, and other characteristics can help to unify your design (Figure B–7), create patterns, or impart a sense of movement. Most Web sites repeat a design theme across all the pages so users know they are on the same site as they navigate from page to page. Repeated colors and layouts help to unify the overall Web site design.

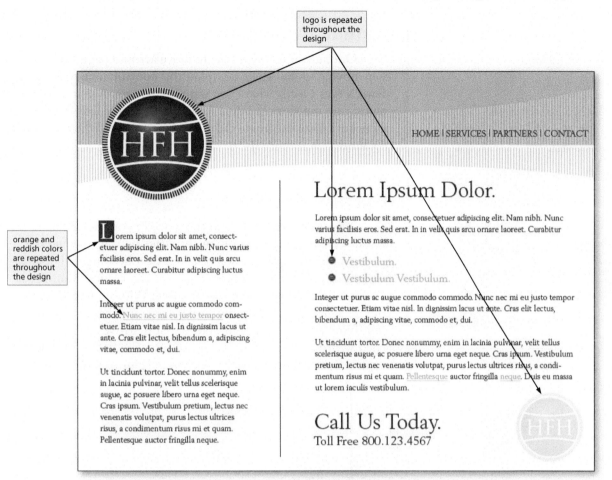

Figure B–7

Closure

Not everything in a design must be composed of solid lines. Composing objects from small parts and spaces allows a design to breathe and creates visual interest. Under the concept of **closure**, the human brain will fill in the blanks to close or complete the object (Figure B–8).

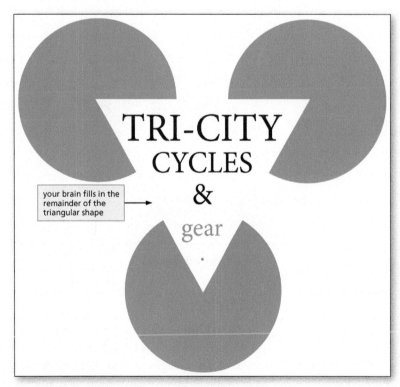

Figure B–8

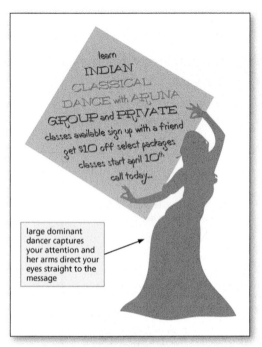

large dominant dancer captures your attention and her arms direct your eyes straight to the message

Figure B–9

Continuance

Once a viewer's eyes start to move across a page, they tend to keep moving — and you can exploit this **continuance** to guide the viewer's eyes exactly where you want them to go. A dominant object can capture the viewer's initial focus, and diagonal lines within that dominant object can guide the viewer's eyes toward the focal point of your design (Figure B–9).

Negative Space

Negative space refers to the space in your design that does not contain information, or the space between elements. For example, the space between the vertical heading and descriptive text or the space between a logo and the vertical heading, as shown in Figure B–10, is negative space. Without negative space, your design will feel cluttered, and viewers will have difficulty identifying on the focal point. Note that negative space, also called **white space**, literally does not translate to "white space," as negative space does not have to be white (Figure B–10).

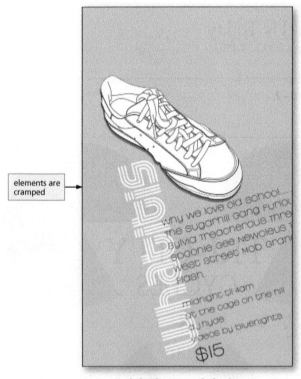

elements are cramped

moving the shoe adds white space and relieves visual tension

(a) Cluttered design   **(b) Uncluttered design**

Figure B–10

Unity
Unity is not limited to elements in a specific piece of work; it can apply to multiple pieces. For example, a business card, Web site, letterhead, and product packaging that feature a similar color and style can help unify a business's identity.

Unity

Unity refers to the concept that all elements within a design work well together to form a whole. The individual images, textures, text, and negative space join together to create a single unified message or meaning. Unity can be created by applying a combination of basic design principles. Balanced elements alone do not produce a visually appealing design. The same is true for elements with appropriate proximity and negative space, good contrast, or clear dominance. No single design principle is responsible for a pleasing design. Instead, the combination of these principles creates a single unified design. Without unity, a design degrades into chaos and loses meaning. Of course, that is not a bad thing if chaos is the intentional message.

Layout Grids

A graphic designer needs to know where to place elements within a document or Web page. The use of grids makes it easy to align objects to each other and can help with balance and proximity. You can apply any of the many standard grids to Web page layouts or print layouts for standard paper sizes. One very popular grid system uses thirds, a method that is derived from the golden ratio.

Rule of Thirds and Golden Ratio   The rule of thirds specifies that splitting a segment into thirds produces an aesthetically pleasing ratio. The rule of thirds is derived from a more complex mathematical concept called the golden ratio, which specifies segment ratios of long segment divided by short segment equal to about 1.618 — which is close enough to the rule of thirds that designers typically apply the rule of thirds rather than break out their calculators (Figure B–11).

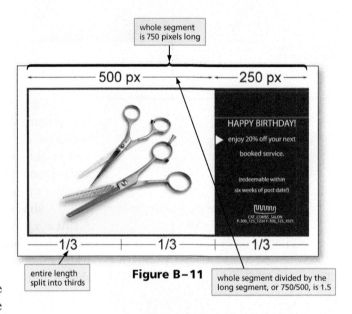

Figure B–11

Color Theory

Color can have a profound effect on the overall message a design conveys. Certain colors evoke specific emotions, and the way colors are combined can make the difference between readable copy and copy that is unable to be read.

Color Properties

Before you begin to work with color, it is important to understand the properties of color, which include hue, saturation, shade, tint, and value.

Hue refers to the tone, or actual color, such as red, yellow, or blue. Many color theorists interpret hue to mean pure color. A pure color, or hue, can be modified to create color variations. A basic color wheel, shown in Figure B–12, displays hue.

Saturation refers to the intensity of a color. As hues become less saturated, they create muted tones and pastels as they approach gray. As hues become more saturated, they appear very bright (Figure B–13).

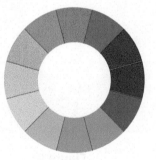

Figure B–12

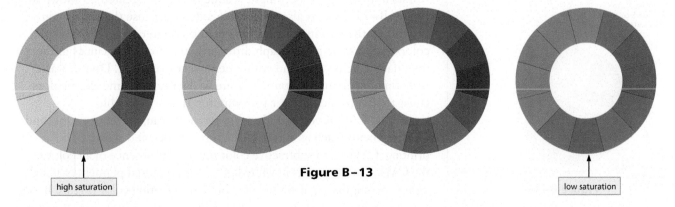

high saturation

low saturation

Figure B–13

desaturated hues can have calming effect

Figure B–14

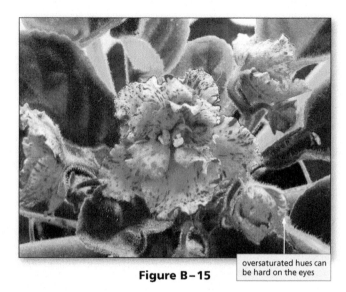

oversaturated hues can be hard on the eyes

Figure B–15

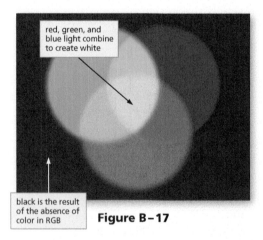

shades ← → tints

← value →

Figure B–16

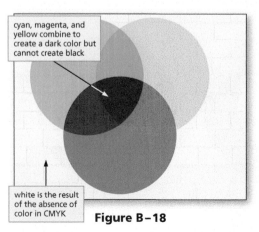

red, green, and blue light combine to create white

black is the result of the absence of color in RGB

Figure B–17

cyan, magenta, and yellow combine to create a dark color but cannot create black

white is the result of the absence of color in CMYK

Figure B–18

Desaturated colors can produce mellow tones and evoke calm feelings (Figure B–14). Oversaturated colors can produce neon-like colors and cause excitement (Figure B–15). Sometimes it is appropriate to use very bright colors, such as in a picture book for children or a high-energy advertisement for a sports drink. Other times, bright, saturated colors produce the wrong feeling for your work.

A **shade** is a mixture of a hue and black, producing a darker color. A **tint** is a mixture of a hue and white, producing a lighter color. A color's **value** describes its overall lightness or darkness. A tint has a higher value, while a shade has a lower value (Figure B–16). Mixing a hue with its shades, tints, and variations of saturation can lead to very harmonious color combinations.

Color Modes

A color mode describes the way in which colors combine to create other colors. The most commonly used color modes are RGB, CMYK, and LAB. Each mode has its strengths and weaknesses, and each is appropriate for a specific type of work.

The **RGB** color mode mixes red, green, and blue light to create other colors. Computer monitors and TV screens use the RGB color mode. All images used on a Web site must use the RGB color mode because few Web browsers can display CMYK images. RGB is an additive color mode, meaning colored light combines (light waves are added) to create other colors. The absence of all color in the RGB mode results in black. As colored light is added, white is created, as shown in Figure B–17. RGB is also device dependent, because the colors you see depend on the viewing device. Different computer screens will display colors in the same photograph differently because of variances in the manufacturing process and component wear over time. Do not waste your time trying to get your Web site to display the same exact colors consistently from computer to computer. It is not possible.

The **CMYK** color mode mixes physical cyan, magenta, yellow, and black pigments (such as ink) to create other colors, and is used in color printing. CMYK is a subtractive color mode. The absence of all color in the CMYK mode results in white light, and, as colored pigment is added, light wavelengths are absorbed or subtracted, creating color (Figure B–18).

Cyan, magenta, and yellow alone cannot create black; thus, the need for pure black in the CMYK mode.

Unlike RGB and CMYK, which combine individual well-defined colors, the **LAB** color mode combines levels of lightness with two color channels, a and b. One color channel ranges from green to magenta, while the other includes blue through yellow. By combining color ranges with lightness values, LAB is able to closely approximate the true human perception of color and thus is able to produce more colors than either RGB or CMYK. This makes it an ideal color mode for photographers wanting to have access to every possible color in a photograph. LAB typically is used during photographic retouching and color correction. The image then is converted to RGB or CMYK for use with electronic media or print.

BTW

LAB
LAB is sometimes written as L*a*b for lightness, color channel a, and color channel b.

Psychological Considerations of Color

Colors can evoke both positive and negative emotions in people, and the influence of a color can differ among individuals and cultures. While the effect of color on people is not an exact science, there are some generalities.

White often is associated with cleanliness, purity, and hope. Doctors and brides in most Western cultures wear white. However, white is associated with death and mourning attire in some Eastern cultures. White is the most popular background color and offers great contrast for highly readable dark text.

Black often is used to represent evil, death, or mourning, but also mystery, intelligence, elegance, and power. Black text on a white background is the easiest to read.

Red is used in Western cultures to signify love, passion, and comfort — but also is used to represent sin, anger, hell, and danger. Use dark reds to imply indulgence or fine living and brownish reds for designs dealing with Thanksgiving, harvest, or the fall season in general.

Green symbolizes many positives such as growth, tranquility, luck, money, ecology, environmentalism, and health, but it also symbolizes jealousy. Green can have a calming effect.

Blue often is cited as the favorite color by men. Like green, it evokes feelings of calmness and serenity. Blue implies authority, stability, loyalty, and confidence. However, it is one of the least appetizing colors, as there are few naturally blue foods. It also is associated with sadness and bad luck, as evidenced in blues music or phrases like "I've got the blues."

Yellow generally makes people happy. It is a highly visible and active color. However, too much yellow can lead to frustration and eye fatigue. Babies cry more in yellow rooms. Avoid using yellow as a page background and use it instead in smaller areas to draw attention.

Print Considerations for Color

The printing process cannot reproduce every color. Gamut refers to the range of printable colors, and colors that cannot be printed are said to be *out of gamut*. If an out of gamut color exists in your document, the printer you are using simply will get as close to it as it can — but it will not be exact. Depending on the printer you have installed, the actual color produced can vary. Photoshop identifies out of gamut colors in the Color Picker with a small icon. If your document contains out of gamut colors, you have two options: change or replace the out of gamut color with one that is in gamut, or accept that the final print may not be exactly what you expected.

Web Considerations for Color

When working with color for the Web, the most important thing to remember is that colors will appear differently on different computers. Web sites look similar, but not exactly the same, from computer to computer. Years ago, Web designers used only

BTW

Using Web-Safe Colors
Use Web-safe colors if you know the site will be viewed on ancient computer systems; otherwise, allow yourself the full spectrum with the understanding the colors will vary slightly from computer to computer.

the **Web-safe colors**, which were a set of 216 colors that supposedly appear the same on all monitors. This was the result of the limitations of video subsystems at the time, as computer monitors could display only 256 specific colors. Microsoft Windows supported 256 specific colors, and Apple Macintosh supported a different 256 colors. Of the two sets, 216 were the same across both platforms; these 216 became the **Web-safe palette**. However, designers soon realized that only 22 of those 216 were truly the same between Windows and Macintosh; this subset was called the **really Web-safe colors**.

Photoshop displays a warning in the Color Picker for non-Web-safe colors. Modern computers (as well as cell phone browsers) can display millions of distinct colors, so limiting yourself to 216 Web-safe colors is no longer a necessity. In fact, it is extremely limiting, because the 216 Web-safe colors are generally very bright or very dark with few choices for pastels or saturation and value variances. Most designers do not use Web-safe colors for their designs.

Relativity

A color's relative lightness/darkness value can appear different depending on what other color neighbors it. The gray block in Figure B–19 looks lighter against the brown background and darker against the light yellow background. Keep this in mind as you choose background/foreground relationships. A certain hue (or tint or shade) might look great when it is by itself, but you may not be so fond of it when it is used in close proximity to another certain color.

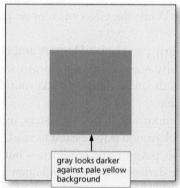

gray looks lighter against brown background

gray looks darker against pale yellow background

Figure B–19

Color Schemes and Matching

Choosing colors that work well together and enforce the design's message can be challenging but worth the effort. Successful color matching requires an understanding of **color schemes**, which simply describes an organized method of matching colors based on their positions on a color wheel. The color scheme can make or break a design.

Figure B–12 on page APP 9 displayed a color wheel. While there are various color wheel models, the most popular uses the primary colors red, blue, and yellow (Figure B–20a). Primary colors combine to create the secondary colors green, orange, and purple (Figure B–20b). A primary and a secondary color combine to create a tertiary (third level) color (Figure B–20c). More complex color wheels can include gradients to show varying saturation, tints, and shades (Figure B–21).

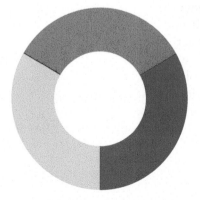
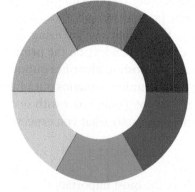
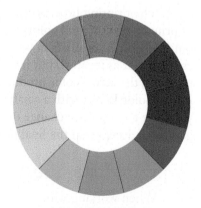

(a) Primary colors   **(b) Secondary colors**   **(c) Tertiary colors**

Figure B–20

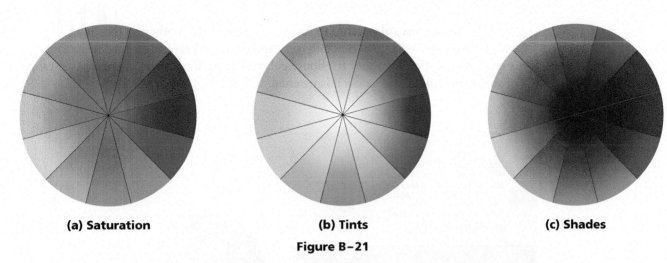

(a) Saturation   **(b) Tints**   **(c) Shades**

Figure B–21

Color Schemes   A **monochromatic color scheme** is one that uses a single hue with a variety of shades and tints (Figure B–22). This is an easy color scheme to create. While a monochromatic color scheme can appear soothing, the lack of hue variance can leave it looking a bit boring.

BTW

Color Scheme Web Sites
Stand-alone color scheme software programs are available for purchase, but Adobe offers a free online service at kuler.adobe.com that lets you browse color schemes created by other users, modify them, and create and save your own.

you are invited...

Figure B–22

A **complementary color scheme** uses colors directly across from each other on the color wheel. Their high contrast can look vibrant but also can be hard on the eyes. Avoid using complementary pairs in a foreground/background relationship, as shown in Figure B–23. Adjusting the saturation or substituting tints and shades makes this color scheme more workable.

bright complementary colors do not work well in a foreground/background relationship

adjusting the arrangement of the colors or using a variety of values or saturation can help

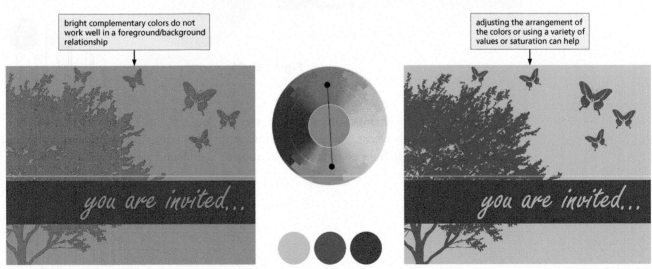

you are invited...   you are invited...

Figure B–23

An **analogous color scheme** uses colors next to each other on the color wheel. This color scheme is generally very appealing and evokes positive feelings (Figure B–24). Be careful not to choose colors that are too far apart. A very wide range of analogous colors can appear mismatched.

Figure B–24

The **split-complementary scheme** uses a base color and, instead of its direct complement, the two colors on either side of its complement (Figure B–25). This scheme offers a lot of hue variance, and therefore excitement. However, if all the hues are overly saturated, split-complementary colors can be very harsh. Try keeping one hue saturated and use tints, shades, or desaturated colors for the rest of the scheme.

Figure B–25

Other color schemes such as triadic, tetradic, neutral, and an infinite number of custom schemes also exist. Using a color-matching resource such as software or a Web site is a good way to help you get started choosing colors and allows you to experiment to see what you and your client like.

Typography

Typography is the art of working with text. Perhaps the two most important factors for graphic designers to address when working with text are visual appeal and readability. A dull text heading will not entice viewers to read the rest of the advertisement, but a text heading that looks beautiful can be useless if it is not readable (Figure B–26).

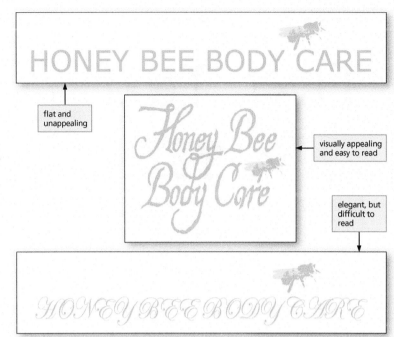

Figure B–26

Readability

Readability is the measurement of how comfortable or easy it is for readers to read the text. Many factors contribute to overall readability. Commonly accepted readability factors include the following:

- Large text passages written in lowercase are easier to read than long text passages in uppercase.

- Regular text is easier to read than italicized text.

- Black text on a white background is easier to read than white text on a black background.

- Legibility affects readability.

- Line length, letterforms, and appearance all influence readability.

Before learning the details of readability, you must understand some type basics. A **font** is a set of characters of a specific family, size, and style. For example, the description Times New Roman, 11 points, italic is a font. What most people consider a font is actually a **typeface** (Times New Roman, in this example). A font represents only a single specific size and style within a family, while a typeface is a set or family of one or more fonts.

Legibility refers to the ease with which a reader can determine what a letter actually is. If readers cannot figure out the letter, they cannot read the text, resulting in low readability and failed message delivery. The difference between legibility and readability is subtle. Figure B–27 shows an exit sign — something that needs to be legible.

Figure B–27

Line length refers to the physical length of a line of text. When lines are too long, the reader's eyes can get lost trying to go all the way back to the left side of the page to find the next line. There is no conclusive magic number for how long a line of text should be. Optimal line lengths differ for adults and children, and for people with dyslexia and without. The best choices for line length differ based on the media of the message; printed newspapers, books, text on a Web site, and the subject lines in an e-mail message all require different line lengths. Some studies recommend line lengths based on physical lengths in inches, while other studies recommend a maximum number of characters per line. However, many designers follow the guideline that line lengths should not exceed 70 characters (about two-and-a-half alphabets' worth of characters).

BTW

PLEASE DO NOT YELL
Not only is typing in all uppercase difficult to read, but it connotes yelling at your reader.

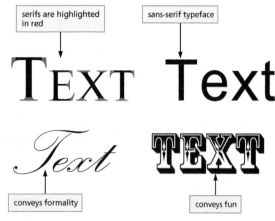

Figure B-28

Typeface Categories

Typefaces are organized into several categories, including serif, sans-serif, script, and display. Serif typefaces include additional appendages, while sans-serif typefaces do not (Figure B–28). It is generally accepted that large passages of serif text in print are easy to read, while sans-serif text is easier to read on a Web page. Because headlines are typically small, either serif or sans-serif is appropriate. Varying the headline typeface style from the body copy typeface style is an effective method of adding some visual excitement to an otherwise dull page of text. Script typefaces look like handwriting, and display typefaces are decorative.

In addition to differences in readability, the choice of a serif, sans-serif, or other typeface can help to create an emotion much like the selection of a color scheme. Wedding invitations often use a script typeface to signify elegance, while headlines using display typefaces can grab a reader's attention. The same phrase written in different typefaces can have different implications (Figure B–29). Similarly, differences in the size, weight (boldness), or spacing of a typeface also can influence emotion or meaning (Figure B–30).

Figure B-29

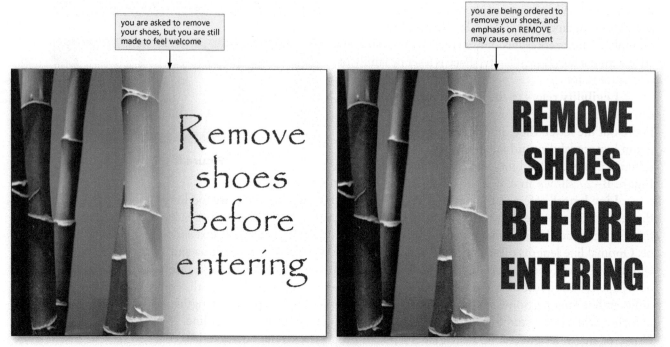

Figure B-30

Designing for Web versus Print

Graphic designers must be aware of subtle differences in how print and Web projects are created and perceived when designing for these media. While many design principles are common to both, it takes a different mindset to successfully create a design for either medium. Print designs are static, as the layout never varies from print to print (though differences in color may appear because of inconsistencies with the printer or printing press). The appearance of Web designs can vary, depending on the device used to view them. Some print designers struggle with the device dependency and fluidity of Web page designs. Some Web designers unnecessarily concern themselves about accommodating fluid or shifting content when designing a print advertisement.

Device Dependency and Fluidity

The main differences between print and Web design are related to device dependency and fluidity. Web pages are **device dependent**, meaning that the appearance of the page varies depending on the device (computer, cell phone, or PDA) on which they are viewed (Figure B–31). Discrepancies in monitor color calibration, screen resolution, and browser window size can affect how a Web page appears to the viewer. Colors can change, objects can shift, and text can wrap to a new line on different words from one device to another. In comparison, a newspaper or magazine looks the same no matter where it is purchased or where it is read. Designers can work with Web programmers to design pages for different devices.

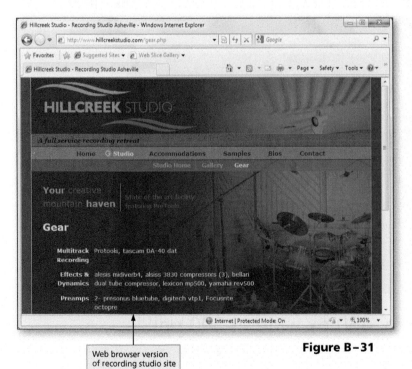

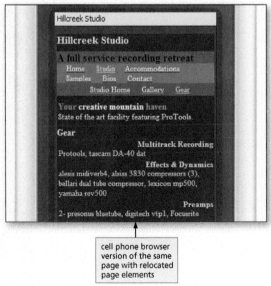

cell phone browser version of the same page with relocated page elements

Web browser version of recording studio site

Figure B–31

Pixels, Dimensions, and Resolution

A pixel is the smallest element of a digital image. Magnifying an image reveals the individual pixels (Figure B–32). A pixel, unlike an inch or centimeter, is not an absolute measurement. The physical size of a pixel can change depending on device resolution.

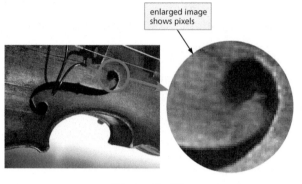

enlarged image shows pixels

Figure B–32

As you learned in Chapter 1, resolution refers to the number of pixels displayed on a computer screen. More pixels gives greater detail. When referring to an image file, the phrase, document dimensions, is used to describe the number of pixels in the file. For example, a document might have the dimensions of 450×337, meaning it contains 450 pixels across and 337 pixels vertically, for a total of 151,650 pixels. File size is directly related to document dimension. The more pixels there are in a document, the larger the file size.

When used to describe an image file, the word, resolution, also is used to describe the printed output. The print resolution is given in pixels per inch (PPI); for example, 72 PPI or 300 PPI. PPI is a linear measurement: 72 PPI means that, when printed, the output will contain 72 pixels across every linear inch. If the document dimensions were 450×337, those 450 horizontal pixels would print in groups of 72 PPI, resulting in a printout just over 6 inches wide (Figure B–33). If the resolution,

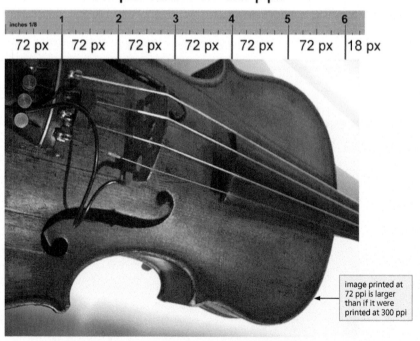

450 px wide at 72 ppi

inches 1/8   1   2   3   4   5   6

72 px | 72 px | 72 px | 72 px | 72 px | 72 px | 18 px

image printed at 72 ppi is larger than if it were printed at 300 ppi

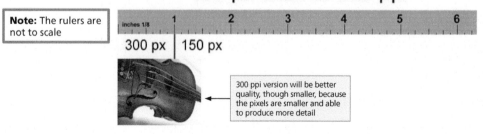

450 px wide at 300 ppi

Note: The rulers are not to scale

inches 1/8   1   2   3   4   5   6

300 px | 150 px

300 ppi version will be better quality, though smaller, because the pixels are smaller and able to produce more detail

Figure B–33

but not the dimensions, were increased to 300 PPI, then those same 450 pixels would print in groups of 300 per inch, producing a final output about 1.5 inches wide.

Key points to remember when working with resolution are:

- A pixel is not a static measurement. Pixels change in size. They get smaller or larger to fill an inch as defined in the PPI setting.

- Changing the resolution of an image file has no effect on the file size. It affects the physical size of the printed output.

- Changing the document dimensions does affect the file size.

When printing documents, printers create each individual pixel with a group of microscopic dots of ink (or toner or other pigment). The number of dots a printer can generate is measured in dots per inch (DPI). People sometimes incorrectly use the term DPI when they really mean PPI. A printer with a resolution of 2400 DPI means it can squeeze 2400 dots of ink (not pixels) into a single inch. The more dots used to create a pixel, the truer color each pixel can have — resulting in a higher-quality print.

A common misconception related to creating image files is that all graphics for use on the Web should be created at a resolution of 72 PPI. However, because PPI affects the output of printing only, the PPI setting has no effect on the screen display of an image.

It is common practice to save Web images at 72 PPI, not because it optimizes images for the Web, but because the 72 PPI myth so widely is believed.

Working as a Graphic Designer

The business world offers many opportunities for people with creativity and an eye for design. From automotive design to fashion to advertising, the need for talented graphic artists is vast. Many industry experts believe there are generally three levels of professionals working in the graphics field: graphic artists, graphic designers, and people who own graphics editing/design software.

Graphic artists typically receive extensive schooling as art majors and know a lot about design principles and art history. However, schooling does not necessarily mean formal education in a school environment. A graphic artist can be self-educated. The key to the "artist" designation revolves around a personal need to creatively express oneself beyond that of producing commercial work for hire. While graphic artists work with software, they typically also produce art with more traditional media such as paints, pencils, fiber, metals, or other physical materials. Graphic artists may hold the same job as a graphic designer, but very often graphic artists will create and sell their own original artwork. This personal drive to create and the resulting independent production of original artwork is what distinguishes graphic artists from graphic designers.

The line separating graphic artists from graphic designers is a fine one. A **graphic designer** often is knowledgeable about design principles and may possess a wealth of information about art history, but not all graphic designers are graphic artists. They usually create design products for others, such as brochures, advertisements, or Web sites, using software, but do not create their own original works.

The third category of graphic designers includes people who own and use graphics design software for various purposes. This category, **software owners**, is not a true graphic design designation. Simply owning a copy of Photoshop or knowing how to use a certain software program does not make you a graphic artist/designer. Whereas artists and designers understand principles of design and effective use of color, and possess a certain degree of artistic ability or raw talent, design amateurs rely on the power of the software to help them create projects. Of course, it is possible for an amateur to become a professional designer or artist — but doing so requires education and training, not just purchasing a software suite.

BTW | **Resolution and Print Quality**
The higher the resolution, the smaller the pixels and the printout, and the better the quality.

BTW | **PPI and Printing**
An image with the dimensions of 800 x 600 at 72 PPI will look exactly the same on screen as the same image at 300 PPI. In fact, the file sizes will be identical. There only will be a difference when printed. For Web images, you can save them at 0 PPI, and they would work just as well, and have the same file size, as if you saved them at 1200 PPI. However, when printed, they will differ.

BTW | **PPI on the Web**
You cannot make an image appear larger on screen by resizing its pixels. Every pixel on the same screen will always be the same size.

Jobs in Graphic Design

An understanding of design principles and software skills opens the door to many opportunities in the professional graphics industry. Jobs for graphic designers range from freelance work and self-employment to full-time careers with advertising agencies, Web design firms, print houses, software companies, or the marketing team within an organization such as a school or commercial or nonprofit business. Perhaps the most important questions to ask yourself when considering a job in this field are:

- Do I want to work for myself or for someone else?
- Am I truly an artist? Am I creative? Or do I simply follow direction well, understand basic design principles, and know how to use graphics software?
- What is my preferred medium — physical (print) or electronic (Web, software interface)?

Once you have secured a position in the graphics field, you will be assigned projects that will call on your design skills and other abilities.

Design Projects

A successful project always begins with solid planning. Proper planning helps you to stay focused and reduces the potential for wasted time and money — both yours and your client's. A project plan must specify the following aspects of the project:

- Scope of design work
- Roles and responsibilities of designer and client
- Expectations and specifications for final product, including time frame

When you and your client agree on the scope of the work and are clear on what the final product should look like, you as the designer know exactly what it is you need to produce. It is better to take the time to plan a project before sitting down with Photoshop, so you have a good idea of what to do once you start the software.

Client and Designer Roles

Both the client and the designer have specific jobs. Defining and agreeing on these roles is crucial for the success of the collaboration.

Simply put, the client must clearly communicate his or her expectations. Clients often need help articulating their wants and needs, and the designer must be able to help draw this information from the client. Additionally, the client must be available to provide feedback when the designer offers a draft for feedback or proofing. A client's responsibilities include the following:

- Clearly communicate the needs of the project
- Provide timely and constructive feedback
- Trust the designer's expertise
- Pay the bills on time

Aside from the obvious (creating the product), the designer also is responsible for making sure the client knows their own responsibilities and avoids poor design choices. Sometimes, a client will request something that is just bad — like certain colors that do not work well together or make text unreadable. The designer is responsible for respectfully steering the client away from the bad options and toward a better alternative.

In a highly competitive job market, you must determine what sets you apart from your competition. A potential client might choose one designer over another not because one is a better or more creative artist, but simply because they like the other designer more.

Customer service is part of your job, as well. Treat your client and your client's time and money with respect, be personable, and appreciate your client, and you will have more to offer than your competitors will. In addition to meeting the responsibilities previously defined, you should do the following:

- Be on time to meetings
- Meet or beat your deadlines so you do not submit work late
- Be able to explain your design choices
- Ensure adherence to copyright law

Defining the Project

As a designer, you must understand you are acting in the role of a hired hand — not an artist with complete creative control. You are being hired to create what your client wants, not what you necessarily prefer. While you need to educate your client as to best practices in design, ultimately the client is paying the bill, so he or she has the final word when it comes to making decisions.

Specifying Project Details

Project details should be discussed with the client and agreed upon before any design work begins. One detail to consider is what the client needs for files. For example, does the client require a 300 PPI TIF file or a layered Photoshop file? How will the files be delivered? Will they be sent by e-mail, burned to a CD and mailed, or downloaded from a Web site or FTP server? Additionally, a timeline of deliverables should be stated. A first draft of the design should be sent to the client for approval by a certain date, and pending timely client feedback, the final version should be delivered by the project deadline. The client may have a desired time frame, and the designer must be able to deliver the work within that time frame. Sometimes a compromise must be reached.

BTW

Photos on CD or DVD
If possible, get photos and images on a CD or DVD. Many times a collection of photographs and other materials are too large to send by e-mail, and even if they are successfully sent, e-mails accidentally get deleted. Having all the materials on CD or DVD also guarantees you always have a backup of the original files as you modify copies with Photoshop or other software.

Collecting Materials

Existing materials help to speed up the design process. If you are hired to create a Web site or brochure, ask your client for copies of their existing promotional materials, such as a business card, letterhead, or logo. Ask your client what they like and dislike about these materials and if the product you are creating should be stylistically similar. This approach can prevent you from going down the wrong path, inadvertently creating something the client does not like or need. Additionally, you will need to collect any photographs your client has earmarked for the project.

Next, you must gather other assets for the project; specifically, high-quality artwork and photographs.

Original Artwork   If you have the raw artistic ability or own high-quality camera equipment, you can create your own original artwork or take your own photographs if you are a professional-level photographer. You can outsource some of this work to professional artists or photographers — just be sure to get your client's approval for the cost. Your other option is to use stock art.

Stock Art   **Stock art** includes existing artwork and photographs that can be licensed for use. The cost of a single picture can range from zero to several thousand dollars, depending on the source and license restrictions. Realistically, you should expect to pay between $5 and $40 for each print-quality digital file if you cannot find free sources.

Public Domain vs. Commercial Stock Art
Public domain stock art sites can be difficult to use because they do not have the funding for the more intuitive style of interface found on the commercial sites. You often can find exactly what you want in the public domain. However, sometimes it is worth the $5 to more easily find exactly what you want on a commercial Web site.

Stock art is commercially available from many companies, most with a Web presence — meaning you can download images or purchase whole collections of stock art on CD or DVD from a Web site. Thousands of companies sell commercial stock art online. Some of the most popular resources are fotosearch.com, corbis.com, and gettyimages.com.

When searching for stock art, be sure to seek out **royalty-free images**. Images that are royalty free can be reused without paying additional fees. For example, you could spend $100 to purchase an image that is not royalty free and use it on a Web site. If you want to use the same image in a brochure or another client's Web site, you might have to pay another fee to reuse the image. Royalty free means that once the initial payment is made, there are no re-usage fees.

If you do not want to pay anything for your images, look into finding **public domain** artwork or photographs. Images in the public domain are completely free to use. The only trick is finding quality artwork in the public domain. Whereas commercial stock art Web sites typically have millions of high-quality images from which to choose, public domain stock art Web sites often have far fewer choices. Public domain stock art sites include Flickr, Morgue File, and Uncle Sam's Photos.

Other Licenses   There are usage licenses allowing free unrestricted use of images, audio, video, text, and other content similar to that of the public domain. These licenses include Copyleft, Creative Commons, education use, fair use, GNU general public license, and open source. The definitions of these alternative licenses read like a law book, but it is helpful to recognize the names. Laws related to these licenses allow for limited use of copyright-protected material without requiring the permission of the copyright owner. If you find images or other content offered as one of these alternatives, there is a good chance it will be completely free to use.

Whatever the source for your images, be sure to read the license and usage rights and restrictions carefully. No matter your source for artwork, you need to document its origin. The documentation serves two important purposes. First, it provides a record of the image's origin in case you need to get additional similar artwork. Second, it provides peace of mind should you or your client ever face legal action for copyright infringement. The documentation does not have to be fancy; it can simply be a list of where an image is used in a project and where that image was acquired.

Summary

Successful design uses the principles of balance, contrast, dominance, proximity, repetition, closure, continuance, negative space, and unity. The properties of color include hue, saturation, shade, tint, and value. Color modes include RGB for Web images, CMYK for images you intend to print, and LAB for access to the largest color space possible when working with digital photographs. Adherence to Web-safe colors is unnecessary. Colors can have emotional implications and should be used in harmony with neighboring colors. Color schemes include monochrome, complementary, analogous, and split-complementary.

Typeface selections can affect text readability, as can line lengths. Typefaces are organized into several categories, including serif, sans-serif, script, and display. The same Web site can look different from one monitor or computer to another.

Pixels per inch (PPI) determines the number of pixels printed per inch and affects the printed size of an image only, not how it appears onscreen or its file size. Higher PPI settings produce better quality printouts but have no effect on how an image appears onscreen. Dots per inch (DPI) refers to printer capabilities and defines how many dots of ink a printer can print in a linear inch. Pixel dimensions, not image resolution, affect how large an image appears on-screen and the size of a file.

Working in graphic design can incorporate a range of creative roles; working with clients in a design role requires specifying project expectations and the responsibilities of both designer and client.

Appendix C
Publishing to a Web Server

Publishing a Web Site

Once you have created a Web site, you need to make it available to its intended audience. The discussion in this appendix is generally appropriate for small business and personal Web sites. Keep in mind that midsize and larger businesses typically publish their sites using their own dedicated Web servers; however, the concepts are the same. Publishing a Web site, also called going live, involves four general steps:

1. Select a Web hosting company
2. Choose and register a domain name
3. Publish your Web site files to a Web server
4. Associate your domain name with your nameserver

Web Hosting Companies

In order for your Web site to be available to users or visitors, it must reside on a special computer called a Web server. A Web server is a computer connected to the Internet, with Web server software installed. It is the Web server software that makes files stored on a computer available as a Web site. While anyone with a computer can download and install Web server software at no cost, configuring Web server software is a complex process best left to experts. A **Web hosting company**, or **Web host**, is a company that offers Web hosting services. Web hosting companies rent space on their Web servers for you to store your Web site.

How to Choose a Web Host

Choosing a Web host begins with research. Read about Web hosts online and in technology publications. Keep in mind, however, that online reviews of Web hosting companies often are biased or sponsored. Reviews are biased negatively as it is human nature to complain when you do not like something, but fewer people take the time and energy to write a review when they are pleased with a product or service. A review is biased positively when the review is sponsored by the Web hosting company itself — meaning either the Web host owns the review Web site or it purchases advertising on the review Web site, potentially influencing the display of positive reviews.

Once you have identified a few potential Web hosts, you should compare their features and test their tech support policies, as described later in this appendix. Recommendations from friends or colleagues are also important to consider when choosing a Web host. Choosing a host is an important consideration that should not be rushed.

Before choosing a Web hosting company, you should decide whether you need shared hosting or dedicated hosting and review the services and features outlined in the section that follows.

Dedicated and Shared Hosting

When a single Web server hosts a single Web site, the arrangement is called **dedicated hosting**. Dedicated hosting allows the client and the Web site full access to all of the server's resources, such as the processor, memory, and hard drive space (Figure C–1a). Unfortunately, dedicated hosting is expensive, sometimes costing several hundred dollars or more per month.

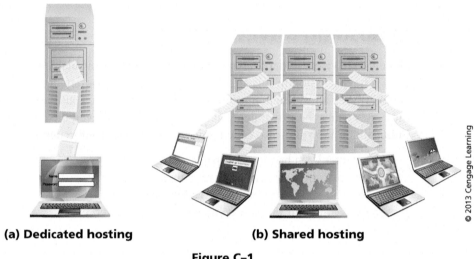

(a) Dedicated hosting   **(b) Shared hosting**

Figure C–1

© 2013 Cengage Learning

Shared hosting refers to multiple Web sites sharing a single Web server or a bank of Web servers (Figure C–1b). Shared Web servers host many, sometimes thousands of individual Web sites that reside on the same server. Those Web sites share the server's processor, memory, hard drive space, and other computer resources. A reputable Web host has powerful Web server computers that can handle this kind of load, as well as the expert staff to configure the computers and Web server software. The disadvantage to shared hosting is that you do not get all the power of the server to yourself, as you do with dedicated hosting. The advantage is that shared hosting is very inexpensive, often just a few dollars a month. Most small business and personal Web sites use shared hosting.

Hosting Services and Features

The following paragraphs outline some of the more important features to consider when choosing a Web host (Figure C–2).

Disk Space   Web site pages (HTML documents) are small files that do not take up much storage space, but other files, such as images, Flash movies, or other video and audio files, used on your site may be quite large. A typical image file used on a Web site may be as large as 50 kilobytes. A Flash movie file might be several thousand kilobytes. If your Web site files are larger than the disk space available to you, your Web site will not fit on the server. Choose a Web hosting plan that offers unlimited disk space.

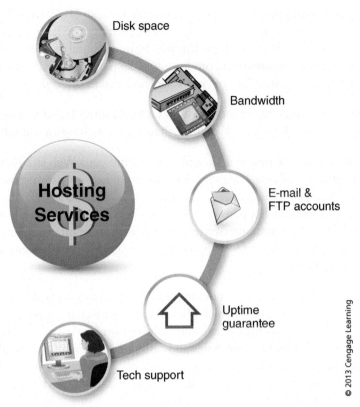

Figure C–2

Bandwidth   Every time a user connects to your Web site, your files are transferred across the Internet to the user. **Bandwidth** refers to the number of bytes your Web site is sending across the Internet. A **byte** is approximately equivalent to one character — a **kilobyte** is 1,024 bytes. The more users that connect to your site, or the larger your files are, the more bandwidth you use. Some Web hosts disable your Web site if you exceed the allotted bandwidth for your account, while other Web hosts charge you additional fees for overages. Choose a Web hosting plan that offers unlimited bandwidth.

E-Mail Accounts   To maintain professionalism, it is best to have an e-mail address that uses the same name as your Web site. For example, if your Web site is www.MyWebSite.com, it is best to have e-mail addresses such as info@MyWebSite.com or contact@MyWebSite.com rather than MyWebSite@hotmail.com or MyWebSite@gmail.com. Having an e-mail address that uses the same name as your Web site increases brand and name recognition, and is more likely to drive people to your site. Some hosting plans offer fewer than five e-mail accounts, which can be problematic if you need e-mail addresses for more many employees, for example. Choose a Web hosting plan that offers an adequate number of e-mail accounts for your site's needs.

FTP Accounts   To copy your Web site to a Web server, you must connect to the Web server using software called an FTP client. **FTP** stands for **file transfer protocol**, which is a method of copying files between computers across the Internet. Because multiple people may be working on the Web site and updating files, each person should have his or her own FTP account for security purposes. If several people use the same FTP account, passwords might be changed inadvertently, making it impossible for the others to log on. Individual FTP accounts also help track who added, updated, or deleted files from the Web site. Choose a Web hosting plan that offers an unlimited number of FTP accounts.

BTW

Other Hosting Considerations
You might want to ask potential Web hosting companies about their financial strength, their physical security, their disaster recovery plan, and how long they have been in business.

Cost   Shared hosting plans typically cost anywhere from $0.99 to $15 per month. The most expensive plans are not necessarily the best, nor are the least expensive always the best value. You can find excellent features from a reputable Web host such as webhostinghub.com or hostgator.com for about $6 per month. Choose a Web hosting company whose costs offer the best value for the services offered.

Setup Fee   Some Web hosting companies charge a setup fee of $20 or more just to set up a new account. Choose a Web host that does not charge a setup fee.

Uptime Guarantee   Uptime is the amount of time your Web site is available. Ideally, you want your site available 100 percent of the time; however sometimes computers crash, hard drives become damaged, or other components in a computer cause it to stop working. When this happens on a Web server, Web sites residing on that server are not available. The reliability of the service is an important consideration. Choose a Web host that offers at least a 99.9 percent uptime guarantee to ensure that your Web site always is available.

Tech Support   Tech support can be offered in a variety of ways. Make sure you choose a Web host that offers e-mail, phone, and online chat support 24 hours a day, 7 days a week. It is a good idea to test the tech support service of a hosting company before signing up for an account. Sales and billing departments are usually excellent about taking phone calls and responding to e-mails, but you are not likely to need to reach those people once your account is active. Call tech support and see how long it takes them to answer. E-mail tech support and see how long it is until you receive a response. Ask a basic question such as, "What is the typical wait time before receiving a response from your tech support?" Some $0.99 per month hosting plans seem like a good deal until you encounter a problem. If you cannot reach tech support or they reply with a generic programmed response as if they are reading from a script, that $0.99 per month cost may not be such a great deal after all. Choose a Web hosting company that offers 24-hour support, short wait times, and quick turnaround for e-mail questions.

Domain Names

Every computer connected to the Internet is assigned a unique number, called an **Internet Protocol (IP) address**, which identifies the computer. An IP address is used when one computer needs to contact another computer. For example, when a user opens a Web browser and types the name of a Web site, such as cengage.com, his or her computer actually connects to the Web server by using the IP address of the Web server. Because IP addresses are difficult to remember, most sites use a domain name such as cengage.com. A **domain name** is a combination of letters and numbers that names a Web site for locating purposes; it is the part of the URL that follows the **protocol designation** such as http:// and any **subdomain** listing such as www (Figure C–3). The user's computer automatically matches the domain name with the IP address in order to connect to the Web server. You need to choose a domain name carefully, and purchase, or register, your domain name to work in conjunction with your Web hosting company. You will learn how to register a domain name later in this appendix.

BTW

IP Addresses
An IP address typically is four decimal numbers separated by periods. However, as these numbers are being exhausted rapidly, a new eight-number IP address, using a hexadecimal notation, is being advocated by the Internet Assigned Numbers Authority (IANA).

protocol designation   subdomain   domain name   top-level domain

Figure C–3

Choosing a Domain Name

Choose a domain name that is easy to spell, easy to type, and easy to remember. Your domain name might have to fit on a business card, and some users will need to type it into their Web browser's Address bar. Avoiding domain names that are lengthy or complicated is a good approach. A **top-level domain (TLD)** is the last part of a Web site's name. For example, .com, .org, .net, and .edu are all top-level domains. When choosing a domain name, you need to decide which top-level domain is best for your site. Table C–1 describes a few of the more popular top-level domains that you are likely to use.

Table C–1 Top-Level Domains

Top-Level Domain	Eligibility	Description
.biz	Anyone can register	Intended for businesses as an alternative to .com
.com	Anyone can register	Originally intended for for-profit businesses, .com has become the most popular top-level domain
.edu	Only educational institutions may register	Used by educational institutions
.info	Anyone can register	No prescribed theme or orientation
.org	Anyone can register	Originally intended for nonprofit organizations

In most cases, you should choose to use .com if possible, because it is the most familiar to people.

BTW

Domain Availability
After you choose a domain name, you need to make sure that no one has chosen that domain name already. You can use a Web site that will check for you, such as godaddy.com or checkdomain.com, or you can type the domain name with its subdomain and top-level domain into a browser's URL text box and see similar Web sites. Keep in mind that some sites may be registered but are not up and running yet.

Registering a Domain Name

You **register**, or purchase, a domain name through a company called a domain name registrar service. Many registrars can be found online. Some of the most popular registrar services include register.com, godaddy.com, and networksolutions.com. By registering a domain name, you become the registrant, or official owner of the site name (Figure C–4).

Figure C–4

Expect to pay anywhere from $10 to $30 per year for domain name registration. After the domain name is registered, you must renew it yearly. If your domain name registration expires, your Web site no longer will be available to the public.

Many registrars also offer Web hosting, and conversely most Web hosting companies offer free domain name registration. However, avoid this temptation to consolidate services. It is best to keep them separate. Register your domain through one company, and host your Web site with a different company. For any number of reasons, you might want to change Web hosting companies. By registering the domain name with a company other than your Web host, you easily can associate your domain name with any current hosting company.

DNS

The **Domain Name System** (**DNS**) is a system that associates or connects a domain name with a Web server (Figure C–5). Computers on the Internet called DNS servers, or **nameservers**, store these associations in a database. The final step in making your Web site available is associating your domain name with the Web server so that when someone opens their browser and types www.YourWebSite.com, that user's computer can find the Web server that hosts your site.

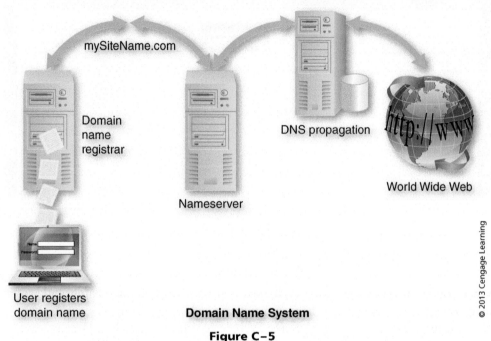

mySiteName.com

Domain name registrar

DNS propagation

World Wide Web

Nameserver

User registers domain name

Domain Name System

Figure C–5

© 2013 Cengage Learning

Some hosting companies associate your domain name for you; others require you to do it yourself. To associate your domain name with your Web server, obtain the name of your nameserver from your Web hosting company. Then go into your domain name registrar service account and update your domain name with the name of the nameserver. As every registrar's Web site is different, you might need to contact the registrar's tech support to learn where to make the nameserver change. Once you have updated your domain name to use a specific nameserver, your domain name will be **associated** with your Web server. This allows the user's Web browser to link to your Web site when a visitor types your domain name in his or her Web browser.

DNS Propagation

There are thousands of nameservers all over the world, and when one is updated, all of the other nameservers receive an update with the new information. The updating process of the nameserver database, across all DNS servers on the Web, is called **DNS propagation**. After you make a change to your nameserver setting, it can take up to 72 hours for that change to propagate, meaning that your Web site might not be available during those three days. Several companies, including whatsmydns.net and viewdns.info, offer instant checking of DNS propagation (Figure C–6 on the next page). DNS propagation is a feature to consider when evaluating potential Web hosts.

BTW

Web Address Forwarding
Web forwarding, also known as domain forwarding, allows you to associate or redirect multiple domain names to a single Web address. For example, if you mistakenly type `google.org` or `google.biz`, domain forwarding will take you to `google.com` automatically. You can increase the number of hits to your Web site by including multiple extensions, misspellings, and common typos in your domain name forwarding.

Figure C–6

Copying Files using FTP

Once you have contracted with a Web host, registered your domain name, and associated your domain name with a nameserver, you need to copy your files to the Web server using FTP client software. Some Web design software, such as Dreamweaver, includes a built-in FTP client (Figure C–7). You also can purchase FTP client software, or use free software such as FileZilla or SmartFTP.

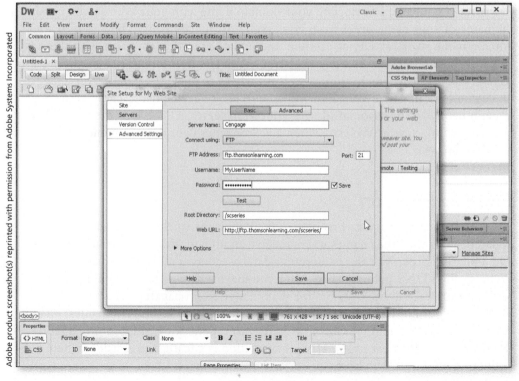

Figure C–7

Copying Files

The process of copying files to the Web server is straightforward, but first you must have four pieces of information from the Web hosting company. Although all FTP clients have slightly different interfaces, they all allow you to specify these four pieces of information:

1. Host name: the name of the Web server. This is usually the same as your domain name, but your Web host should provide an alternate name to use until DNS propagation is complete.
2. Username: the name you use to log on to the Web server.
3. Password: the password you use in conjunction with the username.
4. Remote folder: the name of the folder on the Web server to which you copy your files.

The Web hosting company should provide all this information in an e-mail message. If this information is not provided to you by e-mail, you should contact the hosting company's tech support.

Once the information is entered, you can connect to the Web server and copy your files from your computer to the Web server, either by dragging and dropping or by clicking a Move button. The process of copying files from your computer to another computer, such as a Web server, is called **uploading**. Copying files from another computer to your computer is called **downloading**. With FTP software and the proper user permissions, you can upload your Web files to publish them and download your Web files to edit them as necessary.

BTW

Viewing Server Files
Your Web hosting service may allow Windows Explorer-based copy and paste techniques for copying files to your Web server. With the correct FTP URL, you can use a browser to log into your files. Your browser may display a message such as, "On the menu, click View, and then click Open FTP Site in Windows Explorer."

Summary

Publishing a Web site to a Web server requires research and preparation. Prior to publishing you must select and hire a Web hosting company. Consider both technical and support offerings provided by the Web host before you decide on a company. You must acquire a domain name through a domain name registrar, and associate it with a Web server for DNS propagation. Finally, publishing the Web files involves uploading files to your Web server using FTP.

Publishing to a Web Server

1: Choosing a Web Hosting Company

Instructions: This appendix recommends several features and characteristics to measure when choosing a Web hosting company. Research Web hosts — online at reputable sources and in technology publications. Find at least four different Web Hosting companies and create a table similar to the following, using the criteria described in the appendix.

Company name				
Web site				
Dedicated or shared?				
Disk space				
Bandwidth				
E-mail accounts				
FTP accounts				
Cost				
Setup fee				
Uptime guarantee				
Tech support				

Publishing to a Web Server

2: Choosing a Domain Name

Instructions: You have taken a job as an intern with a consulting firm that helps start-up businesses create a Web presence. Your boss has asked you to recommend three appropriate domain names for a small hobby store named Hobby Express. Their specialty is model railroading, but they also sell puzzles, craft kits, art supplies, and strategy games.

Using the recommendations in this appendix, research domain names that are not currently used. Choose an appropriate top-level domain and an effective domain name that is easy to spell, easy to type, and easy to remember. Write a paragraph for each of the three recommendations explaining why you chose the domain.

Appendix D
Using Photoshop Help

This appendix shows you how to use Photoshop Help. At anytime, whether you are accessing Photoshop currently or not, there are ways to interact with Photoshop Help and display information on any Photoshop topic. The help system is a complete reference manual at your fingertips.

Photoshop Help

Photoshop Help documentation for Photoshop CS6 is available in several formats, as shown in Figure D–1 on the next page. The first format is a Web-based help system that was introduced in Chapter 1. If you press the F1 key or choose Photoshop Online Help on the Help menu, Adobe Community Help appears in your default browser. You then can use the Web page to search for help topics. The Adobe Community Help page also contains many other kinds of assistance, including tutorials and videos. Your computer must be connected to the Web to use this form of Photoshop Help.

A second form of Photoshop Help is available as a PDF file. Again, pressing the F1 key or choosing Photoshop Online Help on the Help menu opens the Adobe Community Help page on the Web. Then, you can click the Help PDF link to open a searchable help documentation, called Using Adobe Photoshop CS6, in book format. You can save this help file on your storage device, or continue to use it on the Web. If you prefer to view documentation in print form, you can print the Photoshop Help PDF file.

Photoshop Help displays two main panes. The left pane displays a search system. The right pane displays help information on the selected topic. Using Adobe Photoshop CS6 displays a chapter navigation system on the left, and pages from Photoshop Help documentation on the right.

Using Help

The quickest way to navigate the Photoshop help system is by clicking topic links on the Help pages. You also can search for specific words and phrases by using the **Search box** in the upper-left corner of the Adobe Community Help Web page. Here you can type words, such as *layer mask, hue,* or *file formats,* or you can type phrases, such as *preview a Web graphic,* or *drawing with the Pen Tool.* Adobe Community Help responds by displaying search results with a list of topics you can click.

Here are some tips regarding the words or phrases you enter to initiate a search:

1. Check the spelling of the word or phrase.
2. Keep your search specific, with fewer than seven words, to return the most accurate results.
3. If you search using a specific phrase, such as *shape tool,* put quotation marks around the phrase — the search returns only those topics containing all words in the phrase.
4. If a search term does not yield the desired results, try using a synonym, such as Web instead of Internet.

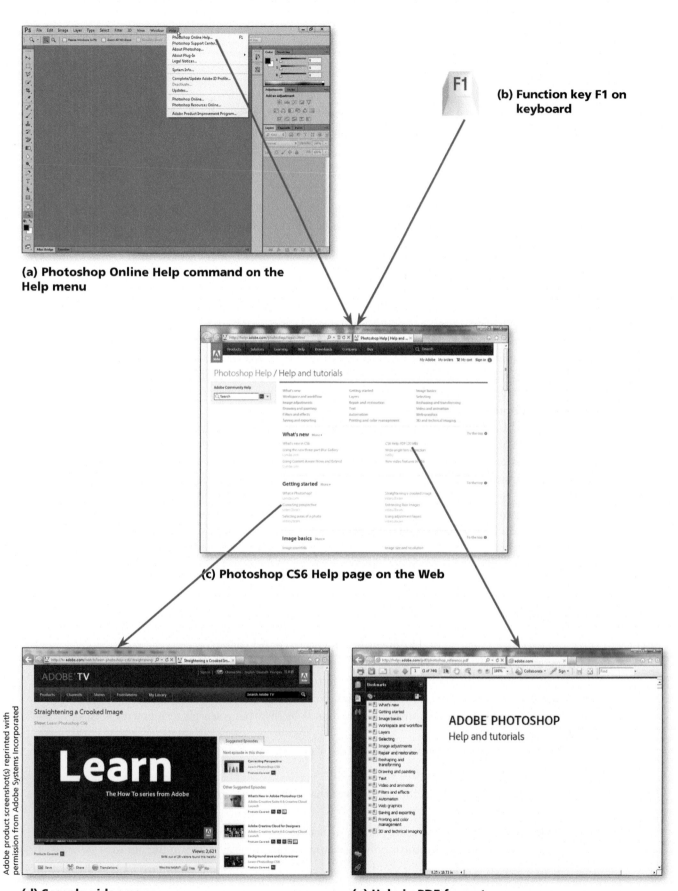

(a) Photoshop Online Help command on the Help menu

(b) Function key F1 on keyboard

(c) Photoshop CS6 Help page on the Web

(d) Sample video page

(e) Help in PDF format

Figure D–1

To Access Photoshop Online Help

The following step shows how to open Photoshop Online Help.

- With Photoshop running on your system, press the F1 key to display the Photoshop Help window.

- When the Adobe Community Help window is displayed, double-click the title bar to maximize the window, if necessary (Figure D–2).

Figure D–2

To Use the Topics List

The Topics List is similar to a table of contents in a book. Because Adobe updates the topics on a regular basis, your Topics List will look different. The following steps use the topics list to look up information about what is new in CS6.

1

- Click the topic, What's new in CS6 to display its contents (Figure D–3).

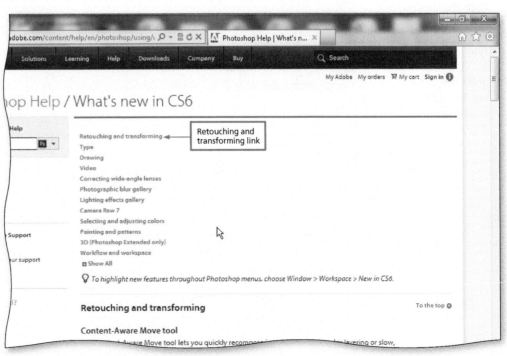

Figure D–3

● Click the link, Retouching and transforming, to display information about the new retouching tools (Figure D–4).

Figure D–4

To Use the Adobe Community Help Search Box

The following steps use the Search box to obtain useful information by entering the keywords, ruler origin.

● Click the Search box.

● Type `ruler origin` and then press the ENTER key to display the search results (Figure D–5).

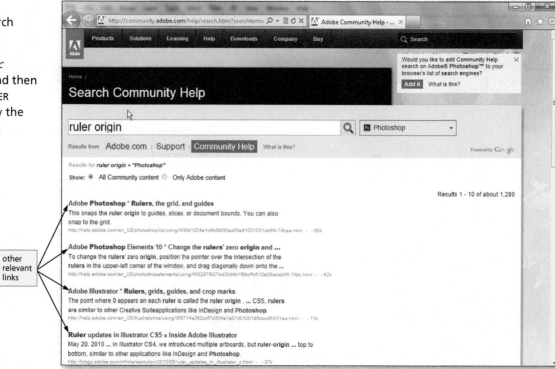

Figure D–5

2

- When the list of Help topics is displayed, click Adobe Photoshop* Rulers, the grid, and guides, or a similar topic in your list.

- Scroll as necessary to display the Change a ruler's zero origin topic (Figure D–6).

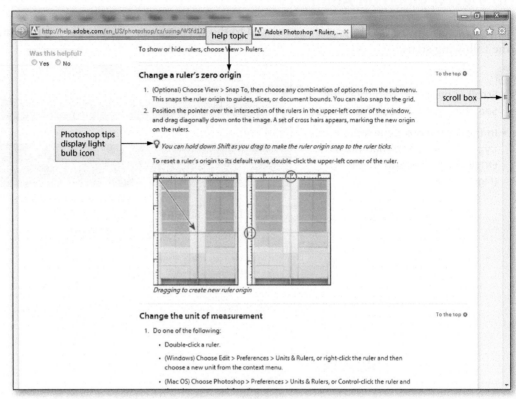

Figure D–6

On the right, Photoshop Help displays information about the topic, instructions, and a graphic. A light bulb icon indicates a Photoshop tip.

If none of the topics presents the information you want, you can refine the search by entering another word or phrase in the Search box.

To View a Video on Adobe TV

Using Photoshop Help while connected to the Web, you can view online videos and tutorials, as done in the following steps.

- Scroll as necessary to display the Search box at the top of the page.
- In the Search box, type adobe tv type styles, and then press the ENTER key to perform the search (Figure D–7).

Figure D–7

- Click the link named Type Styles in Photoshop CS6 to open the page and start the video (Figure D–8).

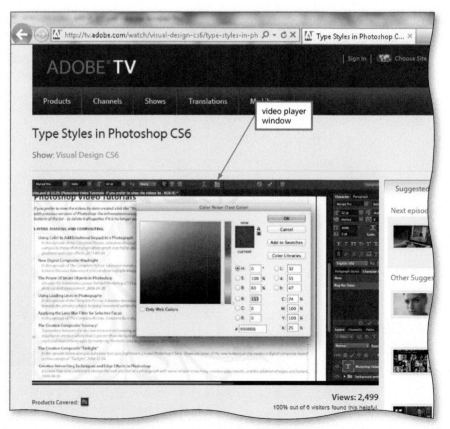

Figure D–8

3

● When the video is finished playing, click the Close button on the title bar of the browser window to quit Help (Figure D–9).

Figure D–9

Using Help PDF Documentation

The PDF file, Adobe Photoshop Help and Tutorials, is a complete set of documentation for using Photoshop CS6. The PDF file is organized into chapter topics with a table of contents like a regular book. You can access Adobe Photoshop Help and Tutorials by clicking the link on the Photoshop Online Help page.

To Open Adobe Photoshop Help and Tutorials

The following step opens the PDF file, Adobe Photoshop Help and Tutorials, from the Photoshop Online Help page. You will use Adobe Acrobat to view the documentation.

1

- Start Photoshop if necessary.

- Press the F1 key to access Photoshop online Help.

- Click the Help PDF link to open the Adobe Photoshop Help and Tutorials documentation. (Figure D–10).

The file would not open because I do not have Adobe Acrobat on my system.

See your instructor for ways to access the file.

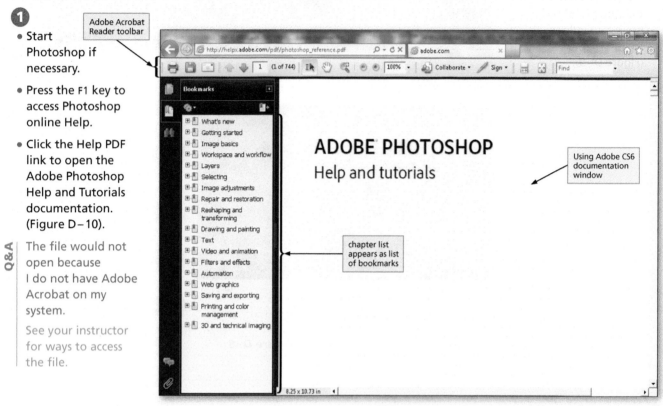

Figure D–10

To Navigate the Documentation by Chapter Topic

The following steps use the left pane of the documentation window to find information related to color.

1

- With the Adobe Photoshop Help and Tutorials documentation file still displayed, click the plus sign next to the words, Image Basics, and then click About color, to display the topic (Figure D–11).

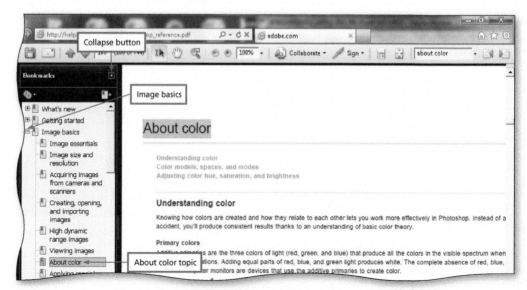

Figure D–11

2

- Click the words, Understanding color, to display the information on the right side of the window.

- Click the Collpase button to hide the Search pane (Figure D–12).

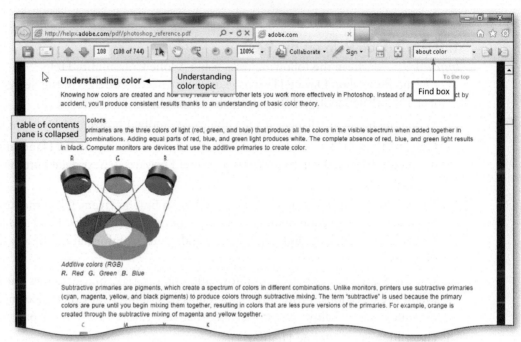

Figure D–12

To Use the Find Box

The following step searches the documentation for information about the topic, knockout, using the Adobe Acrobat Find box.

1

- With the Adobe Photoshop Help and Tutorials documentation window still displayed, click the Find box in the Adobe Acrobat toolbar and then type **knockout options**.

- Press the ENTER key to search for the term (Figure D–13).

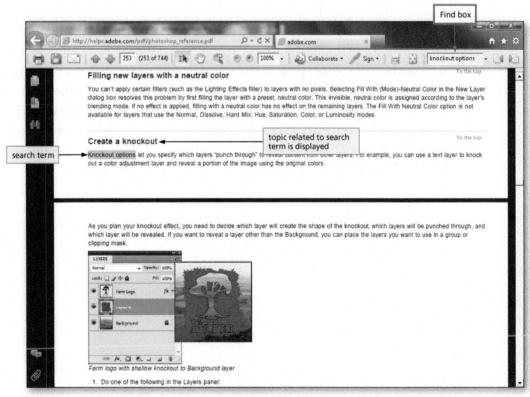

Figure D–13

Use Help

1: Using Adobe Help on the Web

Instructions: Perform the following tasks using Adobe Community Help.

1. On the Photoshop Online Help page, type `pencil tool` in the Search box to obtain help on using the Pencil tool, and then press the ENTER key.

2. When the topics are displayed, click the topic, Adobe Photoshop* Drawing with the Pen tools.

3. One at a time, click two additional links and print the information. Hand in the printouts to your instructor. Use the Back to previous page and Forward to next page buttons to return to the original page.

4. Use the Search box to search for information on linking layers. Click the Adobe Photoshop* Selecting, grouping, and linking layers topic in the search results. Read and print the information. One at a time, click the links on the page and print the information for any new page that is displayed.

5. Use the Search box to search for information on tutorials. Navigate to a tutorial of your choice and follow the directions. Write three paragraphs describing your experience, including how easy or difficult it was to follow the tutorial and what you learned. Turn in the paragraphs to your instructor.

6. Close Photoshop Online Help.

Use Help

2: Using Adobe Photoshop CS6 Documentation

Instructions: Use the Adobe Photoshop CS6 documentation to understand the topics better and answer the questions listed below. Answer the questions on your own paper, or hand in the printed Help information to your instructor.

1. Open the PDF file, Adobe Photoshop Help and Tutorials from the Photoshop Online Help page.

2. Use the Adobe Photoshop Help and Tutorials documentation to find help on snapping. Use the Find box, and enter `use snapping` as the term. Click the search result entitled, Use snapping, and then print the page. Hand in the printouts to your instructor.

3. Use the Adobe Photoshop Help and Tutorials documentation and expand the bookmarks, if necessary. Navigate to Chapter 10: Drawing, and then click the plus sign to expand the topic. Click the plus sign next to Drawing Shapes. One at a time, click each link and print the page. Hand in the printouts to your instructor.

Appendix E

Using Adobe Bridge CS6

This appendix shows you how to use Adobe Bridge CS6. Bridge is a file exploration tool similar to Windows Explorer, but with added functionality related to images. Bridge replaces previous file browsing techniques, and now is the control center for the Adobe Creative Suite. Bridge is used to organize, browse, and locate the assets you need to create content for print, the Web, and mobile devices with drag-and-drop functionality.

Adobe Bridge

You can access Bridge from Photoshop or from the Windows 7 Start menu. Bridge can run independently from Photoshop as a stand-alone program.

To Start Bridge Using Windows

The following steps start Bridge from the Windows 7 Start menu.

1

- Click the Start button on the Windows 7 taskbar to display the Start menu.

- Type **Bridge CS6** as the search text in the 'Search programs and files' text box, and watch the search results appear on the Start menu (Figure E–1).

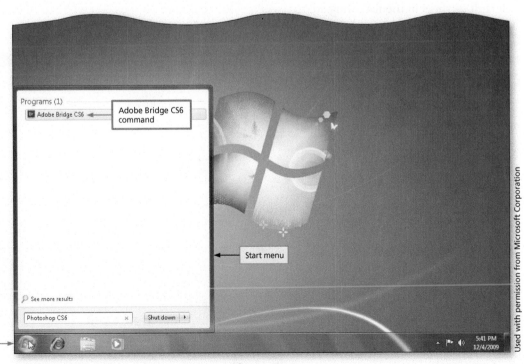

Figure E–1

- Click Adobe Bridge CS6 in the search results on the Start menu to start Bridge.

- When the Bridge window is displayed, double-click its title bar to maximize the window, if necessary.

- Click Computer on the Favorites panel, if necessary (Figure E–2).

Other Ways

1. In Photoshop, click File on menu bar, click Browse in Bridge
2. Press ATL+CTRL+O

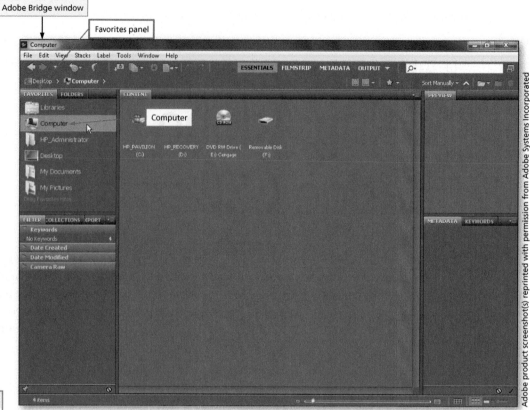

Figure E–2

To Reset the Workspace

To make your installation of Bridge match the figures in this book, you will reset the workspace to its default settings in the following step.

- Click Window on the menu bar, and then point to Workspace to display the Workspace submenu (Figure E–3).

- Click Reset Workspace on the Workspace submenu.

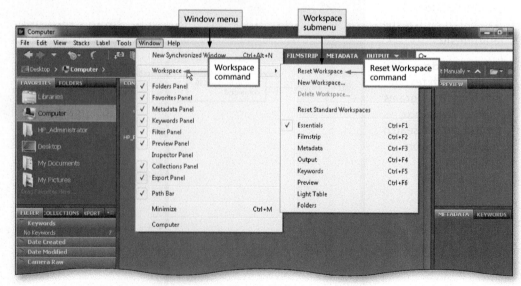

Figure E–3

Other Ways

1. Press CTRL+F1

The Bridge Window

The parts of the Bridge window are displayed in Figure E–4. The window is divided into panels and includes a menu bar, a toolbar, and a status bar.

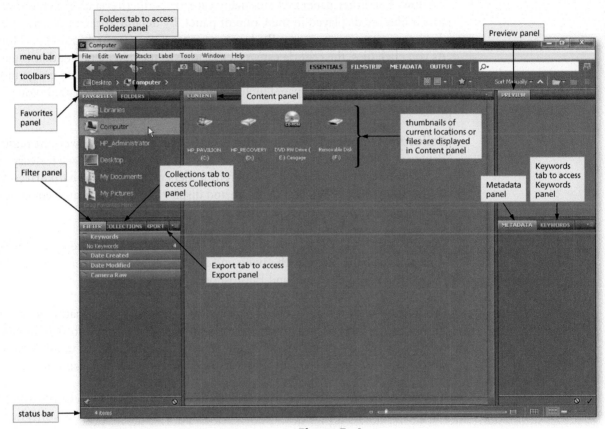

Figure E–4

The Panels

Several panels are displayed in the Bridge workspace in default view. To select a panel, click its tab. You can change the location of the panels by dragging their tabs. You can enlarge or reduce the size of the panels by dragging their borders. Some panels include buttons and menus to help you organize displayed information.

Favorites Panel   The Favorites panel allows quick access to common locations and folders, as well as access to other Adobe applications. You can click a location to display its contents in the Content panel.

Folders Panel   The Folders panel shows the folder hierarchy in a display similar to that of Windows Explorer. You can click the plus sign to expand folders and the minus sign to collapse them.

Content Panel   The Content panel is displayed in a large pane in the center of the Bridge window. The content panel includes a view of each file and folder, its name, the creation date, and other information about each item. The Content panel is used to select files and open folders. To select a file, click it. To open a folder, double-click it. You can change how the Content panel is displayed on the Bridge status bar.

Preview Panel   The Preview panel displays a preview of the selected file that is usually larger than the thumbnail displayed in the Content panel. If the panel is resized, the preview also is resized.

Filter Panel   The Filter panel is displayed in the lower-left region of the Bridge window. The Filter panel includes many categories of criteria used to filter or control which files are displayed in the Content panel. By default, three categories are displayed when you first start Bridge: Keywords, Date Created, and Date Modified. As you click files, the criteria categories change to include metadata that is generated dynamically depending on the file type. For example, if you click an image in the Content panel, the Filter panel includes criteria such as camera data. If you click an audio file, the criteria include artist, album genre, and so on.

Collections Panel   The Collections panel is displayed in the lower-left region of the Bridge window. **Collections** are a way to group photos in one place for easy viewing, even if the images are located in different folders or on different hard drives. The Collections panel allows you to create and display previously created collections, by identifying files or by saving previous searches.

Export Panel   The Export panel is displayed in the lower-left region of the Bridge window. The panel helps with saving and uploading to photo-sharing Web sites, including Facebook, Flickr, and Photoshop.com.

Metadata Panel   The Metadata panel contains metadata information for the selected file. Recall that metadata is information about the file including properties, camera data, creation and modification data, and other pieces of information. If multiple files are selected, shared data is listed such as keywords, date created, and exposure settings.

Keywords Panel   The Keywords panel allows you to assign keywords using categories designed by Bridge, or you can create new ones. The keywords help you organize and search your images.

Toolbars and Buttons

Bridge displays several toolbars and sets of buttons to help you work more efficiently (Figure E–5).

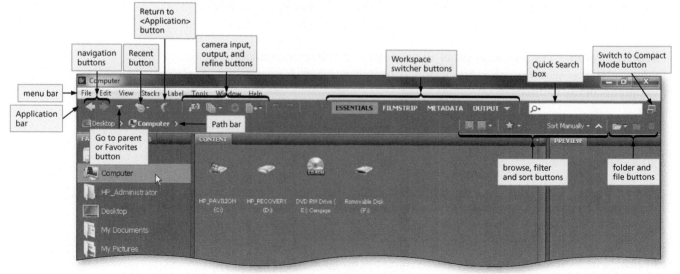

Figure E–5

Menu Bar   The menu bar is displayed at the top of the Bridge window and contains commands specific to Bridge.

Application Bar   Below the menu bar is the Application bar, which includes the navigation buttons, file retrieval and output buttons, buttons for switching workspaces, and other buttons to search for files.

Path Bar   The Path bar displays the path for the current file. To the right of the Path bar are shortcut buttons to help you work with your files. Browse, filter, and sort buttons change the display in the Content panel. The 'Create a new folder' button inserts a new folder in the current location. The rotate buttons are active when an image file is selected in the Content panel. The Delete item button deletes the selected item.

Status Bar   At the bottom of the Bridge window, the status bar displays information and contains buttons (Figure E–6). On the left side of the status bar is information regarding the number of items in the current location and how many files are selected, if any. On the right side of the status bar, the Thumbnail slider sets the size of the thumbnails. To the right of the slider are four buttons used to change the display of the Content panel, including the 'Click to lock thumbnail grid' button, the 'View content as thumbnails' button, the 'View content as details' button, and the 'View content as list' button.

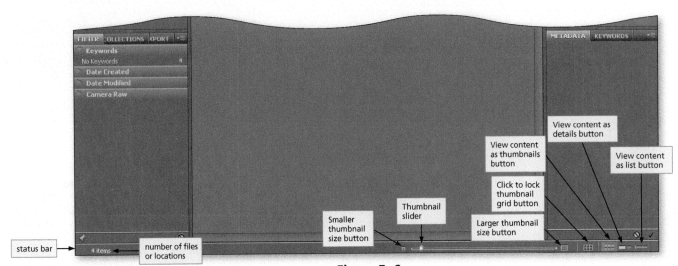

Figure E–6

Bridge Navigation and File Viewing

The advantages of using Bridge to navigate through the files and folders on your computer system include an interface that looks the same in all folders, the ability to see the images quickly, and the ease with which you can open the files in Photoshop or other image editing software. Besides the four kinds of displays represented by the Workspace switcher buttons on the right side of the status bar, Bridge offers several other configurations or layouts of the workspace accessible on the Workspace submenu on the Window menu (Figure E–3 on page APP 44).

To Navigate and View Files Using Bridge

The following step navigates to the Data Files for Students in order to view files. Visit www.cengage.com/ct/studentdownload for detailed instructions or contact your instructor for information about accessing the required files. You then will use the Workspace switcher buttons to view the Content panel in different styles.

- In the Content panel, double-click the drive associated with the Data Files for Students.

- When the folders and files are displayed, double-click the Photoshop folder, and then double-click the Chapter 01 folder to display the files (Figure E–7).

 **Experiment**

- One at a time, click each of the workspace buttons on the options bar and note how the Content panel changes.

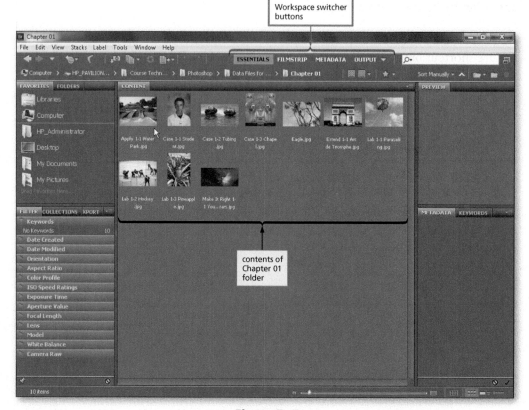

Figure E–7

Other Ways
1. To view Filmstrip workspace, press CTRL+F2   4. To view Keywords workspace, press CTRL+F5
2. To view Metadata workspace, press CTRL+F3   5. To view Preview workspace, press CTRL+F6
3. To view Output workspace, press CTRL+F4

BTW

Duplicating Files
Bridge also offers a Duplicate command on the Edit menu (Figure E–8) that makes a copy in the same folder. Bridge renames the second file with the word, Copy, appended to the file name.

Managing Files

If you want to move a file to a folder that currently is displayed in the Content panel, you can drag and drop the file. The right-drag option is not available. If you want to copy a file, you can choose Copy on the Edit menu, navigate to the new folder and then choose Paste on the Edit menu. At anytime, you can press the DELETE key to delete a file or folder, or right-click and then click Delete on the context menu. To rename a photo in Bridge, right-click the file and then click Rename. Type the new name.

To Copy a File

The following steps copy a file from the Data Files for Students to a USB flash drive using Bridge.

- With the Chapter 01 folder contents still displayed in the Content panel, click the Case 1-2 Tubing thumbnail to select it.

- Click Edit on the menu bar to display the Edit menu (Figure E–8).

 **Experiment**

- Choose a picture and then use one of the rotate commands on the Edit menu to rotate the image. Press CTRL+Z to cancel the rotation. When you are done, click Edit on the menu bar.

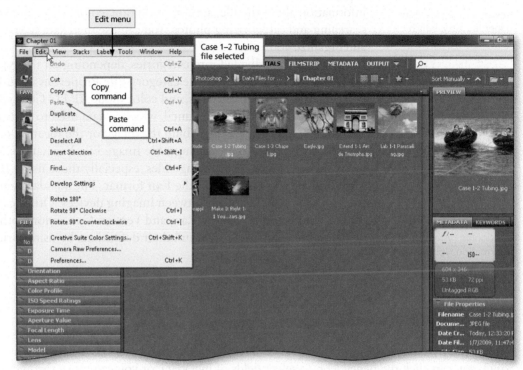

Figure E–8

- Click Copy on the Edit menu.

- In the Favorites panel, click Computer.

- When the Computer locations are displayed in the Content panel, double-click Removable Disk (F:) or the drive associated with your USB flash drive.

- Click Edit on the menu bar, and then click Paste to display the copy in its new location (Figure E–9).

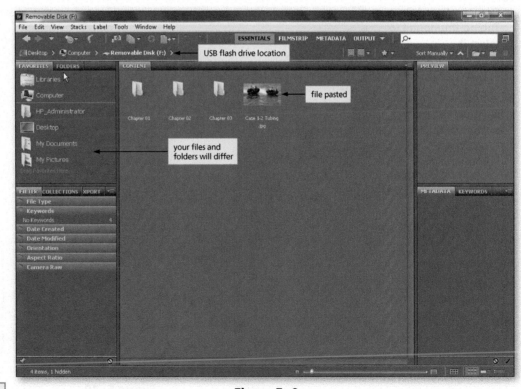

Figure E–9

Other Ways

1. To copy, press CTRL+C
2. To paste, press CTRL+V

Metadata

A popular use for Bridge allows you to assign metadata to files. Metadata, such as information about the file, author, resolution, color space, and copyright, is used for searching and categorizing photos. You can use metadata to streamline your workflow and organize your files.

Metadata is divided into categories, depending on the type of software you are using and the selected files. The category File Properties includes things like file type, creation date, dimensions, and color mode. IPTC Core stands for International Press Telecommunications Council, which is data used to identify transmitted text and images, such as data describing the image or the location of a photo. Camera Data (Exif) refers to the Exchangeable Image File Format, a standard for storing interchange information in image files, especially those using JPEG compression. Most digital cameras now use the Exif format. The standardization of IPTC and Exif encourages interoperability between imaging devices. Other categories may include Audio, Video, Fonts, Camera Raw, and Version Cue, among others. You can see a list of all the metadata categories and their definitions by using Bridge Help.

To Assign and View Metadata

The Metadata Focus workspace makes it easier to assign or enter metadata for photos. In the Metadata panel, you can click the pencil icon to select fields of metadata, or you can move through the fields by pressing the TAB key. The following steps enter description and location information for the selected file.

- Click the Case 1-2 Tubing thumbnail to select it.

- In the Metadata panel, move the mouse pointer to a location just right of the field names. When the mouse pointer changes to a double-headed arrow, drag to the right to display more of the words.

- Drag the left border of the Metadata panel to widen the panel itself.

- In the Metadata panel, scroll down to the IPTC Core area.

- Click the arrow next to the heading, IPTC Core to expand the area if necessary (Figure E–10).

Figure E–10

2

- Scroll down to the Description field and then click the pencil icon to the right of the Description field. Type **Tubing Adventure** as the description.

- Scroll as needed and then click the pencil icon to the right of the Sublocation field. Type **Raccoon Lake** as the location.

- Press the TAB key, Type **Rockville** as the city.

- Press the TAB key. Type **Missouri** as the state (Figure E–11).

Figure E–11

3

- Click the Apply button at the bottom of the Metadata panel to assign the metadata to the photo.

- Click File on the menu bar and then click File Info to display the Case 1-2 Tubing.jpg dialog box, and verify the information in the Description field (Figure E–12).

- Click the OK button to close the dialog box.

 Experiment

- Click each of the thumbnail buttons on the Bridge status bar to see how they change the display.

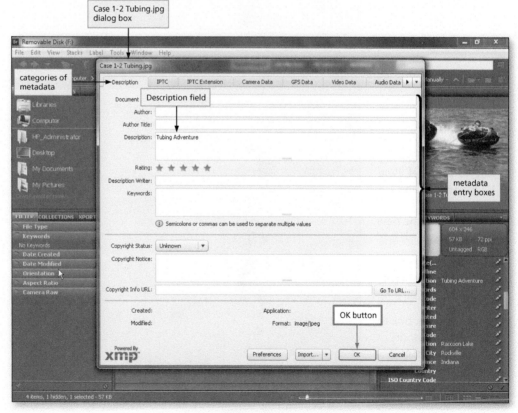

Figure E–12

To Enter a New Keyword

The Keywords panel lets you create and apply Bridge **keywords** to files. Keywords can be organized into categories called **sets.** Using keywords and sets, you identify and search for files based on their content. To assign keywords, you click the box to the left of the keyword in the Keywords panel, as shown in the following steps.

1

• With the Case 1-2 Tubing image still selected, click the Keywords tab to display the Keywords panel.

• Right-click the word, Places, to display the context menu (Figure E–13).

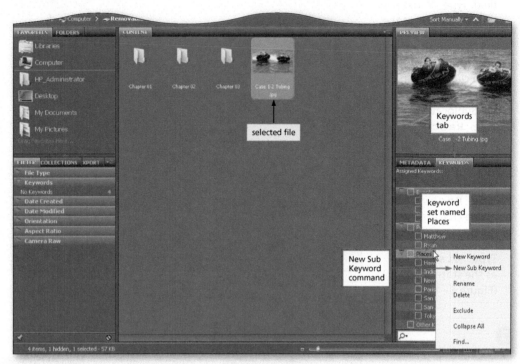

Figure E–13

2

• Click New Sub Keyword on the context menu.

• When the new field is displayed in the Keywords panel, type **Missouri** and then press the ENTER key to create the new item in Places.

• Select the photo again in the Content panel, if necessary.

• Click the check box to the left of Missouri to assign a Missouri keyword to the picture (Figure E–14).

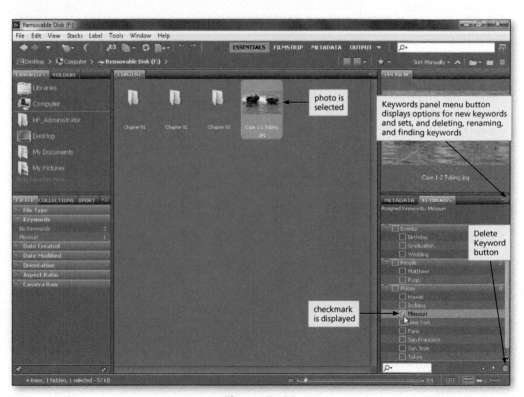

Figure E–14

To Rate a Photo

A rating system from zero stars to five stars is available in Bridge to rate your images and photos. A rating system helps you organize and flag your favorite or best files. Many photographers transfer their digital photos from a camera into Bridge and then look back through them, rating and grouping the photos. You can rate a photo using the Label menu or using shortcut keys. Once the photo is rated, stars are displayed below or above the file name depending on the workspace view. To change a rating, click Label on the menu bar and then either increase or decrease the rating. To remove all stars, click Label on the menu bar and then click No Rating. In some views, you can change a rating by clicking stars or dots that display below the thumbnail. You can remove the rating by clicking left of the stars.

The following step adds a rating to a photo file in Bridge.

1

- With the Case 1-2 Tubing image still selected in the Content panel, press CTRL+3 to assign a three star rating (Figure E–15).

Q&A

How do you remove the stars if you change your mind?

Click to the left of the stars in the Content panel, or press CTRL+0 (zero) to remove the stars.

Figure E–15

Other Ways

1. On Label menu, select desired rating

To Label a Photo with Color Coding

Another way to group photos in Bridge is to use a color coding system. Bridge provides five colors with which users can label or group their photos. Each color has a category keyword that can be used to group photos. Keywords such as Approved, Second, or Review are used in photojournalism to indicate the status of the photo for future usage. Some companies use the colors for sorting and selecting only. The steps on the next page add a green color indicating approval to the Case 1-2 Tubing image using the menu system. Shortcut keys also are available for labeling photos with color coding. You can edit the words associated with the various colors. To do so, press CTRL+K to enter Preferences and then click Labels in the left navigation pane.

1

- With the Case 1-2 Tubing image still selected in the Content panel, click Label on the menu bar to display the Label menu (Figure E–16).

 Q&A Can I change the colors associated with each label status?

No. Beginning with the Select command on the Label menu and going down, the colors are red, yellow, green, blue, and purple, respectively.

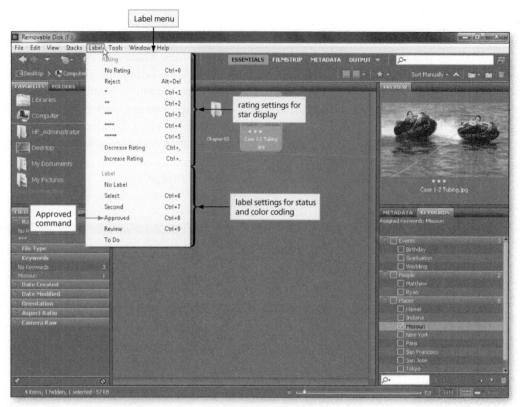

Figure E–16

2

- Click Approved to choose a label status.

- If Bridge displays a dialog box, click its OK button to apply the color (Figure E–17).

Q&A Where will I see the word, Approved, that I chose from the Label menu?

In the Essentials workspace, you only see the green color around the rating. If you click the Metadata workspace switcher button, the status itself is displayed.

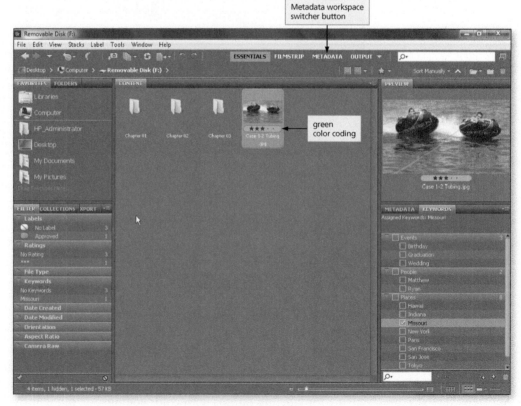

Figure E–17

Other Ways

1. For green color coding, press CTRL+8

Searching Bridge

Searching is a powerful tool in Bridge, especially as the number of stored image files increases on your computer system. It is a good idea to enter keywords, or meta-data, for every image file you store, to make searching more efficient. Without Bridge and the search tool, you would have to view all files as filmstrips in Windows, and then look at them a screen at a time until you found what you wanted.

Using the Find Command

In Bridge, you can enter the kind of data or field that you want to search, parameters for that field, and the text you are looking for using the Find command. For example, you could search for all files with a rating of three stars or better, for files less than 1 megabyte in size, files with Missouri as their location, or files that begin with the letter, m.

To Use the Find Command

The Find dialog box displays many boxes and buttons to help you search effectively. In the following steps, you will look for all files with metadata that includes the word, lake.

1
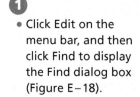

- Click Edit on the menu bar, and then click Find to display the Find dialog box (Figure E–18).

Q&A

How do I search in other locations?

Click the Look in box arrow and choose a preset location, or click the Browse command in the list to navigate to the desired location.

Figure E–18

2

- If necessary, click the first Criteria box arrow, scroll down as necessary, and then click All Metadata to search all of the metadata fields.

- Press the TAB key twice, and then type **lake** in the Enter Text box to enter the criteria (Figure E–19).

Experiment

- Click the second Criteria box arrow to view the choices for delimiting the criteria. When you are finished, click contains.

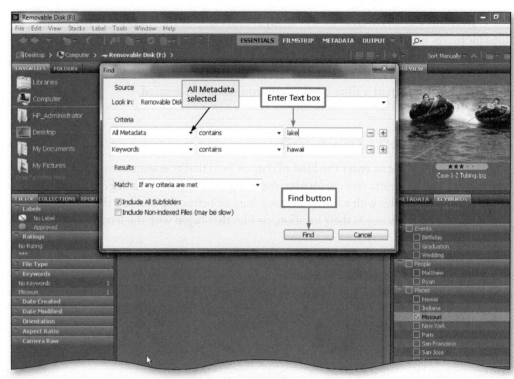

Figure E–19

3

- Click the Find button to display all files that have the word, lake, in any part of their metadata (Figure E–20).

- Click the Cancel button in the Search title bar.

Q&A

Can I search for types of images?

Yes, click the first Criteria box arrow, and then click Document Type. The third Criteria box then lists types of images from which you can choose.

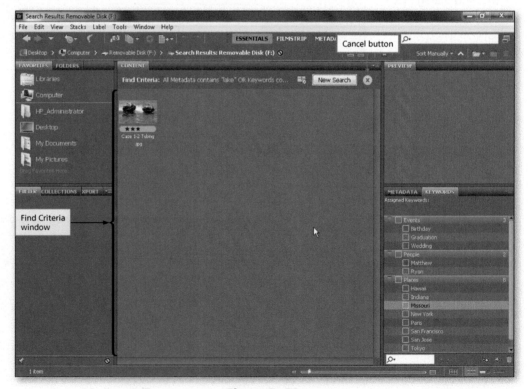

Figure E–20

Other Ways

1. Press CTRL+F, enter search criteria, click Find button

The plus sign to the right of the search boxes in the Find dialog box allows you to search multiple fields. You can add additional criteria by clicking the plus sign. For example, if you needed to find photos that were created last winter from your vacation in the Rockies, you could search for the date in the first line of boxes, and then enter a description in the second line of criteria boxes to narrow your search even further in the second line of boxes (Figure E–21). When clicked, the Match box arrow allows you to match any or all criteria.

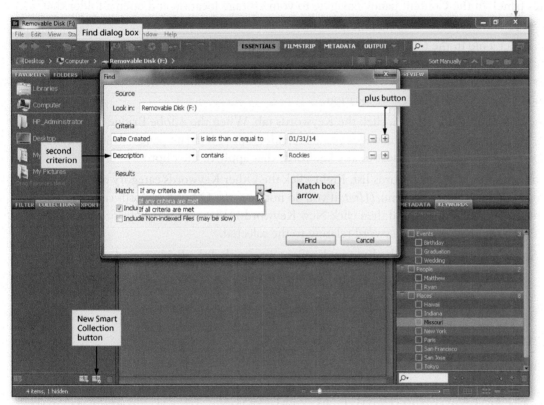

Figure E–21

Bridge offers you a way to save common searches as a **collection** for use later. For example, if you were working for a grocery wholesaler who stores many files for artwork in advertising, searching for pictures related to dairy products would be a common search. Looking through folders of images for pictures of milk or cheese would be very time consuming. To create a stored search collection, click the New Smart Collection button and enter your criteria. Bridge then allows you to name the search. To display stored collections, click Collections in the Favorites panel. Then to perform the search again, double-click the collection. With metadata and collection searches, Bridge saves a lot of time.

To Quit Bridge

The final step quits Bridge.

1 Click the Close button on the Bridge title bar.

Using Bridge

1: Assigning Metadata

Instructions: You would like to assign metadata to some of the photos you worked on in previous chapters in this book.

1. Start Bridge on your system. When the Bridge window is displayed, click Computer on the Favorites panel. In the Content panel, navigate to your storage location and open a folder that contains a photo or image file.

2. Click to select a file in the folder. In the Metadata panel, scroll down and click the pencil icon next to the word, Description. In the description box, enter a short description of the image. Scroll as necessary to click the Description Writer box. Enter your name. Enter Metadata for two other fields such as your e-mail address or location.

3. With the first photo still selected, click the Keywords tab. When the Adobe Bridge dialog box appears, click Apply to apply the changes you just made in the Metadata panel. On the Keywords tab, click to place a check mark next to any keywords that apply to the photo.

4. Scroll to the bottom of the keywords list. Right-click the Other Keywords category and then click New Keyword on the context menu. (*Hint:* if you do not have the Other Keywords category, click the Keywords panel menu button, and then click New Keyword.) When the new keyword box appears at the top of the panel, type a new keyword relating to the selected.

5. Repeat Steps 2 through 4 for each photo in the Content panel of the Bridge window.

Using Bridge

2: Rating and Categorizing Photos

Instructions: You would like to rate and categorize some of the photos you have created.

1. Start Bridge. Navigate to the location of a Photoshop file you created in a previous chapter.

2. Select the file. Assign a rating to the file on a scale from 1 to 5. On the Label menu, click the number of stars that corresponds to your rating. Repeat the process for other photos as directed by your instructor.

3. Click the file again to select it. Click Label on the menu bar. Choose a label setting, such as Approved. Repeat the process for the previous file you rated, choosing a different label setting.

4. Choose your favorite photo in the folder and right-click the file in the Content panel. Click Add to Favorites on the context menu.

5. Consult with at least three other members of your class to compare your ratings.

Appendix F

Changing Screen Resolution and Editing Preferences

This appendix explains how to change the screen resolution in Windows 7 to the resolution used in this book. It also describes how to customize the Photoshop window by setting preferences and resetting user changes.

Screen Resolution

Screen resolution indicates the number of pixels (dots) that the computer uses to display the graphics, text, and background you see on the screen. The screen resolution usually is stated as the product of two numbers, such as 1024×768. That resolution results in a display of 1,024 distinct pixels on each of 768 lines, or about 786,432 pixels on the screen or monitor. The figures in this book were created using a screen resolution of 1024×768.

To Change Screen Resolution

The following steps change your screen's resolution to 1024×768 pixels. Your computer already might be set to 1024×768 or some other resolution.

1

- If necessary, minimize all programs so that the Windows 7 desktop is displayed.

- Right-click the Windows 7 desktop to display the desktop shortcut menu (Figure F–1).

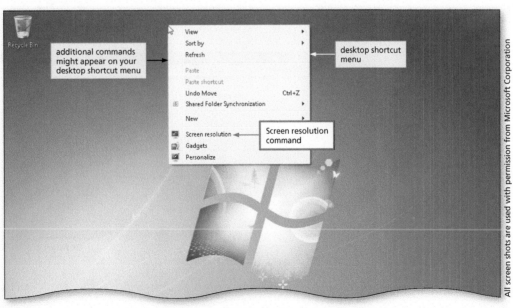

Recycle Bin

View
Sort by
Refresh

additional commands might appear on your desktop shortcut menu

desktop shortcut menu

Paste
Paste shortcut
Undo Move   Ctrl+Z
Shared Folder Synchronization

New

Screen resolution
Gadgets
Personalize

Screen resolution command

Figure F–1

2

- Click Screen resolution on the shortcut menu to open the Screen Resolution window. Maximize the window if necessary (Figure F–2).

Screen Resolution window →

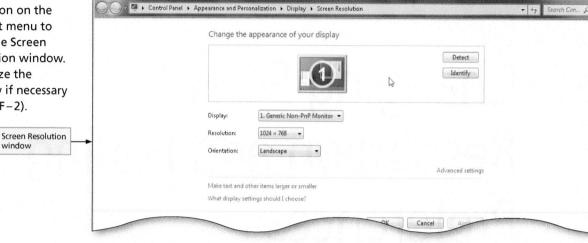

Figure F–2

3

- Click the Resolution button to display the list of available resolutions (Figure F–3).

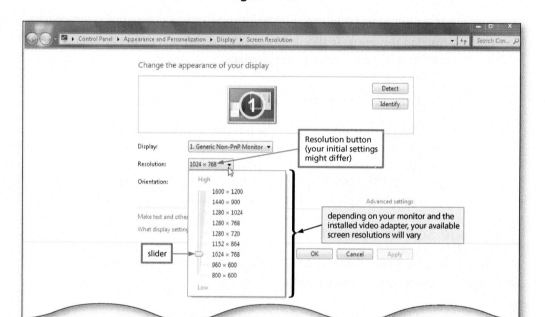

Figure F–3

4

- Drag the slider in the Resolution list so that the screen resolution changes to 1024 × 768, if necessary (Figure F–4).

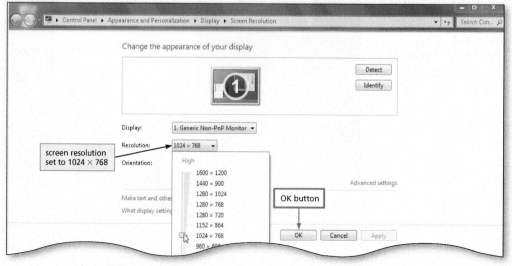

Figure F–4

5

- Click outside of the list to close the list.

- Click the OK button to change the screen resolution (Figure F–5).

6

- If Windows displays the Display Settings dialog box, click the Keep changes button to accept the changes.

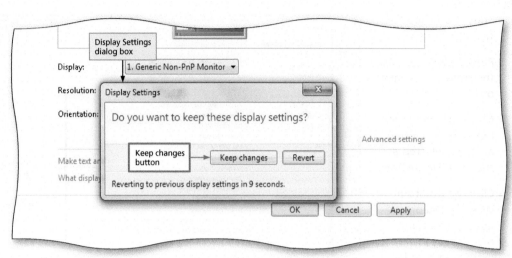

Figure F–5

Editing Photoshop Preferences

In Chapter 1, you learned how to start Photoshop and reset the default workspace, select the default tool, and reset all tools to their default settings. Photoshop has other preferences and settings you can edit to customize the workspace and maximize your efficiency.

Editing General Preferences

General preferences include how Photoshop displays and stores your work. For example, you can change how many states are saved in the History panel, change the number of files shown on the Open Recent menu, or reset the display and cursors.

To Edit General Preferences

In the steps on the next page, you will navigate through several Preferences dialog boxes to reset values and change preferences. You can access this set of dialog boxes by pressing CTRL+K or by clicking Preferences on the Edit menu.

BTW

Screen Resolutions
When you increase the screen resolution, Windows displays more information on the screen, but the information decreases in size. The reverse also is true; as you decrease the screen resolution, Windows displays less information on the screen, but the information increases in size.

①

- Start Photoshop CS6 for your system.

- Press CTRL+K to display the Preferences dialog box.

- Make sure the check boxes in the Options area are selected as shown in Figure F–6.

- Click the Reset All Warning Dialogs button, so your dialog boxes will match the ones in this book.

- When Photoshop displays a Preferences dialog box, click the OK button.

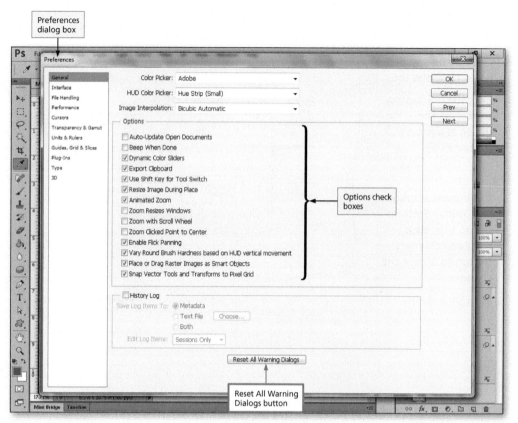

Figure F–6

②

- Click File Handling in the list of Preferences.

- Click the File Extension box arrow and then click Use Lower Case, if necessary, so Photoshop will use lowercase letters when saving.

- Make sure your check boxes are selected as shown in Figure F–7.

- Click the Maximize PSD and PSB File Compatibility box arrow and then click Ask, if necessary, so that Photoshop asks about saving files in PSD format.

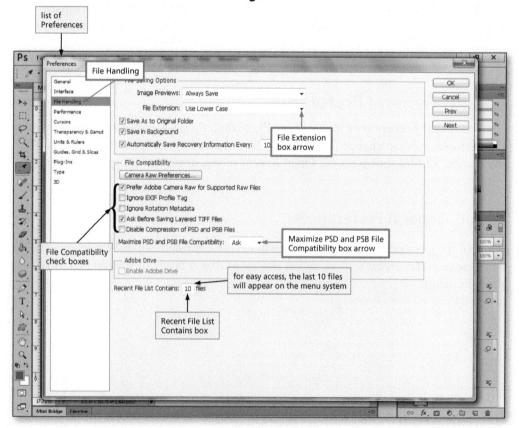

Figure F–7

- Type 10 in the Recent File List Contains box, if necessary, to specify that Photoshop will display the last 10 files.

Photoshop Appendix F

3
- Click Performance in the list of Preferences.

- If necessary, type 2 0 in the History States box, so Photoshop will allow you to back up through the last 20 steps of any editing session (Figure F–8).

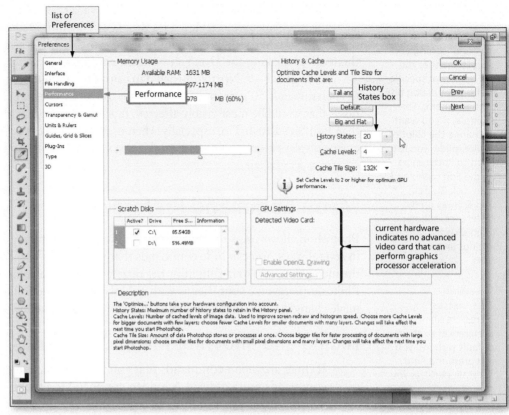

Figure F–8

4
- Click Cursors in the list of Preferences.

- If necessary, select Normal Brush Tip in the Painting Cursors area and Standard in the Other Cursors area, to reset those options back to their default values (Figure F–9).

5
- When you are finished, click the OK button to close the Preferences dialog box.

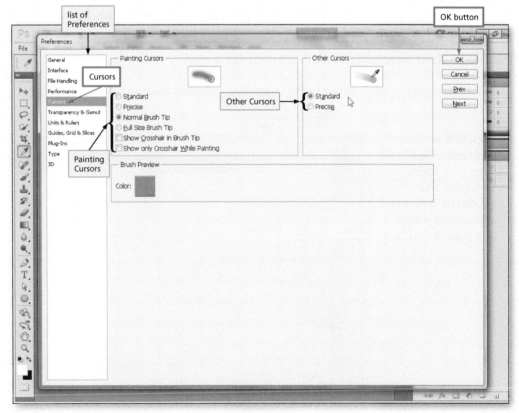

Figure F–9

Other Ways

1. On Edit menu, point to Preferences, click General, select individual preferences

Changing Preferences
If there is one particular setting you wish to change, you can open that specific Preferences dialog box from the menu. For example, if you want to change the color of a ruler guide, you can point to Preferences on the Edit menu and then click Guides, Grid & Slices on the Preferences submenu to go directly to those settings and make your edits.

Resetting Preferences
To restore all preferences to their default settings, you can press and hold ALT+CTRL+SHIFT as you start Photoshop, which causes the system to prompt that you are about to delete the current settings.

The Preferences dialog boxes contain a variety of settings that can be changed to suit individual needs and styles. The Reset All Warning Dialogs button in Figure F–6 on page APP 62 especially is useful to display the dialog boxes if someone has turned them off by clicking the Don't show again check box.

In Figure F–9, Normal Brush Tip causes the mouse pointer outline to correspond to approximately 50 percent of the area that the tool will affect. This option shows the pixels that would be most visibly affected. It is easier to work with Normal Brush Tip than Full Size Brush Tip, especially when using larger brushes. A Standard painting cursor displays mouse pointers as tool icons; a Precise painting cursor displays the mouse pointer as a crosshair.

Menu Command Preferences

Photoshop allows users to customize both the application menus and the panel menus in several ways. You can hide commands that you seldom use. You can set colors on the menu structure to highlight or organize your favorite commands. Or, you can let Photoshop organize your menus with color based on functionality. If another user has made changes to the menu structure, you can reset the menus back to their default states.

Hiding and Showing Menu Commands

If there are menu commands that you seldom use, you can hide them to access other commands more quickly. A hidden command is a menu command that does not appear currently on a menu. If menu commands have been hidden, a Show All Menu Items command will be displayed at the bottom of the menu list. When you click the Show All Menu Items command or press and hold the CTRL key as you click the menu name, Photoshop displays all menu commands, including hidden ones.

To Hide and Show Menu Commands

The following steps hide a menu command and then redisplay it.

1
• Click Edit on the Application bar, and then click Menus to display the Keyboard Shortcuts and Menus dialog box (Figure F–10).

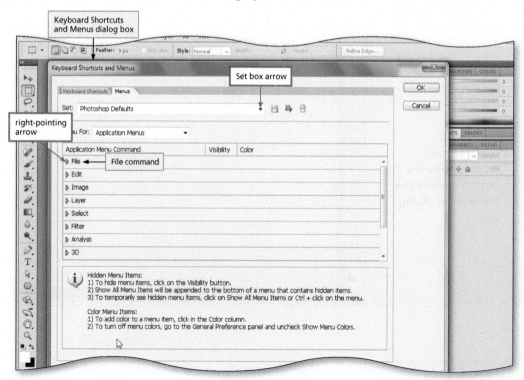

Figure F–10

2

- If necessary, click the Set box arrow and then click Photoshop Defaults.

- Click the right-pointing arrow next to the word File to display the File commands (Figure F–11).

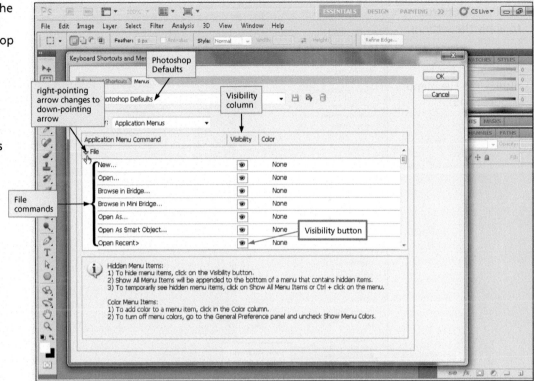

Figure F–11

3

- In the Visibility column, click the Visibility button next to the Open Recent command so it no longer displays the eye icon (Figure F–12).

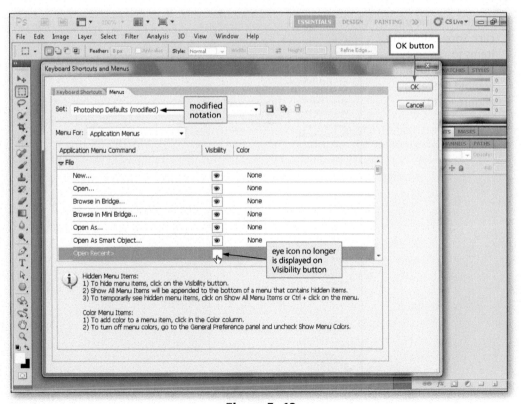

Figure F–12

- Click the OK button to apply the settings.

- Click File on the Application bar to display the File menu (Figure F–13).

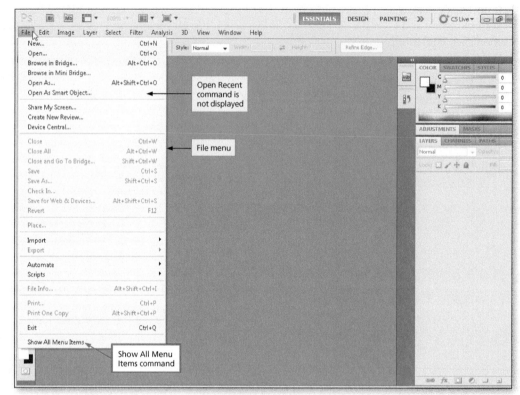

Figure F–13

- On the File menu, click Show All Menu Items to redisplay the command that you hid in Step 3 (Figure F–14).

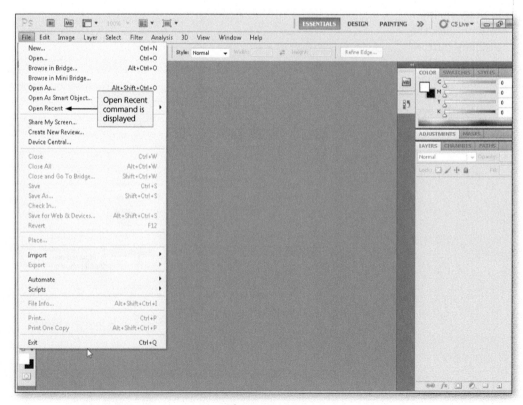

Figure F–14

6

- Click Edit on the Application bar and then click Menus to display the Keyboard Shortcuts and Menus dialog box again.

- If the arrow next to the word, File, is pointing to the right, click it to display the File list.

- Click the Visibility button next to the Open Recent command so it again is displayed (Figure F–15).

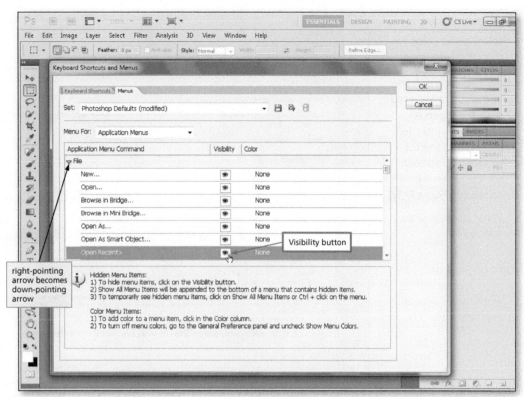

Figure F–15

Other Ways
1. On Window menu, point to Workspace, click Keyboard Shortcuts & Menus   2. Press ALT+SHIFT+CTRL+M

To Add Color to Menu Commands

You can add color to menu commands to help you find them easily or to organize them into groups based on personal preferences. The following steps change the color of the Open and Open As commands.

1

- With the Keyboard Shortcuts and Menus dialog box still displayed, click the word, None, in the row associated with the Open command to display a list of colors (Figure F–16).

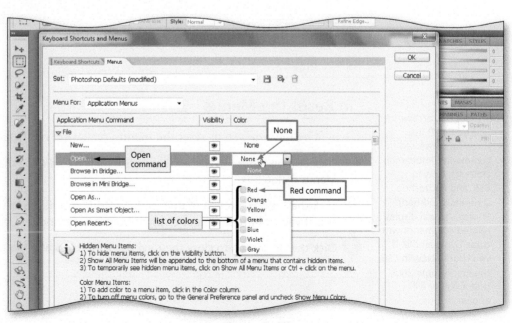

Figure F–16

2

- Click Red in the list to select a red color for the Open command.

- Click the word, None, in the row associated with the Open As command, and then click Red in the list to select a red color for the Open As command (Figure F–17).

Q&A

What other menus are available?

If you click the Menu For box arrow, you can choose Application Menus or Panel Menus.

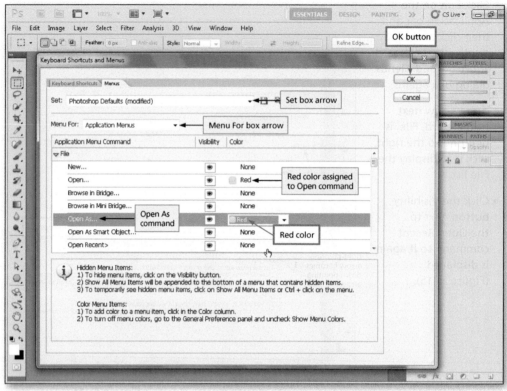

Figure F–17

3

- Click the OK button to close the Keyboard Shortcuts and Menus dialog box.

- Click File on the Application bar to display the new color settings (Figure F–18).

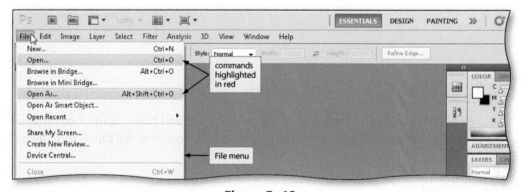

Figure F–18

BTW

Stored Menu Sets
The Set box arrow (Figure F–17) lists three sets of stored commands: Photoshop Defaults, New in CS6, and Photoshop Defaults (modified). Photoshop will display related commands with color. For example, if you choose New in CS6, the menu commands that are new will appear in blue.

To Reset the Menus

The following steps reset the menus, removing red from the Open commands.

1 Click Edit on the menu bar and then click Menus to display the Keyboard Shortcuts and Menus dialog box.

2 Click the Set box arrow and then click Photoshop Defaults in the list. When Photoshop asks if you want to save your changes before switching sets, click the No button.

3 Click the OK button to close the Keyboard Shortcuts and Menus dialog box.

Resetting the Panels, Keyboard Shortcuts, and Menus

A **tool preset** is a way to store settings from the options bar. Besides the default settings for each tool, Photoshop contains tool presets for many of the tools that automatically change the options bar. In a lab situation, if you notice that some tools are not working they way they are supposed to, or some presets are missing, it might be because another user changed the settings. The following steps reload all of the default tool presets.

To Reset Tool Presets

- On the options bar, click the current tool's Preset picker and then click the menu button to display the Tool Preset menu (Figure F–19).

- Click Reset Tool Presets to reset the tool's preset list.

- If Photoshop displays a dialog box, click the OK button to reload all the default tool presets.

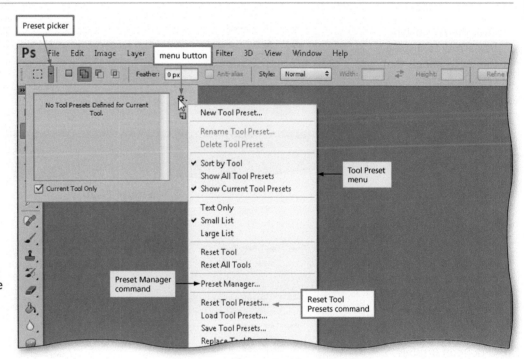

Figure F–19

Other Ways

1. From any panel menu, click Reset Tool Presets, click OK

Resetting Panel Components

Many panels, including the Brushes, Swatches, and Styles panels, display preset samples with preset shapes, colors, and sizes. A few options bars, including the Gradient and Shape options bars, as well as the Contours box in the Layer Style dialog box, also display similar components — all of which may need to be reset at some time.

You can reset these presets using the Preset Manager (Figure F–19), or each panel menu.

To Reset Panel Presets

The steps on the next page reset all panels that use presets.

- On the options bar, click the current tool's Preset picker and then click the menu button to display the Tool Preset menu.

- Click Preset Manager to display the Preset Manager dialog box.

- Click the Preset Type box arrow to display the list of panels that contain presets (Figure F–20).

- Click Brushes to select the Brush presets.

Figure F–20

- Click the Preset Manager menu button to display the list of commands and preset libraries (Figure F–21).

- Click Reset Brushes to reset the Brush presets. When Photoshop displays a confirmation dialog box, click the OK button.

- Repeat Steps 1 and 2 for each of the other panels that appear on the Preset Type box arrow list.

- When you are finished resetting all panels, click the Done button to close the dialog box.

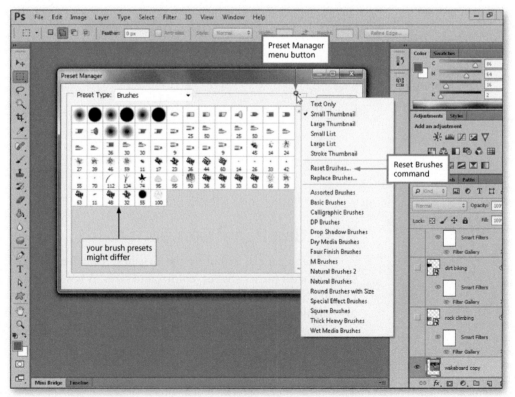

Figure F–21

1. On each panel menu, click Reset command, click OK button

Changing Preferences

1: Changing the color and style of guides, grids, and slices

Instructions: You would like to use some different colors and styles for grids and guides because the current colors are very similar to the colors in your image, making them hard to see. You decide to change the color and style preferences on your system as described in the following steps.

1. Start Photoshop CS6.
2. On the Edit menu, point to Preferences, and then click Guides, Grid & Slices.
3. When the Preferences dialog box is displayed, change the Color and Style settings as shown in Figure F–22.
4. Click the OK button.

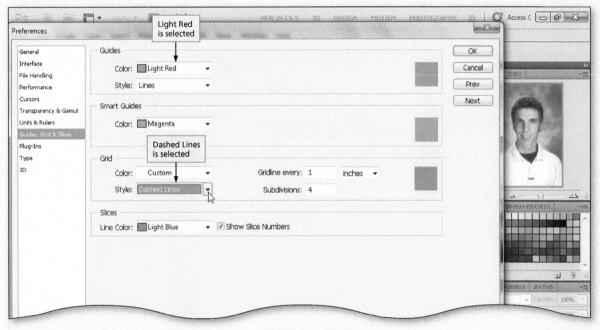

Figure F–22

5. Open any image file you have saved on your system and drag a guide from the horizontal ruler. Note the Light Red colored line.
6. On the View menu, point to Show, and then click Grid. Note the grid with dashed gray lines.
7. To clear the guides, on the View menu, click Clear Guides.
8. To hide the grid, on the View menu, point to Show and then click Grid.
9. To reset the colors and styles, either change the guide color back to Cyan and the grid style back to Lines, or quit Photoshop and then restart Photoshop while pressing ALT+CTRL+SHIFT. If Photoshop asks if you wish to delete the previous settings, click the Yes button.
10. Quit Photoshop.

Resetting Styles

Instructions: Someone has loaded many styles into the style box, making it difficult to find the common styles you prefer. You decide to reset the styles using the following steps.

1. Start Photoshop CS6.
2. On the Edit menu, point to Presets, and then click Preset Manager to display the Preset Manager dialog box.
3. Click the Preset Type box arrow to display the Preset list, and then click Styles in the list (Figure F–23).
4. Click the Preset Manager menu button to display a list of commands about the Styles Presets. Click Reset Styles in the list.
5. When Photoshop asks if you want to replace the styles with the default set, click the OK button.
6. Click the Done button to close the Preset Manager dialog box.
7. Quit Photoshop.

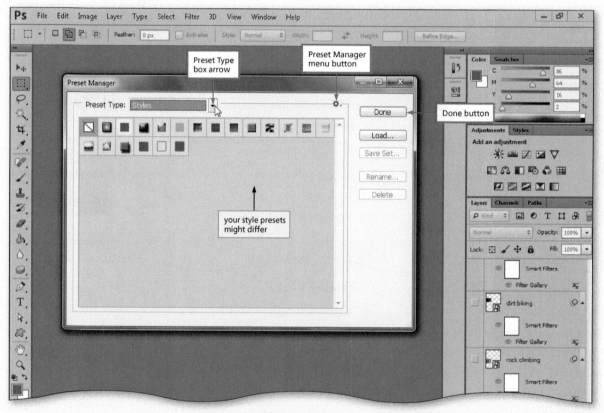

Figure F–23

Searching the Web

Instructions: You want to learn more about optimizing Photoshop settings and your computer system's memory by setting preferences for file size, history states, and cached views. Perform a Web search by using the Google search engine at google.com (or any major search engine) to display and print three Web pages that pertain to optimizing Photoshop CS6. On each printout, highlight something new that you learned by reading the Web page.

Appendix G

For Mac Users

For the Mac User of this Book

For most tasks, little difference exists between using Photoshop CS6 with the Windows 7 operating system and using it with the Mac OS X Lion 10.7 operating system. With some tasks, however, you will see some differences, or you might need to complete the tasks using different steps. This appendix demonstrates how to start an application, open a file, create a folder and save a file, close a file, display the application menu, and quit an application, using Photoshop CS6 and the Mac operating system.

Keyboard Differences

One difference between a Mac and a PC is in the use of modifier keys. **Modifier keys** are special keys used to modify the normal action of a key when the two are pressed in combination. Examples of modifier keys include the SHIFT, CTRL, and ALT keys on a PC and the SHIFT, CMD, and OPT keys on a Mac (Figure G–1). The CMD key sometimes is referred to as the APPLE key.

PC modifier keys

(a) PC keyboard

Mac modifier keys

(b) Mac keyboard

Figure G–1

Table G–1 explains the keystroke equivalencies. For instance, if PC instructions tell you to press CTRL+T to perform a task, Mac users would press CMD+T. In addition, many Mac menus display shortcut notations, using symbols to represent the modifier key.

Table G–1 PC vs. Mac Keystroke Equivalencies		
PC	**Mac**	**Mac Symbol**
CTRL key	CMD key	⌘
ALT key	OPT key	⌥
SHIFT key	SHIFT key	⇧

To Start an Application

The following steps, which assume Mac OS X Lion 10.7 is running, start an application based on a typical installation. You might need to ask your instructor how to start Photoshop for your computer.

1

- Click the Spotlight button on the Mac desktop to display the Spotlight box.

- Type Photoshop CS6, as the search text in the Spotlight text box and watch the search results appear (Figure G–2).

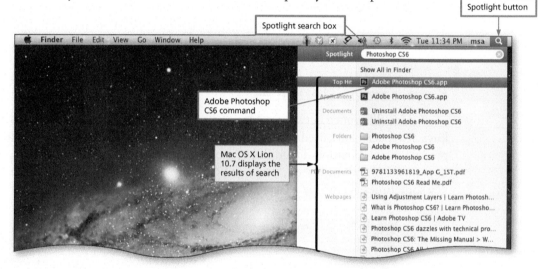

Figure G–2

2

- Click Adobe Photoshop CS6 in the list to start the application.

- If the window is not maximized, click the green Zoom button on the application title bar to maximize the window (Figure G–3).

Figure G–3

Adobe product screenshot(s) reprinted with permission from Adobe Systems Incorporated

Q&A

Does the PC version of Photoshop have a title bar?

No. On the PC platform, Photoshop has an Application bar that combines the menu and clip controls. The clip control functions — minimize, maximize, and close — are inherited from the operating system, and are placed where the system user would expect to find them.

Other Ways

1. Click Finder icon in Dock, navigate to applications, locate Adobe Photoshop CS6, double-click icon

2. Click Photoshop icon on dock

Customize the Workspace on a Mac

In general, customizing the Photoshop workspace on a Mac is the same as customizing it on a PC. Chapter 1 covers selecting the Essentials workspace, selecting the default tool, and resetting the option bar. When using the Mac OS X operating system, the Preferences submenu is located on the Photoshop menu, rather than the Edit menu. Figure G–4 displays the Preferences submenu, which you use to reset the interface color.

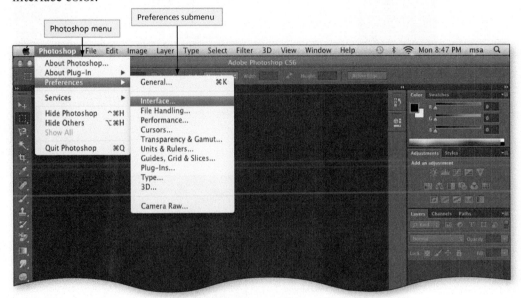

Figure G–4

To Open a File

The following steps open a file from the Data Files for Students. To complete this assignment, you will be required to use the Data Files for Students. Visit www.cengage.com/ct/studentdownload for detailed instructions or contact your instructor for information about accessing the required files.

1

- Start your application, if necessary, and reset the preferences.

- Click File on the title bar to display the File menu (Figure G–5).

Q&A What does it mean when Adobe includes multiple symbols in the shortcut key notation?

Multiple symbols mean that you must hold down several keys. For example, a notation of ⌥ ⌘ ○ on the menu would mean to press and hold the option and command keys while you press the o key. Written instructions might say press OPT+CMD+O.

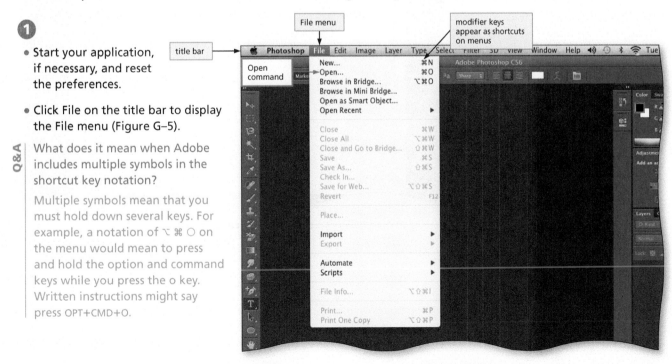

Figure G–5

2

- Click Open on the File menu to display the Open dialog box.

- Click the Where button to display a list of the available storage locations on your system (Figure G–6).

 **Experiment**

- Click a location on the Favorites panel on the left side of the Open dialog box and watch the Where button change. Click the Where button.

Figure G–6

3

- Click the drive associated with the location of the Data Files for Students.

- Navigate to the Photoshop folder, and then the Data Files for Students folder (Figure G–7).

What is the default location shown in the Open dialog box?

By default, the Open dialog box shows the first 10 items in the folder or volume last used during an open or save process. You can use the Icon view, List view, Column view, or Cover Flow view buttons to change the way the contents are presented. Cover Flow view allows you to see the contents of a file as a thumbnail.

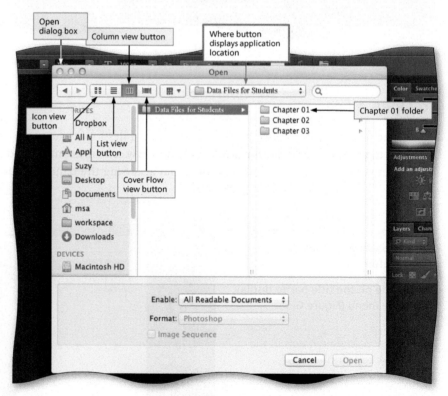

Figure G–7

- Double-click the Chapter 01 folder.
- Click the file, Eagle.jpg, to select it (Figure G–8).

5

- Click the Open button to open the selected file and display the open file in the Photoshop workspace.

Figure G–8

Other Ways

1. Press CMD+O, select file, click Open button

To Create a Folder and Save a File

After editing a file, you should save it. The following steps create a folder on a USB flash drive and save a file.

1

- Start Photoshop and open a file, if necessary.
- With a USB flash drive connected to one of the computer's USB ports, click File on the title bar to display the File menu and then click Save As to display the Save As dialog box.
- Type the name of your file, such as Eagle Edited, in the Save As box to change the file name. Do not press the RETURN key after typing the file name.
- Click the Where button to display the list of available drives (Figure G–9).

Figure G–9

2

- Click Removable Disk (F:), or the name of your USB flash drive, in the list of devices to select that drive as the new save location.

- Click the New Folder button to create a new folder on the selected storage device.

- When the new folder appears, type a new folder name such as Appendix G, to change the name of the folder, and then press the RETURN key (Figure G–10).

Figure G–10

3

- If necessary, click the new folder to open it.

- If necessary, click the Format button to display the list of available file formats. Choose the format appropriate for your application and purpose, in this case, the JPEG format (Figure G–11).

4

- Click the Save button to save the document on the selected drive with the new file name.

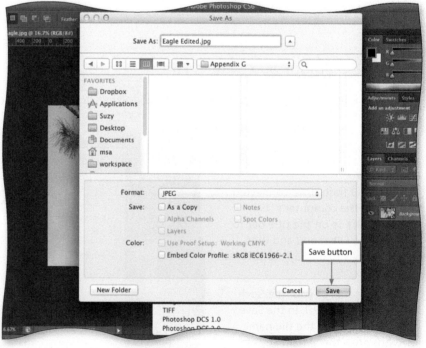

Figure G–11

Other Ways

1. Press SHIFT+CMD+S, choose settings, click Save button

To Close a File

The following steps close an open file.

1

- Start Photoshop and open a file, if necessary.

- Click File on the title bar to display the File menu (Figure G–12).

Q&A

Is the File menu different on a Mac?

The File menu is essentially the same. The commands might be grouped in a slightly different manner. The File menu does not contain the Exit command as it does on a PC. You will learn in the next steps that the Quit command is on the Photoshop menu.

2

- Click the Close command on the File menu to close the current open file without quitting the application.

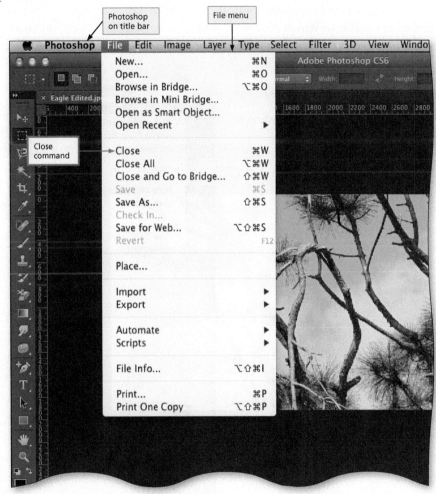

Figure G–12

To Display the Application Menu and Quit the Application

Using the Mac operating system, Photoshop CS6 includes a Photoshop menu to the left of the typical menu used in Windows. This application menu includes commands that you find in different locations on a PC, the most notable of which are the preferences, services, and the Quit command for each application. The following steps open the Photoshop menu to quit the application.

1

- Start Photoshop, if necessary.

- On the title bar, click Photoshop to open the Photoshop menu (Figure G–13).

Q&A What does the Services command do?

Mac OS X includes a Services submenu in many applications for tasks such as looking up a word in the dictionary, rotating an image, sending an e-mail, or compressing a video. Any Service installed on your Mac that manipulates files related to your application will be displayed on the Services submenu.

2

- Click Quit Photoshop to quit the application.

Q&A Can I click the red Close button to quit the application?

The red button closes the application window, but the application will continue to run until you quit the application.

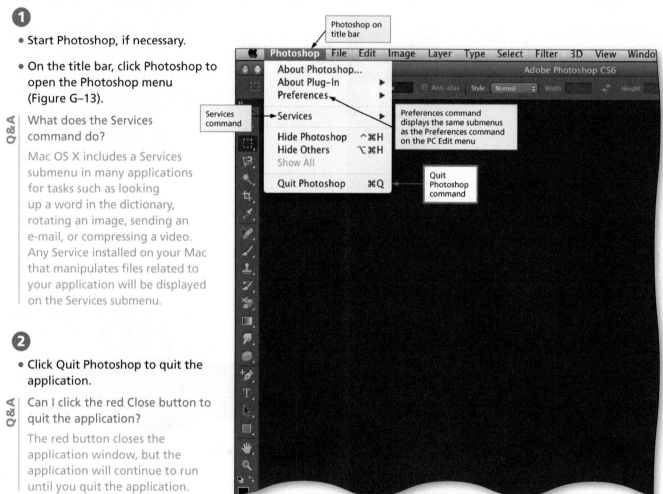

Figure G–13

Other Ways

1. Press CMD+Q
2. On Dock, click and hold mouse button, on context menu, click Quit

Index

Quick Reference Summary

Adobe Photoshop CS6 Quick Reference Summary

Task	Page Number	Mouse	Menu	Context Menu	Keyboard Shortcut
Action Set, Append	PS 442	Actions panel menu button, select action set, select subset to append			
Action Set, Create	PS 445	'Create new set' button on Actions panel status bar			
Action Set, Save	PS 450	Select actions set on Actions panel, Actions panel menu button, Save Actions button			
Action, Create	PS 446	'Create new action' on Actions panel status bar			
Action, Play	PS 450	Play selection button on Actions panel status bar			
Action, Record	PS 446	Record button (New Action dialog box), record action keystrokes, 'Stop playing/ recording' button			
Actions Panel, Display	PS 442		Window | Actions		
Adjustment Layer	PS 182	Clip to Layer button on Adjustments panel	Layer | New Adjustment Layer		CTRL+L
Align and Distribute Layers	PS 359	Align and Distribute buttons on Move tool options bar			
Alpha Channel, Create from Scratch	PS 417			Duplicate Channel	
Alpha Channel, Create from Selection	PS 412	Create selection in channel, click 'Save selection as panel' button			
Anchor Points, Add	PS 499			Pen Tool button | Add Anchor Point Tool | click in document window	
Animation, Optimize	PS 607		Timeline panel menu | Select All Frames, Timeline panel menu | Optimize Animation		
Animation, Preview	PS 602	Plan animation button on Timeline status bar			
(Animation) Timing, Set	PS 600	'Selects frame delay time' button on Animation panel			

Adobe Photoshop CS6 Quick Reference Summary *(continued)*

Task	Page Number	Mouse	Menu	Context Menu	Keyboard Shortcut
Append a Brush Library	PS 239	Preset Picker button on Brush options bar; menu button on panel			
Append Shape Presets	PS 259	Preset Picker button on Custom Shape options bar; menu button on panel			
Background Eraser Tool	PS 171	Background Eraser Tool button on Tools panel			SHIFT+E
Blending Mode, Apply	PS 384	Click Mode box arrow on Layers panel, click Overlay			
Blur Filter	PS 348, PS 366–368		Filter | Blur		
Border, Create	PS 36		Select | Select All; Edit | Stroke		
Border, Modify	PS 37		Select | Modify | Border		
Bridge Output Panel	PS 571	Workspace picker button, click Output	Window | Workspace | Output	Output	CTRL+F4
Brightness/Contrast, Adjust	PS 186	Brightness/Contrast icon on Adjustments panel or Create new fill or adjustment layer button on Layers panel; Brightness/Contrast	Layer | New Adjustment Layer | Brightness/Contrast		
Brush Panel, Display	PS 235	Click Brush button on vertical dock	On Window menu, click Brush, on Brush options bar, click Toggle the Brush panel button, on Brush Presets panel, click Toggle the Brush panel button, press F5		
Brush Presets, Append	PS 231	Click Brush Presets panel menu button, click Assorted brushes, click Append button	Click Brush Preset picker, click menu button, click desired set of brush presets		
Brush Tool, Select	PS 229			Right-click current brush tool on Tools panel, click Brush Tool	B
Brush, Select using Brush Preset Picker	PS 240	On Brush Preset panel, select brush or on Brush options bar, click Brush Preset picker, click panel menu button, select brush		Document window; choose brush	
Character Style, Create	PS 247	Create new Character Style button on Character Styles panel status bar			
Character Style, Show Panel	PS 247		Window |Character Styles		
Clone Stamp Tool	PS 192	Clone Stamp Tool button on Tools panel	Window | Clone Source		S
Close	PS 42	Close button on document window tab	File | Close		CTRL+W
Color Separations, Print	PS 468		File | Print, click Color Handling box arrow, select Separations, click Print button		

Adobe Photoshop CS6 Quick Reference Summary *(continued)*

Task	Page Number	Mouse	Menu	Context Menu	Keyboard Shortcut
Color Sliders, Change on Color Panel	PS 343	Click Color panel menu button, click CMYK sliders			
Color, Choose on Swatches Panel	PS 230	Click Swatches panel tab, select color			
Colors, Reset Default	PS 51	Default Foreground/Background Colors button on Tools panel			D
Colors, Switch Between Background and Foreground	PS 40	Switch Between Background and Foreground Colors button on Tools panel			X
Commit Change (transformation)	PS 160	Commit transform (Enter) button on options bar			ENTER
Commit Edits (text)	PS 49	Commit any current edits button on options bar			
Content-Aware	PS 291			Right-click Quick Selection Tool button, click Magic Wand Tool, click missing area of image, press DELETE key, click Use box arrow (Fill dialog box), click Content-Aware, click OK button	
Content-Aware Move Tool	PS 295	Content-Aware Move Tool on Tools panel			Press J or SHIFT+J
Convert to Duotone	PS 458		Image | Mode | Grayscale, click OK button, click Discard button | Image | Mode | Duotone | click Type box arrow, click Duotone, Preset box arrow, select color to use as Duotone		
Convert to LAB Color	PS 463		Image | Mode | Lab Color		
Copy File in Bridge	APP 49		Edit | Copy; navigate to copy location; Edit | Paste	Copy; Paste	CTRL+C to copy CTRL+V to paste
Curves	PS 285	Curves button on Adjustment panel	Layer | New Adjustment Layer | Curves		
Custom Shape Tool	PS 258, PS 527	Custom Shape button on Tools panel			U
Darken using Burn Tool	PS 311			Create selection using marquee tool, right-click Dodge Tool button, click Burn Tool, adjust brush size, click selection as needed	Press O or SHIFT+O

Adobe Photoshop CS6 Quick Reference Summary *(continued)*

Task	Page Number	Mouse	Menu	Context Menu	Keyboard Shortcut
Decontaminate Colors	PS 433	Select Brush Tool, D key to set colors to default settings, X key to reverse colors, 'Lock transparent pixels' button, Mode button, set brush to Color mode, drag brush over contaminated pixels			
Desaturate	PS 453		Select layer on Layers panel | Image | Adjustments | Desaturate		
Direction Points, Use	PS 501			Path Selection Tool button | Direct Selection Tool | click path, click anchor point, drag endpoint of direction line in desired direction	
Document Windows, Arrange	PS 150, 151		Window | Arrange		
Download Speed, Choose	PS 54	Select download speed button (Save for Web dialog box)	File | Save for Web		ALT+SHIFT+ CTRL+S
Draw using Brush Tool	PS 237, PS 241	Select brush, drag in document window or SHIFT+drag to draw straight lines			
Elliptical Marquee Tool	PS 76, 105	Elliptical Marquee Tool button on Tools panel			SHIFT+M
Eraser Tools	PS 163, 167	Eraser Tool button on Tools panel			E
Essentials Workspace, Select	PS 6	Essentials button on Application bar	Window | Workspace | Essentials		
Eyedropper Tool, Use	PS 254			On Tools panel, right-click Eyedropper Tool button, click Eyedropper Tool, click desired color to sample	
Filter, Apply with Filter Gallery	PS 360–365	Select layer to edit, click Filter on Application bar, click Filter Gallery, click desired filter category folder, click desired filter, adjust settings, click OK button		On Filter menu, point to folder, click filter, adjust settings, click OK button	
Find File in Bridge	APP 55		Edit | Find		CTRL+F
Fit on Screen	PS 110, 184	Fit screen button on Zoom Tool options bar	View | Fit on Screen		CTRL+0 (zero)
Folder, Create in Bridge	PS 567		File | New Folder		
Font Options, Set	PS 244	On options bar, click 'Set the font family' box arrow, select font from list, click 'Set the font size' box arrow, select size, click 'Set the anti-aliasing method' box arrow, select anti-aliasing method, click desired alignment button, click 'Set the text color' box, click to select desired color			

Adobe Photoshop CS6 Quick Reference Summary *(continued)*

Task	Page Number	Mouse	Menu	Context Menu	Keyboard Shortcut
Gradient, Create	PS 222	Gradient button on Tools panel			G
Gradient, Draw	PS 224	With Gradient Tool selected, drag in document window			
Gradient Tool and Style, Select	PS 220			Right-click Gradient Tool button, click Gradient Tool, select gradient style on Gradient Options bar	
Grid, Hide or Show	PS 96		View | Show | Grid		CTRL+ APOSTROPHE (')
Guides, Create	PS 97	Drag from ruler	View | New Guide		
Guides, Hide or Show	PS 97		View | Show | Guides		CTRL+SEMICOLON (;)
Hand Tool	PS 28	Hand Tool button on Tools panel			H
Hard Proof, Print	PS 389		Click View on Application bar, point to Proof Setup, click Working CMYK check box, close menu, click CTRL+P, click Scale to Fit Media check box, click Proof option button, click Color Handling box arrow, click Photoshop Manages Colors, click Print Settings button, turn off color management, click OK button or Print button		
Healing Brush Tool	PS 301			Right-click current healing tool on Tools panel, click Healing Brush Tool, ALT+click to sample, drag across damage to repair	Press J or SHIFT+J
Help	PS 58, Appendix D		Help | Photoshop Help		F1
History, Step Backward	PS 86	Click state on History panel	History panel menu | Step Backward		CTRL+ALT+Z
History, Step Forward	PS 87	Click state on History panel	History panel menu | Step Forward		CTRL+SHIFT+Z
Horizontal Type Tool	PS 244			Right-click current type tool, click Horizontal Type Tool	
Hue/Saturation, Adjust	PS 184	Hue/Saturation icon on Adjustment panel or Create new fill or adjustment layer button on Layers panel; Hue/ Saturation	Layer | New Adjustment Layer | Hue/Saturation		CTRL+U
Image, Crop	PS 33	Crop Tool button on Tools panel	Image | Crop		C

Adobe Photoshop CS6 Quick Reference Summary *(continued)*

Task	Page Number	Mouse	Menu	Context Menu	Keyboard Shortcut
Image, Flatten	PS 195		Layer | Flatten Image or Layers panel menu | Flatten Image	Flatten Image	
Image, Resize	PS 45		Image | Image Size		ALT+CTRL+I
Keyboard Shortcuts, Create	PS 114		Edit | Keyboard Shortcuts		ALT+SHIFT+ CTRL+K
Keyboard Shortcuts, Reset Default	PS 118	Set Photoshop Defaults in Keyboard Shortcuts and Menus dialog box	Edit | Keyboard Shortcuts | Photoshop Defaults		
Lasso Tool	PS 100	Lasso Tool button on Tools panel			L
Layer From Background, Create	PS 285			Right-click Background layer on Layers panel, click Layer From Background, name new layer, click OK button	
Layer Group, Create	PS 523	Select layers in Layers panel, click Layers panel menu button, New Group from Layers			
Layer Groups, Nest	PS 526	On Layers panel, drag nested layer onto layer group			
Layer Mask, add from Alpha Channel	PS 428		Select layer on Layers panel | Select | Load Selection, select channel from Channel menu, click OK button, click 'Add layer mask' button		
Layer Mask, Create	PS 176	Add layer mask button on Layers panel			
Layer Mask, Create from Alpha Channel	PS 424		Select | Load Selection, Channel box arrow, select channel, click OK button, select layer to mask on Layers panel, click 'Add layer mask' button		
Layer Style, Add	PS 189	Add a layer style button on Layers panel	Layer | Layer Style		
Layer Style, Copy	PS 252			Indicates layer effects button on Layers panel; copy Layer Style	
Layer Via Cut, Create	PS 143		Layer | New | Layer via Cut	Layer Via Cut	SHIFT+CTRL+J
Layer, Assign a Color	PS 146		Layers panel menu	Indicates layer visibility button | color	
Layer, Create	PS 151		Layer | New | Layer or Layers panel menu | New Layer		SHIFT+CTRL+N
Layer, Display Current	PS 164	ALT+click layer visibility icon on Layers panel			
Layer, Hide	PS 147	Indicates layer visibility icon on Layers panel	Layer | Hide Layers	Indicates layer visibility button | Hide this layer	

Adobe Photoshop CS6 Quick Reference Summary *(continued)*

Task	Page Number	Mouse	Menu	Context Menu	Keyboard Shortcut
Layer, Move	PS 152	Select Move Tool, drag layer in document window			
Layer, Rename	PS 145	Double-click layer name | enter new name	Layers panel menu | Layer Properties | enter new name	Layer Properties | enter new name	
Layer, Show	PS 147	Indicates layer visibility icon on Layers panel	Layer | Show Layers		
Layer, Show Only Current	PS 164	ALT+click layer visibility icon on Layers panel			
Layers and Slices, Hide	PS 592				CTRL+H
Layers Panel Options, Change	PS 142		Layers panel menu | Panel Options		
Layers, Lock	PS 490	Select layer to lock, click Lock All button			
Layers, Rearrange	PS 174	Drag layer on Layers panel			CTRL+[or CTRL+]
Layers, Rotate	PS 594				CTRL+T, drag
Lens Correction Dialog Box	PS 317		Click Filter on Application bar, click Lens Correction		SHIFT+CTRL+R
Levels, Adjust	PS 182	Levels icon on Adjustments panel or Create new fill or adjustment layer button on Layers panel; Levels	Image | Adjustments | Levels		CTRL+L
Lighten using Dodge Tool	PS 312			Create selection using marquee tool, right-click Dodge Tool button, click Dodge Tool, adjust brush size, click selection as needed	Press O or SHIFT+O
Liquify Filter	PS 356		Filter | Liquify		SHIFT+CTRL+X
Lock Transparent Pixels	PS 288	On Layers panel, click 'Lock transparent pixels' button			
Magic Eraser Tool	PS 164	Magic Eraser Tool button on Tools panel			SHIFT+E
Magic Wand Tool	PS 102	Magic Wand Tool button on Tools panel			SHIFT+W
Magnetic Lasso Tool	PS 99	Magnetic Lasso Tool button on Tools panel			SHIFT+L
Magnification, Change	PS 29	Enter number in Magnification box on status bar			
Masking Error, Correct	PS 178		Layer | Layer Mask | Reveal All	Disable Mask	
Menus, Hide or Show	APP 7		Edit | Menus		ALT+SHIFT+CTRL+M
Metadata, Add	APP 50	Description field on Metadata panel, enter description			
Move Tool	PS 80	Move Tool button on Tools panel			V
Navigate Files using Bridge	APP 48	Double-click file location, click workspace buttons			

Task	Page Number	Mouse	Menu	Context Menu	Keyboard Shortcut
New Adjustment Layer, Create	PS 284	Click 'Create new fill or adjustment layer' button on Layers panel status bar, click Levels, click 'Clip to layer' button		On Layer menu, point to New Adjustment Layer, click Levels, click OK button (Levels dialog box)	
New Photoshop File, Start	PS 216	Click File on Application bar, click New			CTRL+N
Note, Create	PS 540			Eyedropper Tool | Note Tool, click document window, type note content	
Note, View	PS 541	Double-click note in document window			
Opacity, Change	PS 180	Drag Opacity scrubby slider on Layers panel			
Open	PS 11		File | Open	Document tab | Open Document	CTRL+O
Open Recent	PS 43		File | Open Recent		
Out of Gamut Error	PS 344	Out of Gamut warning icon on Color panel			
Paint Bucket Tool	PS 345–346	Right-click Gradient Tool button on Tools panel, click Paint Bucket Tool, click selection to apply color			
Painting Workspace, Select	PS 214	Click Painting on Application bar or click Show More Workspaces and Options button, click Painting			
Panel, Collapse	PS 18, 27	Collapse to Icons button on panel		Panel tab | Collapse to Icons	
Panel, Open	PS 26	Panel button on vertical docking of panels	Window | panel name		
Paste	PS 102		Edit | Paste	Paste	CTRL+V
Patch	PS 303			Right-click current healing tool on Tools panel, click Patch Tool, click Source option button, draw patch shape, click Destination option button, drag selection to cover damage	Press J or SHIFT+J
Path, Create using Pen Tool	PS 510	Select Pen Tool, click 'Pick tool mode' button, click Path, click in document window to create path			
Path, Save	PS 513	Double-click Work Path on Paths panel, type new name, press ENTER			
Paths Panel, Display	PS 512	Click Paths panel tab			
Paths, Merge	PS 514			Direct Selection Tool | Path Selection Tool | select first path to merge, CTRL+C, select second path to merge on Paths panel, CTRL+V	

Adobe Photoshop CS6 Quick Reference Summary *(continued)*

Task	Page Number	Mouse	Menu	Context Menu	Keyboard Shortcut
Pattern, Define	PS 375		Create selection around pattern source, click Edit on Application bar, click Define Pattern, name pattern, click OK button		
Pattern Stamp Tool	PS 190	Pattern Stamp Tool button on Tools panel			SHIFT+S
Pattern, Use	PS 375	Create selection in layer, G key, click 'Set source for fill area' box arrow, click Pattern, click Pattern Picker box, select pattern, click in selection to apply pattern			
Perspective, Change	PS 169			Perspective	
Perspective Errors, Correct	PS 318	In Lens Correction dialog box, click Custom tab, double-click Vertical Perspective box, enter a negative value to bring top of image closer			
Polygonal Lasso Tool	PS 93	Polygonal Lasso Tool button on Tools panel			SHIFT+L
Preferences, Edit	APP 62		Edit | Preferences | General		CTRL+K
Preview, Web	PS 55	Preview button (Save for Web & Devices dialog box)	File | Save for Web & Devices		ALT+CTRL+ SHIFT+S
Print	PS 52		File | Print		CTRL+P
Print One Copy	PS 52		File | Print One Copy		ALT+SHIFT+ CTRL+P
Quick Selection Tool	PS 83	Quick Selection Tool button on Tools panel			W
Quit Photoshop	PS 60	Close button	File | Exit		CTRL+Q
Rate File in Bridge	APP 53				CTRL+1 through CTRL+5
Rectangular Marquee Tool	PS 79	Rectangular Marquee Tool button on Tools panel			M
Red Eye, Correct	PS 307			Right-click current healing tool button, click Red Eye Tool, click red portion of eye	Press j or SHIFT+J
Refine Edge	PS 89	Refine Edge button on options bar	Select | Refine Edge	Refine Edge	ALT+CTRL+R
Refine Mask Tool	PS 432		Select mask thumbnail | Select, Refine Mask command, View box arrow, adjust settings, Output To box arrow, New Layer		
Reselect	PS 108		Select | Reselect		
Reset All Tools	PS 9			Reset All Tools	
Resize File with Resampling	PS 466		Image | Image Size		

Task	Page Number	Mouse	Menu	Context Menu	Keyboard Shortcut
Rule of Thirds Overlay, Position	PS 33	Drag overlay			
Rulers, Show or Hide	PS 30	View Extras button on Application bar	View | Rulers		CTRL+R
Save	PS 20		File | Save		CTRL+S
Save for Web	PS 56		File | Save for Web & Devices		ALT+SHIFT+ CTRL+S
Save in PDF Format	PS 112		File | Save As; Format box arrow | Photoshop PDF (*.PDF; *.PDP)		
Save with New Name	PS 51		File | Save As | enter new name		SHIFT+CTRL+S
Screen Mode, Change	PS 30	Screen Mode button on Applications bar	View | Screen Mode | select mode		F
Select All	PS 36		Select | All		CTRL+A
Select using a Channel	PS 411	Click channel on Channels panel, create selection using Zoom or Lasso tool			
Selection, Add To	PS 76–77	Add to selection button on options bar			SHIFT+drag
Selection, Deselect	PS 91		Select | Deselect		CTRL+D
Selection, Distort	PS 157, 169	Enter rotation percentage on options bar	Edit | Transform | Distort	Free Transform mode | Distort	
Selection, Duplicate	PS 82		Edit | Copy | Edit Paste		CTRL+ALT+drag
Selection, Flip Horizontal	PS 88, 157		Edit | Transform | Flip Horizontal	Free Transform mode | Flip Horizontal	
Selection, Flip Vertical	PS 88, 157		Edit | Transform | Flip Vertical	Free Transform mode | Flip Vertical	
Selection, Free Transform	PS 156		Edit | Free Transform	Free Transform	CTRL+T
Selection, Grow	PS 94		Select | Grow		
Selection, Intersect with	PS 77, 102	Intersect with selection button on options bar			
Selection, Rotate	PS 156	Enter degree rotation on options bar	Edit | Transform | Rotate	Free Transform mode | Rotate	
Selection, Rotate 180°	PS 156	Enter degree rotation on options bar	Edit | Transform | Rotate 180°	Free Transform mode | Rotate 180°	
Selection, Rotate 90° CCW	PS 156	Enter degree rotation on options bar	Edit | Transform | Rotate 90° CCW	Free Transform mode | Rotate 90° CCW	
Selection, Rotate 90° CW	PS 156	Enter degree rotation on options bar	Edit | Transform | Rotate 90° CW	Free Transform mode | Rotate 90° CW	
Selection, Scale	PS 156	SHIFT+drag corner sizing handle	Edit | Transform | Scale	Free Transform mode | Scale	
Selection, Skew	PS 157		Edit | Transform | Skew	Free Transform mode | Skew	
Selection, Snap	PS 98	Drag selection near object or guide			
Selection, Subtract From	PS 102	Subtract from selection button on options bar			ALT+drag
Selection, Transform Perspective	PS 157, 169		Edit | Transform | Perspective	Free Transform mode | Perspective	
Selection, Warp	PS 157	Warp button on Transform options bar	Edit | Transform | Warp	Free Transform mode | Warp	

Adobe Photoshop CS6 Quick Reference Summary *(continued)*

Task	Page Number	Mouse	Menu	Context Menu	Keyboard Shortcut
Sepia Image, Create	PS 456	Selective Color icon on Adjustments panel, click Colors box arrow, click Neutrals			
Set Tracking	PS 379, PS 381	Select text to track, click Toggle the Character and Paragraph panels button, click 'Set the tracking' box arrow, type a positive number to move characters further apart or a negative number to bring characters closer together, click 'Commit any current edits' button			
Shape Layer, Create	PS 495	Click Pen Tool button, click in document window to create shape, click starting point to close shape			
Shape Layer, Create from Path	PS 516		Select path | Layer | New Fill Layer, select layer type | specify layer settings		
Shape Layer, Duplicate	PS 261	Right-click layer on Layers panel, click Duplicate Layer, click OK button, activate Move Tool			
Shape Tool in Pixel Mode	PS 505			Shape tool | Line Tool | 'Pick tool mode' button on options bar, select Pixels, drag in document window to draw	
Shape, Create	PS 260			Right-click current shape tool, select desired shape	
Shape, Fill with a Pattern	PS 534	Select shape layer on Layers panel, click 'Add a layer style' button, click Pattern Overlay, select pattern from Pattern Picker			
Sharpen Tool	PS 325	Sharpen Tool button on Tools panel			
Single Column Marquee Tool	PS 76	Single Column Marquee Tool button on Tools panel			
Single Row Marquee Tool	PS 76	Single Row Marquee Tool button on Tools panel			
Slice Select Tool	PS 587			Slice Select Tool	
Slices, Create	PS 585		Layer | New Layer Based Slice	Slice Tool	
Smart Filter, Apply	PS 362–365	Select layer to edit, click Filter on Application bar, click Filter Gallery, click desired folder, click desired filter, adjust settings, click OK to apply filter	On Filter menu, point to folder, click filter, adjust settings, click OK button		

Adobe Photoshop CS6 Quick Reference Summary *(continued)*

Task	Page Number	Mouse	Menu	Context Menu	Keyboard Shortcut
Smart Filter, Create	PS 361	Select layer to edit, click Filter on Application bar, click Convert to Smart Filter			
Smart Object, Create using Place Command	PS 227	Click File on Application bar, click Place, navigate to file, open file to Place		Right-click layer, click Convert to Smart Object	
Smart Object, Layer	PS 153		Layer | Smart Objects | Convert to Smart Object or Layers panel menu | Convert to Smart Object	Convert to Smart Object	
Smooth, Modify	PS 88, 89		Select | Modify | Smooth		
Smudge	PS 321	Right-click Blur Tool button, click Smudge Tool, adjust brush size, drag over image to create smudge area			
Snapping, Turn On	PS 96, 98		View | Snap		SHIFT+CTRL+ SEMICOLON (;)
Solid Gradient, Edit	PS 223	Click Gradient Editor box, double-click left Color Stop button (Select Stop Color dialog box), choose color, click OK button			
Sponge Tool	PS 313	Sponge Tool button on Tools panel			Press O or SHIFT+O
Spot Healing Brush Tool	PS 298			Right-click current healing tool on Tools panel, click Spot Healing Brush Tool, point to damaged area, adjust brush size, click to repair	Press J or SHIFT+J
Straighten a Photo	PS 318	In Lens Correction dialog box, click Straighten Tool button, drag across horizontal image element to straighten, drag across vertical image element or click Custom tab (Lens Correction dialog box), drag Angle icon			
Stroke Layer, Create	PS 251	With text layer selected, click 'Add a layer style' button, click Stroke, adjust stroke settings, click OK button			
Templates and Styles	PS 572	Click Web Gallery button on Output panel, click Template button, select template, click Style button, select style to apply			
Text, Create within a Shape	PS 529	Select Type Tool, click shape in document window, type text, click 'Commit any current edits' button			

Adobe Photoshop CS6 Quick Reference Summary *(continued)*

Task	Page Number	Mouse	Menu	Context Menu	Keyboard Shortcut
Text, Insert	PS 244	With Type Tool selected, drag bounding box, type text, click 'Commit any current edits' button			
Timeline Panel, Display	PS 579		Window | Timeline		
Transform Controls, Display	PS 158, 159	Show Transform Controls checkbox on options bar	Edit | Free Transform		CTRL+T
Tween	PS 603	'Tweens animation frames' button on Animation pane status bar or select frames, click Tween on panel menu			
Undo	PS 34	Click previous state in History panel	Edit | Undo		CTRL+Z
View Channels	PS 409	Click Channels panel tab, click individual channels			
View Corrections	PS 305	Display Background layer, hide corrections layer			
Warp Text	PS 436	Horizontal Type Tool, 'Create warped text' button			
Web Gallery, Preview	PS 574	Click Preview in Browser button on Output panel			
Web Gallery, Save	PS 574	Click Browse button on Output panel, navigate to save location, click OK button, click Save button			
Web Page, View Interactively	PS 610	Double-click HTML file			
Windows, Consolidate	PS 151		Window | Arrange | Consolidate All to Tabs	Document tab | Consolidate All to Here	
Yellowed Portions of a Document, Correct	PS 284		Click Image on Application bar, point to Mode, click Grayscale		
Zoom by Dragging	PS 410	Click Zoom Tool button, drag around selection			
Zoom In	PS 24	Zoom In button on Navigator panel	View | Zoom In	Zoom In	CTRL+PLUS SIGN (+)
Zoom Out	PS 24	Zoom Out button on Navigator panel	View | Zoom Out	Zoom Out	CTRL+MINUS SIGN (−)
Zoom Tool	PS 24	Zoom Tool button on Tools panel			Z
Zoomify	PS 53		File | Export | Zoomify